Gender and Economics

The International Library of Critical Writings in Economics

Series Editor: Mark Blaug

Professor Emeritus, University of London
Professor Emeritus, University of Buckingham
Visiting Professor, University of Exeter

This series is an essential reference source for students, researchers and lecturers in economics. It presents by theme an authoritative selection of the most important articles across the entire spectrum of economics. Each volume has been prepared by a leading specialist who has written an authoritative introduction to the literature included.

A full list of published and future titles in this series is printed at the end of this volume.

Gender and Economics

Edited by

Jane Humphries

*Lecturer in the Faculty of Economics and Politics
and Fellow of Newnham College
University of Cambridge*

THE INTERNATIONAL LIBRARY OF CRITICAL WRITINGS IN ECONOMICS

An Elgar Reference Collection

Published by
Edward Elgar Publishing Limited
Gower House
Croft Road
Aldershot
Hants GU11 3HR
England

Edward Elgar Publishing Company
Old Post Road
Brookfield
Vermont 05036
USA

British Library Cataloguing in Publication Data
Gender and Economics. – (International
Library of Critical Writings in Economics;
No. 45)
  I. Humphries, Jane II. Series
  331.4

Library of Congress Cataloguing in Publication Data
Gender and economics / edited by Jane Humphries.
      p. cm. — (The international library of critical writings in
  economics; 45) (An Elgar reference collection)
    Includes index.
    1. Sexual division of labor. 2. Sex discrimination in employment.
  3. Sex discrimination against women. 4. Sex role in the work
  environment. I. Humphries, Jane, 1948–   . II. Series.
  III. Series: An Elgar reference collection.
  HD6060.6.G447 1995
  306.3'615—dc20   94–40794
                                                                    CIP

ISBN 1 85278 843 7

Printed in Great Britain by Galliard (Printers) Ltd, Great Yarmouth

Contents

Acknowledgements

The editor and publishers wish to thank the following who have kindly given permission for the use of copyright material.

Academic Press Ltd for article: Michèle Pujol (1984), 'Gender and Class in Marshall's Principles of Economics', *Cambridge Journal of Economics*, **8** (3), September, 217–34.

American Economic Review for articles: Robert H. Pollak (1985), 'A Transactions Cost Approach to Families and Households', *Journal of Economic Literature*, **XXIII** (2), 594–608; Morley Gunderson (1989), 'Male–Female Wage Differentials and Policy Responses', *Journal of Economic Literature*, **XXVII**, March, 46–72.

Basil Blackwell Ltd for articles: F.Y. Edgeworth (1923), 'Women's Wages in Relation to Economic Welfare', *Economic Journal*, **33**, December, 487–95; Gary S. Becker (1965), 'A Theory of the Allocation of Time', *Economic Journal*, **LXXV** (299), September, 493–517; R. Layard, M. Barton and A. Zabalza (1980), 'Married Women's Participation and Hours', *Economica*, **47** (185), February, 51–72; Robert E. Wright and John F. Ermisch (1991), 'Gender Discrimination in the British Labour Market: A Reassessment', *Economic Journal*, **101** (406), May, 508–21.

Cambridge University Press for article: Julie A. Nelson (1992), 'Gender, Metaphor, and the Definition of Economics', *Economics and Philosophy*, **8** (1), April, 103–25.

Eastern Economic Association for article: Barbara R. Bergmann (1974), 'Occupational Segregation, Wages and Profits when Employers Discriminate by Race or Sex', **1** (2/3), April/July, 103–10.

Elsevier Science Publishers BV for article: William G. Shepherd and Sharon G. Levin (1973), 'Managerial Discrimination in Large Firms', *Review of Economics and Statistics*, **LX** (4), November, 412–22.

Frances R. Woolley for her own article: (1993), 'The Feminist Challenge to Neoclassical Economics', *Cambridge Journal of Economics*, **17**, 485–500.

Industrial and Labor Relations Review for article: Henry Sanborn (1964), 'Pay Differences between Men and Women', *Industrial and Labor Relations Review*, **17** (4), July, 534–50; Dennis J. Aigner and Glen G. Cain (1977), 'Statistical Theories of Discrimination in Labor Markets', *Industrial and Labor Relations Review*, **30** (2), January, 175–87; Marianne A. Ferber and Helen M. Lowry (1976), 'The Sex Differential in Earnings: A Reappraisal', *Industrial and Labor Relations Review*, **29**, April, 377–87.

International Labour Office for article: Christine Craig, Elizabeth Garnsey and Jill Rubery (1985), 'Labour Market Segmentation and Women's Employment: A Case-Study from the United Kingdom', *International Labour Review*, **124** (3), May–June, 267–80.

Macmillan Publishing Company for article: Gary S. Becker (1968), 'Discrimination, Economic', *International Encyclopedia of the Social Sciences*, **4**, 208–10.

M E Sharpe Inc. Publishers for article: Mary E. Corcoran and Paul N. Courant (1987), 'Sex-Role Socialization and Occupational Segregation: An Exploratory Investigation', *Journal of Post Keynesian Economics*, **IX** (3), Spring, 330–46.

National Bureau of Economic Research for article: Jacob Mincer (1962), 'Labor Force Participation of Married Women: A Study of Labor Supply', in H.G. Lewis (ed.), *Aspects of Labor Economics*, 63–105.

Transaction Publishers for article: Paula England (1989), 'A Feminist Critique of Rational-Choice Theories: Implications for Sociology', *The American Sociologist*, **20** (1), Spring, 14–28.

University of Chicago Press for articles: Jacob Mincer and Solomon Polachek (1974), 'Family Investments in Human Capital: Earnings of Women', *Journal of Political Economy*, **82** (2), S76–S108; Heidi I. Hartmann (1981), 'The Family as the Locus of Gender, Class, and Political Struggle: The Example of Housework', *Signs: Journal of Women in Culture and Society*, **6** (3), Spring, 366–94; Gary S. Becker (1985), 'Human Capital, Effort, and the Sexual Division of Labor', *Journal of Labor Economics*, **3** (1), January, Supplement, S33–S58; Heather E. Joshi, Richard Layard and Susan J. Owen (1985), 'Why are more Women Working in Britain?', *Journal of Labor Economics*, **3** (1), January, Supplement, S147–S76; Nancy Folbre (1991), 'The Unproductive Housewife: Her Evolution in Nineteenth-Century Economic Thought', *Signs: Journal of Women in Culture and Society*, **16** (3), Spring, 463–84.

University of Wisconsin Press for articles: Andrea H. Beller (1982), 'Occupational Segregation by Sex: Determinants and Changes', *Journal of Human Resources*, **XVII** (3), Summer, 371–92; Paula England (1982), 'The Failure of Human Capital Theory to Explain Occupational Sex Segregation', *Journal of Human Resources*, **XVII** (3), Summer, 358–70.

Work, Employment & Society for articles: Sara Horrell, Jill Rubery and Brendan Burchell (1990), 'Gender and Skills', *Work, Employment and Society*, **4** (2), June, 189–216.

In addition the publishers wish to thank the Library of the London School of Economics and Political Science, the Marshall Library of Economics, Cambridge University and the Photographic Unit of the University of London Library for their assistance in obtaining these articles.

Introduction

Economics without gender is like *Hamlet* without Ophelia. Now Ophelia is an important character in the play. She familiarizes us with a woman's experience of the medieval Danish court. She broadens our vision because she sees the events of sixteenth-century domestic homicide from a distinct perspective and understands them differently. While our hero, the Prince, knows only through fact and logic (indeed this could be said to be his downfall), Ophelia reasons with metaphor and story. She represents 'feminine' ways of knowing: through intuition, emotion and a holistic vision. But she is not central to the main plot. And the same could be said of gender to economics.

Economics has been socially constructed. The agents involved have been mainly men. Women have been notably absent as researchers, and issues to do with women have been neglected as the subject-matter of research. The significant exceptions, the New Household Economics, women's labour supply and male–female pay differentials, are discussed extensively below. Most economists agree with this liberal feminist critique of economics and endorse an affirmative action response. Here the problem is the underrepresentation of women and not necessarily anything to do with the way economics is done. The policy prescription is for a professional pressure group to monitor gender proportions and encourage women to become economists. The increasing representation of women will carry with it a broadening of the empirical domain of economics to include more topics relevant to women as the new recruits work on issues they see as important. Advocates of affirmative action within economics can point to patchy growth in the proportions of women (Committee on the Status of Women in the Economics Profession, 1990), and a new level of attention to women-orientated issues such as the family (see Pollak, 1985). But affirmative action carries with it no necessary challenge to the methodology of mainstream economics.

Yet from the outset feminists expressed reservations about the work of neoclassical economists when their attention *did* turn to gender issues and the family. All too often this work seemed to rationalize and reinforce traditional gender stereotypes (for surveys see: Amsden, 1980; Blau and Ferber, 1986; Ferber and Nelson, 1993). Feminists traced their dissatisfaction to economists' neglect of the sources of preferences (Sawhill, 1977; Woolley, 1993, and Chapter 1), their failure to understand the particular constraints which women faced (Bergmann, 1987; Boserup, 1987), and their gendered concept of rationality (England, 1989, and Chapter 3; Nelson, 1992 and Chapter 2; and Feiner and Roberts, 1990). These criticisms went beyond worries about the representation of women in the profession. Drawing on feminist criticism of other disciplines, particularly the natural sciences (Harding, 1986), feminist critics detected male bias in the way that topics were approached and in the inter-pretation of results. They began to question the neutrality and objectivity of researchers.

Several remedial strategies have been proposed. The first involves the self-conscious intro-duction and highlighting of women's experience: a feminist standpoint. Feminist-standpoint epistemology is not simply intended to reach a better understanding of 'marginal lives' but to use this perspective in order to explain the whole social order (Harding, 1992a, 1992b).

The second involves an evermore determined pursuit of neutrality and objectivity as traditionally understood: a feminist empiricism. The biases of the discipline can be eliminated by an even stricter adherence to the alleged methodological norms of scientific inquiry. More dispassion, less involvement, a *purer* scientific approach will purge andocentrism.

These strategies alone are not enough for yet other critics who have gone so far as to charge that gender bias is not incidental to their enterprise, caused by bad practice and flawed objectivity, but that it is embedded in what has been embraced as good practice and 'scientific detachment'. These deeper feminist critiques branch off in different directions. But they share common ground. Postmodernism has had a heavy influence by its exposure of the artifice inherent in categories such as 'nature' and 'gender', by its understanding of the multiple determinants that figure in a person's identity, and, by its dismantling of binary thinking (Poovey, 1988). In other fields feminist criticism at this level has long been acknowledged and solutions to gender bias sought. In economics feminist revisionism has been laggard. Why?

The answer lies in the uncompromising attachment economists have to their methodology. Economics is peculiar among the empirical sciences in being defined by an approach, a way of looking at the world, rather than by a subject matter. Economists practise by applying constrained maximization in models peopled by rational, calculating, self-interested individuals. This *methodological* definition of economics has had significant implications for the development of feminist and other criticisms. It makes economists particularly reluctant to admit dissent which challenges their approach, for this would threaten a methodological unravelling that would leave them naked in the world. Moreover economics remains doggedly (though usually implicitly) Popperian. The idea of data representing an independent reality unrelated to the theories is still widely accepted. Feminist critiques which focus on the role of language and gender metaphor, and seek progress through the deconstruction of hierarchical dualisms which structure the discipline and the world, seem exotic and irrelevant. Recently, however, feminist critics have found allies in critics with different origins but similar revisionist designs on mainstream methodology. Progress is slow but there have been significant developments. Feminists have seen the appearance of several important articles, some reproduced below, the publication of a collection of essays covering a variety of feminist critiques (Ferber and Nelson, 1993), the organization of a conference exclusively devoted to feminist perspectives on economic theory ('Out of the Margin: Feminist Perspectives on Economic Theory', held in Amsterdam, 2–5 June 1993), and plans for the appearance of a journal devoted to feminist economics. In the present collection the reader is thrown immediately into this debate in the first section of readings.

Frances Woolley's lead-off essay (Chapter 1) describes a feminist empiricist response to neoclassical economics. She details a three-point feminist agenda: to document differences in the well-being of men and women; to advocate policies which promote equity; and to conduct research free of andocentric bias. The first target is the closest to being achieved. There is a large body of evidence suggesting that in terms of income, household sharing and hours worked, women, on average, are disadvantaged. Relevant articles have been published in major journals, and their findings incorporated into the corpus of widely shared views which constitute economic 'knowledge' (Chapters 11–27).

Where feminist economics encounters less support is in advocation of policies which promote equity. The obstacle here is that policy prescription derives not from the documentation of gender inequality but from the analysis of its causes. Economists have not reached agreement as to causation, and, as Woolley shows, feminists interested in anything more than a superficial analysis of causation are led to challenge the axiomatic foundations of their discipline.

Woolley sketches three well-known models of explanation of male–female earnings differentials: discriminating tastes; statistical discrimination; and error discrimination. Discriminating tastes, despite doubts about its compatibility with competitive markets, is the longest standing explanation. Clearly 'tastes' can be only an intermediate variable in any feminist analysis. Feminists are drawn to ask how such discriminating tastes originated and are reproduced. In seeing the formation of tastes as part of the economic project they join forces with other critics of neoclassical economics to question the core assumption of stable preferences.

On the other hand, statistical discrimination can only accommodate behaviour which is, on average, correct, and so seems inconsistent with empirical analyses which persistently find some part of the male–female wage differential 'unexplained' by individual character- istics commonly associated with productivity. This has led feminists to postulate the importance of 'error discrimination' whereby agents mistakenly overestimate the differences between an average man and an average woman. While consistent with the empirical evidence, error discrimination again leads feminists to question a basic and useful assumption of orthodox economics: the assumption of individual rationality and its identification with the avoidance of systematic mistakes.

Andocentric bias is also evident in terms of the choice of stylized facts from which to develop models, the abstract representations of the world with which economists work, and the way in which orthodox models and measurements often omit women. Thus feminist economists must correct mistaken stylized facts, incorporate both men and women into economic analysis, ascertain what shapes the institutions which privilege men or disadvantage women, and develop a better economic model of caring, as well as endogenize preferences and recognize that people make systematic mistakes. Feminist revisionism involves the modification of basic assumptions, the inclusion of some variables traditionally neglected, and the self-conscious incorporation of women into analyses which have been too male-orientated. Is this possible within neoclassical economic theory and is it enough? Woolley seems to think so (see also Ferber and Teiman, 1981). But other feminists are beginning to doubt whether a patched-up neoclassical economics will ever serve their purposes (Sap, Cuelenaere and Schreurs, 1993).

Paula England's essay (Chapter 3) sets out a feminist critique of rational choice theory. She begins with four assumptions common to neoclassical theory: selfishness; the impossibility of interpersonal comparisons of utility; the exogeneity and stability of tastes; and rationality. These assumptions, she argues, flow from a separative model of human nature, a model which has been a focus of feminist criticism in other disciplines. A separative self contrasts with a self that is emotionally connected to others. Emotional connections and the skill and work involved in maintaining them are seen as feminine. Rational economic man is not merely generically masculine but displays a masculinized selfhood. Thus both the assumptions and the separative selfhood with which they harmonize are not gender neutral.

The separation/connection dualism is not only gendered but hierarchical. The elevation of separation and therefore masculinity and the deprecation of connection and therefore femininity, and the distorted view of women and their experience that this produces, is seen in political theory, developmental psychology, science and the philosophy of science. The feminist critique is of both the claim that all selves are unconnected and the endorsement of the separative self as more valued. So although the asymmetry in men being separative and women emphasizing connection contributes to women's subordination, this cannot be corrected by elevating the separative self for both men and women. Instead connection must be valued for both.

To the extent that a separative-self model more accurately describes men than women, the neoclassical assumptions are masculinized and not universally applicable. To challenge the assumption of rationality, England extends the critique of separativeness from separation between individuals to polar separations between human qualities and so reaches the feminist postmodern opposition to misleading dualisms like reason *vs.* emotion and its offshoot within neoclassical economics – rationality *vs.* tastes. The problem is that although breaking down this false dichotomy might well promote a more realistic comingling of cognition and emotion, it changes the meaning of rationality and introduces a new level of indeterminacy into conventional economic analysis. Readers must decide for themselves whether or not this improves economic theory.

Recent pioneering efforts to establish the importance of language and metaphor within economics (McCloskey, 1983; McCloskey, 1985; Klamer, McCloskey and Solow, 1988) make room for Julie Nelson's critique of the masculinized ways of reasoning, definition of rationality and specification of subject matter characteristic of neoclassical economics (Chapter 2). Drawing on feminist analysis of science, Nelson argues that the definition and properties of economics have been intertwined with those of gender. Well-known hierarchical dualisms, mind *vs.* nature, reason *vs.* emotion, objectivity *vs.* subjectivity, figure importantly in the intellectual structure of economics and in the cultural understanding of gender. Economics has been socially constructed as hard, logical, scientific and precise, as it has been constructed as masculine. As long as masculinity is associated with superiority, the idea that economics could be improved by becoming more 'feminine' makes little sense. But orthogonal gender and value dimensions identify what has been excluded from economics by the concentration on masculinity and reveal its worth. For example, reasoning in economics is identified with formal logic, mathematics and masculinity. A simple dualism collapses other forms of reasoning into 'illogic'. But a more sophisticated view might complement logic with 'feminine' ways of reasoning such as by analogy or by pattern recognition, and recognize a masculine-negative dimension in terms of (say) a sterile and impoverished formalism. To confine reasoning to formal logic alone, a Cartesian masculinization of thought, reduces economics. More generally the admission of feminine ways of knowing would make economics more flexible, intuitive, humanistic and rich (see also McCloskey, 1993).

The expanded metaphor for gender and value is also applied to the concept of rational economic man. The conception of human nature here is of an individual radically separate from other human beings and from nature. Nelson, like England, focuses on the significance of gender in the privileging of separation over connection. Again the masculine-positive/ feminine-negative metaphor (here say individuated/embedded) has its orthogonal dimension of masculine-negative/feminine-positive (here say isolated/connected). A feminist economics requires the central character be changed from the autonomous, isolated agent who needs no social contacts to a socially and materially situated human being.

Changes in the ways of reasoning and in the conception of individual agency promote changes also in the definition of economics in terms of its subject matter, currently dominated by the concept of the market. A feminist economics would broaden out to concern itself more with concrete issues of provisioning and less with abstract analyses of hypothetical choice. This seems to coincide with Woolley's plea for a more realistic and inclusive economics which includes a less masculinized model of human behaviour and a broader empirical domain. Whereas tampering with the assumptions and broadening the focus of economics may well be tolerated, Nelson's demand that economics break free of positivism and admit as legitimate 'feminine' ways of reasoning, although sharing a ground with other (not necessarily feminist) critics of mainstream methodology, may be less easily forborne. The reasons are clear from Nelson's own work. Economics is not well-defined by its subject matter. Markets may be identified everywhere and anywhere. What has distinguished economics has been its *method* which is exactly the target of Nelson's attack. Economics may be improved by an exploration of feminine ways of knowing and being, and the excising of masculine perversions of scholarly method, but the methodological readjustment which this involves is very threatening in a discipline defined by its masculine method. As Nelson notes, 'nobody wants to be called a sissy' (Chapter 2, p. 36). Hamlet could have learned from Ophelia's ways of knowing but he was too much of a hero.

In Part II, we turn from the recent feminist critiques of contemporary neoclassical theory, to trace the development of gender analyses and andocentric bias in the history of economic thought. Michèle Pujol (1984 and Chapter 4) searches Marshall's *Principles of Economics* to piece together his views on women and show how they impacted the structure of neoclassical theory, while Nancy Folbre (1991 and Chapter 5) exposes the fundamental influence of gender bias on the construction of data in terms of the treatment of women in national censuses. Edgeworth, a founding father of modern neoclassical economics, is allowed to speak for himself through one of his several articles on women's wages (1923 and Chapter 6).

Marshallian economics introduced many of the hallmark characteristics of neoclassicism. It was positivist and sciential: characteristics which rested on the measurability of economic phenomena by the use of money in economic transactions and on the logic and precision which marginalism promised. The key assumption of individualistic rational economic decision making via marginalism brought new legitimation to market processes by establishing their outcomes as optimal in welfare terms. Pujol shows that Marshall repeatedly failed to live up to the scientific canons of methodological positivism. Far from being a detached, objective researcher testing the predictions of his newly determinate theories, Marshall, in his treatment of women and gender issues, was prejudiced and unscientific. Time and time again he presents opinions reflecting the gender stereotypes of the late Victorian upper class without even cursory empirical validation.

Yet what is astounding is not only the way in which Marshall falls away from detachment and objectivity, but the extent of Marshall's concern with gender issues. Remember this essay is based not on work specifically concerned with gender such as equal pay or family wages, but on Marshall's reflections on these issues within his major theoretical contribution. What contemporary exposition of the *principles* of economics would contain so much commentary on such issues? Marshall's definition of economics seems more consistent with the ideas of the feminist critics discussed above than with the methodological definition common today.

Marshall's treatment of women incorporated hierarchical conceptions of gender into economic theory. In particular it contributed to the invisibility of women. Turning this around, the gender-biased political economy then became a cultural production through which nineteenth-century men and women made sense of their experiences. The nineteenth century has been understood as the period associated with the domestication of women, that is, the creation of a separate sphere of feminine influence and importance in the home, and indeed the definition of womenhood in these terms (Davidoff and Hall, 1987). Marshall's political economy was not only influenced by these images and ideas but it contributed to them. Political economy was not only made by gendered subjects but it made gendered subjects.

Nancy Folbre's essay (Chapter 5) again links the feminist critique with an attack on positivism. Census data appear as objective and value free. But census categories, which mould and structure the statistical information, embody contemporary cultural and political values. Folbre's example is the statistical construction of the unproductive housewife in successive nineteenth-century censuses in both the USA and Great Britain, which she sees as harmonizing with the cult of domesticity, and Trade Unionists' campaigns for a family wage, and with the (gender biased) definitions of productive work and dependence emerging in contemporary political economy (enter Marshall again!). Folbre's view is unique in highlighting the politics surrounding the emerging gendered categories and complements existing work exposing the biased stories which emerge from a naive interpretation of the unreconstructed data (Higgs, 1987; Folbre and Abel, 1989; Horrell and Humphries, 1994). Here too notice the historical dialectic involved in the emergence of gender: gender roles were one of the important influences on census designers but their categories in turn exerted widespread direct and indirect influence on peoples' self-understanding and behaviour, in turn producing and reproducing gendered identities.

In his 1923 article on women's wages, Francis Edgeworth (Chapter 6) does not so much fail to follow his discipline's established procedures to produce gender-biased results, as revolt against the results that he does obtain from his 'good science by existing standards' (see Harding, 1993). In an earlier paper (1922) Edgeworth, captured by the logic of the competitive model, had argued in favour of reducing the cultural and social constraints on the operation of the labour market which he argued would eliminate pay differentials and maximize wealth. A year later he hedges his position. He appeals to the different family circumstances of men and women to justify arrangements which support wage differentials. He argues that the infringements of free competition involved are so minor that the resulting welfare loss would be negligible. His main point is to use the new techniques of marginalism to deduce that for any total quantity of work, given women are comparatively weak, the disutility minimizing allocation of work should involve a smaller burden for women. None of this is good science by existing standards though the last point is dressed up to be. Indeed Edgeworth remains committed to greater freedom of competition though not on such a scale as to change wage relativities of single women and married men to the detriment of families. Combination and regulation are usually seen as metaphorical manacles on the workings of the market, but in this instance they 'gentle that jostle of competition' (Chapter 6, p. 104). Edgeworth's final policy recommendation is feminist friendly by the standards of the times: some labour market liberalization and family allowances payable to mothers. The idea that it is anything other than a political position is patently false.

Part III brings us to more familiar ground. The articles reproduced here represent milestones in neoclassical economists' treatments of gender-related issues: the family, household production and paid work (for surveys see Amsden, 1980; Blau and Ferber, 1986; Dex, 1985).

Economists' interests in topics such as the use of time and goods within the family, marriage and divorce, and fertility, date from the mid-1960s and were heavily influenced by the development of human capital theory and the theory of the allocation of time between alternative uses (see, Becker, 1965 and Chapter 7). The New Household Economics established a formal framework to analyse households' combination of time and purchased goods to produce outputs which yield utility. The New Household Economics was not new in terms of its approach or method. The novelty lay in the domain: the application of standard microeconomics to choices made within the household. What might be understood as a broadening of economics, in terms of its subject matter, ironically involved a narrowing in terms of the identification of economics with a *method*: the use of constrained maximization to analyse choice in conditions of scarcity. The dissatisfaction feminists subsequently felt with economic theory was only reinforced (Strassman, 1993).

But at least the approach highlighted the importance of households as the relevant unit of decision making with significant implications for the analysis of labour supply. A series of applications of the New Household Economics can be found in Levy-Garboua (1979) and Gronau (1973) and a review in Joseph (1983). Kahne and Kohen (1975) discuss the implications of the New Household Economics for women.

From the tentative sketch of the implications of the scarcity of time within a household production model for the division of labour in families included in 'A Theory of the Allocation of Time' (1965 and Chapter 7), Gary Becker went on to develop a fully fledged economic theory of marriage (Becker, 1973, 1974). The first problem was to explain the existence of marriage as an institution. People marry because by so doing they increase their welfare. The gain from marriage, compared with remaining single, is positively related to the incomes of the two individuals, to the difference in their wage rates, and to the level of non-market productivity enhancing variables such as beauty. The gains from marriage are greater the more complementary are the inputs of husband and wife. Complementarity is acute in the case of children; so the gains from marriage are positively related to the importance of children. Divorce can be handled symmetrically. Marriage-specific capital which increases productivity within the household but is worthless if the particular marriage dissolves, stabilizes marriage and reduces the risk of investment in further marriage-specific capital (Becker, Landes and Michael, 1977; Becker, 1981). Childen are the archetypal marriage-specific investment, though Becker, Landes and Michael (1977) also regard working in the home as in this category.

What of the division of labour in these economically constituted families? Marriage, according to one of the most widely quoted phrases in economics, is conceptualized as 'a two person firm with either member being the "entrepreneur" who "hires" the other' (Becker, 1974). Specialization in market or household activities is an efficient outcome of the allocation of time by family members but the theory cannot of itself explain why women specialize in domestic labour and men in paid work. The form that specialization takes is in turn explained by comparative advantage. But the gendered outcomes require gendered comparative advantage. Then either the argument is circular, women hire men as breadwinners because they earn more, while women earn less because they opt out of market work to rear children, or it relies on women's comparative advantage in childrearing following from their biological (absolute) advantage in childbearing. The result is biological determinism disguised as economic analysis: pregnancy is a prior investment which gives women a greater stake in their children and encourages further investment (Becker, 1981; for objections here see Humphries, 1982).

More recently, Becker (1985, and Chapter 9) has turned to other factors to ensure the consistency of his model with the gendered division of labour characteristic of the real world. Again the starting point is 'intrinsically identical household members' (Chapter 9, p. 155). Once the traditional division of labour is adopted, and Becker is deliberately vague about why this occurs (perhaps because of high fertility, or even because of discrimination against women which reduces their relative market earnings), increasing returns to specialized human capital becomes a powerful force maintaining and exaggerating the division of labour. Moreover since housework is more labour intensive than leisure, given again an initial division of labour and a fixed amount of total effort available, married women spend less energy on each hour of market work than married men working the same number of hours. As a result they have lower hourly earnings and will not only work less than they would have otherwise but will reduce their investment in market capital even when they work the same number of hours as married men.

In either vintage of explanation, comparative advantage is deduced from the existing sexual division of labour and then used to explain that division. Most critics have agreed that despite its claims to use one behavioural principle to explain all human activity, the New Household Economics does little more than describe the *status quo* in a society where sex roles are given (Bell, 1974; Ferber and Birnbaum, 1977; Sawhill, 1977; Humphries and Rubery, 1984; Dex, 1985).

Another theoretical problem for the New Household Economics, is in the idea of *household decision making*. The difficulty involved in aggregating individual preferences into a collective preference ordering has been widely discussed in economic theory (Arrow, 1951). The aggregation of family members' preferences into a household ordering poses the same problem on a smaller scale, and bedevils all analyses which posit a household decision maker (see below p. xxi). Early references cut through this problem by simply postulating a family social welfare function (Samuelson, 1956). But Becker, explicitly concerned with allocation and distribution within the family, developed an alternative 'altruist model' (1981). A household is understood to contain one 'altruistic' member whose preferences reflect concern with the welfare of the others. Purely selfish but rational family members will then behave altruistically too ('the Rotten Kid Theorem') and the intrafamily allocation will be the one which reflects the altruist's utility function subject to the family's resource constraints. Becker concludes that individual differences can be ignored and the family treated as a single harmonious unit with consistent preferences, those of the altruist. But this result is *deduced* not *asserted* as in the older approach (see Pollak, 1985 and Chapter 8; and for doubts about the argument see Manser and Brown, 1980).

Although simple, this solution fails to live up to the accepted norms of scientific inquiry which would require discussion of the criteria most appropriate for aggregating preferences: the feminist empiricist point again. The dichotomous assumptions of perfect selfishness in the marketplace and perfect altruism in the home, go back, of course, to Adam Smith (1776) and are only formally elaborated in Becker (1981). But feminist unease with economists' model of human agency is surely exacerbated by this bifurcation of behavioural norms: all altruism in the family; all selfishness in the marketplace (Strassman, 1993). Not surprisingly feminists have suspected masculine self-interest as underlying the traditional acceptance of this model (Folbre and Hartmann, 1988). What is most objectionable is the way in which the model debars from the discussion issues of power and control, issues that alternative bargaining approaches, which explicitly embed the problems of intrafamily allocation and distribution in a game-theoretic context, promise to highlight.

Robert Pollak's article (1985 and Chapter 8) compares the New Household Economics with such alternative approaches, while simultaneously locating the analysis of the family in the new institutional economics. The latter highlights the importance, obfuscated in the New Household Economics, of studying the internal organization of families as a governance structure for economic activities. Initially developed to understand the emergence of hierarchy in the firm, transaction–cost models are readily adapted to explain the existence and stability of marriage. Complex, continuing relationships are difficult to govern via contracts, hence agents resort to a more complete form of integration. Marriage is just such an institution: 'flexible enough to allow adaptive, sequential decisionmaking in the face of unfolding events and rigid enough to safeguard each spouse against opportunistic exploitation by the other' (Chapter 8, p. 139).

Bargaining models abandon the concept of a joint preference ordering and model household decisions as a result of intra-family bargaining (Manser and Brown, 1980; McElroy and Horney, 1981; Pollak, 1985, reproduced in this volume; Lundberg and Pollak, 1992). Formal game-theoretic models and non-formalized bargaining frameworks have been applied to a range of household issues, including topics such as domestic violence, fertility decisions, divorce, divorce settlements, dowry and excess female mortality, but the most common is the allocation and distribution within the family.

In the altruist model allocations within households are determined by total income not the contributions of individuals; in bargaining models and the transaction–cost approach, the allocation depends systematically on the wealth, income and earning power of individual family members as well as on their sum. Empirical tests of altruistic versus other models of household decision making can be developed on the basis of whether individual alternatives influence allocations. But direct econometric implementation of any model of allocation depends on identifying and measuring goods and activities desired by one partner but not the other. While difficult this has not proved impossible (for example see, Klasen, 1993). Moreover as Pollak notes, indirect testing which focuses on the implications of the transaction–cost approach for marital instability, labour force participation, or other variables for which data is readily available, is possible. Nor does empirical work have to be econometric and quantitative (Pollak, 1985 and Chapter 8).

The problems which remain are not just in rendering the alternative models amenable to empirical testing. One-period games are clearly inappropriate for analysing the ongoing interaction and decision making families undertake. But both the multi-period bargaining models and the more general transaction–cost approach seem to require a sacrifice in determinacy: 'one in effect abandons the sharp testable implications of . . . [the conventional model] . . . without necessarily putting alternative clearcut predictions in their place' (Killingsworth and Heckman, 1986). Moreover the technical characteristics of game theory and the constraints they impose may well limit the insights about gender relations inside and outside the family that this approach can produce (Seiz, 1991). The looser framework imposed by the transaction–cost approach may be preferred by feminists anxious, for example, to integrate institutional and cultural variables into their analyses (see Woolley, 1993 and Chapter 1). A bigger question for feminists is whether the way forward is to pursue analysis of power relations within the household using models of this kind, or to use structural models in which men as a socioeconomic group oppress women. An example is patriarchy theory which combines men's oppression of women with a historically specific form of economic organization to explain gender divisions.

Although its influence on mainstream economics has been only marginal, patriarchy theory has had a major impact in related disciplines such as sociology and history (recent surveys include Walby, 1986; Fine, 1992; Charles, 1993). Much debate has concerned the precise nature of the structural relationship between patriarchal social relations and the economy (Humphries and Rubery, 1984). Hartmann (1979) provides an influential account suggesting that patriarchy exists in articulation with capitalism and that men have organized to ensure that they maintain patriarchal power within the workforce and the home. The essay reproduced here (Hartmann, 1981 and Chapter 10) links this interpretation to an older feminist theme: that women's responsibility for unpaid domestic labour is the key to their oppression (for a recent summary of the 'domestic labour debate' see Fine, 1992). The gendered division of labour in the household is not the rational and neutral outcome of an ahistorical comparative advantage but a manifestation of male power in a form functional for the reproduction of the capitalist system. Unpaid domestic workers provide crucial services less expensively than could the state or private enterprise. But the status and nature of this work both denigrates the women who undertake it and handicaps them in their pursuit of paid employment. Housework is a source of conflict between men and women and its potential for generating discord has increased historically as women's entry into paid work has not been accompanied by a parallel reallocation of work in the home.

Heidi Hartmann's paper (Chapter 10) represents an attempt in the feminist standpoint tradition to unravel the complex relationships between capital and labour and between men and women beginning from housework, that onerous but 'marginal' activity of 'marginal lives'. In so doing it inverts social scientists' emphasis on the home as the domain of altruism by underlining its potential as the site for exploitation and conflict. The relative openness of structural analysis may prove attractive to feminists disillusioned with the restrictions of neoclassical economics. The same openness has also proved frustrating to authors unable to establish a hierarchy of determinations in the articulation of patriarchy and capitalism (Humphries and Rubery, 1984).

There is a considerable literature in neoclassical economics on female labour supply (for recent surveys see: Killingsworth, 1983; Joseph, 1983; Dex, 1985; Killingsworth and Heckman, 1986; Dex, 1988; Fallon and Verry, 1988). Significantly economists' emphasis on the distinction between paid and unpaid work is at odds with feminist claims that the distinction is blurred and artificial and that the two types of work are interrelated (Dex, 1988). In the traditional ungendered analysis, labour supply, in terms of hours of work, is derived from an individual's rational allocation of his time between work which via wages and consumption affords utility, and leisure, which is deemed directly rewarding, in a way which maximizes happiness. The analysis involves time, as the ultimate scarce resource (24 hours in the day), and the individual's preferences for goods versus leisure, a subjective trade-off which has to be brought into line with the market rate of exchange which depends on wage rates and goods prices. At an optimum the individual cannot increase his happiness by a marginal reallocation of time (unless prices or his preferences change). The optimum can be characterized by equality between the ratio of relative utilities and relative prices. Labour supply depends on the wage rate, non-labour income and product prices. Particular attention was paid to decomposing the effects of a change in the net wage on hours worked into an income and a substitution effect. In addition to the simple comparative statics of changes in wage rates, goods prices, even preferences, the model can be extended to look at the effects of unearned income, taxes on earnings, transfers, etc.

The model is easily converted into linear form to be tested empirically. Early empirical work on men's labour supply functions (reviewed in Cain and Watts, 1973) found, as theory suggested, that men's hours of work depended on wage rates, unearned income and proxies for personal tastes such as marital status, although the elasticity estimates varied widely and even by sign in the case of the own wage elasticity.

The basic model has been extended in several ways (Killingsworth and Heckman, 1986; Fallon and Verry, 1988). What is seldom appreciated is that several significant extensions originated in attempts to make the model a more reasonable representation of *women's* labour supply. Realism is obtained through a feminist standpoint.

First, it was recognized that labour supply decisions are often not taken on an individual basis but where there is interdependence between individuals' decisions, in particular, labour supply is often determined by family decision making. Thus analysts of labour supply were forced to confront the problems of modelling family decision making discussed above. Various approaches have been tried. One approach assumes a common utility function; another specifies separate utility functions for the spouses, each function defined over common consumption and leisure (Leuthold, 1968); and more complex models introduce the husband's leisure into the wife's utility function and *vice versa*, and allow for some private consumption (Ashworth and Ulph, 1981). Generality is only obtained at the price of greatly increased complexity. The specification of the utility function to be maximized was shown to be a crucial factor in determining the analytical results (Fallon and Verry, 1988). Bargaining models can also be used to analyse labour supply and commodity demand (McElroy and Horney, 1981).

Second, the model was extended by abandoning the assumption that time is used either for paid work or for leisure. When other time uses and different time intensities of different utility-yielding activities are included, a richer set of implications can be drawn (Gronau, 1977). The relative productivities of home and market time become an important determinant of labour supply, though the source of any systematic gender variation in relative productivities is beyond the scope of the model. In terms of both extensions it is easy to see how the analysis of labour supply was influenced by the theory of the allocation of time and the New Household Economics.

Early empirical work on female labour supply was conducted within the basic model described above. The elasticity estimates reported varied even more widely than did those emerging from the work on male participation (Killingsworth, 1983). On the whole the labour supply elasticities were greater than those of men which economists explained in terms of women's marginal productivity in the home being less sensitive to hours spent in domestic work than is the case with men.

Jacob Mincer's article (1962 and Chapter 11) represents a milestone in the empirical analysis of female labour supply. Mincer recognized that married women's choice was not between paid work and leisure but included a third option: work in the home. Mincer's analysis also includes variables which stand for allegedly exogenous tastes. But completion of high school education, for example, could just as well be a response to market opportunities as an independent event.

Mincer was motivated to study married women's participation by a seeming contradiction between cross-section analyses and historic trends in female participation rates. Cross-section studies showed an inverse relationship between husbands' income and wives' participation; time series implied a positive relation. Mincer argued that in addition to her husband's earnings a wife's own potential wage rate would influence her time allocation. Ecological regressions of labour force participation rates of married women across a sample of the 57 largest standard metropolitan areas showed that although the effect of husbands' incomes was negative as theoretically expected, the effect of wives' earnings power was positive and indeed stronger than the effect of income. Though not directly applicable to changes over time, Mincer found these results suggestive in terms of the historical changes. The apparent contradiction was partly resolved by projecting the dominance of the own-wage effect over time. Increasing take-home pay for married women in the twentieth century had attracted them into paid employment as it raised the opportunity costs of both leisure and homework.

Innovative as it was, Mincer's model was constrained by the static framework of analysis endemic to the approach. Cross-section studies do not provide a full explanation of the large increases in married women's activity rates observed in almost all advanced industrial economies since the 1950s (see Layard, Barton and Zabalza, 1980, and Chapter 12). Historical changes which cannot be satisfactorily simulated in cross-section, also contribute to the explanation (Joshi, Layard and Owen, 1985, and Chapter 13). Most studies mention a long list of such factors including: changes in attitudes towards married women working, increased availability of and decline in the relative price of substitutes for labour in the home, increased availability of non-familial child care and falling fertility. It is difficult to know whether these are genuinely independent events or are themselves, at least in part, the result of married women's increasing attachment to the labour force (Humphries and Rubery, 1984; Fallon and Verry, 1988). Time series studies are in principle capable of exploring these issues, but are less common than cross-section analyses because of the difficulties involved in securing high-quality historical data.

Labour supply estimation has been refined considerably since these 'first generation' models (Heckman, Killingsworth and MaCurdy, 1981). Indeed labour supply analysis has been a testing ground for new model specifications and econometric techniques. Again what has gone unnoticed in the reviews is the way that several of the most important changes have resulted from a consideration of women's labour supply functions (but see Dex, 1985). One major development stemmed from the view of labour supply decisions as joint decisions made in households and influenced by family circumstances. Household-structure variables as proxies for personal preferences are now routinely included in analyses (Greenhalgh and Mayhew, 1981). Another set of developments are associated with corrections for sample selection bias, a particular problem for the estimation of married women's labour supply ignored in first generation work.

Many early econometric studies of female labour supply specified the labour supply function as a linear equation with one wage, family income and a vector of other (demographic) variables as the independent variables and hours of work as the dependent variable. But how were non-workers to be treated in analyses of hours? One early approach was simply to exclude non-workers. Observations are then systematically not randomly omitted; the error distribution in the sample will differ from that in the population and the estimates will be biased (Fallon and Verry, 1988; Layard, Barton and Zabalza, 1980, and Chapter 12; Killingsworth and Heckman, 1986). Another approach was to include non-workers with their hours set at zero. This implicitly assumes, however, that for non-participants the wage is equal to their subjective trade-off of leisure for goods at zero hours. For most non-participants the reservation wage likely exceeds the real wage, in which case labour supply will be completely insensitive to small changes in wages, exogenous income, or indeed anything else (Killingsworth and Heckman, 1986). In addition to this specification problem, including non-workers raises a measurement difficulty which is also relevant to the analysis of participation. How are the wages of non-participants to be imputed? The usual procedure involved predicting the wages of non-participants from those of participants assuming that wages and potential wages are systematically related to the productivity enhancing characteristics of workers as in a human capital model. Women who participate are likely to have different unmeasured characteristics from those not in the labour force. If the correlation between the measured and unmeasured characteristics differs between the two groups another sample selection bias enters. It is widely held that the unmeasured characteristics which cause a woman to have higher potential earnings also make it more likely she participates. Heckman (1974; 1976) provided statistical procedures for correcting for such bias. More generally a second generation of studies emerged which viewed the decision to participate or not and the supply of hours if participating as interrelated aspects of labour supply, both the result of maximizing the same preferences subject to the same constraints (for a description of procedures see Killingsworth and Heckman, 1986). New models were devised to incorporate both the observed and unobserved aspects of these decisions and new statistical techniques for handling discrete choices were used, for example, logit, probit and tobit (Layard, Barton and Zabalza, 1980, and Chapter 12).

The estimation techniques used in second-generation studies produce results which differ systematically from those of first-generation studies (Killingsworth and Heckman, 1986). But has there been convergence in the estimates of key elasticities? The answer must be no. The range of available estimates from second-generation studies is as bewildering as was that from the more *ad hoc* early work. Initially estimates obtained using recently developed econometric techniques suggested that the wage elasticity of female labour supply was greater than had earlier been thought (Heckman, Killingsworth and MaCurdy, 1981). Work since then seems to have reduced the mean but substantially increased the variance of this estimate (Killingsworth and Heckman, 1986). In contrast to the long-standing consensus that compensated and uncompensated female labour supply wage elasticities are positive and larger in absolute value than those for men, some recent studies appear to show that the wage elasticities of women workers are little different from those of men.

Some disappointment with the practical dividends accruing from the second-generation work has to be set against insights obtained from specific attention to the participation decision and from analyses of panel data. Econometric techniques applied to such life-cycle histories of birth cohorts enable the separate identification of factors which influence women's participation over their life cycles for particular cohorts, from those which cause participation to vary from cohort to cohort, abstracting from life-cycle effects (Smith and Ward, 1985; Joshi, Layard and Owen, 1985 and Chapter 13). Such studies have not resolved questions about elasticity estimates (see for example, Joshi, Layard and Owen, 1985 and Chapter 13). But they impart other insights. For example, they highlight the importance of children in explaining women's life-cycle participation. Most important of all, through their ability to locate the labour supply decision in a dynamic context, these studies respond to the inability of cross-section simulations to explain secular trends and make room for contextualizing variables such as falling prices of domestic appliances, and even long-term changes in the roles women see for themselves (Joshi, Layard and Owen, 1985, and Chapter 13). For these reasons they are the most 'feminist-friendly' of the econometric studies.

Differences between men's and women's pay and the associated issue of employment segregation has probably attracted more attention from neoclassical economists than any other gender-related issue. Most neoclassical economists do not ascribe women's lower earnings to injustice. It is viewed as the outcome of women's free choice: specifically their decision to make smaller investments in productivity-enhancing human capital. Earnings commanded in the labour market depend on an individual's productivity which in turn relates both to his/her innate abilities and to acquired characteristics like education and training, summarized as human capital (Becker, 1964). How much an individual invests in him/herself depends on the costs and benefits. Benefits accrue in the future in the form of enhanced wages. The pay-off is clearly sensitive to lifetime labour force participation: those who work long hours and anticipate many years in the workforce have the highest expected returns. Women then rationally invest less than men in human capital because they spend proportionally less time in the labour force, interrupting paid work to bear and raise children (Mincer and Polachek, 1974 and Chapter 15; and for an update on this argument see Becker, 1985 and Chapter 7). Moreover while women are out of the labour force their human capital usually depreciates, contributing to an earnings gap should they re-enter.

A large number of empirical studies of male–female earnings differentials appeared in the 1960s and early 1970s showing that some, much or virtually all of the differentials observed were caused by factors other than discrimination. For a review of these studies see Ferber and Lowry (1976 and Chapter 22). Sanborn (1964 and Chapter 19) was one of the first studies to appear. Other important studies include: Fuchs (1971); Polachek (1973); Malkiel and Malkiel (1973); and Oaxaca (1973). True to the human capital tradition, the studies used measurable differences between female and male workers to explain women's lower earnings.

Gunderson's survey (1989 and Chapter 23) brings this literature up to date. He describes the now standard procedure for decomposing an overall average male–female wage gap into: (1) a component which is attributable to differences in the endowments of human capital; and, (2) a residual which is identified with discrimination. Summaries of empirical evidence are found in a number of reviews (see Lloyd and Neimi, 1979; Treiman and Hartmann, 1981; Madden, 1985; Willborn, 1986; Cain, 1986; Blau and Ferber, 1987; Gunderson, 1985; Agarwal, 1981). A number of important generalizations emerge, several of which have important policy implications. Here we note first that the greater the number of variables used to control for productivity-related factors, that is the broader the concept of human capital, the smaller the productivity-adjusted wage gap relative to the observed gap, and second that, even when they use extensive lists of control variables, most studies do find some residual that they attribute to discrimination (Gunderson, 1989 and Chapter 23).

The explanatory significance of women's lower accumulation of work experience is highlighted in Wright and Ermisch's (1991 and Chapter 24) state-of-the-art estimation of pay discrimination in the British labour market. Although potential experience in terms of age minus age at leaving full-time education is a good proxy for men's actual experience, the same is not true for women. Hence economists have developed a way to impute women's work experience by backwards projection from a cross-section participation equation, as pioneered by Zabalza and Arrufat (1985). Wright and Ermisch's data set includes measures of actual experience and so allows them to compare women's earnings functions and summary measures of discrimination using imputed experience with those based on actual experience. The measures appear similar. The success of imputation relates to the predictive power of child-bearing patterns for work experience, underlining one more time the links between women's disadvantaged status in the labour market and their assumption of domestic responsibilities.

Wright and Ermisch's study also raises the question of sample selection bias, occurring here in the female wage equation estimated as part of the decomposition of the earnings gap. Their results confirm the importance of controlling for sample selection bias in this context (see also, Berger and Glenn, 1986; Dolton and Makepeace, 1986, 1987).

Wright and Ermisch estimate that women's pay would be about 20 per cent higher in the absence of discrimination, which is four times the 'highest' comparable estimate in the influential study by Zabalza and Arrufat (1985). The latter appears to have underestimated the level of gender discrimination and exaggerated the impact of the anti-discrimination legislation of the 1970s. It remains unclear why the Zabalza and Arrufat estimates are so low in comparison with other studies, which must raise doubts about measurement and methods. Certainly it seems premature to rely on single studies to indicate the success or failure of policy measures.

Ferber and Lowry's essay, (1976 and Chapter 22), written in response to the early literature but continuing to be relevant, provides a good example of feminist reactions to work on pay differentials between men and women within the neoclassical framework. They perceive the latter as constraining the range and method of research so as to rationalize the inequality observed and deflect attention from the charge of discrimination. They doubt that the existing differences between male and female workers explain as much of the earnings gap as alleged, and they point out that these differences themselves, particularly the educational and occupational patterns of the female workforce, are likely caused by discrimination. Consequently, the explanations of the earnings differentials involve circular reasoning. What the neoclassical economist sees as free choice, a feminist standpoint theorist understands as the cumulative moulding of behavioural response produced by a history of difference and discrimination.

Discrimination, as defined in neoclassical economics, relates only to that portion of the observed wage gap which cannot be attributed to differences in the endowment of wage generating characteristics (Becker, 1968 and Chapter 18). One interpretation of the residual is that it represents differences in the returns that males and females get for the same human capital (Gunderson, 1989 and Chapter 23).

Once attention is focused on explanations of these residuals the structural incompatibility between neoclassical economics and discrimination becomes apparent. Discriminatory outcomes are not easily deduced from the standard axioms and usual behavioural assumptions (Becker, 1968 and Chapter 18). Hence the vigour with which economists have pursued the human capital explanation, including, on occasion, insistence that even different returns for the same measured characteristics might signal not discrimination but bad measurement! Neoclassical economists' preference for reading male–female earnings differentials as the consequences of traditional divisions of labour around childcare, cultural stereotypes and 'pre-market' (non-economic) discrimination, may be more an unintended consequence of their disciplinary loyalty than a reflection of male chauvinism.

Consideration of theories of discrimination brings us back to Woolley's survey (1993 and Chapter 1). In addition to the two main neoclassical approaches to discrimination, discriminating tastes and statistical discrimination, approaches which foreground the structure of the labour market or the cultural production of gender roles are also considered.

Taste-based models of discrimination begin with the assumption that the utility of some or all the relevant agents is affected by association with members of other identifiable groups (Becker, 1957; Becker, 1968 and Chapter 18; Arrow, 1971). This is a rather different kind of taste from that usually taken as given by economists and its interjection as axiomatic devalues the analysis. Economic analysts have generally concluded that customer discrimination plays a minor part in the differences observed in earnings. If customers prefer to avoid contact with a certain group, workers in that group will specialize in the production of goods which have no customer contact, to avoid being paid a lower wage which would be the outcome if they competed with non-group workers in an occupation with customer contact. As long as the number of workers in the group which is discriminated against is small relative to the jobs that do not have customer contact, the result is some degree of job segregation but no group earnings differences.

Employer discrimination is taken more seriously. The traditional deduction of labour demand in the context of one group of employers having an aversion to (say) female labour implies that discriminating employers will employ higher ratios of men to women than non-discriminating employers and will employ only men if men and women are perfect substitutes. The final equilibrium depends on the product market structure. Average production costs are greater the greater the employer's discrimination coefficient. With free entry in the product market, competition among firms will ensure that discriminating employers are eventually driven out of business (Arrow, 1972). An important corollary of the no-discrimination equilibrium is that unless one group of workers has monopoly power in the labour market, workers with the same human capital must earn the same wages. Pay differentials unrelated to human capital are incompatible with robust competition. An important policy implication is that equal pay legislation acts as a brake on the market processes which eliminate discrimination as described above, as discriminators can indulge their tastes without any penalty. Non-discriminators are forced to pay the same wages to their female employees and so lose their competitive advantage.

The situation is different if market structure is imperfectly competitive, since excess profit can buffer employers' discrimination costs. Discriminating firms are still threatened in the long run since non-discriminators can buy them out and earn even larger profits. There are ways in which discrimination can be reconciled with competition, even in the long run (Cain, 1986). But these usually involve assumptions which are themselves threatening to competition, such as non-constant costs, inelastic supplies of entrepreneurship, and inelastic supplies of non-labour factors of production.

The most important empirical prediction from the analysis is that discrimination will be more prevalent in highly concentrated industries. Empirical studies have concentrated on correlating measures of discrimination with measures of concentration, with mixed results. US studies have found a positive relationship between the proportion of blacks in total employment and industrial employment (Comador, 1973; Medoff, 1980). Shepherd and Levin (1973 and Chapter 20) fail to detect any clear structure/discrimination relationship in their sample of large US firms (see also Oster, 1975). They conclude that 'Except for a few "women's" industries, the management of large corporations is in fact a distinctively white male preserve' (Chapter 20, p. 415). Studies focused on relative wages by race and sex produce mixed results (Haessell and Palmer, 1978; Fuji and Trapani, 1978). For the UK, Chiplin and Sloane (1976) found no relationship between male/female wage differentials and industrial structure, and seemed to find that as far as the proportion of women is concerned this was *higher* in the more concentrated industries!

Becker also considers the case where groups of employees dislike working with each other. In this case if members of the two groups are identical as workers, the employment structure will become segregated with both types of workers getting the same pay. If there are skill complementarities, employment will be mixed but workers will have to be compensated for this violation of their preferences by higher pay and so there will be lower levels of employment. Unfortunately this intuitively more realistic hypothesis has attracted less attention probably because it is not easily subjected to formal quantitative investigation (but see Chiswick, 1973).

If competition in the labour market causes difficulties for neoclassical theories of discrimination, market power makes things easier. The classic case of employers paying a wage less than the worker's productivity occurs under monopsony where a single buyer of labour faces an upward sloping supply curve (Robinson, 1933). Where two kinds of labour are involved the degree of exploitation is greater for the workers whose labour supply is more inelastic. But this classic case seems to have little empirical purchase (but see Manning, 1992). Not only is monopsony empirically infrequent, in the case of gender discrimination there is also a good deal of empirical evidence and theoretical support for the finding that women's labour supply is more elastic than that of men (see above), which is the opposite of the requisite condition for the relative underpayment of women.

In Becker's model of discrimination, men's prejudice against women workers was not a sufficient condition to sustain a discriminatory wage differential. However, by forming a monopoly in the sale of labour to employers, male workers could enforce their tastes *and* raise their wage above the competitive level. Overall however, despite many individual cases of discrimination by unions, research suggests that labour monopoly is not a major source of the observed gender earnings gap (see Cain, 1986 for a survey of important studies). Perhaps a distinction should be made between the role of unions in sustaining existing differential and their historic role in the gendering of jobs as suggested in structural models of patriarchal-capitalism (see p. xxii) and in some radical descriptions of segmented labour markets. Elements of employee prejudice, combined with male-dominated trade unions' exercise of market power, and perhaps with 'within-sex altruism' operating between male employees and employers, provide persuasive analyses of historical developments in labour markets (for a discussion of within-sex altruism see England, 1993; relevant historical analyses include: Hartmann, 1979; Cockburn, 1986).

Simple models of the labour market assume that employers are able directly to observe the productivity of job applicants. Greater realism is introduced in models which have employers using observed characteristics such as education as a screen or signal. If such characteristics include innate attributes, such as race or gender, then they can ground a theory of discrimination based on imperfect information. Unfortunately statistical discrimination has been widely misunderstood (see Aigner and Cain, 1977 and Chapter 21). Statistical discrimination does not involve employers mistakenly believing that the average abilities of men are greater than those of women and so mistakenly overpaying men relative to women, though such 'error discrimination' has been hypothesized in the feminist literature and is discussed briefly above (see, p. xv). While it is a trivial matter to see how error discrimination explains observed differences in men's and women's pay, seemingly unrelated to their human capital, as an explanation of discrimination it sits uncomfortably with neoclassical economics. The problem is again to explain the persistence of such mistaken behaviour in competitive markets. Indeed, as an explanation of discrimination, a theory based on employers' mistakes is even harder for neoclassical economics to accept than an explanation based on employers' 'tastes for discrimination', because the tastes are at least presumed to provide utility to the discriminator.

One factor in the confusion is that the basic model, developed by Phelps (1972), cannot explain discrimination between groups as defined in neoclassical economics. The model assumes that employers hire on the basis of a skill indicator, y, which is an unbiased predictor of a worker's true productivity, q. Thus for the ith job applicant:

$$y_i = q_i + u_i$$

where u_i is a random error term independent of q_i. An employer's hiring decision is based on the predicted value of q_i given y_i. Suppose the employer regressed q_i on y_i, for a large sample of workers for whom q_i was known, then the fitted equation would be

$$\hat{q}_i = (1\text{-}b)a + b\ y_i$$

where a is the group mean of q (and y) and b is a measure of the strength of association theoretically equal to the square of the correlation coefficeint between y and q in a sufficiently large sample. In other words the conditional expectation is a linear combination of a group component, a, and an individual component, y_i.

Suppose there are two differentiated groups of worker, men and women. Suppose first that mean productivity is the same for both groups of worker but that the skill indicator is more reliable for men. Then a male worker will be paid a higher wage than a woman worker if his skill indicator was above average and *vice versa*. High quality women workers will earn lower wages than their male counterparts while the opposite will be true for low quality workers. Male workers will be more dispersed around the mean than women workers, simply because more weight will be given to individual performance. Workers will receive different pay for the same y scores which Phelps associated with discrimination. But as each worker is paid in accordance with expected productivity based on an unbiased predictor and the two groups which have the same average ability receive the same average wages, this situation does not constitute discrimination as usually defined (Aiger and Cain, 1977, and Chapter 21). Nor is it capable of generating the kind of empirical phenomenon described above in terms of group differences in earnings unrelated to measured attributes.

Phelps also considered a model in which the average abilities differed between groups. Assume that mean ability of men exceeds that of women. Here the systematic effect of femaleness leads to a lower predicted value of q for women than men even if the y scores are equal because y is by assumption a fallible indicator. Competitive market forces lead employers to pay workers according to their expected productivity, thus male workers will be preferred and receive higher wages than female workers with the same y score. But again a proportional relation will exist between the average compensation for the groups and their average ability, and the outcome is not discrimination as usually understood.

But although the Phelps model does not explain sex discrimination, extensions which incorporate risk aversion on the part of employers can be shown to be consistent with empirical patterns in pay (see Aigner and Cain, 1977 and Chapter 21). In another model the combination of lesser reliability for women on tests with truncation of lower-scoring applicants also produces a kind of discrimination. Neither model appears sufficient as an explanation of discrimination.

An outcome in which segregation reduces market discrimination occurs in several versions of Becker's model of discrimination. Competition enables segregation to accommodate demand side prejudice costlessly. But again this seems inconsistent with the empirical evidence. Differences in the occupational distribution of males and females account for a substantial portion of the earnings gap. A divide exists in the literature as to whether differences in occupational distributions are the outcome of the (free) choices of men and women, and so legitimately viewed as exogenous determinants of earnings differentials, or whether they are manifestations of discrimination. Job choice, as well as productivity-related characterisics acquired by workers, may reflect discrimination in the labour market or in society more generally or it may occur as a rational response to wage discrimination and occupational segregation. Again investigation of gendered outcomes requires opening up the black box of preferences which neoclassical economics leaves closed. Instead neoclassical economics offers a more comfortable explanation for occupational choice.

Human capital theory is used not only to explain differences in human capital formation and so in earnings, but is extended to explain the concentration of women and men in different occupations and industries (Polachek, 1976 and 1979). Different occupations convey different opportunities for on-the-job acquisition of human capital. But training involves current costs (earnings foregone, disutility, time) and only pays off in the future. Again it may not be worthwhile if the individual anticipates a relatively short working career. So women choose jobs which combine current returns and capital formation in an optimal way given their anticipated shorter life-time work experience, and which impose lower penalties for depreciation, given their greater employment intermittency (again see Becker, 1985 for a development of this model).

One logical problem with Polachek's extension of the human capital model to explain the occupational segregation of women workers concerns the assumption that women will choose occupations with low rewards for experience. Even if only intermittent experience is planned, greater lifetime earnings accrue in a job which rewards what little experience has been accumulated (England, 1982). For women to avoid jobs with high rates of appreciation, these *jobs* must exhibit unattractively low starting salaries, an inverse correlation commonly assumed in the human capital literature but not made explicit in Polachek's analysis. On a deeper level the human capital model of either earnings differences or employment segregation share the circularity of the New Household Economics' explanations of gender divisions: women invest less in human capital or choose a less demanding job because they anticipate spending more time than their spouses out of the labour force, but they spend more time out of the labour force because their potential earnings are lower. Predictions from the human capital model about the pattern of concentration of women workers have not proved robust (for example, see, Zellner, 1975; England, 1982 and Chapter 17); Beller, 1982 and Chapter 16; Polachek, 1985; England, 1985).

Human capital theory does not provide the only explanation of the commonly observed increase of earnings with experience or earnings penalties for intermittent participation.

Institutionalist analyses see some of the relationship between employment continuity and earnings as a result of legal, contractual and traditional agreements in the workplace which have little to do with productivity (England, 1982). Institutionalist analyses too can be readily extended to explain employment segregation by sex not only in terms of the incentive structures confronting women in their job choice but also in terms of institutional barriers to women's entry into certain occupations. These explanations of employment segregation shift attention from the supply side (women's choices) back to demand (employment discrimination).

In general institutional theories of discrimination make more room for historical contexts, pre-labour market discrimination, group bargaining and monopoly elements. Neoclassical economists often view them with a combination of impatience and condescension: arguing, first, that they implicitly misrepresent neoclassical models which, for example, are not synonymous with perfect competition, and second, that they are complements not substitutes for neoclassical analysis, contextualizing and shading rather than usurping the latter (see Cain, 1986). Such insouciance is unjustified. Neoclassical economists have found it difficult to explain the persistence of discrimination and occupational segregation and alternatives deserve to be taken seriously.

Bergmann's 1974 classic article Chapter 14 represents a hybrid model: neoclassical in the sense that workers receive their marginal products, but institutional in the sense that certain workers are restricted in terms of their employment opportunities and 'crowded' into jobs where their presence is acceptable. Like the human capital model, the crowding hypothesis is an attempt to explain both women's lower earnings and their employment segregation within the same framework. Unlike other demand side models of discrimination, discriminators here do not automatically make lower profits. When they discriminate against one group of workers they raise the wages of other groups but lower the wages of the group discriminated against. The paper constitutes a seminal contribution to a tradition which links the unequal treatment of workers to non-competing segments within the labour market.

Piore's (1975) model conceptualizes the labour market as containing a primary and a secondary sector. The primary sector offers jobs with relatively high wages, good working conditions, opportunities to advance and employment security. Jobs in the secondary sector pay low wages, have poor working conditions, offer few opportunities for advancement, and afford little security. The challenge is to explain how such segmentation withstands the self-interested mobility and hiring of agents in the market and persists in the face of competitive pressures. Proponents of segmented labour markets argue that, in the context of changing industrial structure and technology, their development benefited both (some) workers and (some) employers who together had the power to structure employment in their interests.

Segmented labour market theories seek to explain the divisions among groups of jobs. But they do not explain how it is that different kinds of workers occupy different segments of the labour market. Women fit the description of secondary workers: they have lower pay and are concentrated in less-skilled, dead-end and insecure jobs (Barron and Norris, 1976). Why is this? For some authors women's occupancy of the secondary segment comes out of the historical moment in which they were incorporated into the workforce, others see patriarchy as structuring the supply side of the labour market, yet others see patriarchy as structuring demand in terms of employers and unionized male workers in alliance controlling access to primary jobs. Early work in this tradition involved grand theoretical overviews with rather unspecific independent variables such as capitalism, patriarchy and industrialization. Recent work has involved detailed case studies. The aim is to use such microanalysis to demonstrate how earnings differentials come into being and are maintained in firms or industries. Craig, Garnsey and Rubery (1985 and Chapter 25) provide a study of women's pay and employment in the United Kingdom which suggests that pay inequalities are rooted in the system of industrial organization *and* the system of social reproduction of the labour force. Labour supply conditions *interact* with product market and technical conditions to mould the segmented employment structure.

Quantitative analyses suggest that factors exogenous to the labour market itself, such as differences in household responsibilities, are an important source of earnings differences between men and women (Gunderson, 1989, and Chapter 23). Feminist critics have long been irritated by neoclassical economists' depiction of these factors as reflecting preferences perhaps moulded by pre-market discrimination, and demand that they be studied as important contributors to economic discrimination. Mary Corcoran and Paul Courant (1987 and Chapter 26) show the importance of pre-market discrimination and sex-role socialization. It is necessary to discover more about the interaction between what goes on in the labour market and what happens before employment because an adequate policy response to inequalities in pay and occupational segregation must reach into these areas.

Similarly, feminists have long demanded that closer attention be paid to the nature of variables commonly viewed as unproblematic indicators of productivity. Research has suggested that the conceptualization and measurement of these characteristics may not be gender-neutral. In particular, the meaning of *skill* has been shown to be socially constructed within a gendered culture. Activities and processes done by women tend to be defined as 'unskilled' simply because they are done by women (see Craig, Rubery, Tarling and Wilkinson, 1982; Phillips and Taylor, 1980; Game and Pringle, 1983; Coyle, 1982). Male-dominated trade unions have played a part in the establishment and maintenance of skill divisions on gendered lines. Horrell, Rubery and Burchell (1990 and Chapter 27) contribute to this discussion through an analysis of workers' own perceptions of the content and skills associated with their jobs. Their analysis suggests that mapping from job content to perceived skill depends not just on gender but also whether the job is full or part time.

Focusing on preferences as the trojan horse introducing gender bias into otherwise objective economic analysis makes it easy for economists to side-step the issue: they work with given tastes and it is for other social scientists to understand the formation of preferences. But this kind of work forces recognition that even standard economic variables in both conceptualization and measurement have already been contaminated by being socially constructed.

It should now be clear why, as Woolley (1993 and Chapter 1) noted, there is less agreement about policies to eliminate economic inequality between men and women than there is about its extent. This is partly because sensible policy response requires understanding of the causes of inequality, and here consensus is not yet achieved. Empirical evidence has provided some guidelines. For example, evidence that occupational segregation accounts for more of the earnings gap than does discriminatory pay differentials within the same job, implies a larger potential role for equal employment opportunity and comparable worth as opposed to conventional equal pay policies. Here there is a second problem. The former are much more difficult to design and monitor than the latter. As Gunderson says '. . . given the importance of comparable worth . . . more effort – especially on the part of economists – will have to be placed on the technical issues and program design and implementation features so as to help attain the objectives of the legislation with a minimum of adverse consequences' (1989 and Chapter 23, p. 462). In view, for example, of the feminist problematization of variables considered standard exogenous determinants of pay, such as skill, some of that energy could be well spent considering critiques hitherto brushed onto the sidelines or relegated to the footnotes of mainstream economics.

Ophelia is not the prince. *Hamlet* would survive if she was written out. Similarly economics will survive if gender is never written in. But, without Ophelia *Hamlet* as a play would be much diminished. So in the absence of a response to the feminist critique, contemporary neoclassical economics will remain stunted and picayune in its treatment of the family, women's work and the gender division of labour. Moreover it is not simply a question of how best to deal with gender-related subject matter. An economics which went beyond economic man would be a richer and more useful discipline.

References

Agarwal, Naresh (1981) 'Pay Discrimination: Evidence, Policies and Issues', in *Equal Employment Issues: Race and Sex Discrimination in the United States, Canada and Britain*, Harish Jain and Peter Sloan (eds), New York: Praeger.

Aigner, Dennis J. and Cain, Glen C. (1977) 'Statistical Theories of Discrimination in Labor Markets', *Industrial and Labor Relations Review*, **30** (2), 175–87.

Amsden, Alice H. (ed.) (1980) *The Economics of Women and Work*, Harmondsworth, Middlesex: Penguin.

Arrow, Kenneth J. (1951) *Social Choice and Individual Values*, New York:

Arrow, Kenneth J. (1971) 'Some Models of Racial Discrimination in the Labor Market', Santa Monica, California: RAND document No. RM-6253-RC.

Arrow, Kenneth J. (1972) 'Models of Job Discrimination', in *Racial Discrimination in Economic Life*, Anthony H. Pascal (ed.), Lexington, Mass.: D.C. Heath and Co.

Ashworth, J.S. and Ulph, D.T. (1981) 'Household Models', in *Taxation and Labour Supply*, C.V. Brown (ed.), London: George Allen and Unwin.

Barron, R.D. and Norris, G.M. (1976) 'Sexual Divisions and the Dual Labour Market', in *Dependence and Exploitation in Work and Marriage*, D.L. Barker and S. Allen (eds), London: Longman.

Becker, Gary S. (1957) *The Economics of Discrimination*, Chicago: University of Chicago Press.

Becker, Gary S. (1964) *Human Capital*, New York: Columbia University Press.

Becker, Gary S. (1965) 'A Theory of the Allocation of Time', *Economic Journal*, **75** (200), 493–517.

Becker, Gary S. (1968) 'Discrimination, Economic', *International Encyclopedia of the Social Sciences*, 208–10.

Becker, Gary S. (1973) 'A Theory of Marriage: Part I', *Journal of Political Economy*, **81** (4), 813–46.

Becker, Gary S. (1974) 'A Theory of Marriage: Part II', *Journal of Political Economy*, **82** (2), S11–12.

Becker, Gary S. (1981) *A Treatise on the Family*, Cambridge, Massachusetts: Harvard University Press.

Becker, Gary S. (1985) 'Human Capital, Effort, and the Sexual Division of Labor', *Journal of Labor Economics*, **3** (1), S33–58.

Becker, Gary S., Landes, Elisabeth M. and Michael, Robert T. (1977) 'An Economic Analysis of Marital Instability', *Journal of Political Economy*, **85** (6), 1141–87.

Bell, Carolyn Shaw (1974) 'Economics, Sex, and Gender', *Social Science Quarterly*, **55** (3), 615–31.

Beller, Andrea (1982) 'Occupational Segregation by Sex: Determinants and Changes', *Journal of Human Resources*, **17** (3), 358–70.

Berger, Mark C. and Glenn, Darrell E. (1986) 'Selectivity Bias and Earnings Differences by Gender and Race', *Economic Letters*, **21** (3), 291–6.

Bergmann, Barbara R. (1974) 'Occupational Segregation, Wages, and Profits When Employers Discriminate by Race and Sex', *Eastern Economic Journal*, **1** (1–2), 103–10.

Bergmann, Barbara R. (1987) 'The Task of a Feminist Economics: A More Equitable Future', in *The Impact of Feminist Research in the Academy*, Christie Farnham (ed.), Bloomington: Indiana University Press, pp. 131–47.

Blau, Francine and Ferber, Marianne A. (1986) *The Economics of Women, Men and Work*, Englewood Cliffs NJ: Prentice Hall.

Blau, Francine and Ferber, Marianne A. (1987) 'Discrimination: Empirical Evidence from the United States', *American Economic Review*, **77** (2), 316–20.

Boserup, Esther (1987), 'Inequality between the Sexes', in *The New Palgrave: A Dictionary of Economic Theory*, 4 Vols. John Eatwell, Murray Milgate and Peter Newman (eds), New York: The Stockton Press.

Cain, Glen C. (1986) 'Labor Market Discrimination', in *Handbook of Labor Economics*, Orley Ashenfelter and Richard Layard (eds), Amsterdam: North Holland.

Cain, Glen C. and Watts, H.W. (eds) (1973) *Income Maintenance and Labor Supply*, New York: Academic.

Charles, Nickie (1993) *Gender Divisions and Social Change*, Hemel Hempstead: Harvester Wheatsheaf.

Chiplin, Brian and Sloane, Peter (1976) *Sex Discrimiantion in the Labour Market*, London: Macmillan.

Chiswick, B.R. (1973) 'Racial Discrimination and the Labor Market: A Test of Alternative Hypothesis', *Journal of Political Economy*, **81**, 1330–52.

Cockburn, Cynthia (1986) 'The Relations of Technology: What Implications for Theories of Sex and Class', in *Gender and Stratification*, Rosemary Crompton and Michael Mann (eds), Cambridge: Polity.

Comador, W.S. (1973) 'Racial Discrimination in American Industry', *Economica*, **40**, 363–78.

Committee on the Status of Women in the Economics Profession (1990) 'Report', *American Economic Review*, **80** (2), 486–9.

Corcoran, Mary E. and Courant, Paul N. (1987) 'Sex-role Socialization and Occupational Segregation: An Exploratory Investigation', *Journal of Post Keynesian Economics*, **9** (3), 330–47.

Coyle, A. (1982) 'Sex and Skill in the Organisation of the Clothing Industry', in *Work, Women and the Labour Market*, Jackie West (ed.), London: Routledge and Kegan Paul.

Craig, Christine, Rubery, Jill, Tarling, Roger and Wilkinson, Frank (1982) *Labour Market Structure, Industrial Organisation and Low Pay*, Cambridge: Cambridge University Press.

Craig, Christine, Garnsey, Elizabeth and Rubery, Jill (1985) 'Labour Market Segmentation and Women's Employment: A Case Study from the United Kingdom', *International Labor Review*, **124** (3), 267–80.

Davidoff, Leonore and Hall, Catherine (1987) *Family Fortunes*, London: Hutchinson.

Dex, Shirley (1985) *The Sexual Division of Labour*, Brighton: Wheatsheaf.

Dex, Shirley (1988) 'Gender and the Labour Markets, in *Employment in Britain*, Duncan Gallie (ed.), Oxford: Blackwells.

Dolton, P.J. and Makepeace, G.H. (1986) 'Sample Selection and Male Female Earnings Differentials in the Graduate Labour Market', *Oxford Economic Papers*, **38** (2), 317–41.

Dolton, P.J. and Makepeace, G.H. (1987) 'Interpreting Sample Selection Effects', *Economic Letters*, **24** (4), 373–9.

The Economic Report of the President (1974) Washington D.C.: G.P.O.

Edgeworth, Francis, Y. (1922) 'Equal Pay to Men and Women for Equal Work', *Economic Journal*, **32** (4), 431–57.

Edgeworth, Francis, Y. (1923) 'Women's Wages in Relation to Economic Welfare', *Economic Journal*, **33** (4), 487–95.

England, Paula (1982), 'The Failure of Human Capital Theory to Explain Occupational Sex Segregation', *Journal of Human Resources*, **17** (3), 358–70.

England, Paula (1985) 'Occupational Segregation: Rejoinder to Polachek', *Journal of Human Resources*, **20** (3), 441–2.

England, Paula (1989) 'A Feminist Critique of Rational Choice Theories: Implications for Sociology', *The American Sociologist*, **20** (1), 14–28.

England, Paula (1993) 'The Separative Self: Andocentric Bias in Neoclassical Assumptions', in *Beyond*

Economic Man: Feminist Theory and Economics, Marianne A. Ferber and Julie A. Nelson (eds), Chicago: University of Chicago Press.

Fallon, Peter and Verry, Donald (1988) *The Economics of Labour Markets*, Oxford: Philip Allan.

Feiner, Susan F. and Roberts, Bruce B. (1990), 'Hidden by the Invisible Hand: Neoclassical Economic Theory and the Textbook Treatment of Race and Gender', *Gender and Society*, **4** (2), 159–81.

Ferber, Marianne A. and Birnbaum, Bonnie G. (1977) 'The "New Home Economics": Retrospects and Prospects', *Journal of Consumer Research*, **4**, 19–28.

Ferber, Marianne A. and Lowry, Helen M. (1976) 'The Sex Differential in Earnings: A Reappraisal', *Industrial and Labor Relations Review*, **29**, 377–87.

Ferber, Marianne A. and Nelson, Julie A. (eds) (1993) *Beyond Economic Man: Feminist Theory and Economics*, Chicago: University of Chicago Press.

Ferber, Marianne A. and Teiman, Michelle L. (1981) 'The Oldest, the Most Established, the Most Quantative of the Social Sciences – and the Most Dominated by Men: The Impact of Feminism on Economics', in *Men's Studies Modified: The Impact of Feminism on the Academic Disciplines*, Dale Spender (ed.), New York: Pergamon.

Fine, Ben (1992) *Women's Employment and the Capitalist Family*, London: Routledge.

Folbre, Nancy and Hartmann, Heidi (1988) 'The Rhetoric of Self-Interest: Ideology and Gender in Economic Theory', in *The Consequences of Economic Rhetoric*, Arjo Klamer, Donald N. McCloskey and Robert M. Solow (eds), Cambridge: Cambridge University Press.

Folbre, Nancy and Abel, Marjorie (1989) 'Women's Work and Women's Households: Gender Bias in the US Census', *Social Research*, **56** (3), 545–70.

Folbre, Nancy (1991) 'The Unproductive Housewife: Her Evolution in Nineteenth-Century Economic Thought', *Signs: Journal of Women in Culture and Society*, **16** (3), 463–84.

Fuchs, Victor R. (1971) 'Differences in Hourly Earnings Between Men and Women', *Monthly Labor Review*, **94** (5), 9–15.

Fuji, E.T. and Trapani, J.M. (1978) 'On Estimating the Relationship Between Discrimination and Market Structure', *Southern Economic Journal*, **45**, 556–67.

Game, R. and Pringle, A. (1983) *Gender at Work*, London: Allen and Unwin.

Greenhalgh, Christine and Mayhew, K. (1981) 'Labour Supply in Great Britain: Theory and Evidence', *The Economics of the Labour Market*, Z. Horstein, J. Grice and A. Webb (eds), London: HMSO.

Gronau, Reuben (1973) 'The Intra-Family Allocation of Time: The Value of the Housewives' Time', *American Economic Review*, **63** (4), 634–51.

Gronau, Reuben (1977), 'Leisure, Home Production and Work – The Theory of the Allocation of Time Revisited', *Journal of Political Economy*, **85** (6), 1099–123.

Gunderson, Morley (1985) 'Discrimination, Equal Pay, and Equal Opportunities in the Labour Market', in *Work and Pay: The Canadian Labour Market*, Craig Riddell (ed.), Toronto: University of Toronto Press.

Gunderson, Morley (1989) 'Male–Female Wage Differentials and Policy Responses', *Journal of Economic Literatue*, **27** (1), 46–72.

Haessell, W. and Palmer, J. (1978) 'Market Power and Employment Discrimination', *Journal of Human Resources*, **13**, 545–60.

Harding, Sandra (1986) *The Science Question in Feminism*, Ithaca NY: Cornell University Press.

Harding, Sandra (1992a) 'After the Neutrality Ideal: Science, Politics, and "Strong Objectivity"', *Social Research*, **59**, 3, 567–87.

Harding, Sandra (1992b) 'Rethinking Standpoint Epistemology: What is "Strong Objectivity"', in *Feminist Epistemologies*, Linda Alcoff and Elizabeth Potter (eds), New York: Routledge.

Harding, Sandra (1993) 'Feminist Philosophy of Science: The Objectivity Question', *Out of the Margin: Book of Abstracts*, Amsterdam: International Scientific Conference.

Hartmann, Heidi (1979) 'The Unhappy Marriage of Marxism and Feminism: Towards a More Progressive Union', *Capital and Class*, **8**, 1–33.

Heckman, James J. (1974) 'Shadow Prices, Market Wages and Labor Supply', *Econometrica*, **42** (4), 679–94.

Heckman, James J. (1976) 'The Common Structure of Statistical Models of Truncation, Sample Selection and Limited Dependent Variables and a Simple Estimator for such Models', *Annals of Economic and Social Measurement*, **5**, 511–44.

Heckman, James J., Killingsworth, M.R. and MaCurdy, T.E.M. (1981) 'Empirical Evidence on Static Labour Supply Models: A Survey of Recent Developments', in *The Economics of the Labour Market*, Z. Hornstein, J. Grice and A. Webb (eds), London: HMSO.

Higgs, Edward (1987) 'Women's Occupations and Work in the Nineteenth-Century Censuses', *History Workshop*, **23**, 59–80.

Horrell, Sara, Rubery, Jill and Burchell, Brendan (1990) 'Gender and Skills', *Work, Employment and Society*, **4** (2), 189–216.

Horrell, Sara and Humphries, Jane (1995) 'Women's Labour Force Participation and the Transition to the Male-Breadwinner Family, 1790–1865', *Economic History Review*, **48** (1).

Humphries, Jane (1982) 'Review' of *A Treatise on the Family*, by Gary S. Becker, *Economic Journal*, **92** (374), 739–40.

Humphries, Jane and Rubery, Jill (1984) 'The Reconstitution of the Supply Side of the Labour Market: The Relative Autonomy of Social Reproduction', *Cambridge Journal of Economics*, **8** (4), 331–46.

Joseph, George (1983) *Women at Work*, Oxford: Blackwells.

Joshi, Heather E., Layard, Richard and Owen, Susan J. (1985) 'Why Are More Women Working in Britain?', *Journal of Labor Economics*, **3** (1), S147–S176.

Kahne, H. and Kohen, A.I. (1975) 'Economic Perspectives on the Role of Women in the American Economy', *Journal of Economic Literature*, **13** (4), 1249–92.

Killingsworth, Mark R. (1983) *Labor Supply*, Cambridge: Cambridge University Press.

Killingsworth, Mark R. and Heckman, James J. (1986) 'Female Labor Supply', *Handbook of Labor Economics*, Vol. 1, Orley Ashenfelter, and Richard Layard (eds), Amsterdam: North Holland.

Klamer, Arjo, McCloskey, Donald N. and Solow, Robert M. (eds) (1988) *The Consequence of Economic Rhetoric*, New York: Cambridge University Press.

Klasen, Stephan (1993) 'Marriage, Bargaining, and Intrahousehold Resource Distribution: Excess Female Mortality among Adults during Early German Development', Mimeo, Department of Economics, Harvard University.

Layard, R., Barton, M. and Zabalza, A. (1980) 'Married Women's Participation and Hours', *Economica*, **47** (185), 51–72.

Leuthold, J.H. (1968) 'An Empirical Study of Formula Income Transfers and the Work Decision of the Poor', *Journal of Human Resources*, **3** (3), 312–23.

Levy-Garboua, L. (ed.) (1979) *Sociological Economics*, London: Sage.

Lloyd, Cynthia and Neimi, Beth (1979) *The Economics of Sex Differentials*, New York: Columbia University Press.

Lundberg, Shelly and Pollak, Robert A. (1992) 'Separate Spheres, Bargaining and the Marriage Market', Mimeo, Department of Economics, University of Washington.

Madden, Janice (1985) 'The Persistence of Pay Differentials: The Economics of Sex Discrimination', in *Women and Work: An Annual Review*, Laurie Larwood, Ann Stromberg, and Barbara Gutek (eds), Beverly Hills: Sage.

Malkiel, Burton and Malkiel, Judith (1973) 'Male–Female Pay Differentials in Professional Employment', *American Economic Review*, **63** (4), 693–705.

Manning, Alan (1992) 'The Equal Pay Act and the Workings of Labour Markets', mimeo.

Manser, Marilyn and Brown, Murray (1980) 'Marriage and Household Decision-Making: A Bargaining Analysis', *International Economic Review*, **21** (1), 31–44.

McCloskey, Donald N. (1983) 'The Rhetoric of Economics', *Journal of Economic Literature*, **21** (2), 481–517.

McCloskey, Donald N. (1985) *The Rhetoric of Economics*, Madison: University of Wisconsin Press.

McCloskey, Donald N. (1993) 'Some Consequences of a Conjective Economics', in *Beyond Economic Man: Feminist Theory and Economics*, Marianne A. Ferber and Julie A. Nelson (eds), Chicago: University of Chicago Press.

McElroy, Marjorie B. and Horney, Mary J. (1981) 'Nash-Bargained Household Decisions: Towards a Generalization of the Theory of Demand', *International Economic Review*, **22** (2), 333–49.

Medoff, M.H. (1980) 'On the Relationship Between Discrimination and Market Structure: A Comment', *Southern Economic Journal*, **46**, 1227–34.

Mincer, Jacob (1962) 'Labor Force Participation of Married Women: A Study of Labor Supply',

Aspects of Labor Economics, A Report of the National Bureau of Economic Research, H.G. Lewis (ed.), Princeton: Princeton University Press.

Mincer, Jacob and Polachek, Solomon (1974) 'Family Investments in Human Capital: Earnings of Women', *Journal of Political Economy*, **82** (2), S76–S108.

Nelson, Julie A. (1992) 'Gender, Metaphor, and the Definition of Economics', *Economics and Philosophy*, **8** (1), 103–26.

Oaxaca, Ronald (1973) 'Male–Female Wage Differentials in Urban Labor Markets', *International Economic Review*, **14** (3), 693–709.

Oster, S.M. (1975) 'Industry Differences in the Level of Discrimination Against Women', *Quarterly Journal of Economics*, **89** (2), 215–29.

Phelps, Edmund S. (1972) 'The Statistical Theory of Racism and Sexism', *American Economic Review*, **62** (4), 659–61.

Phillips, Ann and Taylor, Barbara (1980) 'Sex and Skill: Notes Towards a Feminist Economics', *Feminist Review*, **6**, 79–88.

Piore, Michael J. (1975) 'Notes for a Theory of Labor Market Stratification', in *Labor Market Segmentation*, Richard Edwards, Michael Reich and David Gordon (eds), Lexington, Mass.: D.C. Heath and Co.

Polachek, Solomon (1973) 'Work Experience and the Difference Between Male and Female Wages', Unpublished Ph.D. Dissertation, Department of Economics, Columbia University.

Polachek, Solomon (1976) 'Occupational Segregation: An Alternative Hypothesis', *Journal of Contemporary Business*, **5**, 1–12.

Polachek, Solomon (1979) 'Occupational Segregation Among Women: Theory, Evidence, and a Prognosis', in *Women in the Labour Market*, Cynthia Lloyd, Emily Andrews and Curtis Gilroy (eds), New York: Columbia University Press.

Polachek, Solomon (1985) 'Occupational Segregation: A Defence of Human Capital Predictions', *Journal of Human Resources*, **20** (3), 437–40.

Pollak, Robert A. (1985) 'A Transactions Cost Approach to Families and Households', *Journal of Economic Literature*, **XXIII** (2), 581–608.

Poovey, Mary (1988) 'Feminism and Deconstruction', *Feminist Studies*, **14** (1), 51–66.

Pujol, Michele (1984) 'Gender and Class in Marshall's Principles of Economics', *Cambridge Journal of Economics*, **8** (3), 217–34.

Robinson, Joan (1933) *The Economics of Imperfect Competition*, London: Macmillan.

Samuelson, Paul A. (1956) 'Social Indifference Curves', *Quarterly Journal of Economics*, **70** (1), 1–22.

Sanborn, Henry (1964) 'Pay Differences between Men and Women', *Industrial and Labor Relations Review*, **17** (4), 534–50.

Sap, Jolande, Cuelenaere, Boukje and Schreurs, Petra (1993) 'Economic Theory: Assumptions, Contents and Concepts', *Out of the Margin: Book of Abstracts*, Amsterdam: International Scientific Conference.

Sawhill, Isabel V. (1977), 'Economic Perspectives on the Family', *Daedalus, Journal of the American Academy of Arts and Sciences*, **106** (2), 115–25.

Seiz, Janet A. (1991) 'The Bargaining Approach and Feminist Methodology', *Review of Radical Political Economy*, **23**, 22–9.

Shepherd, William G. and Levin, Sharon G. (1973) 'Managerial Discrimination in Large Firms', *Review of Economics and Statistics*, **60** (4), 412–22.

Smith, Adam (1776) *An Enquiry into the Wealth of Nations*, London: W. Strahan and T. Cadell.

Smith, J.P. and Ward, M.P. (1985) 'Time Series Growth in the Female Labor Force', *Journal of Labor Economics*, **3** (1), Part 2, 559–90.

Strassmann, Diana (1993) 'Not a Free Market: The Rhetoric of Disciplinary Authority in Economics', in *Beyond Economic Man: Feminist Theory and Economics*, Marianne A. Ferber and Julie A. Nelson (eds), Chicago: University of Chicago Press.

Treiman, Donald and Hartmann, Heidi (eds) (1981) *Women, Work, and Wages: Equal Pay for Jobs of Equal Value*, Washington D.C.: National Academy Press.

Walby, Sylvia (1986) *Patriarchy at Work*, Oxford: Polity.

Willborn, Steven A. (1986) *A Comparable Worth Primer*, Lexington, Mass: D.C. Heath and Co.

Woolley, Frances R. (1993) 'The Feminist Challenge to Neoclassical Economics', *Cambridge Journal of Economics*, **17** (1), 485–500.

Wright, R.E. and Ermisch, J.F. (1991) 'Gender Discrimination in the British Labour Market: A Reassessment', *Economic Journal*, **101** (406), 508–22.

Zabalza, A. and Arrufat, J.L. (1985), 'The Extent of Sex Discrimination in Great Britain', in *Women and Equal Pay: The Effects of Legislation on Female Employment and Wages in Britain*, A. Zabalza and Z. Tzannatos (eds), Cambridge: Cambridge University Press.

Zellner, Harriet (1975) 'The Determinants of Occupational Segregation', in *Sex, Discrimination, and the Division of Labor*, Cynthia Lloyd (ed.), New York: Columbia University Press.

Part I
Gender and Methodology

[1]

Cambridge Journal of Economics 1993, 17, 485–500

COMMENTARY

This section is designed for the discussion and debate of current economic problems. Contributions which raise new issues or comment on issues already raised are welcome.

The feminist challenge to neoclassical economics

Frances R. Woolley*

1. Introduction

There are economists who are feminists. Working within economics, we address feminist concerns, such as gender inequality and androcentric research strategies. This essay is a report on our progress, describing our research agenda, how some of the research priorities have been accommodated within neoclassical economics, and how others fundamentally challenge the neoclassical economic paradigm.

As Michèle Pujol notes (1992, p. 10), feminist economics is not a homogeneous concept. The diverse positions within feminist scholarship as a whole are echoed in feminist economics. A liberal vision of feminist economics can be found in the writings of Barbara Bergmann. She writes: 'what really distinguishes feminist economists is their view that the present assignment of economic duties based on sex is unfair and should be eliminated' (Bergmann, 1983, p. 25). Feminist economists recognise that women are disadvantaged and are committed on equity grounds to improving women's well-being. Brown (1989), like Bergmann, emphasises the fact of women's inferior position: 'Another unifying theme of feminism is the view that in most societies and throughout most of recorded history, women as a group have been in a socially, economically, and politically inferior position to men as a group' (p. 4).

Feminist economists, influenced by critiques of the natural sciences (Harding, 1986), have also begun to question the objectivity of economics. Paula England (1990) asks 'What can economics learn from feminism?' and answers: 'To be more attentive to gender biases in economic work and in the world' (p. 1). More generally, Sandra Harding (1986) has identified two ways in which feminist perspectives expand scientific thought. Feminist empiricism eliminates sexism and androcentrism by applying the tools of scientific investigation in an unbiased way to both women's and men's behaviour. Feminist standpoint theory argues that women's experiences, particularly as a disadvantaged group and as a group engaged in caring labour, give women (or feminists) a different and valuable perspective in their scientific investigations.

Manuscript received 15 November 1991; final version received 20 November 1992.

*Carleton University, Ottawa. An earlier version of this paper was presented in Carleton University's Women's Studies seminar. I have benefited from discussions with the participants in that seminar, my colleagues at Carleton, and participants at the University of Manitoba conference on Feminist Criticisms of Economic Theory. Fiona Coulter, T. K. Rymes and a referee provided written comments. David Long provided intellectual support throughout.

0309–166X/93/040485 + 16 $08.00/0

486   F. R. Woolley

These views form an agenda for feminist neoclassical economics:

  (i) to document differences in the well-being of men and women;
 (ii) to advocate policies which will promote equity; and
(iii) to conduct research free from androcentric bias.

The first two items on the agenda correspond to the active, policy-oriented feminism advocated by Bergmann. The third relates to Harding's feminist empiricism and feminist standpoint perspectives. In this essay I make a progress report on the feminist economics agenda, highlight the challenges feminism raises for neoclassical economics, and discuss the relationship between feminist and other challenges to the neoclassical framework. The main point of the paper is to argue that advocating equity-promoting policies and attempting to eliminate bias leads feminist neoclassical economists to challenge their discipline.[1]

Before we consider how feminists challenge neoclassical economics, however, we need to define neoclassical economics. The definition proposed by Robbins—the study of the allocation of scarce resources among different and competing ends—is too broad. Marxist, Austrian, and other varieties of non-neoclassical economics also study the allocation of resources. Alternatively, neoclassical economics can be characterised by the assumptions of methodological individualism, that is, 'individuals are assumed to behave self-interestedly' and 'the analysis is built on the individual' (Nicolaides, 1988, p. 315). While methodological individualism drives much economic research, it does not define the subject, primarily because substantial areas of study lack microfoundations, for example, much of macroeconomics, or theories which aggregate families or firms into individuals or entrepreneurs. Perhaps the most fruitful approach is simply to define neoclassical economics as 'mainstream, orthodox economics' (Blaug, 1980, p. 160) or to 'think of traditional or neoclassical economics as that which is presented in intermediate text books' (Nicolaides, 1988, p. 313). In this essay we shall attempt to take into account both traditional neoclassical views and the new, more institutional, research which is currently entering the economic mainstream.

2. Documenting the well-being of women

The first item on the feminist agenda is documenting differences in the well-being of men and women. Levels of well-being are determined in part by non-monetary factors, such as health, ties of family and friendship, and disposition. At the same time, money matters. Two major determinants of a woman's well-being are her own income and her share of any family income. A third factor contributing to her well-being is the amount of time she spends working. Let us examine, for earnings, sharing, and time, the absolute position of women, and their position relative to men.

The majority of women in most industrialised countries work. Yet women working full time earn less than two-thirds of men's salaries (Blau and Ferber, 1986, p. 70, US figures). Part of the pay differential is structural. Most women are in poorly paid, predominately female jobs, and many women have less education and training than men. A factor of major importance is that women bear the primary responsibility for child care.

[1] Other varieties of economics, such as Marxian or post-Keynesian economics, might benefit from feminist scrutiny. I confine my attention to neoclassical economics. In part this is because the neoclassical paradigm is the one dominant in much of English-speaking economic thought. In part it is because I am trained as a neoclassical economist.

Gunderson (1989, p. 51) concludes that: 'Factors originating from outside the labour market (e.g. differences in household responsibilities ...) are an important source of the overall earnings gap ...' Finally, women face discrimination: '... most studies do find *some* residual wage gap that they attribute to discrimination' (Gunderson, 1989, p. 51).

Women's own wages are an important determinant of women's well-being, particularly for the large number of women who are unmarried, divorced, single parents or widows. But earnings do not tell the whole story. A woman living with a partner benefits from that partner's income. If we take into account sharing within the family, how does the position of women change? Sen (1984) concludes that there is inequality in the distribution of food within the family. Evidence from rural Bangladesh and West Bengal suggests that women generally receive less calories than men, and, in times of famine, suffer from more malnutrition. More recent studies have confirmed Sen's results. For example, Haddad and Kanbur (1990) conclude on the basis of Philippine data that 'the neglect of intra-household inequality is likely to lead to a considerable understatement of the levels of inequality and poverty' (p. 866). We should not simply project the experience of developing countries onto developed ones, but it is fair to say that we should not assume wage inequalities are cancelled out by sharing in the family.

Women earn less than men, and perhaps they have a smaller share of household income. Yet their lower income may be compensated for by greater leisure time. The evidence does not support this hypothesis. In the US, men on average spend more time working (including both market and housework) than do women (Juster and Stafford, 1991). However, if one compares men and women with similar labour market commitments, women devote more time to work than do men (Juster and Stafford, 1985, pp. 147–8). Women pay for greater equality in earnings with their leisure time.[1]

If feminist economics fails to take root, it will not be because of a failure to achieve the first item on the agenda, to document differences in the well-being of men and women. There is a large body of evidence to suggest that in terms of income, household sharing, and hours worked, certain women are in a disadvantaged position. The evidence is published in the leading journals of the profession. Where feminist economics encounters less support is in its normative agenda, that is, the commitment to advocate policies which will promote equity.

3. Policies to promote equity

In section 1 we identified inequities in three areas: earned income, share of household income, and leisure time. In this section I shall focus on income inequality, for two reasons. First, government policies, such as affirmative action or equal pay for comparable worth legislation, have aimed at remedying income inequality. Second, other inequalities, particularly inequality in the share of household income, may be alleviated by greater equality in earned income.

How to promote equity depends upon our hypothesis as to what causes inequality between men and women. In this section I shall outline three explanations of the male/female earnings differential, namely taste, statistical, and error discrimination. I consider the implications of each explanation for the choice of government policy, and

---

[1] When we turn from industrialised to agricultural societies, women's relative access to leisure falls. One study of rural Botswana in 1975 found that women worked on average 12 hours per week more than men; a 1981 study of Nepalese villages found that women worked 23 hours per week more than men (Juster and Stafford, 1991).

the challenges each raises for neoclassical economics. These three forms of discrimination are by no means the only models of discrimination. I choose them, first, because they are frequently advanced explanations of discrimination and, second, because they illustrate the point I want to make in this section: *a policy-oriented feminism is not sufficient. It leads to more research or to challenges to neoclassical economics.*

Taste discrimination
The idea behind taste discrimination is that employers, coworkers or customers have a 'taste' for discrimination, that is, they prefer to hire, work with or be served by, say, men. These preferences translate into lower wages and fewer employment opportunities for women. For example, if employers prefer men to women, they will give male candidates preference when hiring, and offer males higher salaries. Although taste discrimination was originally advanced by Becker (1971) as an explanation for racial discrimination, feminist economists are now using men's preferences to explain occupational segregation (Bergmann, 1986, 1989).

According to the Becker (1971) taste model of discrimination, government policies can increase equity, but at a cost in terms of efficiency. Equal pay combined with affirmative action legislation will improve women's pay and employment opportunities, improving equity. However, it will have two efficiency costs. First, it will make discriminating individuals worse off. The very fact that they discriminate means that they are less well off in a mixed environment than in a gender-segregated one. Second, when employers have a strong preference against hiring women, they may substitute capital for labour instead of hiring a gender-mixed work force, which would cause a departure from the efficient, competitive equilibrium.

However, this efficiency costs story is unsatisfactory, since it suggests that, in a world with taste discrimination, a non-discriminating employer would be able to make substantial profits. S/he could hire women instead of men, pay them slightly less than the going male wage rate, and because s/he had lower costs than other firms, would make profits. With these profits s/he would be able to expand, generating more employment for women, and so on. Just a few non-discriminating employers can, in a competitive market, bid away taste discrimination. The persistence of discrimination over long periods of time is hard to explain in the Becker model.

Bergmann (1989) draws on efficiency wage theory to explain the survival of discriminatory firms in a competitive environment. Efficiency wage theory suggests that increasing wages reduces shirking and turnover, creating efficiency gains which offset the costs of the higher wages groups not discriminated against receive. With this story, discriminating firms will not necessarily be at a substantial disadvantage *vis-à-vis* non-discriminating firms.

The fundamental issue raised by taste discrimination models is the origin of discriminatory tastes. Feminist and other economists are beginning to answer this question. Paula England and Irene Brown (1990) apply Nancy Chodorow's feminist psychoanalytic theory to labour market segregation. Chodorow argues that because boys are raised by women and have little opportunity to interact with men, they forge their masculine identity out of a rejection of things feminine (England and Brown, 1990, p. 10). Men's identities are threatened if women enter traditionally male occupations as equals. Nancy Folbre (1992, forthcoming) discusses how the process of evolution may have favoured societies in which men and women shared a preference for male control. Geoff Hodgson (1986) stresses the role of institutions in shaping individual's purposes.

The feminist challenge to neoclassical economics 489

Variables such as child-rearing practices, cultural evolution or institutions contrast sharply with the variables used to explain tastes in strongly neoclassical models.[1] For example, Stigler and Becker (1977) explain taste changes in terms of prices and incomes. Employers have stable underlying meta-preferences, but will cultivate tastes which are more cheaply satisfied, for example, for immigrant workers. Feminists do not reject price or income explanations of taste changes but add other, less conventional, explanatory variables.

Changing tastes are crucial for feminist economics because many strategies to increase gender equality within and outside the workplace involve changing discriminatory preferences. Yet neoclassical welfare economic policy evaluation almost invariably assumes stable underlying preference orderings.[2] Dropping the assumption of given tastes is problematic. For example, how do we evaluate an affirmative action policy which is expected to increase the acceptance of female employees: in terms of current tastes, in terms of future tastes, or in terms of what tastes would be in a world characterised by gender equality? Or perhaps the notion of welfarism is suspect when tastes are variable? These questions do not have straightforward answers.[3] They raise the first feminist challenge to economics:

Challenge no. 1: To develop models to explain and evaluate endogenous preference changes

Statistical discrimination: a human capital approach

An alternative to the taste discrimination explanation of inequality between men and women is statistical discrimination. There is a body of evidence to suggest that, given two candidates identical in every respect except gender, potential employers, referees and others will rate the performance of the woman as inferior to that of the man. Numerous studies have simulated hiring situations, presenting employers with equivalent male and female candidates, and have found that male candidates are more likely to be hired, or were offered a higher starting salary, in universities, and for managerial, scientific and semi-skilled positions (see Nieva and Gutek, 1980, for a survey). To take another example, Ferber and Teiman found that women are more likely to have their articles accepted in journals where the referees do not know the sex of the author (Ferber and Teiman, 1981, pp. 126–7).[4] A third example is a study in which groups of students, both male and female, were asked to value two paintings, one attributed to a male and the other to a female. On average the 'male' painting received the higher appraised value (Nieva and Gutek, 1980, p. 268). There is a large body of evidence suggesting that identical work by women is valued less than the same work by men. The question is: why?

One explanation which fits in well with economic theory is that of statistical discrimination. Perhaps women's paintings are, on average, inferior to men's and so worth less in the market. Given two paintings, one will be right more often than not in guessing that the woman's painting has a lower market value. Assigning a lower value to the woman's artwork may be a rational way of reducing the odds of making costly evaluation errors, given the tremendous difficulty of measuring the inherent merit of a work of art.

---

[1] Nicolaides (1988, pp. 321–22) provides a discussion of this literature.
[2] Notable exceptions include Gintis (1974) and Hahnel and Albert (1990).
[3] I address these issues in more detail in Woolley (1992).
[4] Although Blank (1991) is more cautious in her appraisal of the evidence: 'While the data are consistent with an argument that women fare better under a double-blind reviewing system, the estimated effects are small and show no statistical significance'.

490   F. R. Woolley

Economists such as Aigner and Cain (1977) have argued that statistical discrimination
need not lead to economic discrimination. Although excellent female artists' work may be
undervalued, that of unskilled females will be overvalued. On average the evaluation will
be correct.

   Is there any empirical evidence to support the statistical discrimination hypothesis? As
was described in section 1, even after controlling for age, work experience, education, and
other variables, most studies find some residual wage differential which they attribute to
discrimination. If the statistical discrimination hypothesis is correct, that wage differential represents some unobserved productivity or human capital differential, not proxied by
education and so on. What is this variable which employers find so easy to observe and
econometricians so elusive? One possibility is women's higher turnover rates. However, as
Gronau (1988) has noted, turnover is a 'chicken or egg' problem—are women in relatively
low-paid jobs requiring little training because they have high turnover, or do women's
higher turnover rates result from their low occupational status? Gronau (1988) deciphers
this interrelationship, and finds that 'if women were to reduce their quit rate, increase
their labour force experience and tenure, and change their occupational composition,
they would obtain only marginally better jobs, and the wage gap would not narrow
appreciably'. He concludes: 'Closing the gap therefore requires a structural change'. A
range of other factors have been proposed to explain the male–female wage differential,
including the greater variability of women (Aigner and Cain, 1977), or that women,
exhausted by their household responsibilities, devote less effort to work than men (Becker,
1985), but there is little empirical evidence in support of these factors. Given the number
of econometric studies which have found male–female wage differentials not explained by
observed productivity or human capital differentials, it seems reasonable to turn to other
models of discrimination to explain the wage inequality.

Error discrimination
A final explanation for the under-rating of women's work is error discrimination
(England, forthcoming). People mistakenly over-estimate the difference between an
average man and an average woman and, therefore, assign women's work too low a value.
Error discrimination can become enshrined in institutional structures, for example,
Victorian laws forbidding women from working underground (preventing them, for
example, from driving subway trains) remained in force in the UK in the 1980s.
Moreover, error discrimination creates self-fulfilling prophecies—women are hired for
low-grade jobs because they are perceived to be less skilled, they do not learn skills because
they are in jobs with no possibility of advancement.

   Error discrimination and statistical discrimination have radically different policy
implications. If women are disadvantaged because of employers' errors, policies such as
affirmative action or pay equity simply correct employers' errors, benefiting women at no
cost in terms of economic efficiency. If there is statistical discrimination, requiring
employers to change their hiring or pay practices will lower the average quality of the work
force (recall—if more men are hired than women it is because men are more productive)
decreasing productivity and leading to a fall in economic efficiency. Error discrimination
implies that affirmative action and pay equity can be costless, statistical discrimination
that they are costly.

   The systematic mistakes explanation of discrimination is not one that is universally
accepted by feminist economists. First, feminist economists are economists, and are
reluctant to dispense with the notion of rationality. Behaviour which produces systematic

The feminist challenge to neoclassical economics 491

mistakes, that is, outcomes which are wrong on average, or which are not the best choice given current information and the cost of making decisions (i.e. not satisfying), is evidence of irrationality. Second, systematic mistakes suggest that intervening in markets can improve both equity and efficiency. Feminists might consider this an unrealistically rosy view of the consequences of policy intervention. Finally, it seems almost naive to think that those who support discriminatory institutions are honestly mistaken, and are completely uninfluenced by any benefits they might receive from the current *status quo*.

Yet at the same time, when we look at the history of female subordination, it does seem that economists have held mistaken beliefs about the capabilities of women (Pujol, 1992). If the error discrimination hypothesis is true, it fundamentally challenges neoclassical economics, because it suggests that people may not act rationally, and that the outcome of competitive markets may not be optimal.

Challenge no. 2: To allow that people may make systematic mistakes

The reason for considering policies which promote equity was to show how economists advocating such policies are led away from textbook neoclassical models and towards models where tastes can be endogenised and where judgement errors can persist over time. What, now, for the third item on the feminist agenda? Will moving towards research free from androcentric bias also challenge neoclassical economics?

4. Towards research free from androcentric bias

How does bias enter into economic research? The feminist agenda of creating economic research free from androcentric bias is developing in a number of directions. First, feminists aim to do better economics. Economists appeal to 'stylised facts' to motivate their models. Gender bias can cause people to be mistaken about stylised facts. Second, many feminists are concerned that the economic issues affecting women have not been addressed by the profession, or have been marginalised. Economists at times appear unable to 'see' women- or gender-related issues. In this section we shall discuss each of these feminist critiques.

Stylised facts
Economic models, like maps, are abstract representations which are simpler and more tractable than the real world, yet at the same time do not capture all of the real world's complexity. For a feminist to argue convincingly that her colleagues are using the wrong stylised facts, she cannot simply demonstrate that the assumptions of their models do not correspond to the real world, since no model is ever perfectly realistic. The London Underground map's stylised simplicity is what makes it so easy to use and remember. A feminist also has to show that relaxing a model's assumptions provides predictions which correspond more closely to the real world than those of alternative models.

In this paper I shall take one fairly straightforward but, I think, significant example of a mistaken stylised fact. Economists generally assume, as Gary Becker (1981A) puts it, 'altruism in the family and selfishness in the market place'. Yet it can be argued, that the family-altruism/market place-selfishness dichotomy is in fact incorrect. First, altruism can be found in the market. Paula England (1990, p. 12) argues that male collusion to keep women out of 'their' jobs can be thought of as selective within-sex altruism. Don McCloskey (1989) gives war as an example of a situation where men are public spirited. Second, there is little discussion of why conflict is absent from families. One of the few

492   F. R. Woolley

rigorous analyses that conclude there is indeed altruism within the family (Becker, 1974) relies on the assumption that one household member has a large enough share of the household income that all others are supported by him. This is not true for couples where the wife works full- or part-time.[1] Even in 1974 many women worked; today the majority of women work.

Selfishness in the family and altruism in the market place has implications which matter to economists. For example, in the conventional model of the altruistic family, we are unable to explain why it might make a difference to pay family allowance payments to mothers rather than to fathers. The family-altruism/market place-selfishness dichotomy passes the two tests for a mistaken stylised fact. It does not correspond to the real world, and it is unable to explain certain observations, such as the idea that it matters who receives the family allowance cheque, about the real world. This brings us to our third challenge:

Challenge no. 3: To correct mistaken stylised facts

In a sense mistakes about stylised facts are the easiest form of gender bias to combat. One simply has to gather the appropriate data and present evidence which shows that a particular view is mistaken. A mistaken view is a public view.

At the same time, correcting mistaken stylised facts is not entirely straightforward. First, women and men have different experiences of the world, and a stylised fact that seems perfectly reasonable to one sex may seem strange or outrageous to the other. Second, as McCloskey (1983) has argued, an overwhelming body of econometric evidence has to be assembled before a model can be considered to be 'disproved'. Take, for example, the statistical discrimination model of the previous section. Advocates of the model can always maintain that there are economically relevant differences between men and women, it is just that econometricians have not yet found out what they are. Refutation of a model is highly problematic.

The invisible woman
While mistaken stylised facts may be difficult to correct, one can at least argue about an assumption which is in the public domain. The form of gender bias which is hardest to counter is the invisibility of women. Females can disappear from economic analysis in a number of ways. First, results derived on the basis of a male sample are presented as if they applied to all individuals. For example, a recent article on 'The occupational choice of British children' studied only the occupational choice of British boys (Robertson and Symons, 1990). Second, the productive and reproductive activities of women are not recognised as part of economic activity. As Marilyn Waring (1988) points out, the value of household production is not recognised in the national accounts. Third, even when men and women are incorporated into economic models, relationships between men and women rarely are. For example, Robert Barro's celebrated (1974) analysis of the effect of government debt is based on a model of individuals who reproduce themselves asexually. As Bernheim and Bagwell (1988) have shown, if the model is expanded to allow for marriage, it produces absurd results. This brings us to the fourth challenge:

Challenge no. 4: To incorporate both men and women into economic analysis

There has been progress made in countering the first two aspects of women's invisibility. Women are beginning to appear in economics texts. A survey of the introductory chapters

---

[1] To be strictly accurate, Becker's result holds when the wife's earnings are less than the income transfer from husband to wife.

The feminist challenge to neoclassical economics   493

of six intermediate microeconomics textbooks[1] found only one (Gould and Lazear, 1989) which used exclusively male pronouns and characters. The latest planned revisions of the UN system of national accounts meets a number of the feminist criticisms raised by Marilyn Waring (Postner, 1992), and there is a growing literature on the value of household production, which is surveyed by Goldschmidt-Clermont (1982, 1987).

However, there is more work to be done. The major problem now is to incorporate women as women, and to describe the constraints and relationships particular to this gender. Women spend much of their time in what feminists refer to as the private sphere, doing housework, caring for children, and so on. Economics tends to regard the private sphere as a black box. This places sources of women's disadvantage, such as long hours spent in housework, unequal sharing of household income, or inability to influence family spending decisions, outside the scope of economic analysis. I shall now consider the economics of the private sphere.

The private sphere
Economists usually finesse the private sphere by assuming that the family maximises a single utility function. Family members act as if they all have the same preferences for food, children's clothing, or individual family members enjoying leisure. The family utility function assumption is unsound for feminist and for methodological reasons.

A consequence of the family utility function is that conflict within the family cannot be addressed. Marshall's treatment of the family is not unrepresentative:

. . . the family affections generally are so pure a form of altruism, that their action might have shown little semblance of regularity, had it not been for the uniformity of the family relations themselves. As it is, their action is fairly regular and it has always been fully reckoned with by economists, especially in relation to the distribution of the family income between the various family members, the expenses of preparing children for their future career, and the accumulation of wealth to be enjoyed after the death of him by whom it has been earned (Marshall, 1920, p. 20).

Since families are regulated by a uniform altruism, economics can be assured that family income is distributed equitably between the various family members, and there is no need to enquire into intra-family equity. Conflict disappears. A fundamental question on the feminist research agenda, namely, the position of women in the private sphere, cannot be answered. The family enters a 'black box'.

Treating the family as a single unit is also methodologically unsound. A number of writers have noted the inconsistency between the notion of a single family utility function and neoclassical economics' standard of methodological individualism. Neoclassical (micro-) economics takes as the basic explanatory device the behaviour of a rational individual. As Chiappori (1992) puts it 'Modelling a *group* (even reduced to two partici-pants) as if it were a single individual . . . should be seen as a . . . holistic deviation'. What are the justifications for this deviation?

Early economists such as James Mill justified treating the household as a single individual on the grounds that the interests of women and children were subsumed in the interests of the male household head. Folbre and Hartmann (1988) quote James Mill's *Encyclopedia Britannica* article arguing against the emancipation of women to illustrate this view:

One thing is pretty clear, that all those individuals whose interests are indisputably included in those of other individuals may be struck off without inconvenience. In this light may be viewed all

[1] Salvatore (1991), Hirschleifer (1988), Frank (1991), Eaton and Eaton (1991), Gould and Lazear (1989), Hyman (1989).

494   F. R. Woolley

children, up to a certain age, whose interests are involved in those of their parents. In this light also, women may be regarded, the interests of almost all of whom is involved either in that of their fathers or in that of their husbands (quoted in Folbre and Hartmann, 1988, p. 188).

The household is treated as a single unit, and the interests of women and children are thereby rendered invisible.

There are few modern defences given for the family utility function assumption. Samuelson (1956) gives the rather weak argument that families reach a 'consensus' because 'blood is thicker than water'. The problem with his argument is that, even if we agree that families are cooperative, there is no reason to believe that the outcome of family cooperation will be a utility function which has all the properties of an individual utility function, that is, that a harmonious family will be as consistent and rational as a single individual. Betts (1991) derives a family utility function using assumptions which guarantee that everyone marries someone with tastes identical to his or her own. Even if we accept this vision of marital harmony, we must admit that it does not include women as distinct individuals, it does not allow any analysis of the private sphere, and is open to the objections advanced to Samuelson's model. Becker's theory of social interactions is the most rigorous justification of the family utility function assumption. Becker showed that, under certain conditions, the household has a single utility function which is identical to that of the head of the household, that is the male income earner (Becker, 1974). Women and children count only to the extent of their husbands' and fathers' caring.

Alternative models of family decision-making which do not arrive at a single family utility function have been developed by Leuthold (1968), Manser and Brown (1980), Apps (1981), Apps and Savage (1989), Ashworth and Ulph (1981), McElroy and Horney (1981), Sen (1985B, 1987), Ulph (1988), Lommerud (1989), Chiappori (1992), Bragstad (1989), Woolley (1990), and Lundberg and Pollak (1992).[1] Feminist critiques have been provided by Janet Seiz (1991), Julie Nelson (1991) and Elaine McCrate (1987). A brief description of the new models of the household gives a guide to their general flavour.

All the models of family decision-making model interaction between two people. One fundamental question that each modeller has to face is: 'How are the asymmetries between men and women captured in this model?' If one is to stay within the neoclassical method-ological mainstream, the fundamental explanatory variables must be individuals' tastes, capacities and endowments. So, in Jane Leuthold's (1968) pioneering work, there are asymmetries between men's and women's labour supply, and these arise from differences in their wage rates and in the preferences for leisure versus market work, which may in turn be influenced by the presence of children. In Torunn Bragstad's (1989) model, each member of the household has a 'threshold', which is the maximum amount of untidiness, dirty dishes, and so on he or she can tolerate. Small differences in the thresholds of family members can lead to large differences in the amount of housework performed. McElroy and Horney (1981) argue that a woman will enjoy a greater command over household income the higher her fall-back position, that is, the level of well-being in case of marital breakdown, the greater her partner's concern for her consumption and the lower the price of the goods which she likes to consume.

Does the presence of alternative models of household decision-making provide evidence that it is possible to fight the traditional invisibility of women within the neoclassical economic paradigm? In an obvious sense, it does. The models discussed above are

---

[1] There is not sufficient space here to describe the literature in detail; those interested will find a survey in Woolley (1990).

neoclassical models with rational, visible, women. They allow us to answer questions such as: 'Do working women enjoy a greater level of well-being than housewives?'. Apps and Savage (1989) actually estimate the extent of inequality within the household. So, in one sense, the models do provide a non-gendered neoclassical economics.

Yet building models of the family according to the standard economic rules, that is, people maximise their own well-being (which may depend upon the well-being of other people) subject to some set of constraints, fails to yield explanations or predictions about family behaviour which are convincing to all economists. Traditional economists and feminists might agree that there is something missing from the models of the family, but would differ in the preferred candidate for the missing element. Ben-Porath (1982) attacks the notion of rationality within the household: maximisation of utility 'is less compelling in household behaviour where those who fail to maximise are not necessarily eliminated' (p. 58). In my own experience, traditional economists often react to models which view the family as two rational utility maximisers by saying something along the lines of 'My marriage isn't like that. We cooperate and make decisions together'. Samuelson's idea that families reach a consensus has broad popular appeal. But there is an infinite variety of possible consensuses—we could agree to go on a cycling holiday or we could agree to visit New York city, but cannot afford to do both. What determines which consensus is reached? The question is rarely asked, so I can only speculate as to likely answers, such as, love, commitment, or perhaps the longevity of family relations which make people sacrifice short-term interest to the long-run good of the family. In a way the real challenge is for traditional economists to articulate clearly the problems with models of family decision-making.

Feminists are fundamentally concerned with how gender is incorporated within economic models of the family. What makes the models apply to a man and a woman living together, instead of to, say, college roommates? One difference between men and women is in the institutional constraints the genders face. Family relations, particularly marriage, are what legal scholars call a 'status', not a freely negotiated contract. The state imposes limits on the terms of, on entry to, and exit from marriage. For example, homosexuals cannot marry. Conventions surround the roles of 'husband', 'wife' and 'mother', and determine socially acceptable behaviour. Feminist economists are now beginning the vast enterprise of explaining the emergence of institutions which disadvantage women. For example, Nancy Folbre (1992) discusses how evolution has shaped institutional 'structures of constraint'. This brings us to another challenge.

Challenge no. 5: To find out what shapes the institutions which privilege or disadvantage women

The literature explaining economic institutions has grown rapidly in the last decade, and has a number of divergent strands. A number of writers connect the search for an individualistic explanation of institutions with political individualism or libertarianism (see, for example, Rowe, 1989). The transaction cost approach provides insights into the evolution of firms and families (Pollak, 1985). What feminists can add to this literature is a feminist standpoint. Women's experiences of economic institutions are not always the same as men's, and neither are their stylised facts, or reasonable explanations. A feminist economics would draw from non-feminist writers, but would be informed by a feminist perspective.

A second way in which gender enters the new economic models of the family is through tastes. For example, in Bragstad's model, women have a lower threshold for household

496   F. R. Woolley

mess than do men.[1] Recognising that tastes may be endogenous brings us back to our first challenge: endogenising tastes may be necessary if we are to find satisfactory explanations of women's disadvantage.[2]

A third aspect of gender difference is that women have children. Yet, as Julie Nelson (1991) points out, models of 'families' too often become models of adult individuals in which children play no role. Indeed, my own work (Woolley, 1990) essentially models a 'household' as two childless adults. Nelson (1991) argues that: 'A view of families that focuses only on the prime-age adults makes invisible—unimportant, part of 'nature', not amenable to study—exactly those activities which have traditionally been of foremost importance to women'.

Does incorporating children into models of the family pose a fundamental challenge to neoclassical economics? Children can be included within models of the family as, say, a public good (Lundberg and Pollak, 1992). Children's welfare or consumption enters as an argument in the parents' utility functions. This approach generates a number of interesting predictions about, for example, the potential effect of differentials in caring on the distribution of household income or the division of household labour. However, as Nelson (1991) has argued, it is open to feminist critiques. First, it treats children as objects not ends in themselves. Second, women's caring for children at times seems a commitment, a responsibility, or even a constraint.

A feminist perspective on children could fundamentally challenge neoclassical economics. First, if, as Nelson suggests, we choose to look after children because of responsibility or commitment, we may want to reconsider our welfare economic evaluation of these choices, perhaps along the lines developed in Sen in his classic essay, 'Rational Fools' (1982). Second, inclusion of children as economic agents and not consumer durables would radically change the new home economics. This brings us to our sixth challenge:

> Challenge no. 6: To develop a better economic model of caring and reproductive
>   activity

Perhaps a feminist might not want to tie herself to one particular view of the family. The models developed by Bragstad, McElroy and Horney, and others within the economic paradigm yield insights as to the effect of mess thresholds, divorce laws, and other factors on the well-being of women within the private sphere. At the same time, a richer modelling of institutional structures might allow a better understanding of family relations. Feminists would not deny the traditional economists' view that loving is part of family life—but only one part. People in families can be nurturing and giving, and they can be motivated by their own self-interest. We are best off taking a part from each view of the family, rather than committing ourselves to one.

5. Conclusions

We are now in a position to appraise each item on the feminist economics agenda.

To document differences in the well-being of men and women. The first agenda item is the one which is the closest to being achieved. There is a substantial literature documenting

---

[1] It is interesting to note that Becker's (1974) model of the family also incorporates asymmetric tastes. The head (male) is altruistic and the dependent (female) is selfish. The motivation for this assumption is unclear.

[2] John Stuart Mill, an early feminist economist, recognised how women's tastes were shaped by their cultural conditioning: 'If women are better than men at anything, it surely is in individual self-sacrifice for those of their own family. But I lay little stress on this, so long as *they are universally taught that they are born and created for self-sacrifice*' (Mill, 1970, p. 172, emphasis added).

The feminist challenge to neoclassical economics   497

differentials in women's and men's earnings, leisure time and, most recently, share of household income. The research is published in mainstream economic journals.

To advocate policies which will promote equity. The second agenda item is more problematic. In many neoclassical economic models, policies which promote equity have efficiency costs. Hence a feminist economist has two options. First, to do unbiased research which establishes the relative magnitude of equity gains and efficiency losses. Second, to push back the boundaries of neoclassical economics by endogenising preference structures and institutions. A policy-oriented feminism is not sufficient unto itself.

To conduct research free from androcentric bias. There are two types of gender bias in economics. The first, the use of mistaken stylised facts, is easier to combat than the second, the invisibility of women. Invisibility is more pervasive, more persistent, and harder to fight. I suggested that the most serious example of women's invisibility is the subsuming of women's preferences into the household utility function, but this may reflect my own particular biases as a micro-economist. Certainly, the attempts which have been made to model the household explicitly provoke fundamental questions about neoclassical economics.

Carrying out the feminist economics agenda raises challenges for neoclassical economics. First, inequality between men and women in the labour market and in the household appears to be partially attributable to tastes and institutions. Feminist economists' commitment to greater gender equality brings with it a hope that tastes and institutions can be changed in ways that will promote greater equality between men and women, and a corresponding need for a welfare economic framework within which to evaluate changing preferences and institutions. Second, a feminist economics would make visible traditional areas of female concern, such as household production, child rearing, and caring.

Feminist economists are not alone in examining the origin of tastes, modelling the household, or calling for a more institutional economics. On the one hand, the questions raised by feminists have been addressed by economists trained in the Chicago tradition. Stigler and Becker (1977) endogenise preferences, Becker (1974) models the household, and Landes (1978) and Becker and Murphy (1988) discuss the evolution of marriage and divorce institutions. There are, I think, two reasons why this work is not feminist. First, the stylised facts of these Chicago models seem to many feminists to be wrong. Second, the models encourage an almost complacent acceptance of the status quo. For example, Becker and Murphy (1988, p. 18) conclude 'It is remarkable how many state interventions in the family appear to contribute to the efficiency of family arrangements'. To be a feminist is to believe that it would in some sense be better if the world was characterised by a greater degree of gender equality than is presently the case.

On the other hand, there is an emerging 'neo-neoclassical' economics which is meeting many of the challenges raised by feminist economists. Amartya Sen has suggested that economic man is a rational fool if he does not take time to think about the preference function he is maximising. Sen's work on meta-preference orderings (1982) and capabilities (1987) provides promising avenues for the development of a welfare economics which incorporates feminist ideas of endogenous preferences (Woolley, 1992). Sheila Dow's (1990) idea of moving 'beyond dualism' is thought-provoking from a feminist perspective. The division between self and other permeates economic thinking. Dow's 'Babylonian

498   F. R. Woolley

thinking' provides a way of breaking down this division, recognising that at times we think in terms of self-interest, at times in terms of our children's interests, or our family's interests, or social interests. Geoff Hodgson's (1986) insightful critique of methodological individualism, and his call for a synthesis of explanations, involving both individual agency and social structure (p. 219) is very welcome.

Feminist economics can draw from all of these new economic thinkers. What feminism can add to the literature is, first and foremost, a focus on economic justice between men and women, which unifies an otherwise disparate literature, and gives a compelling motivation for continuing to challenge traditional economic thinking. Second, feminists bring new prespectives and experiences which allow them to see, and to seek to explain, economic facts about male-female wage differentials, household production, or family decision-making.

Bibliography

Aigner, D. J. and Cain, G. C. 1977. Statistical theories of discrimination in labour markets, *Industrial and Labour Relations Review*, vol. 30

Apps, P. 1981. *A Theory of Inequality and Taxation*, Cambridge, Cambridge University Press

Apps, P and Savage, E. 1989. Labour supply, welfare rankings and the measurement of inequality, *Journal of Public Economics*, vol. 39

Ashworth, J. S. and Ulph, D. 1981. Household models, in Brown, C. V. (ed.), *Taxation and Labour Supply*, London, George Allen and Unwin

Barro, R. 1974. Are government bonds net wealth?, *Journal of Political Economy*, vol. 82

Becker, G. S. 1971. *The Economics of Discrimination*, 2nd edn, Chicago, IL, University of Chicago Press

Becker, G. S. 1974. A theory of social interactions, *Journal of Political Economy*, vol. 82

Becker, G. S. 1981A. Altruism in the family and selfishness in the market place, *Economica*, vol. 48

Becker, G. S. 1981B. *A Treatise on the Family*, Cambridge, Harvard University Press

Becker, G. S. 1985. Human capital, effort, and the sexual division of labour, *Journal of Labor Economics*, vol. 3

Becker, G. S. and Murphy, K. 1988. The family and the state, *Journal of Law and Economics*, vol. 31

Ben-Porath, Y. 1982. Economics and the family—match or mismatch? A review of Beckers *A Treatise on the Family*, *Journal of Economic Literature*, vol. 22

Bergmann, B. 1983. Feminism and economics, *Academe* September/October

Bergmann, B. 1986. *The Economic Emergence of Women*, New York, Basic Books

Bergmann, B. 1989. Does the market for womens labor need fixing, *Journal of Economic Perspectives*, vol. 3

Bernheim, B. and Bagwell, K. 1988. Is everything neutral?, *Journal of Political Economy*, vol. 96

Betts, J. 1991. Technological change and the intra-family division of labour, paper presented to the Canadian Economics Association meetings, Kingston, Ontario, June, 1991

Blank, R. 1991. The effects of double-blind versus single-blind reviewing: experimental evidence from the American economic review, *American Economic Review*, vol. 81

Blau, F. and Ferber, M. A. 1986. *The Economics of Women, Men and Work* Englewood Cliffs, NJ, Prentice Hall

Blaug, M. 1980. *The Methodology of Economics or How Economists Explain*, Cambridge, Cambridge University Press

Bragstad, T. 1989. 'On the significance of standards for the division of work in the household', mimeo, University of Oslo

Brown, L. J. 1989. 'Gender and economic analysis: a feminist perspective', mimeo, Eastern Washington University

Chiappori, P. A. 1992. Collective labour supply and welfare, *Journal of Political Economy*

Dow, S. C. 1990. Beyond dualism, *Cambridge Journal of Economics*, vol. 14, no. 2

Eaton, B. C. and Eaton, D. F. 1991. *Microeconomics*, 2nd edn, New York, W. H. Freeman

England, P. 1990. What can economics learn from feminism, paper presented at the AEA annual meetings, December, 1990

The feminist challenge to neoclassical economics 499

England, P. *Comparable Worth: Theories and Evidence,* New York, Aldine, forthcoming

England, P. and Brown, I. 1990. Internalization and constraint in theories of women's oppression, forthcoming in Ben Agger (ed.), *Current Perspectives on Social Theory*

Ferber, M. and Teiman, M. 1981. The oldest, the most established, the most quantitative of the social sciences—and the most dominated by men: the impact of feminism on economics, in Spender, D. (ed.), *Men's Studies Modified; The Impact of Feminism on the Academic Disciplines,* Oxford, Pergamon Press

Folbre, N. and Heidi, H. 1988. The rhetoric of self-interest: ideology of gender in economic theory in Klamer, A., McCloskey, D. N. and Solow, R. M. (ed.), *The Consequences of Economic Rhetoric,* Cambridge, Cambridge University Press

Folbre, N. 1992. *Who Pays for the Kids? Gender and the Structure of Constraint,* London, Routledge

Frank, R. H. 1991. *Microeconomics and Behavior,* New York, McGraw Hill

Fuchs, V. R. 1986. His and hers: gender differences in work and income, 1959–1979, *Journal of Labor Economics,* vol. 4

Gintis, H. 1974. Welfare criteria with endogenous preferences: the economics of education, *International Economic Review,* vol. 13

Goldschmidt-Clermont, L. 1982. *Unpaid Work in the Household: A Review of Economic Evaluation Methods,* Geneva, International Labour Office

Goldschmidt-Clermont, L. 1987. *Economic Evaluations of Unpaid Household Work: Africa, Asia, Latin America and Ocean,* Geneva, International Labour Office

Gould, J. P. and Lazear, E. P. 1989. *Microeconomic Theory,* 6th edn, Homewood, IL, Irwin

Gronau, R. 1988. Sex-related wage differentials and women's interrupted labor careers—the chicken or the egg, *Journal of Labor Economics,* vol. 6

Gunderson, M. 1989. Male-female wage differentials and policy responses, *Journal of Economic Literature,* vol. 27

Haddad, L. and Kanbur, R. 1990. How serious is the neglect of intra-household inequality, *Economic Journal,* vol. 100

Hahnel, R. and Albert, M. 1990. *Quiet Revolution in Welfare Economics,* Princeton, NJ, Princeton University Press

Harding, S. 1986. *The Science Question in Feminism,* Milton Keynes, Open University Press

Hirshleifer, J. 1988. *Price Theory and Applications,* 4th edn, Englewood Cliffs, NJ, Prentice Hall

Hodgson, G. 1986. Behind methodological individualism, *Cambridge Journal of Economics,* vol. 10, no. 2

Hyman, D. N. 1989. *Modern Microeconomics: Analysis and Applications,* 2nd edn, Homewood, IL, Irwin

Juster, F. T. and Stafford, F. D. 1985. *Time, Goods and Well-Being,* Ann Arbor, MI, Institute of Social Research, University of Michigan

Juster, F. T. and Stafford, F. D. 1991. The allocation of time: empirical findings, behavioural models and problems of measurement, *Journal of Economic Literature,* vol. 29

Lam, D. 1988. Marriage markets and assortative mating with household public goods, *Journal of Human Resources,* vol. 23

Landes, E. 1978. The economics of alimony, *Journal of Legal Studies*

Leuthold, J. 1968. An empirical study of formula income transfers and the work decisions of the poor, *Journal of Human Resources,* vol. 3

Lommerud, K. 1989. Marital division of labor with risk of divorce: the role of 'voice' enforcement, *Journal of Labor Economics,* vol. 7

Lundberg, S. and Pollak, R. A. 1992. 'Separate spheres bargaining and the marriage market' mimeo, Department of Economics, University of Washington

Manser, M. and Brown, M. 1980. Marriage and household decision-making, *International Economic Review,* vol. 21

Marshall, A. 1920. *Principles of Economics,* 8th edn, London and Basingstoke, MacMillan

McCloskey, D. 1983. The rhetoric of economics, *Journal of Economic Literature,* vol. 23

McCloskey, D. 1989. 'Some consequences of a feminine economics', published as Some consequences of a conjective economics, in Ferber, M. A. and Nelson, J. A. (eds), *Beyond Economic Man: Feminist Theory and Economics,* Chicago, IL, University of Chicago Press

McCrate, E. 1987. Trade, merger and employment: economic theory on marriage, *Review of Radical Political Economics,* vol. 19

for

500   F. R. Woolley

McElroy, M. J. and Horney, M. B. 1981. Nash bargained household decision making, *International Economic Review*, vol. 22

Mill, J. S. 1970. The subjection of women in John Stuart Mill and Harriet Taylor Mill, *Essays on Sex Equality* in Rossi, A. (ed.), Chicago, IL, University of Chicago Press

Nelson, J. 1991. Towards a feminist theory of the family, paper presented at the AEA annual meetings, January 3–5, 1992

Nicolaides, P. 1988. Limits to the expansion of neoclassical economics, *Cambridge Journal of Economics*, vol. 12, no. 3

Nieva, V. F. and Gutek, B. A. 1980. Sex effects of evaluation, *Academy of Management Review*, vol. 5

Peters, H. E. 1986. Marriage and divorce: informational constraints and private contracting, *American Economic Review*, vol. 76

Pollak, R. A. 1985. A transaction cost approach to families and households, *Journal of Economic Literature*, vol. 23

Postner, H. 1992. Review of *If Women Counted: A New Feminist Economics, Review of Income and Wealth*, vol. 38

Pujol, M. A. 1992. *Feminism and Anti-Feminism in Early Economic Thought*, Edward Elgar, Aldershot, England

Robb, R. E. 1978. Earnings differentials between males and females in Ontario, *Canadian Journal of Economics*, vol. 11

Robertson, D. and Symons, J. 1990. The occupational choice of British children, *Economic Journal*, vol. 100

Rowe, N. 1989. *Rules and Institutions*, Hemel Hempstead, Herts, Allan

Salvatore, D. 1991. *Microeconomics*, New York, Harper Collins

Samuelson, P. 1956. Social indifference curves, *Quarterly Journal of Economics*, vol. 52

Seiz, J. A. 1991. The bargaining approach and feminist methodology, *Review of Radical Political Economics*, vol. 23

Seiz, J. A. 1991. Gender and economic research, forthcoming in de Marchi, N. (ed.), *The Methodology of Economics*, Boston, MA, Kluwer Nijhoff

Sen, A. K. 1966. Labour allocation in a cooperative enterprise, *Review of Economic Studies*, vol. 33

Sen, A. K. 1982. *Choice, Welfare, and Measurement*, Oxford, Basil Blackwell

Sen, A. K. 1984. Family and food: sex bias in poverty, *Resources, Values, and Development*. Cambridge, MA, Harvard University Press

Sen, A. K. 1985A. Well-being, agency and freedom: the Dewey lectures 1984, *The Journal of Philosophy*, vol. 82

Sen, A. K. 1985B. Women, technology and sexual divisions, *Trade and Development: An UNCTAD Review*, vol. 6

Sen, A. K. 1987. Gender and cooperative conflicts, WIDER Working Paper 18

Shakespeare, W. 1986. *The Complete Works*, Wells, S. and Taylor, G. (eds), Oxford, Clarendon Press

Stigler, G. J. and Becker, G. S. 1977. De Gustibus Non Est Disputandum, *American Economic Review* vol. 67

Ulph, D. 1988. 'A general noncooperative Nash model of household behaviour', mimeo, University of Bristol

Waring, M. 1988. *If Women Counted: A New Feminist Economics*, San Francisco, CA, Harper and Row

Woolley, F. R. 1990. *Economic Models of Family Decision Making, with Applications to Intergenerational Justice*, unpublished Ph.D. dissertation, London School of Economics

Woolley, F. R. 1992. 'Welfare economics and its critics: a feminist reappraisal mimeo', Carleton University

[2]

Economics and Philosophy, **8** (1992), 103–125. Printed in the United States of America.

GENDER, METAPHOR, AND THE DEFINITION OF ECONOMICS

JULIE A. NELSON

University of California, Davis

1. INTRODUCTION

Let me make it clear from the outset that my main point is *not* either of the following: one, that there should be more women economists and research on "women's issues" (though I think there should be), or two, that women as a class do, or should do, economics in a manner different from men (a position with which I disagree). My argument is different and has to do with trying to gain an understanding of how a certain way of thinking about gender and a certain way of thinking about economics have become intertwined through metaphor – with detrimental results – and how a richer conception of human understanding and human identity could broaden and improve the field of economics for both female and male practitioners.

My thesis is that dualistic, hierarchical metaphors for gender have permeated the way we think about what economics is, and how it should be done, and that an alternative metaphor provides a more adequate base of understanding. I owe a debt to the pioneers of the rhetorical understanding of economics, Donald McCloskey and Arjo Klamer, for

This is a revision of an article entitled "Sex, Gender and Economic Research," prepared for presentation at the American Economic Association meetings in Atlanta, Georgia, December 28–30, 1989. I am grateful for the comments on the earlier draft received from Severin Borenstein, Marianne Ferber, Diane Felmlee, Kevin Hoover, Cathy Kling, Peter Lindert, Tom Mayer, Don McCloskey, Janet Seiz, Linda Shaffer, Steve Sheffrin, and participants in a seminar at Rice University sponsored by the Center for the Study of Institutions and Values and the Women's Studies program. I am also grateful for comments on a portion of the earlier draft received from Alison Berry, Evelyn Fox Keller, Judith Newton, Stephanie Shields, Evelyn Silvia, and participants in a Faculty Women's Research Support Group discussion at the University of California, Davis. Daniel M. Hausman and referees of this journal provided helpful comments. All positions expressed are my own and should not be taken as representing the views of these individuals or organizations.

103

104   JULIE A. NELSON

creating a niche in which the discussion of language and metaphor is possible (though still not entirely respectable) among economists. I warn sympathizers of this school, however, that I intend to use this niche for subversive purposes (Solow, 1988) – to tear down as well as to build up and improve.

2. THE DEFINITION OF ECONOMICS IS BASED IN DUALISTIC GENDER METAPHORS

Definitions

As the concepts of metaphor and gender are not in the typical economist's "toolbox," and the definition of economics may be a point of contention, I must start with brief definitions of my "variables."

"The essence of metaphor is understanding and experiencing one kind of thing in terms of another," as George Lakoff and Mark Johnson say in their work *Metaphors We Live By* (1980, p. 5). According to Lakoff and Johnson, and numerous other researchers in the areas of cognition, philosophy, rhetoric, and linguistics, metaphor is not merely a fancy addition to language, but is instead the fundamental way in which we understand our world and communicate our understanding from one person to another (e.g., Grassi, 1980, cited in Weinreich-Haste, 1986; Margolis, 1987; McCloskey, 1985; Ortony, 1979). Lakoff and Johnson give many examples of how the language we use reflects metaphorical elaborations of more abstract concepts on the foundation of basic physical experiences. Our perception of "up/down," for example, forms the basis for "good is up, bad is down" and "reason is up, emotion is down." Richer meanings can be found in more complex metaphors such as "argument is war" (reflected in language like "win," "lose," "defend," "attack"), "argument is a journey" (e.g., "step by step," "arrive at conclusions"), or "argument is a building" (e.g., "groundwork," "framework," "construct," "buttress," "fall apart"). These metaphors affect our understanding and our action; for example, if we perceive ourselves as engaged in an argument, how we interpret what we hear and how we respond depends in good part on which metaphor we use. Metaphorical understanding is also culturally variable. For example, there could exist another culture that uses the metaphor "argument is dance" and so uses language of esthetics, style, and synchronization. All of these examples are given by Lakoff and Johnson. Echoes of a similar understanding of cognition and communication can be found in works that speak about cognition in terms of "webs of connection" (C. Keller, 1986), "patterning" (Margolis, 1987; Wilshire, 1989), "cognitive schema" (Bem, 1981), gestalts, or analogies, instead of "metaphor." I will use the word "metaphor" loosely, to mean all these things.

I use "gender," as do most feminist scholars, to refer to the patterning a culture *constructs* on the base of actual or perceived differences

GENDER, METAPHOR, AND THE DEFINITION OF ECONOMICS 105

between males and females. Gender is then the metaphorical connection of nonbiological phenomena with a bodily experience of biological differentiation. One of the major breakthroughs in feminist analysis has been the discovery that many (if not most) of the traits assumed to be "essentially" male or female related, in a biological sense, actually have very strong cultural components. Take, for example, the idea that men are more suited for intellectual work than are women. The smaller size of the female brain was taken as scientific proof of intellectual inferiority in the nineteenth century (Bleier, 1986). While the lack of connection between size and power has since removed this craniometric argument, the undermining of such supposed biological proofs does not necessarily carry with it a cessation of gender attribution. The cultural salience of the idea of men as intellectual and women as emotional may persist in spite of a lack of supporting theory and even in the face of evidence to the contrary. To say something has the masculine gender, then, is not to say that it necessarily relates to intrinsic characteristics of actual men, but rather to say that it is cognitively (or metaphorically) associated with the category "man." A male person is biologically masculine; a pair of pants (as on the stick figures that adorn restroom doors) is only metaphorically so; an angular abstract shape may also be understood through the metaphor of masculinity, as contrasted to a curvy abstract shape. The attribution of masculinity to pants or angular shapes clearly reflects an imposition of a tendency to organize what we see according to gender, rather than a perception of any femaleness or maleness inherent in the object itself. There is general agreement within a particular culture, at a particular time, in a particular context, about what objects, activities, personality attributes, skills, etc. are perceived to be masculine, which are understood as being feminine, and which are more or less ungendered. As the functioning of gender categories varies historically and cross-culturally, I need to clarify here that when I talk about "our" conceptions of gender, I will be referring, with all due apologies to non-Western readers, to dominant conceptions held in the modern Western and English-speaking world. When I refer to "masculine" or "feminine" traits, I do not mean traits that are essentially "more appropriate for" or "more' likely found in" persons of one sex or the other, but rather traits that have been culturally, metaphorically gendered.[1]

1. The question of what significance to give to biological differences between the sexes is currently being debated in the feminist literature. On one side are those who tend to minimize the difference between the sexes, looking to a vision of "androgynous" humans who take on traditionally masculine or feminine traits as needed. On the other side are those who do not downplay difference, but rather emphasize the need for "revalorization" (i.e., increasing the perceived social value) of distinctly female bodily experiences such as childbearing. See Nelson (1992) and citations therein. As the issues involved tend to be subtle as well as politically charged (Ruddick, 1987), the position I take in this article is one of simply withholding judgment about any claimed link between gender categories and biological nature.

The dominant conception of gender is as a hierarchical dualism.
That is, to the metaphorical connections outlined by Lakoff and Johnson
of up-in-center-control-rational we can add "superior" and "masculine,"
and to the connections of down-out-periphery-submission-emotional we
can add "inferior" and "feminine." I will have much more to say on
this subject later in the article. To a reader who would question the
asymmetry of what I argue is the dominant conception of gender (who
would, perhaps, prefer to think of the actual social meaning of gender
differences in terms of a more benign complementarity), I need only
point out some obvious manifestations of asymmetry in the social domain. Rough "tomboy" girls are socially acceptable and even praised,
but woe to the gentle boy who is labeled a "sissy"; a woman may wear
pants, but a man may not wear a skirt. The hierarchical nature of the
dualism – the systematic devaluation of females and whatever is metaphorically understood as "feminine" – is what I identify as sexism.
Seen in this way, sexism is a cultural and even a cognitive habit, not
just an isolated personal trait.

Turning to the definition of economics, the diversity of endeavors
undertaken by economists suggests that there is no easy, definitive description of what economics is, and what projects are outside its realm.
I will limit my comments to mainstream North American economics
(often referred to as "neoclassical," in a broad sense) as I am not myself
familiar enough with other branches such as Marxism or modern insti-
tutionalism. Clearly, the central concept in mainstream economics is that
of "the market." On this, even economists as diverse as Robert Heilbroner and Gary Becker agree: Heilbroner traces the historical beginning
of the field of economics to the ascendance of the market system over
systems of "custom or command" (1986, p. 20); Becker simply carries
this conception to its logical extreme in seeing markets in all aspects of
human behavior (1976). The idealized market is a place where rational,
autonomous, anonymous agents with stable preferences interact for the
purposes of exchange. The agents make their choices in accordance with
the maximization of some objective function subject to resource constraints, and the outcome of their market interactions is the determination of an efficient allocation of goods along with a set of equilibrium
prices. The prototypical market is one in which tangible goods or labor
services are exchanged, with money facilitating the transactions, and in
which the agents are individual persons. The prototypical scholarly work
in economics is an article that studies market behavior using sophisticated mathematics to formalize the model in a "theory" section, accompanied by econometric analysis of data in an "empirical" section. Few
works in economics follow the prototype exactly – the "agent" may be
a household, firm, or even a country, for example, instead of an individual, or the empirical work may be left "for further research" or be
ignored entirely – but for a work to be accepted as "being economics,"

it must bear a family resemblance to the core model. This definition of economics is wide enough to include research on dual labor markets, intrafirm behavior, satisficing, bargaining, cooperative aspects of markets, the role of government, aspects of finance, the distribution of wealth, human capital, fertility, and many other areas – but some areas are considered more central than others. The less a work has in common with the prototype, the more it will be considered to be "on the fringe" or "not economics at all." Discussions of comparable worth, for example, violate the centrality of the idea of allocation by market forces, and thus the subject is usually demoted to the realm of politics. Articles that consist of "just words" are rarely recognized as "economics" – you might see them in the *American Economic Review* as presidential addresses or in clearly suspect journals such as those that deal with history or philosophy.

The definition of economics is not immutable. Some working economists may, of course, see themselves as working in an age-old process of creating ever-closer approximations to Truth. The idea that economics is socially constructed should not, however, be novel to anyone with an interest in methodology or the philosophy of science or who ever heard of Thomas Kuhn (1962). In the words of economists Bruce Caldwell and A. W. Coats (1984), " . . . reality is everywhere dense. Observation thus requires selection. All description is from a point of view." Economics, as a human endeavor, reflects human limitations in understanding a reality that is always just beyond our grasp. Economics, as a social endeavor, reflects some points of view, favored by the group that makes the rules for the discipline, and neglects others.

My argument begins with the point that while diversity does exist around the fringes of economics, the central program of economics is metaphorically linked with the hierarchical, dualistic conception of gender and a "privileging" of a particular conception of masculinity.

Economics as Embedded and Distinct

The role of the conception of gender as a hierarchical dualism in the construction of economics can be elaborated on two different margins: the way in which economics is defined as being embedded in a multitude of projects that together constitute "science," and the way in which economics is differentiated from other scientific disciplines, and especially the other social sciences.

The historical and contemporary links between thinking about science and thinking about gender have been explored in a plethora of recent works by feminist scholars, including the books *Reflections on Gender and Science* by Evelyn Fox Keller (1985) and *The Science Question in Feminism* by Sandra Harding (1986), as well as numerous articles and anthologies (Bleier, 1986; J. Harding, 1986; S. Harding and O'Barr, 1987). Harding argues that

> Mind vs. nature and the body, reason vs. emotion and social commitment, subject vs. object and objectivity vs. subjectivity, the abstract and the general vs. the concrete and particular – in each case we are told that the former must dominate the latter lest human life be overwhelmed by irrational and alien forces, forces symbolized in science as the feminine. All these dichotomies play important roles in the intellectual structures of science, and all appear to be associated both historically and in contemporary psyches with distinctively masculine sexual and gender identity projects. (1986, p. 25)

That is, science has been socially constructed to conform to a particular image of masculinity. A parallel idea of dualism, though with less emphasis on gender, can be found in Donald McCloskey's work on *The Rhetoric of Economics*. McCloskey asserts that "modernism" stresses the strict demarcation between scientific and humanistic, fact and value, truth and opinion, objective and subjective, hard and soft, rigorous and intuitive, precise and vague, male and female (1985, p. 42).

The connection of science with masculinity is blatant in some of the language and metaphors used by scientists to describe their endeavor. For example, an early Secretary of the Royal Society stated that the intent of the Society was to "raise a Masculine Philosophy . . . whereby the Mind of Man may be ennobled with the knowledge of Solid Truths" (E. Keller, 1985, p. 52). The relation of masculine science with feminine nature is often expressed in terms of domination, as in Francis Bacon's words, "I am come in very truth leading to you Nature with all her children to bind her to your service and make her your slave" (E. Keller, 1985, p. 39). The experience of sexual intercourse from the male point of view is often reflected in historical and contemporary language with imagery of penetration, probing, and piercing of nature, and the "overpowering rush" of scientific advance. While at times the metaphors suggest a loving intercourse, or at least a willing seduction of nature, at others times the combination of imagery of domination and of heterosexual intercourse suggests rape (E. Keller, 1985, chap. 2; Weinreich-Haste; Easlea, 1986).

The definition of economics is embedded in the definition of modern science, but economics is also differentiated from science-in-general. As *social* science, economics takes a "feminine" role vis a vis mathematics and the physical sciences. Human behavior is a "softer" subject than abstract math or the natural world, less amenable to quantitative (as opposed to qualitative) description or formulation in terms of "laws." This presents a problem for those economists who, perhaps to maintain a clear-cut gender self-image, need to see their work as consistently masculine. Consider the language used in the statement of purpose of the Econometric Society, which can be found inside the back cover of every issue of *Econometrica*:

> The Society shall operate as a completely disinterested, scientific organization, without political, social, financial or nationalistic bias. Its main object shall be to promote studies that aim at the unification of the theoretical-quantitative and the empirical-quantitative approach to economic problems and that are penetrated by constructive and rigorous thinking similar to that which has come to dominate in the natural sciences.

Translated, I suggest that this says, "Hey guys, we want to penetrate and dominate, too!"

Among social sciences, the masculine identity of economics is more secure. A favorite pastime of economists is dumping on, expressing bewilderment about, or ridiculing the lack of "rigor" in the other social sciences. Classifying a work as "sociology" is an especially quick and sure-fire way of silencing it by removing it from the territory of serious conversation of economists. The hierarchical relations between the social sciences is especially evident in the ranking of journals within academic culture: having an article accepted for publication in an economics journal seems to be considered a coup for a sociologist or political scientist, but a publication in a political science or sociology journal by an economist (or in a sociology journal by a political scientist) is no harbinger of professional advancement. It may even be seen as an embarrassment.

Why is economics perceived as more masculine? One reason may be that economics is blessed with a natural unit of measure – money – which makes quantitative analysis easier. Another may be that economics as a profession has managed (whether by conscious intent or, more likely, by subtle gender structuring) to hold the line more strongly against the influx of women. Marianne Ferber (1990) notes that the fields of sociology, psychology, anthropology, and political science all have a substantially higher percentage of women among new Ph.D.s than has economics. One would think that this might be tied in with the first reason, in that women in general tend to have less mathematical training than men. However, Ferber also points out that mathematics also has more women as a percentage of new Ph.D.s than economics.

I suspect that other reasons going beyond the association of mathematics and masculinity can be found by looking at more subtle gendered aspects of the differentiation of economics from the other social sciences. It has been said, for example, that economics is about how people make choices, while sociology is about why people have no choices to make. The economist's conception of a person as an autonomous agent (consistent with the centrality of the market metaphor) is quite different from the sociologist's idea of persons as acting out social roles (consistent with a central metaphor of functional society). Economics deals with concepts of the individual, activity, choice, and competition that are identified in our culture with masculinity; the domain of sociology might be seen, from the economist's point of view, as involving the more feminine-identified concepts of the collective, passivity, determinism, and cooperative social relations. This is not to say that sociology is immune from criticism that within its own structure it contains masculine biases, but only that vis à vis economics it takes the more "feminine" role.

Have the properties associated with the "masculine" identity of economics served any useful purpose? I believe that they have and do not want to leave the impression that I consider neoclassical economics to be evil incarnate. The emphasis on rigor can be seen as an attempt to avoid sloppiness, the use of mathematical formalism as a way of catching errors that might go unnoticed in ordinary language, and the emphasis on self-interest and competition as a way of avoiding a mushy sentimentality. So far, so good. But is sloppiness the only alternative to rigor? Empty rhetoric the only alternative to precise mathematics? Is mushy sentimentality the only alternative to heartless competition? Within the dualistic metaphors for gender and economics, these are the only alternatives, and a "less masculine" economics could only be "emasculated." However, metaphors, while highlighting certain aspects of experience, hide others. I argue that the simple dualistic model of gender hides very important aspects of reality; a more encompassing way of thinking about gender can contribute to a definition of science and of economics that is more fully human, rather than distinctly masculine.

3. "NEW METAPHORS HAVE THE POWER TO CREATE A NEW REALITY"[2]

Thinking about Gender and Value

As long as masculinity is associated with superiority, the idea that economics could be improved by becoming less one-sidedly masculine makes little sense. But can the metaphorical associations between masculine/feminine and positive/negative be broken? Experience suggests that metaphors are not immutable; in fact the phenomenon of discovery in science (as well as the power of certain kinds of poetry) has sometimes been attributed to the creation of a new metaphorical association (Ortony, 1979).

One way of changing the understanding of gender and value might be to assert simply that "feminine is good, too." While one might be able to gain some ground by this route, looking at the roles that stereotypically feminine concepts and traits might play in a different defi-

2. Lakoff and Johnson (1980, p. 145).

nition of knowledge, sooner or later it becomes clear that some of these factors are quite unattractive. For example, as mentioned, McCloskey (1985) contrasts the quality of "precision," associated with maleness, with "vagueness," associated with femaleness. Can "vagueness" really be elevated to the status of a virtue?

Another way of challenging the association of masculinity with superiority and femininity with inferiority might be to decide to do away with gender associations entirely. Perhaps we can just talk about good and bad ways of doing economics, and leave gender out of the discussion. While some may hope for such a case as an ultimate goal, it seems premature to throw away gender categories if they still are actively used as cognitive and social organizers. The line between overcoming gender distinctions and simply suppressing (or, the more psychoanalytic might say, repressing) them is one that can be too easily crossed.

I propose here an analysis that retains both culturally shared gender constructs and many common judgments about what is desirable in economics. In particular, I propose that we accept that terms like "hard," "logical," "scientific," "precise," are both masculine-identified and describe legitimate goals of economic practice. But I also propose that we think of gender and value as orthogonal dimensions and actively seek out what has been *excluded* from economics by the concentration on masculinity. This exercise is not definitive of gender in any sense, nor does it cover every possible term that could be used to describe economics. The idea of orthogonality is simply proposed as an alternative metaphor to the usual hierarchical dualism. As with any metaphor, it hides as well as exposes some aspects of the reality it is meant to describe.[3]

If we draw a picture of orthogonal gender and value dimensions, like this,

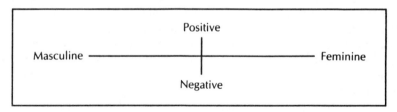

it is immediately obvious that two categories have been left out of the usual, masculine-up-positive and feminine-down-negative, metaphor.

3. By describing "hard," "logical," etc., as *culturally defined as masculine*, I by no means mean to imply that, for example, women are less logical than men. (See the discussion of gender in Section 2.) Also, while it is possible that the association of these terms with gender categories is stronger in the thinking of some individuals than in others (Bem, 1981), this does not negate the idea that these associations are culturally dominant.

The old metaphor has room neither for positive femininity or negative masculinity. Yet, with some thought, these gaps can sometimes be filled in.

As an example, take the idea that economic argument should be "hard," in the sense of "strong." The feminine-negative correspondent term, indicating a lack of hardness or strength is "soft," in the sense of "weak." This fills up one diagonal of the diagram:

M + strong-hard	
	F – weak-soft

But hardness can also mean a lack of flexibility, rigidity, a lack of malleability needed to adapt to changing conditions. "Softness" also has other connotations besides weakness. The aspect of feminine "softness" that needs elevation here is not weakness, but rather flexibility or resilience:

M + strong-hard	F + flexible-soft
M – rigid-hard	F – weak-soft

Each of the positive terms now in the diagram can be seen as one-half of a necessary balance to achieve a "durable" argument. This suggests that while economics should be masculine-hard, it should also be feminine-soft (each understood in their positive sense). It suggests that rigidity is a potential hazard for a discipline that concentrates too much on the achievement of masculinity rather than the achievement of good argument.[4]

The association of economics with formal, logical reasoning can be addressed in the same framework. In the simple dualistic view, reason is conceived of as identical with formal logic and masculinity; any exposition not conforming to the laws of logic is identified as being illogical and, by implication, inferior. Economics seminars, for example, often

4. I have elsewhere described in more detail the role of relationships of "complementarity," "lack," and "perversion" in the structure of this diagram (Nelson, 1992). The formalization is omitted here; the point is simply to suggest that important insights might be hidden by the usual masculine-positive, feminine-negative dualism.

GENDER, METAPHOR, AND THE DEFINITION OF ECONOMICS   **113**

showcase a presentation of a formal model and its formal implications, and bring in as an aside an explanation of the "intuition" behind the result. These "intuitive" explanations (quite in contrast to the alternative meaning of "intuition" in terms of a flash of inspiration) often include long and elaborate chains of verbal reasoning, carefully constructed analogies, and concrete examples. These explanations, however, are considered "softer" than the formal models and, like the proverbial "feminine intuition," unreliable and unrelated to true rationality. A more sophisticated idea of what it means "to reason" and "to know," suggested in the works on metaphor and cognition previously cited, identifies reason, instead, with a complementarity of logic, on the one hand, and reasoning by other means, such as analogy or pattern recognition, on the other. For example, Howard Margolis (1987) expresses cognition as the combination of "reasoning why," or step-by-step critical analysis, with "seeing that," which involves a no less important perception of the bigger pattern. Georgescu-Roegen's (1971) distinction between "arithmomorphic" and "dialectical" concepts is helpful in suggesting terms for the missing feminine-positive, masculine-negative diagonal in the gender value compass. He calls "arithmomorphic" those concepts that can be manipulated by formal logic. Most of our thoughts, however (he argues), are concerned with forms and qualities and concepts that overlap with their opposites, and dealing with these requires "dialectical" thought.[5] The "position that dialectical concepts should be barred from science because they would infest it with muddled thinking" he labels "arithmomania" (1971, p. 52). Such a richer understanding of the nature of rationality can be summarized in a gender-value diagram as

logical reasoning	"dialectical" reasoning
"arithmomania"	illogic

The extensive verbal explanations economists often call "intuition" are examples of dialectical reasoning, not merely cases of degraded or diluted logic. The identification of reasoning with logical reasoning alone

5. Georgescu-Roegen's examples of dialectical concepts include "good," "justice," "likelihood," and "want" (1971, p. 45). Another example of the contrast between logical and dialectical thinking is given by Howard Margolis's discussion of the meanings of the word "or" (1987, p. 94). In formal logic, "or" means "either or both, and not neither." But in common usage, its meanings are contradictory: in "Cream or sugar?" it means "either, both, or neither"; in a judicial decision of "$100 or 10 days" it means "either, but not neither and not both"; in a waiter's question of "soup or salad" it means "either or neither, but not both," Yet, in context, these are all meaningful and reasonable statements. It is hard to imagine any discussion of economic issues that would not rely heavily on such understanding of context.

ends up, in Georgescu-Roegen's words, "giving us mental cramps" (1971, p. 80). The usefulness of two-dimensional over one-dimensional thinking comes from the exposition of relationships that are hidden by the usual pairing of reason-masculine-superior with intuitive-feminine-inferior. That simple dualism can be seen to involve the too-easy collapsing of reason into logic and the false identification of other valid forms of reasoning with illogic.

Similarly, the idea that there are different kinds of knowledge can be pictured as

scientific	humanistic
inhuman	unscientific

where I use the term "scientific" in the sense of instrumental, technological ("how to") knowledge, systematically gathered from observation of phenomena "external" to the researchers own consciousness, and "humanistic" in the sense of affective, introspective knowledge focusing on the "why" and "for what purpose" questions of human existence. Humanistic knowledge without at least a touch of the practical, outward-focusing approach I have labeled "scientific" is at best sterile (because it can have no effect on what actually happens) and at worst the ravings of a lunatic (if unique to a single person). But the elevation of scientific knowledge (implicit in the project of "demarcation" of science) without attention to human values could very well lead to the very efficient destruction of life on earth.

The emphasis on mathematics as the key to "rigorous" understanding in economics, and the downplaying of language as having any importance to the business of knowledge seeking, can be understood using the diagram:

precise	rich
thin	vague

The left side highlights aspects of mathematical language and the right side aspects of common language. The advantage of use of mathematics is the precision it supplies, as opposed to the vagueness or ambiguity that may be associated with words in all their diverse meanings. On the other hand, pure mathematics is precisely content-free; the application of mathematics to problems of human behavior can come only through the explanation of mathematical formulas as metaphors for some real world phenomenon, and this drawing of analogies involves the use of words. In the process, meanings beyond that immediately present in the mathematical analogy will also be suggested. Mathematics can certainly be helpful in overcoming the failings of imprecise words, but, if concentration is put on maintaining the gender boundary rather than on recognizing the value boundary, the failure of thin, empty mathematics may sneak in unobserved. Empty math, or "rhetorical math" in the pejorative sense, is described by Philip J. Davis and Reuben Hersh (1987) as math that neither brings forth any new mathematical idea nor "leads back to the phenomenon being modeled" (p. 58). "Precision" is a virtue in economics; this analysis suggests we also consider "richness" to be good, too, and furthermore that we recognize the pursuit of precision alone, without richness, as a vice.

Gender, Value, and "Economic Man"

While the previous analysis can aid in developing new and broader understandings of rationality, knowledge, rigor, and numerous other concepts that come into play in the definition of economics, this section applies the expanded metaphor for gender and value to the concept of individual agency. The point at issue here is not whether the assumption of individual agency can lead to fruitful hypotheses: there is no doubt that the assumption of "economic man" has been fruitful, especially as contrasted to the alternative hypotheses that human behavior is completely socially determined, as assumed in my caricature of sociology, or that it is materially determined, as in some variants of Marxism or perhaps in sociobiology. The problem is that when we limit the choices to an autonomy/determinism dualism, we limit ourselves to playing with only half a deck.

The conception of human nature underlying neoclassical economics is of an individual human as radically separate from other humans and from nature; the emphasis is on separation, distance, demarcation, autonomy, independence of self. *Homo economicus* is the personification of individuality run wild. "Economic man," the "agent" of the prototypical economic model, springs up fully formed, with preferences fully developed, and is fully active and self-contained. He has no childhood or old age, no dependence on anyone, no responsibility for anyone but himself. The environment has no effect on him, but rather is merely the passive material, presented as "constraints," over which his rationality has play. He interacts in society without being influenced by society: his mode of interaction is through an ideal market in which prices form the only, and only necessary, form of communication.[6] *Homo economicus*

6. I use the pronoun "he" intentionally: the gender biases in economics would by no means be overcome by replacing or alternating with the pronoun "she," in an attempt at cheap gender neutrality. See Frank and Treichler, editors, 1989, for the difference between gender-neutral and nonsexist language.

is the central character in a romance of individuality without connection to nature or to society.

The idea that this conception of selfhood as radically separate from our fellow humans could be misleading and indeed dangerous is not unique to feminist scholarship. The way in which it leads us to ignore the sociality of our thought and existence is pointed out by, among others, McCloskey and other scholars who investigate the role of rhetoric (McCloskey, 1985). The way it causes us to neglect the physical basis of our thought has been pointed out by Lakoff and Johnson, who stress the "bodily basis of meaning, imagination and reason" (Johnson, 1987). Not all criticism of this solipsistic view of individuality is this recent: Alfred North Whitehead wrote about the dehumanizing and self-defeating aspects of the modernist view in 1925.

Recently, however, a rich line of feminist scholarship developed that has focused on the *gendered* meaning of the Cartesian view. The relation of gender to the "privileging" of separation over connection has been traced through history by Sandra Harding (1986) and Susan Bordo (1986); through psychological development by Nancy Chodorow (1980); through personal ethical development by Carol Gilligan (1982, 1986); through myth and religion by Catherine Keller (1986). The projection of autonomy onto masculinity and connection to nature and society onto femininity is "embarrassingly empirical," to borrow a phrase from Catherine Keller (1986, p. 201). Abstract philosophy connects with gendered experience in everyday distinctions between who does the thinking versus who does the dishes; who writes the journal articles versus who writes the Christmas cards; the man who envisages "man" as individual and autonomous versus the woman who changes her name to Mrs. John Jones when she marries. What could be a recognition of physical embodiment and social connectedness, as well as individuality, within each person becomes a negative complementarity. The male's "transcendence" of nature and society is made possible only through the subjection of the female to full-time maintenance of the social and physical connections that are, after all, indispensable for human existence (C. Keller, 1986; Fee, 1983).

To this familiar dualistic contrasting of individual to social identity, and individual agency to social or material determinism, the scholarship on gender adds complementary contrasts of connection and isolation, "influenced" action and radical autonomy. The various conceptions of human nature, particularly in regard to the relation of the self to other humans and to nature, can be encompasssed in:

individuated	connected
isolated	engulfed

That is, the conventional idea of identity stresses the northwest-south-east diagonal: the lack of any individuality or differentiation implies the dissolving or engulfing of the individual into the larger whole of nature or society. The gender connotations are "masculine" for the positively valued individuality and "feminine" for the undifferentiated state. But differentiation can go too far, into radical separation or isolation. And the message of a certain strain of current feminist scholarship is that connection and relation do not necessarily imply the dissolving of individual identity. The positive complementarity of the upper two terms in the diagram refers to the recognition of selfhood as including both individuality and connectedness or relatedness. Or, in Alfred North Whitehead's words, we are "organisms" who require "an environment of friends" (1925, p. 206). The boundaries between oneself and others and oneself and nature are *not* strict, but neither does this imply that one is therefore swallowed up. The separation of the gender/value dimensions creates a way of seeing that individuality is not definitive of the human condition.

Similarly, for the question of the locus of decision-making, the separation of the dimensions suggests alternatives to individual agency and social or material determinism:

individually agenic	influenced
radically autonomous	determined

The radically autonomous decision-maker admits no influence from society or nature: as the sociopath whose psychological development lacks the interactive aspects shared by the rest of society, or the anorexia nervosa patient who claims that eating is a "lifestyle" habit that she can do without. Or Economic Man, whose behavior can be described purely in terms of individual preferences, without recourse to any description of social context, preference formation, or physical need. The feminist approach to economics that I am suggesting is by no means only "more sociological" than current economics, if what is meant by that is a turn to analysis assuming that agency lies entirely outside the individual. It means rejecting both radical autonomy and social determinism as paradigmatic stand-alone models of agency.

4. GENDER, VALUE, AND THE DEFINITION OF ECONOMICS

If we were to change the central character in our economic story from the radically autonomous, isolated agent, who is unneedful of social contact and uninfluenced by physical concerns, to the socially and materially situated human being, what effect would this have on the definition of economics? As pointed out earlier, the central concept of modern economics is that of the market, the locus of exchange activity.

One direction might be to promote the study of markets with an eye to their social and institutional character, instead of always starting from the view that they are more or less corrupted versions of idealized (perfectly competitive, perfect information, etc.) markets. Arjo Klamer's (1989) project on "interpretive" economics, for example, captures some of this approach. Another direction is suggested by the dimension of physical connection. Kenneth Boulding has remarked on the loss of an ecological understanding of economics, as concerned with the biosphere. He argues that part of what he sees as the "failure" of modern economics results from the loss of an earlier understanding of economic life as being both about "how society was organized by exchange" *and* about "how society was 'provisioned'" (Boulding, 1986).

An understanding of economics as centrally concerned with pro-visioning, or providing the necessaries of life, has quite different implications from the idea of economics as centrally concerned with exchange. In the exchange view, the primary distinguishing characteristic of a good is whether or not it can be exchanged on a market, not what human needs or wants it may satisfy or what role it may play in a more global, ecological system. The choice of goods depends only on abstract preferences. This radical conceptual separation of humans from their physical environment implies, among other things, sterility of economics about questions of human welfare. In the provisioning view, on the other hand, there are qualitative differences between different goods and services. Cooter and Rappoport (1984) explain how the pre-1930s material welfare school considered needs for survival and health to be more economic than desires for goods more at the luxury end of the spectrum. While the dividing line between "needs" and "wants" may be far from distinct (the concept of "need" being clearly in Georgescu-Roegen's "dialectical" category), the admittance of a category of "need" implies the recognition of an inescapable dependence of human bodies on their physical environment, which is lacking in the modern view. The tie of the deprecation of need to the deprecation of the feminine has been expressed by Muriel Dimen (in another context) as "Wanting, associated with adulthood, active will, and masculinity, is better than need, linked to infancy, passive dependency, and femininity" (1989, p. 42).

The primacy within market-oriented economics of the focus on "want," to the neglect of any consideration of the provisioning-related concept of "need," suggests the following gender/value diagram:

ability to choose actively	ability to discern what is needed
unlimited wants	neediness

GENDER, METAPHOR, AND THE DEFINITION OF ECONOMICS **119**

The masculine quadrants suggest interpretation of the world as a world of scarcity, hostile to human purposes, or the standard Lionel Robbins definition of economics as the study of human choices in context of unlimited wants and scarce resources (1935). The feminine-positive quadrant, missing from economic analysis, is the sensitivity about one-self and one's relation to the environment that allows one to determine what is *useful*, not merely what gives the highest rating on some immediate pleasure/pain calculus. Anyone who has been a parent should recognize the skill involved in this activity in discerning the needs of one's children: all I suggest is that we also focus such "maternal thinking" (the term is Ruddick's, 1989) on ourselves. Note also that while resources are by definition scarce in relation to wants conceived of as unlimited, resources might (still) be abundant in relation to human needs. The closest work in economics I have seen to this conception of how humans are actually involved in their natural environment is Amartya Sen's notion of "capability" ("a feature of a person in relation to goods," 1984, p. 316). Without this understanding of material connection, we have the scandal of professional economists working out endless theoretical yarns about preferences, while a majority of people in the world live in a state of neediness apparent to any observer who has not lost her or his humanity. With an understanding that incorporates both choice and material connection, comes the possibility of abundance and a hospitable nature, if we choose wisely.

In highlighting the connections as well as the distinctions between humans and between humans and nature, does a wider, "encompassing" view of economics then imply that economics has to be about "life, the universe, and everything"? I do not think so. The relationship of economics with other social sciences could be closer and more cooperative, of course, and based on shared understanding of the multiple dimensions of human experience (rather than imperialistic, based on imposition of the model of radical separativeness). But economics need not be undifferentiated. As a practical matter, I tentatively suggest that our discipline take as its organizational center the down-to-earth subject matter of how humans try to meet their need for material goods and services. This core corresponds better to the common sense use of the term "economics" (and to the etymological roots of the term in the Greek words meaning "household management") than does the present central concept of the idealized market. This core grounds the discipline both socially and materially. Economic provision becomes the center of study, whether it be through market, household, or government action, or whether it be by symmetric exchange, coercion, or gift. This definition dethrones choice, scarcity, and rationality as central concepts, and relegates them to the status of potentially useful tools. It brings previously taboo or fringe subjects like power and poverty into the core.

5. IS *GENDER* REALLY SO IMPORTANT?

This article is not, of course, the first to suggest that economics should be flexible, intuitive, humanistic, and rich, as well as hard, logical, scientific, and precise; or that the notion of Economic Man is seriously deficient as a model of actual human behavior in relation to nature and society; or that economics should concern itself more with concrete issues of provisioning and less with abstract analysis of hypothetical choice.[7] What this article does suggest, perhaps for the first time, is a systematic basis for the biases that have grown up in economics: nobody wants to be called a sissy.

As a devil's advocate position, suppose we argue for the moment that gender, or more specifically, the protection of a particular "masculine" conception of economics, is *not* an important factor in these internal debates within the discipline. Suppose that these are all real debates, but I am making a mountain out of a molehill by drawing out masculine/feminine associations. The major counter-argument to this comes directly from the sociology of knowledge: does not this argument also suggest that the exclusion of *women* from economics is of negligible importance? If sexism, on the social and intellectual levels, is simply incidental and suitable as the subject of drawing- (or seminar-) room jokes, then the debate about the definition of economics can presumably be carried on without any discussion of gender and even entirely by men. If on the other hand sexism (manifested, among other ways, in the exclusion of women from the community of scholars who define economics) is a pervasive social fact, is it not likely that it has had some influence on the construction of the intellectual foundations of the discipline? Note that my argument does not rest, as does Donald Mc-Closkey's (1988), on the claim that women think differently, and so would "bring" something different to economics. Most female economists I know do research that is indistinguishable from that of their male colleagues. Rather, I claim that it is systematic sexism – the systematic devaluation of women as part of a systematic devaluation of "the feminine" on many levels – that is the most important link between women and the disparaged ways of knowing. The historic exclusion of women, combined with evidence of the one-sided recent development of economics and the (limited) proof-texting that I engaged in earlier (with quotes from Bacon and *Econometrica*), is, I believe, at least suggestive of the idea that the protection of the "masculinity" of economics has played a role in the construction of the discipline.

---

7. See, for examples of some of such points raised within the mainstream, addresses by American Economic Association presidents in Gordon (1976) and quoted in Heller (1975), or the original statement of principles of the American Economic Association – later rescinded (Ely, 1936). Articles and books expressing these points of view from somewhat outside the mainstream are legion.

It might also be argued that while gender is important, other social and conceptual ways of dividing the world – such as white/nonwhite – might also be influential. I take no issue with this argument. Sandra Harding (1987) pointed out that interesting similarities can be found between feminist analysis and work on an "Afro-centered" view by the economist Vernon J. Dixon (1970, 1977). It may be that the defense of the privileged status of masculinity is only a part of a defense of privilege on many fronts.

The direction I suggest for economics is "feminist" in that it revalues the concepts metaphorically associated with femaleness. It is, however, distinct from what some might call a "feminine" approach to economics, in which one simply emphasizes those stereotypically feminine characteristics that have been neglected in the current construction of science. Such an approach runs the risks of reifying masculine/feminine categories, glorifying feminine-negative aspects, neglecting the task of distinguishing the positive and negative aspects of masculinity, and, just like the current masculine construction of economics, viewing economic phenomena through one lens when encompassing vision would be more appropriate. For example, it might be considered more "feminine" to model a particular phenomenon in terms of its aspects of cooperation rather than in terms of its aspects of competition or conflict or to focus on social constraints instead of on individual agency. I would argue, however, that while aspects of cooperation have in general been unjustly neglected, substantial *feminist* insights into the understanding of the economics of the household have been accomplished by *denying* the existence of total cooperation within the household and, instead, noting the actual presence of conflict and by rejecting common dictatorship models of the household (mislabeled as "altruistic" is a particularly glaring example of blindness to issues of power) in favor of attributing some form of agency to female actors (Folbre and Hartmann, 1988). A feminist approach, while revaluing the positive aspects of femininity, does not then limit one to using these categories of analysis that happen to be in the socially created cognitive category of feminine.

6. WHY PROGRESS IS SLOW

I have laid out in this article some hints as to how economics might look if it were to be based in an understanding of balanced humanity rather than in a perverse image of masculinity. These are only hints, and the lack of indications of what a more fully worked-out research program would look like presents an even more glaring lack to me than it, perhaps, presents to the reader. It is natural to want to know what "the bottom line" would be or "what difference it would make" in each specific area of research if an encompassing view were adopted.

Let me suggest two reasons why progress up to this point has been very limited. The first is a very real and significant problem that underlies not only a feminist transformation of economics but the whole endeavor of speaking and writing in a feminist mode: the problem of language. That is, the hierarchical dualism that links femininity with all things inferior is so ingrained in our cognition and our language that a feminist writer is often at a literal loss for words to express what she (or he) means. It is much easier to fill in the masculine-positive and feminine-negative quadrants in the gender/value diagram than to think of adequate expressions for the strengths associated with femininity and the dangers of unbalanced masculinity. One example of this problem was given earlier, where recourse had to be made to special terms coined by Georgescu-Roegen in discussing the question of rationality. To see this problem of language in a larger framework, consider how one would complete a gender-value diagram with the term "virile" (meaning "manly vigor") as its masculine-positive term. The lack of virility is "emasculation," which is a term in common use and which belongs in the feminine-negative quadrant. There exists a term, "muliebrity," whose definition is "womanliness" or the feminine "correlative of virility," but this is a very obscure word, to say the least. There exists no term suited for the masculine-negative quadrant: by analogy to "emasculation," the term that belongs there should be "effemination," but the word "effeminate" already exists and signifies an abundance of feminine (presumably negative) traits, not the lack of feminine positive traits. Even when one does come up with positive complementarities, one finds oneself dealing with expressions like "embodied rationality" or "social individuality" that sound awkward and vague in a society used to thinking in terms of dualisms and clear demarcations. Extend this problem to all areas of discourse, and it becomes obvious why much feminist scholarship is devoted to analysis of language and why at times the process of communication is frustrating and slow.

The second reason for not having a clear program worked out is that very few economists are as yet working along this line. While conversation within economics about women has a couple of decades of history, and discussion about feminism and economics has been carried on by a dedicated few, conversation about the ties between the social construction of gender and the social construction of economics is still in its infancy.[8] Economics is far behind other disciplines in looking at the implications of gender; there is more scholarship on gender not only in such fields as history, literary criticism, philosophy, psychology, and sociology but also in areas such as biology and the sociology and history of science. Several fields have one or more scholarly journals devoted

8. For other examples from these literatures, see Bergman (1987), Brown (1989), England and Kilbourne (1990), Feiner and Roberts (1990), Ferber and Birnbaum (1977), Folbre (1992), Harrison and Strassmann (1989), and Seiz (1991). Ferber and Nelson (1991) contains a collection of essays.

GENDER, METAPHOR, AND THE DEFINITION OF ECONOMICS   **123**

entirely to gender issues. As latecomers, economists could benefit from the analysis that has already been done. I especially see interesting parallels to economics in feminist scholarship on evolutionary biology (E. Keller, 1988a,b) and to work on alternatives to contractarian notions of justice (Gilligan, 1986; Benhabib, 1987).

Economics could be improved by an exploration of feminine-positive ways of knowing and being and the excising of masculine-negative perversions of the choice of subject and scholarly method. The positive-negative dualism should be the salient schema for judging the adequacy of economic research rather than the feminine-masculine schema. An approach based on a new understanding of gender and value would incorporate all aspects of knowledge that are helpful in approaching a problem, whatever they may be, and would extend the possible subject matter beyond simply those areas that can be "squeezed and moulded" (the words are Francis Bacon's, in Weinreich-Haste, 1986) into the form of a mathematically tractable model of an idealized market.

REFERENCES

Becker, Gary S. 1976. *The Economic Approach to Human Behavior*. Chicago: University of Chicago Press.

Bem, Sandra Lipsitz. 1981. "Gender Schema Theory: A Cognitive Account of Sex Typing." *Psychological Review* 88:354–64.

Benhabib, Seyla. 1987. "The Generalized and the Concrete Other: The Kohlberg-Gilligan Controversy and Moral Theory." In *Women and Moral Theory*, edited by Diana Meyers and Eva Feder Kittay, pp. 154–77. Totowa, NJ: Rowman and Littlefield.

Bergmann, Barbara R. 1987. "The Task of a Feminist Economics: A More Equitable Future." In *The Impact of Feminist Research in the Academy*, edited by Christie Farnham, pp. 131–47. Bloomington: Indiana University Press.

Bleier, Ruth (editor). 1986. "Sex Differences Research: Science or Belief?" In *Feminist Approaches to Science*, pp. 147–64. New York: Pergamon.

Bordo, Susan. 1986. "The Cartesian Masculinization of Thought." *Signs: Journal of Women in Culture and Society* 11:439–56.

Boulding, Kenneth E. 1986. "What Went Wrong with Economics." *American Economist* 30:5–12.

Brown, Lisa Jo. 1989, December. "Gender and Economic Analysis: A Feminist Perspective." Paper prepared for the annual meetings of the American Economic Association, Atlanta.

Caldwell, Bruce J., and A. W. Coats. 1984. "The Rhetoric of Economists: A Comment on McCloskey." *Journal of Economic Literature* 22:575–78.

Chodorow, Nancy Julia. 1980. "Gender, Relation, and Difference in Psychoanalytic Perspective." In *The Future of Difference*, edited by Hester Eisenstein and Alice Jardine, pp. 3–19. New Brunswick: Rutgers University Press.

Cooter, Robert, and Peter Rappoport. 1984. "Were the Ordinalists Wrong about Welfare Economics?" *Journal of Economic Literature* 22:507–30.

Davis, Philip J., and Reuben Hersh. 1987. "Rhetoric and Mathematics." In *The Rhetoric of the Human Sciences*, edited by John S. Nelson et al., pp. 53–68. Madison: University of Wisconsin Press.

Dimen, Muriel. 1989. "Power, Sexuality, & Intimacy." In *Gender/Body/Knowledge: Feminist Reconstructions of Being and Knowing*, edited by Alison M. Jaggar and Susan R. Bordo, pp. 34–51. New Brunswick: Rutgers University Press.

Dixon, Vernon. 1970. "The Diunital Approach to 'Black Economics.'" *American Economic Review* 70:424–29.

———. 1977. "African-Oriented and Euro-American-Oriented World Views: Research Methodologies and Economics." *Review of Black Political Economy* 7:119–56.

Easlea, Brian. 1986. "The Masculine Image of Science with Special Reference to Physics: How Much Does Gender Really Matter?" In *Perspectives on Gender and Science*, edited by Jan Harding, pp. 132–58. London: The Falmer Press.

Ely, Richard T. 1936. "The Founding and Early History of the American Economic Association." *American Economic Review* 26:141–50.

England, Paula, and Barbara S. Kilbourne. 1990. "Feminist Critiques of the Separative Model of Self: Implications for Rational Choice Theory." *Rationality and Society* 2:156–71.

Fee, Elizabeth, 1983. "Women's Nature and Scientific Objectivity." In *Women's Nature: Rationalizations of Inequality*, edited by Marian Lowe and Ruth Hubbard, pp. 9–27. New York: Pergamon.

Feiner, Susan F., and Bruce Roberts. 1990. "Hidden by the Invisible Hand: Neoclassical Economic Theory and the Textbook Treatment of Race and Gender." *Gender and Society* 4:159–81.

Ferber, Marianne A. 1990. "Gender and the Study of Economics." In *The Principles of Economics Course: A Handbook for Instructors*, edited by Phillip Saunders and William Walstad, pp. 44–60. New York: McGraw-Hill.

Ferber, Marianne A., and Bonnie G. Birnbaum. 1977. "The 'New Home Economics': Retrospects and Prospects." *Journal of Consumer Research* 4:19–28.

Ferber, Marianne A., and Julie A. Nelson (editors). 1991. "Beyond Economic Man: Feminist Theory and Economics." Manuscript.

Folbre, Nancy. 1992. "How Does She Know? Feminist Theories of Gender Bias in Economics." Forthcoming in *History of Political Economy*.

Folbre, Nancy, and Heidi Hartmann. 1988. "The Rhetoric of Self-Interest: Ideology and Gender in Economic Theory." In *The Consequences of Economic Rhetoric*, edited by Arjo Klamer, Donald N. McCloskey, and Robert M. Solow, pp. 184–203. Cambridge: Cambridge University Press.

Frank, Francine Wattman, and Paula A. Treichler. 1989. *Language, Gender and Professional Writing: Theoretical Approaches and Guidelines for Nonsexist Usage*. New York: The Modern Language Association of America.

Georgescu-Roegen, Nicholas. 1971. *The Entropy Law and the Economic Process*. Cambridge: Harvard University Press.

Gilligan, Carol. 1982. *In a Different Voice*. Cambridge: Harvard University Press.

Gilligan, Carol. 1986. "Reply." *Signs* 11:324–33.

Gordon, Robert Aaron. 1976. "Rigor and Relevance in a Changing Institutional Setting." *The American Economic Review* 66:1–14.

Grassi, Ernesto. 1980. *Rhetoric as Philosophy: The Humanist Tradition*. University Park: Pennsylvania State University Press.

Harding, Jan (editor). 1986. *Perspectives on Gender and Science*. London: The Falmer Press.

Harding, Sandra. 1986. *The Science Question in Feminism*. Ithaca: Cornell University Press.

———. 1987. "The Curious Coincidence of Feminine and African Moralities: Challenges for Feminist Theory." In *Women and Moral Theory*, edited by Diana Meyers and Eva Feder Kittay, pp. 296–315. Totowa, NJ: Rowman and Littlefield.

Harding, Sandra, and Jean F. O'Barr (editors). 1987. *Sex and Scientific Inquiry*. Chicago: University of Chicago Press.

Harrison, Karey, and Diana Strassmann. 1989, November. "Gender, Rhetoric and Economic Theory." Paper prepared for the annual meetings of the Southern Economic Association, Orlando.

Heilbroner, Robert L. 1986. *The Worldly Philosophers: The Lives, Times and Ideas of the Great Economic Thinkers*. New York: Simon & Schuster.

GENDER, METAPHOR, AND THE DEFINITION OF ECONOMICS 125

Heller, Walter W. 1975. "What's Right with Economics." *The American Economic Review* 65:1–26.

Johnson, Mark. 1987. *The Body in the Mind: The Bodily Basis of Meaning, Imagination, and Reason.* Chicago: University of Chicago Press.

Keller, Catherine. 1986. *From a Broken Web: Separation, Sexism, and Self.* Boston: Beacon Press.

Keller, Evelyn Fox. 1985. *Reflections on Gender and Science.* New Haven: Yale University Press.

———. 1988a. "Demarcating Public from Private Values in Evolutionary Discourse." *Journal of the History of Biology* 21(2. Summer):195–211.

———. 1988b. "Feminist Perspectives on Science Studies." *Science, Technology, and Human Values* 13:235–49.

Klamer, Arjo. 1989, November. "On Interpretive and Feminist Economics." Paper prepared for presentation at the annual meetings of the Southern Economic Association, Orlando.

Kuhn, Thomas, 1962 (2nd edition 1970). *The Structure of Scientific Revolutions.* Chicago: University of Chicago Press.

Lakoff, George, and Mark Johnson. 1980. *Metaphors We Live By.* Chicago: University of Chicago Press.

Margolis, Howard. 1987. *Patterns, Thinking, and Cognition.* Chicago: University of Chicago Press.

McCloskey, Donald N. 1985. *The Rhetoric of Economics.* Madison: University of Wisconsin Press.

———. 1988. "Some Consequences of a Feminine Economics." Mimeo, Project on the Rhetoric of Inquiry. December 1989 version prepared for presentation at the annual meetings of the American Economic Association, Atlanta.

Nelson, Julie A. 1992. "A Picture of Gender." Forthcoming in *Hypatia: A Journal of Feminist Philosophy.*

Ortony, Andrew. 1979. "Metaphor: A Multidimensional Problem." In *Metaphor and Thought,* edited by Andrew Ortony, pp. 1–16. Cambridge: Cambridge University Press.

Robbins, Lionel. 1935. *An Essay on the Nature and Significance of Economic Science.* London: Macmillan. (Excerpted in *The Philosophy of Economics: An Anthology,* edited by Daniel M. Hausman, 1984, chap. 4, pp. 113–40. Cambridge: Cambridge University Press.)

Ruddick, Sara. 1987. "Remarks on the Sexual Politics of Reason." In *Women and Moral Theory,* edited by Diana Meyers and Eva Feder Kittay, pp. 237–60. Totowa, NJ: Rowman and Littlefield.

———. 1989. *Maternal Thinking: Toward a Politics of Peace.* Boston: Beacon Press.

Seiz, Janet A. 1991. "Gender and Economic Research." Forthcoming in *The Methodology of Economics,* edited by Neil de Marchi. Boston: Kluwer-Nijhoff.

Sen, Amartya. 1984. *Resources, Values, and Development,* chap. 13. Boston: Harvard University Press.

Solow, Robert M. 1988. "Comments from inside Economics." In *The Consequences of Economic Rhetoric,* edited by Arjo Klamer et al., pp. 31–36. Cambridge: Cambridge University Press.

Weinreich-Haste, Helen. 1986. "Brother Sun, Sister Moon: Does Rationality Overcome a Dualistic World View?" In *Perspectives on Gender and Science,* edited by Jan Harding, pp. 113–31. London: The Falmer Press.

Whitehead, Alfred North. 1925. *Science and the Modern World.* New York: Macmillan.

Wilshire, Donna. 1989. "The Uses of Myth, Image, and the Female Body in Re-visioning Knowledge." In *Gender/Body/Knowledge: Feminist Reconstructions of Being and Knowing,* edited by Alison M. Jaggar and Susan R. Bordo, pp. 92–114. New Brunswick: Rutgers University Press.

J16
A12

[3]

A *Feminist Critique of Rational-Choice Theories: Implications for Sociology*

PAULA ENGLAND

I consider the relationship between two currents affecting sociology, rational-choice theory and interdisciplinary feminist theory. In particular, I consider how the feminist critique of the separative model of self applies to one version of rational-choice theory, neoclassical economics. In discussing this I identify four assumptions of neoclassical economics: selfishness; interpersonal utility comparisons are impossible; tastes are exogenous and unchanging; and individuals are rational. I argue that each of these harmonizes best with a view of separate rather than connected selves, and that this imbalance distorts theories, particularly those that claim to understand women's experience. These distorting assumptions are less prevalent in sociology than in economics, but some of them are implicit in some versions of sociological rational-choice and exchange theories. I conclude by using research on marital power to illustrate how removing distorting assumptions and bringing questions about separation/connection to center stage can help illuminate sociological research.

The topical arena of sociology overlaps with that of economics, psychology, history, and political science. This breadth gives sociologists special needs and opportunities for dialogue with other fields. Here I consider the relationship between two currents affecting sociology, rational-choice theory and interdisciplinary feminist theory. In particular, I consider how the feminist critique of the separative model of self applies to one version of rational-choice theory, neoclassical economics. In discussing this I identify four assumptions of neoclassical economics: selfishness, that interpersonal utility comparisons are impossible, that tastes are exogenous and unchanging, and that individuals are rational. I argue that each of these harmonizes best with a view of separate rather than connected selves, and that this imbalance distorts theories, particularly those that claim to understand women's experience. I argue that these distorting assumptions are less prevalent in sociology than in economics, but that some of them are present

Paula England is a professor of sociology and political economy at the University of Texas-Dallas. Her forthcoming book, *Comparable Worth: Theories and Evidence* (New York: Aldine deGruyter), discusses this controversial policy issue from a perspective that draws upon sociology, economics, and feminist theory. Please address correspondence to: Programs in Sociology & Political Economy, The University of Texas-Dallas, Box 688, Richardson, TX 75080-0688.

in some parts of sociology, particularly in rational-choice and exchange theories. I conclude by using research on marital power as an example to illustrate how removing distorting assumptions and bringing questions about separation/ connection to center stage can help illuminate sociological research.

The "ideal-type" or rational-choice theory is neoclassical economics. This perspective is creeping into other disciplines through two related processes. First, economists are becoming "imperialists," applying the neoclassical paradigm to topics formerly thought beyond their purview, such as crime (Becker 1968; Witte 1980), the family (Becker 1981; Pollak 1985), and the authority structure within firms (Williamson 1985, 1988). Second, some sociologists adopt some of economists' assumptions in their work (Hechter 1987; Hechter et al. forthcoming). Thus, I will take the assumptions of neoclassical theory to be the assumptions of rational-choice theory, while realizing that even sociologists who call themselves rational-choice theorists may be selective in borrowing these assumptions from economists.

Another current affecting sociology is feminist theory. Feminists in a number of disciplines have argued that a large share of social science thinking is limited by seeing things through male eyes, by glorifying the roles and traits traditionally associated with males, by deprecating the roles and traits traditionally associated with females, and by a failure to consider gender inequality and its sources. There is no one unified feminist theory; but one way to summarize positions is to distinguish between liberal feminism, socialist feminism, and radical-cultural feminism (Donovan 1985; Jaggar 1983; England forthcoming, Chapter 6). Here I focus upon one strand of radical-cultural feminist theory that I believe to make the most interesting and important criticisms of assumptions of rational-choice theory. The theme from feminist theory with this promise is the distinction between a *separative self* and an *emotionally connected self*.

A Feminist Critique of the Separative Model of Self

Several feminist authors have noted that tendency in Western thought to assume and glorify a *separative* self. The separative self also has been seen as masculine rather than feminine. To introduce the reader to this theme, I trace it through recent writings in several disciplines.

Theologian Catherine Keller (1986) provides a sketch that begins with Greek philosophers and the early Christians. Aristotle and the early Christians associated women with water, animal nature, and monsters that are composites of others. Men, on the other hand, were seen as more like God, a unified substance separated from the primal womb. In short, men's superiority over women was seen to involve being *separate*, homogeneous forms, while women's inferiority was related to their *connection to the heterogeneous*, primal slime. Here already we see separation revered and connection deprecated.

Benhabib (1987) traces the importance of the ideal of separation and autonomy through classical liberalism in political philosophy. The contractarian tradition (whether the version of Hobbes, Locke, Rousseau, or Kant) discusses moving from a "state of nature" to the contractual cooperative state. Both before and after the contract men are presumed to be separative and autonomous; what changes with the contract is the degree of civility or justice wrought out of their separative selves. Nurturance and connection were presumed available to men through women, yet the moral sphere was not seen to hinge on nurturing emotional connections. Women's nurturing did not count as moral since it was seen as "natural." Men's nurturing or receipt of nurture was ignored. Thus, the separative self of bourgeois autonomy was valued, whereas nurturant connection either was ignored or deprecated.

This glorification of separation can be seen in modern developmental psychology as well. Developmental and clinical psychology have never been able to sanitize their discourse of normative statements to the extent that experimental psychology has, because models of healthy maturation imply values. As Gilligan (1982) points out, a long line of psychologists including Freud, Jung, Erikson, Piaget, and Kohlberg have seen individuation as synonymous with maturing. Gilligan's (1982) contribution was to provide a feminist critique of Kohlberg's (1976) stage-theory of moral development. Gilligan's empirical research suggested that women's moral reasoning is often based on an ethic of responsibility and caring which flows from an *emotional connection* between self and other. By contrast, men's moral reasoning is more often based on an ethic of principled noncoercion, which presumes and seeks to honor the other's *separateness*. When women are measured on Kohlberg's scale, they tend to score lower, particularly if they have been in nurturing roles. (For debate on whether Gilligan's or Kohlberg's empirical contentions about gender differences have been replicated, see Walker 1986; Baumrind 1986; Lifton 1985). Gilligan thinks women's lower scores on Kohlberg's scales reveal a bias in the conception of morality rather than a defect of women. She believes that women's conception of morality is as valuable as that of men, and hints that some combination of the two views might be best for both men and women to learn. One part of Gilligan's analysis is the empirical assertion of a gender difference in morality, while a second part of it is the normative claim that we should value ethics of care as much as ethics of noncoercion. This normative argument has been explored more fully by philosophers in a volume devoted to consideration of Gilligan's ethic of caring as a moral principle (Kittay and Meyers 1987).

Like Gilligan, sociologist Nancy Chodorow (1978) was struck by the twin facts that men are more "separative" than women and that psychological theories have seen separation as synonymous with development, thus glorifying the male pattern. Chodorow devised a feminist revision of the object-relations tradition in psychoanalytic theory to account for gender differences in separativeness. Chodorow argues that a key aspect of childhood socialization flows unintentionally from the fact that women are almost always the primary caretakers of young children. This means that females have their primary bond with a same-sex person, whereas males are bonded to a person of a different sex. As a result, males become more individuated than females because defining themselves as a male requires separation from, rather than identity with, their caretaker. In contrast, among females, such separation is not required, allowing females to retain more permeable psychological boundaries that encourage emotional closeness, empathy, and altruism. Of course, less psychodynamic and more cultural and structural forces may also be at work affecting sex differences in orientation to separation/connection.

Glorification of a separative self appears in science and the philosophy of science as well, according to Evelyn Fox Keller (1983, 1985). She argues that objectivity has been defined in terms of a radical separation between the subject (the scientist) and the object (of study), and that this choice of how to define science tells us more about male psychology than about how we might best come to know the world. Part of Keller's work is an explanation of why she thinks men glorify this separative mode of knowing; her thesis here borrows heavily from Chodorow (1978). Keller also argues that it is bad science to eschew emotional connection with one's subject matter when this can aid understanding, as she claims it did for Nobel Prize winner, biologist Barbara McClintock. Keller is thus arguing against the glorification of separativeness that has been present in science and the philosophy of science.

The prevalence of this theme of separation/connection in recent feminist writing is striking. It suggests several things: 1) Models assuming a separative self more accurately describe men than women. 2) But men, too, are embedded in emotional bonds of connection that separative-self theories have denied. 3) To the extent that gender differences in orientation to separation/connection are socially constructed, social theories that assume a separative self are inaccurate models of some possible and actual social arrangements, though they claim to be completely generic. For example, emotional connections may produce empathy and altruism, and these may be sources of group solidarity. The feminist position above is a critique of both the positive claim that all selves are unconnected as well as the normative glorification of the separative rather than connected self. Although this feminist position calls attention to current gender differences, most of its proponents see no necessity or virtue in men being separative while women emphasize connection. Indeed, they see the asymmetry to contribute to women's subordination. But while liberal feminists would correct this asymmetry by glorifying the separative self for both men and women, this strand of radical-cultural feminism sees an equal and prominent valuation of connection for both men and women as a goal (England forthcoming, Chapter 6).

Evaluating the Assumptions of Neoclassical Rational-Choice Theory

Neoclassical economic theory has four major assumptions: 1) that individuals act on the basis of self-interest, 2) that interpersonal utility comparisons are impossible, 3) that tastes are exogenous to economic models, and 4) that individuals are rational. Below I consider whether and in what ways the feminist critique of the separative model of self provides a critique of each of these assumptions.

The Assumption that Individuals are Selfish

Neoclassical economic theory assumes self-interested actors. However, the theory says nothing explicit about what gives people utility, and most economists presume that this varies from person to person according to tastes. Thus, it is not inconsistent with neoclassical assumptions for some individuals to have a taste for social approval or for altruism. Despite the consistency of status consciousness or altruism with economists' *formal* assumptions, in *practice*, most economists assume selfishness without explicitly stating the assumption, as Frank (forthcoming) has pointed out. One reason the assumption of selfishness is "snuck" in is that, without such an assumption, in a model where individuals are sometimes selfish and sometimes altruistic, determinant predictions of the type economists derive mathematically are often impossible. This is particularly true if individuals vary in their altruism, and if altruism is encouraged by some situations and not others. If selfishness were not assumed, economists couldn't presume that consumers will choose the best good at the lowest price or that workers will prefer a raise for themselves to a raise for others.

In the unusual case where economists do posit altruism, they often do it with very unrealistic, restrictive assumptions so that mathematically driven deductive conclusions can be preserved. For example, in Becker's (1981) analysis of the family, he posits a family "head" who is an altruist in the sense that he takes the utility functions of family members as arguments of his own utility function. (Becker uses masculine pronouns for the altruist and head throughout his discussion, while using feminine pronouns for the "beneficiary.") This allows Becker the mathematical simplicity of a single family utility function, while allowing him to avoid examining problems of family power and conflict (England and Farkas 1986, Chapter 3).

The assumption that individuals are selfish is related to the separative model of self. I suggest that this is true because emotional connection can breed empathy, altruism, and social solidarity (though when it is asymmetric it may also breed domination). If this is true, then separative selves are more likely to be selfish than are connected selves. Thus, if separation/connection is variable, selfishness is as well, and it should not be assumed to be more prevalent than altruism.

The Assumption That Interpersonal Utility Comparisons Are Impossible

An assumption made explicitly by neoclassical economists is that interpersonal utility comparisons are impossible. That is, we cannot know which of two persons gained more from a given exchange or who is more advantaged, overall, before or after the exchange. This is because the relevant "currency" in which we measure gain or advantage is utility, but utility is conceived as radically subjective. It is thus seen as able to be measured ordinally within persons through their revealed preferences, but not on an interval-ratio scale that would provide a common metric with which to compare between individuals (Hirshleifer 1984, p. 476).

Any voluntary exchange is said to lead to a Pareto-superior distribution of utility, and a sequence of as many voluntary exchanges as are desired leads to a Pareto-optimal result in neoclassical terms. But Pareto-optimality does not imply equal utility before or after the exchanges; equality or inequality of utility between parties is not believed to be knowable.

The closest concept in neoclassical theory to what we think of in commonsense terms as "someone getting a bad deal" is the notion of trading with a monopolist or monopsonist. Monopoly refers to a situation where there is only one seller for a particular good or service; monopsony refers to only one buyer. In either situation there is an absence of competition. In this case, economists recognize that the monopolist or monopsonist derives more from the exchange than she or he would derive under competition. But this is not the same as arguing that the monopolist or monopsonist gets more from the exchange than did the other party to the exchange. Thus, even in this case, interpersonal utility comparisons are avoided.

When we apply this principle—that interpersonal utility exchanges are impossible—to the comparison of structural positions or groups, we see why economists never conclude that the group in one structural position is more advantaged than is another. Such a conclusion requires averaging across various rewards. Economists assume it impossible to do such averaging precisely because individuals may weight rewards differently in their utility functions. This explains why neoclassical economics harmonizes with conservative positions on distributional issues. A paradigm that assumes we can never be sure if those at the bottom of hierarchies average less "utility" overall than others, that sees all free-market exchanges as Pareto-optimal by definition, and that sees all collectivistic redistribution as non-Pareto-optimal must be conservative on distributional issues.

Economists' belief that interpersonal utility comparisons are impossible reveals that they assume a separative model of the self. Emotional connection would seem a facilitator of empathy. Empathy, in turn, should facilitate the making of interpersonal utility comparisons, since being able to imagine how another feels in a given situation implies a possibility of translating between one's own and another's metric for utility. If our model allows the possibility of interpersonal utility comparisons between the individuals we study, then the notion that the economist/sociologist can make such comparisons among individuals and groups under study becomes more plausible. Thus, the assumption of the utterly subjective nature of utility is one more example of basing models on a socially constructed specific of male psychology, while presenting them to rest on a constant of human nature.

The Assumption That Tastes are Exogenous to Economic Models and Unchanging

Economists take individuals who are trying to maximize utility as their analytic building blocks. Tastes are seen as inputs into such a model, since each individual's tastes determine the amount of utility provided by different combinations of leisure, job conditions, consumer goods, household arrangements, friendship, and other factors. Economists do not attempt to explain the origin of these tastes. Stigler and Becker (1977) have argued that there is little variation in tastes, and thus that most behavior can be explained by prices or endowments. Other economists assume that tastes vary across individuals and see a role for disciplines such as sociology in explaining variation in tastes (Hirschleifer 1984). But whether they see tastes to vary or not, economists' see tastes as exogenous inputs to their models. Accordingly, an individual's tastes are not seen to change as she or he interacts with economic forces. For example, one's preferences for job attributes is not seen to be affected by what jobs one has held. Indeed, if economic models purport to explain family behavior, as in Becker's (1981) *Treatise on the Family*, this would imply that tastes cannot be affected even by socialization in one's family of origin, since otherwise tastes would not be exogenous to the behavior of parents that Becker purports to model. Assuming fixed and exogenous rather than changing and endogenous preferences radically simplifies neoclassical models.

The feminist critique of the separative model of self provides one way to think about the unreasonableness of such an assumption. Only a self cleanly emotionally separated from others could move through social interaction, exchange, and structural roles with no effect on his or her tastes. Such a degree of emotional separation and atomism is highly unrealistic.

The Rationality Assumption

The rationality assumption in economics, as in all rational-choice theories, refers to the cognitive assessments individuals make about the relationships between means and ends. Ultimate ends are chosen by tastes. Intermediate goals (those that are ends with respect to some means and means with respect to more ultimate ends), as well as lower-level means, are chosen according to one's cognitive assessment of whether and at what cost they will achieve one's taste-defined ends. The ability to make such assessments accurately is the essence of the rationality assumption.

Most critiques of the rationality assumption focus on the fact that people often lack the necessary information to make correct calculations, or on the limitations of cognitive ability to make them. Economists have responded to the first problem with the development of search theory, which posits that people will incur costs to obtain information only if the cost of obtaining the information is less than the expected gain from obtaining the information. Thus, making a decision without full information *is* often rational. (For a nontechnical introduction to search theory, see England and Farkas 1986, pp. 36-42, 123-126). The second problem, lack of cognitive ability to make optimizing calculations has led to the concept of "bounded rationality" (Simon 1982; Hogarth and Reder 1987; Williamson 1985, 1988). In the case of either limited information or bounded rationality, if the limitations lead merely to *random* errors in individuals' optimizing, the effect of this on rational-choice models is to lower their explanatory power (e.g. their R-square), not to make them wrong-headed. Neither of these critiques seem related in any clear way to the feminist critique of the separative-self model.

The question to be explored here is how the feminist critique of the separative self relates to the rationality assumption. To see this, we need to extend the critique beyond application to a separation between persons, and apply it to the tendency to *separate human qualities into oppositionally defined dichotomies* (England forthcoming, Chapter 6). The term dichotomy, as used here, does not imply a discrete rather than continuous concept. Rather, it implies that the two poles of the scale, whether discrete or continuous, are radically separate opposites. For example, much of Western thought features a dichotomy between reason and emotion, with a privileging of reason and a deprecation of emotion. While the liberal feminist protest against seeing this dichotomy as inherently linked to gender is well understood, less well known is the radical-cultural feminist critique of the dichotomization itself. (For a discussion of the distinction between the liberal and radical-cultural feminist positions, see Donovan 1985; England forthcoming, Chapter 6). This rejection of separating human capacities into opposites bears considerable similarity to a rejection of glorifying the separation between individuals.

Since the radical-cultural feminist position argues against a false dichotomization of reason and emotion, it judges the rationality assumption by the extent to which such a dichotomization is entailed in how rationality is conceptualized. Thus, this feminist position would find economists' conception of rationality problematic to the extent that rationality is seen as radically separate from emotion. To examine whether this is the case in economists' conception of rationality, it is important to note that desires or "emotions" appear in economic theory only in the realm of tastes that are seen as exogenous. The theory thus creates a radical separation between two spheres of subjective events. In one sphere are the "tastes" (preferences, emotions, desires, values) that determine one's ends. In the other sphere are the cognitions, the calculations about what means will achieve the ends satisfying the demands of the first sphere. The rationality principle resides in this second sphere. In this way, economists have reproduced the reason/emotion dichotomy so common to Western thought. Cognition (rationality) and emotion (tastes) have been separated from each other so that rationality serves the interest of tastes but is not distorted by them, and so that ultimate tastes are not changed by the constraints or by the rational calculations of what is possible for what cost within these constraints. It is this radical separation of tastes from everything else that distorts the conceptualization of rationality. In reality, there is probably much more commingling of the realms of emotion and cognition, so this conceptual separation is artificial. In this sense, the general feminist critique of false separations requires a revision of our concept of rationality. This would not preclude assuming rationality, but would change what we mean by it in a way that would make deductions less determinate.

England   **21**

Implications for Sociology

How does the feminist critique of the separative-self model apply to contemporary sociology? Of course, sociology is more heterodox than economics, so no one answer to the question will describe all of sociology. One approach to the question is to examine whether sociologists have made each of the four assumptions made by neoclassical economists. After discussing how various theoretical strands of sociology accept or reject neoclassical assumptions, I conclude by presenting one example of how sociological research might be improved by removing the distorting effects of these assumptions.

The Variability of Selfishness

For the most part, sociologists have not assumed selfishness. Most sociologists recognize that sometimes people show group solidarity that can't be explained entirely by atomistic selfishness, but that such group "altruism" cannot be assumed as unproblematic either. The interesting question for sociologists is to investigate the circumstances under which solidarity based on altruism is most and least likely to occur. One way to view the debates in sociology between functionalism, with its conservative overtones, and conflict theory, with its critical view of the status quo, is to see them as disagreeing over the relative amounts of normatively or altruistically based orientations to societal solidarity of elites and nonelites. In the conservative view, elites are quite more "trustworthy" than nonelites as regards societal interests, whereas in the critical view the opposite is the case.

However, selfishness *is* generally assumed in the two sociological perspectives that are closest kin to the neoclassical economic paradigm, exchange theory (Cook 1987) and rational-choice theory (Hechter et al. forthcoming). For example, Hechter's (1987) work on determinants of group solidarity assumes selfishness of individuals and posits group cohesion on the basis of the benefits to individuals of group conformity combined with the ability of the group to create the sanctions to monitor such conformity. The solidarity he describes is not based on empathy, altruism, or emotional connection, and thus is fully consistent with the separative model of self. What I find admirable about sociological rational-choice work is that it is more inventive than economists have been about how the "free-rider" problem (that each person wants the gains from group cooperation without having to contribute to the effort) can be overcome *even by selfish actors* (Hechter et al. forthcoming). However, ignoring the possibility that group solidarity ever arises from connection and feelings like altruism is hardly defensible. It is also inconsistent with the feminist critique of denying and deprecating connection.

Possible but Problematic Interpersonal Utility Comparisons

Few sociologists have explicitly discussed whether interpersonal utility comparisons are possible. (For exceptions, see Emerson et al. 1983; Emerson 1987;

Friedman 1987.) But sociologists *implicitly* assume that such comparisons are possible when they use terms like subordination, disadvantage, or oppression. For example, most textbooks on stratification convey the impression that (to translate into economists' terms) the poor have less utility, overall, than the rich. Even some exchange theorists have differentiated their view from neoclassical economics to allow such comparisons in their models dealing with power (Emerson et al. 1983; Emerson 1987; Friedman 1987). I would characterize the implicit view of most sociologists as seeing such comparisons as a practical, if difficult, measurement problem, not an impossibility. This allows sociologists not to lose sight of disadvantage and its structural and cultural roots.

Tastes or Values as Changeable and Endogenous

In general, sociologists also eschew the assumption that tastes are exogenous and unchanging. Indeed, the "social structure and personality" school of sociology has demonstrated that many features of social psychology are affected by one's structural position (e.g. Kohn and Schooler 1983), using a level of methodological sophistication able to counter the complaint economists likely would make of selection bias. That is, this research shows that psychological characteristics of individuals (which we could think of as tastes) are altered by being in jobs with certain characteristics, and this relationship is demonstrated to exist net of prior differences between the individuals who are selected into different jobs.

Rationality

Sociologists vary in adopting the rationality assumption. It is adopted most fully by rational-choice theorists and exchange theorists. Marxist and other theories focusing on the interest-based collective action of classes or other groups assume a kind of collective rationality—that classes or groups will act rationally in their interests. But these latter theories depart from the *individual* rationality assumed in economics, since it may be individually rational for one to be a "free rider" on the efforts of other members of one's class. Sociologists generally push the rationality assumption less far than economists, believing that imperfect information and humans' finite cognitive powers limit optimization. As well, sociologists sometimes consider how social structural positions systematically affect/distort the kinds of information one receives. This is an improvement over economists' search theory which sees imperfect information as a random disturbance term.

Implications for Sociology: The Example of Research on Marital Power

Let me suggest, by way of example, how research on one topic, marital power, could become more illuminating by questioning the assumptions discussed earlier and bringing the question of separative versus connected selves to center stage. This example will involve self-critique since I will use my own earlier interpretations of research on marital power as the focus of the discussion.

Research on marital power has measured power a number of ways, one of which is to ask survey respondents to identify areas of conflict in their marriage, and then report who usually gets their way in these areas. Whatever their method of measurement, sociological studies generally find that husbands get their way more often than wives, that this male power is stronger when the wife is exclusively a homemaker than when she is employed outside the home, and that male power is less extreme when women have higher earnings (Blumstein and Schwartz 1983; Scanzoni 1970).

Farkas and I (England and Farkas 1986, Chapter 3) interpreted these findings using a combination of sociological exchange theory and implicit contract theory from neoclassical economics. We pointed out that both earners and homemakers contribute resources (domestic labor or the earnings from other labor) to the marital exchange relationship, though much of the literature reads as though women's lesser power results from contributing no resources to the exchange. The interesting question is why the earner role yields more power. The essence of our argument was that while the activities of homemakers do benefit their husbands, fewer of the investments made by homemakers (for example, in learning a husband's idiosyncratic preferences, or forging connections with his kin) than earners will bear fruit outside this particular marriage should it end. In contrast, earnings are both of benefit within the marriage and portable to another exchange relationship outside this marriage. Because the partner with more earnings would lose less if the marriage dissolves she or he (usually he) has greater bargaining power within the relationship. Though other interpretations of these research findings have differed somewhat from ours (mainly in ignoring the fact that women are contributing anything to exchange without explaining why household labor and emotional work don't "count"), most have in common with our perspective the fact of being guided by exchange theory (e.g. Scanzoni 1970).

I continue to believe that the described interpretation has merit. However, I now believe that an unwitting acceptance of some of the assumptions discussed earlier precluded a fuller understanding of marital power. Let us consider what position such an exchange-based interpretation implicitly takes on each of the four assumptions. Our exchange-oriented perspective assumed that selfishness prevails such that people generally use their resource-based bargaining power to get their way in conflicts. We failed to consider that the same empirical results might be generated if the typical marriage contains one partner who behaves according to the individual maximization principles of exchange theory while the other partner does not. Our analysis did permit interpersonal utility comparisons, or we could not have concluded that, overall, husbands get more of what they want than wives. However, we left undiscussed the question of why husbands' ability to assess their wives' utility does not lead to greater empathy and altruism on their part. Tastes about the issues over which spouses feel conflict (e.g. how to spend money, where to live, how much to share feelings) were presumed exogenous to the exchange model since nothing was said about how outcomes of exchange change tastes. Tastes for altruism or selfishness were implicitly assumed constant or randomly varying around a mean tilted toward selfishness. Finally, spouses were assumed to be individually rational, using whatever bargaining power flowed from their portable resources.

Let us now consider a more complex model to interpret the findings on marital power that relaxes more neoclassical assumptions and takes advantage of feminist insights regarding separation/connection. Suppose that there are two kinds of dispositions toward self and other coexisting in the social world: 1) Model "S" (for separative) deemphasizes empathy, sees self-interested behavior as natural, and takes advantage of being in a "power-over" bargaining position when it occurs. 2) Model "C" (for connective) emphasizes the rewards of emotional connection, and takes both one's own and a connected other's utility as roughly of equal importance, regardless of who is in a stronger bargaining position. One way to put this is that those who practice model S fit economic and exchange theories better than those who practice model C. Suppose further that existing social structures and socialization practices produce more males practicing S and more females practicing C. To oversimplify for the clarity of exposition, let us assume all men practice S and all women practice C.

Under these assumptions, marriage would feature men pressing their bargaining harder and getting more of what they wanted as a function of the amount of their earnings relative to their wives' earnings. The extent to which wives pushed for their own way at the expense of a partner's would be uncorrelated with their earnings. Yet overall, the fit of men's behavior with exchange theory would be sufficient to produce the correlation between earnings and power observed in the literature, though the correlation is less than it would be if women, too, practiced S. This model does not imply that women like getting their way less than men. Indeed, the fact that women count their own utility as equally important to their partners' implies that they do not like this state of affairs. But in such an asymmetric situation, there are only two ways for women to rectify the power imbalance, and each has perils. The first way is through increasing their earnings and using them for bargaining power. Of course, using earnings for bargaining power requires that they abandon model C, which they do not want to do. Their second option is to persuade men to adopt model C with them, but this is a "hard sell" to men already thinking in S terms. We might think of the situation as the connective self's version of the prisoner's dilemma.

A recent study by Blumstein and Schwartz (1983) produced findings consistent with this view. They interviewed four types of cohabiting couples: married couples, unmarried heterosexuals, gay men, and lesbians. They found that the magnitude of the relationship between relative earnings and power varied across the four types of couples. Disparities in earnings produced the greatest disparities in power among gay male couples. The effects were of intermediate magnitude among heterosexual couples (married or not), and nonexistent among lesbians (Blumstein and Schwartz 1983, p. 53-63). I want to suggest a possible interpretation of these findings that does not see sexual preference as the important thing differentiating these groups. Rather, we might see the numerical presence of

males versus females in each type of couple as indicative of the numerical pre-
ponderence of practitioners of models S and C. On that assumption, it is striking
that the strongest correlation of earnings to power is in the couples containing
two practicing S, the intermediate correlation is in the group where couples have
one S and one C, and there is no relationship between relative earnings and power
in the group with both partners practicing C.

These findings make sense: If both partners eschew the separative/selfish S
model, exchange theory predictions are no longer true, hinging as they do on the
assumption of selfishness. At the other extreme, when both parties adopt S, exchange theory is true in spades. But when one party practices C and one S the
correlation between earnings and power is intermediate but still positive. Thus
exchange theory appears to be validated even though it only describes one partner of each couple. Yet, there are ways to distinguish the empirical predictions of
exchange theory and the model of separative and connective selves coexisting.
Blumstein and Schwartz's findings (1983), for example, could not have been
predicted from exchange theory.

So far the discussion has focused on the merits of relaxing the selfishness
assumption and replacing it with a model where selfishness varies systematically
across the population. But our understanding will also be enriched by reconsid-
ering two other assumptions. In the England-Farkas formulation presented earlier,
tastes concerning selfishness and empathy were implicitly treated as exogenous
to the exchange process. But we should also consider the possibility that women
and men's experiences with marital exchange may be simultaneously shaping
their tastes for selfishness and intimacy. Let us return to our stylized case of a wife
practicing C and a husband practicing S where the husband has higher earnings.
Suppose the wife wants to move to a new city where she has a job offer, but she
fails to get her way because of the husband's higher earnings. As a result, she is
unemployed and takes on more of the child rearing responsibilities than she
would have had they moved to the new city. The experience of nurturing children may further skew her tastes toward connection and empathy, which may
further disadvantage her in the bargaining situation. Or, she may abandon some of
the valuation she places on C because of the disadvantage it causes her in the
relationship, and redouble her efforts to increase her earnings to increase her
bargaining power. This may be true despite the fact that, initially (given her
socialization) she would have preferred a relationship in which each partner
practices C. Or, to take yet a third possibility, she may glimpse the "prisoner's
dilemma" of her situation, leave her marriage, and resolve to have intimate relationships only with those practicing model C, perhaps becoming a lesbian. Such
relationships may further reinforce her tastes for empathy (i.e. for making interpersonal utility comparisons) and for responding altruistically. In any of these
cases, tastes and proclivity to make interpersonal utility comparisons have changed
due to the results of the exchange situation.

Let us end by considering where the rationality assumption fits into all of this.
Either separative or connective individuals can be rational in the sense of rea-

soning about what ends will reach what goals. But the rationality assumption has more force in a model in which selves are also separative in a way embodied in the other three assumptions. Once one accepts the feminist critique of the other three neoclassical assumptions, even if one fully retains the rationality assumption, the changes in other assumptions blunt the power of the rationality assumption to lead to deductively generated predictions. For example, a model in which people are rational in the service of utility functions that may or may not include empathy for another's level of utility and altruism has less clear predictions than a model in which one's rationality is always in the service of one's self, separatively construed. Similarly, a model in which individuals are rational in the service of their tastes loses some of its predictive power when placement in a social structural role or network can change those tastes. In sum, rationality tells us less about the way people will behave when we don't know a priori if they are selfish, they feel and respond to another's suffering ("lack of utility"), and their tastes sometimes change.

Thus, even if sociology sees people as rational, relaxing the other three assumptions—as I have done in this example of marital power—of necessity produces a less deductively determinate model. This is probably the single most important reason that economists and rational-choice theorists cling to simplifying assumptions: they create more determinate conclusions. Thus economists often fault sociologists for being empiricists without a strong deductively generated theory. This poses a dilemma for sociology. We would like theories that make sense of the world. Yet economists' assumptions are often unrealistic, and distorted in a way that in our cultural heritage is masculinist. As I see it, the challenge for sociology is to determine the social and cultural forms that flow from and make possible either separative or connected selfhood. This allows us to reject distorting assumptions while not giving up the search for systematic patterns. This yields complex models that themselves can change as the world changes. Some price in deductive determinacy has to be paid, but the gain is a reduction of masculinist distortion.

References

Baumrind, Diana. 1986. "Sex Differences in Moral Reasoning: Response to Walker's (1984) Conclusion that There Are None." *Child Development* 57:511-21.
Becker, Gary. 1968. "Crime and Punishment: An Economic Approach." *Journal of Political Economy* 76:169-217.
_____. 1981. *A Treatise on the Family*. Cambridge, MA: Harvard University Press.
Benhabib, Seyla. 1987. "The Generalized and the Concrete Other: The Kohlberg-Gilligan Controversy and Moral Theory." Pp. 154-78 in *Women and Moral Theory*, edited by Eva Feder Kittay and Diana T. Meyers. Totowa, NJ: Rowman & Littlefield.
Blumstein and Schwartz. 1983. *American Couples: Money, Work, Sex*. New York: William Morrow.
Chodorow, Nancy. 1978. *The Reproduction of Mothering*. Berkeley, CA: University of California Press.
Cook, Karen. 1987. *Social Exchange Theory*. Beverly Hills, CA: Sage.
Donovan, Josephine. 1985. *Feminist Theory: The Intellectual Traditions of American Feminism*. New York: Ungar.
Emerson, Richard. 1987. "Toward a Theory of Value in Social Exchange." Pp. 11-46 in *Social Exchange Theory*, edited by Karen Cook. Beverly Hills CA: Sage.
_____, Karen Cook, Mary Gillmore, and Toshio Yamagishi. 1983. "Valid Predictions from Invalid Comparisons: Response to Heckathorn." *Social Forces* 61:1232-47.

England, Paula. Forthcoming. *Comparable Worth: Theories and Evidence.* New York: Aldine de Gruyter.
_____ and George Farkas. 1986. *Households, Employment, and Gender: A Social, Economic, and Demographic View.* New York: Aldine.
_____ and Peter Lewin. Forthcoming. "Economic and Sociological Views of Employment Discrimination: Persistence or Demise?" *Sociological Spectrum.*
Frank, Robert. Forthcoming. "Patching Up the Rational-Choice Model." In *Beyond the Marketplace: Society and Economy Revisited,* edited by R. Friedland and S. Robertson. New York: Aldine.
Friedman, Debra. 1987. "Notes on 'Toward a Theory of Value in Social Exchange.'" Pp. 47-48 in *Social Exchange Theory,* edited by Karen Cook. Beverly Hills, CA: Sage.
Gilligan, Carol. 1982. *In A Different Voice: Psychological Theory and Women's Development.* Cambridge, MA: Harvard University Press.
Hechter, Michael. 1987. *Principles of Group Solidarity.* Berkeley: University of California Press.
Hechter, Michael, Karl-Dieter Opp, and Reinhard Wippler, eds. Forthcoming. *Social Institutions: Their Emergence, Maintenance, and Effects.* New York: Aldine de Gruyter.
Hirshleifer, Jack. 1984. *Price Theory and Applications.* Third Edition. Englewood Cliffs, NJ: Prentice-Hall.
Hogarth, Robin and Melvin Reder. 1987. *Rational Choice: The Contrast Between Economics and Psychology.* Chicago: University of Chicago Press.
Jaggar, Allison. 1985. *Feminist Politics and Human Nature.* Totowa, NJ: Rowman and Allanheld.
Keller, Catherine. 1986. *From A Broken Web: Separation, Sexism, and Self.* Boston: Beacon Press.
Keller, Evelyn Fox. 1983. *A Feeling for the Organism: The Life and Work of Barbara McClintock.* New York: W.H. Freeman.
_____. 1985. *Reflections on Gender and Science.* New Haven, CT: Yale University Press.
Kittay, Eva Feder and Diana T. Meyers. 1987. *Women and Moral Theory.* Totowa, NJ: Rowman & Littlefield.
Kohlberg, Lawrence. 1976. "Moral Stages and Moralization: The Cognitive-Developmental Approach." Pp. 31-53 in *Moral Development and Behavior: Theory, Research, and Social Issues,* edited by T. Lickona. New York: Holt, Rinehart and Winston.
Kohn, Melvin and Carmi Schooler (with J. Miller, K. Miller, and R. Schoenberg). 1983. *Work and Personality: An Inquiry into the Impact of Social Stratification.* Norwood, NJ: Ablex.
Lifton, Peter. 1985. "Individual Differences in Moral Development: The Relation of Sex, Gender, and Personality to Morality." *Journal of Personality* 53:307-34.
Pollak, Robert. 1985. "A Transaction Cost Approach to Families and Households." *Journal of Economic Literature* 23:581-608.
Scanzoni, John. 1970. *Opportunity and the Family.* New York: Macmillan.
Simon, Herbert. 1982. *Models of Bounded Rationality.* Volumes 1 and 2. Cambridge, MA: MIT Press.
Stigler, C.J. and Gary Becker. 1977. "De Gustibus non est Disputandum." *American Economic Review* 67:76-90.
Walker, Lawrence. 1986. "Sex Differences in the Development of Moral Reasoning: A Rejoinder to Baumrind." *Child Development* 57:522-26.
Williamson, Oliver. 1985. *The Economic Institutions of Capitalism.* New York: Free Press.
Williamson, Oliver. 1988. "The Economics and Sociology of Organization: Promoting a Dialogue." Pp. 159-86 in *Industries, Firms, and Jobs: Sociological and Economic Approaches,* edited by G. Farkas and P. England. New York: Plenum.
Witte, Ann. 1980. "Estimating the Economic Model of Crime with Individual Data." *Quarterly Journal of Economics* 94:57-84.

Part II
Gender and the History of Economics

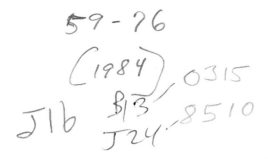

Cambridge Journal of Economics 1984, **8**, 217–234

Gender and class in Marshall's *Principles of Economics*

Michèle Pujol*

Marshall. held that economics is a positive and not a normative science[1] and emphasised the scientificity imported to the discipline's approach and object by the measurability of the phenomena observed,[2] this measurability being afforded (and limited) by the use of money in economic transactions and decision-making.[3]

Marshall's marginalist model rests on the assumption of individualistic rational economic behaviour, a behaviour directed at 'the attainment and . . . the use of the material requisites of well being' (p. 1) involving marginal calculations by the individual to reach a welfare optimum. In this model, income shares—and wages—are determined by the marginal product of the individual factors of production. Market mechanisms allow the maximisation of economic returns and the optimal state of economic welfare at the level of the nation and beyond.

Yet Marshall departs from that model in at least two instances. In particular, the unit to be considered for consumption, welfare decisions, income levels, etc. . . in many cases is not the individual, but the family. Interestingly, individualistic (selfish) economic motivations break down within the family unit, especially in the case of inter-generational transfers (p. 24). Elsewhere, Marshall breaks with the market-orientated *laissez-faire* tradition when he approves of state intervention (Factory Acts) and advocates further state involvement in the economy (education, family wage . . .). As we shall see, these divergences from the model find a unity in the economist's treatment of the role of women in a capitalist economy.

Marshall's argument about women rests on his development of a 'human capital' theory in Book IV of his *Principles*. His intent there is to provide advice on how to improve the productivity of the working class. Education is a major element in his proposal. But, to enhance the environment in which male workers and their children live, and to generate greater health, 'character and ability', working-class women are required to build a 'true home'. Marshall therefore opposes employment for married women and advocates a 'family

---

University of Manitoba. I wish to acknowledge the invaluable criticisms and advice of Joseph Dolecki. All my thanks to Lynne Slobodian and Betty McGregor for their clerical skills and their patience.

[1]'Scientific inquiries are to be arranged with reference not to the practical aims which they subserve, but to the nature of the subjects with which they are concerned' (Marshall, *Principles of Economics*, Macmillan, 1930, eighth ed. rep. p 39. All references are to this edition).

[2]'The *raison d'etre* of economics as a separate science is that it deals chiefly with that part of man's action which is most under the control of measurable motives; and which therefore lends itself better than any other to systematic reasoning and analysis' (pp. 38–39).

[3]'The methods and tests of science' are made possible 'as soon as the forces of a person's motives can be approximately measured by the sum of money which he will just give up in order to secure a desired satisfaction; or again by the sum which is just required to induce him to undergo a certain fatigue' (p. 15).

0309–166X/84/030217 + 18 $03.00/0

218   M. Pujol

wage' paid to male workers to cover the subsistence requirement of a housebound wife and children. He consistently applies bourgeois Victorian values to the working class in a system where women are assigned to contributing their time to investments in the human capital of male workers without receiving a direct return for it.

Marshall's human capital theory

Marshall states that, of the factors of production, labour has superior properties: it creates capital.[1] As such it deserves special study for so much of production and the welfare of society depends on it.

> The growth of mankind in number, in health and strength, in knowledge, ability, and in richness of character is the end of all our studies... We cannot avoid taking account of the direct agency of man in production, and of the conditions which govern his efficiency as a producer (p. 139).

The labour force of a country is clearly seen as its most important asset and as such requires proper investment to be maintained and augmented: 'The most valuable capital is that invested in human beings' (p. 564). At the same time, this asset has to be shaped in a specific way, to meet the production requirements of an industrial society. The requisite qualities of the labour force are listed by Marshall:

> To be able to bear in mind many things at a time, to have everything ready when wanted, to act promptly and show resource when anything goes wrong, to accommodate oneself quickly to changes in detail of the work done, to be steady and trustworthy, to have always a reserve of force which will come out in emergency, these are the qualities which make a great industrial people. They are not peculiar to any occupations, but are wanted in all (p. 206–207).

In essence, for Marshall, the workers must show adaptable intelligence.[2]

Marshall's approach to the study of labour, its characteristics and the determining factors of labour supply becomes more prescriptive than analytical, more normative than positive. The role of the economist, in his view, is to enlighten society as to how this asset (the labour force) must be maintained and improved through 'human capital investment'. Marshall's proposals include the following elements.

First of all, poverty must be eradicated to allow a better use of the labour potential of the poor.

> Prompt action is needed in regard to the large.... 'Residuum' of persons who are physically, mentally or morally incapable of doing a good day's work with which to earn a good day's wage (p. 714)
> ... there are vast numbers of people both in towns and country who are brought up with insufficient food, clothing, and house-room; whose education is broken off early in order that they may go to work for wages; who thenceforth are engaged during long hours in exhausting toil with imperfectly nourished bodies, and have therefore no chance to develop their higher mental faculties (p. 2).

---

[1] 'In a sense there are only two agents of production, nature and man. Capital and organisation are the results of the work of man aided by nature' (p. 139).

[2] It is interesting to note here that Marshall's argument about the education of workers leads him to speculate on a transformation of the class structure of society and the feasibility of 'worker self management': 'Ought we to rest content with the existing form of division of labour? Is it necessary that large numbers of people should be exclusively occupied with work that has no elevating character? Is it possible to educate gradually among the great mass of workers a new capacity for the higher kinds of work; and in particular for undertaking cooperatively the management of the business in which they are themselves employed?' (p. 4). He does not, however, answer these questions.

This eradication of poverty requires the increase in incomes and wages of the poorer classes which will lower the death rate (p. 529) and provide the poor with the subsistence levels required to improve their working ability: '.... there is a certain consumption which is strictly necessary for each grade of work in this sense, that if any of it is curtailed the work cannot be done efficiently' (p. 529). Marshall writes at length on the food requirements of various types of labourer (pp. 529–530) and on the other 'necessaries': clothing, shorter hours and more healthy surroundings.

Rest is essential for the growth of a vigorous population. . . . Overwork of every form lowers vitality; while anxiety, worrying, and excessive mental strain have a fatal influence in undermining the constitution, impairing fecundity and diminishing the vigour of the race (p. 197).

At the beginning of this century the conditions of factory work were needlessly unhealthy and oppressive for all, and especially for young children (p. 198).

Marshall argues that such improvement will have cumulative effects on the workforce: '. . . an increase in wages unless earned under unwholesome conditions, almost always increases the strength, physical, mental, and even moral, of the coming generations' (p. 532).

Marshall prescribes direct government intervention to achieve the above-stated goals. This includes the upholding of Factory Acts (p. 198), the establishment of a 'minimum wage . . . fixed by authority of government below which no man may work, and another below which no woman may work' (p. 715), and control by the state of childrearing in the Residuum class:

The case of those, who are responsible for young children would call for greater expenditure of public funds, and a more *strict subordination of personal freedom to public necessity.* The most urgent among the first steps towards causing the Residuum to cease from the land, is to insist on regular school attendance in decent clothing, and with bodies clean and well fed. In case of failure the parents should be warned and advised: as a last resource the homes might be closed or regulated with some *limitation of the freedom of the parents.* The expense would be great: but there is no other so urgent need for bold expenditure. It would remove the great canker that infects the whole body of the nation (pp. 714–715 n., emphasis added).

The second set of measures proposed by Marshall to improve the country's supply of labour concerns the education of the working classes. Education is necessary to improve the supply of skilled labour: 'the children of unskilled workers need to be made capable of earning the wages of skilled work: and the children of skilled workers need similar means to be made capable of doing still more responsible work' (p. 718). The main goal of education is clearly identified by Marshall as serving the needs of industry for a skilled labour force, to make the future workers 'efficient producers' (p. 720). To that effect,

Education must be made more thorough. The schoolmaster must learn that his main duty is not to impart knowledge, for a few shillings will buy more printed knowledge than a man's brain can hold. It is to educate character, faculties and activities (p. 717–718).

Providing education is 'a national investment' (p. 216). 'To this end, public money must flow freely' (p. 718) as it is 'the most imperative duty of this generation . . . to provide for the young' (p. 720) and as 'the wisdom of expanding public and private funds on education is not to be measured by its direct fruits alone' (p. 216). In effect, the benefits of working-class education will be cumulative over time as it will generate among more educated parents a greater willingness to educate their children and more resources to devote to that goal (pp. 516–563, 718).

For, although benefits from education go in a great part to society at large and to private

220   M. Pujol

industry, the decision whether children should receive an education, and what particular education rests with the parents.

... the investment of capital in the rearing and early training of the workers of England is limited by the resources of parents on the various grades of society, by their power of forecasting the future, and by their willingness to sacrifice themselves for the sake of their children (p. 561).

While Marshall recognises that this 'willingness to sacrifice' oneself for the sake of one's children does exist 'now even among the poorer classes, so far as their means and the limits of their knowledge will allow' (p. 563), he perceives that the propensity to provide education for their offspring is stronger in 'the higher grades' who have more information on employment opportunities, who 'are generally willing and able to incur a considerable expense for the purpose',[1] and who are more able to 'distinctly realise the future', and 'discount it at a low rate of interest' (pp. 561–562).[2]

Human capital investment by parents in their children is obviously complicated by the generational transfers involved. Unlike the case of physical capital where 'he who bears the expenses of production' receives all the returns,

Those who bear the expenses of rearing and educating [the worker] receive but very little of the price that is paid for his services in later years... Consequently, the investment of capital in him is limited by the means, the forethought, and the unselfishness of his parents (pp. 560–561).

Consequently, the proper habits and attitudes of parents must be generated within society. In a capitalist society, human capital investment depends entirely on the unselfishness of parents *vis à vis* their children, on their willingness to sacrifice themselves for their future, a behaviour quite contrary to the individual greed and selfishness that is assumed, in the marginalist model, to motivate rational economic decisions, yet entirely essential to the requirements of reproduction and growth of a capitalist society.

While Marshall takes for granted that the 'willingness' to insure the 'wellbeing of their children' is present among parents, 'even among the poorest classes' (p. 563), he makes it clear that this propensity should be increased through the education of the working classes, which, beyond providing greater incomes, some of which might be available for their children's education, will also generate the required 'moral qualities' to instill proper behaviour (pp. 561–563). What is to be obtained through education is a sense of social duty, of responsibility *vis à vis* the next generation's welfare: 'Education is a *duty* of parents' (p. 216, emphasis added).

Women's duty to their family

This sense of duty is particularly required of women; mothers more than fathers are called upon to sacrifice themselves for the sake of their children. One thing women have to give up is employment: Marshall constantly maintains that women's employment is detrimental because 'it tempts them to neglect their duty of building up a true home, and investing their efforts in the personal capital of their children's character and abilities' (p. 685).

---

[1]'The professional classes especially, while generally eager to save some capital *for* their children, are even more on the alert for opportunities of investing it *in* them' (p. 562).

[2]'Most parents are willing enough to do for their children what their own parents did for them; and perhaps even to go a little beyond it if they find themselves among neighbours who happen to have a rather high standard. But to do more than this requires, in addition to the moral qualities of unselfishness and a warmth of affection that are perhaps not rare, a certain habit of mind which is as yet not very common. It requires the habit of distinctly realising the future, of regarding a distant event as of nearly the same importance as if it were close at hand (discounting the future at a low rate of interest); this habit (... is a product and a cause) of civilisation, and is seldom fully developed except among the middle and upper classes of the more cultivated nations' (p. 216–217).

In Marshall's opinion, a mother's care of her children is one of the most essential elements in the production of the human capital that is required by modern industry:

> If we compare (countries, regions, trades) we find that the degradation of the working-classes varies almost uniformly with the amount of rough work done by women. The most valuable of all capital is that invested in human beings; and of that capital, the most precious part is the result of the care and influence of the mother, so long as she retains her tender and unselfish instincts, and has not been hardened by the strain and stress of unfeminine work (p. 564).

While Marshall exposes his sympathies for the 'cult of the Home' and the 'cult of true womanhood', he does not attempt to back up his assertions on the relation between 'the degradation of the working classes' and the employment of women with any specific data. Neither does he try to correlate other variables (e.g. wage levels, length of the working day, diet) to that 'degradation' to test whether it could be attributed to women's employment alone.

The same criticism applies to Marshall's argument that infant mortality is directly linked to women's employment: infant mortality is higher in towns 'especially where there are many mothers who neglect their parental duties in order to earn money wages' (p. 198); '... an increase of wages is almost certain to diminish the death rate, unless it has been obtained at the price of the neglect by mothers of their duties to their children' (p. 529). Here again, Marshall is found to depart significantly from his positivist posture.[1]

Furthermore, work interferes with an efficient use of women's reproductive capacity: on the one hand over-work impairs fecundity (p. 197), on the other hand 'the birth of children who die early from the want of care and adequate means is a useless strain to the mother' (p. 202).

Work, especially if 'unfeminine' (no example provided), is seen by Marshall as destructive of these qualities (tenderness and unselfishness) required for the building of a 'true home' and the nurturing of children.[2] These feminine qualities are an essential ingredient of the human capital investment in children: 'general ability', i.e. the faculties and general knowledge and intelligence that must be developed among workers, 'depends largely on the surroundings of childhood and youth. In this the first and far the most powerful influence is that of the mother' (p. 207).[3]

One further requirement is the mother's full-time presence in the home. 'Able workers and good citizens are not likely to come from homes from which the mother is absent during a great part of the day' (p. 721). In this respect, the son of the artisan enjoys an advantage over the son of the unskilled worker:

---

[1]Contrast the above statements with the following methodological remark: 'It must ... always be remembered that though observation or history may tell us that one event happened at the same time as another, or after it, they cannot tell us whether the first was the cause of the second ... wider experience, more careful inquiry, may show that the causes to which the event is attributed could not have produced it unaided; perhaps even that they hindered the event, which was brought about in spite of them by other causes that have escaped notice' (p. 774).

[2]Although there were no children in the Marshall household, Marshall himself benefited from the nurturing and the building of a true home by his wife Mary Paley Marshall. According to Keynes, 'During fourty-seven years of married life his dependence upon her devotion was complete. Her life was given to him and to his work ...' (Pigou (ed.) 1956, p. 15). Elsewhere he says: 'Neither in Alfred's lifetime nor afterwards did she ever ask, or expect, anything for herself' (Keynes, 1944).

[3]Marshall notes here that great men had great mothers; 'an earnest mother leads her child to feel deeply about great things; and a thoughtful mother does not repress, but encourages that childish curiosity which is the raw material of scientific habits of thought' (p. 207n).

222   **M. Pujol**

He generally lives in a better and cleaner house. . . . His parents are likely to be better educated . . . ; and, last but not least, his mother is likely to be able to give more of her time to the care of her family (pp. 563–564).

While Marshall holds that women have a 'tender and unselfish instinct' to give priority to the care of their children, he does not seem to trust this natural character of women to be sufficient to generate in them the qualities and behaviour that will benefit industrial society the most. This can be helped by some form of state intervention.

In the first place, education is needed to make women better mothers and housewives. Better educated *parents* are, generally, more likely to generate a more adequate environment for their children (p. 563). Women in particular require education, not for the purpose of improving their skills as workers, but for the purpose of contributing to the human capital investment in their children.[1]

Marshall insists that the need to educate men cannot be separated from the need to educate women, as a part of the social design of improving the workforce as a whole:

. . . in estimating the cost of production of efficient labour, we must take as our unit the family. At all events, we cannot treat the cost of production of efficient men as an isolated problem; it must be taken as part of the broader problem of the cost of production of efficient men together with the women who are fitted to make their home happy, and to bring up their children vigorous in body and mind, truthful and cleanly, gentle and brave (p. 564).

The education of women must be directed towards developing specific skills and knowledge. The mother and housewife must know how best to take care of her family. To this end, she requires, besides a knowledge of, among other things, healthcare and nutrition, some notion of household economy to make the best of the tight working-class household budget:

. . . a skilled housewife with ten shillings a week to spend on food will often do more for the health and strength of her family than an unskilled one with twenty. The great mortality of infants among the poor is largely due to the want of care and judgement in preparing their food; and those who do not entirely succumb to this want of motherly care often grow up with enfeebled constitutions (pp. 195–196).

The value of the housewife's skills to society seem therefore to be great. On the one hand they allow the production of a stronger, healthier and better prepared workforce; they prevent the social waste of infant and child mortality. On the other hand they allow industry to obtain a quality workforce at reduced expense: subsistence wages paid to male workers can be lowered without negative consequences for their productivity.

---

[1]This applies to both male and female children. The educational investment in the male child is to prepare him for industrial work, the investment in the female child to prepare her for the future duties of housewife and mother. Marshall did not agree that women should have the same educational opportunities as men. Edgeworth points out in his 'Reminiscences' of Alfred Marshall that 'concern for the practice of family duties was the ground of Marshall's opposition to the granting of degrees to women' in a submission Marshall made to the Cambridge Senate in 1896 (Pigou (ed.), 1956, p. 72). The paradox in this is that Mary Paley Marshall was one of the first women to receive an education at Cambridge and taught economics to women at Oxford and Cambridge (Newnham College) after marrying Marshall. She also co-authored with him the book *Economics of Industry* which she had actually been commissioned to write. Keynes comments that, by 1896, Marshall had come 'increasingly to to conclusion that there was nothing useful to be made of women's intellect' (Keynes, 1944). Yet all his life he benefited from the partnership, advice and help (particularly for the proof reading and indexing of his writings) of his educated and intelligent companion.

Gender and class in Marshall's *Principles*   223

In spite of this, Marshall does not prescribe any system to recognise socially the value of the housewife's contribution to industrial society, to reward it, or to induce the development of such skills by women. While, for instance, male workers benefit from the human capital invested in them as they earn better wages, women get no return from their education (and *a fortiori* from their contribution to the 'investment' of human capital in their children). The 'virtue of those who have aided [the worker in acquiring better skills] must remain for the greater part its *own* reward' (p. 564).[1] For Marshall, 'virtue', or the accomplishment of motherly or housewifely 'duties', is a sufficient reward for women's contribution to society. He holds that women's 'neglect of their duty' is reprehensible but refuses to devise an economic explanation for this 'neglect' or an economic solution (monetary incentive) to it.

Women's employment

The only kind of monetary incentive prescribed by Marshall to generate the appropriate social behaviour among women is negative (and punitive). Women can be induced to stay home, discouraged from seeking the employment opportunities that will lead them to 'neglect their duties', if the wages offered to women workers on the job market are kept low.[2]

Marshall implicitly advocates low wages for women when he calls for women's minimum wage to be set at a different level from that of men (p. 715) and when he describes as 'injurious' a rise of women's wages relative to men's: such a rise is detrimental not only to men's employment and relative earning capacity but also to the performance of household duties by women (p. 685).[3]

Besides keeping women's wages low, another way to discourage and restrict their access to the job market is through the Factory Acts. The Acts fit with Marshall's overall proposal on the improvement of the working classes. The restriction of women's and children's employment will give the latter a better chance to be educated and enjoy improved physical health while it will prevent the disastrous effect of over-work on women's fecundity and increase the amount of time women will consecrate to their 'family duties'.

To appease the opponents of the Acts Marshall reassures them that 'the temporary material loss' they might generate 'should be submitted to for the sake of a higher and ultimate greater gain'. No doubt he is talking about production (The National Dividend) rather than the incomes of women and children.[4] Yet, his official justification for the Acts is chivalrous:. 'the coming generation is interested in the *rescue* of men, and still more in that of women, from excessive work' (p. 694, emphasis added). The Factory Acts

are imposed not as means of class domination; but with the purpose of *defending the weak*, and especially children and the *mothers* of children, in matters in which they are not able to use the forces of competition in their own defence (p. 751, emphasis added).

---

[1]This quotation actually refers to the 'virtue' of employers who undertake to train their workers to new skills while knowing that they will not keep all the returns from their investment (other employers will benefit). Marshall does not even acknowledge the similar (and greater) 'virtue' of women who are called upon to sacrifice self-interest for the future of their children and expect no return whatsoever from their 'investment'.

[2]But, according to the hypothesis of a backward-bending supply curve for labour, low wages could in fact induce women to spend even more time in the job market.

[3]Marshall, in the same argument and for similar reasons, opposes high relative wages for children: they would deter school attendance and human capital investment. However, children are eventually to benefit from abstention from work, through higher future earnings. Women's exclusion from the job market will not bring them a similar future recompense.

[4]See next page.

224   M. Pujol

Marshall does not say what renders women so 'weak' once they become mothers; nor whether he feels that women are better protected in the home (e.g. against a tyrannical husband); nor whether they are more able 'to use the forces of competition in their own defence' in that environment; nor whether they will certainly work shorter hours and perform less strenuous tasks when engaging full-time in household drudgery.

His concern for the weak does not lead him, for instance, to advocate some form of state intervention to ensure fair rates of pay (i.e. equal to men's) for children and women. He is here simply appealing to the Victorian ideology (which equates women with children) to support his proposal that women should dedicate themselves to their 'household duties'.

The level and determination of women's wages are not specifically investigated in the *Principles*. By contrast, in *The Economics of Industry*, (jointly written with Mary Paley Marshall), a couple of pages are devoted to this question. In particular, the authors observe:

In England, many women get low wages, not because the value of the work they do is low, but because both they and their employers have been in the habit of taking it for granted that the wages of women must be low. Sometimes even when men and women do the same work in the same factory, not only the Time-wages, but also the Task-wages of the women are lower than those of the men (p. 175–176).

The Marshalls do not comment on this departure from a marginal productivity determination of wages. They only speculate on some of the possible reasons for the differential treatment of women. In particular, they note that the employer's demand price for women's labour is influenced by his perception that 'the woman is of less service in the long run' owing to her responsibility for her family, and this influences the 'general opinion' on the value of women's work.[1]

With respect to the question of the minimum wage, Marshall actually proposed 'to adjust the minimum wage to the family instead of to the individual' (p. 715). A nationally-set minimum wage for each sex is too rigid a concept as regional variations in the demand for the labour of each sex will create variations in the sexes' wage levels, which will 'naturally' compensate one another if the family and not the individual is taken as the income unit.

---

[1] *The Economics of Industry* was first published in 1879 whereas the first edition of the *Principles* was in 1890. In contrast with the later developed opinions of Marshall on women's education, this early work identifies the education of women as one element that will fit 'women to do more difficult work . . . making them more ready to demand, and employers more ready to grant them higher wages for it' (p. 176).

'These are precisely what Harriet Martineau had in mind when opposing the Acts. But Marshall disregards this particular element. Although Marshall never conducts specific calculations to prove the gain in production that is supposed to result from keeping women and children away from employment, he tries to discredit the opponents to the Factory Acts, and in particular Harriet Martineau who is considered a precursor of sociologists and published numerous essays, treaties and pamphlets (e.g. Martineau 1832, 1833, 1834, 1838, 1855 and 1858). Marshall proclaims that her position is prompted by her ignorance of economics: 'Miss Martineau was not an economist in the *proper* sense of the word: she confessed that she never read more than one chapter of an economic book at a time before writing a story to illustrate economic principles, *for fear that pressure on her mind should be too great*; and before her death she expressed a just doubt whether the principles of economics (as understood by her) had any validity' (p. 763 n, emphasis added). Curiously, Marshall's treatment of Martineau grew harsher with time. In the earlier editions of the *Principles*, he quotes Martineau's own words: 'In order to save my nerves from being overwhelmed by the thought of what I had undertaken, I resolved not to look beyond the department on which I was engaged' (*Principles*, Guillebaud Edition, MacMillan, 1961, Vol. II, p. 759). His paraphrasing and interpretation of that quote from the Fifth edition is an attempt to discredit her completely. By that time it seems that Marshall's opinion of women's intellectual ability had overcome the requirements of honest scholarship. Curiously he never formulated similarly scathing commentaries on J. S. Mill's or N. Senior's position on the Factory Acts.

The family is, in the main, a single unit as regards geographical migration: and therefore the wages of men are relatively high, and those of women and children low where heavy iron or other industries preponderate, while in some other districts less than half the money income of the family is earned by the father, and men's wages are relatively low. This natural adjustment is socially beneficial; and rigid national rules as to minimum wages for men and for women, which ignore or oppose it, are to be deprecated (p. 715n).

This approach asserts that all women should be in families and that their earnings—if any— have the sole purpose of complementing men's earnings towards a subsistence level of income for the family unit. One can further deduce from Marshall's statement that women's wage needs not be related to her own subsistence requirements or to her own productivity but is only to be related to the prevailing male wage rate in the area considered.[1]

Marshall's theory of wages

Marshall's theory of wages deserves notice here:

... demand and supply exert co-ordinate influences on wages; neither has a claim to predomi-nance ... wages tend to equal the net product of labour; its marginal productivity rules the demand price for it; and, on the other side, wages tend to retain a close though indirect and intricate relation with the cost of rearing, training, and sustaining the energy of efficient labour. The various elements of the problem mutually determine (in the sense of governing) one another;... this secures that supply-price and demand-price tend to equality (p. 532).

That 'intricate relation' referred to above is in fact a very close relation of the supply price of labour to subsistence wage levels:

... the earnings that are got by efficient labour are *not much above the lowest earnings that are needed* to cover the expenses of rearing and training efficient workers, and of sustaining and bringing into activity their full energies (p. 531, emphasis added).

Wages cannot go below that subsistence level, except at a cost to society: '... there is a certain consumption which is strictly necessary for each grade of work in this sense, that if any of it is curtailed, the work cannot be done efficiently' (p. 529).[2] Yet, if wages go beyond subsistence, industrial society suffers too. Labour is used efficiently and economi-cally if its cost does not exceed the exact wage required to maintain its optimum pro-ductivity. In this context, consumption by workers beyond subsistence levels is considered wasteful. Talking about non-subsistence 'conventional necessaries and customary com-forts', Marshall states: 'the greater they are, the less economical is man as an agent of production' (p. 530). Another argument in favour of subsistence-level wages is that wages kept at this level will generate a more elastic supply of labour: '... the question of how closely the supply of labour responds to the demand for it, is ... resolved into the question how great a part of the present consumption of the people at large consists of necessaries, strictly so called' (p. 530).

---

[1]Pigou states this more explicitly than Marshall: 'women are the less likely to work at industry the more money their husbands are earning'. He thus makes men's wages one of the arguments in his mathematical formulation of women's labour supply (1952, pp. 565–566).

[2]See also p.69: '... the income of any class in the ranks of industry is below its *necessary* level, when any increase in their income would in the course of time produce a more than proportionate increase in their efficiency. ... any stinting of necessaries is wasteful.'

226   **M. Pujol**

Overall, even though Marshall states his full acceptance of the marginal productivity theory of wages,[1] he cannot depart from a subsistence theory. He goes on at length parsimoniously listing the food and non-food requirements of a representative working class family in different categories of employment:

.. the necessaries for the efficiency of an ordinary agricultural or of an unskilled town labourer and his family, in England, in this generation ... consist of a well-drained dwelling with several rooms, warm clothing, with some changes of underclothing, pure water, a plentiful supply of cereal food, with a moderate allowance of meat and milk, and a little tea, etc., some education and some recreation, and lastly, *sufficient freedom for his wife from other work to enable her to perform properly her maternal and her household duties* (p. 69, emphasis added).[2]

Clearly, Marshall is advocating a family wage here, one which arises out of and is consistent with the view that the most efficient organisation for a capitalist society involves the household—made up of a nuclear family composed of a sole (male) bread-winner, a non-employed wife, and children pursuing education until adolescence—as a basic economic and reproduction unit.

The concept of 'necessaries' in Marshall's argument requires clarification. Why should it be a 'necessary' for the male worker that his wife be house-bound full-time?[3] And for the woman herself? Does Marshall subscribe to Veblen's theory and suggest that workers should accede to the leisure-class status by being able to afford and enjoy the luxury of the conspicuous leisure of the female household members? Far from it. This 'necessary' conveys a benefit to industrial society by ensuring full-time supervision of and contribution to the human capital investment in working-class children as well as a more efficient and economical use of the family income to reproduce the family members.

These 'necessaries' are socially determined. They comprise what is required—from the 'efficient' point of view of the capitalists' interests—to reproduce the labour power of the worker and the working class as a whole. They benefit the worker and his wife and children only insofar as he remains capable of earning a wage and insofar as the household is kept alive, and—for children—insofar as they will be able to work in the future.

One may wonder why Marshall takes such trouble determining exactly what the working class family's consumption basket should hold. His concern raises the question of whether he believes that workers can act rationally and maximise their own welfare. Although he does not explicitly address that question, he seems to hold that workers would pursue their

---

[1]Marshall for instance states that 'every worker will in general be able with the earnings of a hundred days' labour to buy the net products of a hundred days' labour of other workers in the same grade with himself' (p. 539). One can note a possible oversight in Marshall's argument on the demand price for labour: while it is clear that no rational employer would hire–or continue to hire–a worker if her/his contribution to production is less than her/his wage, nothing, except particular market circumstances or the bargaining strength of the worker, will actually force the employer to pay a wage exactly equivalent to the marginal product contributed by the worker.

[2]In a footnote, Marshall goes further and evaluates the necessaries for different classes of households: ' ... the strict necessaries for an average agricultural family are covered by fifteen or eighteen shillings a week. ... For the unskilled labourer in the town, a few shillings must be added. ... For the family of the skilled workman living in town, we may take twenty-five or thirty shillings for strict necessaries. ... For a man whose brain has to undergo great and continuous strain, the strict necessaries are perhaps two hundred or two hundred and fifty pounds per year if he is a batchelor (p. 70 n). Unfortunately, Marshall does not list the commodities he considers to be 'strict necessaries' for any but the lowest classes.

[3]Presumably, the 'sufficient freedom for his wife from other work' enters into the worker's consumption and utility function, and is hence the object of a utility maximising decision on his part. Unfortunately, Marshall does not explore the point.

own enjoyment by, for instance, engaging in drinking and smoking, and will even 'sacrifice some things which are necessary for efficiency' to indulge in the 'consumption of alcohol and tobacco' (p. 70). Such indulgence in wasteful commodities, and in frivolous expenses when access to luxury goods is permitted by the workers' wage level, contradicts the interests of industrial society by rendering labour an uneconomical factor of production.

Consequently, workers have to be guided (i.e. forced) towards the appropriate (non-wasteful) level of consumption and mix of consumption goods.[1] To achieve this objective, wages have to be kept at the subsistence level required for efficiency—a level carefully calculated to cover the necessaries listed. In Marshall's view, this will ensure 'rational' spending by workers within the constraint of subsistence wages, rational from the perspective of the maximisation of the 'welfare' of industrial society.

Working-class women are given even less opportunity to make their own utility-maximising decisions. They are not even allowed to choose the type of economic activity they want to engage in and, should they—just in case—decide to become independent and seek employment, they would soon find that their wages could not assure their own subsistence. In short, women have access to the utility-maximising marginal calculus only insofar as they have to allocate the meagre family budget among the various 'necessaries'.[2]

Housework and the national dividend

While Marshall recognises and commends the great skill deployed by the housewife in getting the most necessaries out of a thin budget, and while he maintains that women are more useful to a capitalist society as mothers and housewives than as wage workers, he evades both the issue of whether their household activities ought to be considered productive, and the question of the valuation of women's economic contribution—in the form of household, motherly, or family 'duties'—to society.

'If we had to make a fresh start', states Marshall, 'it would be best to regard all labour as productive except that which failed to promote the aim towards which it was directed and so produced no utility' (p. 65). However, he quickly abandons this concept and defines productive labour as labour which produces 'means of production and durable sources of enjoyment', or labour 'productive of necessaries', the latter being defined as 'all things required to meet wants which *must* be satisfied for existence and efficiency' (pp. 67–68).[3] But while he contends that a house-bound wife is part of the 'necessaries' which the wage should afford the male worker, Marshall avoids—at this poing—determining whether housework and mothering are to be classed as 'labour' and whether these activities are to be considered 'productive'.

Marshall also defines labour as any activity which contributes to 'income', and he notes that income can be defined in two ways. On the one hand, it can be understood in the wide sense, as real income, that includes 'all the benefits which mankind derive at any time from their efforts in the present, and in the past, to turn nature's resources to their best account' (p. 76). Under this definition, it is possible to recognise the social contribution of housework activities—a point which Marshall acknowledges when he observes that,

---

[1] As he recognises that workers may sacrifice some of the strict necessaries to obtain these commodities, Marshall will—for the sake of efficiency—make an allowance for them.

[2] Is it ironic that Marshall uses the particular example of a 'primitive housewife' allocating yarn between different uses to illustrate the principle of utility maximisation at the margin for, as he admits, this 'illustration belongs indeed properly to domestic production rather than to domestic consumption' (p. 117).

[3] Is the labour producing housewife productive?

228   M. Pujol

should a housewife work, 'the loss resulting from any consequent neglect by the wife from her household duties' must be deducted from the family income (p. 556). On the other hand, income can be defined in the narrow sense, including only 'those incomings which are in the form of money' (p. 71). By this definition, which Marshall (in deference to 'common practice') adopts in his analysis of National Income Accounts, the contribution of housework (to which no 'money forms' attach) cannot be recognised.

With respect to services performed for self (and presumably for one's household), Marshall observes that: 'no services that (a person) performs for himself are commonly reckoned as adding to his nominal income. But, though it is best generally to neglect them when they are trivial, account should for consistency be taken of them, when they are of a kind which people commonly pay for having done for them' p. 72).[1] He does not address the question of whether all housework should be considered trivial (his example of a trivial service is the brushing of one's hat, p. 79n) or whether it should be considered as a service commonly paid for. In fact, such service is 'commonly paid for' in the upper classes (when it is performed by domestics) but not in the lower classes. Perhaps this distinction is enough—for Marshall—to keep household services unacknowledged in the lower classes.

Be that as it may, the question of household activities 'productiveness' does seem to trouble him. On the one hand, he does not hesitate to declare (in opposition to Adam Smith) that domestic workers are productive.[2] 'The work of domestic servants is always classed as 'labour' in the technical sense . . . and can be assessed *en bloc* at the value of their remuneration in money and in kind' and, hence, it can be included in national income. At the same time, however, he notes that there is ' . . . some inconsistency in omitting the heavy domestic work which is done by women and other members of the household, where no servants are kept' (pp. 79–80). Curiously, the resolution of this inconsistency by accounting for the work of the housewife by means of, e.g., 'remuneration in kind' estimates is not explored by him.

Rather than seeking to establish consistency between work performed and goods and services produced, Marshall seeks to establish it by using the mode of measurement of economic activity, i.e. accounting for only that which has a monetary counterpart.[3]

It is *best* here to follow the *common practice*, and not count as part of the national income or dividend anything that is not *commonly* counted as part of the income of the individual. Thus . . . the services which a person renders to himself, and those which he renders gratuitously to members of his family or friends, the benefits which he derives from using his own personal goods, or public property . . . are not reckoned as parts of the national dividend, but are left to be accounted for separately' (p. 524, emphasis added).

Unfortunately, Marshall does not indicate how all these services and benefits can 'be accounted for separately' and his followers quickly ignored his recommendation.

[1]Elsewhere, Marshall considers the situation where 'a landowner with an annual income of £10,000, hires a secretary at a salary of £500, who hires a servant at wages of £50'. All of these incomes are to be included in the Net National Income without encountering the problem of double counting because they represent real services performed. 'But if the landlord makes an allowance of £500 to his son, that must not be counted as an independent income; because no services are rendered for it' (p. 80). Unfortunately, Marshall does not consider the situation of services rendered without monetary compensation in the home (housework, childrearing, etc.) nor does he even consider the case where the landlord gives an allowance to his wife. Here, would Marshall argue that the wife, like the son, renders or performs no 'real services' for the landlord and, hence, her allowance should not be counted as income?

[2]Is it because they receive a wage?

[3]Other non-monetary incomes are, besides payments in kind to domestics, the services rendered by a house to its owner, and the production for use by farm households.

Notice that, in the end, Marshall abandons all pretense of 'scientific method' in arriving at his National Income accounting scheme. Instead, he is guided by the views of 'the world at large' and by 'popular convention' as enshrined, in particular, in 'the practice of the [British] income tax commissioners' (pp. 77, 78) when determining what should and what should not be included in the National Income.[1] In this way, Marshall helps to institution-alise in marginalist literature, as well as in national and international standards of income accounting, the practice of excluding from consideration (at the level of theory as well as practice) an important share of total production,[2] viz. that share which is carried out for no monetary compensation by women in the home.

Marshall's decision to follow the tax collectors and include in the national dividend at least part of the value of household production in the middle and upper classes—*via* the inclusion of domestics' income in monetary and kind—and not to include the value of that production when it is carried out in households that cannot afford paid servants also reveals a definite class bias. Thus, the value of services to bourgeois households is recognised as being valuable to society while the services of working class women to the members of their households (and, through them, to capital) are not given any definite monetary or social recognition.

Bourgeois Victorian values and the working class

The class bias is also present in Marshall's suggestion that what is appropriate for middle-class and upper-class women (gentility, protection, and, above all, house-boundedness) is also appropriate for working-class women. It is present as well in his belief that working-class children should be cared for in the same manner as middle-class or upper-class children (*viz.* with a great deal of individual attention), and that the standards of home-care that apply in middle-class and upper-class households (*re* cleanliness, houseroom, fresh air, hygiene, and so on) should apply in the working-class home, etc.

In advocating the working-class woman's 'return' to the household, Marshall does not seem to worry about whether it is economically feasible for the working-class family to live on the single salary of the male member of the household. Indeed, at no point does he address the question of whether the wage levels extant at the time of his writing would 'permit' such a return (i.e. he doesn't compare the 'going' level of men's wages to his notion of the appropriate level of the family wage). He rather seems to assume that the house-wife's skills (acquired immediately upon being transferred from full-time employment to full-time housework?) will palliate the (inevitable, at least in the immediate term) decrease in family money income.[3]

---

[1] In so doing, Marshall forgets that the serviceability of the practice of the income tax commissioners in relation to the task of meeting the revenue needs of the British state in no way guarantees the appropriateness of that practice in relation to the theoretical needs of economic analysis. Indeed, had economic theorists consistently deferred to such 'common conventions' in their analytical constructions, the discipline would–by its own standards of scientificity–be judged a mere collection of superstitious beliefs.

[2] Recent surveys estimate that housework yields a total product equivalent to 30–40% of total GNP (depending on estimating methods). One can surmise that, in Marshall's time, housework probably yielded an even greater total product in relation to GNP. Although a much greater proportion of housework was performed by domestics (and included in GNP), capitalist production had made little headway (compared to today) into the traditional fields of household production.

[3] Marshall could have argued that the decrease in the supply of labour caused by the massive withdrawal of women and children from the labour market should induce a rise in men's wages; but he does not.

230   **M. Pujol**

When he argues that women and children should stay at home for the purpose of the future improvement in workers' welfare (and, of course, the future welfare of industry) he does not seem to notice that this involves a cost in terms of the present welfare of the working-class family (a cost that could show up, e.g., as a decline in the health and welfare of future generations). In fact, however, the only costs that 'should be submitted to' in Marshall's view are those incurred by industry which result from the loss of a cheap supply of labour.

At the beginning of his *Principles*, Marshall argues that economists should not 'defend class privileges' (p. 47); he declares that 'economic studies call for and develop the faculty of *sympathy*, and especially that rare sympathy which enables people to put themselves in the place, not only of their comrades, but also of other classes' (p. 46, emphasis added). But can sympathy replace, in serious scientific enquiry, the *real practice* of attempting to feed a whole family on ten shillings a week?

The intent of Marshall's sympathy (as well as his concern for the weak and for the future welfare of workers) is specific: it is needed to study 'the ways in which the efficiency of a nation is strenthened by and strengthens the confidences and affections which hold together the members of each economic group—the family, employers and employees in the same business, citizens of the same country' (p. 46). One wonders if the expression of Marshall's sympathy, i.e. his defence of a subsistence wage and his prescription that working-class women should be made into unpaid servants to their class, will reassure the poor and the working class that he does not defend the interests of the capitalist class, but that he is speaking for the interest of all.

It is perhaps this 'sympathy' for members of the lower classes which guides Marshall in applying to them bourgeois standards or, more correctly, prescribing for them some of the canons of bourgeois behaviour without worrying about the financial consequences of their being followed. Such is Marshall's wish that the working class acquire 'the habit of distinctly realising the future' (i.e. 'discounting the future at a low interest rate') as well as an eagerness to invest capital 'in' their children, both of which he argues prevail among the middle and upper classes.

It seems that Marshall's use of such terminology as 'human' or 'personal' capital invest-ment *in* human beings, etc. arises out of an attempt to apply a similar, 'symmetrical', theoretical approach to the two basic factors of production in the capitalist economy. Indeed, he contends that the two factors obey the same rules—rules which originate in the predominant social relations of the capitalist market.[1] The motivations of the owners of the two factors of production and their behaviour can, in Marshall's view, be therefore treated in the same way, since they arise from such market phenomena as demand, supply, and prices. It is this 'symmetry' which provides the basis for the development of Marshall's 'human capital theory.'[2]

The similarity between the two factors, according to Marshall, is revealed by the 'general correspondence between the causes that govern the supply prices of material and personal capital':[3]

---

[1] It is obvious that this treatment is actually not symmetrical—but biased, since a capital-oriented terminology is applied to labour. Could the bias have been inverse? Probably not, since Marshall here is merely being a 'reflector' of the tendency of capital to objectify labour, to appropriate it, to dominate and control it, to transform it into part of itself, i.e. the secular tendency for capital to subsume labour. Hence, the 'essential' intent of Marshall's human capital theory is not only to fit labour into a capital framework, but also to transform it ultimately into capital.

[2] and [3] See next page.

Wages and other earnings of effort have much in common with interest on capital . . . the motives which induce a man to accumulate personal capital *in* his son's education are similar to those which control his accumulation of material capital *for* his son (p. 660–661).[1]

In his attempt to render the two factors of production identical, Marshall implies that *all* acts of investment are governed by a single motive, *viz.* providing returns to the next generation (or, more precisely, to the male element in that generation). While the motive has to be such in the case of human capital, since the return of a wage reflecting the amount of education, etc. received accrues only to the 'son' of the worker, artisan, etc., this is not the case for physical capital. Here, the investor can—and expects to—receive all the returns during his lifetime. The bequeathing of physical capital to one's son is an action separate (and responds to a motivation different) from the action of investment proper. Indeed, there is sufficient motivation for capital investment in the prospect of immediate personal returns; the capitalist will invest regardless of whether he has a son to provide for.

Marshall is aware of this difference, and at one point he contradicts himself by saying that 'parents are governed by motives different from those which induce a capitalist undertaker to erect a new machine' (p. 571). He also acknowledges that the intergenerational transfer necessarily involved in the case of human capital investment will generate a less than optimal level of human capital stock (p. 560–561). This suboptimality also arises from the length of time required between the initial investment decision and the availabilty of the new skill developed (p. 474). From all this, one can infer that in fact the supplies of human and physical capital do not follow the same rules.

Moreover, Marshall is aware of another basic difference between the two factors, one which he sees as inherent in the character of labour, *viz.* it is human. '[H]uman agents of production are not bought and sold as machinery and other material agents of production are . . . [the worker] remains his own property (p. 560). From this perspective, it becomes doubtful whether the concept of investment is applicable at all to human beings.

---

[1]This point is further developed by Marshall when he applies to this matter his own view of economic gradualism: 'There is a continuous transition from the father who works and waits in order that he may bequeath to his son a rich and firmly established manufacturing or trading business, to the one who works and waits in order to support his son while he is slowly acquiring a thorough medical education, and ultimately to buy for him a lucrative practice . . . to one who works and waits in order that his son may stay long at school' (p. 661). These 'continuous transitions' permit Marshall a wide generalisation of investment behaviour across social classes. At all levels of society, fathers 'work and wait'—even if there is more 'waiting' at the top and more 'working' at the bottom. This generalisation gives the appearance that the sacrifices of all fathers are of the same 'essential nature' and magnitude.

---

[2]Although Marshall is a precursor of the modern human capital theorists, his approach is slightly different than that of Becker. For Becker, human capital is an asset for only a sole individual, *viz.* its owner, while Marshall has a more traditional (i.e. classical) view that human capital (population/labour force) is an asset to a particular country, i.e. a social asset. Becker denies the existence of externalities in the cost of production of and the returns from human capital. For him, all costs are borne by the individual (foregone earnings) and all benefits (income streams) acrue to him/her. On the other hand, Marshall acknowledges the existence of externalities arising from the social character of the 'asset,' regardless of how these externalities might be confusing for his treatment and might lead to inconsistencies in his paradigm. Thus he jettisons the assumption of selfishness to explain the intergenerational transfers of welfare, and abandons the notion that individuals—as opposed to families—are the basic economic units. Becker retains the assumption of individualism and selfishness, and generates consistency within his model by introducing psychic, non-consumption-induced benefits as a motivation for the sacrifice of consumption-oriented welfare by the present generation (see Becker 1964).

[3]Does Marshall mean that the supply-price of capital is also governed by the cost of rearing, training, and sustaining (its) energy' (p. 532) i.e. its subsistence level of consumption?

232   **M. Pujol**

What returns for women?

A final and, for the present purpose, most significant difference between human and physical capital—one which Marshall does not take into explicit account—is that all the transactions involved in physical capital investment are done through the capitalist market framework, whereas practically none of the elements of human capital investment (except the payment of a wage in exchange for work and skill once the investment has reached 'maturity') take place in the market. Along with this goes the complete absence of women as agents in physical capital investment while their role is of supreme importance in human capital formation.

Marshall is, characteristically, ambiguous on the exact role played by women in human capital investment. Whereas he clearly states that women have the duty of 'investing their efforts in the personal capital of their children' (p. 685), and that 'the most precious part of the capital invested in human beings is the result of the care and influence of the mother' (p. 564), Marshall forgets all this when he compares human and physical capital. Here, the father 'works and waits' and invests *in* and *for* his son. Women, it seems, have no part in this process of working and waiting. The emphasis on the monetary element involved in 'investment' is decisive: since the mother does not 'work' to earn the family income, she is not seen to partake in the sacrifice involved in not using that income for consumption, but instead to develop the childrens' education.

There is, of course, a definite 'cost' involved for the woman: she has to sacrifice—not only her consumption of goods bought on the family budget—but also her whole being. She has to spend her whole life-activity 'investing her efforts' into the human capital of her children. Her life and self-purpose is taken from her in the process. And, for that reason, it can be said that she bears the bulk of the costs involved in this 'investment'.

In terms of returns, it is clear that only male children receive benefits from human capital investment, since only male children are called to become wage earners in Marshall's scheme. Female children must instead devote their adult life to the human capital investment of the next generation of males. Moreover, in Marshall's writings, the form of human capital investment women receive—to become skilled housewives and good mothers—does not yield them any 'real' return in the 'form of money'. Indeed, the only 'payment' associated with their efforts is self-denial.

If male workers get a return in the form of higher wages, industry also benefits from human capital investment by getting an improved, healthier, more skilled and adaptable supply of labour. In fact, in some cases, it seems that industry benefits more than workers do. As Marshall notes, an aggregate increase in human capital investment

has resulted [in a] largely increased supply of trained abilities. . . . but it has taken away from these trained abilities much of that scarcity value which they used to possess, and has lowered their earnings not indeed absolutely, but relatively to the general advance; and it has caused many occupations, which not long ago were accounted skilled and which are still spoken of as skilled, *to rank with unskilled labour as regards wages* (p. 681–682, emphasis added).

While industry was supplied in the process with increased quantities of skilled labour at a lower relative wage, it is not clear that the workers benefited since their wages failed to increase proportionately with the increase in their human capital. As for the parents of these workers, it seems that they 'worked and waited' to see industry subsidised by their own earnings. Marshall, unfortunately, does not investigate the frequency of such occurrences and the distribution of the returns between capital and labour.

Gender and class in Marshall's *Principles* 233

To recapitulate, in Marshall's scheme of human capital investment, fathers are seen to be the main investors but mothers happen to bear a large share of the investment cost; male children are seen to receive the returns but capital potentially receives a large proportion of these returns; women get no return from the human capital invested in them, and *a fortiori* from that they invest in their children; their sole reward for a life of toil is virtue and abnegation; men do bear some of the costs of investment and they do receive some of the benefits on an intergenerational basis; capital bears none of the costs, or only in so far as some of the training may happen on the shop floor; its labour costs are subsidised by the workers, but it gets benefits from a more productive workforce—this however is not seen by Marshall, as his marginalist myopia leads him to recognise only the factor returns going to the individual factor owners.[1]

In this paper we have seen how Alfred Marshall, the leading British economist of his time and founder of the marginalist school, approaches the question of women's role in the economy and of the production of the factor labour. It is clear that his approach not only reflects the influence of Victorian ideology but also contributes directly to its propagation by offering economic justifications for seemingly purely social propositions.

Thus, he proposes and justifies the extension of the Victorian bourgeois sexual division of labour to the working class and to the poor. Working-class women are assigned to the home to nurture male human capital while men have to earn a 'family wage' in the labour market. In addition, a national human capital investment policy and a minimum wage policy are advocated. But the economic justification advanced by Marshall for these proposals does not focus on the maximisation of individual utility and on the returns to individual factors of production. Rather, what is stressed is the economic benefits arising from such policies for capitalist society as a whole.

In a striking departure from the *laissez-faire* dogma that permeated the economic doctrines of his time, Marshall supports existing state intervention in the economy (e.g. the Factory Acts) and advances and constructs new proposals to expand such intervention into the autonomy of the labour market, into the autonomy of the family and of individuals, and into the mechanisms of determination and distribution of incomes. His proposals contribute to the development and reinforcement of socio-economic structures based on the institution of the nuclear family and economic dependence of women within that family— structures wherein appeals to 'duty' rather than 'economic motivation' serve as a basis for the allocation of women's labour to specific activities.

In Marshall's *Principles,* beneath the image of weakness and gentility projected on to working-class women—following the model set in higher classes—appears a heavy taxing of their life-activity. Under the categories of his national income, this activity appears to contribute nothing to the national dividend,[2] whereas his entire capital investment mechanism is fundamentally dependent upon its performance. Under the guise of protection, women are assigned to the home and given the major responsibility of care for the family and human capital investment in children while constrained by a budget set at the minimum

[1]The question raised by this complicated system of welfare transfer is: how can the appropriate level of human capital investment be insured? Given that the recipients of benefits and returns differ from those who bear the costs, and that most of the 'investment activity' does not happen through a market, marginal calculations and market mechanisms cannot be relied on to yield this appropriate level. This leads to some considerations of state intervention through the education system and its state financing, factory legislation, minimum wages laws and through these, the setting and maintenance of an adequate family structure. State involvement in itself indicates that the social benefits from such a scheme are greater than individual benefits.

[2]But then, how can one compute the value of virtue?

234   M. Pujol

level for capitalist efficiency. Even though this requires a skilled exercise of economic rationality, women are not considered by Marshall to be economic beings.

It might be that the question of whether women are economic beings is irrelevant to Marshall because he carefully removes them from the economic sphere and turns them, in this theory, from economic *actors* into mere *parameters* in the decisions taken by other economic agents. It is more likely, however, that Marshall's position results from his careful calculation of the most economical (from whose point of view?) place for women in capitalist society.

Bibliography

Becker, G. S. 1964. *Human Capital*, New York, Columbia University Press

Keynes, J. M. 1944. Obituary. Mary Paley Marshall, *Economic Journal*, June–September

Marshall, A. 1930. *Principles of Economics*, (8th edition reprinted), London, Macmillan

Marshall, A. and Marshall, M. P. 1881. *The Economics of Industry*, (2nd edition), London, Macmillan

Martineau, H. 1832. *Illustrations of Political Economy*, (9 vols), London, Charles Fox

Martineau, H. 1833A. *Society in America*, (3 vols), London, Saunders and Otley

Martineau, H. 1833B. *Poor Laws and Paupers*, (4 parts), London, Charles Fox

Martineau, H. 1834. *Illustrations of Taxation*, London, Charles Fox

Martineau, H. 1838. *A Restrospect of Western Travel*, (3 vols), London, Saunders and Otley; New York, Harper and Bros

Martineau, H. 1855. *The Factory Controversy; a Warning Against 'Meddling Legislation'*, Manchester, National Association of Factory Occupiers

Martineau, H. 1858. *The Positive Philosophy of Auguste Comte*, freely translated and condensed, (2 vols), New York, C. Blanchard (first published 1853, London)

Pigou, A. C. 1952. *The Economics of Welfare*, (4th edition), London, Macmillan (first published 1920, London)

Pigou, A. C. (ed.) 1956. *Memorials of Alfred Marshall*, New York, Kelley and Millman (first published 1925, London)

[5]

THE UNPRODUCTIVE HOUSEWIFE:
HER EVOLUTION IN NINETEENTH-CENTURY ECONOMIC THOUGHT

USA
UK
N30
J16
D13

NANCY FOLBRE

In 1878 the officers of the Association for the Advancement of Women (AAW) protested the U.S. Census's notion that "home-keepers" were not gainful workers. In a letter to Congress they wrote, "We pray your honorable body to make provision for the more careful and just enumeration of women as laborers and producers." They complained that women's domestic efforts were "not even incidentally named as in any wise affecting the causes of increase or decrease of population or wealth."[1] (See Appendix.) In short, the AAW quarreled with the official assumption that housewives were unproductive workers because they earned no pay.

Census data consist of ordered sets of numbers. They appear objective and value free, but their meaning grows out of socially constructed concepts that are laden with cultural and political values. "Statistical reports exemplify the process by which visions

My collaboration with Marjorie Abel on related topics inspired this article; Margo Anderson kept me going. Daniel Scott Smith provided many helpful suggestions, including one that led me to the expertise of archivist Susan Grigg, director of the Sophia Smith Collection at Smith College. David Alexander, Donald McCloskey, and Robert Solow offered invaluable encouragement. Two anonymous reviewers of *Signs* suggested important revisions in the exposition of the arguments. Thanks to all.
    [1] Memorial of Mary F. Eastman, Henrietta L. T. Woolcott, and others . . . Senate Miscellaneous Documents, 45th Congress, 2d Session, vol. 2, no. 84 (Serial Set, 1786). For full text, see Appendix.

[*Signs: Journal of Women in Culture and Society* 1991, vol. 16, no. 3]

of reality, models of social structure, were elaborated and revised," writes Joan Scott.[2] Other recent feminist scholarship details the androcentric focus of many conventional census categories.[3]

Gender bias in the definition of economically productive activity has important implications for the analysis of changes in female labor-force participation. One aspect of such gender bias—the concept of the unproductive housewife—gradually coalesced in the nineteenth-century censuses of population in England and the United States. In 1800, women whose work consisted largely of caring for their families were considered productive workers. By 1900, they had been formally relegated to the census category of "dependents," a category that included infants, young children, the sick, and the elderly.

Several factors shaped the changing attitudes toward household labor during the nineteenth century. A new enthusiasm for female domesticity soothed apprehensions about the impact of capitalist development on the family, and the growth of paid domestic service relieved upper-class women from the most onerous domestic chores. But gender interests were also influential. When male trade unionists argued that hardworking housewives were—or should be—"dependents," they obscured the benefits men enjoyed from women's domestic labor.

Political economists and statisticians played an important role in the deployment of a new vocabulary that complemented the idealization of family life and men's demands for a family wage. While they seldom explicitly discussed household labor, they addressed related topics, and their influence on official terminology can be traced through the evolution of census categories. In Great Britain, the initial assumption that housewives were gainful workers was gradually displaced, with the assistance of economist Alfred Marshall. The prominent Francis Amasa Walker, who took charge of the U.S. census after the Civil War, ignored the productive contributions of housewives, despite strong feminist criticisms. In Massachusetts, the liberal Carroll Wright encouraged attention to

[2] Joan Scott, "A Statistical Representation of Work," in her *Gender and History* (New York: Columbia University Press, 1988), 113–38, esp. 115.

[3] In addition to Scott, see Desley Deacon, "Political Arithmetic: The Nineteenth Century Australian Census and the Construction of the Dependent Woman," *Signs: Journal of Women in Culture and Society* 11, no. 1 (Autumn 1985): 27–47; Margo Anderson, *The American Census: A Social History* (New Haven, Conn.: Yale University Press, 1988); Marilyn Waring, *If Women Counted: A New Feminist Economics* (New York: Harper & Row, 1988); Nancy Folbre and Marjorie Abel, "Women's Work and Women's Households: Gender Bias in the U.S. Census," *Social Research* 56, no. 3 (Autumn 1989): 545–70.

Spring 1991 / **SIGNS**

household work, but the census in his state gradually, if reluctantly, relinquished the concept of the productive housewife.

Domesticity and devaluation

Praise of domesticity and the unique character of the family home played a widely recognized role in nineteenth-century social thought. The "cult of domesticity" contributed to the emergence of a distinctively female culture and became an important strand of nineteenth-century feminism. While feminist scholarship has focused on the social and cultural aspects of this phenomenon, the economic implications have been largely ignored.[4]

Ironically, the moral elevation of the home was accompanied by the economic devaluation of the work performed there. The growth of wage labor, which separated individuals from traditional family-based productive units, almost inevitably wrought new concepts of productive labor. Goods that could be bought and sold, quantities that could be expressed in dollar terms, became the new arbiters of value. Indeed, the growing enthusiasm for social statistics, reflected in new census-taking efforts, deflected attention from activities that could not easily be reduced to a money metric.

Over the course of the nineteenth century, work once performed within patriarchal households under the authority of fathers and husbands was gradually, but only partially, supplanted by the growth of an impersonal marketplace in which the labor power of individuals was bought and sold like any other commodity. Single women entered the paid labor force in large numbers, but most left upon marriage. As late as 1900, 40 percent of single women, but only 6 percent of married women, over age ten in the United States were designated "occupied" by the U.S. Census. In England and Wales in 1901, about 10 percent of married women were listed with occupations.[5]

These figures understate the contributions that women made to their families' economic welfare. Numerous social historical studies show that married women not only performed domestic labor

[4] Barbara Welter, "The Cult of True Womanhood," *American Quarterly* 18, no. 2 (1966): 151–74; Linda Kerber, "Separate Spheres, Female Worlds, Woman's Place: The Rhetoric of Women's History," *Journal of American History* 75, no. 1 (June 1988): 9–39.

[5] *Twelfth Census of the United States: 1900*, Special Reports, Supplementary Analysis and Derivative Tables (Washington, D.C.: Government Printing Office); *Census of England and Wales*, 1901.

but also garnered significant amounts of market income.[6] The wives of farmers, merchants, and craftsmen participated in family enterprises. Many women took in boarders and lodgers, exchanging household services such as cooking and cleaning for money. Housewives provided their own families with an even wider range of domestic services—meal preparation, laundry, child rearing, care of the sick and elderly, household management, and general nurturance.

During the late eighteenth and early nineteenth centuries, domestic work was recognized as a productive and valuable contribution. Despite a strict sexual division of labor, many men as well as women produced goods and services for household use, including housing, furniture, and food grown for the family table. As male participation in the market economy expanded, however, production for use rather than exchange became identified as a distinctly female activity.[7] The home was often described in feminine terms—stable, reassuring, altruistic. The market, by contrast, was a masculine, dynamic realm, characterized by competition and the pursuit of economic self-interest.

A new emphasis on domestic virtue, rather than domestic work, was rooted in genuine fears about the impact of a new emphasis on profits and personal gain that conflicted with traditional religious values. Catherine Beecher's *Treatise on Domestic Economy,* first published in 1841, strictly banished the logic of economic self-interest and laissez-faire from the home. The great mission of the "family state," she wrote, "is self denial and in training its members to self-sacrificing labors for the ignorant and weak."[8] Beecher consistently argued that women's allegiance to home and family was a necessary counterbalance to the competitive anarchy of the market economy.[9]

[6] Alice Clark, *Working Life of Women in the Seventeenth Century* (1919; reprint, New York: Kelley, 1967); Edith Abbott, *Women in Industry: A Study in American Economic History* (1910; reprint, New York: Appleton, 1924); Joan Jensen, *Loosening the Bonds: Mid-Atlantic Farm Women, 1750–1850* (New Haven, Conn.: Yale University Press, 1986); Claudia Goldin, "The Female Labor Force and American Economic Growth, 1890–1980," in *Long-Term Factors in American Economic Growth,* ed. Stanley L. Engerman and Robert E. Gallman, National Bureau of Economic Research Studies in Income and Wealth, vol. 51 (Chicago: University of Chicago Press, 1986), 557–604.

[7] Glenna Matthews, *Just a Housewife: The Rise and Fall of Domesticity in America* (New York: Oxford University Press, 1987); Ruth Schwartz Cowan, *More Work for Mother: The Ironies of Household Technology from the Open Hearth to the Microwave* (New York: Basic, 1983).

[8] Catherine Beecher, *A Treatise on Domestic Economy* (1841; reprint, New York: Source Book Press, 1974), 19.

[9] Kathryn Kish Sklar, *Catherine Beecher: A Study in American Domesticity* (New York: Norton, 1976).

Spring 1991 / **SIGNS**

She developed her philosophy further in *The American Woman's Home*, published in 1869 and coauthored with her sister, Harriet Beecher Stowe.[10] The book embodies the contradictory character of Victorian domesticity. On the one hand, it provides a wealth of technical details regarding the efficient management and performance of household labor. On the other hand, it treats this work as a moral responsibility, not an economically important activity that might be organized along different, less gendered lines. This was family labor, not domestic labor—its aim, the fulfillment of God-given responsibilities, not economic efficiency; its motive not self-interest, but love.

Most political economists reinforced this distinction between the moral (or private) and the economic (or public) world, neatly assigning women and the family to one, men and the market to the other.[11] Even the prominent English neoclassicals, well known for their emphasis on the competitive marketplace, were reluctant to allow economic self-interest to disrupt the home. Stanley Jevons, an otherwise loyal advocate of laissez-faire, proposed that mothers with children under age three should be banned from factories and workshops.[12] Alfred Marshall cautioned against increases in women's wages that might tempt wives and mothers to neglect their household duties.[13]

Growing class differences also contributed to a new view of married women's roles. The "lady," long the ideal of English aristocratic society, began to supplant the housewife as a cultural ideal in the United States during the 1830s.[14] With the increased availability of domestic servants, middle- and upper-class families redefined the role of wives, emphasizing their qualities of personal nurturance and their civilizing influence on husbands and children. By 1880, more than fifteen domestic servants were enumerated per 100 families in many major cities.[15]

---

[10] Catherine Beecher and Harriet Beecher Stowe, *The American Woman's Home* (New York: J. B. Ford, 1869).

[11] Nancy Folbre and Heidi Hartmann, "The Rhetoric of Self Interest and the Ideology of Gender," in *The Consequences of Economic Rhetoric*, ed. Arjo Klamer, Donald McCloskey, and Robert Solow (New York: Cambridge University Press, 1988), 184–206.

[12] Stanley Jevons, "Married Women in Factories," in *Methods of Social Reform and Other Papers* (London: Macmillan, 1883).

[13] Alfred Marshall, *Principles of Economics*, 8th ed. (London: Macmillan, 1930: 685, 715.

[14] Sarah Eisenstein, *Give Us Bread but Give Us Roses: Working Women's Consciousness in the United States, 1890 to the First World War* (Boston: Routledge & Kegan Paul, 1983).

[15] David Katzman, *Seven Days a Week: Women and Domestic Service in Industrial America* (New York: Oxford University Press, 1978), 286. See also Faye

Victorian culture promoted new, refined ideals that working-class women, busy keeping their families fed and clothed, could seldom afford.[16] Yet these ideals proved appealing partly because they helped stabilize a traditional patriarchal system that was being shaken by women's new economic opportunities outside the home. Wally Seccombe persuasively describes the emergence of the "male breadwinner norm" in England as an expression of the economic interests of skilled male trade unionists who feared competition from women who would work for a lower wage.[17] Men also benefited economically from the cheap domestic services that women provided for them in the home.[18]

In both England and the United States, predominantly male trade unions couched their demands in terms of a "family wage" that only men should earn.[19] Economic vocabulary played an important part in such arguments. Consider the words of a member of the National Typographer's Union who protested the seating of Susan B. Anthony at a National Labor Union Conference in 1869: "The lady goes in for taking women away from the wash tub, and in the name of heaven, who is going there, if they don't? I believe in a woman's doing her work, men marrying them and supporting them."[20] The gentleman's concern with his laundry hints at the stake men had in reinforcing women's domestic responsibilities, a self-interest that this speaker obscured with the concept of male economic "support." When male trade unionists argued that they should earn enough money so their wives would not have to work,

---

Dudden, *Household Service in Nineteenth-Century America* (Middletown, Conn.: Wesleyan University Press, 1983); and Theresa McBride, *The Domestic Revolution: The Modernization of Household Service in England and France, 1820–1920* (New York: Holmes & Meier, 1976).

[16] Gerda Lerner, "The Lady and the Mill Girl: Changes in the Status of Women in the Age of Jackson," *Midcontinent American Studies Journal* 10, no. 1 (Spring 1969): 5–15.

[17] Wally Seccombe, "Patriarchy Stabilized: The Construction of the Male Breadwinner Wage Norm in Nineteenth-Century Britain," *Social History* 2, no. 1 (January 1986): 53–76.

[18] Heidi Hartmann, "Capitalism, Patriarchy, and Job Segregation by Sex," *Signs* 1, no. 3 (Spring 1976): 137–69; Phillip Foner, *Women and the American Labor Movement: From Colonial Times to the Eve of World War I* (New York: Free Press, 1979); Sonia Rose, "Gender and Work: Sex, Class and Industrial Capitalism," *History Workshop Journal* 21 (Spring 1986): 557–604; Sidney Webb, "Women's Wages," in *Problems of Modern Industry*, by Sidney Webb and Beatrice Webb (New York: Longmans Green, 1989), 46–81.

[19] Martha May, "Bread before Roses: American Workingmen, Labor Unions and the Family Wage," in *Women, Work and Protest: A Century of U.S. Women's Labor History*, ed. Ruth Milkman (Boston: Routledge & Kegan Paul, 1985), 113–31.

[20] Foner, 136.

Spring 1991 / **SIGNS**

they clearly defined "work" as labor performed outside the home for wages. By describing themselves as the sole support of the family, men undervalued the services they received in return for the wages they contributed.

The exaltation of domestic virtue, growing class inequalities, patriarchal interests—all of these factors contributed to new characterizations of household labor. But the most specific evidence of literal devaluation lies in the history of Anglo-American political economy. In both theory and practice, this emerging science showed a distinct tendency to treat women's household work in moral rather than economic terms. The result was a new statistical categorization of housewives that gradually found expression in the censuses of population.

England and Wales

England was home to the classics of political economy, and her censuses provided a model for the data-gathering practices of her colonies and, later, her Commonwealth. Unlike the United States, where the Constitution mandated a decennial census that helped determine political representation, the early censuses of Great Britain were incorporated into the existing vital registry system and, as such, were heavily influenced by medical concerns such as the measurement of infant mortality.[21] Perhaps as a result, early census practices reflected physicians' appreciation of the difficulties of rearing children, rather than economists' lack of interest in such forms of work.

From the very outset, political economy was preoccupied with the distinction between productive and unproductive labor. In the eighteenth century, the French Physiocrats suggested that agriculture was the only true source of surplus and described profits earned in manufacturing as a mere redistribution. But the Scottish economist Adam Smith offered a spirited defense of manufacturing and called for a new definition of productive labor, based on the addition of "net value" to a vendible commodity.[22] He argued that services were unproductive because they did not contribute to the accumulation of physical wealth. Domestic servants, for example, merely enhanced their employers' standard of living.

[21] J. M. Eyler, *Victorian Social Medicine: The Ideas and Methods of William Farr* (Baltimore: Johns Hopkins University Press, 1979).

[22] Mark Blaug, *Economic Theory in Retrospect*, 4th ed. (Cambridge: Cambridge University Press, 1985).

Smith used the term "productive" primarily to distinguish activities that he believed contributed to economic growth. Most of his immediate successors in the field, including David Ricardo, Thomas Robert Malthus, and John Stuart Mill, followed suit. But none agreed completely with the terms of Smith's definitions. Mill, in particular, argued that some services, such as the training of workers, contributed to economic growth and should be deemed productive.[23] Partly because the issue was never resolved, the classical dichotomy between productive and unproductive labor was gradually replaced by a new distinction between market and nonmarket labor.

By the end of the nineteenth century, most economists had come to agree that all paid services should be considered productive, and many advocated that the term "unproductive" be dropped from the language of their discipline.[24] Yet, almost to a man, they also agreed that nonmarket services lay outside the realm of economics and therefore did not contribute to economic growth. While paid domestic servants were considered part of the labor force, unpaid domestic workers were not. Nonmarket production—a wife's work in the home, for instance—was implicitly defined as unproductive.

This sharp distinction between the household and the market was not reflected in the early censuses of Great Britain. Following an unsuccessful attempt in 1801 to collect information on the occupations of individuals, the censuses of 1811, 1821, and 1831 inquired after the occupations of families as productive units. As Catherine Hakim points out, "The idea of an individual male wage-earner supporting his family was unfamiliar in the first half of the nineteenth century. It was assumed that all members of the household contributed to the family enterprise in agriculture, trade, or handicraft (unless they had independent means)."[25] In 1831 occupations of males age twenty or older were enumerated separately, as were those of female servants of all ages. In 1851, for the first time, general female occupations were enumerated.[26] The list of categories to which they could be assigned included nonmarket household work as well as paid occupations such as teacher or dressmaker.

[23] William J. Barber, *A History of Economic Thought* (New York: Penguin, 1979), 97.

[24] Joseph Schumpeter, *History of Economic Analysis* (New York: Oxford University Press, 1954), 628; *The New Palgrave: A Dictionary of Economics*, ed. John Eatwell, Murray Milgate, and Peter Newman (London: Macmillan, 1987), 1008.

[25] Catherine Hakim, "Census Reports as Documentary Evidence: The Census Commentaries, 1801–1951," *Sociological Review* 28, no. 3 (August 1980): 551–80, esp. 554.

[26] *Census of Great Britain, 1851*, vol. 1, *Population*, British Parliamentary Papers (Dublin: Irish University Press, 1970), lxix.

Spring 1991 / **SIGNS**

Under the influence of the physician William Farr, the 1851 census placed "wives, mothers and mistresses" in a category by themselves, the "Fifth Class" among the occupations. Women with occupations outside the home were grouped accordingly in different classes. Still another class (the "Seventeenth," to be precise) was reserved for "dependents," or those supported by the community: "children, the sick and infirm, gypsies and vagrants, and certain ladies and gentlemen of independent means."[27] The official discussion of the tabulations conveyed a strong appreciation of domestic work: "The most important production of a country is its population."[28] The text went on to deplore women's employment outside the home.

In their critical analyses of the early English censuses, Desley Deacon and Edward Higgs both emphasize the influence of Farr's medical orientation.[29] But Farr was by no means immune to the predominant opinions of political economists. The tenor of the discussion of women's work in the census volumes he supervised changed over time. In the 1861 Census of England and Wales, wives and widows "not otherwise described" were included in class 2, the "Domestic Class," along with scholars, paid domestic workers, entertainers, and people who performed personal services, such as barbers. But the census discussion seemed somewhat apologetic: "These women are sometimes returned as of no occupation. But the occupation of wife and mother and housewife is the most important in the country, as will be immediately apparent if it be assumed for a moment to be suppressed."[30]

The 1871 census used similar categories, but more openly confronted its nomenclatural dilemma. The notes comment that the occupation of wife and mother is "a noble and essential" one, but they also call attention to the increase in women's factory employment, a rapid increase in "the proportion of women engaged specifically in productive work."[31] The language suggests that unpaid domestic labor, however noble, was not truly productive.

Still, the suggestion remained just that; wives and mothers could have been but were not included in the new category termed "Indefinite and Non-productive," which included people without

[27] Celia Davies, "Making Sense of the Census in Britain and the U.S.A.: The Changing Occupational Classification and the Position of Nurses," *Sociological Review* 28, no. 3 (August 1980): 581–609.

[28] *Census of Great Britain, 1851,* lxxxviii.

[29] Deacon (n. 3 above); see also Edward Higgs, "Women, Occupations, and Work in the Nineteenth-Century Censuses," *History Workshop* 23 (Spring 1987): 59–80.

[30] *Census of England and Wales, 1861 and 1871,* British Parliamentary Papers (Dublin: Irish University Press, 1970) 33.

[31] Ibid., xlii.

specified occupations and those whose occupations were described in general or vague terms. William Farr retired shortly after the 1871 census appeared, and terminology shifted more decisively in the 1881 census. Wives and other women engaged in domestic duties were explicitly placed in the "Unoccupied Class," which apparently replaced the earlier "Indefinite and Non-productive" category. The discussion noted that many of the "unoccupied" were women, "of whom by far the greater part were married and engaged in the management of domestic life, and who can only be called unoccupied, when that term is used in the limited sense that it bears in the Census Returns. Many more of these women, though unmarried, were also engaged in domestic duties, or were assisting their fathers or other near relatives in the details of business."[32] Having previously apologized for counting wives and mothers occupied, the registry now apologized for doing just the opposite.

In 1890, a parliamentary committee was convened to consider improvements to the census. The prominent neoclassical economist Alfred Marshall, who was called to testify, held up a recent German census as an example of superior methodology. Marshall complained that the English occupational categories failed to explain the distinctions between skilled and unskilled labor.[33] He was also dissatisfied with the large numbers in the "Unoccupied" column and urged the committee to eliminate it. "In other countries," he explained, "you see the dependents upon anybody who is occupied are entered as dependent, and therefore the figures in this column (unoccupied) are very small."[34]

Marshall clearly agreed with the German convention of describing married women as "dependents," a description far more consistent with the tradition of English political economy than previous census practices. According to the diaries of the prominent social reformer Beatrice Webb, who opposed women's suffrage at the time she met him, Marshall strongly disliked and disapproved of the prospect of female independence.[35] His classic *Principles of Eco-*

[32] *Census of England and Wales, 1881*, British Parliamentary Papers (Dublin: Irish University Press, 1970), 63.

[33] Report of the Committee Appointed by the Treasury to Inquire into Certain Questions Connected with the Taking of the Census, British Parliamentary Papers (c. 6071), LVIII, 13, 68.

[34] Ibid., 66.

[35] *Glitter Around and Darkness Within*, vol. 1 (1873–92) of *The Diary of Beatrice Webb*, ed. Norman and Jeanne McKenzie (Cambridge, Mass.: Harvard University Press, 1982), 273. The entire passage follows: "Conversation with Professor Marshall, he holding that woman was a subordinate being, and that, if she ceased to be subordinate, there would be no object for a man to marry, that marriage was a sacrifice of the masculine freedom and would only be tolerated by male creatures so

Spring 1991 / **SIGNS**

nomics mentioned only in passing the problematic character of the new definition of productive labor: "There is however some inconsistency in omitting the heavy domestic work which is done by women and other members of the household, where no servants are kept."[36]

At least one of Marshall's lesser-known contemporaries devoted slightly more attention to the economic significance of women's household work: "What this income really amounts to may be guessed if we imagine what we should have to pay to servants for doing work now done by wives, sisters, and daughters, and how entirely impossible it would be to get similar work done for money," wrote economist William Smart. "If such women went to the factory or into professional life, we should have to withdraw probably a much greater number from the factory or professions to take their place, and should lose something with it all."[37] Unfortunately, by the time Smart registered these concerns, a new census terminology had limited the prospects for empirically assessing them.

In 1891 the Census of England and Wales restricted the "Domestic Class" to those employed in paid domestic service. The "Unoccupied Class" simply disappeared from the categories, as Marshall had recommended. Polite mention was still made of wives and mothers: "The most important, however, of all female occupations . . . is altogether omitted from the reckoning, namely the rearing of children and the management of domestic life." If these were included, the notes continue, the proportion of occupied women would approach that of men.[38]

Australia, a major Commonwealth country, shifted its terminology in a similar way in 1890. Advocates of a clear emphasis on men as "breadwinners" and women as "dependents" won a decisive victory when, in the absence of a clear statement to the contrary,

---

long as it meant the devotion, body and mind, of the female and no longer. Hence the woman must develop in no way unpleasant to the man: that strength, courage, independence were not attractive in women, that rivalry in men's pursuits was positively unpleasant. Therefore masculine strength and masculine ability in women must be firmly trampled on and 'boycotted' by men. Contrast was the essence of the matrimonial relation: feminine weakness contrasted with masculine strength, masculine egotism with feminine self-devotion. Naturally enough I maintained the opposite argument; viz. that there was an ideal of character in which strength, courage, sympathy, self-devotion, persistent purpose were united to a clear and far-seeing intellect: that this ideal was common to the man and the woman."

[36] Marshall (n. 13 above), 80.
[37] William Smart, *The Distribution of Income* (New York: Macmillan, 1899), 69.
[38] *Census of England and Wales, 1891*, British Parliamentary Papers (Dublin: Irish University Press), 58.

women's work was classified as domestic and they were labeled "dependents." The chief director of the New South Wales census "argued that both women's contributions to family economies and their competition for jobs lowered the wages of men and the community's standard of living."[39] National statistics showing a low rate of female labor-force participation would, he believed, enhance Australia's image as a prosperous colony worthy of English investment.

The United States

The grand tradition of English political economy shaped the U.S. federal censuses from the outset. The lack of connection with a vital statistics registry may have deflected attention from child rearing and other domestic activities. The standard occupational categories consistently ignored women's household labor, and protests by feminists, however articulate, had no apparent impact.

In the United States, political economists never fully endorsed Smith's distinction between productive and unproductive labor.[40] Yet they were remarkably unanimous in their low opinion of women's capacity for important work. The absence of discussion before the 1880s was perhaps more significant than the few remarks that were made. Noteworthy, however, was the well-known political economist Amasa Walker's insistence that women's wages should be low because "the prevailing ideas of the community restrict them to easily dispensible occupations."[41] The eminent southerner Thomas Dew held that women's qualities of mind fitted them for subservient roles.[42]

Such ideas had little discernible influence on the early censuses of population, which, as in England and Wales, focused on families rather than individuals. In 1820, the first year that economic activities became a topic of concern, the federal census tallied the number of families engaged in agriculture, commerce, and manufacturing.[43] The 1830 census included no reference to occupations, but the 1840 census basically followed the 1820 format.

[39] Deacon (n. 3 above), 35.
[40] Paul K. Conkin, *Prophets of Prosperity: America's First Political Economists* (Bloomington: Indiana University Press, 1980), 147.
[41] Joseph Dorfman, *The Economic Mind in American Civilization* (New York: Kelley, 1969), 750.
[42] Ibid., 908.
[43] Still, even at this early date "household manufactures" were explicitly distinguished from others as "only incidental, and not the profession properly marking the class of society to which such individual belongs." These words, attributed to John Quincy Adams, suggests that the census was more interested in "properly marking" class (broadly construed to include the class of housewives) rather than counting the

Spring 1991 / **SIGNS**

As industrial employment grew, so did interest in individual occupations. In 1850 the census inquired after the "profession, occupation, or trade of each male person over 15 years of age."[44] In 1860 and thereafter, this inquiry was extended to women. Unlike the Census of England and Wales, the U.S. Census did not officially recognize the occupation of housewife.

The influence of political economic theory became particularly apparent in 1870, when Francis Amasa Walker, son of Amasa Walker, took charge of the census. Of all the nineteenth-century stewards of official statistics, Walker was by far the most academically prestigious. President of the Massachusetts Institute of Technology, he also presided over the American Economics Association from 1885 to 1892.[45]

Under his aegis, the census explicitly stipulated a wage/salary criterion for women's occupations: "The term 'housekeeper' will be reserved for such persons as receive distinct wages or salary for the service. Women keeping house for their own families or for themselves, without any other gainful occupation, will be entered as 'keeping house.' "[46] This wording implies that keeping house was a gainful occupation, despite its lack of inclusion in the aggregate tabulations.

Francis Walker supported women's right to vote and argued that they should have greater access to jobs outside the home—to a degree. Like his father, who described women as "incapable of self support," Walker had a low opinion of women's productive capacities.[47] His views on the family were distinctly Malthusian. Men undertook the support of women in "obedience to a natural instinct second only, in the demand it makes on men, to the craving for food."[48] Having distinguished himself in the Civil War, Walker was often addressed as "General." His description of women's assigned role in primitive economies reads like a list of military directives: "She will spin and weave . . . she will bring water. . . . She will

---

true extent of manufacturing. See Carroll Wright, *The History and Growth of the U.S. Census* (Washington, D.C.: Government Printing Office, 1900), 135.

[44] Ibid., 147.

[45] James Phinney Munroe, *A Life of Francis Amasa Walker* (New York: Henry Holt, 1923), 328; Robert Solow, "What Do We Know That Francis Amasa Walker Didn't?" *History of Political Economy* 19, no. 2 (Summer 1987): 183–90.

[46] Wright, *The History and Growth of the U.S. Census*, 159.

[47] Amasa Walker, *The Science of Wealth, A Manual of Political Economy, Embracing the Laws of Trade, Currency, and Finance* (1874; reprint, Boston: Little, Brown, 1969).

[48] Francis Walker, *Political Economy* (1883; reprint, New York: Henry Holt, 1911), 297.

keep the hut or tent in a certain order and decency." He went on to make it absolutely clear that women in such economies were not productive workers: "We may assume that speaking broadly, she does not produce as much as she consumes."[49]

Walker's conviction that women's household work was unproductive spilled over into the census's measurement of women's participation in the market economy. By Walker's own account, women with occupations outside the home were underenumerated. He attributed this largely to social custom and enumerator bias. In the 1870 U.S. Census, Walker wrote, "it is taken for granted that every man has an occupation, and the examination of tens of thousands of pages of schedules returned in the present census has satisfied the superintendent that only in rare cases . . . have assistant marshals failed to ask and obtain the occupation of men, or boys old enough to work with effect. It is precisely the other way with women and young children. The assumption is, as the fact generally is, that they are not engaged in remunerative employments. Those who are so engaged constitute the exception, and it follows from a plain principle of human nature, that assistant marshals will not infrequently forget or neglect to ask the question."[50] Women who took in boarders and lodgers, helped with the family farm or business, or contracted industrial homework from factories were not counted among the gainfully occupied, even though they were earning money.[51]

The depreciation of women's domestic labor had long been a theme of feminist protest. Early socialist feminists such as William Thompson and Frances Wright raised the issue in England during the 1830s, and so-called material feminists in the United States called for more efficient organization of domestic labor, including collective facilities for meals that could take full advantage of new cooking technologies.[52] In the 1860s, as the National Women's Suffrage Association explored the possibility of alliances with progressive trade unions, many of its members emphasized the

[49] Ibid.

[50] Ibid., 375.

[51] For a more detailed discussion of the underenumeration of women's market work, see Christine Bose, "Devaluing Women's Work: The Undercount of Women's Employment in 1900," in *Hidden Aspects of Women's Work*, ed. Christine Bose, Roslyn Feldberg, and Natalie Sokoloff (New York: Praeger, 1987); and Nancy Folbre and Marjorie Abel, "Women's Work and Women's Households: Gender Bias in the U.S. Census," *Social Research* 56, no. 3 (Autumn 1989): 545–70.

[52] Barbara Taylor, *Eve and the New Jerusalem: Socialism and Feminism in the Nineteenth Century* (New York: Pantheon, 1983); Dolores Hayden, *The Grand Domestic Revolution: A History of Feminist Designs for American Homes, Neighborhoods, and Cities* (Cambridge, Mass.: MIT Press, 1981).

Spring 1991 / **SIGNS**

drudgery of household work and the exploitation of women who performed it. Elizabeth Cady Stanton declared that women's domestic work differed from that of men only because it was "unpaid, unsocialized, and unrelenting."[53] Elizabeth Blackwell wrote, "The theory that a wife who . . . bears her fair share of the joint burdens, is yet 'supported' by her husband has been the bane of all society."[54] Some progressive trade unionists within the Knights of Labor fully agreed.[55]

Explicit feminist criticism of the census originated with the Association for the Advancement of Women, a group founded in 1873 that included many of the most highly educated women of the day. The Commonwealth of Massachusetts was particularly well represented by Julia Ward Howe, a prominent feminist activist; Melusina Fay Pierce, famous for her advocacy of the collectivization of housework; and Maria Mitchell, a Harvard astronomer. Sometimes affectionately dubbed the "Ladies' Social Science Association," the group held annual conferences throughout the 1890s and helped design the Women's Exhibit for the Centennial Exposition of 1876.[56]

The AAW's concerns were hardly limited to the "twelve millions of American women being overlooked as laborers or producers" (see Appendix). Consonant with their own professional interests, the members pointed out that the census could improve the quality of its statistics on women and children by hiring intelligent women as enumerators. Summaries of the conference proceedings included no mention of a response until a short retrospective essay was published in 1893. Apparently, Walker had invoked the cult of domesticity in his own defense. Ladies themselves, he argued, were reluctant to acknowledge that they worked for a living.[57]

In 1900, the U.S. Census adopted a new use for the term "breadwinner," cautioning that "it must be understood in a sense somewhat different from its usual one . . . it does not include a person who has retired from practice or business or a wife or daughter living at home and assisting only in the household duties

[53] *The Revolution*, ed. Susan B. Anthony and Elizabeth Cady Stanton (December 24, 1868), 393.

[54] Cited in William Leach, *True Love and Perfect Union* (New York: Basic, 1980), 193.

[55] Susan Levine, *Labor's True Woman: Carpet Weavers, Industrialization and Labor Reform in the Gilded Age* (Philadelphia: Temple University Press, 1984).

[56] Leach, 292–322.

[57] American Association for the Advancement of Women, *Historical Account of the Association for the Advancement of Women, 1873–1893*, Twenty-first Women's Congress, World's Columbian Exposition, Chicago (Dedham, Mass.: Transcript Steam Job Print, 1893), 9.

without pay."[58] Wives and daughters without a paying job were officially designated "dependents." State censuses became increasingly common in the late nineteenth century, and most of them conformed to federal format and terminology.[59] The Commonwealth of Massachusetts, however, proved an important exception.

The Massachusetts anomaly

The 1875 State Census of Massachusetts, probably the most ambitious of its day, collected and compiled an unusual variety of social statistics. Its complexity may have obscured its English-style categorization of women's domestic work, which received little or no attention. Its terminological anomalies represent an interesting detour from federal census practices that only gradually converged with the main road.

In 1875, housewives and unmarried women who performed housework without remuneration were included in the larger category of "Domestic and Personal Office," along with subcategories for paid employment such as housekeepers, servants, nurses, and washerwomen. The introduction to the first volume makes it clear that a housewife's work was considered productive: "The terms non-productive and unemployed are applied to all who take no part in the work of life."[60] Indeed, a separate occupational category was reserved for the "non-productive and propertied."

Traces of the old-fashioned Smithian emphasis on production of material goods remained. The introductory notes observe that only occupations in agriculture, fisheries, manufacturing, and mechanical industries, as well as apprentices and laborers, actually produced things. All services, though they may have been performed for pay, were seen as distinct from agriculture and manufacturing— and were, by implication, somewhat suspect.

Married women were not automatically assumed to be housewives. Some were described as "having nothing to do but superintend the households," and there were those who did even less than that. In the census's own words, "there are 4,786 wives of heads simply ornamental."[61] These amounted to less than 2 percent of all wives.

[58] *Twelfth Census of the United States, 1900* (n. 5 above), 225.
[59] This generalization is based on scrutiny of nineteenth-century censuses from states in which more than eight censuses were taken: New York, Michigan, and Iowa, as well as the western states of Texas and Colorado. The majority of states did not conduct systematic censuses during the nineteenth century, and interest in occupational categories was limited to the most industrialized states.
[60] *The Census of Massachusetts: 1875* (Boston: Albert J. Wright, 1876), xlix.
[61] Ibid., 1.

Spring 1991 / **SIGNS**

The 1885 State Census of Massachusetts dropped the "non-productive and propertied" category and introduced a variety of new categories in its place, including "retired"—"those possessed of a competency, inherited or acquired, or for some reasons, do not need to be actively engaged in order to obtain a subsistence, as distinguished from those persons classified as 'dependents,' mostly in private families, who are more or less dependent upon relatives or friends for their support."[62] Similarly, the term "non-productive" was reserved for "those afflicted persons, homeless children, paupers, prisoners, and convicts, who by reason of their disabilities, etc., have no productive occupations." This census used the terms "dependent" and "non-productive" quite restrictively. They were not used to label housewives.

But the text that accompanied the tabulations in 1885 reflected a major concession to the emerging conventional wisdom. Housewives and women who performed unpaid housework, along with scholars and students, were subtracted from the total to arrive at "remunerative occupations." The definition of the word "housewife" itself shifted away from one based on actual work performed to more general, social terms: "By housewives are meant the female heads of household, that is, the wife or some person in the family who has general charge of the domestic affairs."[63] "Housework," used to describe the work of unmarried people who performed unpaid domestic labor, retained a specific meaning at least somewhat independent of gender. Of 89,062 people so engaged, seventy-seven were males.

The apparent contradictions persist in the 1895 Massachusetts census. Housewives and housework are tabulated in "Domestic Service," rather than in the "not gainful," "not productive," or "dependent" categories. But in 1905, the Massachusetts census surrendered its eccentricities and placed housewives and housework in the "not gainful" class, along with scholars, students, retirees, those unemployed for twelve months, and dependents. The "Domestic and Personal Service" category was limited to those who received a wage or salary for their work.

This terminological shift was discussed in the twentieth annual report of the Massachusetts Bureau of Statistics of Labor (1889), which summarized the findings of the 1885 census regarding women in industry. The lengthy explanation of why women were excluded from the "remunerative occupations" had an apologetic

---

[62] *The Census of Massachusetts: 1885*, prepared under the direction of Carroll D. Wright, vol. 1, *Population and Social Statistics* (Boston: Wright & Potter, 1888), xxi.
[63] Ibid., xxv.

tone reminiscent of that found in the Census of England and Wales after 1880. But the discussion, far more assertive in its criticism of the conventional wisdom, anticipated William Smart's questions regarding the implicit value of unpaid domestic labor—in short, what it could cost, were it paid for:

> To be sure, [housewives] receive no stated salary or wage, but their work is surely worth what it would cost to have it done, supposing that the housewife, as such, did no work at all. There were 372,612 housewives in Massachusetts in 1885, and only 300,999 women engaged in all other branches of industry. If a housewife were not expected nor required to work, then for the labor of 372,612 women paid service would have to be substituted. Such a demand for labor could not be supplied by the inhabitants of the State itself. Consequently, as the labor of the housewives was absolutely necessary to allow society to exist in its present form, the housewife is certainly "in industry." As has been stated, she is excluded from the previous tables in this Part for conventional and arbitrary reasons alone. The housewife is as much a member of the army of workers as the clerk or cotton weaver, and too often supplements the toil of the day, "in industry" with household duties performed at home, but outside of the "in industry" classification.[64]

The author of this prescient explanation remains a mystery, although Horace Wadlin, director of the Boston Public Library, was in command of the Massachusetts Bureau of Labor at the time. Responsibility for the more generous English-style terminology of the 1875 and 1885 censuses lies almost certainly with then-director Carroll Wright, who had a unique, if undeveloped, theoretical perspective on women's household work. The 1875 Massachusetts census represented his official debut as one of the most influential statisticians of the late nineteenth century. Wright, who also served as a special agent for the 1880 U.S. Census, was appointed U.S. Commissioner of Labor in 1885 and served until 1905. During his tenure, he presided over the 1890 U.S. Census and many important census-sponsored studies and reports.

James Leiby's classic study of Wright's lifework describes him as an autodidact lacking in intellectual stature, who relied heavily

---

[64] Massachusetts Bureau of Labor Statistics, *Twentieth Annual Report of the Bureau of the Statistics of Labor* (Boston: Wright & Potter, December 1889), 579.

on the advice of Francis Walker.[65] Yet the data that Wright collected
may have had a far greater impact on subsequent economic research
than Walker's theoretical or empirical contributions. Wright had an
uncanny instinct for the systematic exploration of politically important issues. His classic study, *The Working Girls of Boston*, was one
of the first efforts to examine the implications of factory employment. In it, Wright argued that the length of the working day for
women should be limited to ten hours in part because, according to
his survey, they did much of their own domestic labor and had little
time for rest.[66]

Wright eventually became far more sympathetic to feminism
than most of his male counterparts, as evidenced by his article
"Why Women Earn Less Than Men," which acknowledged the
discrimination women faced.[67] His Massachusetts background
meant that he almost inevitably came into contact with some of the
more prominent members of the Association for the Advancement
of Women. But Wright's adherence to the concept of the productive
housewife, though admirable, was neither strong nor persistent.
His voluminous writings were largely preoccupied with relations
between labor and capital. Even his published address to the
American Social Science Association on "Problems of the Census"
in 1887 omitted any consideration of household labor.

The implications of a new terminology

The censuses of England, the United States, and Massachusetts
reveal the emergence of a new terminology that clearly labeled
housework unproductive. What do these examples tell us about the
coevolution of political economy and its more pragmatic language
of measurement? The concept of the unproductive housewife was
a by-product of a new definition of productive labor that valorized
participation in the market and devalorized the nonmarket work
central to many women's lives. The terminological shift formalized
the assumptions of androcentric political economy.

This shift was not unique to one country. Given Alfred Marshall's
recommendation that England import the German practice of cat-

[65] James Leiby, *Carroll Wright and Labor Reform: The Origin of Labor Statistics*
(Cambridge, Mass.: Harvard University Press, 1960).
[66] Carroll Wright, "The Working Girls of Boston," *Fifteenth Annual Report of the
Bureau of the Statistics of Labor* (Boston: Wright & Potter, July 1884), 129.
[67] Carroll Wright, "Why Women Earn Less Than Men," *Forum* (July 1892),
629–39.

egorizing housewives as dependents, it cannot be attributed simply to Victorian ideology writ large. Nor did the shift go unnoticed. William Farr and Carroll Wright both resisted it initially. The Association for the Advancement of Women actively protested it.

Why, then, did it not stir more discussion and debate? Part of the answer lies in the ease with which upper-class men could arrive at a comfortable consensus concerning women's capacities and contributions. The evolution of census terminology resonates with the story that social historians have told about the functional aspects of the "breadwinner/dependent ideal."[68] Indeed, it suggests that historians may have underestimated the importance of new cultural conceptions of work by failing to recognize the ways that gender bias influenced "objective" measurements of women's productive work.

Political pressures influenced the way in which late nineteenth-century social statistics were collected in the United States. The Massachusetts Bureau of Labor was created largely in response to agitation by a labor group, the Knights of Saint Crispin. The Knights of Labor successfully demanded a Federal Bureau of Labor.[69] The Divorce Reform League prompted the Federal Bureau's study of marriage and divorce statistics in the United States, which Carroll Wright conducted in 1889. When Wright first assumed his responsibilities at the new Federal Bureau of Labor, his interest in developing a major study of African-American workers was discouraged because of concern that southern Congressmen would be offended.[70] If African-Americans or women had had more political power, even an effective right to vote, U.S. census categories might have evolved differently.

A mélange of theoretical, political, and practical concerns influenced census designers. Yet their categories, in turn, exerted tremendous influence on both everyday politics and economic theory. By 1900, the notion that married women without paying jobs outside the home were "dependents" had acquired the status of a scientific fact. Women's economic dependence commonly was used to explain their lower wages—they did not *need* a living wage. Indeed, men demanded a higher wage so that they might support their dependent wives.[71]

[68] See Hartmann (n. 18 above); Seccombe (n. 17 above); and Rose (n. 18 above).
[69] Carroll Wright, "The Working of the Department of Labor," in *Monographs on Social Economics*, ed. Chas. H. Verrill (U.S. Department of Labor Exhibit, Pan American Exhibition, 1901), 1.
[70] Leiby, 105.
[71] Carroll Wright, *The Industrial Evolution of the United States* (New York: Charles Scribner's, 1901), 212; Sidney Webb (n. 18 above), 78; Barbara Meyer

Spring 1991 / **SIGNS**

The result was a certain symmetry between private, public, and academic assumptions. The new terminology made it difficult to explain how a married man benefited from his wife's household labor or, similarly, how the larger economy benefited from nonmarket work. Those few scholars who remained interested in household production stepped outside the traditions of political economy to found the new discipline of home economics. In that sphere, the productive housewife lived on, in theory as well as in practice.

Department of Economics
University of Massachusetts—Amherst

Appendix

Memorial of Mary F. Eastman, Henrietta L. T. Woolcott, and others, officers of the Association for the Advancement of Women, praying that the tenth census may contain a just enumeration of women as laborers and producers.

To the Senate and House of Representatives of the United States in Congress assembled:

Whereas the acknowledged errors, discrepancies, and incompleteness of the Ninth Census render it an unsatisfactory and unreliable record of the population, wealth, industry, and physical, mental and moral conditions of the American people; and

Whereas the home and woman as a home-keeper have no place in the report, only the occupations called "gainful" being noted, and more than twelve millions of American women being overlooked as laborers or producers or left out, in common with those pursuing disreputable employments, and not even incidentally named as in any wise affecting the causes or increase or decrease of population or wealth; and

Whereas gross errors in enumerating the births, ages, diseases, and deaths of children are the inevitable result of the natural barriers in the way of men as collectors of social and vital statistics, who frequently obtain information, in the language of the report, from "fathers, nurses, servants, and unsympathetic fellow-boarders"; and

Whereas there is obvious justice and propriety in the employment of intelligent women to collect vital statistics concerning women and children:

Therefore we pray your honorable body, in enacting a law providing for the taking of the Tenth Census, to make provision for the more careful

---

Wertheimer, *We Were There: The Story of Working Women in America* (New York: Pantheon, 1977), 207.

Folbre / UNPRODUCTIVE HOUSEWIFE

and just enumeration of women as laborers and producers; for a record of the wages of men and women in all occupations; for a record of causes of pauperism, vagrancy, vice and crime, insanity, idiocy, blindness, deformity, and disease; for the enumeration of all men and women engaged in disreputable occupations, for full statistics concerning all reformatory institutions; and

We further pray that you will enact such laws or amendments as may be requisite to secure the employment of a fair ratio of suitable women as collectors of the centennial census.

Mary T. Eastman, Massachusetts, Secretary Association for Advancement of Women, et al.

[6]

WOMEN'S WAGES IN RELATION TO ECONOMIC WELFARE [1]

A PRECEDING inquiry was directed to the question what relation between the wages of men and women is most conducive to production of wealth in the narrower sense of that term.[2] In this sequel there is substituted for *wealth* a higher aim, *economic welfare*. Welfare is related to wealth as inward feeling to outward means. Economic welfare is distinguished from other kinds of happiness in that it depends more on external means, enters easily into relation with the measuring rod of money, as Professor Pigou defines (*ante*, § 2).[3] As a property of this essential difference it seems that propositions respecting economic welfare possess one characteristic of positive science, general consent, in a greater degree than beliefs concerning higher kinds of well-being. There is more agreement about the conditions of material prosperity than about the first principles of ethics and politics.

A distinctive feature of welfare which especially concerns us here is the postulate that the satisfactions felt by different persons admit of comparison. It thus becomes possible to consider the aggregate economic welfare of a community as the sum of satisfactions enjoyed by the individual members. By the law of diminishing utility the addition of wealth to those who have already abundance tends to increase the aggregate welfare less than if the same amount of means were applied to the relief of pressing wants. Accordingly, if the wealth of a community is increased or diminished, the gain or loss of aggregate welfare depends not only on the amount of wealth added or subtracted, but also on the distribution of the benefits or privations among the members of the community. The negative case of this proposition forms the basis of a now generally accepted principle of taxation. If a given amount is to be raised by taxation, the

---

[1] Read before Section F of the British Association, 1923.

[2] See article on "Equal Pay to Men and Women for Equal Work" in the ECONOMIC JOURNAL, December, 1922.

[3] The references of this type are to the previous article in the ECONOMIC JOURNAL, December, 1922.

burden should be distributed among the contributors in such
wise that the aggregate sacrifice incurred may be a minimum.[1]

The only question is whether we should stop at the amount
of revenue required for the public services, or whether taxation
should be applied beyond this limit for the express purpose of
equalising incomes. There are those who think that such equal-
isation would be theoretically *per se* desirable, and are deterred
only by the consideration that production would be discouraged.
It is as if a force tending to cause movement in a certain direction
is held in check by an opposite force. Then, if the counteracting
force is lessened, the ever-present tendency will spring into action.
Upon this principle it was forcibly argued in the year 1916 that
the burden of " special taxes levied on an exceptional occasion
for the purpose of financing an unprecedented war " should be
distributed with less regard than usual to counteracting considerations.[2]

Similar statements would hold good if taxes consisted of
services exacted for the benefit of the State. For the analogy
between taxation and *corvée* is very close. Quite philosophically
the taxes collected for the kings of ancient Egypt were named
" labour." [3] So on the supposition that imposts were exacted in
the form of work, as pointed out by Sir Josiah Stamp, more would
be expected from the more powerful man.[4] *Prima facie* the principle should be applicable, beyond the sphere of public services,
to the distribution of labour and remuneration in general. It
would seem to follow that if one class is less capable of work than
another, but equally capable of enjoyment, the former class shall
do less work, but enjoy equal remuneration. But of course such
an arrangement would be impracticable. The numbers of the
less capable class would increase to the detriment of production.
The survival of the inefficient would be encouraged. These
results would not equally follow if the privileged class consisted
of the weaker sex. *Prima facie* the case would resemble one just
now instanced in that first principles spring into action, counteracting considerations being withdrawn. It would seem to be
opportune to discuss and apply a problem which Mr. and

---

[1] Cp. Cannan : " Minium aggregate sacrifice in the long run is the principle
which all good ministers of finance and Parliament endeavour to the best of their
abilities (often poor) to adopt. Under its ample folds equity, ability, benefit,
and all other good things drop into their proper places."—ECONOMIC JOURNAL,
1921, p. 350.

[2] Pigou, *Economy and Finance of the War*, referred to in the ECONOMIC
JOURNAL, 1916, p. 227.

[3] Breasted, *History of Ancient Egypt*.

[4] *Fundamental Principles of Taxation*, 1919, p. 8.

Mrs. Webb cite as interesting.[1] Whereas on a certain slave plantation equal tasks were imposed on men and women, the latter accordingly, in consequence of their comparative weakness, suffering much more fatigue; supposing the employer to insist only on a certain quantity of work being done, and to leave the distribution of the burden to the philanthropist, what would be the most beneficent arrangement?[2] But a regime so socialistic is not here contemplated. It is supposed that the forces of competition can only be slightly modified by combination. It is not proposed to defy the ruling of competition. But, as pointed out before (*ante*, § 10), the determinations effected by competition are often not minutely graduated. It is as if the *integers* of economic quantities that are in dispute were determined by the play of competition; while the *fractions* are left to be settled by collective bargaining and utilitarian considerations (*ante*, § 10). Even as regards the integers, if one or two units are changed in the interest of one set of workers, no appreciable economic loss to the community is

---

[1] *Industrial Democracy*, p. 505, ed. 1902.

[2] Let X be the amount of work to be done by the average man, and x the corresponding task of the woman; where $X + x$ is given, the numbers of the sexes being supposed equal. Let $F(X)$ represent the disutility experienced by the average man doing the amount of work denoted by X; where $F'(X)$ and $F''(X)$ are both continually positive. And let $f(x)$ likewise represent the analogous subjective quantity for the woman. Then the sum-total of disutility, $F(X) + f(x)$ is to be a minimum; *subject to the condition* that $X + x =$ constant. Whence $F'(X) = f'(x)$. Now let it be granted that for any quantity z (of the order of the quantities X and x with which we have to do), $f(z) > F(z)$, and also ($f(z) - F(z)$ continually increasing) $f'(z) > F'(z)$. Then when $F'(X) = f'(x)$, X must be greater than x.

To adapt this reasoning to the distribution of work and produce in an ideal community regulated according to utilitarian (or as some may prefer to say, socialistic) principles; let X denote the amount of goods produced by the average man—amount measured in money or some even more appropriate index; and let Ξ be the portion of goods assigned for his consumption. Let the corresponding quantities for women be x and ξ. Then, if N is the number of the men, n of the women, $NX + nx = N\Xi + n\xi$. Let $F(X)$ be the disutility accruing to the man from the production of X; and let $f(x)$ be the corresponding expression for the woman worker. Also let $\Phi(\Xi)$ be the satisfaction accruing to the average man from the consumption of goods amounting to Ξ ($\Phi' > 0$, $\Phi'' < 0$) and let the corresponding expression for the women be $\phi(\xi)$. There is then to be maximised the sum-total of welfare $N\Phi((\Xi) - F(X)) + n(\phi(\xi) - f(x))$; *subject to the condition* $N\Xi + n\xi = NX + nx$. Whence $F'(X) = f'(x) = \Phi'(\Xi) = \phi'(\xi)$. Now let it be granted that, as before, for any quantity z (of the order of the quantities with which we have to do) $f(z) > F'(z)$; while there is no corresponding datum with respect to the quantities and functions designated by the Greek symbols. Then it follows, as before, that X shall be greater than x. It does not follow that Ξ (the man's portion of goods) should be greater than (the woman's) ξ; it being understood that there is not deducted from Ξ any special charge for the support of families (or other public purpose).

to be apprehended. For the economic equilibrium which is determined by competition may be considered as realising the *maximum* of advantage (attainable in the existing state of things). So by the theory of maxima a slight modification of the arrangements which secure maximum advantage will be attended with only a *very slight* diminution of the total advantage (*ante*, § 8). There would not be an appreciable loss *in globo*, but a transference conducive to economic welfare.

But the gain to the women-workers would not always involve an equal loss to the men. For many of the concessions demanded would consist of increased facilities for work; and so would result in an increase of the wealth to be distributed (*ante*, § 19). The war has shown that there is much room for improvement in this direction. We read of " processes which by some reorganisation, or the introduction of labour-saving appliances, could be made suitable for them " (women). The difficulty of employing women on heavy work may often be got over by mechanical means—" lifting tackle, trolleys, runways for bogies, lighter tools and trucks," and so on. " There would appear to be a fairly large new field of possible activity for women." [1] Arrangements to suit those who cannot work many hours may be foreseen. The removal of hindrances to the entrance of employments and to the training required for their exercise has already been claimed as conducive to wealth (*ante*, § 9). On the ground of economic welfare it is now further demanded that women-workers should at least have the benefit of any doubt that may arise with regard to the apportionment of industries between the sexes (*ante*, § 12). If in effect, however masked by the wording of awards and agreements, there comes in an element of chance in determinations about work and wages—as Dido apportioned the labour of her workpeople not simply by just partition, but also by drawing lots [2]—let us weight the chances somewhat in favour of the weaker sex.

These concessions may be demanded and granted without indulging the fantastic sentiments of Don Quixote, without accepting Michelet's old-fashioned objection to the employment of women in industry : " L'ouvrière mot impie et sordide ! " [3] There would be demanded only a little more than Francis Walker

---

[1] *Memorandum on Substitution of Women in Non-Munition Factories.* Home Office, 1919.

[2] " Operumque laborem
Partibus æquabat justis, aut sorto trahebat."
                              Æneid, 1, 507-8.

[3] *La Femme*, ch. 2.

claims in his eminently sane observations upon women's wages.[1] Impressed with the advantages of free competition he demands "mobility" for women-workers, free access to the labour market to which they have been driven by the changed conditions of production.

Walker enforces this claim by appealing to the well-known chivalry of American men. And certainly if chivalry in the general sense of knightly virtue has been shown by another great economist to be compatible with modern industry,[2] why whould not this be true also of chivalry in that special sense which was the crown and glory of the knightly character? Yet here appeal is not made to so refined a motive. For economic welfare is considered as depending on characteristics of human nature that are very general, almost as universal—and so nearly as amenable to scientific treatment—as the motives commonly ascribed to the "economic man." It is hardly consistent with this definition to include a sentiment which is far from universal, not common to the Eastern or the ancient civilisations. To secure the validity of our conclusions there is not postulated any particular code of manners and customs. It is not necessary to dispute the views of Mr. Belfort Bax, who in his unpleasant book, *Frauds of Feminism*, complains that "women are iniquitously privileged at the expense of men"; denounces the rule of the sea, that the women should have priority of exit from a sinking ship, as "an abominable piece of sex favouritism," which "cries aloud in its irrational injustice." Nor, on the other hand, need we accept the Comtist doctrine that female relatives have a claim to be supported by the men of their household on the analogy of priests and magistrates "maintained by those for whom their lives are devoted."[3] The premises of our argument are more general, containing more of the *quod semper, quod ubique;* such as the laws of diminishing utility and increasing fatigue, the fact of unequal capacities—differences in the relation between work done and fatigue felt.

Nevertheless it is not irrelevant to the argument that its practical conclusions are in harmony with the manners of Christendom. If most Englishmen and many other men regard as detestable opinions of the kind professed by Belfort Bax, this is a fact favourable to the application of our reasoning. Consider

---

[1] *The Wages Question*, p. 381 and context.

[2] Marshall, "The Social Possibilities of Economic Chivalry," ECONOMIC JOURNAL, Vol. XVII (1907).

[3] Cp. Frederic Harrison, *Realities and Ideals.*

the opinion of a late Lord Chancellor which Mr. Bax quotes with disapprobation, the dictum that " our laws taken as a whole are more merciful to women than to men, and are more mercifully administered." If this discrimination is generally approved, there may be presumed a predisposition to admit a similar discrimination with respect to the laws of political economy. But the tendency is held in check by the supposed rigidity of those laws, by the conception of competition as necessary and beneficent. It is, therefore, not without consequence to point out that some discrimination of the slight yet appreciable degree which is admitted in the sphere of law is possible in the sphere of industry. The supposed predisposition would secure a response to Walker's appeal for the removal of obstructions. It would secure attention to the subtler arguments which are based on the " elasticity of the demand for labour " and the nature of economic equilibrium (*ante*, § 19 and § 8). There would at least be rendered more gentle that jostle of competition from which Frederic Harrison apprehended that " the great majority of men and women would sink into the relative position of big and little boys at school." [1] Why should not the relation be, rather, like that of the young men and maidens at our Universities who compete in work tested by examinations without being related as fag and bully ? May not Competition in industry, tempered by Combination (*ante*, § 10) work equally smoothly ? Altogether, under the favourable conditions supposed—the action of reason quickened by a predisposing sentiment—the pursuit of economic welfare may avert the reproach conveyed in Burke's tremendous words : " The age of chivalry is gone. That of sophisters, economists, and calculators has succeeded ; and the glory of Europe is extinguished for ever." [2] Rather, the economists, if aiming at economic welfare, the sophisters and calculators, if so named because, in accordance with the utilitarian philosophy, they seek to calculate the course that is conducive to the greatest quantity of happiness, will cultivate a certain species of chivalry, wanting, it may be, the glory of the older virtue, but still a precious element of civilisation. It might not be so dearly prized as its romantic prototype by those who form its object, in benefiting whom consists its virtue ; but the benefit would be more widely diffused, less confined to aristocratic circles.

The concessions now advised on the ground of economic welfare, unlike those before admitted (*ante*, § 16 *et seq.*), are not based on the incidents of family life. The fresh considerations,

---

[1] *Op. cit.*   [2] *Reflections on the French Revolution.*

however, do not contravene those admissions; the concessions
advocated, not being on such a scale as seriously to alter the
balance between the wage of spinsters and that of married
men to the detriment of families.

In this part of the subject not only is the present sequel in
keeping with, but it also lends support to, the preceding
argument. It will be remembered that the presumption
in favour of equal pay to men and women encountered the
objection that the bulk of men are subject to a charge from
which the bulk of women are exempt, the support of families
(*ante*, §§ 16–18). This circumstance much weakens the force of
appeals to the justice which is inherent in *laissez-faire*, the " system
of natural liberty." [1] The case for equal pay is not so strong as it
has been represented by ardent champions of woman's rights,
Olive Schreiner for example in passages like the following : "The
fact that for equal work equally well performed by a man and a
woman it is ordained that the woman on the ground of her sex
alone shall receive a less recompense is the nearest approach to
a wilful and unqualified ' wrong ' in the whole relations of women
to Society to-day. . . . That males of enlightenment and equity
can for an hour tolerate the existence of this inequality has seemed
to me always incomprehensible." [2] There is certainly a " wrong "
of the kind which consists in the infraction of *laissez-faire*.
But it is not " unqualified " in so far as it is calculated to correct
another sort of wrong. If with equal pay for equal work one
of the parties is to be subject to unequal deductions from his
pay; it seems not unreasonable that the said party should have
some advantage in the Labour Market (*ante*, § 18 par 1). Moreover, those barriers against the entrance of women workers into
certain occupations which are the main cause of different remuneration for the same effort appear to subserve the purpose of
preventing the *débâcle*, ultimately ruinous alike to wealth and
family life, which the hasty substitution of low-paid female
operatives for well-paid men threatens to bring about (*ante*, § 5).
Accordingly the case for unrestricted competition, without any
provision for the endowment of families, is not so strong as it
has been represented by advocates of equal pay. Even with
such provision as recommended in the preceding article the
case is not so strong but that it may be strengthened by the
considerations adduced in the sequel. The man who is hesitating
between the older policy of exclusion and greater freedom of
competition (safe-guarded by subsidy to families) is exhorted

[1] *Wealth of Nations*, Book IV.   [2] Introduction, p. 24.

to give the benefit of the doubt to the course which makes for the higher remuneration and larger independence of the woman worker. To thwart her wishes and degrade her status would not be consistent with economic chivalry.

Altogether these considerations are calculated to strengthen the reasons before given for some sort of subsidy to mothers of families, whether on the part of the State or of unmarried fellow-workmen (*ante*, § 21). Such are the institution of family allocations which, as described in the publications of the Family Endowment Council, are coming into vogue in France and other countries; and the kindred German arrangements which are described by Dr. Heimann in this issue of the ECONOMIC JOURNAL.[1] If there could be a doubt whether, in case of a money subsidy being granted, it should be paid into the hands of the mother, the preceding considerations would be decisive in her favour.

But while the arguments in favour of family endowment are strengthened, the objections to its injudicious use are nowise weakened. The reader is requested to consider carefully the long list of disadvantages and dangers enumerated in the preceding paper (*ante*, § 20). It is true that all those objections would not attend all schemes of State support. In particular the evil effects on the future of population are not to be attributed to all such schemes. Thus Professor Pearson in his original and outspoken *Ethic of Free Thought*, while recommending the support of mothers by the State or Commune, seems only to guarantee that support in case of births sanctioned by the authorities.[2] Mr. H. G. Wells, too, accompanies his drastic provisions for the State support of mothers with State regulation of births.[3] But it may be doubted whether this platonic regulation will in practice be embodied in schemes for the endowment of motherhood. Consideration for the quantity and quality of population cannot be counted on. Nor, even if it could be, would it secure the wealth and welfare of a people dependent on the State for the support of families. It is a fearfully rash assumption that, because each man now generally works hard for the sake of his own wife and children, all men will work equally hard for all wives and children collectively.

The danger of this assumption is by no means confined to the

---

[1] p. 509 below. Cp. Douglas on "The Project of Child-Endowment in Australia," *Quarterly Journal of Economics*, August, 1923. See also *Revue de Travail*, Belgium, May, 1923.

[2] *Op. cit.*, p. 443 *et seq.*, ed. 1.   [3] *Socialism and the Family.*

common Socialist intent upon material gains. The main facts of life are even more easily forgotten by the idealist. The Swedish sentimentalist, Ellen Key, for instance, expects that when a " profounder culture " becomes prevalent " it will seem as natural for society to maintain its women as it was natural to maintain its army and navy." They will receive a "subsidy from the community for the bringing up of children," " the economic appreciation of her (their) domestic work." They will thus be free to cultivate a " soulful sensuousness or sensuous soulfulness "; in accordance with " a new morality." [1] Naturally conditions of wealth and economic welfare are not considered by reformers intent upon some object of a higher or at least a different order. The greatest of such innovators has characterised his proposal in terms which may be cited as quaintly expressing the spirit in which the economist at least should *not* approach such matters. Milton, when, galled by the yoke of an ill-assorted marriage, he proposed as a remedy for marital troubles freedom of divorce, thus reflected complacently on that proposal : " I doubt not but with one gentle stroking to wipe away ten thousand tears out of the life of man." [2] But the economist, remembering how often the appearance of easy remedies for human ills, in his sphere at least, has proved deceptive, will not expect much from a stroke, gentle or violent, intended to revolutionise established institutions which have worked well for the production of wealth and economic welfare. The only reforms of such institutions which the economist can approve are tentative and gradual.

[1] *Love and Ethics*, p. 54. *Love and Marriage*, p. 20, ch. xi. Cp. *The Woman Worker*, ch. vi.
[2] *Doctrine and Discipline of Divorce*, second edition.

F. Y. EDGEWORTH

Part III
The Family, Household Production, and Market Work

A
Household Production and the Allocation of Time

[7]

THE ECONOMIC JOURNAL

SEPTEMBER 1965

113-37

[1965]

Gary S. Becker

J22

D11

A THEORY OF THE ALLOCATION OF TIME

I. Introduction

THROUGHOUT history the amount of time spent at work has never consistently been much greater than that spent at other activities. Even a work week of fourteen hours a day for six days still leaves half the total time for sleeping, eating and other activities. Economic development has led to a large secular decline in the work week, so that whatever may have been true of the past, to-day it is below fifty hours in most countries, less than a third of the total time available. Consequently the allocation and efficiency of non-working time may now be more important to economic welfare than that of working time; yet the attention paid by economists to the latter dwarfs any paid to the former.

Fortunately, there is a movement under way to redress the balance. The time spent at work declined secularly, partly because young persons increasingly delayed entering the labour market by lengthening their period of schooling. In recent years many economists have stressed that the time of students is one of the inputs into the educational process, that this time could be used to participate more fully in the labour market and therefore that one of the costs of education is the forgone earnings of students. Indeed, various estimates clearly indicate that forgone earnings is the dominant private and an important social cost of both high-school and college education in the United States.[1] The increased awareness of the importance of forgone earnings has resulted in several attempts to economise on students' time, as manifested, say, by the spread of the quarterly and tri-mester systems.[2]

Most economists have now fully grasped the importance of forgone earnings in the educational process and, more generally, in all investments in human capital, and criticise educationalists and others for neglecting them. In the light of this it is perhaps surprising that economists have not been

---

[1] See T. W. Schultz, " The Formation of Human Capital by Education," *Journal of Political Economy* (December 1960), and my *Human Capital* (Columbia University Press for the N.B.E.R., 1964), Chapter IV. I argue there that the importance of forgone earnings can be directly seen, *e.g.*, from the failure of free tuition to eliminate impediments to college attendance or the increased enrolments that sometimes occur in depressed areas or time periods.

[2] On the cause of the secular trend towards an increased school year see my comments, *ibid.*, p. 103.

equally sophisticated about other non-working uses of time. For example, the cost of a service like the theatre or a good like meat is generally simply said to equal their market prices, yet everyone would agree that the theatre and even dining take time, just as schooling does, time that often could have been used productively. If so, the full costs of these activities would equal the sum of market prices and the forgone value of the time used up. In other words, indirect costs should be treated on the same footing when discussing all non-work uses of time, as they are now in discussions of schooling.

In the last few years a group of us at Columbia University have been occupied, perhaps initially independently but then increasingly less so, with introducing the cost of time systematically into decisions about non-work activities. J. Mincer has shown with several empirical examples how estimates of the income elasticity of demand for different commodities are biased when the cost of time is ignored;[1] J. Owen has analysed how the demand for leisure can be affected;[2] E. Dean has considered the allocation of time between subsistence work and market participation in some African economies;[3] while, as already mentioned, I have been concerned with the use of time in education, training and other kinds of human capital. Here I attempt to develop a general treatment of the allocation of time in all other non-work activities. Although under my name alone, much of any credit it merits belongs to the stimulus received from Mincer, Owen, Dean and other past and present participants in the Labor Workshop at Columbia.[4]

The plan of the discussion is as follows. The first section sets out a basic theoretical analysis of choice that includes the cost of time on the same footing as the cost of market goods, while the remaining sections treat various empirical implications of the theory. These include a new approach to changes in hours of work and " leisure," the full integration of so-called " productive " consumption into economic analysis, a new analysis of the effect of income on the quantity and " quality " of commodities consumed, some suggestions on the measurement of productivity, an economic analysis of queues and a few others as well. Although I refer to relevant empirical

---

[1] See his " Market Prices, Opportunity Costs, and Income Effects," in *Measurement in Economics: Studies in Mathematical Economics and Econometrics in Memory of Yehuda Grunfeld* (Stanford University Press, 1963). In his well-known earlier study Mincer considered the allocation of married women between " housework " and labour force participation. (See his " Labor Force Participation of Married Women," in *Aspects of Labor Economics* (Princeton University Press, 1962).)

[2] See his *The Supply of Labor and the Demand for Recreation* (unpublished Ph.D. dissertation, Columbia University, 1964).

[3] See his *Economic Analysis and African Response to Price* (unpublished Ph.D. dissertation, Columbia University, 1963).

[4] Let me emphasise, however, that I alone am responsible for any errors.

I would also like to express my appreciation for the comments received when presenting these ideas to seminars at the Universities of California (Los Angeles), Chicago, Pittsburgh, Rochester and Yale, and to a session at the 1963 Meetings of the Econometric Society. Extremely helpful comments on an earlier draft were provided by Milton Friedman and by Gregory C. Chow; the latter also assisted in the mathematical formulation. Linda Kee provided useful research assistance. My research was partially supported by the IBM Corporation.

work that has come to my attention, little systematic testing of the theory has been attempted.

II. A REVISED THEORY OF CHOICE

According to traditional theory, households maximise utility functions of the form

$$U = U(y_1, y_2, \ldots, y_n) \quad \cdots \quad (1)$$

subject to the resource constraint

$$\sum p_i' y_i = I = W + V \quad \cdots \quad (2)$$

where y_i are goods purchased on the market, p_i' are their prices, I is money income, W is earnings and V is other income. As the introduction suggests, the point of departure here is the systematic incorporation of non-working time. Households will be assumed to combine time and market goods to produce more basic commodities that directly enter their utility functions. One such commodity is the seeing of a play, which depends on the input of actors, script, theatre and the playgoer's time; another is sleeping, which depends on the input of a bed, house (pills?) and time. These commodities will be called Z_i and written as

$$Z_i = f_i(x_i, T_i) \quad \cdots \quad (3)$$

where x_i is a vector of market goods and T_i a vector of time inputs used in producing the ith commodity.[1] Note that, when capital goods such as refrigerators or automobiles are used, x refers to the services yielded by the goods. Also note that T_i is a vector because, *e.g.*, the hours used during the day or on weekdays may be distinguished from those used at night or on week-ends. Each dimension of T_i refers to a different aspect of time. Generally, the partial derivatives of Z_i with respect to both x_i and T_i are non-negative.[2]

In this formulation households are both producing units and utility maximisers. They combine time and market goods via the " production functions " f_i'to produce the basic commodities Z_i, and they choose the best combination of these commodities in the conventional way by maximising a utility function

$$U = U(Z_i, \ldots Z_m) \equiv U(f_1, \ldots f_m) \equiv U(x_1, \ldots x_m; T_1, \ldots T_m) \quad (4)$$

---

[1] There are several empirical as well as conceptual advantages in assuming that households combine goods and time to produce commodities instead of simply assuming that the amount of time used at an activity is a direct function of the amount of goods consumed. For example, a change in the cost of goods relative to time could cause a significant substitution away from the one rising in relative cost. This, as well as other applications, are treated in the following sections.

[2] If a good or time period was used in producing several commodities I assume that these "joint costs" could be fully and uniquely allocated among the commodities. The problems here are no different from those usually arising in the analysis of multi-product firms.

subject to a budget constraint

$$g(Z_t, \ldots Z_m) = Z \qquad \cdot \quad \cdot \quad \cdot \quad \cdot \quad (5)$$

where g is an expenditure function of Z_t and Z is the bound on resources. The integration of production and consumption is at odds with the tendency for economists to separate them sharply, production occurring in firms and consumption in households. It should be pointed out, however, that in recent years economists increasingly recognise that a household is truly a " small factory ":[1] it combines capital goods, raw materials and labour to clean, feed, procreate and otherwise produce useful commodities. Undoubtedly the fundamental reason for the traditional separation is that firms are usually given control over working time in exchange for market goods, while " discretionary " control over market goods and consumption time is retained by households as they create their own utility. If (presumably different) firms were also given control over market goods and consumption time in exchange for providing utility the separation would quickly fade away in analysis as well as in fact.

The basic goal of the analysis is to find measures of g and Z which facilitate the development of empirical implications. The most direct approach is to assume that the utility function in equation (4) is maximised subject to separate constraints on the expenditure of market goods and time, and to the production functions in equation (3). The goods constraint can be written as

$$\sum_1^m p_t x_t = I = V + T_w \bar{w} \qquad \cdot \quad \cdot \quad \cdot \quad \cdot \quad (6)$$

where p_t is a vector giving the unit prices of x_t, T_w is a vector giving the hours spent at work and $\bar{w}$ is a vector giving the earnings per unit of T_w. The time constraints can be written as

$$\sum_1^m T_t = T_c = T - T_w \qquad \cdot \quad \cdot \quad \cdot \quad \cdot \quad (7)$$

where T_c is a vector giving the total time spent at consumption and T is a vector giving the total time available. The production functions (3) can be written in the equivalent form

$$\left. \begin{array}{l} T_t \equiv t_t Z_t \\ x_t \equiv b_t Z_t \end{array} \right\} \qquad \cdot \quad \cdot \quad \cdot \quad \cdot \quad (8)$$

where t_t is a vector giving the input of time per unit of Z_t and b_t is a similar vector for market goods.

The problem would appear to be to maximise the utility function (4) subject to the multiple constraints (6) and (7) and to the production relations (8). There is, however, really only one basic constraint: (6) is not independent of (7) because time can be converted into goods by using less time

---

[1] See, *e.g.*, A. K. Cairncross, " Economic Schizophrenia," *Scottish Journal of Political Economy* (February 1958).

at consumption and more at work. Thus, substituting for T_w in (6) its equivalent in (7) gives the single constraint [1]

$$\sum p_i x_i + \sum T_i \bar{w} = V + T\bar{w} \quad \ldots \ldots \quad (9)$$

By using (8), (9) can be written as

$$\sum (p_i b_i + t_i \bar{w}) Z_i = V + T\bar{w} \quad \ldots \ldots \quad (10)$$

with
$$\left. \begin{array}{l} \pi_i \equiv p_i b_i + t_i \bar{w} \\ S' \equiv V + T\bar{w} \end{array} \right\} \quad \ldots \ldots \quad (11)$$

The full price of a unit of Z_i (π_i) is the sum of the prices of the goods and of the time used per unit of Z_i. That is, the full price of consumption is the sum of direct and indirect prices in the same way that the full cost of investing in human capital is the sum of direct and indirect costs.[2] These direct and indirect prices are symmetrical determinants of total price, and there is no analytical reason to stress one rather than the other.

The resource constraint on the right side of equation (10), S', is easy to interpret if $\bar{w}$ were a constant, independent of the Z_i. For then S' gives the money income achieved if all the time available were devoted to work. This achievable income is " spent " on the commodities Z_i either directly through expenditures on goods, $\sum p_i b_i Z_i$, or indirectly through the forgoing of income, $\sum t_i \bar{w} Z_i$, i.e., by using time at consumption rather than at work. As long as $\bar{w}$ were constant, and if there were constant returns in producing Z_i so that b_i and t_i were fixed for given p_i and $\bar{w}$ the equilibrium condition resulting from maximising (4) subject to (10) takes a very simple form:

$$U_i = \frac{\partial U}{\partial Z_i} = \lambda \pi_i \qquad i = 1, \ldots m \quad \ldots \quad (12)$$

where λ is the marginal utility of money income. If $\bar{w}$ were not constant the resource constraint in equation (10) would not have any particularly useful interpretation: $S' = V + T\bar{w}$ would overstate the money income achievable as long as marginal wage-rates were below average ones. Moreover, the equilibrium conditions would become more complicated than (12) because marginal would have to replace average prices.

The total resource constraint could be given the sensible interpretation of the maximum money income achievable only in the special and unlikely case when average earnings were constant. This suggests dropping the approach based on explicitly considering separate goods and time constraints and substituting one in which the total resource constraint necessarily equalled the maximum money income achievable, which will be simply called " full income." [3] This income could in general be obtained by devoting all the

---

[1] The dependency among constraints distinguishes this problem from many other multiple-constraint situations in economic analysis, such as those arising in the usual theory of rationing (see J. Tobin, " A Survey of the Theory of Rationing," *Econometrica* (October, 1952)). Rationing would reduce to a formally identical single-constraint situation if rations were saleable and fully convertible into money income.

[2] See my *Human Capital, op. cit.*

[3] This term emerged from a conversation with Milton Friedman.

time and other resources of a household to earning income, with no regard for consumption. Of course, all the time would not usually be spent " at " a job: sleep, food, even leisure are required for efficiency, and some time (and other resources) would have to be spent on these activities in order to maximise money income. The amount spent would, however, be determined solely by the effect on income and not by any effect on utility. Slaves, for example, might be permitted time " off " from work only in so far as that maximised their output, or free persons in poor environments might have to maximise money income simply to survive.[1]

Households in richer countries do, however, forfeit money income in order to obtain additional utility, *i.e.*, they exchange money income for a greater amount of psychic income. For example, they might increase their leisure time, take a pleasant job in preference to a better-paying unpleasant one, employ unproductive nephews or eat more than is warranted by considerations of productivity. In these and other situations the amount of money income forfeited measures the cost of obtaining additional utility.

Thus the full income approach provides a meaningful resource constraint and one firmly based on the fact that goods and time can be combined into a single overall constraint because time can be converted into goods through money income. It also incorporates a unified treatment of all substitutions of non-pecuniary for pecuniary income, regardless of their nature or whether they occur on the job or in the household. The advantages of this will become clear as the analysis proceeds.

If full income is denoted by S, and if the total earnings forgone or " lost " by the interest in utility is denoted by L, the identity relating L to S and I is simply

$$L(Z_1, \ldots, Z_m) \equiv S - I(Z_1, \ldots, Z_m) \quad . \quad . \quad . \quad (13)$$

I and L are functions of the Z_i because how much is earned or forgone depends on the consumption set chosen; for example, up to a point, the less leisure chosen the larger the money income and the smaller the amount forgone.[2] Using equations (6) and (8), equation (13) can be written as

$$\sum p_i b_i Z_i + L(Z_1, \ldots, Z_m) \equiv S \quad . \quad . \quad . \quad . \quad (14)$$

[1] Any utility received would only be an incidental by-product of the pursuit of money income. Perhaps this explains why utility analysis was not clearly formulated and accepted until economic development had raised incomes well above the subsistence level.

[2] Full income is achieved by maximising the earnings function

$$W = W(Z_1, \ldots Z_m) \quad . \quad . \quad . \quad . \quad . \quad . \quad . \quad (1')$$

subject to the expenditure constraint in equation (6), to the inequality

$$\sum_1^m T_1 \leq T \quad . \quad . \quad . \quad . \quad . \quad . \quad . \quad . \quad (2')$$

and to the restrictions in (8). I assume for simplicity that the amount of each dimension of time used in producing commodities is less than the total available, so that (2') can be ignored; it is not

This basic resource constraint states that full income is spent either directly on market goods or indirectly through the forgoing of money income. Unfortunately, there is no simple expression for the average price of Z_i as there is in equation (10). However, marginal, not average, prices are relevant for behaviour, and these would be identical for the constraint in (10) only when average earnings, $\bar{w}$, was constant. But, if so, the expression for the loss function simplifies to

$$L = \bar{w}T_c = \bar{w}\sum t_i Z_i \quad . \quad . \quad . \quad . \quad . \quad . \quad (15)$$

and (14) reduces to (10). Moreover, even in the general case the total marginal prices resulting from (14) can always be divided into direct and indirect components: the equilibrium conditions resulting from maximising the utility function subject to (14) [1] are

$$U_i = T(p_i b_i + L_i), \qquad i = 1, \ldots, m \quad . \quad . \quad . \quad (16)$$

where $p_i b_i$ is the direct and L_i the indirect component of the total marginal price $p_i b_i + L_i$.[2]

Behind the division into direct and indirect costs is the allocation of time and goods between work-orientated and consumption-orientated activities. This suggests an alternative division of costs; namely, into those resulting from the allocation of goods and those resulting from the allocation of time. Write $L_i = \partial L/\partial Z_i$ as

$$L_i = \frac{\partial L}{\partial T_i}\frac{\partial T_i}{\partial Z_i} + \frac{\partial L}{\partial x_i}\frac{\partial x_i}{\partial Z_i} \quad . \quad . \quad . \quad . \quad (17)$$

$$= l_i t_i + c_i b_i \quad . \quad . \quad . \quad . \quad . \quad . \quad (18)$$

where $l_i = \dfrac{\partial L}{\partial T_i}$ and $c_i = \dfrac{\partial L}{\partial x_i}$ are the marginal forgone earnings of using more time and goods respectively on Z_i. Equation (16) can then be written as

$$U_i = T[b_i(p_i + c_i) + t_i l_i] \quad . \quad . \quad . \quad (19)$$

The total marginal cost of Z_i is the sum of $b_i(p_i + c_i)$, the marginal cost of using goods in producing Z_i, and $t_i l_i$, the marginal cost of using time. This division would be equivalent to that between direct and indirect costs only if $c_i = 0$ or if there were no indirect costs of using goods.

---

difficult to incorporate this constraint. Maximising (1') subject to (6) and (8) yields the following conditions

$$\frac{\partial W}{\partial Z_i} = \frac{p_i b_i \sigma}{1 + \sigma} \quad . \quad . \quad . \quad . \quad . \quad . \quad . \quad (3')$$

where σ is the marginal productivity of money income. Since the loss function $L = (S - V) - W$, the equilibrium conditions to minimise the loss is the same as (3') except for a change in sign.

[1] Households maximise their utility subject only to the single total resource constraint given by (14), for once the full income constraint is satisfied, there is no other restriction on the set of Z_i that can be chosen. By introducing the concept of full income the problem of maximising utility subject to the time and goods constraints is solved in two stages: first, full income is determined from the goods and time constraints, and then utility is maximised subject only to the constraint imposed by full income.

[2] It can easily be shown that the equilibrium conditions of (16) are in fact precisely the same as those following in general from equation (10).

The accompanying figure shows the equilibrium given by equation (16) for a two-commodity world. In equilibrium the slope of the full income

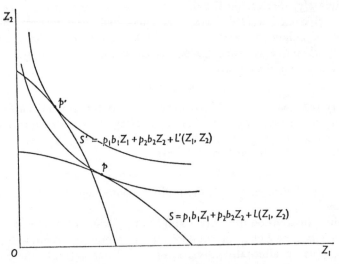

opportunity curve, which equals the ratio of marginal prices, would equal the slope of an indifference curve, which equals the ratio of marginal utilities. Equilibrium occurs at p and p' for the opportunity curves S and S' respectively.

The rest of the paper is concerned with developing numerous empirical implications of this theory, starting with determinants of hours worked and concluding with an economic interpretation of various queueing systems. To simplify the presentation, it is assumed that the distinction between direct and indirect costs is equivalent to that between goods and time costs; in other words, the marginal forgone cost of the use of goods, c_i, is set equal to zero. The discussion would not be much changed, but would be more cumbersome were this not assumed.[1] Finally, until Section IV goods and time are assumed to be used in fixed proportions in producing commodities; that is, the coefficients b_i and t_i in equation (8) are treated as constants.

III. APPLICATIONS

(a) *Hours of Work*

If the effects of various changes on the time used on consumption, T_c, could be determined their effects on hours worked, T_w, could be found residually from equation (7). This section considers, among other things, the effects of changes in income, earnings and market prices on T_c, and thus on T_w,

---

[1] Elsewhere I have discussed some effects of the allocation of goods on productivity (see my "Investment in Human Capital: A Theoretical Analysis," *Journal of Political Economy*, special supplement (October 1962), Section 2); essentially the same discussion can be found in *Human Capital, op. cit.*, Chapter II.

using as the major tool of analysis differences among commodities in the importance of forgone earnings.

The relative marginal importance of forgone earnings is defined as

$$\alpha_i = \frac{l_i t_i}{p_i b_i + l_i t_i} \qquad \cdots \cdots \cdots \quad (20)$$

The importance of forgone earnings would be greater the larger l_i and t_i, the forgone earnings per hour of time and the number of hours used per unit of Z_i respectively, while it would be smaller the larger p_i and b_i, the market price of goods and the number of goods used per unit of Z_i respectively. Similarly, the relative marginal importance of time is defined as

$$\gamma_i = \frac{t_i}{p_i b_i + l_i t_i} \qquad \cdots \cdots \cdots \quad (21)$$

If full income increased solely because of an increase in V (other money income) there would simply be a parallel shift of the opportunity curve to the right with no change in relative commodity prices. The consumption of most commodities would have to increase; if all did, hours worked would decrease, for the total time spent on consumption must increase if the output of all commodities did, and by equation (7) the time spent at work is inversely related to that spent on consumption. Hours worked could increase only if relatively time intensive commodities, those with large γ, were sufficiently inferior.[1]

A uniform percentage increase in earnings for all allocations of time would increase the cost per hour used in consumption by the same percentage for all commodities.[2] The relative prices of different commodities would, however, change as long as forgone earnings were not equally important for all; in particular, the prices of commodities having relatively important forgone earnings would rise more. Now the fundamental theorem of

---

[1] The problem is: under what conditions would

$$\frac{-\partial T_w}{\partial V} = \frac{\partial T_c}{\partial V} = \Sigma t_i \frac{\partial Z_i}{\partial V} < 0 \qquad \cdots \cdots \cdots \quad (1')$$

when

$$\Sigma(p_i b_i + l_i t_i) \frac{\partial Z_i}{\partial V} = 1 \qquad \cdots \cdots \cdots \quad (2')$$

If the analysis were limited to a two-commodity world where Z_1 was more time intensive, then it can easily be shown that (1') would hold if, and only if,

$$\frac{\partial Z_1}{\partial V} < \frac{-\gamma_2}{(\gamma_1 - \gamma_2)(p_1 b_1 + l_1 t_1)} < 0 \qquad \cdots \cdots \cdots \quad (3')$$

[2] By a uniform change of β is meant

$$W_1 = (1 + \beta) W_0(Z_1, \ldots Z_n)$$

where W_0 represents the earnings function before the change and W_1 represents it afterwards. Since the loss function is defined as

$$L = S - W - V$$
$$= W(\hat{Z}) - W(Z),$$

then

$$L_1 = W_1(\hat{Z}) - W_1(Z)$$
$$= (1 + \beta)[W_0(\hat{Z}) - W_0(Z)] = (1 + \beta) L_0$$

Consequently, all opportunities costs also change by β.

demand theory states that a compensated change in relative prices would induce households to consume less of commodities rising in price. The figure shows the effect of a rise in earnings fully compensated by a decline in other income: the opportunity curve would be rotated clockwise through the initial position p if Z_1 were the more earnings-intensive commodity. In the figure the new equilibrium p' must be to the left and above p, or less Z_1 and more Z_2 would be consumed.

Therefore a compensated uniform rise in earnings would lead to a shift away from earnings-intensive commodities and towards goods-intensive ones. Since earnings and time intensiveness tend to be positively correlated,[1] consumption would be shifted from time-intensive commodities. A shift away from such commodities would, however, result in a reduction in the total time spent in consumption, and thus an increase in the time spent at work.[2]

The effect of an uncompensated increase in earnings on hours worked would depend on the relative strength of the substitution and income effects. The former would increase hours, the latter reduce them; which dominates cannot be determined *a priori*.

The conclusion that a pure rise in earnings increases and a pure rise in income reduces hours of work must sound very familiar, for they are traditional results of the well-known labour–leisure analysis. What, then, is the relation between our analysis, which treats all commodities symmetrically and stresses only their differences in relative time and earning intensities, and the usual analysis, which distinguishes a commodity having special properties called " leisure " from other more commonplace commodities? It is easily shown that the usual labour–leisure analysis can be looked upon as a special case of ours in which the cost of the commodity called leisure consists entirely of forgone earnings and the cost of other commodities entirely of goods.[3]

---

[1] According to the definitions of earning and time intensity in equations (20) and (21), they would be positively correlated unless l_i and t_i were sufficiently negatively correlated. See the further discussion later on.

[2] Let it be stressed that this conclusion usually holds, even when households are irrational; sophisticated calculations about the value of time at work or in consumption, or substantial knowledge about the amount of time used by different commodities is not required. Changes in the hours of work, even of non-maximising, impulsive, habitual, etc., households would tend to be positively related to compensated changes in earnings because demand curves tend to be negatively inclined even for such households (see G. S. Becker, " Irrational Behavior and Economic Theory," *Journal of Political Economy* (February 1962)).

[3] Suppose there were two commodities Z_1 and Z_2, where the cost of Z_1 depended only on the cost of market goods, while the cost of Z_2 depended only on the cost of time. The goods-budget constraint would then simply be

$$p_1 b_1 Z_1 = I = V + T_w \bar{w}$$

and the constraint on time would be

$$t_2 Z_2 = T - T_w$$

This is essentially the algebra of the analysis presented by Henderson and Quandt, and their treatment is representative. They call Z_2 " leisure," and Z_1 an average of different commodities. Their

As a description of reality such an approach, of course, is not tenable, since virtually all activities use both time and goods. Perhaps it would be defended either as an analytically necessary or extremely insightful approximation to reality. Yet the usual substitution and income effects of a change in resources on hours worked have easily been derived from a more general analysis which stresses only that the relative importance of time varies among commodities. The rest of the paper tries to go further and demonstrate that the traditional approach, with its stress on the demand for " leisure," apparently has seriously impeded the development of insights about the economy, since the more direct and general approach presented here naturally leads to a variety of implications never yet obtained.

The two determinants of the importance of forgone earnings are the amount of time used per dollar of goods and the cost per unit of time. Reading a book, taking a haircut or commuting use more time per dollar of goods than eating dinner, frequenting a night-club or sending children to private summer camps. Other things the same, forgone earnings would be more important for the former set of commodities than the latter.

The importance of forgone earnings would be determined solely by time intensity only if the cost of time was the same for all commodities. Presumably, however, it varies considerably among commodities and at different periods. For example, the cost of time is often less on week-ends and in the evenings because many firms are closed then,[1] which explains why a famous liner intentionally includes a week-end in each voyage between the United States and Europe.[2] The cost of time would also tend to be less for commodities that contribute to productive effort, traditionally called " productive consumption." A considerable amount of sleep, food and even " play " fall under this heading. The opportunity cost of the time is less because these commodities indirectly contribute to earnings. Productive consumption has had a long but bandit-like existence in economic thought; our analysis does systematically incorporate it into household decision-making.

Although the formal specification of leisure in economic models has ignored expenditures on goods, cannot one argue that a more correct specification would simply associate leisure with relatively important forgone earnings? Most conceptions of leisure do imply that it is time intensive and does not indirectly contribute to earnings,[3] two of the important

equilibrium condition that the rate of substitution between goods and leisure equals the real wage-rate is just a special case of our equation (19) (see *Microeconomic Theory* (McGraw-Hill, 1958), p. 23).

[1] For workers receiving premium pay on the week-ends and in the evenings, however, the cost of time may be considerably greater then.

[2] See the advertisement by United States Lines in various issues of the *New Yorker* magazine: " The S.S. *United States* regularly includes a week-end in its 5 days to Europe, saving [economic] time for businessmen " (my insertion).

[3] For example, *Webster's Collegiate Dictionary* defines leisurely as " characterized by leisure, taking abundant time " (my italics); or S. de Grazia, in his recent *Of Time, Work and Leisure*, says, " Leisure is a state of being in which activity is performed for its own sake or as its own end " (New York: The Twentieth Century Fund, 1962, p. 15).

characteristics of earnings-intensive commodities. On the other hand, not all of what are usually considered leisure activities do have relatively important forgone earnings: night-clubbing is generally considered leisure, and yet, at least in its more expensive forms, has a large expenditure component. Conversely, some activities have relatively large forgone earnings and are not considered leisure: haircuts or child care are examples. Consequently, the distinction between earnings-intensive and other commodities corresponds only partly to the usual distinction between leisure and other commodities. Since it has been shown that the relative importance of forgone earnings rather than any concept of leisure is more relevant for economic analysis, less attention should be paid to the latter. Indeed, although the social philosopher might have to define precisely the concept of leisure,[1] the economist can reach all his traditional results as well as many more without introducing it at all!

Not only is it difficult to distinguish leisure from other non-work [2] but also even work from non-work. Is commuting work, non-work or both? How about a business lunch, a good diet or relaxation? Indeed, the notion of productive consumption was introduced precisely to cover those commodities that contribute to work as well as to consumption. Cannot pure work then be considered simply as a limiting commodity of such joint commodities in which the contribution to consumption was nil? Similarly, pure consumption would be a limiting commodity in the opposite direction in which the contribution to work was nil, and intermediate commodities would contribute to both consumption and work. The more important the contribution to work relative to consumption, the smaller would tend to be the relative importance of forgone earnings. Consequently, the effects of changes in earnings, other income, etc., on hours worked then become assimiliated to and essentially a special case of their effects on the consumption of less earnings-intensive commodities. For example, a pure rise in earnings would reduce the relative price, and thus increase the time spent on these commodities, *including the time spent at work*; similarly, for changes in income and other variables. The generalisation wrought by our approach is even greater than may have appeared at first.

Before concluding this section a few other relevant implications of our

[1] S. de Grazia has recently entertainingly shown the many difficulties in even reaching a reliable definition, and *a fortiori*, in quantitatively estimating the amount of leisure. See *ibid.*, Chapters III and IV; also see W. Moore, *Man, Time and Society* (New York: Wiley, 1963), Chapter II; J. N. Morgan, M. H. David, W. J. Cohen and H. E. Brazer, *Income and Welfare in the United States* (New York: McGraw-Hill, 1962), p. 322, and Owen, *op. cit.*, Chapter II.

[2] Sometimes true leisure is defined as the amount of discretionary time available (see Moore, *op. cit.*, p. 18). It is always difficult to attach a rigorous meaning to the word " discretionary " when referring to economic resources. One might say that in the short run consumption time is and working time is not discretionary, because the latter is partially subject to the authoritarian control of employers. (Even this distinction would vanish if households gave certain firms authoritarian control over their consumption time; see the discussion in Section II.) In the long run this definition of discretionary time is suspect too because the availability of alternative sources of employment would make working time also discretionary.

theory might be briefly mentioned. Just as a (compensated) rise in earnings would increase the prices of commodities with relatively large forgone earnings, induce a substitution away from them and increase the hours worked, so a (compensated) fall in market prices would also induce a substitution away from them and increase the hours worked: the effects of changes in direct and indirect costs are symmetrical. Indeed, Owen presents some evidence indicating that hours of work in the United States fell somewhat more in the first thirty years of this century than in the second thirty years, not because wages rose more during the first period, but because the market prices of recreation commodities fell more then.[1]

A well-known result of the traditional labour–leisure approach is that a rise in the income tax induces at least a substitution effect away from work and towards " leisure." Our approach reaches the same result only via a substitution towards time-intensive consumption rather than leisure. A simple additional implication of our approach, however, is that if a rise in the income tax were combined with an appropriate excise on the goods used in time-intensive commodities or subsidy to the goods used in other commodities there need be no change in full relative prices, and thus no substitution away from work. The traditional approach has recently reached the same conclusion, although in a much more involved way.[2]

There is no exception in the traditional approach to the rule that a pure rise in earnings would not induce a decrease in hours worked. An exception does occur in ours, for if the time and earnings intensities (*i.e.*, $l_i t_i$ and t_i) were negatively correlated a pure rise in earnings would induce a substitution towards time-intensive commodities, and thus away from work.[3] Although this exception does illustrate the greater power of our approach, there is no reason to believe that it is any more important empirically than the exception to the rule on income effects.

(b) *The Productivity of Time*

Most of the large secular increase in earnings, which stimulated the development of the labour–leisure analysis, resulted from an increase in the productivity of working time due to the growth in human and physical capital, technological progress and other factors. Since a rise in earnings resulting from an increase in productivity has both income and substitution

[1] See *op. cit.*, Chapter VIII. Recreation commodities presumably have relatively large forgone earnings.

[2] See W. J. Corbett and D. C. Hague, " Complementarity and the Excess Burden of Taxation," *Review of Economic Studies*, Vol. XXI (1953–54); also A. C. Harberger, " Taxation, Resource Allocation and Welfare," in the *Role of Direct and Indirect Taxes in the Federal Revenue System* (Princeton University Press, 1964).

[3] The effect on earnings is more difficult to determine because, by assumption, time intensive commodities have smaller costs per unit time than other commodities. A shift towards the former would, therefore, raise hourly earnings, which would partially and perhaps more than entirely offset the reduction in hours worked. Incidentally, this illustrates how the productivity of hours worked is influenced by the consumption set chosen.

effects, the secular decline in hours worked appeared to be evidence that the income effect was sufficiently strong to swamp the substitution effect.

The secular growth in capital and technology also improved the productivity of consumption time: supermarkets, automobiles, sleeping pills, safety and electric razors, and telephones are a few familiar and important examples of such developments. An improvement in the productivity of consumption time would change relative commodity prices and increase full income, which in turn would produce substitution and income effects. The interesting point is that a very different interpretation of the observed decline in hours of work is suggested because these effects are precisely the opposite of those produced by improvements in the productivity of working time.

Assume a uniform increase only in the productivity of consumption time, which is taken to mean a decline in all t_i, time required to produce a unit of Z_i, by a common percentage. The relative prices of commodities with large forgone earnings would fall, and substitution would be induced towards these and away from other commodities, causing hours of work also to fall. Since the increase in productivity would also produce an income effect,[1] the demand for commodities would increase, which, in turn, would induce an increased demand for goods. But since the productivity of working time is assumed not to change, more goods could be obtained only by an increase in work. That is, the higher real income resulting from an advance in the productivity of consumption time would cause hours of work to *increase*.

Consequently, an emphasis on the secular increase in the productivity of consumption time would lead to a very different interpretation of the secular decline in hours worked. Instead of claiming that a powerful income effect swamped a weaker substitution effect, the claim would have to be that a powerful substitution effect swamped a weaker income effect.

Of course, the productivity of both working and consumption time increased secularly, and the true interpretation is somewhere between these extremes. If both increased at the same rate there would be no change in relative prices, and thus no substitution effect, because the rise in l_i induced by one would exactly offset the decline in t_i induced by the other, marginal forgone earnings ($i_i t_i$) remaining unchanged. Although the income effects would tend to offset each other too, they would do so completely only if the income elasticity of demand for time-intensive commodities was equal to unity. Hours worked would decline if it was above and increase if it was below unity.[2] Since these commodities have probably on

---

[1] Full money income would be unaffected if it were achieved by using all time at pure work activities. If other uses of time were also required it would tend to increase. Even if full money income were unaffected, however, full real income would increase because prices of the Z_i would fall.

[2] So the " Knight " view that an increase in income would increase " leisure " is not necessarily true, even if leisure were a superior good and even aside from Robbins' emphasis on the substitution effect (see L. Robbins, " On the Elasticity of Demand for Income in Terms of Effort," *Economica* (June 1930)).

the whole been luxuries, such an increase in income would tend to reduce hours worked.

The productivity of working time has probably advanced more than that of consumption time, if only because of familiar reasons associated with the division of labour and economies of scale.[1] Consequently, there probably has been the traditional substitution effect towards and income effect away from work, as well as an income effect away from work because time-intensive commodities were luxuries. The secular decline in hours worked would only imply therefore that the combined income effects swamped the substitution effect, not that the income effect of an advance in the productivity of working time alone swamped its substitution effect.

Cross-sectionally, the hours worked of males have generally declined less as incomes increased than they have over time. Some of the difference between these relations is explained by the distinction between relevant and reported incomes, or by interdependencies among the hours worked by different employees;[2] some is probably also explained by the distinction between working and consumption productivity. There is a presumption that persons distinguished cross-sectionally by money incomes or earnings differ more in working than consumption productivity because they are essentially distinguished by the former. This argument does not apply to time series because persons are distinguished there by calendar time, which in principle is neutral between these productivities. Consequently, the traditional substitution effect towards work is apt to be greater cross-sectionally, which would help to explain why the relation between the income and hours worked of men is less negatively sloped there, and be additional evidence that the substitution effect for men is not weak.[3]

Productivity in the service sector in the United States appears to have advanced more slowly, at least since 1929, than productivity in the goods sector.[4] Service industries like retailing, transportation, education and health, use a good deal of the time of households that never enter into input, output and price series, or therefore into measures of productivity. Incorporation of such time into the series and consideration of changes in its productivity would contribute, I believe, to an understanding of the apparent differences in productivity advance between these sectors.

An excellent example can be found in a recent study of productivity

[1] Wesley Mitchell's justly famous essay " The Backward Art of Spending Money " spells out some of these reasons (see the first essay in the collection, *The Backward Art of Spending Money and Other Essays* (New York: McGraw-Hill, 1932)).

[2] A. Finnegan does find steeper cross-sectional relations when the average incomes and hours of different occupations are used (*see* his " A Cross-Sectional Analysis of Hours of Work," *Journal of Political Economy* (October, 1962)).

[3] Note that Mincer has found a very strong substitution effect for women (see his " Labor Force Participation of Married Women," *op. cit.*).

[4] See the essay by Victor Fuchs, " Productivity Trends in the Goods and Service Sectors, 1929–61: A Preliminary Survey," N.B.E.R. Occasional Paper, October 1964.

trends in the barbering industry in the United States.[1] Conventional productivity measures show relatively little advance in barbers' shops since 1929, yet a revolution has occurred in the activities performed by these shops. In the 1920s shaves still accounted for an important part of their sales, but declined to a negligible part by the 1950s because of the spread of home safety and electric razors. Instead of travelling to a shop, waiting in line, receiving a shave and continuing to another destination, men now shave themselves at home, saving travelling, waiting and even some shaving time. This considerable advance in the productivity of shaving nowhere enters measures for barbers' shops. If, however, a productivity measure for general barbering activities, including shaving, was constructed, I suspect that it would show an advance since 1929 comparable to most goods.[2]

(c) *Income Elasticities*

Income elasticities of demand are often estimated cross-sectionally from the behaviour of families or other units with different incomes. When these units buy in the same market-place it is natural to assume that they face the same prices of goods. If, however, incomes differ because earnings do, and cross-sectional income differences are usually dominated by earnings differences, commodities prices would differ systematically. All commodities prices would be higher to higher-income units because their forgone earnings would be higher (which means, incidentally, that differences in real income would be less than those in money income), and the prices of earnings-intensive commodities would be unusually so.

Cross-sectional relations between consumption and income would not therefore measure the effect of income alone, because they would be affected by differences in relative prices as well as in incomes.[3] The effect of income would be underestimated for earnings-intensive and overestimated for other commodities, because the higher relative prices of the former would cause a substitution away from them and towards the latter. Accordingly, the income elasticities of demand for " leisure," unproductive and time-intensive commodities would be under-stated, and for " work," productive and other goods-intensive commodities over-stated by cross-sectional estimates. Low apparent income elasticities of earnings-intensive commodities and high apparent elasticities of other commodities may simply be illusions resulting from substitution effects.[4]

---

[1] See J. Wilburn, " Productivity Trends in Barber and Beauty Shops," mimeographed report, N.B.E.R., September 1964.

[2] The movement of shaving from barbers' shops to households illustrates how and why even in urban areas households have become " small factories." Under the impetus of a general growth in the value of time they have been encouraged to find ways of saving on travelling and waiting time by performing more activities themselves.

[3] More appropriate income elasticities for several commodities are estimated in Mincer, " Market Prices . . .," *op. cit.*

[4] In this connection note that cross-sectional data are often preferred to time-series data in estimating income elasticities precisely because they are supposed to be largely free of co-linearity

Moreover, according to our theory demand depends also on the importance of earnings as a source of income. For if total income were held constant an increase in earnings would create only substitution effects: away from earnings-intensive and towards goods-intensive commodities. So one unusual implication of the analysis that can and should be tested with available budget data is that the source of income may have a significant effect on consumption patterns. An important special case is found in comparisons of the consumption of employed and unemployed workers. Unemployed workers not only have lower incomes but also lower forgone costs, and thus lower relative prices of time and other earnings-intensive commodities. The propensity of unemployed workers to go fishing, watch television, attend school and so on are simply vivid illustrations of the incentives they have to substitute such commodities for others.

One interesting application of the analysis is to the relation between family size and income.[1] The traditional view, based usually on simple correlations, has been that an increase in income leads to a reduction in the number of children per family. If, however, birth-control knowledge and other variables were held constant economic theory suggests a positive relation between family size and income, and therefore that the traditional negative correlation resulted from positive correlations between income, knowledge and some other variables. The data I put together supported this interpretation, as did those found in several subsequent studies.[2]

Although positive, the elasticity of family size with respect to income is apparently quite low, even when birth-control knowledge is held constant. Some persons have interpreted this (and other evidence) to indicate that family-size formation cannot usefully be fitted into traditional economic analysis.[3] It was pointed out, however, that the small elasticity found for children is not so inconsistent with what is found for goods as soon as quantity and quality income elasticities are distinguished.[4] Increased expenditures on many goods largely take the form of increased quality–expenditure per pound, per car, etc.—and the increase in quantity is modest. Similarly, increased expenditures on children largely take the form of increased expenditures per child, while the increase in number of children is very modest.

---

between prices and incomes (see, *e.g.*, J. Tobin, " A Statistical Demand Function for Food in the U.S.A.," *Journal of the Royal Statistical Society*, Series A (1950)).

[1] Biases in cross-sectional estimates of the demand for work and leisure were considered in the last section.

[2] See G. S. Becker, "An Economic Analysis of Fertility," *Demographic and Economic Change in Developed Countries* (N.B.E.R. Conference Volume, 1960); R. A. Easterlin, " The American Baby Boom in Historical Perspective," *American Economic Review* (December 1961); I. Adelman, " An Econometric Analysis of Population Growth," *American Economic Review* (June 1963); R. Weintraub, "The Birth Rate and Economic Development: An Empirical Study," *Econometrica* (October 1962); Morris Silver, *Birth Rates, Marriages, and Business Cycles* (unpublished Ph.D. dissertation, Columbia University, 1964); and several other studies; for an apparent exception, see the note by D. Freedman, "The Relation of Economic Status to Fertility," *American Economic Review* (June 1963).

[3] See, for example, Duesenberry's comment on Becker, *op. cit.*   [4] See Becker, *op. cit.*

Nevertheless, the elasticity of demand for number of children does seem somewhat smaller than the quantity elasticities found for many goods. Perhaps the explanation is simply the shape of indifference curves; one other factor that may be more important, however, is the increase in forgone costs with income.[1] Child care would seem to be a time-intensive activity that is not " productive " (in terms of earnings) and uses many hours that could be used at work. Consequently, it would be an earnings-intensive activity, and our analysis predicts that its relative price would be higher to higher-income families.[2] There is already some evidence suggesting that the positive relation between forgone costs and income explains why the apparent quantity income elasticity of demand for children is relatively small. Mincer found that cross-sectional differences in the forgone price of children have an important effect on the number of children.[3]

(d) *Transportation*

Transportation is one of the few activities where the cost of time has been explicitly incorporated into economic discussions. In most benefit-cost evaluations of new transportation networks the value of the savings in transportation time has tended to overshadow other benefits.[4] The importance of the value placed on time has encouraged experiment with different methods of determination: from the simple view that the value of an hour equals average hourly earnings to sophisticated considerations of the distinction between standard and overtime hours, the internal and external margins, etc.

The transport field offers considerable opportunity to estimate the marginal productivity or value of time from actual behaviour. One could, for example, relate the ratio of the number of persons travelling by aeroplane to those travelling by slower mediums to the distance travelled (and, of course, also to market prices and incomes). Since relatively more people use faster mediums for longer distances, presumably largely because of the greater importance of the saving in time, one should be able to estimate a marginal value of time from the relation between medium and distance travelled.[5]

[1] In *Ibid.*, p. 214 fn. 8, the relation between forgone costs and income was mentioned but not elaborated.

[2] Other arguments suggesting that higher-income families face a higher price of children have generally confused price with quality (see *ibid.*, pp. 214–15).

[3] See Mincer, " Market Prices . . .," *op. cit.* He measures the price of children by the wife's potential wage-rate, and fits regressions to various cross-sectional data, where number of children is the dependent variable, and family income and the wife's potential wage-rate are among the independent variables.

[4] See, for example, H. Mohring, " Land Values and the Measurement of Highway Benefits," *Journal of Political Economy* (June 1961).

[5] The only quantitative estimate of the marginal value of time that I am familiar with uses the relation between the value of land and its commuting distance from employment (see *ibid.*). With many assumptions I have estimated the marginal value of time of those commuting at about 40% of their average hourly earnings. It is not clear whether this value is so low because of errors in these assumptions or because of severe kinks in the supply and demand functions for hours of work.

Another transportation problem extensively studied is the length and mode of commuting to work.[1] It is usually assumed that direct commuting costs, such as train fare, vary positively and that living costs, such as space, vary negatively with the distance commuted. These assumptions alone would imply that a rise in incomes would result in longer commutes as long as space ("housing") were a superior good.[2]

A rise in income resulting at least in part from a rise in earnings would, however, increase the cost of commuting a given distance because the forgone value of the time involved would increase. This increase in commuting costs would discourage commuting in the same way that the increased demand for space would encourage it. The outcome depends on the relative strengths of these conflicting forces: one can show with a few assumptions that the distance commuted would increase as income increased if, and only if, space had an income elasticity greater than unity.

For let Z_1 refer to the commuting commodity, Z_2 to other commodities, and let

$$Z_1 = f_1(x, t) \quad \cdots \cdots \quad (22)$$

where t is the time spent commuting and x is the quantity of space used. Commuting costs are assumed to have the simple form $a + l_1 t$, where a is a constant and l_1 is the marginal forgone cost per hour spent commuting. In other words, the cost of time is the only variable commuting cost. The cost per unit of space is $p(t)$, where by assumption $p' < 0$. The problem is to maximise the utility function

$$U = U(x, t, Z_2) \quad \cdots \cdots \quad (23)$$

subject to the resource constraint

$$a + l_1 t + px + h(Z_2) = S \quad \cdots \cdots \quad (24)$$

If it were assumed that $U_t = 0$—commuting was neither enjoyable nor irksome—the main equilibrium condition would reduce to

$$l_1 + p'x = 0 \, [3] \quad \cdots \cdots \quad (25)$$

which would be the equilibrium condition if households simply attempt to minimise the sum of transportation and space costs.[4] If $l_1 = kS$, where k

---

[1] See L. N. Moses and H. F. Williamson, "Value of Time, Choice of Mode, and the Subsidy Issue in Urban Transportation," *Journal of Political Economy* (June 1963), R. Muth, "Economic Change and Rural–Urban Conversion," *Econometrica* (January 1961), and J. F. Kain, *Commuting and the Residential Decisions of Chicago and Detroit Central Business District Workers* (April 1963).

[2] See Muth, *op. cit.*

[3] If $U_t \neq 0$, the main equilibrium condition would be

$$\frac{U_t}{U_x} = \frac{l_1 + p'x}{p}$$

Probably the most plausible assumption is that $U_t < 0$, which would imply that $l_1 + p'x < 0$.

[4] See Kain, *op. cit.*, pp. 6–12.

is a constant, the effect of a change in full income on the time spent commuting can be found by differentiating equation (25) to be

$$\frac{\partial t}{\partial S} = \frac{k(\epsilon_x - 1)}{p''x} \qquad \qquad (26)$$

where ϵ_x is the income elasticity of demand for space. Since stability requires that $p'' > 0$, an increase in income increases the time spent commuting if, and only if, $\epsilon_x > 1$.

In metropolitan areas of the United States higher-income families tend to live further from the central city,[1] which contradicts our analysis if one accepts the traditional view that the income elasticity of demand for housing is less than unity. In a definitive study of the demand for housing in the United States, however, Margaret Reid found income elasticities greater than unity.[2] Moreover, the analysis of distance commuted incorporates only a few dimensions of the demand for housing; principally the demand for outdoor space. The evidence on distances commuted would then only imply that outdoor space is a " luxury," which is rather plausible [3] and not even inconsistent with the traditional view about the total elasticity of demand for housing.

(e) *The Division of Labour Within Families*

Space is too limited to do more than summarise the main implications of the theory concerning the division of labour among members of the same household. Instead of simply allocating time efficiently among commodities, multi-person households also allocate the time of different members. Members who are relatively more efficient at market activities would use less of their time at consumption activities than would other members. Moreover, an increase in the relative market efficiency of any member would effect a reallocation of the time of all other members towards consumption activities in order to permit the former to spend more time at market activities. In short, the allocation of the time of any member is greatly influenced by the opportunities open to other members.

IV. Substitution Between Time and Goods

Although time and goods have been assumed to be used in fixed proportions in producing commodities, substitution could take place because different commodities used them in different proportions. The assumption of fixed proportions is now dropped in order to include many additional implications of the theory.

It is well known from the theory of variable proportions that households

[1] For a discussion, including many qualifications, of this proposition see L. F. Schnore, " The Socio-Economic Status of Cities and Suburbs," *American Sociological Review* (February 1963).

[2] See her *Housing and Income* (University of Chicago Press, 1962), p. 6 and *passim*.

[3] According to Reid, the elasticity of demand for indoor space is less than unity (*ibid.*, Chapter 12). If her total elasticity is accepted this suggests that outdoor space has an elasticity exceeding unity.

would minimise costs by setting the ratio of the marginal product of goods to that of time equal to the ratio of their marginal costs.[1] A rise in the cost of time relative to goods would induce a reduction in the amount of time and an increase in the amount of goods used per unit of each commodity. Thus, not only would a rise in earnings induce a substitution away from earnings-intensive commodities but also a substitution away from time and towards goods in the production of each commodity. Only the first is (implicitly) recognised in the labour–leisure analysis, although the second may well be of considerable importance. It increases one's confidence that the substitution effect of a rise in earnings is more important than is commonly believed.

The change in the input coefficients of time and goods resulting from a change in their relative costs is defined by the elasticity of substitution between them, which presumably varies from commodity to commodity. The only empirical study of this elasticity assumes that recreation goods and " leisure " time are used to produce a recreation commodity.[2] Definite evidence of substitution is found, since the ratio of leisure time to recreation goods is negatively related to the ratio of their prices. The elasticity of substitution appears to be less than unity, however, since the share of leisure in total factor costs is apparently positively related to its relative price.

The incentive to economise on time as its relative cost increases goes a long way towards explaining certain broad aspects of behaviour that have puzzled and often disturbed observers of contemporary life. Since hours worked have declined secularly in most advanced countries, and so-called " leisure " has presumably increased, a natural expectation has been that " free " time would become more abundant, and be used more " leisurely " and " luxuriously." Yet, if anything, time is used more carefully to-day than a century ago.[3] If there was a secular increase in the productivity of working time relative to consumption time (see Section III (b)) there would be an increasing incentive to economise on the latter because of its greater expense (our theory emphatically cautions against calling such time " free "). Not surprisingly, therefore, it is now kept track of and used more carefully than in the past.

Americans are supposed to be much more wasteful of food and other

---

[1] The cost of producing a given amount of commodity Z_i would be minimised if

$$\frac{\partial f_i / \partial x_i}{\partial f_i / \partial T_i} = \frac{P_i}{\partial L / \partial T_i}$$

If utility were considered an indirect function of goods and time rather than simply a direct function of commodities the following conditions, among others, would be required to maximise utility:

$$\frac{\partial U / \partial x_i}{\partial U / \partial T_i} \equiv \frac{\partial Z_i / \partial x_i}{\partial Z_i / \partial T_i} = \frac{p_i}{\partial L / \partial T}$$

which are exactly the same conditions as above. The ratio of the marginal utility of x_i to that of T_i depends only on f_i, x_i and T_i, and is thus independent of other production functions, goods and time. In other words, the indirect utility function is what has been called " weakly separable " (see R. Muth, " Household Production and Consumer Demand Functions," unpublished manuscript).

[2] See Owen, *op. cit.*, Chapter X.   [3] See, for example, de Grazia, *op. cit.*, Chapter IV.

goods than persons in poorer countries, and much more conscious of time: they keep track of it continuously, make (and keep) appointments for specific minutes, rush about more, cook steaks and chops rather than time-consuming stews and so forth.[1] They are simultaneously supposed to be wasteful—of material goods—and overly economical—of immaterial time. Yet both allegations may be correct and not simply indicative of a strange American temperament because the market value of time is higher relative to the price of goods there than elsewhere. That is, the tendency to be economical about time and lavish about goods may be no paradox, but in part simply a reaction to a difference in relative costs.

The substitution towards goods induced by an increase in the relative cost of time would often include a substitution towards more expensive goods. For example, an increase in the value of a mother's time may induce her to enter the labour force and spend less time cooking by using pre-cooked foods and less time on child-care by using nurseries, camps or baby-sitters. Or barbers' shops in wealthier sections of town charge more and provide quicker service than those in poorer sections, because waiting by barbers is substituted for waiting by customers. These examples illustrate that a change in the quality of goods [2] resulting from a change in the relative cost of goods may simply reflect a change in the methods used to produce given commodities, and not any corresponding change in *their* quality.

Consequently, a rise in income due to a rise in earnings would increase the quality of goods purchased not only because of the effect of income on quality but also because of a substitution of goods for time; a rise in income due to a rise in property income would not cause any substitution, and should have less effect on the quality of goods. Put more dramatically, with total income held constant, a rise in earnings should increase while a rise in property income should decrease the quality chosen. Once again, the composition of income is important and provides testable implications of the theory.

One analytically interesting application of these conclusions is to the recent study by Margaret Reid of the substitution between store-bought and home-delivered milk.[3] According to our approach, the cost of inputs into the commodity " milk consumption at home " is either the sum of the price of milk in the store and the forgone value of the time used to carry it home or simply the price of delivered milk. A reduction in the price of store relative to delivered milk, the value of time remaining constant, would reduce the cost of the first method relatively to the second, and shift production towards the first. For the same reason a reduction in the value of time, market prices

---

[1] For a comparison of the American concept of time with others see Edward T. Hall, *The Silent Language* (New York: Doubleday, 1959), Chapter 9.

[2] Quality is usually defined empirically by the amount spent per physical unit, such as pound of food, car or child. See especially S. J. Prais and H. Houthakker, *The Analysis of Family Budgets* (Cambridge, 1955); also my " An Economic Analysis of Fertility," *op. cit.*

[3] See her " Consumer Response to the Relative Price of Store versus Delivered Milk," *Journal of Political Economy* (April 1963).

of milk remaining constant, would also shift production towards the first method.

Reid's finding of a very large negative relation between the ratio of store to delivered milk and the ratio of their prices, income and some other variables held constant, would be evidence both that milk costs are a large part of total production costs and that there is easy substitution between these alternative methods of production. The large, but not quite as large, negative relation with income simply confirms the easy substitution between methods, and indicates that the cost of time is less important than the cost of milk. In other words, instead of conveying separate information, her price and income elasticities both measure substitution between the two methods of producing the same commodity, and are consistent and plausible.

The importance of forgone earnings and the substitution between time and goods may be quite relevant in interpreting observed price elasticities. A given percentage increase in the price of goods would be less of an increase in commodity prices the more important forgone earnings are. Consequently, even if all commodities had the same true price elasticity, those having relatively important forgone earnings would show lower apparent elasticities in the typical analysis that relates quantities and prices of goods alone.

The importance of forgone earnings differs not only among commodities but also among households for a given commodity because of differences in income. Its importance would change in the same or opposite direction as income, depending on whether the elasticity of substitution between time and goods was less or greater than unity. Thus, even when the true price elasticity of a commodity did not vary with income, the observed price elasticity of goods would be negatively or positively related to income as the elasticity of substitution was less or greater than unity.

The importance of substitution between time and goods can be illustrated in a still different way. Suppose, for simplicity, that only good x and no time was initially required to produce commodity Z. A price ceiling is placed on x, it nominally becomes a free good, and the production of x is subsidised sufficiently to maintain the same output. The increased quantity of x and Z demanded due to the decline in the price of x has to be rationed because the output of x has not increased. Suppose that the system of rationing made the quantity obtained a positive function of the time and effort expended. For example, the quantity of price-controlled bread or medical attention obtained might depend on the time spent in a queue outside a bakery or in a physician's office. Or if an appointment system were used a literal queue would be replaced by a figurative one, in which the waiting was done at "home," as in the Broadway theatre, admissions to hospitals or air travel during peak seasons. Again, even in depressed times the likelihood of obtaining a job is positively related to the time put into job hunting.

Although x became nominally a free good, Z would not be free, because the time now required as an input into Z is not free. The demand for Z would be greater than the supply (fixed by assumption) if the cost of this time was less than the equilibrium price of Z before the price control. The scrambling by households for the limited supply would increase the time required to get a unit of Z, and thus its cost. Both would continue to increase until the average cost of time tended to the equilibrium price before price control. At that point equilibrium would be achieved because the supply and demand for Z would be equal.

Equilibrium would take different forms depending on the method of rationing. With a literal " first come first served " system the size of the queue (say outside the bakery or in the doctor's office) would grow until the expected cost of standing in line discouraged any excess demand;[1] with the figurative queues of appointment systems, the " waiting " time (say to see a play) would grow until demand was sufficiently curtailed. If the system of rationing was less formal, as in the labour market during recessions, the expected time required to ferret out a scarce job would grow until the demand for jobs was curtailed to the limited supply.

Therefore, price control of x combined with a subsidy that kept its amount constant would not change the average private equilibrium price of Z,[2] but would substitute indirect time costs for direct goods costs.[3] Since, however, indirect costs are positively related to income, the price of Z would be raised to higher-income persons and reduced to lower-income ones, thereby re-distributing consumption from the former to the latter. That is, women, the poor, children, the unemployed, etc., would be more willing to spend their time in a queue or otherwise ferreting out rationed goods than would high-earning males.

V. Summary and Conclusions

This paper has presented a theory of the allocation of time between different activities. At the heart of the theory is an assumption that house-holds are producers as well as consumers; they produce commodities by combining inputs of goods and time according to the cost-minimisation rules of the traditional theory of the firm. Commodities are produced in quantities determined by maximising a utility function of the commodity set subject to prices and a constraint on resources. Resources are measured by what is called full income, which is the sum of money income and that forgone or " lost " by the use of time and goods to obtain utility, while commodity prices are measured by the sum of the costs of their goods and time inputs.

---

[1] In queueing language the cost of waiting in line is a " discouragement " factor that stabilises the queueing scheme (see, for example, D. R. Cox and W. L. Smith, *Queues* (New York: Wiley 1961)).

[2] The social price, on the other hand, would double, for it is the sum of private indirect costs and subsidised direct costs.

[3] Time costs can be criticised from a Pareto optimality point of view because they often result in external diseconomies: *e.g.*, a person joining a queue would impose costs on subsequent joiners. The diseconomies are real, not simply pecuniary, because time is a cost to demanders, but is not revenue to suppliers.

The effect of changes in earnings, other income, goods prices and the productivity of working and consumption time on the allocation of time and the commodity set produced has been analysed. For example, a rise in earnings, compensated by a decline in other income so that full income would be unchanged, would induce a decline in the amount of time used at consumption activities, because time would become more expensive. Partly goods would be substituted for the more expensive time in the production of each commodity, and partly goods-intensive commodities would be substituted for the more expensive time-intensive ones. Both substitutions require less time to be used at consumption, and permit more to be used at work. Since the reallocation of time involves simultaneously a reallocation of goods and commodities, all three decisions become intimately related.

The theory has many interesting and even novel interpretations of, and implications about, empirical phenomena. A few will be summarised here.

A traditional " economic " interpretation of the secular decline in hours worked has stressed the growth in productivity of working time and the resulting income and substitution effects, with the former supposedly dominating. Ours stresses that the substitution effects of the growth in productivity of working and consumption time tended to offset each other, and that hours worked declined secularly primarily because time-intensive commodities have been luxuries. A contributing influence has been the secular decline in the relative prices of goods used in time-intensive commodities.

Since an increase in income partly due to an increase in earnings would raise the relative cost of time and of time-intensive commodities, traditional cross-sectional estimates of income elasticities do not hold either factor or commodity prices constant. Consequently, they would, among other things, be biased downward for time-intensive commodities, and give a misleading impression of the effect of income on the quality of commodities consumed. The composition of income also affects demand, for an increase in earnings, total income held constant, would shift demand away from time-intensive commodities and input combinations.

Rough estimates suggest that forgone earnings are quantitatively important and therefore that full income is substantially above money income. Since forgone earnings are primarily determined by the use of time, considerably more attention should be paid to its efficiency and allocation. In particular, agencies that collect information on the expenditure of money income might simultaneously collect information on the " expenditure " of time. The resulting time budgets, which have not been seriously investigated in most countries, including the United States and Great Britain, should be integrated with the money budgets in order to give a more accurate picture of the size and allocation of full income.

GARY S. BECKER

Columbia University.

[8]

II. *Internal Organization of Families*

The family's internal organization is a determinant of its effectiveness as a governance structure for economic activities and for distribution within the family. I begin in Section A by examining marriage from a contracting perspective, emphasizing the difficulties of using contracts to structure complex, ongoing relationships. In Section B I turn to allocation and distribution within the family, bargaining models of marriage, and the roles of marriage- or family-specific capital. In Section C I discuss social exchange theory, arguing that it is broadly consistent with approaches emphasizing bargaining. Section D summarizes the case for bargaining models.

A. *Marriage and Contract*

Individuals desire secure long-term family relationships to provide a stable environment in which to live and to rear children and, in Becker's terminology, to reduce the risks associated with accumulating marital-specific or marriage-specific capital.[32] This requires an institutional structure that is both flexible enough to allow adaptive, sequential decisionmaking in the face of unfolding events and rigid enough to safeguard each spouse against opportunistic exploitation by the other. Marriage is a governance structure which, more or less satisfactorily, accommodates these requirements.

In *Ancient Law* (1861) Sir Henry Sumner Maine identified the progress of civilization with a movement *"from Status to Contract."* He argued that modern society is founded on obligations that individuals create for themselves by voluntary agreements and promises rather than on obligations involuntarily and automatically imposed on them because of their status within the family. Maine's thesis provides a starting point for several recent discussions of marriage. Tony Tanner (1979), for example, begins by quoting several long passages from Maine and views adultery against this background: ". . . adultery can be seen as an attempt to establish an extracontractual contract, or indeed an anticontract . . ." (p. 6) that threatens the

fabric of society. "For bourgeois society marriage is the all-subsuming, all-organizing, all-containing contract. It is the structure that maintains the Structure . . ." (p. 15). For this reason ". . . the problem of transgressing the marriage contract . . . is at the center . . ." of the late eighteenth- and early nineteenth-century novel (p. 12).

Like Tanner, Lenore J. Weitzman (1981) begins with Maine but she denies that his thesis applies to family law: ". . . marriage has not moved from status to contract" (p. xix). The tension between the status and the contract views of marriage is summarized in a recent family law case book by Walter O. Weyrauch and Michael B. Katz (1983):

> *Maynard, Ponder,* and *Ryan* relate to the nature of marriage as seen in the light of Sir Henry Sumner Maine's famous statement, 'that the movement of the progressive societies has been a movement *from Status to Contract.*' In legal practice this statement has never had the same significance it has had for scholarship, but relational and contractual aspects of marriage have lived side by side relatively undisturbed. These cases illustrate that legal practice can live with and accommodate apparent contradictions with ease. *Maynard* stands today for the proposition that marriage is something more than a mere contract, that it is a status or a relationship and, as such, subject to regulation by the government.
>
> *Ponder,* on the other hand, . . . , continues to be relied on for the seemingly opposite proposition that marriage is contract rather than a mere relationship, and that legislation regulating marriage could conceivably impair the obligation of contract if it affects vested rights. . . . *Maynard* can be cited whenever an argument in support of the police power of the state to regulate marriage is made, while *Ponder* can be cited in support of the contractual autonomy of marital parties to regulate their own affairs. In an extreme case this may be done within the same case, and *Ryan* demonstrates this capacity to draw from contradictory sources for support [p. 59].

Firms do not marry, but transaction cost analysis argues that they often resort to merger or vertical integration to avoid us-

---

[32] Becker uses the phrase "marital-specific capital" to refer to capital that would be "much less valuable" if the particular marriage dissolved (Becker, Landes and Michael 1977, p. 338). "Children are the prime example, especially young children, although learning about the idiosyncrasies of one's spouse is also important . . ." (Becker 1981, p. 224). Becker, Landes and Michael also include "working exclusively in the nonmarket sector" (pp. 1142, 1152), as marriage-specific capital. I return to marriage-specific capital in Section B.

596   *Journal of Economic Literature, Vol. XXIII (June 1985)*

ing contracts to structure complex, ongoing relationships. Short-term contracts require frequent renegotiation, making it risky to accumulate capital whose value is contingent on the relationship continuing and discouraging investment in such specific capital. Complete long-term contracts which specify every possible contingency are costly or impossible to write, a reflection of bounded rationality and asymmetric information. Incomplete long-term contracts which fail to specify every possible contingency are perilous because uncovered contingencies must be dealt with through bilateral negotiations under circumstances that may give one party or the other a strategic advantage. While the parties have some control over how complete their contract is to be, more complete contracts are relatively expensive to write and relatively rigid to apply. To avoid these contracting hazards firms often rely on some more complete form of integration such as merger. Since bureaucratic structures have their own characteristic disabilities, internal governance does not eliminate all difficulties associated with a transaction or exchange. Nevertheless, replacing a market relationship by an organization with an appropriate governance structure often safeguards the interests of both parties.

Comparing marriage and merger calls attention to the difference between individuals and firms. When two firms merge, at least one of them loses its legal identity and disappears. When two individuals marry, this is not the case, or, more precisely, this is no longer the case. Sir William Blackstone (1765), describing marriage under eighteenth-century common law, wrote:

> By marriage, the husband and wife are one person in law . . . [T]he very being or legal existence of the woman is suspended during marriage, or at least is incorporated and consolidated into that of the husband, under whose

wing, protection, and cover she performs everything; and is therefore called . . . a femme-covert; and her condition during her marriage is called her coverture.[33]

Thus under the eighteenth-century English common law the parallel between marriage and merger was striking: the wife's legal personality was merged with and submerged in her husband's.

Recent legal scholarship that emphasizes the diversity of contracting modes provides a closely related analysis of these issues. Ian R. Macneil (1978) distinguishes among "classical," "neoclassical," and "relational" contracting.[34] The classical paradigm ignores any relationship between the parties other than that established by the contract itself: The parties' identities are irrelevant, since they may be viewed as trading with the market rather than with each other. The classical paradigm thus adopts a discrete transactions view that is very close to the economist's stereotype of contract law. Neoclassical and relational contracting arose in response to the difficulties of using contracts to structure complex, long-term relationships. Neoclassical contracting introduces a governance structure, often involving third-party arbitration, to reduce these hazards. Relational contracting goes a step further in this direction by treating the ongoing relationship between the parties rather than the contract as central. Collective bargaining is the leading example. Thus, the disabilities of contracts for structuring complex, long-term relationships apply to both commercial and personal contracts.

In Macneil's terminology marriage is a relational contract. The feature that

---

[33] After quoting this passage Weitzman (1981) goes on to quote Justice Black: "this rule has worked out in reality to mean that though the husband and wife are one, the one is the husband" (p. 1). U.S. v. Yazell, 382 U.S. 341, 359 (1966).

[34] Williamson (1979) develops the implications of Macneil's analysis for the transaction cost approach. See also Macneil (1974, 1980).

makes classical and neoclassical contracting inappropriate for structuring labor relations agreements—their inability to view specific disputes in the context of a continuing relationship requiring adaptive, sequential decisionmaking—makes them at least equally inappropriate for structuring marriage. Relational contracting provides a more instructive model.

Weitzman (1981) and others have recently urged that privately negotiated marriage contracts be treated like other contracts, enforceable through the courts, but not accorded special treatment.[35] The contracting analysis of Williamson and Macneil draws attention to the range of contracting modes and implies that relational contracts, because they are likely to be less complete than other contracts, are more dependent on legal rules and on institutions for their interpretation and articulation. This dependence on rules and institutions signals a larger role for the state, organized religion, or custom, and a correspondingly smaller role for the contracting parties than is typical in classical and neoclassical contracting.[36] This is evident in labor law, where relational contracting is most fully developed: Special rules and institutions have been created to circumvent the perceived defects of classical and neoclassical contracting.[37] Treating marriage contracts "like any other contract" is to treat them as classical contracts. But marriage contracts, because they are relational contracts, do require "special treatment": Dispute resolution would require special rules and perhaps special institutions.[38] Privately negotiated marriage contracts articulated through public rules and institutions that reflect society's values and mores might yield results not very different from those obtained through a system of family courts.[39]

[35] Weitzman describes marriage as a contract whose terms are imposed by the state rather than negotiated privately by the parties and examines the terms of that state-imposed contract. She then offers examples of privately negotiated marriage contracts and argues that such "intimate" contracts provide a means of redressing the sexual imbalance which she believes remains present in family law and of providing the certainty, clarity, and assurance that are often absent in family courts. Her argument relies heavily on an analogy between personal relationships and business or commercial ones: Our legal system recognizes the advantages of allowing individuals and firms considerable latitude in structuring business relationships by privately negotiated contracts; why not allow individuals similar latitude in structuring their personal, intimate relationships? This analogy provides some support for the use of contracts to structure personal relationships, but it also draws attention to the difficulties of doing so. Privately negotiated contracts can increase individuals' abilities to determine the duties and obligations of their personal relationships. Using contracts to structure complex, long-term relationships, whether commercial or personal, is intrinsically hazardous, however, and certainty, clarity, and assurance are not to be found in relational contracts.

[36] Because all contracts are subject to certain general rules of law, this distinction is one of degree. Although economists sometimes assume that contracting parties are free to strike any mutually advantageous bargain, this assumption is unwarranted: In the United States some contract provisions are unenforceable because they have been prohibited by statute; others are unenforceable because the courts have held them "contrary to public policy."

[37] These rules affect not only dispute resolution under existing collective bargaining agreements but also the conditions under which collective bargaining takes place in the absence of a prior contract or after the expiration of an existing agreement. Recently some U.S. courts have held that, even absent a collective bargaining agreement or an individual contract, "employers cannot dismiss employees arbitrarily or in bad faith." In Europe protection against dismissal without cause is provided through legislation (William B. Gould 1982, p. 7). Clyde W. Summers (1983) provides a brief overview in his introduction to a recent symposium on "employment at will." Mark R. Kramer (1984, pp. 243–47) summarizes recent developments in this rapidly changing area of the law.

[38] This would be true even absent children and the third-party effects associated with them. The presence of children provides a further rationale for state regulation of marriage and the family.

[39] As Becker (1981, p. 27, fn. 6) notes, Chinese, Japanese, and Christians have generally relied on oral and customary rather than written marriage contracts. In Christian Europe marriage was historically governed not by the state but by the Church through canon law and ecclesiastical courts. The Jewish marriage contract, the Ketuba, is traditionally written. In Islamic law marriage is a civil contract

B. *Allocation and Distribution within Families*

Economists have considered three models of allocation and distribution within families: Samuelson's family consensus model, Becker's altruist model, and recent bargaining models. Although these models usually focus on husbands and wives, they also provide a framework for examining relationships between parents and children. Samuelson's consensus model, explicitly articulated in Samuelson (1956), resolves the problem of intrafamily allocation and distribution by postulating a family social welfare function. Samuelson begins by noting that "the fundamental unit on the demand side is clearly the 'family' " (p. 9), and goes on to pose what he terms the "Mr. Jekyll and Mrs. Jekyll" problem: How can we expect family demand functions to obey any consistency conditions? This question, a crucial one from the standpoint of revealed preference theory, provided the motivation for Samuelson's theory of intrafamily allocation:

> Of course, we might try to save the conventional theory by claiming that one titular head has sovereign power within the family and all of its demands reflect his (or her) consistent indifference curves. But as casual anthropologists we all know how unlikely it is in modern Western culture for one person to "wear the pants." It is perhaps less unrealistic to adopt the hypothesis of a consistent "family consensus" that represents a meeting of the minds

or a compromise between them. (Perhaps Arrow will produce a proof that such a consensus is impossible.) [p. 9].

Samuelson goes on to consider what he characterizes as "one extreme polar case of family organization":

> This family consists of two or more persons: each person consumes his own goods and has indifference curves ordering those goods, and his preferences among his own goods have the special property of being independent of the other members' consumption. But since blood is thicker than water, the preferences of the different members are interrelated by what might be called a "consensus" or "social welfare function" which takes into account the deservingness or ethical worths of the consumption levels of each of the members. The family acts *as if* it were maximizing their joint welfare function [p. 10].

While Samuelson's approach determines allocation and distribution within the family, this is not his principal concern even in the section of "Social Indifference Curves" entitled "The Problem of Family Preference." His primary point is the logical parallel between distribution in the family and distribution in society. His secondary point, crucial for demand analysis, is that the Mr. Jekyll and Mrs. Jekyll problem can be finessed: The consensus or family social welfare function approach provides a rationale for treating family demand functions as if they were individual demand functions. But because Samuelson's "consensus" is postulated, not derived, his family is simply a preference ordering. Samuelson's concern is to keep the lid on the "black box," not to look inside.

The second model of allocation and distribution within the family is the altruist model articulated in Becker (1974, 1981).[40] Becker, unlike Samuelson, is primarily concerned with intrafamily allocation. He begins by postulating that the

---

(John L. Esposito 1982, p. 16) but the parties' latitude to specify its terms is circumscribed (N. J. Coulson 1964, pp. 189–91; Esposito 1982, pp. 23–24).

The special legal rules and institutions governing marriage and the family in the U.S. may be viewed as society's response to the difficulties inherent in structuring such relationships. Four features deserve attention. A standard form marriage "contract" is imposed on the parties to avoid problems of overreaching and unconscionability; specialized courts are responsible for administering family law; courts generally refuse to intervene in ongoing marriages; and the legal system provides a complex and unsatisfactory set of rules in the one area in which they cannot escape involvement: marital dissolution.

[40] Becker (1973) proposes an alternative model of allocation and distribution within the family in which outcomes are essentially determined by the market.

family contains one "altruistic" member whose preferences reflect concern with the welfare of the others.[41] Becker then argues that the presence of one altruist in the family induces purely selfish but rational family members to behave altruistically and that the resulting intrafamily allocation is the one that maximizes the altruist's utility function subject to the family's resource constraint. He concludes that individual differences can be submerged and the family treated as a single harmonious unit with consistent preferences, those of the altruist, without arbitrarily postulating Samuelson's family social welfare function: "In my approach the 'optimal reallocation' results from altruism and voluntary contributions, and the 'group preference function' is identical to that of the altruistic head, even when he does not have sovereign power" (1981, p. 192, footnote omitted).

Becker's claims have been challenged. Marilyn Manser and Murray Brown (1980, p. 32) argue that Becker's conclusion depends not merely on the presence of an altruist but also on implicitly introducing a particular bargaining rule, the rule that the household maximizes the altruist's utility function. Manser and Brown are correct that Becker's analysis is seriously flawed, although Becker is correct that his result does not depend on the altruist having sovereign power. Neither Becker nor Manser and Brown have analyzed the conditions under which Becker's results hold. In addition to the dictatorial case, it also holds when the altruist is a player in an asymmetric bargaining game in which he can offer the others all-or-nothing choices.[42,43]

Bargaining models of allocation and distribution within families, developed independently by Manser and Brown (1980) and by McElroy and Mary J. Horney (1981), treat marriage as a cooperative game.[44,45] These models do not require that either spouse be altruistic, although one or both may be. Spouses are assumed to have conflicting preferences and to resolve their differences in the manner prescribed by some explicit bargaining model.[46] The utility payoffs to the spouses if they fail to reach agreement—called

---

vant when the altruist does not have enough resources to move the others to his preferred allocation by offering them an all-or-nothing choice. To see that Becker's solution does not follow from altruism alone, consider a family with two altruists. Alternatively, consider a family with one altruist and one egoist, but suppose that the egoist has dictatorial power or that the egoist can offer the altruist an all-or-nothing choice. Becker's result depends not on altruism, but on implicit assumptions about power or, equivalently, about the structure of the bargaining game.

[44] A cooperative game is one in which "the players have complete freedom of preplay communication to make joint *binding* agreements"; a non-cooperative game is one in which "absolutely no preplay communication is permitted . . ." (R. Duncan Luce and Howard Raiffa 1957, p. 89; emphasis in original). Simone Clemhout and Henry Y. Wan, Jr. (1977) is the only paper I know that models marriage as a non-cooperative game.

[45] Manser and Brown and McElroy and Horney are specifically concerned with marriage rather than the family, but the analytical issues are similar. The differences between models of allocation between husbands and wives and between parents and children are twofold. First, marriage can be treated as a two-person game, while allocation between parents and children may involve more than two players and, hence, raises the possibility of coalition formation. Second, timing issues, which deserve more attention than they have thus far received in models of marriage, become crucial in models involving parents and children.

[46] Alvin E. Roth (1979) provides a survey of alternative bargaining models. Manser and Brown and McElroy and Horney consider the Nash solution (John F. Nash 1950) to the bargaining problem, and Manser and Brown also consider the Kalai and Smorodinsky solution (Ehud Kalai and Meir Smorodinsky 1975). Sharon C. Rochford (1984) analyzes the implications for assignment or matching in the marriage market of a model in which allocations within marriages are determined by Nash bargaining with transferable utility.

---

[41] Becker's use of the term "altruism" differs from its meaning in sociobiology, although Becker (1976) claims they are closely related.

[42] And in which the others are not allowed to form coalitions.

[43] Becker mentions that his result need not hold in the case of "corner solutions" (1981, pp. 191–92). Under my interpretation, corner solutions are rele-

"threat points" in cooperative game theory—play a dual role in bargaining models. They are essential both to determining the negotiation set—the set of utility payoffs which are Pareto optimal and individually rational (i.e., better for both parties than failing to reach agreements)—and to determining a particular solution, often a unique solution, within the negotiation set. In some bargaining models the threat point corresponds to the payoffs associated with clearly defined "next best" alternatives for each party; in a bargaining model of marriage, for example, the next best alternative for one or both spouses to remaining in a particular marriage might be becoming and remaining single. Usually, however, the threat point corresponds to the expected utility taken over some set of alternatives, for example, the expected utility associated with leaving the present marriage and searching for another spouse.[47]

Bargaining models of intrafamily allocation, in contrast to Becker's model, emphasize the role played by threat points or alternatives in determining allocation and distribution within the family. Thus, investigating whether threat points or alternatives affect intrafamily allocation and distribution may permit us to distinguish empirically between bargaining models and Becker's model.[48]

Bargaining models explicitly embed the problem of intrafamily allocation and distribution in a game-theoretic context, and therefore they provide an intellectually satisfying framework for addressing these issues. Game-theoretic models serve a similar function in industrial organization: Posing the duopoly or bilateral monopoly problem in game-theoretic terms does not resolve the difficulties inherent in modeling the interaction of two firms that recognize their mutual interdependence. For both families and firms, however, the game-theoretic formulation exposes the fundamental nature of the analytical problem.

The transaction cost approach, although broadly consistent with the spirit of the bargaining models, implies that one-period bargaining models are seriously deficient. Neither adaptive sequential decisionmaking, required to deal with new information and unfolding events, nor a governance structure, required to protect each spouse against changes in threat points that strengthen the bargaining position of the other and leave the disadvantaged spouse vulnerable to opportunistic exploitation, has any place in one-period models. Formulation of multiperiod bargaining models depends, however, on developments in the theory of cooperative games.[49]

Focusing on opportunism and the need for a governance structure that limits its

---

[47] In bargaining models the threat point almost never involves the threat of physical violence. Economists' models of conflict, whether between husbands and wives or between workers and firms, seldom recognize even the possibility of violence. Ann D. Witte, Helen V. Tauchen and Sharon K. Long (1984) summarize the sociological literature on family violence, which distinguishes between "expressive" violence (i.e., violence as an end in itself) and "instrumental" violence (i.e., violence as a means of coercion). They then propose a game-theoretic model in which violence and credible threats of violence can be instruments of social control and can affect allocation within the family.

[48] This is too simple. In the market-determined model of Becker (1973) alternatives outside the marriage completely determine allocation within marriage. That model, however, implies a negotiation set which reduces to a single point and, not surpris-

ingly, all models give identical predictions in this case. In Becker (1974, 1981) the negotiation set is determined by the alternatives available to each spouse, but the altruist chooses the point in the negotiation set he prefers. Thus, unless the altruist chooses a "corner solution," changes in alternatives which do not eliminate the allocation chosen by the altruist from the negotiation set cannot force him to a less preferred allocation. Finally, there remains the empirical problem of identifying threat points or alternatives.

[49] If marriage is modeled as a non-cooperative game, then the multiperiod formulation is a supergame in which the constituent game changes from one period to another.

scope allows us to understand better the dual role of family- or marriage-specific capital. Marriage-specific capital is defined by two characteristics: It increases productivity in the household and it is worthless if the particular marriage dissolves.[50] Thus, other things being equal, an increase in marriage-specific capital widens the gap between remaining in a particular marriage and leaving it, either to become and remain single or to search for a better marriage. By widening this gap the accumulation of marriage-specific capital stabilizes the marriage and reduces the risk of further investment in productive marriage-specific capital.[51]

Becker, Landes and Michael (1977, p. 1142) characterize "working exclusively in the nonmarket sector" as a form of marriage-specific investment. This characterization fails to recognize the two distinct channels through which working exclusively in the nonmarket sector affects both marital stability and intrafamily allocation. Working in the home creates nontransferable skills that increase productivity in the marriage; these skills represent marriage-specific capital which increases the payoff associated with remaining in a particular marriage. But a decision to work exclusively in the nonmarket sector is also a decision not to acquire market human capital. Thus the effects of such a decision on the payoffs are twofold: Because marriage-specific capital has been accumulated, it increases the "married payoff"—the payoff associated with remaining in the marriage; and, because market human capital has not been accumulated, it de-

creases the "divorced payoff"—the payoff associated with leaving the marriage and starting work in the market sector.[52]

The relative importance of the married payoff and divorced payoff depends on the rates at which marriage-specific and market human capital accumulate. There are two polar cases. In the first, productivity in the home depends on the accumulation of marriage-specific human capital while wages are independent of experience in the market sector: In this case, working exclusively in the nonmarket sector affects marital stability and intrafamily allocation only by increasing the married payoff; the divorced payoff at a given future date will be the same regardless of whether the intervening period has been spent exclusively in the nonmarket sector. In the second polar case, productivity in the home is independent of experience in the nonmarket sector while wages depend on accumulated experience in the market sector: In this case working exclusively in the nonmarket sector affects marital stability and intrafamily allocation solely by decreasing the divorced payoff; the married payoff will be the same regardless of whether the intervening period has been spent exclusively in the nonmarket sector. In this second case working exclusively in the nonmarket sector involves no accumulation of marriage-specific human capital. Between these poles lies a continuum of cases in which marriage-specific capital and market capital both accumulate at nonzero rates. It is an unresolved and virtually unexplored empirical issue whether

---

[50] In some respects a spouse acquiring marriage-specific capital is analogous to a worker acquiring firm-specific human capital. A major difference is that in labor markets workers are protected by the firm's need to maintain its reputation so it can hire workers in the future, while in marriage markets this protection is attenuated.

[51] Becker is well aware that marriage-specific capital plays both of these roles (Becker, Landes and Michael 1977, p. 1152; Becker 1981, p. 224).

[52] The bases for these comparisons are the payoffs that would be realized at a particular future date in each of the two states—remaining in the marriage and leaving it—if the individual had not worked exclusively in the nonmarket sector. The married payoff refers to the total to be divided between the spouses; in a bargaining model the division of this total depends on the threat point (i.e., the divorced payoff). The "total to be divided between the spouses" is a problematic notion without special assumptions such as transferable utility.

working exclusively in the nonmarket sector increases marital stability primarily by increasing marriage-specific capital, thus increasing the married payoff, or primarily by failing to increase market capital, thus decreasing the divorced payoff.[53]

Becker, Landes and Michael (1977, p. 1152) also characterize children as marriage-specific capital "since one parent usually has much less contact with the children after dissolution."[54] This characterization is misleading for two reasons. First, unlike marriage-specific capital, children do not disappear when a marriage dissolves; typically one parent or the other is granted custody of the children. The observation that one parent usually has much less contact with the children after dissolution suggests that children are like public goods within the marriage, not that they are marriage-specific capital. Second, like working exclusively in the nonmarket sector, children increase the payoff associated with remaining in a marriage and reduce the payoff associated with leaving it.[55,56] Hence, the presence of children affects both marital stability and intrafamily allocation through two distinct channels. The increased payoff associated with remaining in the marriage reflects the "productivity" of children as sources of satisfaction in the intact marriage. The reduced payoff associated with leaving reflects the role of children as "hostages."[57,58]

The transaction cost approach suggests a number of empirically implementable research projects on allocation within the family—between husbands and wives, between parents and children, and among children. Allocation between husbands and wives is difficult to investigate empirically because of the pervasiveness of public goods within the household. Neglecting corner solutions, Becker's altruism model implies that the allocation between spouses depends on the sum of their resources, but not on each spouse's individual wealth, income, and earning power except as they affect this total: The altruist's utility function is maximized subject to the family's resource constraint. The transaction cost approach, like the bargaining models, suggests that the allocation between spouses depends systematically on the individual wealth, income, and earning power of the spouses as well as on their sum. Although the transaction cost approach does not imply a specific

---

[53] Marriage-specific capital is, by definition, idiosyncratic to a particular marriage. The discussion could be generalized, however, to consider the role of human capital which is specific to the household sector but not to a particular marriage. This distinction is analogous to that in the labor market literature between firm-specific and industry-specific human capital.

[54] Becker (1974, p. S23, fn. 36) notes that children "would be a specific investment if the pleasure received by a parent were smaller when the parent was (permanently) separated from the children."

[55] Pollak and Wachter (1975, p. 273–76) criticize the new home economics literature for failing to distinguish between "household production processes" that produce observable and measurable commodities and those that produce "satisfaction" or unmeasurable commodities such as "child services."

[56] Utility payoffs to each spouse in the event of dissolution are conceptually unambiguous. Utility payoffs to each spouse when the marriage remains intact presuppose a particular solution to the problem of distribution within marriage.

[57] Williamson (1983) discusses the use of hostages to lend stability to bilateral governance structures. He argues that reciprocal selling arrangements and product exchanges among rival firms, practices usually condemned as anticompetitive, under certain conditions may represent exchanges of hostages that facilitate socially beneficial trading.

[58] The hostage effect has two components. The first is psychological: Even if leaving a marriage with children entailed no financial obligations, leaving such a marriage would be different from leaving a childless marriage. The second is financial: To the extent that parents retain child support obligations after leaving a marriage, the payoff to leaving a marriage with children is less than the payoff to leaving a childless marriage. These costs may be magnified if there are "economies of scale in consumption" that are lost with dissolution. The financial effect on the payoffs of the parents depends on the extent to which child support is borne by the state and how the portion of it not borne by the state is divided between the parents.

bargaining model, by viewing marriage as a governance structure which permits some flexibility while protecting the parties against the hazards of unconstrained bilateral bargaining, it does suggest that alternatives and threat points affect allocation within marriage.

Direct econometric implementation of any model of allocation within marriage depends on identifying and measuring goods, commodities, or activities desired by one spouse but not the other.[59] For example, contributions of husbands and wives to their respective undergraduate colleges are likely to fall into this category. Or, if either or both spouses have children by previous marriages, then the consumption of these children or expenditures on their education are likely to be of more interest to the children's parent than to the other spouse: An uncluttered case would be one in which a widow with children married a widower with children. Using data from a developing country, one might investigate whether the nutrition of a child in such a family depended only on the family's total resources or whether those of the child's parent had an independent effect on the child's consumption. Using contemporary U.S. data, one might investigate whether the educational attainment of a child depended only on the new family's total resources, or whether the resources of the child's parent had a systematic, independent effect. Although the data needed to estimate models based on the transaction cost approach are diffi-

cult to obtain, in the long run data availability is endogenous. Data collection by government agencies or by individual researchers—a practice less common in economics than in other disciplines—depends in large part on the apparent demand for such data by the research community.

C. *Social Exchange Theory*

Social exchange theory, a framework developed by sociologists and social historians which draws heavily on economics, has been used to analyze a wide range of social phenomena, including intrafamily allocation.

Greven's *Four Generations* (1970), a study of colonial Andover, explains the changing relationships between successive generations in terms of changing economic opportunities and alternatives:

> With abundant land for themselves and their off-spring, the first generation established extended patriarchal families, in which fathers maintained their authority over their mature sons, mainly by withholding control over the land from them until late in their lives. The delayed marriages of sons testified to their prolonged attachment to paternal families . . . [p. 268].

Greven argues that age at marriage is a sensitive indicator of the assumption of adult status and responsibility (pp. 31–32), that marriage required parental support (p. 75), and that the first-generation fathers retained legal control of their lands until their deaths (p. 78). In the middle decades of the eighteenth century, the fourth generation "married younger, established their independence more effectively and earlier in life, and departed from the community with even greater frequency than in earlier generations" (p. 272). Many sons in the fourth generation acquired land from their fathers by deeds of gift or sale during the father's lifetime, rather than by bequest at the father's death (p. 241).

Greven explains these changes in terms

[59] Empirical implementation need not be either direct or econometric. At least two other strategies are available. The first, which I have already discussed, is indirect and focuses on the implications of the transaction cost approach for marital stability, labor force participation, or other variables for which data are widely available. The second is direct but non-econometric and uses qualitative rather than quantitive evidence. Appealing to narrative case studies does not solve the problem of econometric implementation, but challenges the importance of doing so by implicitly raising the question of what types of evidence are admissible in economics.

generally consistent with a bargaining framework in which threat points (i.e., alternatives or opportunities) play a significant role:

A combination of circumstances probably fostered the relatively early autonomy of many fourth-generation sons and encouraged their fathers to assume that their sons ought to be on their own as soon as possible. The rapid expansion of settlements and the emigration of many third-generation Andover men had amply demonstrated the opportunities which existed outside Andover for those willing and able to leave their families and begin life for themselves elsewhere. The diminished landholdings of many families and the constantly rising prices of land in Andover during the first half of the century also put great pressure upon sons who wished to remain as farmers in Andover and made it imperative that many sons take up trades instead or move elsewhere for the land they needed [p. 222].

If patriarchalism was not yet gone, it had been made less viable by the changing circumstances. The earlier economic basis which had sustained the attempts by fathers to establish and to maintain their control and influence over the lives of their sons no longer was to be found among the majority of families living in Andover. Only the wealthy and only those with sons who were willing to accede to their fathers' wishes regarding the possession and ownership of the land could still consider themselves to be patriarchs [p. 273].

Anderson (1971) utilizes an explicit conceptual framework for analyzing the impact of urbanization and industrialization on family structure in nineteenth-century Lancashire. His framework is an elaboration of "social exchange theory," which postulates that individuals engage in exchange to maximize "psychic profit."[60] Anderson, however, stresses two considerations that exchange theory neglects: whether reciprocation is immediate or in the distant future, and whether reciprocation is certain or uncertain (p. 9). The ex-

[60] The basic social exchange theory framework is borrowed from social psychology. The seminal works are George C. Homans (1961) and Peter M. Blau (1964); for an analytical survey and references to the literature see Anthony F. Heath (1976).

change theory foundation of Anderson's analysis is consonant with a bargaining approach, and the two additional considerations he introduces, timing and uncertainty, suggest modifying social exchange theory in the same general directions as transaction cost analysis suggests modifying bargaining models.

Anderson documents the effect of children's employment opportunities on their relationships with their parents:

. . . children's high individual wages allowed them to enter into relational bargains with their parents on terms of more or less precise equality. If, as was usually the case, a bargain could be struck which was immediately favourable to both parties, then all was well, and the relationship continued, though the degree of commitment to such a relationship must often have been low. If a better alternative was obtainable elsewhere the child could take it. The contrast between the choice element in these relationships between urban children and their parents, and the situation in rural areas . . . is very marked. In the rural areas even in the short run, child and father entered a bargaining situation with the child at a very considerable disadvantage, because the father had complete control over the only really viable source of income [pp. 131–32].

Summarizing his findings, Anderson writes:

. . . one crucial way in which urban-industrial life in the nineteenth century affected family cohesion was by offering to teenage children wages at such a level that they were able to free themselves from total economic dependence on the nuclear family. Because normative controls were weak and because housing, food, and other day to day necessities could be obtained on the open market, many could . . . live as well or better than they could with kin or parents. Some children did desert their families and I have presented some evidence which suggested that even where they did not do so many children were conscious of the existence of this possibility and the alternatives it offered, and used it as a way of bargaining a highly independent relationship with their families [p. 134].

Social exchange theory provides an analytical framework for sociology and social history which appeals strongly to economists; its appeal to sociologists and social historians is somewhat less powerful. For example, Michael Katz (1975), a social historian, contrasts Anderson's work on nineteenth-century Preston with his own analysis of nineteenth-century Hamilton, emphasizing the narrowness of Anderson's exchange theory approach. He argues that it "constricts the range of human motivation," and "it assumes a greater degree of rationality than probably underlies ordinary behavior" (p. 302).[61]

D. *The Case for Bargaining Models*

Even without the contracting problems emphasized by the transaction cost approach, bargaining models would often be required to analyze intrafamily allocation. There are three exceptions: (1) there is a family consensus on resource allocation, (2) some "altruistic" family member has the power to choose an allocation from the negotiation set and impose his choice on the others, and (3) the negotiation set is a single point, so there is no surplus over which to bargain. Virtually any other circumstances require a bargaining analysis to determine an equilibrium allocation within the negotiation set.

The negotiation set corresponding to a particular marriage depends on the next-best alternative of each spouse. When the negotiation set is small, determining an equilibrium allocation within it becomes uninteresting: The well-being of each spouse is essentially determined by the negotiation set, not by bargaining within the marriage to determine an allocation within the negotiation set. In the limit, when the negotiation set shrinks to a single point, the well-being of each spouse is uniquely determined by his or her alternatives outside the marriage.[62]

[61] Katz also argues that Anderson's theory "is not supported by the data in his book" (p. 302).
[62] The limit is a limit for the marriage to continue. If the bargaining set is empty, the marriage will presumably dissolve.

A bargaining approach to intrafamily allocation is required because negotiation sets in ongoing marriages are often large and because intrafamily allocation cannot be resolved at the outset. The emergence of a surplus in ongoing marriages can be ascribed to the accumulation of idiosyncratic or marriage-specific capital or, more simply, to a random process in which marriages with empty negotiation sets dissolve while those with nonempty negotiation sets continue. Because bounded rationality precludes complete long-term contracts which specify intrafamily allocations under every possible contingency, intrafamily allocation must be dealt with in an adaptive, sequential way—in short, through bargaining.

III. *Conclusion*

Although the metaphor of household production can usefully be applied to a wide range of activities, the formal framework of the household production model is best suited to analyzing processes that combine household time and purchased inputs to produce well-defined and measurable outputs. The family's role in many economic activities, however, is explicable not in terms of technology but of governance.

The transaction cost approach provides a new perspective on families and households. Unlike the new home economics, which focuses exclusively on household production, it recognizes the importance of household organization and family structure. The transaction cost approach views marriage as a "governance structure," emphasizes the role of "bargaining" within families, and draws attention to the advantages and disadvantages of family organization in terms of incentives and monitoring, and to the special roles of "altruism" and "family loyalty." It also recognizes the disadvantages of family governance: conflict spillover, the toleration of inefficient personnel, inappropriate ability match, and inability to realize economies of scale. If activities are assigned to institutions in an efficient or cost-minimizing fashion, the balance of these advantages and disadvantages plays a major role in determining which activities are carried out within families and which are performed by firms, nonprofit institutions, or the state.

A principal defect of the transaction cost approach is its failure to provide a structure for rigorous econometric investigations. Developing such a framework requires incorporating the insights of the transaction cost approach into formal models and specifying such models in sufficient detail to permit estimation. The present essay represents a first step toward that goal.

REFERENCES

AKERLOF, GEORGE A. "The Market for 'Lemons': Quality Uncertainty and the Market Mechanism," *Quart. J. Econ.,* Aug. 1970, *84*(3), pp. 488–500.

ALCHIAN, ARMEN A. AND DEMSETZ, HAROLD. "Production, Information Costs, and Economic Organization," *Amer. Econ. Rev.,* Dec. 1972, *62*(5), pp. 777–95.

ANDERSON, MICHAEL. *Family structure in nineteenth century Lancashire.* London: Cambridge U. Press, 1971.

ARROW, KENNETH J. "Uncertainty and the Welfare Economics of Medical Care," *Amer. Econ. Rev.* Dec. 1963, *53*(5), pp. 941–73.

———, AND HAHN, FRANK, H. *General competitive analysis.* San Francisco: Holden-Day, Inc., 1971.

BANFIELD, EDWARD C. *The moral basis of a backward society.* Glencoe, IL: Free Press, 1958.

BARNUM, HOWARD N. AND SQUIRE, LYN. *A model of an agricultural household: Theory and evidence.* Baltimore, MD: Johns Hopkins U. Press, 1979.

BECKER, GARY S. "A Theory of the Allocation of Time," *Econ. J.,* Sept. 1965, *75*(299), pp. 493–517.

———. "A Theory of Marriage: Part I," *J. Polit. Econ.,* July/Aug. 1973, *81*(4) pp. 813–46.

———. "A Theory of Marriage: Part II," *J. Polit. Econ.,* Mar./Apr. 1974, *82*(2), pp. S11–26.

———. "Altruism, Egoism, and Genetic Fitness," *J. Econ. Lit.,* Sept. 1976, *14*(3), pp. 817–26.

———. *A treatise on the family.* Cambridge: Harvard U. Press, 1981.

———; LANDES, ELISABETH M. AND MICHAEL, ROBERT T. "An Economic Analysis of Marital Instability," *J. Polit. Econ.,* Dec. 1977, *85*(6), pp. 1141–87.

BENEDICT, BURTON. "Family Firms and Economic Development," *Southwestern J. Anthro.,* Spring 1968, *24*(1), pp. 1–19.

BEN-PORATH, YORAM. "The F-Connection: Families, Friends, and Firms and the Organization of Exchange," *Population Devel. Rev.,* Mar. 1980, *6*(1), pp. 1–30.

———. "Economics and the Family—Match or Mismatch? A Review of Becker's *A Treatise on the Family,*" *J. Econ. Lit.,* Mar. 1982, *20*(1), pp. 52–64.

BINSWANGER, HANS P. AND ROSENZWEIG, MARK R. "Behavioral and Material Determinants of Production Relations in Agriculture." Research Unit, Agriculture and Rural Development Department, Operational Policy Staff, World Bank, Report No.: ARU 5, June 1982. Revised, Oct. 5, 1983.

———. "Contractual Arrangements, Employment and Wages in Rural Labor Markets: A Critical Review," in *Contractual arrangements, employment and wages in rural labor markets in Asia.* Eds.: HANS P. BINSWANGER AND MARK R. ROSENZWEIG. New Haven: Yale U. Press, 1984.

BLACKSTONE, SIR WILLIAM. *Commentaries on the laws of England.* Oxford: Clarendon Press, 1765.

BLAU, PETER M. *Exchange and power in social life.* NY: John Wiley & Sons, Inc., 1964.

CHRISTENSEN, LAURITS R.; JORGENSON, DALE W. AND LAU, LAWRENCE J. "Transcendental Logarithmic Utility Functions," *Amer. Econ. Rev.,* June 1975, *65*(3), pp. 367–83.

CLEMHOUT, SIMONE AND WAN, HENRY Y., JR., "Symmetric Marriage, Household Decision Making and Impact on Fertility." Working Paper No. 152, Cornell U., Sept. 1977.

COASE, RONALD H. "The Nature of the Firm," *Economica, N.S.,* Nov. 1937, *4,* pp. 386–405.

COULSON, N. J. *A history of Islamic law.* Edinburgh: Edinburgh U. Press, 1964.

DAVIS, PETER. "Realizing the Potential of the Family Business," *Organizational Dynamics,* Summer 1983, pp. 47–56.

DEBREU, GERARD. *Theory of value: An axiomatic analysis of economic equilibrium.* NY: John Wiley & Sons, 1959.

DEMOS, JOHN AND BOOCOCK, SARANE SPENCE, eds. *Turning points: Historical and sociological essays on the family. Amer. J. Soc.,* Supplement. 1978, *84.*

DEOLALIKAR, ANIL B. AND VIJVERBERG, WIM P. M. "The Heterogeneity of Family and Hired Labor in Agricultural Production: A Test Using District-Level Data from India," *J. Econ. Devel.,* Dec. 1983a, *8*(2), pp. 45–69.

———. "Heterogeneity of Family and Hired Labor in Agriculture: A Test Using Farm-Level Data from India and Malaysia." Economic Growth Center, Yale U., Discussion Paper No. 444, Sept. 1983b.

EASTERLIN, RICHARD A.; POLLAK, ROBERT A. AND WACHTER, MICHAEL L. "Towards a More General Economic Model of Fertility Determination: Endogenous Preferences and Natural Fertility," in *Population and economic change in developing*

Pollak: Transaction Cost and Families 607

countries. Ed.: RICHARD A. EASTERLIN. Chicago: U. of Chicago Press, 1980.

EHRLICH, ISAAC AND BECKER, GARY S. "Market Insurance, Self-Insurance and Self-Protection," *J. Polit. Econ.*, July/Aug. 1972, *80*(4), pp. 623–48.

ESPOSITO, JOHN L. *Women in Muslim family law.* Syracuse: Syracuse U. Press, 1982.

FENOALTEA, STEFANO. "Slavery and Supervision in Comparative Perspective: A Model," *J. Econ. Hist.*, Sept. 1984, *44*(3), pp. 635–68.

FØRSUND, FINN R.; LOVELL, C. A. KNOX AND SCHMIDT, PETER. "A Survey of Frontier Production Functions and of Their Relationship to Efficiency Measurement," *J. Econometrics*, May 1980, *13*(1), pp. 5–25.

FUCHS, VICTOR R. *How we live.* Cambridge: Harvard U. Press, 1983.

GOLDBERG, VICTOR P. "Regulation and Administered Contracts," *Bell J. Econ.*, Autumn 1976, *7*(2), pp. 426–48.

GOULD, WILLIAM B. *A primer on American labor law.* Cambridge: MIT Press, 1982.

GREVEN, PHILIP J., JR. *Four generations: Population, land, and family in colonial Andover, Massachusetts.* Ithaca, NY: Cornell U. Press, 1970.

GRIFFEN, SALLY AND GRIFFEN, CLYDE. "Family and Business in a Small City: Poughkeepsie, New York, 1850–1880," in *Family and kin in urban communities, 1700–1930.* Ed.: TAMARA K. HAREVEN. NY: New Viewpoints, 1977, pp. 144–63.

GRILICHES, ZVI. "Household and Economy: Towards a New Theory of Population and Economic Growth: Comment," *J. Polit. Econ.*, Mar./Apr. 1974, 82(2, Part II), pp. S219–21.

HANNAN, MICHAEL T. "Families, Markets, and Social Structures: An Essay on Becker's *A Treatise on the Family*," *J. Econ. Lit.*, Mar. 1982, *20*(1), pp. 65–72

HANSMANN, HENRY B. "The Role of Nonprofit Enterprise," *Yale Law J.*, Apr. 1980, *89*(5), pp. 835–901.

HAREVEN, TAMARA K. "Family Time and Industrial Time: Family and Work in a Planned Corporation Town, 1900–1924," in *Family and kin in urban communities, 1700–1930.* Ed.: TAMARA K. HAREVEN. NY: New Viewpoints, 1977a.

———, ed. *Family and kin in urban communities, 1700–1930.* NY: New Viewpoints, 1977b.

———. "The Dynamics of Kin in an Industrial Community," in *Turning points: Historical and sociological essays on the family.* Ed.: JOHN DEMOS AND SARANE SPENCE BOOCOCK. *Amer. J. Soc.*, Supplement 1978, *84*, pp. S151–82.

HEATH, ANTHONY F. *Rational choice and social exchange: A critique of exchange theory.* NY & Cambridge: Cambridge U. Press, 1976.

HIRSCHMAN, ALBERT O. *Exit, voice, and loyalty: Responses to decline in firms, organizations and states.* Cambridge: Harvard U. Press, 1970.

HOMANS, GEORGE C. *Social behavior: Its elementary forms.* NY: Harcourt Brace & World, 1961.

KALAI, EHUD AND SMORODINSKY, MEIR. "Other Solutions to Nash's Bargaining Problem," *Econometrica.* May 1975, *43*(3), pp. 513–18.

KATZ, MICHAEL B. *The people of Hamilton, Canada West: Family and class in a mid-nineteenth-century city.* Cambridge: Harvard U. Press, 1975.

KINKEAD, GWEN. "Family Business Is a Passion Play," *Fortune*, June 30, 1980, pp. 70–75.

KLEIN, BENJAMIN; CRAWFORD, ROBERT G. AND ALCHIAN, ARMEN A. "Vertical Integration, Appropriable Rents, and the Competitive Contracting Process," *J. Law Econ.*, Oct. 1978, *21*(2), pp. 297–326.

KRAMER, MARK R. "The Role of Federal Courts in Changing State Law: The Employment at Will Doctrine in Pennsylvania," *U. of Penn. Law Rev.*, Dec. 1984, *133*(1), pp. 227–64.

KUHN, THOMAS S. *The structure of scientific revolutions.* 2nd ed., enlarged. Chicago: U. of Chicago Press, [1962] 1970.

LANDA, JANET T. "A Theory of the Ethnically Homogeneous Middleman Group: An Institutional Alternative to Contract Law," *J. Legal Stud.*, June 1981, *10*(2), pp. 349–62

LANDA, JANET T. AND SALAFF, JANET W. "The Socioeconomic Functions of Kinship and Ethnic Networks in Promoting Chinese Entrepreneurship in Singapore: A Case Study of the Tan Kah Kee Firm." Mimeo. Oct. 1982.

LASLETT, PETER assist. by WALL, RICHARD. *Household and family in past time.* Cambridge: Cambridge U. Press, 1972.

LUCE, R. DUNCAN AND RAIFFA, HOWARD. *Games and decisions: Introduction and critical survey.* NY: John Wiley & Sons, 1957.

MACNEIL, IAN R. "The Many Futures of Contracts," *Southern Calif. Law Rev.*, May 1974, *47*(3), pp. 691–816.

———. "Contracts: Adjustment of Long–Term Economic Relations under Classical, Neoclassical, and Relational Contract Law," *Northwestern U. Law Rev.*, Jan./Feb. 1978, *72*(6), pp. 854–905.

———. *The new social contract: An inquiry into modern contractual relations.* New Haven, CT: Yale U. Press, 1980.

MAINE, SIR HENRY SUMNER. *Ancient law: Its connection with the early history of society and its relation to modern ideas.* London: J. Murray, 1861.

MANSER, MARILYN AND BROWN, MURRAY. "Marriage and Household Decision-Making: A Bargaining Analysis," *Int. Econ. Rev.*, Feb. 1980, *21*(1), pp. 31–44.

MCELROY, MARJORIE B. The Joint Determination of Household Membership and Market Work: The Case of Young Men," *J. Labor Econ.*, forthcoming.

MCELROY, MARJORIE B. AND HORNEY, MARY J. "Nash-Bargained Household Decisions: Toward a Generalization of the Theory of Demand," *Int. Econ. Rev.*, June 1981, *22*(2), pp. 333–49.

MICHAEL, ROBERT T. AND BECKER, GARY S. "On the New Theory of Consumer Behavior," *Swedish J. Econ.*, Dec. 1973, *75*(4), pp. 378–96.

———; FUCHS, VICTOR R. AND SCOTT, SHARON R. "Changes in the Propensity to Live Alone: 1950–1976," *Demography*, Feb. 1980, *17*(1), pp. 39–56.

608   *Journal of Economic Literature, Vol. XXIII (June 1985)*

MURRELL, PETER. "The Economics of Sharing: A Transactions Cost Analysis of Contractual Choice in Farming," *Bell J. Econ.*, Spring 1983, *14*(1), pp. 283–93.

NASH, JOHN F. "The Bargaining Problem," *Econometrica*, Apr. 1950, *28*(1), pp. 155–62.

NERLOVE, MARC. "Household and Economy: Toward a New Theory of Population and Economic Growth," *J. Polit. Econ.*, Mar./Apr. 1974, *83*(2, Part II), pp. S200–18.

PAULY, MARK. "Overinsurance and Public Provision of Insurance: The Roles of Moral Hazard and Adverse Selection," *Quart. J. Econ.*, Feb. 1974, *81*(1), pp. 44–62.

POLLAK, ROBERT A. AND WACHTER, MICHAEL L. "The Relevance of the Household Production Function and Its Implications for the Allocation of Time," *J. Polit. Econ.*, Apr. 1975, *83*(2), pp. 255–77.

_____ AND WALES, TERENCE J. "Estimation of Complete Demand Systems from Household Budget Data: The Linear and Quadratic Expenditure System," *Amer. Econ. Rev.*, June 1978, *68*(3), pp. 349–59.

_____. "Comparison of the Quadratic Expenditure System and Translog Demand Systems with Alternative Specifications of Demographic Effects," *Econometrica*, Apr. 1980, 48(3), pp. 595–612.

POSNER, RICHARD A. "Theories of Economic Regulation," *Bell J. Econ. Manage. Sci.*, Autumn 1974, *5*(2), pp. 335–58.

_____. "Anthropology and Economics," *J. Polit. Econ.*, June 1980, *88*(3), pp. 608–16.

ROCHFORD, SHARON C. "Symmetrically Pairwise-Bargained Allocations in an Assignment Market," *J. Econ. Theory*, Dec. 1984, *34*(2), pp. 262–81.

ROSENZWEIG, MARK R. AND WOLPIN, KENNETH I. "Specific Experience, Household Structure and Intergenerational Transfers: Farm Family Land and Labor Arrangements in Developing Countries," *Quart. J. Econ.*, forthcoming.

ROTH, ALVIN E. *Axiomatic models of bargaining.* Lecture Notes in Economics and Mathematical Systems, No. 170. Berlin: Springer-Verlag, 1979.

ROTHSCHILD, MICHAEL AND STIGLITZ, JOSEPH E. "Equilibrium in Competitive Insurance Markets: An Essay on the Economics of Imperfect Information," *Quart. J. Econ.*, Nov. 1976, *90*(4), pp. 629–49.

SAMUELSON, PAUL A. *Foundations of economic analysis.* Cambridge: Harvard U. Press, 1947.

_____. "Social Indifference Curves," *Quart. J. Econ.*, Feb. 1956, *70*(1), pp. 1–22.

SIMON, HERBERT A. *Models of man: Social and rational.* NY: John Wiley & Sons, 1957.

STIGLER, GEORGE J. AND BECKER, GARY S. "De Gustibus Non Est Disputandum," *Amer. Econ. Rev.*, Mar. 1977, *67*(2), pp. 76–90.

SUMMERS, CLYDE W. "Introduction. Individual Rights in the Workplace: The Employment-At-Will Issue," *U. of Michigan J. Law Reform*, Winter 1983, *16*(2), pp. 201–05.

TANNER, TONY. *Adultery in the novel: Contract and transgression.* Baltimore, MD: Johns Hopkins U. Press, 1979.

VANEK, JAROSLAV. "Decentralization under Workers' Management: A Theoretical Appraisal," *Amer. Econ. Rev.*, Dec. 1969, *59*(5), pp. 1006–14.

WEITZMAN, LENORE J. *The marriage contract: Spouses, lovers and the law.* NY: Free Press, 1981.

WEYRAUCH, WALTER O. AND KATZ, SANFORD N. *American family law in transition.* Wash., DC: The Bureau of National Affairs, 1983.

WILLIAMSON, OLIVER E. *Markets and hierarchies: Analysis and antitrust implications.* NY: Free Press, 1975.

_____. "Franchise Bidding for Natural Monopolies—in General and with Respect to CATV," *Bell J. Econ.*, Spring 1976, 7(1), pp. 73–104.

_____. "Transaction-Cost Economics: The Governance of Contractual Relations," *J. Law Econ.*, Oct. 1979, *22*(2), pp. 223–61.

_____. "The Modern Corporation: Origins, Evolution, Attributes," *J. Econ. Lit.*, Dec. 1981, *19*(4), pp. 1537–68.

_____. "Credible Commitments: Using Hostages to Support Exchange," *Amer. Econ. Rev.*, Sept. 1983, *73*(4), pp. 519–40.

WILSON, CHARLES A. "A Model of Insurance Markets with Incomplete Information," *J. Econ. Theory*, Dec. 1977, *16*(2), pp. 167–207.

_____. "The Nature of Equilibrium in Markets with Adverse Selection," *Bell J. Econ.*, Spring 1980, *11*(1), pp. 108–30.

WINSTON, GORDON C. *The timing of economic activities: Firms, households, and markets in time-specific analysis.* Cambridge: Cambridge U. Press, 1982.

WITTE, ANN D.; TAUCHEN, HELEN V. AND LONG, SHARON K. "Violence in the Family: A Non-random Affair." Working Paper no. 89. Dept. of Econ., Wellesley College, Oct. 1984.

[9]

Human Capital, Effort, and the Sexual Division of Labor

Gary S. Becker, *University of Chicago and*
National Opinion Research Center

Increasing returns from specialized human capital is a powerful force creating a division of labor in the allocation of time and investments in human capital between married men and married women. Moreover, since child care and housework are more effort intensive than leisure and other household activities, married women spend less effort on each hour of market work than married men working the same number of hours. Hence, married women have lower hourly earnings than married men with the same market human capital, and they economize on the effort expended on market work by seeking less demanding jobs. The responsibility of married women for child care and housework has major implications for earnings and occupational differences between men and women.

This research has been supported by grant no. HD14256-03 from the National Institutes of Health and no. SES-8208260 from the National Science Foundation. I received very helpful comments from Robert Michael, Jacob Mincer, John Muellbauer, Sherwin Rosen, Yoram Weiss, and participants in the Applications of Economics Workshop of the University of Chicago. Much of Section III was worked out jointly with H. Gregg Lewis. Gale Mosteller provided valuable assistance.

[*Journal of Labor Economics*, 1985, vol. 3, no. 1, pt. 2]

S33

I. Introduction

The labor force participation of married women in Western countries has increased enormously during the last 30 years. Initially, the increase was concentrated among older women, but it eventually spread to younger women with small children. Although this paper will not be primarily concerned with the causes of the increase, it will be useful first to sketch out briefly an "economic" explanation (based on Becker 1981, chap. 11) that can be tested against the evidence in other papers in this issue.

The major cause of the increased participation of married women during the twentieth century appears to be the increased earning power of married women as Western economies developed, including the rapid expansion of the service sector. The growth in their earning power raised the forgone value of their time spent at child care and other household activities, which reduced the demand for children and encouraged a substitution away from parental, especially mothers', time. Both of these changes raised the labor force participation of married women.

The gain from marriage is reduced, and hence the attractiveness of divorce raised, by higher earnings and labor force participation of married women, because the sexual division of labor within households becomes less advantageous. Consequently, this interpretation also implies the large growth in divorce rates over time. The decline in the gain from marriage is reflected also in the increased number of "consensual unions" (unmarried couples living together), the large increase in families headed by women, and even partly in the large growth in illegitimate birth rates relative to legitimate rates during recent decades.

Divorce rates, fertility, and labor force participation rates of women also interact in various other ways. For example, fertility is reduced when divorce becomes more likely, because child care is more difficult after a marriage dissolves. There is evidence that couples who anticipate relatively high probabilities of divorce do have fewer children (see Becker, Landes, and Michael 1977). The labor force participation of women is also affected when divorce rates increase, not only because divorced women participate more fully, but also because married women will participate more as protection against the financial adversity of a subsequent divorce.

One difficulty with this explanation is that economic progress and the growth in earning power of women did not accelerate in developed countries after 1950, yet both divorce rates and labor force participation rates of married women have risen far more rapidly since then. I tentatively suggest that threshold effects of increased female earning power on labor force participation rates, fertility, and divorce rates are responsible for much of the acceleration. As the earning power of women continued to grow, fertility continued to fall until the time spent in child care was reduced enough so that married women could anticipate spending appreciable time in the labor force prior to their first child and subsequent to their last child. Women then had much greater incentive to invest in market-oriented human capital, which accelerated the increase in their earning power, participation, and divorce rates, and accelerated the reduction in fertility.

The modest increase in the hourly earnings of women relative to men during the last 30 years in the United States and many other Western countries (but not all; see Gregory, McMahon, and Whittingham [1985]; Gustafsson and Jacobsson [1985]) has been an embarrassment to the human capital interpretation of sexual earnings differentials, since this interpretation seems to imply that increased participation of married women would induce increased investment in earnings-raising market human capital. However, the increased participation may have temporarily reduced the earnings of women because increased supply generally lowers price, the average labor force experience of working women would be initially reduced, and observed earnings are temporarily reduced by increased on-the-job investments (see O'Neill 1985; Smith and Ward 1985).

Nevertheless, the evidence still suggests, although it does not demonstrate, that the earnings of men and women would not be equal even if their participation were equal. Some have inferred substantial discrimination in the marketplace against women, perhaps supported by the evidence in Zabalza and Tzannatos (1983) for Great Britain. This paper argues that responsibility for child care, food preparation, and other household activities also prevents the earnings of women from rising more rapidly.

Child care and other housework are tiring and limit access to jobs requiring travel or odd hours. These effects of housework are captured by a model developed in this paper of the allocation of energy among different activities. If child care and other housework demand relatively large quantities of "energy" compared to leisure and other nonmarket uses of time by men, women with responsibilities for housework would have less energy available for the market than men would. This would reduce the hourly earnings of married women, affect their jobs and occupations, and even lower their investment in market human capital when they worked the same number of market hours as married men. Consequently, the housework responsibilities of married women may be the source of much of the difference in earnings and in job segregation between men and women.

Section II sets out a model of the optimal division of labor among intrinsically identical household members who invest in different kinds of activity-specific human capital. Increasing returns from investments in specific human capital encourage a division of labor that reinforces differences in market and household productivity of men and women due to other forces, including any discrimination against women.

Section III models an individual's optimal allocation of energy among different activities. Many implications are derived, including a measure of the value of time in different activities, the forces encouraging the production of energy, and especially a very simple equation for the optimal supply of energy per hour of each activity.

Section IV applies the analysis of specialized investment and of the allocation and production of energy to earnings and occupational differentials between married men and women. It shows that married women with responsibility for child care and other housework earn less than men, choose "segregated" jobs and occupations, and invest less in market human capital even when married men and women work the same number of market hours.

Section V provides a summary and concluding remarks.

II. Human Capital and the Division of Labor

The human capital approach has recognized from the beginning that the incentive to invest in human capital specific to a particular activity is positively related to the time spent at that activity (see Becker 1964, pp. 51–52, 100–102). This recognition was early used to explain empirically why married women have earned significantly less than married men since women have participated in the labor force much less than married men (see Oaxaca 1973; Mincer and Polachek 1974).

It was not recognized immediately, however, that investments in specialized human capital produce increasing returns and thereby provide a strong incentive for a division of labor even among basically identical persons. This is recognized in chapter 2 of my book on the family (1981), where economies of scale from investments in activity-specific human capital are shown to encourage identical members of a household to specialize in different types of investments and to allocate their time differently. I also suggest there that the advantages of specialized investments provide more insights into comparative advantage in international trade than does the conventional emphasis on differences in factor supplies. These increasing returns to scale and advantages of specialization are illustrated in this section with a simple model heavily influenced by discussions with and examples in Rosen (1982) and Gros (1983).

Assume that a person's earnings in each of m market activities are proportional to his time spent at the activity and to his stock of human capital specific to the activity:

$$I_i = b_i t_{w_i} h_i, \qquad i = 1, \ldots, m, \tag{1}$$

where h_i is capital completely specific to activity i. To simplify further, assume that h_i is produced only with investment time (t_{h_i}):

$$h_i = a_i t_{h_i}, \qquad i = 1, \ldots, m. \tag{2}$$

If the total time spent at all work and investment activities is fixed, then

$$\sum_{i=1}^{m} (t_{w_i} + t_{h_i}) = \sum t_i = T, \tag{3}$$

where $t_i = t_{w_i} + t_{h_i}$. By summing over earnings in all activities, and substituting from (2),

$$I = \sum I_i = \sum c_i t_{w_i} t_{h_i}, \tag{4}$$

where $c_i = a_i b_i$.

Since earnings in each activity are determined by the product of work and investment time, total earnings are maximized when these times are equal:

$$I = \frac{1}{4} \sum c_i t_i^2, \tag{5}$$

when $t_{h_i} = t_{w_i}$. The increasing returns from the total time allocated to an activity (t_i) arise from the independence between the cost of accumulating human capital and the amount of time spent using the capital. These increasing returns imply that earnings are maximized when all time is spent on just one activity:

$$I^* = \frac{c_k}{4} T^2, \tag{6}$$

where $c_k \geq c_i$, all i. Examples of complete specialization in human capital specific to a single "activity" include doctors, dentists, carpenters, economists, and so on.

The same formulation is applicable to time allocated among consumption activities produced under constant returns to scale, where the effective time input is proportional both to consumption-specific human capital and consumption time, as in

$$Z_i = b_i t_{z_i} h_i. \tag{7}$$

If $h_i = a_i t_{h_i}$, then

$$Z_i = c_i t_{z_i} t_{h_i}, \tag{8}$$

and the output of each commodity is maximized by equating the time spent on production and investment:

$$Z_i^* = \frac{c_i t_i^2}{4}, \tag{9}$$

where $t_i = t_{z_i} + t_{h_i}$.

If the utility function is a simple Leontief function of these commodities,

$$U = \min(Z_i, \ldots, Z_m), \tag{10}$$

and if $c_i = c$, for all i, utility would be maximized by allocating equal time to each commodity:

$$U^a = Z_i^* = \frac{cT^2}{4m^2}. \tag{11}$$

This indirect utility function depends positively on the total time available and negatively on the number of commodities produced and consumed in fixed proportion.

The link between production and consumption would be severed if other persons also produced these commodities. To eliminate any *intrinsic* comparative advantage, I assume that all persons are basically identical. Even though all commodity production functions have constant returns to scale in effective time, there is still a gain from trade because each person can concentrate his investment and production on a smaller number of commodities and trade for the others. By reducing the number of commodities produced, advantage can be taken of the increasing returns to the *total* time spent on a commodity (see eq. [9]). For example, if two persons each produce half the commodities and trade their excess production unit for unit, the output of each commodity would equal

$$Z_i^1 = \frac{cT^2}{4(m/2)^2}, \qquad i = 1, \ldots, \frac{m}{2}$$

$$Z_j^2 = \frac{cT^2}{4(m/2)^2}, \qquad j = \frac{m}{2} + 1, \ldots, m. \tag{12}$$

Since they trade half the production, the indirect utility function of each person becomes

$$U^t = \frac{1}{2} \frac{cT^2}{4(m/2)^2} > \frac{cT^2}{4m^2} = U^a. \tag{13}$$

Increasing returns from investments in specialized human capital are

Division of Labor   S39

the source of the gains from increasing the "extent of the market." Trade permits a division of labor in investments that effectively widens the market and thereby raises the welfare even of basically identical traders. The gain from specialization and trade in this example is simply proportional to the number of traders; each of p traders, $p \le m$, would specialize in m/p commodities, and produce

$$Z_j^k = \frac{c}{4}\frac{T^2}{m^2}p^2, \qquad j \in \frac{m}{p}, \qquad k = 1, \dots, p \le m. \tag{14}$$

If $(p - 1)/p$th of the output were traded unit for unit, the level of utility would be proportional to the number of traders:

$$U' = \frac{1}{p}Z_j^k = \frac{c}{4}\frac{T^2}{m^2}p, \qquad p \le m. \tag{15}$$

The effect of specialization and trade on welfare is shown in figure 1 (suggested by John Muellbauer). A person without access to trade has a

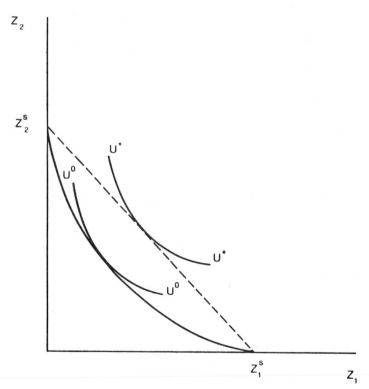

FIG. 1.—The gains from specialization and trade

convex opportunity boundary between Z_1 and Z_2 because of increasing returns from specific investments; his utility is maximized at the point of tangency with an indifference curve (U^0). A market with many basically identical persons has better opportunities and can obtain by specialization and trade any point on the straight line joining the intercepts, Z_1' and Z_2'. If b persons specialize completely in Z_1 and $n - b$ specialize in Z_2, trading provides each person with $(b/n)Z_1'$ units of Z_1 and $(1 - b/n)Z_2'$ units of Z_2. This defines a straight-line opportunity boundary between Z_1' and Z_2' as b varies from zero to n. The improvement in welfare from trade (U^*/U^0) is determined by the degree of increasing returns or by the convexity of the opportunities for a person without trade.

The analysis is readily generalized to permit substitution among a continuum of commodities. The number of commodities consumed along with the degree of specialization in production by any trader would then also depend on the extent of the market (see the analysis in Gros [1983]). Moreover, goods and services as well as time can be inputs into the production of commodities and human capital. The following proposition survives all reasonable generalizations.

PROPOSITION:—If n basically identical persons consume in equilibrium $m \ll n$ commodities produced under constant or increasing returns to scale with specific human capital, each person will completely specialize in producing only one commodity and accumulate only the human capital specific to that commodity. The other $m - 1$ commodities will be acquired by trades with other specialized producers. If $n > 1$ is smaller or not much larger than m, or with decreasing returns to scale, specialization may be incomplete, but *some* commodities *must* be produced by only one person.[1]

This analysis is applicable to the division of labor and specialization within households and families because the production of children, many aspects of child care and investments in children, protection against certain risks, altruism, and other "commodities" are more efficiently produced and consumed within households than by trades among households (see Becker [1981] for a further discussion). Most societies in all parts of the world have had a substantial division of labor, especially by age and sex, in the activities of household members. Although the participation of women in agriculture, trade, and other nonhousehold activities varies greatly throughout different parts of the world, women are responsible for the lion's share of housework, especially child care and food preparation, in essentially all societies. Moreover, even when they participate in market activities, women tend to engage in different

[1] This proposition essentially combines theorems 2.2, 2.3, and 2.4 in Becker (1981, chap. 2).

activities than men do (see Boserup [1970] for evidence from less developed countries that supports these statements).

The advantages of investments in specific human capital encourage a sharp division of labor among household members but do not in and of themselves say anything about the *sexual* division of labor. I suggested in my book on the family that men and women have intrinsically different comparative advantages not only in the production of children, but also in their contribution to child care and possibly to other activities (Becker 1981, pp. 21–25). Such intrinsic differences in productivity would determine the direction of the sexual division by tasks and hence sexual differences in the accumulation of specific human capital that reinforce the intrinsic differences.

Some have objected to the presumption that intrinsic differences in comparative advantage are an important cause of the sexual division of labor, and have argued instead that the sexual division is mainly due to the "exploitation" of women. Yet a sexual division of labor according to intrinsic advantage does not deny exploitation. If men have full power both to determine the division of labor and to take all household output above a "subsistence" amount given to women (a competitive marriage market would divide output more equally), men would impose an efficient division of labor because that would maximize household output, and hence their own "take." In particular, they would assign women to child care and other housework *only if* women have a comparative advantage at such activities.[2]

This argument is suggestive but not conclusive because it assumes that sexual differences in comparative advantage are independent of the exploitation of women. Yet exploited women may have an "advantage" at unpleasant activities only because the monetary value of the disutility tends to be smaller for exploited (and poorer) persons, or because exploited persons are not allowed to participate in activities that undermine their exploitation.[3]

No definitive judgment has to be made for the analysis in this paper (and in my book on the family), because it does not depend on the *source* of the comparative advantage of women at household activities, be it discrimination or other factors. It only requires that investments in specific human capital reinforce the effects of comparative advantage. Indeed, the analysis does not even require that the initial difference in comparative advantage between men and women be large: a small initial

[2] Presumably, the advantages to slaveowners of an efficient division of labor explain why slaves have sometimes been assigned to highly skilled activities (see Finley 1980).

[3] However, Guity Nashat pointed out to me that even slaves sometimes had major military responsibilities (see, e.g., Inalcik [1970] for a discussion of the Janissaries).

difference can be transformed into large observed differences by the reinforcing effects of specialized investments.

This conclusion is highly relevant to empirical decompositions of earnings differentials between men and women. Suppose, for example, that men and women have the same basic productivity, but that discrimination reduces the earnings of women 10% below their market productivity. Given the advantage of specialization, such discrimination would induce a sexual division of labor, with most women specialized to the household and most men specialized to the market. As a result, earnings of the average woman would be considerably less than those of the average man, say only 60%. A decomposition of the 40% differential would show that sexual differences in investments in human capital explain 30 percentage points, or 75%, and that only 25% remains to be explained by discrimination. Yet in this example, the average earnings of men and women would be equal without discrimination, because there would be no sexual division of labor. More generally, discrimination and other causes of sexual differences in basic comparative advantage can be said to explain the *entire* difference in earnings between men and women, even though differences in human capital may appear to explain most of it.

This magnification of small differences in comparative advantage into large differences in earnings distinguishes differences between men and women from those between blacks and whites or other groups. A little market discrimination against blacks would not induce a large reduction in their earnings, because there is no racial division of labor between the market and household sectors. (However, even slightly greater market discrimination against black men compared with black women could be magnified into much larger reduction in the earnings of black men than black women, because black women would be induced to spend more time in the labor force than white women, and black men would spend less time than white men.) Consequently, the empirical decomposition of earnings differences into discrimination and other sources should be interpreted more cautiously for men and women than for other groups because of the division of labor between men and women.

III. The Allocation of Effort

The huge increase in the labor force participation of married women in developed countries should have encouraged much greater investment by women in market capital, which, presumably, would raise their earnings relative to men's. Yet sexual differences in earnings are very large (perhaps 40%) in the Soviet Union, where women participate almost as much as men (see Ofer and Vinokur 1981), and they have not declined much in the United States. The persistence of these large differences may be evidence of substantial market discrimination against women

Division of Labor   S43

(see the evidence for Great Britain in Zabalza and Tzannatos [1983]) or of a countervailing temporary depression in the earnings of women due to the entrance of many women with little market experience (see Mincer 1983; O'Neill 1985; Smith and Ward 1985).

An additional factor is the continuing responsibility of women for housework. For example, married women in the Soviet Union have responsibility for most of the child care and other housework even though they participate in the labor force almost as much as married men, and Ofer and Vinokur (1981) argue that the earnings of married Soviet women are much lower than the earnings of married men in good part because of these responsibilities. O'Neill (1983) has a similar argument regarding the lower earnings and segregated occupations of married women in the United States. Time budget studies clearly show that women have remained responsible for a large fraction of the child care and other housework even in advanced countries (see, e.g., Gronau [1976] for Israel, Stafford [1980] for the United States, and Flood [1983] for Sweden).

The earnings of women are adversely affected by household responsibilities even when they want to participate in the labor force as many hours as men, because they become tired, must stay home to tend to sick children or other emergencies, and are less able to work odd hours or take jobs requiring much travel. Although many effects of these responsibilities on the earnings and occupations of women have been frequently recognized, apparently the only systematic analysis is in my unpublished paper (Becker 1977). A model of the allocation of energy (or effort) among various household and market activities is developed there, and many implications are obtained, including some relating to differences in earnings and the allocation of time between husbands and wives.

This section further develops that model, and shows how the allocation of energy is affected by the energy intensities of different activities, and also how its allocation interacts with the allocation of time and with investments in market and nonmarket human capital. The incentive to increase one's supply of energy is shown to depend positively on market human capital and other determinants of wage rates.

Firms buy a *package* of time and effort from each employee, with payment tied to the package rather than separate payments for units of time and effort. Earnings depend on the package according to

$$I = I(t_m, E_m) \tag{16}$$

with $\partial I/\partial E_m$ and $\partial I/\partial t_m > 0$, and $I(0, t_m) = I(E_m, 0) = 0$, where E_m is effort and t_m is time. By entering E_m explicitly, I am assuming that firms can monitor the effort supplied by each employee, perhaps indirectly (see, e.g., Mirrlees 1976; Shavell 1979). If firms were indifferent to the distribution of hours among identical workers, earnings would be proportional to hours worked for a given effort per hour:

$$I = w(e_m)t_m, \tag{17}$$

with $w' > 0$ and $w(0) = 0$, where $e_m = E_m/t_m$ is effort per hour. A simple function that incorporates these properties is

$$I = \alpha_m e_m^{\sigma_m} t_m = \alpha_m E_m^{\sigma_m} t_m^{1-\sigma_m} = \alpha_m t_m', \tag{18}$$

with $t_m' = e_m^{\sigma_m} t_m$, and $\alpha_m = \beta_m h_m$, where h_m is market human capital, and σ_m, the effort intensity of work, is assumed to be constant and measures the elasticity of earnings with respect to effort per hour.

Clearly, an increase in hours would raise earnings when total effort (E_m) is held constant only when $\sigma_m < 1$. However, $\sigma_m < 1$ implies that equal effort (e_m) is used with each hour, because increases in effort per hour then have diminishing effects on earnings. Equation (18) implies that earnings are proportional to an "effective" quantity of time (t_m') that depends on effort per hour as well as number of hours.

Each firm chooses σ_m and α_m to maximize its income, subject to production functions, competition from other firms, the methods used to monitor employees, and the effect of σ_m and α_m on the effort supplied by employees. An analysis of these decisions and of market equilibrium is contained in Becker (1977). Here I only indicate that the trade-off between α_m and σ_m depends on the cost to firms of monitoring effort (perhaps indirectly), and by the effect of these parameters on the effort supplied by employees.

Time and effort not supplied to firms are used in the household (or nonmarket) sector. Each household produces a set of commodities with market goods and services, time, and effort:

$$Z_i = Z_i(x_i, t_i, E_i), \qquad i = 1, \ldots, n. \tag{19}$$

If time and effort in the household sector also combine to produce "effective" time, the production function for Z_i can be written as

$$Z_i = Z_i(x_i, t_i'), \tag{20}$$

with $t_i' = w_i(e_i)t_i = \alpha_i e_i^{\sigma_i} t_i = \alpha_i E_i^{\sigma_i} t_i^{1-\sigma_i}$, with $0 < \sigma_i < 1$, and $\alpha_i = \beta_i h_i$, where h_i is human capital that raises the productivity of time spent on the ith commodity, and σ_i is the effort intensity of that commodity. The sum of the time spent on each commodity and the time spent at market activities must equal the total time available:

Division of Labor

$$\sum_{i=1}^{n} t_i + t_m = t_h + t_m = t, \tag{21}$$

where t_h is the total time spent in the household sector.

The total energy at the disposal of a person during any period can be altered by the production of energy and by reallocation of energy over the life cycle. I first assume a fixed supply of energy that must be allocated among activities during a single period:

$$\sum_{i=1}^{n} E_i + E_m = E, \tag{22}$$

where E is the fixed available supply. This equation can be written as

$$\sum_{i=1}^{n} e_i t_i + e_m t_m = \bar{e}t = E, \tag{23}$$

where $\bar{e}$ is the energy spent per each of the available hours. Since the decision variables, e_j and t_j, enter multiplicatively rather than linearly, the allocation of time directly "interacts" with the allocation of energy.

Total expenditures on market goods and services must equal money income:

$$\sum p_i x_i = w_m(e_m)t_m + v = I + v = Y, \tag{24}$$

where Y is money income and v is income from transfer payments, property, and other sources not directly related to earnings. Money income is affected not only by the time but also by the energy allocated to the market sector. Full income (S) is achieved when all time and energy is spent at work since earnings are assumed to be independent of the time and energy spent on commodities:

$$w_m(\bar{e})t + v = S. \tag{25}$$

Full income depends on four parameters: property income (v), the wage rate function (w_m), the available time (t), and the supply of energy per unit of time ($\bar{e}$).

Each household maximizes a utility function of commodities

$$U = U(Z_1, \ldots, Z_n), \tag{26}$$

subject to the full income constraint in equation (25) and to the production functions given by equation (20). The following first-order conditions are readily derived:

$$\frac{\partial U}{\partial x_i} = U_{x_i} = \tau p_{x_i}$$

$$\frac{\partial U}{\partial t_i'} w_i = U_{t_i} = \mu + \varepsilon e_i$$

$$\tau w_m = \mu + \varepsilon e_m \qquad (27)$$

$$\frac{\partial U}{\partial t_i'}\left[t_i \frac{dw_i}{de_i} \right] = U_{e_i} = \varepsilon t_i$$

$$\tau t_m \frac{dw_m}{de_m} = \varepsilon t_m,$$

where τ, μ, and ε are the marginal utilities of income, time, and effort, respectively.

The interpretation of these conditions is straightforward. The second and third indicate that the marginal utility of an additional hour spent at any activity must equal the sum of the opportunity cost of this hour in both time (μ) and effort (εe_i). An additional hour has an effort as well as a time cost because some effort is combined with each hour. The fourth and fifth conditions simply indicate that the marginal utility of effort per hour must equal the opportunity cost of effort (εt_j).

Each household selects the combination of goods and effective time that minimizes the cost of producing commodities. Effective time can be substituted for goods by reallocating either time or effort from work to commodities. Costs of production are minimized when the marginal rate of substitution between goods and effective time equals the cost of converting either time or effort into market goods.

On substituting the third into the second condition, one obtains

$$U_{t_i} = \tau\left[w_m - \frac{\varepsilon}{\tau}(e_m - e_i) \right] = \tau\hat{w}_i, \qquad (28)$$

where $\hat{w}_i$ is the shadow price or cost of an additional hour at the *i*th activity. Another expression for the marginal cost of time is obtained by combining the last two conditions, and using the relation between U_{t_i} and U_{t_i}:

$$U_{t_i} = \frac{\tau w_m' \cdot w_i}{w_i'} = \frac{\tau w_m(1 - \sigma_m)}{(1 - \sigma_i)} = \tau\hat{w}_i, \qquad (29)$$

where $w_j' = \partial w_j/\partial e_j$.

The marginal cost of time is below the wage rate for all activities with effort intensities less than the effort intensity of work because the saving

Division of Labor   S47

in energy from reallocating time away from work is also valued. Equation (28) shows that the marginal cost is the difference between the wage rate and the money value of the saving in (or expenditure on) energy: ε/τ is the value of an additional unit of energy, and $e_m - e_i$ is the saving in (or expenditure on) energy.

Consequently, the marginal cost of time would be least for commodities using the least energy per hour. Moreover, the marginal cost is not the same even for persons with the same wage rate, if the money value of energy and the saving in energy differ. Note also that the cost of time *exceeds* the wage rate for highly effort-intensive activities (e.g., the care of young children).

The second and fourth optimality conditions immediately imply that

$$e_i = \frac{\mu}{\varepsilon} \frac{\sigma_i}{1 - \sigma_i} \tag{30}$$

(I am indebted to John Muellbauer for pointing this out). The optimal amount of energy allocated to an hour of any activity is proportional to the marginal cost of time in terms of energy, and also is positively related to the effort intensity of the activity. The cost of time in terms of energy is a sufficient statistic for other variables, including effort intensities of other activities, investments in human capital, property income, and the allocation of time, because they can affect the energy allocation per hour of any activity only by affecting this statistic.

A remarkably simple relation for the ratio of the optimal allocation of energy to any two activities is immediately derived from (30), or from (29) and the fourth condition in (27):

$$\frac{e_j}{e_i} = \frac{\sigma_j(1 - \sigma_i)}{\sigma_i(1 - \sigma_j)}, \tag{31}$$

for all i, j, including m. The optimal ratio of energy per hour in any two activities depends only on their effort intensities, and will be constant as long as these intensities are constant, regardless of changes in other effort intensities, the utility function, the allocation of time, and so on.

The ratio of efforts per hour in equation (31) does not depend on utility, the allocation of time, and other variables, because it is a necessary condition to produce efficiently, that is, to be on the production possibility frontier between commodities in the utility function. A change in the effort intensity of an activity might change the absolute amount of energy per hour in all activities, but would not change the ratio between the energies per hour in any two other activities. The simple relations in equations (30) and (31) are of great use in determining the effects of different parameters on the allocation of energy.

A few things can be surmised about the ordering of effort intensities in different activities. Sleep is obviously closely dependent on time but not energy; indeed, sleep is more energy producing than energy using. Listening to the radio, reading a book, and many other leisure activities also depend on the input of time but less closely on energy. By contrast, many jobs and the care of small children use much energy. Available estimates of the value of time are usually much below wage rates, one-half or less, which suggests by equation (29) that the effort intensity of work greatly exceeds the intensities of many household activities.[4]

A change in property income, human capital, the allocation of time, or other variables that do not change effort intensities would change the effort per hour in all activities by the same positive or negative proportion, equal to the percentage change in the energy value of time (see eq. [30]). This proportionality, and constant energy ratios in different activities, is a theorem following from utility maximization (and other assumptions of our model) and should not be confused with the assumption of a constant effort per hour in each activity (an assumption made, for example, by Freudenberger and Cummins [1976]).

A decrease in hours worked and an increase in "leisure," induced perhaps by a rise in property income, would save on energy and raise the energy value of time, because work is more effort-intensive than leisure.[5] Then the energy spent on each hour of work and other activities would increase by the same proportion, which would raise hourly earnings and the productivity of each hour spent on other activities. Conversely, a compensated increase in market human capital that raised hours worked would reduce the energy value of time, and hence also the energy spent on each hour of work.

The effect of increased market human capital on wage rates, a major determinant of the return to investments in market capital, is positively related to the energy spent on each hour of work. Therefore, the incentive to invest in market capital is greater when the energy per hour

---

[4] However, practically all estimates of the value of time refer to time spent on transportation. Beesley's estimates for commuting time (1965) rise from about 30% of hourly earnings for lower-income persons to 50% for higher-income persons; similar results were obtained by Lisco (1967) and McFadden (1974). Becker (1965) estimates the time spent in commuting at about 40 percent of hourly earnings. Gronau (1970) concludes that business time during air travel is valued at about the hourly earnings of business travelers, while personal air travel time is apparently considered free.

[5] By equation (23), $e_m t_m + e_h t_h = E$, where $e_h = E_h/t_h$. If $e_h = \gamma e_m$, where $\gamma < 1$ because $\sigma_m > \sigma_h$, then

$$\frac{\partial e_m}{\partial t_m} = \frac{-e_m(1 - \gamma)}{\gamma t + t_m(1 - \gamma)} < 0.$$

as well as number of hours of work (see Sec. II) is greater,[6] since costs of investing in human capital are only partly dependent on wage rates. The same conclusion applies to investments in capital specific to any other activity.

Earnings in some jobs are highly responsive to changes in the input of energy, while earnings in others are more responsive to changes in the amount of time. That is, some have larger effort intensities, and others have larger time intensities. Persons devoting much time to effort-intensive household activities like child care would economize on their use of energy by seeking jobs that are not effort intensive, and conversely for persons who devote most of their household time to leisure and other time-intensive activities.

The stock of energy varies enormously from person to person, not only in dimensions like mental and physical energy,[7] but also in "ambition" and motivation. Although equation (30) implies that an increase in the stock of energy, and hence in the energy value of time, increases the energy per hour by the same percentage in all activities, the productivity of working time would increase by a larger percentage if work is more effort intensive than the typical household activity. Then persons with greater stocks of energy would excel at work not only

---

[6] These variables have opposite effects when hours of work change if work is more effort intensive than the competing household activities. Since

$$MP = \frac{\partial l}{\partial h_m} = w_m t_m,$$

then

$$\frac{\partial MP}{\partial t_m} = (1 + n_m \sigma_m) w_m,$$

where

$$n_m = \frac{\partial e_m}{\partial t_m} \frac{t_m}{e_m}.$$

Given that $0 < \sigma_m < 1$, and that $-1 \le n_m \le 1$, then $0 < \partial MP/\partial t_m$ and $(\partial MP/\partial t_m) \gtrless w_m$ as $n_m \gtrless 0$. A change in hours worked always changes the marginal product of human capital in the same direction (as argued in Sec. II), but the effect can be substantially attenuated if n_m is quite negative, because work is *much* more effort intensive than the competing household activities, and conversely, if n_m is positive, because work is less effort intensive than these activities.

[7] The inequality in energy is dramatically conveyed in the following preface to a biography of Gladstone: "Lord Kilbracken, who was once his principal private secretary, said that if a figure of 100 could represent the energy of an ordinary man, and 200 that of an exceptional man, Gladstone's energy would represent a figure of at least 1,000" (see Magnus 1954, p. xi). I owe this reference to George Stigler.

because their wage rates would be above average, but also because the productivity of their working time would be especially high.

If the (full) income effect of greater energy is weak,[8] persons with greater energy also tend to work longer hours and at more effort-intensive jobs because their time is relatively more productive at work than at household activities. Consequently, more energetic persons would both work longer hours and earn more per hour.

Since the elasticity of output with respect to energy per hour is less than unity ($\sigma_m < 1$), a given increase in the stock of energy would raise output by a smaller percentage if hours worked were unchanged. However, the induced increase in hours would raise output by more than the increase in the stock of energy. Several experimental studies do find that an increase in the consumption of calories by workers doing physically demanding work, where calories are an important source of "energy," apparently raises their output by a larger percent (see UN Food and Agriculture Organization 1962, pp. 14–15, 23–25).

Since a person's health affects his energy, ill health reduces hourly earnings (see the evidence in Grossman [1976]), because a lower energy level reduces the energy spent on each working (and household) hour. Ill health also reduces hours worked because work is relatively effort intensive; that is, sick time is spent at home rather than at work because rest and similar leisure activities use less energy than work. Therefore, more energetic persons can be said to work longer hours and earn more per hour partly because they are "healthier."

The energy available to a person changes not only because of illness and other exogenous forces, but also because of the expenditure of time, goods, and effort on exercise, sleep, physical check-ups, relaxation, proper diet, and other energy-producing activities. At the optimal rate of production, the cost of additional inputs equals the money value of additional energy:

---

[8] The sign of the income effect is ambiguous even when leisure is a superior good. The elasticity of working hours with respect to an increase in the stock of energy equals

$$\frac{\partial t_m}{\partial E} \frac{E}{t_m} = \eta_{t_m E} = R[x\delta_c(\sigma_m - \sigma_h) - \sigma_m(x - v)N_t + x\sigma_h N_x],$$

where t_h and x are the total time and goods used in the household ($p_x = 1$), N_t and N_x are the *full* income elasticities of t_h and x respectively, δ_c is the elasticity of substitution between x and t_h in the utility function, and R is positive. The substitution effect is essentially given by $x\delta_c(\sigma_m - \sigma_h) > 0$ if $\sigma_m > \sigma_h$. The income effect is given by $x\sigma_h N_x - \sigma_m(x - v)N_t \gtrless 0$. It is greater than zero if $(\sigma_h/\sigma_m) > k_c(N_t/N_x)$, where k_c is the share of earnings in money income. This footnote is based on notes by H. Gregg Lewis.

Division of Labor S51

$$\dot{w}'_m = \beta_m \sigma_m e_m^{\sigma_m - 1} h_m = \frac{\varepsilon}{\tau} = w'_m t_s \frac{de_s}{dE} + p_s \frac{dx_s}{dE} + w_m \frac{(1 - \sigma_m)}{1 - \sigma_s} \frac{dt_s}{dE}, \quad (32)$$

where e_s, x_s, and t_s are inputs into the production of energy.[9] The term on the right is the cost of inputs used to produce an additional unit of energy; the money value of an additional unit equals the effect on hourly earnings of an increase in energy per hour (see the last condition in [27]).

An increase in the marginal wage rate increases the optimal production of energy because marginal benefits increase relative to marginal costs. An increase in market human capital and a decrease in energy per hour of work (perhaps resulting from an increased number of working hours) both encourage the production of energy by raising benefits relative to cost of production; indeed, costs could decline when energy per hour decreased because the value of time would decrease. Increased production of energy would also improve health, given the positive relation between health and energy.

Many have argued that long hours of work substantially reduce productivity because of "fatigue."[10] This argument is questionable for differences among persons because more energetic persons work longer. Moreover, even if longer working hours by any given person directly reduce his energy (and productivity) per hour of work, longer hours also encourage his production of energy and of market human capital. Since more energy and market capital raise the productivity of each working hour, longer hours could even indirectly *raise* his productivity per hour.

The incentive to invest in energy varies over the life cycle as the stock of market human capital and other determinants of the value of energy vary. Therefore, hourly earnings rise at younger ages probably partly because of increased production of energy, and conversely for declines in earnings at older ages. The stock of energy at a particular age might also be augmentable by "borrowing" from other ages, perhaps with substantial penalty or interest. In extreme forms, borrowing and repayment of energy produce "overwork" and "burn-out."[11]

[9] I assume that inputs are devoted exclusively to the production of energy, but the analysis is readily extended to "joint production," where, say, a good diet produces both energy and commodities.

[10] In his classic study of the sources of economic growth in the United States, Denison (1962) assumed that each hour of work beyond 43 hours per week reduces productivity by at least 30%.

[11] Bertrand Russell claims that he worked so hard on *Principia Mathematica* that "my intellect never quite recovered from the strain" (1967, p. 230).

IV. Division of Labor in the Allocation of Effort between Husbands and Wives

Since more energetic persons have a comparative advantage at effort-intensive activities, efficient marriage markets match more energetic with less energetic persons (i.e., negative sorting by energy). A larger fraction of the time of energetic spouses would be allocated to effort-intensive activities like work where they have a comparative advantage, and a larger fraction of the time of sluggish spouses would be allocated to the household activities where they have a comparative advantage.

The evidence is much too scanty to argue that a division of labor by energy level helps explain the division of labor between married men and women. Therefore, I assume that women have responsibility for child care and other housework for reasons unrelated to their energy or to the effort intensity of housework. Nevertheless, differences in effort intensities have important implications for sexual differences in earnings, hours worked, and occupations.

To demonstrate this, I follow the brief discussion in the previous section suggesting that housework activities like child care are much more effort intensive than leisure-oriented activities and may be more or less effort intensive than market activities. Married women with primary responsibility for child care and other housework allocate less energy to each hour of work than married men who spend equal time in the labor force. A simple proof uses the assumption that housework is more effort intensive than leisure, and the implication of equation (31) that the ratio of the energy spent on each hour of any two activities depends only on the effort intensities of these activities.[12]

Since married women earn less per hour than married men when they spend less energy on each hour of work, the household responsibilities of married women reduce their hourly earnings below those of married men even when both participate the same number of hours and have the same market capital. These household responsibilities also induce occupational segregation because married women seek occupations and jobs that are less effort intensive and otherwise are more compatible with the demands of their home responsibilities. The same argument explains why students who attend class and do homework have lower hourly earnings than persons not in school when both work the same

---

[12] By equation (31), $e_c = \gamma_1 e_m$ and $e_\ell = \gamma_2 e_m$, where $\gamma_1 > \gamma_2$ because $\sigma_c > \sigma_e$, where c refers to housework and ℓ to leisure. Since $e_m t_m + e_c t_c + e_\ell t_\ell = E$, then $e_m(t_m + \gamma_1 t_c + \gamma_2 t_\ell) = E$, and

$$\left. \frac{de_m}{dt_c} \right|_{dt_m = 0} = \frac{-e_m(\gamma_1 - \gamma_2)}{t_m + \gamma_1 t_c + \gamma_2 t_\ell} < 0.$$

number of hours and appear to have similar characteristics (see the evidence and discussion in Lazear [1977]).

Therefore, the traditional concentration on the labor force participation of women gives a misleading, perhaps a highly misleading, impression of the forces reducing the earnings and segregating the employment of married women. Nor is this all. Married women would invest less in market human capital than married men even when both spend the same amount of time in the labor force. Since the benefit from investment in market human capital is positively related to hourly earnings and hence to the energy spent on each hour of market work (see the previous section), the benefit is greater to married men even when they do not work longer hours than married women.

The lower earnings of married women due both to their lower energy spent on work and their lower investment in market human capital discourages their labor force participation relative to that of their husbands. Of course, their lower participation further discourages their investment in market capital (but see n. 6), and could even lower their energy spent on each hour of work if they substitute toward housework that is more effort-intensive than their market activities. A full equilibrium could involve complete specialization by wives in housework and other nonmarket activities.

Table 1 (brought to my attention by June O'Neill) shows that even married women employed full-time in the United States work much

Table 1
Time Use of Married Men and Married Women in the United States by Hours per Week at Home and at Market Work, 1975–76

Type of Activity	Married Women			Married Men	
	Employed Full Time	Employed Part Time	All*	Employed Full Time	All†
Market work:	38.6	20.9	16.3	47.9	39.2
At job‡	35.7	18.9	15.0	44.0	36.0
Travel to/from job	2.9	2.0	1.3	3.9	3.2
Work at home:	24.6	33.5	34.9	12.1	12.8
Indoor housework	14.6	21.0	20.8	2.8	3.5
Child care	2.8	3.2	4.9	1.7	1.5
Repairs, outside work, gardening	1.6	1.7	2.2	3.8	3.9
Shopping, services	5.6	7.6	7.0	3.8	3.9
Leisure	21.0	25.5	26.7	23.0	27.1
Total work time	63.2	54.4	51.2	60.0	52.0
Sample size	101	51	220	236	307

SOURCE.—Hill (1981), based on data from a national sample of U.S. households collected by the Survey Research Center of the University of Michigan.
* Includes married women with no market work.
† Includes married men with part-time work and no market work.
‡ Includes lunch and coffee breaks.

more at home than do unemployed or part-time employed married men, let alone full-time employed married men. Moreover, married women employed full-time work many fewer hours (about 9 hours per week) in the market than do married men employed full-time, although total hours worked are a little higher for these women. There is considerable other evidence that the occupations and earnings of women are also affected by their demand for part-time employment and flexible hours (see Mincer and Polachek 1974, table 7; O'Neill 1983).

This analysis implies that the hourly earnings of single women exceed those of married women even when both work the same number of hours and have the same market capital because child care and other household responsibilities induce married women to seek more convenient and less energy-intensive jobs. The analysis also can explain why marriage appears to raise the health of men substantially and women's health only moderately (see Fuchs 1975). Since married men accumulate more market human capital and work longer hours than single men (see Kenny 1983), married men produce larger stocks of energy than single men, which improves their health. The effect of marriage on the energy of women is more ambiguous: the value of energy to women not working in the market is measured by the value of additional energy in the household, which can be sizable. However, the value of energy to working women is measured by its value at work, which has been below the value to men because women have invested less in market human capital and have chosen less energy-intensive work.

The large growth in the labor force participation of married women during the last 30 years has been accompanied by a steep fall in fertility and a sharp rise in divorce rates. The fall in fertility clearly raises the hourly earnings of married women because they have more energy and more flexible time to devote to market work instead of child care. The time spent in housework by married women in the United States apparently did decline significantly after 1965 (see Stafford 1980).

The effect of the growth in divorce on the hourly earnings of women is more ambiguous. On the one hand, married women invest more in market human capital when they anticipate working because they are likely to become divorced. On the other hand, since divorced women in the United States and other Western countries almost always retain custody of their children, the demands of child care on their energy and attention might exceed those of married women, for they have no husbands to share any of the housework.[13]

---

[13] Dustin Hoffman lost his job in *Kramer vs. Kramer* after he became responsible for the care of his child.

V. Summary and Concluding Remarks

This paper argues that increasing returns from specialized human capital is a powerful force creating a division of labor in the allocation of time and investments in human capital even among basically identical persons. However, increasing returns alone do not imply the traditional sexual division of labor, with women having primary responsibility for many household activities, unless men and women tend to differ in their comparative advantages between household and market activities. Whatever the reason for the traditional division—perhaps discrimination against women or high fertility—housework responsibilities lower the earnings and affect the jobs of married women by reducing their time in the labor force and discouraging their investment in market human capital.

This paper also develops a model of an individual's allocation of energy among different activities. More energy is spent on each hour of more energy-intensive activities, and the ratio of the energy per hour in any two activities depends only on their effort intensities and not at all on the stock of energy, utility function, money income, allocation of time, or human capital. Other implications are derived about the cost of time to different activities, the effect of hours worked on hourly earnings, the effect of earnings on investment in health, and the effect of an increase in the energy spent on each hour of work on the benefits from investment in market human capital.

Since housework is more effort intensive than leisure and other household activities, married women spend less energy on each hour of market work than married men working the same number of hours. As a result, married women have lower hourly earnings than married men with the same market human capital, and they economize on the energy expended on market work by seeking less demanding jobs. Moreover, their lower hourly earnings reduce their investment in market capital even when they work the same number of hours as married men.

Therefore, the responsibility of married women for child care and other housework has major implications for earnings and occupational differences between men and women even aside from the effect on the labor force participation of married women. I submit that this is an important reason why the earnings of married women are typically considerably below those of married men, and why substantial occupational segregation persists, even in countries like the Soviet Union where labor force participation rates of married men and women are not very different.

The persistence of these responsibilities in all advanced societies may only be a legacy of powerful forces from the past and may disappear or be greatly attenuated in the near future. Not only casual impressions, but also evidence from time-budgets indicate that the *relative* contribution of married men to housework in the United States has significantly increased during the last decade (Stafford 1980; personal communication from Stafford about a 1981 survey). The frequency of partial or complete custody of children by divorced fathers has also increased. A continuation of these trends would increase the energy and time spent at market activities by women, which would raise their earnings and incentive to invest in market human capital. The result could be a sizable increase in the relative earnings of married women and a sizable decline in their occupational segregation during the remainder of this century.

Even if the process continued until married women no longer had primary responsibility for child care and other housework, married households would still greatly gain from a division of labor in the allocation of time and investments if specialized household and market human capital remained important, or if spouses differed in energy. This division of labor, however, would no longer be linked to sex: husbands would be more specialized to housework and wives to market activities in about half the marriages, and the reverse would occur in the other half.

Such a development would have major consequences for marriage, fertility, divorce, and many other aspects of family life. Yet the effect on the inequality in either individual or family earnings would be more modest since all persons specialized to housework would still earn less than their spouses, and the distribution of family earnings would still be determined by the division of labor between spouses, by the sorting of spouses by education and other characteristics, by divorce rates and the custody of children, and so forth.

However, a person's sex would then no longer be a good predictor of earnings and household activities. It is still too early to tell how far Western societies will move in this direction.

References

Becker, Gary S. *Human Capital.* New York: Columbia University Press (for NBER), 1964.
———. "A Theory of the Allocation of Time." *Economic Journal* 75 (1965): 493–517.
———. "A Theory of the Production and Allocation of Effort." NBER Working Paper no. 184. Cambridge, Mass.: NBER, 1977.
———. *A Treatise on the Family.* Cambridge, Mass: Harvard University Press, 1981.
Becker, G. S.; Landes, E. M.; and Michael, R. T. "An Economic Analysis of Marital Instability." *Journal of Political Economy* 85 (1977): 1141–87.

Beesley, M. E. "The Value of Time Spent in Travelling: Some New Evidence." *Economica* 32 (1965): 174–85.

Boserup, Ester. *Women's Role in Economic Development.* London: Allen & Unwin, 1970.

Denison, E. *Sources of Economic Growth in the United States.* Washington, D.C.: Committee for Economic Development, 1962.

Finley, M. I. *Ancient Slavery and Modern Ideology.* New York: Viking, 1980.

Flood, L. "Time Allocation to Market and Non-Market Activities in Swedish Households." Department of Statistics Research Report. Göteborg: University of Göteborg, 1983.

Freudenberger, H., and Cummins, G. "Health, Work, and Leisure before the Industrial Revolution." *Explorations in Economic History* 13 (1976): 1–12.

Fuchs, V. R. *Who Shall Live?* New York: Basic, 1975.

Gregory, R.; McMahon, P.; and Whittingham, B. "Women in the Labor Force: Trends, Causes, and Consequences" (1985), in this issue.

Gronau, R. "The Effect of Traveling Time on the Demand for Passenger Transportation." *Journal of Political Economy* 78 (1970): 377–94.

———. "The Allocation of Time of Israeli Women." *Journal of Political Economy* 84 (1976): S201–S220.

Gros, D. "Increasing Returns and Human Capital in International Trade." Thesis seminar paper. Chicago: University of Chicago, Department of Economics, 1983.

Grossman, M. "The Correlation between Health and Schooling." In *Household Production and Consumption,* edited by N. E. Terleckyj. New York: Columbia University Press (for NBER), 1976.

Gustafsson, S., and Jacobsson, R. "Trends in Female Labor Force Participation in Sweden" (1985), in this issue.

Hill, M. S. "Patterns of Time Use." Mimeographed. Ann Arbor: University of Michigan, Survey Research Center, 1981.

Inalcik, H. "The Rise of the Ottoman Empire." In *The Cambridge History of Islam,* vol. 1, edited by P. M. Holt, A. K. S. Lambton, and B. Lewis. Cambridge: Cambridge University Press, 1970.

Kenny, L. W. "The Accumulation of Human Capital during Marriage by Males." *Economic Inquiry* 21 (1983): 223–31.

Lazear, E. P. "Schooling as a Wage Depressant." *Journal of Human Resources* 12 (1977): 164–76.

Lisco, T. E. "The Value of Commuters' Travel Time: A Study in Urban Transportation." Ph.D. dissertation, University of Chicago, 1967.

McFadden, D. "The Measurement of Urban Travel Demand." *Journal of Public Economics* 3 (1974): 303–28.

Magnus, P. *Gladstone.* London: Murray, 1954.

Mincer, J. "Comment on June O'Neill's 'The Trend in Sex Differential in Wages.'" Presented at the conference on Trends in Women's Work, Education and Family Formation, Sussex, England, May 31–June 3, 1983.

Mincer, J., and Polachek, S. "Family Investments in Human Capital: Earnings of Women." *Journal of Political Economy* 82 (1974): S76–S108.

Mirrlees, J. A. "The Optimal Structure of Incentives and Authority within an Organization." *Bell Journal of Economics* 7 (1976): 105–31.

Oaxaca, R. L. "Male-Female Wage Differentials in Urban Labor Markets." *International Economic Review* 14 (1973): 693–709.

Ofer, G., and Vinokur, A. "Earnings Differentials by Sex in the Soviet Union: A First Look." In *Economic Welfare and the Economics of Soviet Socialism,* edited by S. Rosefielde. Cambridge: Cambridge University Press, 1981.

O'Neill, J. "The Determinants and Wage Effects of Occupational Segregation." Working Paper. Washington, D.C.: Urban Institute, 1983.

———. "The Trend in the Male-Female Wage Gap in the United States" (1985), in this issue.

Rosen, S. "The Division of Labor and the Extent of the Market." Mimeographed. Chicago: University of Chicago, 1982.

Russell, B. *The Autobiography of Bertrand Russell, 1872–1914.* Boston: Little, Brown, 1967.

Shavell, S. "Risk Sharing and Incentives in the Principal and Agent Relationship." *Bell Journal of Economics* 10 (1979): 55–73.

Smith, J. P., and Ward, M. P. "Time-Series Growth in the Female Labor Force" (1985), in this issue.

Stafford, F. P. "Women's Use of Time Converging with Men's." *Monthly Labor Review* 103 (1980): 57–59.

UN Food and Agriculture Organization. *Nutrition and Working Efficiency.* FFHC Basic Study no. 5. Rome: UNFAO, 1962.

Zabalza, A., and Tzannatos, Z. "The Effects of Britain's Anti-discriminatory Legislation on Relative Pay and Employment." Discussion Paper no. 155. London: London School of Economics, 1983. (Forthcoming in *Economic Journal.*)

[10]

The Family as the Locus of Gender, Class, and Political Struggle: The Example of Housework

Selected Countries
D13
J16

Heidi I. Hartmann

Although the last decade of research on families has contributed enormously to our understanding of diversity in family structures and the relationship of family units to various other aspects of social life, it has, it seems to me, generally failed to identify and address sources of conflict within family life. Thus, the usefulness of this research for understanding women's situation has been particularly limited. The persistence and resilience of family forms in the midst of general social change, often forcefully documented in this research, have certainly helped to goad us, as feminists, to consider what women's interests may be in the mainte-

The first draft of this paper was presented at the Rockefeller Foundation Conference on Women, Work, and the Family (New York, September 21–22, 1978) organized by Catharine Stimpson and Tamara Hareven. Many people besides myself have labored over this paper. Among them are Rayna Rapp and Joan Burstyn. Jack Wells, Judy Stacey, Shelly Rosaldo, Evelyn Glenn, and my study group provided particularly careful readings; and Sam Bowles, Mead Cain, Steven Dubnoff, Andrew Kohlstad, Ann Markusen, Katie Stewart, and the staff of the National Academy of Sciences provided helpful comments and aid of various sorts. I thank all of them. The views presented here are my own and do not reflect the opinion of the National Academy of Sciences or the National Research Council.

EDITORS' NOTE: While fully conscious of current theories about the nature and consequences of relationship within the nuclear family, Heidi Hartmann challenges the analytical usefulness of the very concept "family." We should focus, she suggests, not on the family as a unit but on the working lives of individual family members and on the patriarchal and capitalist nature of the relationships that shape family life.

[*Signs: Journal of Women in Culture and Society* 1981, vol. 6, no. 3]
© 1981 by The University of Chicago. 0097-9740/81/0603-0005$01.00

nance of a type of family life that we have often viewed as a primary
source of women's oppression. Historical, anthropological, and
sociological studies of families have pointed to the many ways in which
women and men have acted in defense of the family unit, despite the
uneven responsibilities and rewards of the two sexes in family life. In
failing to focus sufficiently clearly on the differences between women's
and men's experiences and interests within families, however, these
studies overlook important aspects of social reality and potentially decisive sources of change in families and society as people struggle both
within and outside families to advance their own interests. This oversight
stems, I think, from a basic commitment shared by many conducting
these studies to a view of the family as a unified interest group and as an
agent of change in its own right.

Family historians, for example, have explored the role of the family
in amassing wealth; in contributing to population growth or decline; in
providing, recruiting, or failing to provide labor for a new industrial
system; in transmitting social values to new generations; and in providing or failing to provide enclaves from new and rude social orders. They
have consistently aimed to place the family in a larger social arena. The
diversity of findings and the range of their interpretation is great: the
size of the household has been constant before, during, and after industrialization (Peter Laslett); it has decreased as capitalism curtailed
household production (Eli Zaretsky); it has been flexible, depending on
the processes of rural-to-urban migration and wage levels in the new
industrial employments, and has often actually increased (Michael Anderson); industrialization liberated sexuality and women (Edward
Shorter); capitalism destroyed the extended family and created the nuclear (Eli Zaretsky); capitalist industrialization destroyed the nuclear
(Friedrich Engels); the nuclear family facilitated industrialization (William Goode); the family and industrialization were partners in modernization (Tamara Hareven).[1] Yet despite this diversity, the consistent

1. Peter Laslett and R. Wall, eds., *Household and Family in Past Time* (Cambridge:
Cambridge University Press, 1972); Michael Anderson, *Family Structure in Nineteenth-
Century Lancashire* (Cambridge: Cambridge University Press, 1971); Eli Zaretsky,
"Capitalism, the Family, and Personal Life," *Socialist Revolution*, no. 13–14 (January–April
1973), pp. 66–125; Friedrich Engels, *The Condition of the Working Class in England* (Stanford,
Calif.: Stanford University Press, 1958)—of course, Engels was only the first and most
prominent person who made this particular argument; Christopher Lasch, *Haven in a
Heartless World: The Family Besieged* (New York: Basic Books, 1977) is a later adherent;
William Goode, *World Revolution and Family Patterns* (Glencoe, Ill.: Free Press, 1963); Ta-
mara Hareven, "Family Time and Industrial Time: The Interaction between Family and
Work in a Planned Corporation Town, 1900–1924," *Journal of Urban History* 1 (May 1975):
365–89; Edward Shorter, *The Making of the Modern Family* (New York: Basic Books, 1975).
Michael Gordon, ed., *The American Family in Social-Historical Perspective*, 2d ed. (New York:
St. Martin's Press, 1978), provides a good introduction to family history.

focus of the new family history on the interconnection between family and society implies a definition of family. The family is generally seen as a social entity that is a source of dynamic change, an actor, an agent, on a par with such other "social forces" as economic change, modernization, or individualism.[2] Such a view assumes the unity of interests among family members; it stresses the role of the family as a unit and tends to downplay conflicts or differences of interest among family members.[3]

In this essay I suggest that the underlying concept of the family as an active agent with unified interests is erroneous, and I offer an alternative concept of the family as a locus of *struggle*. In my view, the family cannot be understood solely, or even primarily, as a unit shaped by affect or kinship, but must be seen as a *location* where production and redistribution take place. As such, it is a location where people with different activities and interests in these processes often come into conflict with one another. I do not wish to deny that families also encompass strong emotional ties, are extremely important in our psychic life, and establish ideological norms, but in developing a Marxist-feminist analysis of the family, I wish to identify and explore the material aspects of gender relations within family units.[4] Therefore, I concentrate on the nature of the work people do in the family and their control over the products of their labor.

In a Marxist-feminist view, the organization of production both within and outside the family is shaped by patriarchy and capitalism. Our present social structure rests upon an unequal division of labor by class and by gender which generates tension, conflict, and change. These underlying patriarchal and capitalist relations among people, rather than familial relations themselves, are the sources of dynamism in our society. The particular forms familial relations take largely reflect these underlying social forces. For example, the redistribution that occurs within the family between wage earners and non-wage earners is necessitated by the division of labor inherent in the patriarchal and capitalistic

2. Examples of the implicit definition can be found in the special issue of *Daedalus* (Spring 1977), later published as *The Family*, ed. Alice S. Rossi, Jerome Kagan, and Tamara K. Hareven (New York: W. W. Norton & Co., 1978).

3. See Joan Scott and Louise Tilly, "Women's Work and the Family in Nineteenth-Century Europe," *Comparative Studies in Society and History* 17, no. 1 (January 1975): 36–64; and Hareven, "Family Time."

4. In distinguishing between the household—the unit in which people actually live—and the family—the concept of the unit in which they think they should live—Rayna Rapp points to the contradictions that develop because of the juxtaposition of economic and ideological norms in the family/household ("Family and Class in Contemporary America: Notes toward an Understanding of Ideology," *Science and Society* 42 [Fall 1978]: 257–77). In addition, see Lila Leibowitz, *Females, Males, Families, a Biosocial Approach* (North Scituate, Mass.: Duxbury Press, 1978), esp. pp. 6–11, for a discussion of how the family defines ties among its members and to kin beyond it.

organization of production. In order to provide a schema for understanding the underlying economic structure of the family form prevalent in modern Western society—the heterosexual nuclear family living together in one household—I do not address in this essay the many real differences in the ways people of different periods, regions, races, or ethnic groups structure and experience family life. I limit my focus in order to emphasize the potential for differing rather than harmonious interests among family members, especially between women and men.

The first part of this essay explains the family's role as a location for production and redistribution and speculates about the interaction between the family and the state and about changes in family-state relations. The second part uses the example of housework to illustrate the differences in material interests among family members that are caused by their differing relations to patriarchy and capitalism. Since, as I argue, members of families frequently have different interests, it may be misleading to hold, as family historians often do, that "the family" as a unit resists or embraces capitalism, industrialization, or the state. Rather, people—men and/or women, adults and/or children—use familial forms in various ways. While they may use their "familial" connections or kin groups and their locations in families in any number of projects—to find jobs, to build labor unions, to wage community struggles, to buy houses, to borrow cars, or to share child care—they are not acting only as family members but also as members of gender categories with particular relations to the division of labor organized by capitalism and patriarchy.

Yet tensions between households and the world outside them have been documented by family historians and others, and these suggest that households do act as entities with unified interests, set in opposition to other entities. This seeming paradox comes about because, although family members have distinct interests arising out of their relations to production and redistribution, those same relations also ensure their mutual dependence. Both the wife who does not work for wages and the husband who does, for example, have a joint interest in the size of his paycheck, the efficiency of her cooking facilities, or the quality of their children's education. However, the same historical processes that created households in opposition to (but also in partnership with) the state also augmented the power of men in households, as they became their household heads, and exacerbated tensions within households.

Examples of tensions and conflicts that involve the family in struggle are presented in table 1. The family can be a locus of internal struggle over matters related to production or redistribution (housework and paychecks, respectively). It can also provide a basis for struggle by its members against larger institutions such as corporations or the state. Will cooking continue to be done at home or be taken over largely by fast-food chains? Will child care continue to be the responsibility of

Table 1

Conflicts Involving the Family

Sources of Conflict	Conflicts within the Household	Conflicts between Households and Larger Institutions
Production issues	*Housework:* Who does it? How? According to which standards? Should women work for wages outside the home or for men inside the home?	*Household production versus production organized by capital and the state:* Fast-food or home-cooked meals? Parent co-operative child care or state regulated child-care centers?
Redistribution issues ..	*Paycheck(s):* How should the money be spent? Who decides? Should the husband's paycheck be spent on luxuries for him or on household needs?	*Taxes:* Who will make the de-cisions about how to use the family's resources? Family members or representatives of the state apparatus?

parents or will it be provided by the state outside the home? Such questions signal tensions over the location of production. Tax protest, revolving as it does around the issue of who will make decisions for the family about the redistribution of its resources, can be viewed as an example of struggle between families and the state over redistribution. In this essay I intend to discuss only one source of conflict in any depth—housework—and merely touch upon some of the issues raised by tensions in other arenas. As with most typologies, the categories offered here are in reality not rigidly bounded or easily separable. Rather they represent different aspects of the same phenomena; production and redistribution are interrelated just as are struggles within and beyond households.[5]

Production, Redistribution, and the Household

Let me begin with a quote from Engels that has become deservedly familiar: "According to the materialistic conception, the determining factor in history is, in the final instance, the production and reproduction of immediate life. This, again, is of a twofold character: on the one side, the production of the means of existence, of food, clothing and

5. For another typology of struggle, see Gosta Esping-Anderson, Roger Friedland, and Erik Olin Wright, "Modes of Class Struggle and the Capitalist State," *Kapitalistate*, no. 4/5 (Summer 1976), pp. 186–220; and for a critique, see Capitol Kapitalistate Collective, "Typology and Class Struggle: Critical Notes on 'Modes of Class Struggle and the Capitalist State,'" *Kapitalistate*, no. 6 (Fall 1977), pp. 209–15.

Signs   *Spring 1981*   *371*

shelter and the tools necessary for that production; on the other side, the production of human beings themselves, the propagation of the species. The social organization under which the people of a particular historical epoch live is determined by both kinds of production."[6]

Engels and later Marxists failed to follow through on this dual project. The concept of production ought to encompass both the production of "things," or material needs, and the "production" of people or, more accurately, the production of people who have particular attributes, such as gender. The Marxist development of the concept of production, however, has focused primarily on the production of things. Gayle Rubin has vastly increased our understanding of how people are produced by identifying the "sex/gender system" as a "set of arrangements by which a society transforms biological sexuality into products of human activity, and in which these transformed sexual needs are satisfied."[7] This set of arrangements, which reproduces the species—and gender as well—is fundamentally social. The biological fact of sex differences is interpreted in many different ways by different groups; biology is always mediated by society.[8]

From an economic perspective, the creation of gender can be thought of as the creation of a division of labor between the sexes, the creation of two categories of workers who need each other.[9] In our society, the division of labor between the sexes involves men primarily in wage labor beyond the household and women primarily in production within the household; men and women, living together in households, pool their resources. The form of the family as we know it, with men in a more advantageous position than women in its hierarchy of gender relations, is simply one possible structuring of this human activity that creates gender; many other arrangements have been known.[10]

Although recent feminist psychoanalytic theory has emphasized the relations between children, mothers, and fathers in typical nuclear families, and the way these relations fundamentally shape personality along gender lines and perpetuate hierarchical gender relations, the pervasiveness of gender relations in all aspects of social life must be

6. Frederick Engels, *The Origin of the Family, Private Property and the State,* ed. with an introduction by Eleanor Leacock (New York: International Publishers, 1972), "Preface to the First Edition," pp. 71–72.

7. Gayle Rubin, "The Traffic in Women: Notes on the 'Political Economy' of Sex," in *Toward an Anthropology of Women,* ed. Rayna Rapp Reiter (New York: Monthly Review Press, 1975), p. 159.

8. The diverse ways in which sex differences are socially interpreted are well illustrated in both Rubin and Leibowitz.

9. See Claude Lévi-Strauss, "The Family," in *Man, Culture and Society,* ed. Harry L. Shapiro (New York: Oxford University Press, 1971).

10. Leibowitz provides examples of diverse household and family structures, especially in chaps. 4 and 5.

recognized.[11] In particular, the creation and perpetuation of hierarchical gender relations depends not only on family life but crucially on the organization of economic production, the production of the material needs of which Engels spoke. While a child's personality is partly shaped by who his or her mother is and her relations to others, her relations to others are products of all our social arrangements, not simply those evident within the household. Such arrangements are collectively generated and collectively maintained. "Dependence" is simultaneously a psychological and political-economic relationship. Male-dominated trade unions and professional associations, for example, have excluded women from skilled employment and reduced their opportunities to support themselves. The denial of abortions to women similarly reinforces women's dependence on men. In these and other ways, many of them similarly institutionalized, men as a group are able to maintain control of women's labor power and thus perpetuate their dominance. Their control of women's labor power is the lever that allows men to benefit from women's provision of personal and household services, including relief from child rearing and many unpleasant tasks both within and beyond households, and the arrangement of the nuclear family, based on monogamous and heterosexual marriage, is one institutional form that seems to enhance this control.[12] Patriarchy's material base is men's control of women's labor; both in the household and in the labor market, the division of labor by gender tends to benefit men.

In a capitalist system the production of material needs takes place largely outside households, in large-scale enterprises where the productive resources are owned by capitalists. Most people, having no productive resources of their own, have no alternative but to offer their labor power in exchange for wages. Capitalists appropriate the surplus value the workers create above and beyond the value of their wages. One of the fundamental dynamics in our society is that which flows from this production process: wage earners seek to retain as much control as possible over both the conditions and products of their labor, and capitalists, driven by competition and the needs of the accumulation process, seek to wrest control away from the workers in order to increase the amount of surplus value.[13] With the wages they receive, people buy the com-

11. In addition to Rubin, see Nancy Chodorow, *The Reproduction of Mothering: Psychoanalysis and the Sociology of Gender* (Berkeley and Los Angeles: University of California Press, 1978); Dorothy Dinnerstein, *The Mermaid and the Minotaur: Sexual Arrangements and Human Malaise* (New York: Harper Colophon Books, 1977); and Jane Flax, "The Conflict between Nurturance and Autonomy in Mother-Daughter Relationships and within Feminism," *Feminist Studies* 4, no. 2 (June 1978): 171–89.

12. Heidi I. Hartmann, "The Unhappy Marriage of Marxism and Feminism: Towards a More Progressive Union," *Capital and Class* 8 (Summer 1979): 1–33. See also extensions and critiques in Lydia Sargent, ed., *Women and Revolution* (Boston: South End Press, in press).

13. See Harry Braverman, *Labor and Monopoly Capital: The Degradation of Work in the*

modities that they need for their survival. Once in the home these commodities are then transformed to become usable in producing and reproducing people. In our society, which is organized by patriarchy as
well as by capitalism, the sexual division of labor by gender makes men
primarily responsible for wage labor and women primarily responsible
for household production. That portion of household production called
housework consists largely in purchasing commodities and transforming
them into usable forms. Sheets, for example, must be bought, put on
beds, rearranged after every sleep, and washed, just as food must be
bought, cleaned, cooked, and served to become a meal. Household production also encompasses the biological reproduction of people and the
shaping of their gender, as well as their maintenance through housework. In the labor process of producing and reproducing people,
household production gives rise to another of the fundamental
dynamics of our society. The system of production in which we live
cannot be understood without reference to the production and reproduction both of commodities—whether in factories, service centers,
or offices—and of people, in households. Although neither type of production can be self-reproducing, together they create and recreate our
existence.[14]

This patriarchal and capitalist arrangement of production necessi-
tates a means of redistribution. Because of the class and gender division
of labor not everyone has direct access to the economic means of survival. A schematic view of the development of capitalism in Western
societies suggests that capitalism generally took root in societies where
production and redistribution had taken place largely in households and
villages; even though capitalism shifted much production beyond the
household, it did not destroy all the traditional ways in which production
and redistribution were organized. In preindustrial households, people
not only carried on production but also shared their output among
themselves (after external obligations such as feudal dues were met),
according to established patriarchal relations of authority. In the period
of capitalist primitive accumulation, capitalists had to alienate the productive resources that people previously attached to the land had controlled in order to establish the capitalist mode of production based on
"free" wage labor. Laborers became "free" to work for capitalists because
they had no other means of subsistence and therefore required wages to
buy from the capitalists what they had formerly produced in households
and villages and exchanged with each other.

With the development of the capitalist mode of production, the old,
the young, and women of childbearing age participated less in economic

Twentieth Century (New York: Monthly Review Press, 1974), as well as Karl Marx, *Capital*
(New York: International Publishers, 1967), vol. 1.

14. See Susan Himmelweit and Simon Mohun, "Domestic Labour and Capital," *Cambridge Journal of Economics* 1, no. 1 (March 1977): 15–31.

production and became dependent on the wage earners, increasingly adult men. People continued to live in households, however, to reproduce the species and to redistribute resources. Households became primarily income-pooling units rather than income-producing units.[15] The previously established patriarchal division of labor, in which men benefited from women's labor, was perpetuated in a capitalist setting where men became primarily wage laborers but retained the personal services of their wives, as women became primarily "housewives."[16] The interdependence of men and women that arises out of the division of labor by gender was also maintained. The need for the household in capitalism to be an income-pooling unit, a place where redistribution occurs between men and women, arises fundamentally from the patriarchal division of labor. Yet it is income pooling that enables the household to be perceived as a unit with unitary interests, despite the very different relationships to production of its separate members. Because of the division of labor among family members, disunity is thus inherent in the "unity" of the family.

Recent, often speculative, anthropological and historical research, by focusing on the development of households and their role in political arenas, has contributed to my understanding of the family as an embodiment of both unity and disunity. Briefly, this research suggests that women's status has declined as political institutions have been elaborated into state apparata, although the mechanisms that connect these two phenomena are not well understood.[17] One possible connection is that the process of state formation enhanced the power of men as they became heads of "their" households. The state's interest in promoting households as political units stemmed from its need to undermine prior political apparata based on kinship. In prestate societies, kinship groups

15. See Heidi Hartmann and Ellen Ross, "The Origins of Modern Marriage" (paper delivered at the Scholar and the Feminist Conference, III, Barnard College, April 10, 1976). Batya Weinbaum, "Women in Transition to Socialism: Perspectives on the Chinese Case," *Review of Radical Political Economics* 8, no. 1 (Spring 1976): 34–58, shows that the family is also an income-pooling unit in China under socialism.

16. See Heidi Hartmann, "Capitalism, Patriarchy, and Job Segregation by Sex," *Signs: Journal of Women in Culture and Society* 1, no. 3, pt. 2 (Spring 1976): 137–69, for how this came about.

17. See Rayna Rapp, "Gender and Class: An Archaeology of Knowledge concerning the Origin of the State," *Dialectical Anthropology* 2 (December 1977): 309–16; Christine Gailey, "Gender Hierarchy and Class Formation: The Origins of the State in Tonga," unpublished paper (New York: New School for Social Research, 1979); Ruby Rohrlich, "Women in Transition: Crete and Sumer," in *Becoming Visible: Women in European History,* ed. Renate Bridenthal and Claudia Koonz (Boston: Houghton Mifflin Co., 1977); Ruby Rohrlich, "State Formation in Sumer and the Subjugation of Women," *Feminist Studies* 6 (Spring 1980): 76–102; and a symposium in *Feminist Studies,* vol. 4 (October 1978), including Anne Barstow, "The Uses of Archaeology for Women's History: James Mellart's Work on the Neolithic Goddess at Çatal Hüyük," pp. 7–18; Sherry B. Orther, "The Virgin and the State," pp. 19–36; and Irene Silverblatt, "Andean Women in the Inca Empire," pp. 37–61.

made fundamental political and economic decisions—how to share resources to provide for everyone's welfare, how to redistribute land
periodically, how to settle disputes, how to build new settlements. States
gradually absorbed these functions.

For instance, in the process of state formation that took place in
England and Wales roughly between the eighth and fifteenth centuries,
Viana Muller suggests, emerging rulers attempted to consolidate their
power against kin groups by winning the allegiance of men away from
their kin. One means of doing this may have been allowing men to usurp
some of the kin group's authority, particularly over land and women and
children.[18] In this view, the household, with its male head, can be seen to
be a "creation" of the state. George Duby reports that by 1250 the
household was everywhere the basis of taxation in Western society.[19]
Lawrence Stone argues that the state's interests were served by an authoritarian household structure, for it was generally believed that deference shown to the head of household would be transferred to the king:
"The power of kings and of heads of households grew in parallel with
one another in the sixteenth century. The state was as supportive of the
patriarchal nuclear family as it was hostile to the kin-oriented family; the
one was a buttress and the other a threat to its own increasing power."[20]

As Elizabeth Fox-Genovese points out, the authoritarianism of the
new nation-state was incompatible with developing capitalism, and
Locke's concept of authority as derivative from the individual helped to
establish a new legitimating ideology for the state: it serves with the
consent of the propertied individuals. To put forward his theory with
logical coherence, Locke had to assert the authority of all individuals,
including women and children. But by removing the family from the
political sphere, ideologically at least, later theorists solved the contradiction between the elevation of women to the status of individuals
and the maintenance of patriarchal authority. The family became private, of no moment in conducting the politics of social interchange, and

18. Viana Muller, "The Formation of the State and the Oppression of Women: Some
Theoretical Considerations and a Case Study in England and Wales," *Review of Radical
Political Economics* 9 (Fall 1977): 7–21. Muller bases her account on the work of Tacitus,
Bede, Seebohm, Phillpotts, F. M. Stenton, Whitelock, Homans, and McNamara and Wem-
ple.

19. Georges Duby, "Peasants and the Agricultural Revolution," in *The Other Side of
Western Civilization,* ed. Stanley Chodorow (New York: Harcourt Brace Jovanovich, 1979),
p. 90, reprinted from *Rural Economy and Country Life in the Medieval West,* trans. Cynthia
Poston (Columbia: University of South Carolina Press, 1968).

20. Lawrence Stone, "The Rise of the Nuclear Family in Early Modern England: The
Patriarchal Stage," in *The Family in History,* ed. Charles E. Rosenberg (Philadelphia: University of Pennsylvania Press, 1975), p. 55. Also see Ellen Ross, "Women and Family," in
"Examining Family History," by Rayna Rapp, Ellen Ross, and Renate Bridenthal, *Feminist
Studies* 5, no. 1 (Spring 1979): 174–200, who discusses the transition from kin to nuclear
family in more detail than I do here and offers a number of useful criticisms of family
history.

the head of the family came to represent its interests in the world.[21] The ideology of individualism, by increasing the political importance of men beyond their households, strengthened patriarchy at home; it completed the legitimation of male public power begun during the process of state elaboration.

Yet even as the household, and particularly the man within it, became in this view an agent of the state against collectivities organized by kinship, the household also remained the last repository of kin ties. Even the nuclear household continues to tie its members to others through the processes of marriage, childbirth, and the establishment of kinship. These ties to others beyond the household (though much more limited than in the past) coupled with the interdependence of household members stemming from their different relations to production continue to give members of households a basis for common interests vis-à-vis the state or other outside forces. Household members continue to make decisions about pooling incomes, caring for dependent members, engaging in wage work, and having children, but it is important to remember that within the household as well as outside it men have more power. Therefore, viewing the household as a unit which jointly chooses, for example, to deploy its available labor power to maximize the interests of *all* its members (the implicit approach of those historians who discuss family strategies and adaptations and the explicit approach of others) obscures the reality of both the capitalist and patriarchal relations of production in which households are enmeshed.[22] Mutual dependence by no means precludes the possibility of coercion. Women and men are no less mutually dependent in the household than are workers and capitalists or slaves and slaveowners. In environments that are fundamentally coercive (such as patriarchy and capitalism) concepts of choice and adaptation are inevitably flawed—as is the belief that workers and capitalists or men and women have unified interests. This is not to say that such unity can *never* exist.

Housework

Some observers have argued that the family is no longer a place where men exercise their power. If patriarchy exists at all for them, it

21. Elizabeth Fox-Genovese, "Property and Patriarchy in Classical Bourgeois Political Theory," *Radical History Review* 4 (Spring/Summer 1977): 36–59. See also Robert A. Nisbet, *The Sociological Tradition* (New York: Basic Books, 1966).

22. Scott and Tilly (n. 3 above) and Hareven (n. 1 above) use the concepts of choice and adaptation. Louise Tilly, "Individual Lives and Family Strategies in the French Proletariat," *Journal of Family History* 4, no. 2 (Summer 1979): 137–52, employs the concept of family strategies but incorporates an understanding of potential intrafamily conflict. Jane Humphries, "The Working Class Family, Women's Liberation, and Class Struggle: The Case of Nineteenth Century British History," *Review of Radical Political Economics* 9, no. 3 (Fall 1977): 25–41, makes explicit use of the concept of family unity.

does so only on impersonal, institutional levels. For some analysts working in the Marxist traditions, the inexorable progress of capitalism has eliminated patriarchy within the family and has even given rise to the women's movement, because it weakened patriarchal power just enough to enable women to confront it directly.[23] I wish to argue, however, that, although capitalism has somewhat shifted the locus of control, the family nevertheless remains a primary arena where men exercise their patriarchal power over women's labor. In this section, I review some of the empirical findings on time spent on housework by husbands and wives to support this proposition. I believe that time spent on housework, as well as other indicators of household labor, can be fruitfully used as a measure of power relations in the home.

Who Does How Much Housework?

In recent years a number of time-budget studies have measured time spent on housework, as well as other activities such as paid work and leisure. Such studies generally involve having respondents record their activities for specified time intervals (for example, fifteen minutes) for one or two days. The most comprehensively analyzed data on time spent doing housework in the United States are those collected in 1967 and 1968 by Kathryn Walker and Margaret Woods for 1,296 husband-and-wife families in Syracuse, New York.[24] Time diaries were also collected for a representative sample of families in five U.S. cities in 1965 and 1966 as part of the Multinational Comparative Time-Budget Research Project.[25] The University of Michigan Survey Research Center has collected data for representative national samples of families and individuals for 1965–66 and for 1975.[26] Subsequently, a number of

23. Stewart Ewen, *Captains of Consciousness* (New York: McGraw-Hill Book Co., 1976), and Barbara Ehrenreich and Deirdre English, *For Her Own Good: 150 Years of the Experts' Advice to Women* (New York: Anchor Press, 1978), argue that patriarchal control is now exercised by the corporation or the experts, rather than the small guy out there, one to a household. The trenchant review of the weakness of family history by Wini Breines, Margaret Cerullo, and Judith Stacey, "Social Biology, Family Studies and Anti-feminist Backlash," *Feminist Studies* 4, no. 1 (February 1978): 43–67, also suggests that within the family male power over women is declining. Barbara Easton, "Feminism and the Contemporary Family," *Socialist Revolution*, no. 39 (May–June 1978), pp. 11–36, makes a similar argument, as do Linda Gordon and Allen Hunter, "Sex, Family and the New Right: Anti Feminism as a Political Force," *Radical America* 11, no. 6 and 12, no. 1 (November 1977– February 1978): 9–25.

24. Kathryn E. Walker and Margaret E. Woods, *Time Use: A Measure of Household Production of Family Goods and Services* (Washington, D.C.: American Home Economics Association, 1976).

25. Alexander Szalai, ed., *The Use of Time* (The Hague: Mouton, 1972).

26. James N. Morgan, "A Potpourri of New Data Gathered from Interviews with Husbands and Wives," in *Five Thousand American Families: Patterns of Economic Progress*, vol. 6, *Accounting for Race and Sex Differences in Earnings and Other Analyses of the First Nine Years of the Panel Study of Income Dynamics*, ed. Greg J. Duncan and James N. Morgan (Ann Arbor: University of Michigan, Institute for Social Research [hereafter ISR], 1978), pp. 367–401;

smaller studies have been conducted.[27] While the studies all differ in such data collection procedures as sampling (national vs. local, husband-and-wife families vs. individuals) and reporting (interview vs. self-report, contemporaneous vs. retrospective reporting), their findings are remarkably consistent and support rather firm conclusions about who does how much housework.[28] Because Walker and Woods have analyzed their data so extensively, their findings are relied upon here.

Women who have no paid employment outside the home work over fifty hours per week on household chores: preparing and cleaning up after meals, doing laundry, cleaning the house, taking care of children and other family members, and shopping and keeping records. Walker and Woods found that 859 full-time houseworkers (usually labeled "homemakers" or "housewives") worked an average of fifty-seven hours per week. Their husbands, as reported by their wives, spent about eleven hours a week on housework, and children were reported to do about the same amount on average.[29] A study of a national sample of 700 women in 1965 and 1966 found that 357 full-time houseworkers worked an average of 55.4 hours per week.[30] Household production is clearly more than a full-time job according to these time-budget studies.

The way that time spent on housework changes as demands on

Frank Stafford and Greg Duncan, "The Use of Time and Technology by Households in the United States," working paper (Ann Arbor: University of Michigan, ISR, 1977); John P. Robinson, "Changes in Americans' Use of Time: 1965–1975: A Progress Report," working paper (Cleveland: Cleveland State University, August 1977).

27. Among the smaller studies are Martin Meissner et al., "No Exit for Wives: Sexual Division of Labour and the Cumulation of Household Demands," *Canadian Review of Sociology and Anthropology* 12 (November 1975): 424–39; Richard A. Berk and Sarah Fenstermaker Berk, *Labor and Leisure at Home: Content and Organization of the Household Day* (Beverly Hills, Calif.: Sage Publications, 1979); and Joseph H. Pleck, "Men's Family Work: Three Perspectives and Some New Data," working paper (Wellesley, Mass.: Wellesley College Center for Research on Women, 1979). New data collection efforts on a larger scale are already under way in several states, coordinated by Kathyrn Walker at Cornell University, and planned by the Survey Research Center at the University of Michigan under the coordination of Frank Stafford, Greg Duncan, and John Robinson.

28. For a discussion of the reliability of time diaries and their compatibility, see John Robinson, "Methodological Studies into the Reliability and Validity of the Time Diary," in *Studies in the Measurement of Time Allocation*, ed. Thomas Juster (Ann Arbor: University of Michigan, ISR, in press); and Joann Vanek, "Keeping Busy: Time Spent in Housework, United States, 1920–1970" (Ph.D. diss., University of Michigan, 1973). Research on the distribution of families at the extremes (e.g., where men and women may be sharing housework equally) would also be very useful.

29. Kathryn E. Walker, "Time-Use Patterns for Household Work Related to Homemakers' Employment" (paper presented at the 1970 National Agricultural Outlook Conference, Washington, D.C., February 18, 1970), p. 5.

30. John Robinson and Philip Converse, "United States Time Use Survey" (Ann Arbor, Mich.: Survey Research Center, 1965–66), as reported by Joann Vanek, "Household Technology and Social Status: Rising Living Standards and Status and Residence Differences in Housework," *Technology and Culture* 19 (July 1978): 374.

Signs　　　　　　　　　　　　　　　　　　*Spring 1981*　　　*379*

members' time increase is a good indicator of how patriarchy operates in the home, at least with respect to housework. Much has been made of the potentially equalizing effects of women's increased labor-force partici- pation: as women earn wages they may come to exercise more power both within and outside the family. Time-budget studies show, however, that husbands of wives who work for wages do not spend more time on housework than those husbands whose wives do not work for wages. The Walker and Woods data for Syracuse families show that the more wage work women do, the fewer hours they spend on housework but the longer are their total work weeks. Women who worked for wages thirty or more hours per week had total work weeks of seventy-six hours on average, including an average of thirty-three hours per week spent on housework. Yet men whose wives had the longest work weeks had the shortest work weeks themselves (see fig. 1). The lack of responsiveness of men's housework time to women's increased wage work is also shown in time-budget data from cities in twelve industrialized countries collected by the Multinational Comparative Time-Budget Research Project in 1965 and 1966. In all countries wage-working wives worked substantially more hours every day than husbands or full-time houseworkers. Em- ployed wives also spent substantially more time on housework on their days off (about double their weekday time), whereas husbands and even full-time houseworkers had the weekends for increased leisure.[31] These findings are corroborated by two later studies, one of 300 couples in Greater Vancouver in 1971, and one of 3,500 couples in the United States in 1976.[32]

A look at the tasks performed by husbands and wives, as well as the time spent, adds to our understanding of the relative burden of house- work. Meissner and his associates, examining participation rates of hus- bands and wives in various tasks for 340 couples, finds that only 26 percent of the husbands reported spending some time cleaning the house (on either of two days reported, one weekday and one weekend day) while 86 percent of their wives did, and that 27 percent of the husbands contributed 2.5 hours per week to cooking, while 93 percent of

31. John P. Robinson, Philip E. Converse, and Alexander Szalai, "Everyday Life in Twelve Countries," in Szalai, ed., pp. 119, 121.

32. Meissner et al.; Morgan. One recent survey, the national 1977 Quality of Employment Survey, does, however, indicate that husbands of employed wives do more housework than husbands of full-time houseworkers: about 1.8 hours more per week in household tasks and 2.7 more in child care (quoted in Pleck, pp. 15, 16). These findings are based on data gathered by the retrospective self-reports of 757 married men in interviews rather than by time diaries kept throughout the day. Respondents were asked to "estimate" how much time they spent on "home chores—things like working, cleaning, repairs, shop- ping, yardwork, and keeping track of money and bills," and on "taking care of or doing things with your child(ren)." The child-care estimates are probably high relative to those from time-budget studies because the latter count only active care; "doing things with your children" would often be classified as leisure.

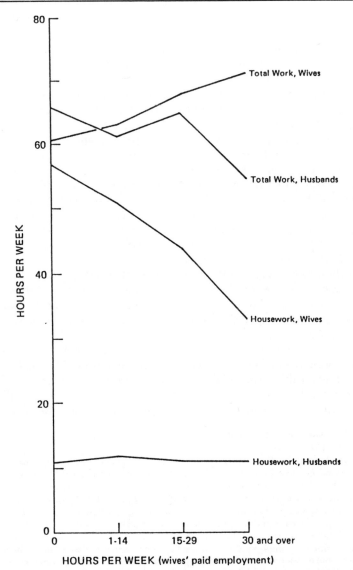

Fig. 1.—Time spent on housework and total work by wives and husbands in 1,296 Syracuse, New York, families (1967–68), by wives' hours of employment. Based on data from Kathryn E. Walker and Margaret E. Woods, *Time Use: A Measure of Household Production of Family Goods and Services* (Washington, D.C.: American Home Economics Association, 1976), p. 45; and Kathryn E. Walker, "Time-Use Patterns for Household Work Related to Homemakers' Employment" (paper presented at the 1970 National Agricultural Outlook Conference, Washington, D.C., February 18, 1970), p. 5.

the wives contributed 8.5 hours. Only seven of the 340 husbands reported doing any laundry, but nearly half their wives did.[33] Meissner
and his associates conclude: "These data indicate that most married
women do the regular, necessary, and most time consuming work in the
household every day. In view of the small and selective contribution of
their husbands, they can anticipate doing it for the rest of their lives."[34]

Walker and Woods, examining the percentage of record days that
wives and husbands, as well as other household members, participated in
various household tasks, conclude that while husbands of employed
wives participated more often than husbands of nonemployed wives in
almost all household tasks, their contributions to the time spent on the
tasks were small.[35] One is forced to conclude that the husbands of
wage-working wives appear to do more housework by participating
more often, but the substance of their contributions remains insignificant.[36] Women are apparently not, for the most part, able to
translate their wages into reduced work weeks, either by buying
sufficient substitute products or labor or by getting their husbands to do
appreciably more housework. In the absence of patriarchy, we would
expect to find an equal sharing of wage work and housework; we find no
such thing.

The burden of housework increases substantially when there are
very young children or many children in the household. The household
time-budget data from Walker and Woods's study indicate that in both
cases the wife's work week expands to meet the needs of the family while
the husband's does not. In families with a child under one year old, the

33. Meissner et al., p. 430.
34. Ibid., p. 431.
35. Husbands of employed wives reported participating in meal preparation on 42
percent of the record-keeping days, while the employed wives participated on 96 percent
of the days. Yet the husbands contributed only 10 percent of the time spent on that task,
while the wives contributed 75 percent. Similarly, 17 percent of the husbands of employed
wives participated in after-meal cleanup, contributing 7 percent of the time. In only two of
the seven tasks constituting regular housework, marketing and nonphysical care of the
family, did husbands contribute as much as 25 percent of the total time spent on the tasks
(tasks defined as nonphysical care of the family are activities that relate to the social and
educational development of other family members, such as reading to children or helping
them with lessons; pet care is also included in this task). For these two tasks, neither the
participation rates nor the proportions of time contributed differed substantially between
those husbands whose wives worked for wages and those whose wives did not. It should be
noted that the percentage of record days husbands were reported as participating in a
particular task is not the same as a straightforward participation rate. For example, a
report that husbands participated on half the days could indicate either that all husbands
participated every other day or that half the husbands participated both days (Walker and
Woods [n. 24 above], pp. 58–59).
36. The unusual finding reported by Pleck, that husbands of employed wives estimate
they spend more time on housework, could be explained by this phenomenon: men *participate* more often, and *think* they are doing more housework. The new time-budget studies
will be useful in confirming or denying this change.

typical full-time houseworker spent nearly seventy hours per week in
housework, nearly thirty of it in family (primarily child) care. The typical
husband spent five hours per week on family care but reduced his time
spent on other housework, so that his total housework did not increase.
When the wife was employed for fifteen or more hours per week, the
average husband did spend two hours more per week on child care, and
his time spent on housework increased to twenty hours (compared to
twelve for the husband whose wife did less wage work). Meanwhile,
however, his employed wife spent over fifty hours on housework, nearly
twenty of them on child care. As figure 2 indicates, the employed wife's
total housework time expands substantially with the presence of young
children, while the husband's increases only moderately. Data from a
national sample of about 3,500 U.S. husband-and-wife families in the
1976 Panel Study of Income Dynamics also show a pattern of longer

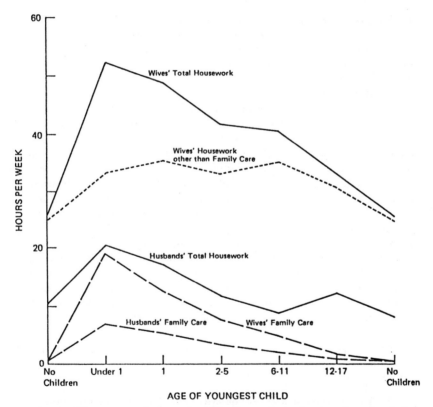

Fig. 2.—Time spent on housework and family care by husbands and employed wives
in 1,296 Syracuse, New York, families (1967–68), by age of youngest child. Based on data
from Walker and Woods (see legend to fig. 1), pp. 50, 126.

housework time for wives with greater family responsibility (indicated by numbers of children) and nearly total lack of variability in the husbands' housework time (see fig. 3).[37]

Meissner and his associates developed a ranked set of four combinations of demands on household time and analyzed the data on changes in the housework time of husbands and wives in response to these increased levels of demands. The first level of demand is represented by households with one job and no children under ten, the second is one job and children under ten, the third is two jobs and no children under ten, and the fourth is two jobs and children under ten. The invariance of time husbands spend on housework is corroborated by their procedure. For the five activities of meals, sleep, gardening, visiting, and watching television, women lose fourteen hours a week from the least to most demanding situation, while men gain 1.4 hours a week.[38] The United States cities survey of 1965–66 found that "among working couples with children, fathers averaged 1.3 hours more free time each weekday and 1.4 hours more on Sunday than mothers."[39]

The rather small, selective, and unresponsive contribution of the husband to housework raises the suspicion that the husband may be a net drain on the family's resources of housework time—that is, husbands may require more housework than they contribute. Indeed, this hypothesis is suggested by my materialist definition of patriarchy, in which men benefit directly from women's labor power. No direct estimates of housework required by the presence of husbands have, to my knowledge, been made. The Michigan survey data, however, in providing information on the housework time of single parents shed some light on this question. Single women spend considerably less time on housework than wives, for the same size families (see fig. 3). They spend less time even when they are compared only to wives who work for wages. It seems plausible that the difference in time spent on housework (approximately eight hours per week) could be interpreted as the amount of increased housework caused by the husband's presence. Unfortunately, because very few time-budget studies solicit information from single women, this estimate of "husband care" cannot be confirmed. Additional estimates can be made, however, from Walker and Woods's data of the minimum time necessary for taking care of a house. For wives who

37. Morgan. These data indicate far fewer hours spent on housework than the Walker and Woods data because they exclude child-care hours and, perhaps as well, because they are based on recall rather than actual time diaries.

38. Meissner et al., p. 433.

39. John Robinson and Philip Converse, "United States Time Use Survey" (Ann Arbor, Mich.: Survey Research Center, 1965–66), as reported in Janice N. Hedges and Jeanne K. Barnett, "Working Women and the Division of Household Tasks," *Monthly Labor Review* (April 1971), p. 11.

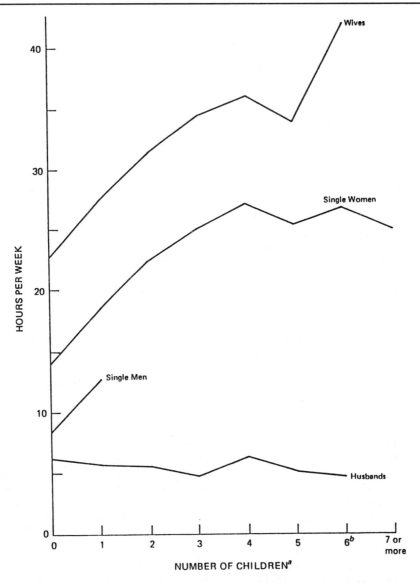

NUMBER OF CHILDREN[a]

[a]Number of other people in household besides husband and wife or single head of household.
[b]Six or more for husbands and wives.

FIG. 3.—Time spent on housework, not including child care, by a national sample of 5,863 families (1976), by number of children. Based on data in James N. Morgan, "A Potpourri of New Data Gathered from Interviews with Husbands and Wives," in *Five Thousand American Families: Patterns of Economic Progress*, vol. 6, *Accounting for Race and Sex Differences in Earnings and Other Analyses of the First Nine Years of the Panel Study of Income Dynamics*, ed. Greg J. Duncan and James N. Morgan (Ann Arbor: University of Michigan, Institute for Social Research, 1978), p. 370.

worked in the labor market less than fourteen hours per week, time
spent on "regular" housework (all housework minus family care) ranged
between forty and forty-five hours for all life-cycle phases (varying ages
and numbers of children), while for wives who worked for wages fifteen
hours per week or more, time spent on regular housework ranged between twenty-five and thirty-five hours per week (see fig. 2).

These studies demonstrate the patriarchal benefits reaped in
housework. First, the vast majority of time spent on housework is spent
by the wife, about 70 percent on the average, with both the husband and
the children providing about 15 percent on average.[40] Second, the wife
is largely responsible for child care. The wife takes on the excess burden
of housework in those families where there are very young or very many
children; the husband's contribution to housework remains about the
same whatever the family size or the age of the youngest child. It is the
wife who, with respect to housework at least, does all of the adjusting to
the family life cycle. Third, the woman who also works for wages (and
she does so usually, we know, out of economic necessity) finds that her
husband spends very little more time on housework on average than the
husband whose wife is not a wage worker. Fourth, the wife spends
perhaps eight hours per week in additional housework on account of the
husband. And fifth, the wife spends, on average, a minimum of forty
hours a week maintaining the house and husband if she does not work
for wages and a minimum of thirty hours per week if she does.

Moreover, while we might expect the receipt of patriarchal benefits
to vary according to class, race, and ethnicity, the limited time data we
have relating to socioeconomic status or race indicate that time spent on
housework by wives is not very sensitive to such differences.[41] The national panel study data, for example, showed no variation in housework
time between racial groups.[42] With respect to class differences, I have
argued elsewhere that the widespread use of household conveniences
(especially the less expensive ones) and the decline in the use of servants
in the early twentieth century probably increased the similarity of
housework across class. In addition, no evidence was found that showed
that the larger appliances effectively reduced housework time.[43] Income
probably has its most important effect on housework through its effect
on women's labor-force participation rates. Wives of husbands with
lower incomes are more likely to be in the labor force and therefore

40. Walker and Woods, p. 64.
41. Hartmann, "Unhappy Marriage."
42. Morgan, p. 369.
43. Heidi I. Hartmann, "Capitalism and Women's Work in the Home, 1900–1930"
(Ph.D. diss., Yale University, 1974 [Temple University Press, in press]). The Robinson-
Converse study found that wives' housework time hovered around forty-two hours per
week at all household incomes above $4,000 per year (1965–66 dollars) but was somewhat
less, thirty-three hours, when household income was below $4,000 (reported in Vanek,
"Household Technology and Social Status," p. 371).

experiencing the "double day" of wage work and housework.[44] Wage work, while it shortens the number of hours spent on housework (compared to those of the full-time houseworker), almost certainly increases the burden of the hours that remain. Even for full-time houseworkers, the number and ages of children appear to be more important than income in effect upon housework time.[45]

The relation of the household's wage workers to the capitalist organization of production places households in class relations with each other and determines the household's access to commodities; yet in viewing and understanding women's work in the home—the rearing of children, the maintenance of the home, the serving of men—patriarchy appears to be a more salient feature than class.[46]

Does It Matter?

I have suggested that women of all classes are subject to patriarchal power in that they perform household labor for men. Some would argue, however, that women's overwhelming share of housework relative to men's and their longer total work weeks should not be perceived as exploitation of one group's labor by another, that the patriarchal division of labor is not like the capitalist division of labor. Some would argue that among the working class, especially, the sexual division of labor is a division of labor without significance. Working-class husbands and wives, it is argued, recognize the fundamental coercion involved in both the homemaker and wage-earner roles.[47] The sexual division of

44. In the Meissner study, fully 36 percent of the wives whose husbands earned under $10,000 (1971 dollars) were in the labor force, whereas no more than 10 percent of those whose husbands earned over $14,000 were in the labor force (Meissner et al., p. 429).

45. Much additional research, both of the already available data and the forthcoming data, is needed to increase our knowledge of potential variations in housework time.

46. The salience of patriarchy over class for women's work could probably be shown for many societies; Bangladesh provides one example. In 1977 Mead Cain and his associates collected data on time use from all members of 114 households in a rural Bangladesh village, where control of arable land is the key to economic survival and position. Dichotomizing people's class position by the amount of arable land owned by their households, Cain found that the work days of men with more than one-half acre of land were substantially shorter than those of men with less than one-half acre of land, whereas women in households with more land worked longer hours. The better-off men probably worked about eleven hours *less* per week than the poorer. The better-off women worked about three hours *more* per week than the poorer. In this rural village, Bangladesh women, unlike the men, did not benefit—at least in terms of lighter work loads—from the higher class position of their households (Mead Cain, Syeda Rokeya Khanam, and Shamsun Naher, "Class, Patriarchy, and Women's Work in Bangladesh," *Population and Development Review* 5, no. 3 [September 1979]: 405–38).

47. Humphries adopts this perspective (see n. 22 above). In reality, the question is not so much whether or not patriarchy is oppressive in the lives of working-class women, but rather what the trade-offs are between patriarchal and class oppression.

labor, it is also argued, has no significance among the middle class, since women's lives are not especially hard.

The argument about the significance of patriarchy in women's lives revolves around whether or not women *perceive* patriarchy as oppressive. The interest behind much of the literature growing out of the women's movement has been to document women's oppression so that they may recognize exploitation when they experience it in their daily lives.[48] The sexual division of labor, so ancient that its unfairness is often accepted as normal, is an example of such oppression. Pat Mainardi, in "The Politics of Housework," captures the essence of the battle between the genders over housework. Her analysis exposes the patriarchal power underlying each response of a radical male to his wife's attempts to get him to share the housework. "The measure of your oppression is his resistance," she warns us, and goes on to point out the husband's typical response: " 'I don't mind sharing the work, but you'll have to show me how to do it.' *Meaning:* I ask a lot of questions and you'll have to show me everything every time I do it because I don't remember so good. Also don't try to sit down and read while I'm doing my jobs because I'm going to annoy hell out of you until it's easier to do them yourself."[49] The women's liberation movement has no doubt changed the perceptions of many middle-class women about the significance of patriarchy. Can the same be said for working-class women? The evidence is more limited, but working-class women are also expressing their recognition of the unfairness of male power within the working class. For example, a Southern white working-class woman recently wrote in response to a column by William Raspberry in the *Washington Post:*

> Men ... live, speak and behave exactly by the slogans and notions of our traditional male "law and the prophets." Their creed and their litany ... is as follows:
> All money and property, including welfare funds and old-age pensions, are "his."
> All wages, no matter who earns them, are "his." ...

48. Beverly Jones, "The Dynamics of Marriage and Motherhood," in *Sisterhood Is Powerful*, ed. Robin Morgan (New York: Vintage Books, 1970), pp. 46–61; Meredith Tax, "Woman and Her Mind: The Story of Daily Life" (Boston: New England Free Press, 1970), 20 pages; Laurel Limpus, "Liberation of Women: Sexual Repression and the Family" (Boston: New England Free Press, ca. 1970), 15 pages; Betty Friedan, *The Feminine Mystique* (New York: Dell Publishing Co., 1963).

49. Pat Mainardi, "The Politics of Housework," in Morgan, ed., pp. 451, 449. Mainardi begins her article with this quote from John Stuart Mill, *On the Subjection of Women:* "Though women do not complain of the power of husbands, each complains of her own husband, or of the husbands of her friends. It is the same in all other cases of servitude; at least in the commencement of the emancipatory movement. The serfs did not at first complain of the power of the lords, but only of their tyranny" (p. 447).

Food, housing, medical and clothing expenses are "her" personal spending money. . . .

Many wives must "steal" food from their own wages! . . .

The sum of it all is a lifetime of ridicule, humiliation, degradation, utter denial of dignity and self-respect for women and their minor children at the hands of husband-father.

We older women took, and take, the male abuse because (1) we thought we had to, (2) we thought rearing our children and keeping our families together was more important than life itself. . . .

Young women can now earn their own and their children's bread, or receive it from welfare, without the abuse, ridicule and humiliation.[50]

The first step in the struggle is awareness, and the second is recognition that the situation can change.

What Are the Prospects for Change?

What is the likelihood that patriarchal power in the home, as measured by who does housework, will decline? What is the likelihood that housework will become equally shared by men and women? Might the amount of time required for housework be reduced? The prospects for change in housework time, while dependent on economic and political changes at the societal level, probably hinge most directly on the strength of the women's movement, for the amount and quality of housework services rendered, like the amount of and pay for wage work, result from historical processes of struggle. Such struggle establishes norms that become embodied in an expected standard of living. Time spent on housework by both full-time houseworkers and employed houseworkers has remained remarkably stable in the twentieth century. Kathryn Walker and Joann Vanek for the United States and Michael Paul Sacks for the Soviet Union report that total time spent on housework has not declined significantly from the 1920s to the 1960s.[51] Although time spent on some tasks, such as preparing and cleaning up after meals, has declined, that spent on others—such as shopping, record keeping, and child care—has increased. Even time spent on laundry has increased, despite new easy care fabrics and the common use of automatic home washing machines. A completely satisfactory explanation for the failure

50. William Raspberry, "Family Breakdowns: A Voice from 'Little Dixie,'" *Washington Post* (June 23, 1978). Lillian Rubin, *Worlds of Pain* (New York: Basic Books, 1976), describes current tensions between the women and men in the working-class families she interviewed.

51. Kathryn E. Walker, "Homemaking Still Takes Time," *Journal of Home Economics* 61, no. 8 (October 1969): 621–24; Joann Vanek, "Time Spent in Housework," *Scientific American* 231 (November 1974): 116–20; Michael Paul Sacks, "Unchanging Times: A Comparison of the Everyday Life of Soviet Working Men and Women between 1923 and 1966," *Journal of Marriage and the Family* 39 (November 1977): 793–805.

of housework time to decline, despite rapid technological change, has
not yet been developed, but part of the answer lies in rising standards of
cleanliness, child care, and emotional support, as well as in the inherent
limitation of technology applied to small decentralized units, that is,
typical homes.[52]

Gender struggle around housework may be bearing fruit. Standards
may in fact be changing, allowing for a reduction in overall time spent on
housework. A recent time-budget study indicates that between 1965 and
1975 housework time may have fallen by as much as six hours per week
for full-time houseworkers and four hours for those also employed outside the house.[53] Such a decrease may also be the result of changing
boundaries between home and market production; production formerly
done by women at home may be increasingly shifted to capitalist production sites. In such cases, the products change as well; home-cooked
meals are replaced by fast food.[54] Over time, the boundary between
home and market production has been flexible rather than fixed, determined by the requirements of patriarchy and capitalism in reproducing themselves and by the gender and class struggles that arise
from these processes.

While women's struggles, and perhaps as well capital's interests, may
be successfully altering standards for housework and shifting some production beyond the home, prospects within the home for shifting some
of the household tasks onto men do not appear to be as good. We have
already seen, in our review of the current time-budget studies, that men
whose wives work for wages do not spend more time than other married
men on housework. This suggests that, even as more women increase
their participation in wage labor and share with men the financial burden of supporting families, men are not likely to share the burden of

52. Technological innovations within the household—the washing machine, the vacuum cleaner, the dishwasher—have not been effective in reducing household time.
Sophisticated robots, microwave ovens, or computer-controlled equipment may yet be able
to reduce the time required for maintaining household services at established levels. Yet
what technology is developed and made available is also the result of historical processes
and the relative strength of particular classes and genders. See Hartmann, *Capitalism and
Women's Work*.

53. Robinson, table 4 (see n. 28 above); Clair Vickry, "Women's Economic Contribution to the Family," in *The Subtle Revolution*, ed. Ralph E. Smith (Washington, D.C.: Urban
Institute, 1979), p. 194.

54. One in four meals is now eaten outside the home (Charles Vaugh, "Growth and
Future of the Fast Food Industry," *Cornell Motel and Restaurant Administration Quarterly*
[November 1976]), cited in Christine Bose, "Technology and Changes in the Division of
Labor in the American Home" (paper delivered at the annual meeting of the American
Sociological Association, San Francisco, September 1978). I suspect that the most effective
means of reducing housework time involves changing the location of production from the
household to the larger economy, but men, acting in their patriarchal interests, may well
resist this removal of production from the home, with its attendant loss of personalized
services.

housework with women. The increase in women's labor-force participation has occurred over the entire course of the twentieth century. Walker's comparison of the 1967–68 Syracuse study with studies from the 1920s shows that husbands' work time may have increased at most about a half hour per week, while the work time of women, whether employed outside the home or full-time houseworkers, may have increased by as much as five hours per week.[55] Interestingly, a similar conclusion was reached by Sacks in his comparison of time-budget studies conducted in several cities in the Soviet Union in 1923 and 1966. He found that women's housework time has decreased somewhat, that men's time has not increased, that women still spend more than twice as much time on housework than do men, and that women have a total work week that is still seventeen hours longer than men's. In 1970, fully 90 percent of all Soviet women between the ages of twenty and forty-nine were in the labor force.[56] We are forced to conclude that the increase in women's wage labor will not *alone* bring about any sharing of housework with men. Continued struggle will be necessary.

People have different interests in the future of household production, based upon their current relation to productive activity outside the home. Their interests are not always unequivocal or constant over time. Some women might perceive their interests to lie in getting greater access to wages by mounting campaigns against employment and wage discrimination, others in maintaining as much control as possible over the home production process by resisting both capitalist inroads on household production and male specifications of standards for it. Some women might reduce housework by limiting childbirth. Some capitalists might seek to expand both the market and mass production of meal preparation if this area appears potentially profitable. Other capitalists may simply need women's labor power in order to expand production in any area or to cheapen labor power.[57] Or their interests might lie in having women in the home to produce and rear the next generation of workers. The outcome of these counteracting requirements and goals is theoretically indeterminate.

My reading of the currently dominant forces and tensions goes as follows: Women are resisting doing housework and rearing children, at least many children; the majority of women increasingly perceive their

55. Walker, "Homemaking Still Takes Time."
56. Sacks, "Unchanging Times," p. 801.
57. In the Marxist perspective, the wage paid to the worker is largely dependent on her or his costs of reproduction, mediated by custom, tradition, and class struggle. When there are two wage workers per family, the family's cost of reproduction can be spread over the wages of both workers; the capitalist can pay two workers the same wage one received previously and get twice as many hours of labor, cheapening the price of labor per hour. See Lise Vogel, "The Earthy Family," *Radical America* 7, no. 4–5 (July–October 1973): 9–50. Jean Gardiner, "Women's Domestic Labor," *New Left Review*, no. 89 (January–February 1975), pp. 47–58, also discusses conflicting tendencies within capitalism.

economic security to lie primarily in being self-supporting. Therefore, they are struggling with men to get out of the house and into decent jobs in the labor market. Given women's restricted access to decent jobs and wages, however, women also maintain their interests in men's continued contribution to family support. Men are relinquishing responsibility for families in some ways but are loathe to give up some of the benefits that go with it. Desertion, informal liaisons, contract cohabitation may be manifestations of this attitude; the attitude itself may be a response to capitalist inroads on patriarchal benefits, as more wives enter the labor force, providing fewer personalized services at home. Men may perceive that part-time wage labor by their wives is useful in contributing to the family's financial support without interfering very much with the provision of household services to them. To make such an arrangement compatible with their continued patriarchal power, men are on the whole struggling fairly hard to keep their better places in the labor market. Capitalists are primarily interested in using women's participation in the labor market to cheapen labor power and to allow expansion on better terms; women workers, for example, are much less unionized than men. Capitalists attempt to pass on most of the social costs—child care, for example—to the state, but the state's ability to provide is limited by a generalized fiscal crisis and by the present difficulties in capital accumulation.[58] The current period of alternating slow growth and actual production setback forces an intensification of class struggle, which in turn may exacerbate gender conflict.

Over the next twenty years, while there will be some change in the sexual division of labor resulting from conflict and struggles, patriarchy will not be eradicated. Despite at least a century of predictions and assertions that capitalism will triumph over patriarchy—a situation in which all production would take place under capitalist relations and all people would be wage earners on equal terms—patriarchy has survived. It has survived otherwise cataclysmic revolutions in the Soviet Union and China.[59] This means that a substantial amount of production will remain in the home. The irreducible minimum from the patriarchal point of view is that women will continue to raise young children and to provide men with the labor power necessary to maintain established standards of living, particularly the decentralized home system.

My assessment is that we are reaching a new equilibrium, or a new form of an old partnership, a judgment supported by data on women's employment in eight countries; these figures suggest that there may be a kind of structural limit on the participation of women in the labor force. As shown in table 2, those countries in which the proportion of women who are in the labor force is largest have the highest proportion of

58. James O'Connor, *The Fiscal Crisis of the State* (New York: St. Martin's Press, 1973).
59. Weinbaum (see n. 15 above).

Table 2

Women's Labor Force Participation and Part-Time Employment in Eight Countries

Country and Year	Women's Labor Force Participation Rate		Women in Labor Force Part Time	
	%	Rank	% of Total Women in Labor Force	Rank
Sweden (1977)	55.2*	1	45.2†	1
United States (1975)	47.3*	2	33.0†	3
Canada (1977)	45.9	3	23.0‡	4
United Kingdom (1975)	45.8*	4	40.9‡	2
France (1975)	43.8*	5	14.1‡	6
Austria (1975)	42.4 .	6	14.0†	7
Federal Republic of Germany (1975)	37.7*	7	22.8‡	5
Belgium (1975)	30.7	8	11.6‡	8

SOURCE.—Ronnie Steinberg Ratner, "Labor Market Inequality and Equal Opportunity Policy for Women, a Cross-national Comparison," paper prepared for Working Party no. 6 on the Role of Women in the Economy (Paris: Organization for Economic Cooperation and Development, June 1979), tables 1, 18.

NOTE.—Women's labor force participation rate is the proportion of all women of working age (usually over fifteen) who are in the labor force (employed or looking for work).

*Figures from 1976.
†Part-time employment defined as less than thirty-five hours per week.
‡Part-time employment defined as ca. thirty hours per week or less.

women working part-time. It is necessary, such findings suggest, that a substantial proportion of women's collective work hours be retained in the home if the patriarchal requirement that women continue to do housework and provide child care is to be fulfilled. In Sweden, it is most often married mothers of young children who work part-time. In the United States, the married mothers of preschool children have unemployment rates more than double those of married women with no children.[60]

We must hope that the new equilibrium will prove unstable, since without question it creates a situation in which a woman's work day is longer than it was when she served as a full-time houseworker, the male as breadwinner. As described earlier, when women's wage labor is greatest their total work weeks (wage work plus housework) are longest and men's are shortest (see fig. 1). Women have entered the labor market in greater numbers, and more husbands consequently have wives who are working for wages and contributing to the family income; the collective work effort of men as a group has decreased since men reduce their total work weeks when their wives work for wages. At the same time the collective contribution of women as a group has increased. This situation will undoubtedly continue to generate gender struggle. As more and more women become subject to the "double burden," more are moved to protest. Yet it is worth noting that husbands may not be the

60. Hedges and Barnett, p. 11 (see n. 39 above).

main beneficiaries of the recent increases in women's labor time. Although their wives' wages contribute to the family income, their wives' labor power is being used to create surplus value for capitalists and not to maintain the previous level of services at home. Eventually the decentralized home system itself may be a casualty of gender and class struggle.

Conclusion

The decentralized home system, which I see as a fundamental result of patriarchy, also meets crucial requirements for the reproduction of the capitalist system.[61] Families can provide crucial services less expensively than does the cash nexus of either the state or capital, especially when economic growth has come to a halt. From capital's point of view, however, the relationship is an uneasy one; capital and the state use the household but do not entirely control it. Despite the spread of capitalism and centralized, bureaucratic states, and their penetration into more and more areas of social life, people in households still manage to retain control over crucial resources and particular areas of decision. Family historians have helped us understand the strength and endurance of family units and their retention of power in many areas. The family historians may not have been sensitive to power relations within the family, but they have focused on another aspect of the same phenomenon—the interdependence of people within households and their common stance as a household against the incursion of forces that would alienate their resources or their control over decision making. Although I have focused on the potential for conflict among family members, particularly between men and women over housework, I want to point out that the same division of labor that creates the basis for that conflict also creates interdependence as a basis for family unity. It is this dual nature of the family that makes the behavior of families so unpredictable and problematic for both capital and the state. In the United States, for example, no one predicted the enormity of the post–World War II baby boom, the size of the subsequent increase in women's labor force participation, the rapid decrease in the birthrate in the late 1960s and early 1970s, or, most recently, the increase in divorce and single parenthood.

With the perspective developed here, these changes in people's household behavior can be understood as responses to conflicts both

61. Ann R. Markusen has extended the notion of decentralized households as characteristic of patriarchy to explain the development of segregated residential areas in cities. See her "City Spatial Structure, Women's Household Work, and National Urban Policy," *Signs: Journal of Women in Culture and Society* 5, no. 3, suppl. (Spring 1980): S23–S44.

within and outside households. As Wendy Lutrell, who has also been working on reconceptualizing the family as a locus of tension and conflict, writes: "People can be seen as historical agents acting both independently as individuals *and* dependently as family members. This dual process, fuels tensions and conflicts within the family arena and creates one potential for social change. . . . When the state, workplace, community, religion, or family are seen as arenas of struggle, we are forced to abandon a static, functional framework which can only see capitalist institutions as maintaining the status quo."[62]

In some cases, family members face capital or state actions together. In the Brookside strike, miners' wives united with their husbands, supporting their demands and even extending them to community concerns. Struggles around community issues are often initiated by women because of their ties to their neighbors and extended kin, and they are sometimes joined by men disaffected with their lot in patriarchy and capitalism. In New York City, both men and women protested government cuts for preschools and hospitals. In other cases, men and women who are in conflict within the family may seek solutions in the capitalist or state sectors. The recent rapid growth of fast-food eateries can be seen in this light, as can English women's fight for milk allowances from the state to redress income inequality within the family.

In our society both class and gender shape people's consciousness of their situation and their struggles to change those situations. At times it may be appropriate to speak of the family or the household as a unit with common interests, but the conditions which make this possible should be clearly spelled out. The conflicts inherent in class and patriarchal society tear people apart, but the dependencies inherent in them can hold people together.

National Research Council
National Academy of Sciences

62. Wendy Lutrell, "The Family as an Arena of Struggle: New Directions and Strategies for Studying Contemporary Family Life" (paper delivered at a Sociology Colloquium, University of California, Santa Cruz, May 30, 1979), pp. 19, 18.

B
Gender and Labour Supply

[11]

Labor Force Participation of Married Women: A Study of Labor Supply

JACOB MINCER

COLUMBIA UNIVERSITY AND NATIONAL BUREAU OF
ECONOMIC RESEARCH

Introductory: Statement of the Problem

ON the assumption that leisure time is a normal good, the standard analysis of work-leisure choices implies a positive substitution effect and a negative income effect on the response of hours of work supplied to variations in the wage rate. An increase in the real wage rate makes leisure time more expensive and tends to elicit an increase in hours of work. However, for a given amount of hours worked, an increase in the wage rate constitutes an increase in income, which leads to an increase in purchases of various goods, including leisure time. Thus, on account of the income effect, hours of work tend to decrease. In which direction hours of work change on balance, given a change in the wage rate, cannot be determined a priori. It depends on the relative strengths of the income and substitution effects in the relevant range. The single assumption of a positive income elasticity of demand for leisure time is not sufficient to yield empirical implications on this matter.

An empirical generalization which fills this theoretical void is the "backward-bending" supply curve of labor. This is the notion that on the average the income effect is stronger than the substitution effect, so that an increase in the wage rate normally results in a decreased amount (hours) of work offered by suppliers of labor. Extreme examples of such behavior have been repeatedly observed in underdeveloped countries. On the American scene, several kinds of empirical evidence apparently point to the same relationship:[1] the historically

NOTE: Research reported in this paper was supported, in part, by a grant from the Social Science Research Council. Data from the 1950 Survey of Consumer Expenditures were made available on punch cards by the Bureau of Labor Statistics. For encouragement and helpful comments I am indebted to Dorothy S. Brady, Gary S. Becker, Zvi Griliches, Mark Leiserson, Phillip J. Nelson, Elliot Zupnick, and to members of the Columbia University Workshop in Labor Economics.

[1] The pioneering works of research and interpretation in this area are well known. See: Paul H. Douglas, *The Theory of Wages*, Macmillan, 1934; John D. Durand, *The Labor Force in the U.S.*, Social Science Research Council, 1948; Clarence D. Long, *The Labor Force under Changing Income and Employment*, Princeton University Press for National Bureau of Economic Research, 1958.

LABOR FORCE PARTICIPATION

declining work week in industry; historically declining labor force participation rates of young and old males; an inverse relation between wages of adult males and labor force participation rates of females by cities in cross sections; an inverse relation between incomes of husbands and labor force participation of wives, by husbands' incomes, in budget studies. Similar phenomena have been reported from the experience of other modern economies.

The secular negative association between the length of the work week, participation rates of males, and rising real incomes is clearly consistent with the backward-bending supply curve.[2] Whether this is also true of cross-sectional data on males is a question which has as yet received little attention. Superficially, the cross-sectional behavior of females seems similarly capable of being rationalized in terms of a backward-bending supply response, or at least in terms of a positive income elasticity of demand for leisure. Such views, however, are immediately challenged by contradictory evidence in time series. One of the most striking phenomena in the history of the American labor force is the continuing secular increase in participation rates of females, particularly of married women, despite the growth in real income. Between 1890 and 1960 labor force rates of all females fourteen years old and over rose from about 18 per cent to 36 per cent. In the same period rates of married women rose from 5 per cent to 30 per cent, while real income per worker tripled.[3]

The apparent contradiction between time series and cross sections has already stimulated a substantial amount of research. The investigation reported in this paper is yet another attempt to uncover the basic economic structure which is, in part, responsible for the observed relations.

The study starts from the recognition that the concepts of work, income, and substitution need clarification and elaboration before they can be applied to labor force choices of particular population groups, in this instance married women. The resulting analytical model, even though restricted to two basic economic factors, seems capable of explaining a variety of apparently diverse cross-sectional behavior patterns. It also, in principle, reconciles time series with cross-section behavior, though further elaboration is needed for a proper explanation

[2] For a rigorous statement, see H. Gregg Lewis, "Hours of Work and Hours of Leisure," *Proceedings of the Industrial Relations Research Association*, 1957.

[3] Based on Long, *The Labor Force*, Table A-6; and *Employment and Earnings*, Bureau of Labor Statistics, 1960.

OF MARRIED WOMEN

of the former. The empirical focus of the paper is a reinterpretation of old cross-section materials, and an investigation of newly available data generated by the 1950 BLS Survey of Consumer Expenditures.

Conceptual Framework

WORK

The analysis of labor supply to the market by way of the theory of demand for leisure time viewed as a consumption good is strictly appropriate whenever leisure time and hours of work in the market in fact constitute an exhaustive dichotomy. This is, of course, never true even in the case of adult males. The logical complement to leisure time is work broadly construed, whether it includes remunerative production in the market or work that is currently "not paid for." The latter includes various forms of investment in oneself, and the production of goods and services for the home and the family. Educational activity is an essential and, indeed, the most important element in the productive life of young boys and girls. Work at home is still an activity to which women, on the average, devote the larger part of their married life. It is an exclusive occupation of many women, and of a vast majority when young children are present.

It is, therefore, not sufficient to analyze labor force behavior of married women in terms of the demand for leisure. A predicted change in hours of leisure may imply different changes in hours of work in the market depending on the effects of the causal factors on hours of work at home. Technically speaking, if we are to derive the market supply function in a residual fashion, not only the demand for hours of leisure but also the demand for hours of work at home must be taken into account. The latter is a demand for a productive service derived from the demand by the family for home goods and services. A full application of the theory of demand for a productive service to the home sector has implications for a variety of socioeconomic phenomena beyond the scope of this paper.

FAMILY CONTEXT

The analysis of market labor supply in terms of consumption theory carries a strong connotation about the appropriate decision-making unit. We take it as self-evident that in studying consumption behavior the family is the unit of analysis. Income is assumed to be pooled, and

LABOR FORCE PARTICIPATION

total family consumption is positively related to it. The distribution
of consumption among family members depends on tastes. It is equally
important to recognize that the decisions about the production of goods
and services at home and about leisure are largely family decisions.
The relevant income variable in the demand for home services and for
leisure of any family member is total family income. A change in income
of some family member will, in general, result in a changed consumption of leisure for the family as a whole. An increase in one individual's
income may not result in a decrease in *his* hours of work, but in those
of other family members. The total amount of work performed at home
is, even more clearly, an outcome of family demand for home goods
and for leisure, given the production function at home. However, unlike the general consumption case, the distribution of leisure, market
work, and home work for each family member as well as among family
members is determined not only by tastes and by biological or cultural
specialization of functions, but by relative prices which are specific to
individual members of the family. This is so, because earning powers
in the market and marginal productivities in alternative pursuits differ
among individual family members. Other things equal (including
family income), an increase in the market wage rate for some family
member makes both the consumption of leisure and the production of
home services by that individual more costly to the family, and will
as a matter of rational family decision encourage greater market labor
input by him (her). Even the assumption of a backward-bending
supply curve would not justify a prediction of a decrease in total hours
of work *for the particular earner*, if wages of other family members
are fixed.

Recognition of the family context of leisure and work choices, and
of the home-market dichotomy within the world of work, is essential
for any analysis of labor force behavior of married women, and perhaps quite important for the analysis of behavior of other family members, including male family heads. For the present purpose of constructing a simple model of labor force behavior of married women it will
be sufficient to utilize these concepts only insofar as they help to select
and elucidate a few empirically manageable variables to represent the
major forces of income and substitution contained in the market supply
function.

OF MARRIED WOMEN

WORK CHOICES

Let us consider the relevant choices of married women as between leisure, work at home, and work in the market. Income is assumed to have a positive effect on the demand for leisure, hence a negative effect on total amount of work. With the relevant prices fixed, increased family income will decrease total hours of work. Since the income effect on the demand for home goods and services is not likely to be negative,[4] it might seem that the increased leisure means exclusively a decrease in hours of work in the market. Such a conclusion, however, would require a complete absence of substitutability between the wife and other (mechanical, or human) factors of production at home, as well as an absence of substitution in consumption between home goods and market-produced goods. Domestic servants, laborsaving appliances, and frozen foods contradict such assumptions. Substitutability is, of course, a matter of degree. It may be concluded therefore that, given the income elasticity of demand for home goods and for leisure, the extent to which income differentially affects hours of work in the two sectors depends on the ease with which substitution in home production or consumption can be carried out. The lesser the substitutability the weaker the negative income effect on hours of work at home, and the stronger the income effect on hours of work in the market.

Change in this degree of substitutability may have played a part in the historical development. At a given moment of time, the degree of substitutability is likely to differ depending on the content of home production. Thus substitutes for a mother's care of small children are much more difficult to come by than those for food preparation or for physical maintenance of the household. It is likely, therefore, that the same change in income will affect hours of market work of the mother more strongly when small children are present than at other times in the life-cycle.

While family income affects the total amount of work, the market wage rate affects the allocation of hours between leisure, the home, and the market. An increase in the real wage rate, given productivity in the home, is an increase in prices (alternative costs) of home production as well as of leisure in terms of prices of wage goods. To the

---

[4] Fragmentary cross-sectional data on food preparation at home indicate a negligible income elasticity. The demand for other home goods and services (including care of children, and their number) may be more income elastic.

LABOR FORCE PARTICIPATION

extent of an existing substitution between home goods and wage goods such a change will lead to an increase in work supplied to the market. Again, the strength of the effect is a matter of the degree of substitution between wage goods and home production.

TEMPORAL DISTRIBUTION OF WORK

In a broad view, the quantity of labor supplied to the market by a wife is the fraction of her married life during which she participates in the labor force. Abstracting from the temporal distribution of labor force activities over a woman's life, this fraction could be translated into a probability of being in the labor force in a given period of time for an individual, hence into a labor force rate for a large group of women.

If leisure and work preferences, long-run family incomes, and earning power were the same for all women, the total amount of market work would, according to the theory, be the same for all women. Even if that were true, however, the *timing* of market activities during the working life may differ from one individual to another. The life cycle introduces changes in demands for and marginal costs of home work and leisure. Such changes are reflected in the relation between labor force rates and age of woman, presence, number and ages of children. There are life-cycle variations in family incomes and assets which may affect the timing of labor force participation, given a limited income horizon and a less than perfect capital market. Cyclical and random variations in wage rates, employment opportunities, income and employment of other family members, particularly of the head, are also likely to induce temporal variations in the allocation of time between home, market, and leisure. It is not surprising, therefore, that over short periods of observation, variation in labor force participation, or turnover, is the outstanding characteristic of labor force behavior of married women.

To the extent that the temporal distribution of labor force participation can be viewed as a consequence of "transitory" variation in variables favoring particular timing, the distinction between "permanent" and current levels of the independent variables becomes imperative in order to adapt our model to family surveys in which the period of observation is quite short.

OF MARRIED WOMEN

An Econometric Model for Cross Sections

"PERMANENT" LEVELS OF VARIABLES AND AREA REGRESSIONS

The simplest specification of a labor-market supply function of married women to which the theoretical considerations lead is:

$$m = \beta_p \cdot y + \gamma w + u \ (1)$$

where m is the quantity of labor supplied to the market, y is a "potential permanent level" of family income[5] computed at a zero rate of leisure and of home production, w is the wife's full-time market wage or market earning power, and u reflects other factors or "tastes." Since family income so computed is a sum of market earning powers of family members plus property income, we may write $y = x_p + w$, where x_p stands for the permanent level of income of the family which does not include earnings of the wife. For empirical convenience we shall identify x_p with income of the husband. This creates some inaccuracy, to the extent that contribution to family income of family members other than head and wife is important.

It is useful to rewrite equation 1 in terms of income of the husband since most data relate labor force behavior of wives to incomes of husbands. Indeed, the use of observed family income in empirical study of the supply relation would be inappropriate. Instead of serving as a determinant of labor force behavior, it already reflects such decisions.

Substituting for y into (1):

$$m = \beta_p (x_p + w) + \gamma w + u = \beta_p x_p + a w + u \ (2)$$

Since $a = \beta_p + \gamma$, equation 1 can be estimated by means of equation 2.

In equation 1 parameter β_p represents the effect of "permanent" family income on the wife's market labor input, keeping her market earning power constant; γ represents the effect of the wife's market earning power, keeping family income constant. The theoretical expectation is that $\beta_p < 0$ and $\gamma > 0$.

The statement of the hypothesis $\beta_p < 0$ in equation 2, when applied to cross sections is: Given a group of women with the same market earning power, and tastes for leisure assumed independent of husbands' earning power, there will be, on the average, a negative relation be-

[5] The definition of "permanent" and "transitory" components of income follows that stated by Friedman in his consumption theory. Permanent income is income in the long-run sense, measuring income status or normal income position. Transitory income is the difference between current and permanent income. See Milton Friedman, *A Theory of the Consumption Function*, Princeton for NBER, 1957.

LABOR FORCE PARTICIPATION

tween husbands' income and hours of market work of wives.[6] This is so because, in this statement, a higher income of husband means a higher family income and, on the assumption that leisure is a normal good, this implies a lesser total amount of work of the wife, at home and in the market.

On the assumption that, in cross sections, productivities of women in the market are unrelated to their productivities in the home, w measures the relative price of labor in the two sectors. In equation 1 γ is therefore a pure substitution effect, hence a positive number reflecting the attractive power of the wage rate in pulling women into the labor market. Parameter a in equation 2 is a relative price effect not compensated by a change in income. The question of its sign can be stated as follows: Given a group of women whose husbands have the same earning power, what is the effect of a difference in the female wage rate on hours of work on the market? Clearly, a higher wage rate will shift women from the home sector and from leisure to the market sector. However, since in this case family income increases as a result of the increase in the wives' earning power, *total* hours of work will tend to decrease. Whether hours of work in the market will increase or decrease depends on whether the job shift from home to market adds more hours of work to the market sector than is subtracted from it by a possibly increased consumption of leisure. Whether the net outcome is a positive or negative sign of a is, therefore, an empirical question. It is certainly incorrect to predict that the income effect of the wage rate on market work exceeds the substitution effect by analogy to the backward-bending supply curve. The two substitution effects involved in this comparison are quite different; the strength of substitution between wage goods and leisure time has no bearing on the strength of substitution between home production and wage goods. If anything, one would intuitively expect the latter to exceed the former.

Equation 2 was specified in terms of long-run magnitudes, such as earning power of husband and wife which also implies a long-run concept of hours of work on the left-hand side. Such specification is inappropriate for most empirical data in which individual families report current annual income and labor force participation of the wife during a survey week, or her work experience during a year. One set

[6] To the extent that women with strong tastes for leisure tend to seek out rich husbands, the true income effect (keeping tastes fixed) is overestimated in cross sections.

70

OF MARRIED WOMEN

of data, however, is usable without adapting the model to the distinction between "permanent" and current magnitudes: These are area statistics which were heavily utilized by Douglas and Long mainly because of the absence of more detailed disaggregations. Even with such data currently available, which are much richer on the individual level, the area averages have special advantages for the purpose of estimating the coefficients of equation 2. First, the data provide information on average earning power of employed females, which can be used as a proxy for w. The second and basic merit of the community averages is that they can be interpreted as approximations to the long-run or permanent levels of the relevant variables.[7] Given that the age and family-type mix in different communities is rather similar at a given time,[8] average income and labor force figures could be considered equivalent to average magnitudes over the life-cycle, when secular trends in population and income are disregarded. At any rate, these averages are free from short-run "transitory" deviations of individual incomes from their normal levels. However, the community averages contain a transitory deviation common to the whole group. In other words, some areas may at a given time be below or above their normal levels of economic activity. The labor force response to such a transitory deviation should be clearly distinguished from the response to an individual difference in a group. Abnormally low or high levels of economic activity in a community create different employment opportunities, and, broadly speaking, cyclical variations in wage rates. On that account, rational timing of market work would be pro-cyclical. On the other hand, a cyclical decline means a loss in husbands' incomes and employment which may induce an opposite labor force response of wives. The controversy centering around the "added worker hypothesis"[9] is a debate about the net outcome of these two different forces for groups over the business cycle. Responses to individual short-run income variations *within* a group at a given time are motivated

[7] This strategy has been employed with some success in the analyses of consumption behavior. See Margaret G. Reid, "Consumption and the Income Effect" (unpublished manuscript); also R. Eisner, "The Permanent Income Hypothesis: Comment," *American Economic Review*, Dec. 1958, pp. 972-980.

[8] Labor force rates by cities, standardized for age, differ negligibly from unstandardized ones.

[9] According to that hypothesis, the labor force increases in depressions because unemployment of the main breadwinner induces other family members to seek employment. See W. S. Woytinsky, *Additional Workers and the Volume of Unemployment in the Depression*, S.S.R.C., 1940. For a critical analysis see Long, *The Labor Force*, Chapter 10.

71

LABOR FORCE PARTICIPATION

by only one of the forces, since the cyclical level is fixed for the whole group. Knowledge of this response to transitory income of the family provides, by itself, no answer to the question posed by the "added worker" controversy.

Table 1 provides estimates of the coefficients of equation 2 as well as coefficients for the equation expanded to include 5 independent

TABLE 1

AREA REGRESSIONS OF LABOR FORCE RATES OF MARRIED WOMEN,
ALL NORTHERN STANDARD METROPOLITAN AREAS OF 250,000
OR MORE POPULATION IN 1950

| | INDEPENDENT VARIABLES | | | | | |
| | X_1 | X_2 | X_3 | X_4 | X_5 | R^2 |
	(thousands of dollars)			(per cent)		
Regression coefficients	−0.62	+1.33	+0.12	−0.41	−0.24	0.62
and standard errors	(0.21)	(0.11)	(0.27)	(0.53)	(0.61)	
Regression coefficients	−0.53	+1.52				0.51
Elasticities at means	−0.83	+1.50				

NOTE: See text for description of independent variables.
SOURCE: *U.S. Census of Population 1950*, Vol. II, *Characteristics of the Population*, Tables 86, 88, 183; Special Report, *General Characteristics of Families*, Table 41; and Gertrude Bancroft, *The American Labor Force, Its Growth and Changing Composition*, New York, Wiley, 1958, Table D-11.

variables. The regression analysis was restricted to 57 largest Standard Metropolitan Areas (population, 250,000 and over) in the North. It was felt that the SMA approximate labor markets more properly than cities. Southern areas were excluded because of the desire to exclude color differentials, which need to be studied separately. The dependent variable is the labor force participation rate (in per cent) of married women with husband present during the census week early in 1950. X_1 is the median income in 1949 of male family heads, wife present; X_2 is the median income of females who worked 50 to 52 weeks in 1949. These are the empirical proxies for x_p and w in equation 2. Three independent variables were added to help in the interpretation. Since areas differ by educational composition, which may affect as well as reflect tastes for market work or for its continuity, this variable was represented by the per cent of population age 25 and over with completed high school education or more (X_3). The position of the community relative to its normal levels of economic activity (group transi-

72

OF MARRIED WOMEN

tory) was represented by the male unemployment rate (X_4). Finally, to take care of the more important differences in demand for work at home, the per cent of families with children under 6 years of age was represented by (X_5).

The coefficients in Table 1 are informative: Judging by the coefficient of determination (R^2), the male income (X_1) and female wage rate (X_2) variables alone explain a half of the observed variation in labor force participation rates among areas in 1950. The effect of husbands' incomes is negative,[10] as theoretically expected. The effect of wives' earning power is positive, and indeed stronger than the effect of income. This result is quite suggestive with regard to time series, though not directly applicable.[11] The introduction of a measure of educational level (X_3) into the equation attenuates the wage rate effect somewhat, though not significantly in a statistical sense. Unemployment (X_4) is seen to have a discouraging effect on labor force participation. This appears to be a contradiction of the added worker hypothesis, though the information is not sufficient to yield statistical significance.[12] Finally, the presence of small children (X_5) has an effect in the expected direction, though again statistical significance is lacking.

ADAPTATION OF THE MODEL TO ANALYSIS OF FAMILY SURVEYS

When labor force behavior (reported for a week or for the preceding year) of wives is related to current income of husbands in family surveys, the observed relation is a compound of two effects which it is important to distinguish: the responsiveness of labor force behavior (1) to husbands' long-run income positions, and (2) to current deviations of that income from its normal level.[13]

[10] This stands in contrast to Long's finding that the negative relation between earnings of males and labor force rates of females, by areas, which was observed by Douglas and Long in other census periods, seems to have vanished in 1950. Such an impression, however, is based on a gross regression between the two variables and is not confirmed, when the other relevant variable, the female wage rate, is included in the equation. Table 1 indicates no basic change in the structure of the labor force relation between 1940 and 1950: A comparable two-variable regression in 1940 showed an income elasticity of -0.91 and a wage rate elasticity of $+1.26$. The change in the *gross* regression from negative to positive is due to a larger positive intercorrelation between male and female earnings in 1950 ($r = +.8$) than in 1940 ($r = +.4$).

[11] See section on cross sections and time series, below, for a discussion of time series.

[12] For a further discussion of the "added worker" question, see section on secular and cyclical effects of transitory components, below.

[13] For present purposes, a similar distinction between current and "permanent"

73

LABOR FORCE PARTICIPATION

How the two factors, if distinct, may affect empirical results is easily discernible: Assume, for example, that, other things equal, wives' market activities are geared to long-run or permanent income, and are not affected in quantity or in timing by current deviations from it. Compare two groups of families, standardized for other characteristics, and with the same observed distribution of husbands' incomes in each. If differences among incomes are purely transitory in one group, and of a lasting nature in the other, an inverse relation between income of husband and participation of wife will be observed in the second group, but not in the first. Exactly the opposite result is obtained if we assume that wives respond to transitory, but not to permanent income. More generally, the observed negative relation will be steeper in the first group, if labor force behavior is more responsive to transitory than to permanent levels of income, and conversely if it is more responsive to permanent levels. Thus, survey observations may yield slopes of varying steepness in different bodies of data, depending on the differential responsiveness of labor force behavior to the two components of income, and on the extent to which the current income variation in the observed groups is "made up" of the two components.

A basic question, at this point, is whether a response to transitory income does exist at all. It is not obvious that temporal variation in family income makes it worthwhile to change the timing of market activities of wives. Such a hypothesis, however, may be derived from several considerations:

According to the simplest version of consumption theory, the absolute income hypothesis, current consumption responds to changes in current income. Hence, as income declines, leisure declines, and work increases. If the temporary change in family income, say a decline, is due to a change in employment (of head), and the family finds itself with an excess amount of "leisure," an attempt is made to restore equilibrium by increased market work of the wife. This is particularly likely, if unemployment is not general, and if the husband to some extent helps out at home.

This theory does not explicitly recognize distinctions between consumption responses to short-run and long-run income variation. Such a distinction is basic to the permanent income theory. According to that

---

levels of the female wage rate is not formally introduced. Short-run variations in it, or rather in employment opportunities, are largely a matter of industry differences among communities. We may assume that such differences are much less important in family surveys than in area comparisons.

74

OF MARRIED WOMEN

theory, aggregate family consumption is determined even in short periods by long-run levels of family income. Adjustment between planned consumption and income received in the short period of observation (current, or measured income) takes place via saving behavior, that is, via changes in assets and debts. However, if assets are low or not liquid, and access to the capital market costly or nonexistent, it might be preferable to make the adjustment to a drop in family income on the money income side rather than on the money expenditure side. This is so because consumption requiring money expenditures may contain elements of short-run inflexibility such as contractual commitments. The greater short-run flexibility of nonmoney items of consumption (leisure, home production) may also be a cultural characteristic of a money economy. Under these conditions, a transitory increase in labor force participation of the wife may well be an alternative to dissaving, asset decumulation, or increasing debt. One useful empirical implication of this hypothesis for labor force behavior is that it should be inversely related to the level of family assets, both in the life-cycle and in the short-run sense.

The proper interpretation of survey data, therefore, requires a specification of transitory income (x_t) in addition to permanent income (x_p) which was included in equation 2. The model becomes:

$$m = \beta_p \cdot x_p + \beta_t \cdot x_t + a \cdot w + u \ (3)$$

Two avenues are open for empirical utilization of equation 3. One is an attempt to estimate the coefficients, particularly the new coefficient β_t. Another is the exploration of the implications of equation 3 for observable relations in various bodies of survey data. Both approaches are used. In both cases the major substantive interest is focused on the relative sizes of β_p and β_t, as well as on those of β_p and a.

Equation 3, if correct, points out two major reasons for the difficulties in understanding the usual cross-sectional findings.[14] No information is available on the extent to which current income represents long-run income. When labor force rates of wives are classified by characteristics of husbands, little or no information is given on characteristics of wives. Since the newly available data from the 1950 BLS Survey of Consumer Expenditures are less deficient in these respects, we turn first to them for an empirical analysis.

[14] Comprehensive summaries of census findings are provided by Gertrude Bancroft, *The American Labor Force, Its Growth and Changing Composition*, New York, Wiley, 1958, and by Long, *The Labor Force*.

LABOR FORCE PARTICIPATION
BLS Survey of Consumer Expenditures

The more systematic testing of the analytical model (equation 3) and estimation of its parameters, particularly of β_t, the coefficient of transitory income, were made possible by cards especially prepared by the Bureau of Labor Statistics from its 1950 Survey of Consumer Expenditures. The cards contain information on economic and other characteristics of individual earners cross-classified by a number of such characteristics of the urban consumer units of which they are members. In what follows, employment status of wives is related to income and work experience of husbands, roughly standardized by age, education, and family type.

For the purpose of this study, the data were restricted to white husband-wife families, excluding units of which heads were self-employed or not gainfully occupied. The excluded population subgroups are known to exhibit differential patterns of labor force behavior. Separate analyses and comparisons are therefore required. The resulting homogeneous sample contained 6,766 consumer units. It was stratified by age and education of head, as well as by presence or absence of young children in the younger age group.[15] The 12 strata so obtained (shown in Table 2) were in turn subdivided into units with heads working full time year-round, and heads not fully employed during the year. Whenever analytically convenient, these subgroups within strata were merged.

The first three columns in Table 3 provide information on average labor force responses of wives to empirical approximations of the permanent levels of the independent variables given by weekly earnings of fully employed heads and by weekly earnings of employed wives. The female labor force rates[16] (column 3) can be interpreted as such response only within each of the four age-family type groups. Differences between groups are influenced by life-cycle phenomena.

Within each of the age-family type groups, except the first, average labor force behavior of wives is consistent with the findings in the area regression. That is, the positive effect of the female wage rate outweighs the negative effect of heads' income power. Indeed, the positive

[15] Preschool children are not important numerically in the older age groups. Unfortunately, time and budget considerations did not permit more detailed stratifications.
[16] Strictly speaking, these are employment rates, that is, the proportion of wives who were employed at any time during the survey year. Labor force rates are, therefore, somewhat underestimated.

TABLE 2

STRATIFICATION AND SAMPLE SIZES OF
HUSBAND-WIFE URBAN CONSUMER UNITS, 1950 BUREAU OF
LABOR STATISTICS DATA

	Education of Head		
Age of Head	Elementary (8 years or less)	High School (9-12 years)	College (13 years or more)
Less than 35, oldest child less than 16	139 75	747 216	283 119
Less than 35, no small children	55 15	258 59	45 43
35-54	851 287	1,308 280	618 139
55 and older	491 221	232 113	117 25

NOTE: Upper figures for each group refer to family units with heads working full time year-round. Lower figures refer to units with heads working less than a full year.

TABLE 3

LABOR FORCE RATES OF WIVES OF FULLY EMPLOYED HEADS, BY HEADS' AGE, EDUCATION, INCOME, AND BY WIVES' WEEKLY EARNINGS

		Heads' Earnings per Week (dollars) (1)	Wives' Earnings per Week (2)	Wives' Labor Force Rate[a]	
Heads' Age	Heads' Education			Average (3)	When Head Earned $2,000-$3,000 (per cent) (4)
Less than 35, oldest child less than 16	Elementary	62.5	41.2	27	19
	High school	71.6	44.2	23	27
	College	83.6	47.1	18	36
Less than 35, no small children	Elementary	63.3	44.7	62	62[b]
	High school	66.7	46.3	69	65
	College	80.1	50.5	69	83[b]
35-54	Elementary	70.0	41.1	31	37
	High school	79.5	45.9	33	45
	College	115.3	52.4	38	56
55 and older	Elementary	65.8	38.6	16	21
	High school	85.6	41.1	20	38
	College	122.5	58.1	23	38[b]

SOURCE: 1950 BLS data.
[a] Husbands employed full time year-round.
[b] Based on less than 20 observations.

LABOR FORCE PARTICIPATION

wage rate elasticity must be more than twice as large as the negative
income elasticity since, moving from lower to higher education and
income levels in each group, the per cent increase in wives' weekly
earnings is less than half the per cent increase in husbands' earnings.
Over the life cycle as a whole, this excess of the wage rate elasticity
over the income elasticity is not so great, since the young group with
small children exhibits what seems to be a stronger negative income
effect or a weaker positive wage rate effect, or both. The theoretical
likelihood of such behavior of units at the time when small children
are present was discussed before.[17]

Differences in labor force behavior between the age-family type
groups are caused largely by life-cycle differences in family responsibilities. The low rates in the open-ended oldest age group probably
reflect retirement age, as well as effects of larger property income and
of greater contributions to family income by members other than head
and wife. This is supported by the fact that the percentage difference
between full time earnings of heads and total family income increases
after age 35 despite the declining labor force rates of wives.[18]

The last column of Table 3 suggests a response of labor force behavior to transitory components of income. At the same low current
earnings of husbands ($2,000-3,000 in this illustration), labor force
rates of wives increase with the heads' education, hence with their
permanent income. The increase in rates is much more pronounced at
the fixed income level than for the group averages. Clearly, the higher
the education of the head, the larger the (negative) difference between
the fixed current income figure and his expected or long-run income
position. In other words, in column 4, negative income transitories increase as we move from lower to higher education levels of heads in
each age-family type group. To sum it up, figures in column 3 reflect
the fact that, in each age group, the discouraging effect of husbands'
normal earning power is more than outweighed by the positive effect
of the female wage rate. The latter effect is augmented in column 4
by the negative transitory components of husbands' income exerting
an additional push into the labor market.

More evidence on the influence of transitory components of family
income on wives' labor force behavior is provided in Table 4. Rates for

[17] See section on Work Choices, above.
[18] See Table III in the author's "Labor Supply, Family Income, and Consumption," *Proceedings of the 1959 Annual Meeting of the American Economic Association, American Economic Review*, May 1960, p. 577.

OF MARRIED WOMEN

TABLE 4
LABOR FORCE RATES OF WIVES, BY EARNINGS AND EMPLOYMENT OF HEADS

EDUCATION OF HEAD

AGE OF HEAD	ELEMENTARY			HIGH SCHOOL			COLLEGE		
	Heads' Earnings	Heads' Weeks[a]	Labor Force Rates of Wives	Heads' Earnings	Heads' Weeks[a]	Labor Force Rates of Wives	Heads' Earnings	Heads' Weeks[a]	Labor Force Rates of Wives
Less than 35, oldest child less than 16	$3,253	52	27%	$3,724	52	23%	$4,346	52	18%
	2,329	38	33	2,772	40	30	2,527	41	39
	−29	−27	+22	−26	−23	+30	−42	−21	+117
Less than 35, no small children	3,291	52	62	3,467	52	69	4,166	52	69
	2,407	38	66	2,385	39	73	1,902	32	88
	−27	−27	+6	−31	−25	+6	−54	−39	+28
35-54	3,636	52	31	4,135	52	33	5,996	52	38
	2,395	36	44	2,871	39	49	3,442	42	52
	−37	−31	+42	−30	−25	+48	−43	−20	+37
55 and older	3,420	52	16	4,450	52	20	6,370	52	23
	1,792	28	27	2,139	30	27	2,950	34	16
	−47	−44	+68	−52	−42	+35	−46	−35	−30

SOURCE: 1950 BLS data.

NOTE: Upper figures for each age-family group refer to heads who worked full time year-round; figures on second line refer to heads who worked part period or part time, or both; figures on third line for each group are the percentage difference between upper and lower lines.

[a] Weeks paid for.

79

LABOR FORCE PARTICIPATION

wives are higher when heads did not work a full year than when they did, in each of the 12 population groups except in the oldest with highest education level. The higher labor force rates in the second line for each group may have been expected in view of the lower annual earnings of heads. However, the differences between earnings within each group are of a quite different nature than those between groups. To the extent that the family units within each group have been made homogeneous by the stratification, income differences within them are of a transitory nature.

The extent to which the families within each group are homogeneous with respect to normal earnings of husbands can be inferred from the third line for each group. If the wage rate (weekly earning rate) were the same for the heads who were not fully employed as for those who were, the percentage "loss" of time worked (weeks not employed) would account for, and would exactly equal, all of the "decline" in the year's earnings. It is clear from Table 4, that (transitory) differences in weeks worked rather than (permanent) differences in wage rates account for the overwhelming part of the differences in the year's earnings between the 2 subgroups, particularly in the strata with elementary and high school education. In the college stratum, however, almost half of the drop is accounted for by permanent differences—the relative decline in earnings is almost twice as large as the relative decline in weeks worked. The heterogeneity of the group with respect to permanent income is not surprising: it lumps people with one year of college together with highly trained professionals.

Table 4 not only shows the existence of a negative labor force response to transitory income, but also suggests orders of magnitude of the elasticity. For each group ratios of percentage difference in labor force rates to percentage difference in earnings and to percentage difference in weeks worked provide rough alternative estimates of this elasticity. These estimates, shown in the last two columns of Table 5, generally exceed the estimate of the elasticity with respect to permanent income levels derived from the area regression (Table 1). A more rigorous test for the hypothesis that the labor force response to transitory income is stronger than the response to permanent income is developed in a procedure (Table 5) which also yields numerical estimates of the elasticities.[19]

[19] The elasticity estimates are equivalent to estimates of regression coefficients of equation 3 stated in terms of logarithms of its variables. They are used for purposes of comparability. In the following discussion the same symbols are used for elasticities as for slopes, but the distinction is made explicit in the text.

OF MARRIED WOMEN

TABLE 5
GROSS AND PARTIAL REGRESSION COEFFICIENTS OF LABOR FORCE RATES OF WIVES ON EARNINGS AND WEEKS WORKED BY HEAD

AGE OF HEAD	EDUCATION	SLOPES[a]			ELASTICITY ESTIMATES OF:			Alternative Elasticity Estimates[b] of β_t	
		$b_{m.e}$ (1)	$b_{m.e}$ (2)	$b_{m.e}$ (3)	β_p (4)	$\beta - \beta_p$ (5)	β_t (6)	(7)	(8)
Less than 35, oldest child less than 16	Elementary	−0.132	+0.035	−0.327	+0.04	−0.61	−0.57	−0.79	−0.82
	High school	−0.604	−0.503	−0.347	−0.80	−0.75	−1.55	−1.19	−1.33
	College	−0.520	−0.423	−0.453	−1.02	−1.26	−2.28	−2.76	−5.60
Less than 35, no small children	Elementary	−0.460	−0.438	−0.071	−0.22	−0.05	−0.27	−0.24	−0.22
	High school	−0.246c	−0.188c	−0.210c	−0.09	−0.15	−0.24	−0.19	−0.24
	College	−0.624	−0.577	−0.190c	−0.35	−0.14	−0.49	−0.51	−0.77
35-54	Elementary	−0.623	−0.568	−0.124	−0.68	−0.20	−0.88	−1.14	−1.35
	High school	−0.511	−0.433	−0.535	−0.61	−0.81	−1.42	−1.61	−1.92
	College	−0.086	−0.338	+0.915	−0.54	+1.21	+0.67	−0.86	−1.85
55 and older	Elementary	−0.402	−0.346	−0.139	−0.73	−0.43	−1.16	−1.45	−1.50
	High school	−0.205	−0.254	+0.213	−0.56	+0.53	−0.03	−0.67	−0.83
	College	−0.092	−0.143	+0.326	−0.40	+0.71	+0.31	+0.66	+0.85

SOURCE: 1950 BLS data.

[a] $b_{m.e}$ = slope of regression of labor force rate (per cent) on earnings of head (thousands of dollars).
$b_{m.e}$ = slope of regression of labor force rate on earnings of head, keeping weeks worked constant.
$b_{m.e}$ = slope of regression of labor force rate on weeks worked, keeping earnings of head constant.

[b] Based on Table 4: Ratios of percentage difference in labor force rates to percentage difference in earnings (col. 7), and to percentage difference in weeks worked (col. 8).

c Not significantly different from zero, under a 5 per cent level.

LABOR FORCE PARTICIPATION

After merging the two employment groups, in each of the cells, a simple and a 2-variable regression of labor force rates of wives on the year's earnings of husbands and on weeks worked by him yielded the gross and partial slopes listed in Table 5. The slope (b_{mx}) of the gross regression of wives' labor force rates on husbands' earnings (column 1) combines the effects of permanent and of transitory income. The partial slope of the same relation ($b_{mx.e}$ in column 2) keeps the number of weeks worked by the head constant. It, therefore, approximates the response to heads' normal earning power, rather than to their current income. Finally, $b_{me.x}$ (in column 3) represents the response to weeks worked by heads, keeping their total earnings constant.

The sign of the slope $b_{me.x}$ (column 3) provides a test for the difference between the strengths of the two income effects on labor force behavior of wives.

If the distinction between permanent and transitory income did not matter, a change in weeks worked by heads, with total earnings constant, would produce no labor force response. This hypothesis is rejected by the data. All slopes in column 3 are statistically significant, except those in the young group without small children. This exception is plausible: the stage in the life cycle represented by this group, namely the period between marriage and first child, is usually short, and during that time most of the wives are employed anyway; thus, there is very little scope for variations in timing of employment within that stage.

Now a decline in weeks, keeping total earnings constant, means a corresponding amount of increase in earning power, which is offset by a transitory loss of income of the same amount. The change in the permanent component of income is expected to bring about a *decrease* in labor force participation. The same change of the transitory component in the opposite direction is expected to stimulate an *increase* in market activities. The direction of the net outcome depends, therefore, on which income effect is stronger. Indeed, the negative sign of $b_{me.x}$ provides evidence that the effect of transitory income outweighs the permanent income effect!

An estimate of the labor force response to transitory income (coefficient β_t in equation 3) is obtained as follows: The partial regression $b_{me.x}$ measures the arithmetic difference in labor force rates of wives due to the equal (but of opposite sign) differences in permanent and in transitory components of income. Converting the arithmetic difference

82

OF MARRIED WOMEN

in labor force rates into a percentage difference (using rates of wives with fully employed husbands as base, column 3 in Table 3), and dividing it by the percentage difference in income, that is, by $(1/52 \times 100)$ we obtain the estimate of the difference $(\beta_t - \beta_p)$ in elasticity terms.[20] This estimate is shown in column 5 of Table 5.

The slope $b_{mx.e}$ which serves as an approximation of the response to permanent income (β_p) is next converted into an elasticity at the mean by the usual procedure[21] using the averages in Table 4. The estimate is shown in column 4 of Table 5. The sum of column 4 and column 5 in Table 5 provides an estimate of the response elasticity to transitory income (β_t), which is shown in column 6. These estimates of transitory income elasticity in column 6 resemble the alternative estimates in columns 7 and 8, though they are somewhat smaller.

Looking at the sizes of parameter estimates in Table 5, we find perhaps most meaningful for purposes of comparisons with aggregates those in the modal population group (age 35-55, high school education). The estimate of the elasticity with respect to permanent income (β_p) in it is not very different from the corresponding estimate in the area regression (Table 1). The estimate of the transitory elasticity (β_t) is more than twice as large.

The estimates vary among population subgroups in a roughly systematic way: Response to permanent income is weaker the higher the educational level of heads 35 years of age and older. Responses to transitory income differ in a similar way. An opposite pattern is discernible in the young groups with small children. In the young but childless groups the magnitudes are either small or statistically unreliable.

It is difficult to say how much substance could be assigned to these differentials, given all the necessary qualifications—about the rata and the estimating procedure. As previously mentioned, small income elasticities in the childless groups are theoretically plausible. But they may also be produced by the arithmetic of elasticities, since levels of partici-

---

[20] $\frac{e}{m} . b_{me . e}$, where e is number of weeks worked by the heads, measures the percentage change in labor force rate per 1 per cent increase in weeks employed, keeping husbands' income constant. But a 1 per cent rise in e, as stated in the text implies a 1 per cent rise in transitory income x_t, *and* a 1 per cent decline in permanent income x_p. Hence: $\frac{e}{m} . b_{me . x}$, in elasticity terms.

[21] Elasticity at the mean of y with respect to x is equal to the slope of the regression of y on x, multiplied by the ratio of the mean of x to the mean of y.

LABOR FORCE PARTICIPATION

pation are high in these groups. The weakening response to transitory income with rising education level in the groups with family heads over 35 years old is consistent with the hypothesis that the availability of assets obviates the need for offsetting temporary income change by means of labor input.

The differential extent to which transitory components in heads' incomes are offset by family labor input in the various population groups is shown in Table 6. In each stratum the regression slope of

TABLE 6

ESTIMATES OF FRACTION OF NEGATIVE TRANSITORY INCOMES OF
HEADS, WHICH IS OFFSET BY FAMILY LABOR INPUT

Age	Education	$b_{y.}$[a]	$b_{z.}$[b]	$1 - \dfrac{b_{y.}}{b_{..}}$
Less than 35, children under 16	Elementary	18.7	39.1	0.52
	High school	27.4	51.2	0.47
	College	33.2	60.5	0.45
Less than 35, no small children	Elementary	13.4	43.8	0.69
	High school	23.1	47.1	0.51
	College	32.4	60.1	0.46
	Elementary	42.1	56.8	0.26
35-55	High school	32.4	60.8	0.47
	College	46.7	75.1	0.38
	Elementary	40.6	54.6	0.25
Over 55	High school	45.1	54.1	0.17
	College	54.9	62.3	0.12

SOURCE: 1950 BLS data.

[a] $b_{y.}$ = slope of regression of family income (dollars) on weeks worked by head.

[b] $b_{z.}$ = slope of regression of heads' income (dollars) on weeks worked by head.

family income (before tax) on weeks worked by heads was divided by the regression slope of heads' earnings on weeks worked by them. This ratio measures the loss in family income relative to the loss in husbands' earnings due to one week's loss of employment. The per cent by which the numerator is smaller than the denominator measures the extent to which a change in head's income was offset by an opposite change in income of other family members.[22]

The results in Table 6 show that the absorption of negative transitory components of heads' income declines with increasing education after

[22] "Loss" and "change" are only figures of speech in a cross-section analysis.

OF MARRIED WOMEN

age 35, and with advancing age in each education group. This absorption is, of course, a net effect of all earners, not just the wife, and is consistent with the hypothesis on alternatives to dissaving.

Census Surveys

Decennial censuses and current population reports of the Census Bureau are the major sources of empirical knowledge about labor force behavior of various population groups. The cross-sectional information on labor force rates of married women is usually contained in one-way or, less frequently, two-way classifications of these rates by variables such as: current or preceding year's income of husbands or of family, education, occupation, age, presence and age of children, color, location, and so forth. These gross relations between labor force rates and the classifying variables are manifold and bewildering. A literal reading of such relations as separate effects of the particular classifying variables is confronted with puzzling differences among various sets of cross-sectional data and leads to apparent contradictions with time series. The purpose of the empirical analysis in this section is to explore the extent to which the economic model presented in this paper (equation 3) is capable of rationalizing some of the observed patterns. Alternatively, this exploration can be viewed as a set of additional tests of the model and of hypotheses concerning sizes of its parameters.

In order to apply equation 3 to the observable gross relations let us deduce the implications of the model for such relations. Starting with the observed gross relation between husbands' income and wives' participation rates (b_{mx}), it can be shown that:[28]

$$b_{mx} = [\beta_p \cdot P + \beta_t \cdot (1\text{-}P)] + a \cdot b_{wx} \quad (4)$$

Specifically, the observed elasticity is a sum of two terms. The first term (in brackets) is an average of permanent (β_p) and transitory (β_t) income elasticities weighted by the ratio (P) of permanent income variance to current income variance. Since both elasticities are negative, this term is negative. The second term is a product of the

[28] From $m = \beta_p \cdot x_p + \beta_t x_t + aw + u$, where the variables are measured as deviations from their means,
$$\Sigma mx = \beta_p \cdot \Sigma x_p \cdot x + \beta_t \cdot \Sigma x_t \cdot x + a\Sigma wx + \Sigma ux$$
Assuming that x_t is independent of x_p and of u, and dividing by Σx^2:
$b_{mx} = \beta_p \cdot P + \beta_t \cdot (1\text{-}P) + ab_{wx}$, where b_{mx} is the least squares regression of m on x, b_{wx} the least squares regression of w on x and P the ratio of variance of X_p to the variance of X. Elasticities replace slopes and relative variances replace variances when the original model is specified in logarithms.

LABOR FORCE PARTICIPATION

female wage rate elasticity (a) and the elasticity of wives' earning power with respect to current income of husband (b_{wx}), that is, of the rate at which a difference in wage rates of wives is associated with a difference in income of husbands. The second term is expected to be positive. It must, therefore, be smaller in absolute size than the first, in order to yield the usually observed negative relation between labor force rates of wives and incomes of husbands, by husbands' current income brackets. This is true for two reasons: b_{wx} is small, thereby weakening the positive effect of the wage rate; and β_t is substantially stronger than β_p, thereby augmenting the negative effect of (permanent) income. That the regression of earning power of wife on income of husband is rather weak is indicated by several sets of data. According to Table 3, the elasticity coefficient is 0.4 to 0.5, by income averages of education groups within age groups. A similar figure was computed from a Census cross-classification of median occupational full-time wages of husbands and wives in 1956.[24] Another computation, which applies full-time average incomes of education classes of males and females[25] to a cross-classification of husbands and wives, by educational background,[26] produced an elasticity coefficient of about 0.5. The inverse regression of the same variables produced an elasticity coefficient of 0.7. Strictly speaking, these are estimates of b_{wx_p} and b_{x_pw} respectively, the regressions with permanent incomes. The term in equation 4 is the regression of *current* income on wives' wage rate (b_{wx}) which is likely to be weaker than b_{wxp}.[27]

When the wage rate of wife is kept fixed, the second term in equation 4 vanishes, and

$$b_{mx.w} = \beta_p \cdot P + \beta_t \cdot (1\text{-}P) \ (4a)$$

If the absolute size of β_t is, in fact, greater than that of β_p, the observed regression $b_{mx.w}$ is steeper than the "long-run" coefficient β_p, so long as the variance of current income exceeds the variance of permanent income ($P < 1$). Also, the negative size of $b_{mx.w}$ increases the smaller P, that is the greater the contribution of transitory components to the current income variance.

[24] Published as Table 2 by Richard N. Rosett in "Working Wives: An Econometric Study," *Studies in Household Economic Behavior*, Yale University Press, 1958, p. 85.
[25] *Current Population Reports*, P-60, No. 27, April 1958, Table 20, p. 37.
[26] *Current Population Reports*, P-20, No. 83, Aug. 1958, Table C, p. 2.
[27] Indeed, a reasonable assumption that X_t is independent of w, yields

$$b_{wx} = b_{wx_p} \cdot P, \text{ since } \frac{\Sigma wx}{\Sigma x^t} = \frac{\Sigma wx_p}{\Sigma x^t_p} \cdot \frac{1}{P}$$

OF MARRIED WOMEN

Looking next at the regression on w, and assuming the X_t is independent of w, we find the expression for the gross relation between wives' earning power and labor force rate is:[28]

$$b_{mw} = \beta_p \cdot b_{x_p w} + a \ (5)$$

It is clear from equation 5 that the observed gross wage rate elasticity of labor force participation (b_{mw}) underestimates the true elasticity (a), because of the negative first term on the right-hand side. It must be positive, however, if $/a/ > /\beta_p/$, and closer to a than to zero, if our previous estimates are roughly correct.

Implications 4 and 5 can be simultaneously put to a test, if labor force rates of wives are cross classified by husbands' income and by a measure of wives' earning power. One such cross-classification in census data provides the opportunity. Table 7 is a two-way tabulation of labor force rates of wives in survey week of March 1957, by income of husbands in 1956 and education level of wife. We use the latter as an index of wives' earning power, assigning to it average full-time incomes of females in these education classes. Empirical results are consistent with the theory.

(1) A comparison of equations 4 and 4a indicates that $/b_{mx.w}/ > /b_{mx}/$. That is to say, the decline in participation associated with increasing income should be stronger when w is held constant than when it is not. Rates of decline are, in fact, more pronounced in the inside columns of Table 7 than in the left-hand marginal column.

(2) The gross relation of participation rates and earning power (measured by education) of wives is positive and strong. This has been repeatedly observed in census data.[29]

(3) When income of husbands is held fixed, the increase in participation with increasing wage rate of wives is stronger than when it is not. Rates of increase are more pronounced in the inside rows of Table 7 than in the left-hand marginal row.

(4) The systematic differences between rows and columns in Table 7 are indicative of the influence of income transitories. From left to right, successive columns correspond to income distributions of groups

[28] Multiply equation 3 by w, sum over all values, and divide by $\Sigma w'$:

$$\Sigma \, mw = \beta_p \cdot \Sigma x_p w + \beta_t \cdot \Sigma x_t w + a \cdot \Sigma w'$$

and

$$b_{mw} = \beta_p \cdot b_{x_p w} + \beta_t \cdot b_{x_t w} + a, \text{ and if } X_t \text{ is independent of } w:$$

$$b_{mw} = \beta_p \cdot b_{x_p w} + a$$

[29] See Long, *The Labor Force*, pp. 94-96, and Bancroft, *The American Labor Force*, pp. 65-69.

LABOR FORCE PARTICIPATION

with higher education and occupation levels. Research in income distribution and consumption[30] indicates that $(1-P)$, the relative importance of transitory components in the income variance, increases with
education and occupation level. Equation 4a, therefore, predicts steeper

TABLE 7

LABOR FORCE RATE OF WIVES, BY OWN EDUCATION, BY INCOME OF
HUSBANDS, URBAN AND RURAL NONFARM, MARCH 1957
(per cent)

INCOME OF HUSBANDS IN 1956	Total	Elementary School	High School 1-3 Years	High School 4 Years	College 1-3 Years	College 4 Years and Over
Total	30.4	26.3	29.9	31.6	35.5	39.4
Under $1,000	33.5	25.6	38.4	48.7	n.a.	n.a.
$1,000-1,999	29.8	24.7	27.1	42.8	n.a.	n.a.
2,000-2,999	36.7	30.3	34.6	47.0	n.a.	n.a.
3,000-3,999	36.3	31.0	34.4	38.8	54.1	n.a.
4,000-4,999	32.3	24.7	33.5	33.4	43.5	n.a.
5,000-5,999	29.1	24.4	26.1	28.6	41.9	50.0
6,000-6,999	27.1	19.3	20.8	28.1	35.1	40.8
7,000-9,999	20.7	16.0	16.2	21.4	22.1	24.7
10,000 and over	11.5	n.a.	n.a.	8.5	9.5	18.3
Median full-year incomes of females, by education		$2,408	$2,583	$3,021	$3,440	$3,809

SOURCE: Labor force rate, *Current Population Reports*, P-50, No. 81, p. 2,
Table 2. Median full-year incomes of females, *Current Population Reports*, P-60,
No. 27, p. 37, Table 20.
n.a. = not available.

slopes at higher education levels, *provided* $/\beta_t/ > /\beta_p/$. The increase
in slopes by columns is clearly visible in Table 7. The systematic differences by rows are, of course, a reflection of the same phenomenon.

(5) A numerical check on the previously estimated parameters
showed them to be rather surprisingly good: Using estimates of β_p from
Table 1, β_t from the modal class in Table 5, a value of 0.8 for P,[31] and
of 0.4 for b_{wx}, equation 4 predicts an average 3 per cent (negative)
difference in participation rates of wives for a 10 per cent (positive)

[30] See the marginal propensities and income elasticities in H. S. Houthakker,
"The Permanent Income Hypothesis," *American Economic Review*, June 1958,
p. 401. Also my "Study of Personal Income Distribution," unpublished Ph.D. dissertation, Columbia University, 1957.
[31] Friedman's estimate of 0.85 relates to family incomes. The value for husbands'
incomes is probably somewhat smaller. The calculations are not sensitive to modest
differences in assumptions.

OF MARRIED WOMEN

difference in current incomes of husbands. This is a good approximation to the actual slope in the marginal column of Table 7.

At the same time, equation 5 predicts an average increase of about 2 per cent in labor force rates of wives for a 10 per cent increase in wives' earning power. This is, again, a remarkably good approximation to the actual value in the marginal row of Table 7.

Equation 4 provides an insight into the nature of bias involved in interpreting the observed gross relation between labor force rates of wives and income of husbands as the "true" income effect. It does not provide a unique answer as to whether such gross regressions under-estimate or overestimate the true income effect. Given the notion that the response to transitory income is stronger than that to permanent income, the expression indicates that the negative elasticity is over-estimated on account of the variability of transitory components in current income ($P < 1$), but a contrary bias is produced by the positive intercorrelation between husbands' income and wives' wage rate.

Since $b_{wx} = b_{wx_p} P$ on the assumption that x_t is independent of w, it follows from equation 4 that the closer the independent variable approximates a permanent income concept, the flatter the gross relation between it and the labor force rate. This is true for two reasons: the negative term in equation 4 decreases, and the positive term increases. It is for these reasons, roughly speaking, that the slope of the relation between labor force rates of wives and education level of husbands,[32] or family rent,[33] is close to zero.[34]

Several other behavior patterns observed in census data can be analyzed in terms of the model presented here.

Labor force rates of wives reported in a survey week, by occupation of husbands, are roughly inversely related to average incomes of husbands in these occupations. However, at the same low income brackets of husbands, participation rates reverse their ranks: they are higher at higher occupational levels[35] (as measured by income). These are effects of transitory components of income of the same kind as shown

---

[32] See, for example, *Current Population Reports*, P-60, No. 27, April 1958, Table F.

[33] Tabulations of the 1940 Census indicate a weak negative slope. The 1950 BLS data used here show a zero or even slightly positive slope.

[34] When $P = 1$ is put into equation 4, it becomes $b_{mx_p} = \beta_p + a \cdot b_{wx_p}$. With the orders of magnitudes of our estimates, b_{mx_p} is close to zero.

[35] See Table F in *Current Population Reports*, P-60, No. 12, also exhibited and discussed by H. P. Miller, *Income of the American People*, pp. 88-89, and by Bancroft, *The American Labor Force*, p. 124.

LABOR FORCE PARTICIPATION

in column 4 of Table 3, where the classification is by education of husband.

Another set of data which suggests a response to temporary income change are classifications of labor force rates of wives by labor force status of husband and by his age. Not being in the labor force is more likely to be a short-run phenomenon for younger husbands (education, temporary disability, etc.) than for older ones. Table 8 shows a strong labor force response in the younger groups and none in the group over

TABLE 8
LABOR FORCE RATES OF WIVES, BY AGE AND LABOR FORCE STATUS OF HUSBANDS

| Age of Husbands | Employment Status of Husbands | | | | | |
| | 1954 | | | 1955 | | |
	Employed	Unemployed	Not in Labor Force	Employed	Unemployed	Not in Labor Force
14-24	26.3	26.6	55.3	29.2	32.0	60.0
25-44	27.3	30.7	54.9	27.4	42.3	44.5
45-64	29.5	34.0	27.3	31.3	35.2	28.0

SOURCE: *Current Population Reports.*

45. The fact that the response to labor force status of husband is stronger than the response to his employment status is also reasonable in view of the short observation period (survey week).

The relation between "transitory" income variability and observed labor force behavior can also be detected by varying the length of the observation period. Extending the period of observation means reducing the importance of transitory income components, hence reducing the negative slope of the income-labor force relation.

In Table 9 a comparison is made between work experience of wives by income level of husbands and by periods of observation. Columns 1 and 2 present the long-run (since marriage) work experience of married women, with husbands and children present, classified by income of husbands as reported at the time of the survey (1955). Over the long run for which the work experience is reported income differences were undoubtedly smaller, but in the same direction.[36] The income-labor

[36] It can be shown that, in general, the correlation between current and permanent income is:

$$r(x,x_p) = \sqrt{P} + r(x_t,x_p) \cdot \sqrt{1-P}$$

This is always positive, with the exception of the case when a negative $r(x_t, x_p)$ exceeds in absolute value the ratio $\sqrt{\dfrac{P}{1-P}} = \dfrac{\sigma(x_p)}{\sigma(x_t)}$

OF MARRIED WOMEN

force relation which is strongly negative for the short observation period (column 3) vanishes in the long period[37] (columns 1 and 2). To repeat the previous argument, this does not mean that the response to permanent income is zero. The permanent elasticity (β_p) which is negative is just about offset by the positive wage rate elasticity (a),

TABLE 9

WORK EXPERIENCE OF WIVES, BY INCOME OF HUSBAND, OBSERVATION PERIOD, AGE, AND PRESENCE OF CHILDREN

| | WORK EXPERIENCE SINCE MARRIAGE[a] | | LABOR FORCE RATE IN SURVEY WEEK, 1956[b] | | | |
| | Age, 25-35 With Children | Age, 18-40 | | Age 20-44 | | |
INCOME OF HUSBAND IN 1955 (dollars)	Average Number of Years at Work (1)	Average Number of Years at Work (2)	All (3)	With Children of Age: Less Than 6 (4)	6-18 (5)	No Children (6)
Less than 3,000	2.67	2.24	38.1	22.4	54.6	59.0
3,000-4,000	2.61	2.49	30.4	16.7	39.0	61.0
4,000-5,000	2.71	2.63	29.6	15.8	38.5	62.6
More than 5,000	2.68	2.64	24.0	11.1	35.9	56.5

[a] From article based on "Growth of American Families Study," *Milbank Memorial Fund Quarterly*, July 1959, Table 5, p. 291.
[b] Based on *Current Population Reports*, P-50, No. 73, Table 9.

even though the effect of the latter is attenuated by the fact that wives' earning power usually rises less than half as fast as that of husbands' when moving up the permanent income brackets of husbands.

Since columns 1 and 2 report for women with children, and column 3 pertains to all women of a similar age group, the latter were further subdivided by presence and age of children for clearer comparison. The contrast between the long-period and the short-period relation is, indeed, stronger for the more appropriate comparison of columns 1 and 2 with columns 4 and 5, rather than with column 3. Moreover, the breakdown by presence of children reveals a phenomenon, previously suggested, and repeatedly observed in census data:[38] When small

[37] The age span in cols. 1 and 2 obscures somewhat the interpretation of results in Table 9. A comparison of cols. 1 and 2 indicates, however, that the quantitative effect is not strong enough to affect the conclusions.
[38] See *Current Population Reports*, P-50, No. 39, Table 6. Also Durand, *The Labor Force in the U.S.*, pp. 91-92.

91

LABOR FORCE PARTICIPATION

children are present the observed negative relation of labor force rates with income is stronger than when they are absent (column 6). Considerations of substitutability between care of children and wage goods and services are consistent with such findings. According to the theoretical argument, the positive wage rate effect (a) is weaker and the negative income effect (β_p) is stronger the lesser the substitutability between wife's labor at home and goods and services obtainable in the market. This is likely to be the case when small children are present.

Implications

CROSS SECTIONS AND TIME SERIES

If the orders of magnitude of the parameter estimates of equation 3 are roughly correct, there is no real contradiction between findings on labor force behavior of married women in cross-sections and in time series. The impression of a contradiction is due to the way cross-sections have been looked at, in terms of gross relations between income of husband and labor force participation of wife. Such gross comparisons yield results (slopes or elasticities) which are sensitive both to the existence of transitory components in income and to the covariation of wives' earning power with husbands' income. The transitory components accentuate the negative effect of income. In their absence, the cross-sectional negative relation would hardly be noticeable. If, in addition, the positive relation between husbands' and wives' incomes were stronger than is usually observed in cross-sections, a positive rather than negative relation would be found between labor force rates of wives and incomes of husbands, even at a point of time.

Thus, if equation 3 is projected onto time series, two facts intervene which convert the negative income relation in cross-sections into a positive secular relation: (1) short-run transitory components of income are not relevant to long-run developments, and (2) the female wage rate has risen over time at least as fast as the male rate.

It is of some interest, at this point, to inquire how much of the quantitative change over time can be "explained" by the use of the supply function estimated from the recent cross sections.

The appropriate equation for this purpose is equation 1,

$$m = \beta_p y + \gamma w + u \text{ where } \gamma = a - \beta_p$$

92

OF MARRIED WOMEN

and y is family income computed as a sum of earning powers of husbands and wives. The estimated equation is (from Table 1):

$$m = -0.53y + 2.05w \ (6)$$

In Table 10 actual secular changes in labor force rates of married women are compared with changes predicted by equation 6. The data used for the comparison are not exactly appropriate. They cover the

TABLE 10

ACTUAL AND "PREDICTED" SECULAR CHANGES IN LABOR FORCE
RATES OF MARRIED WOMEN, 1890-1959

	1889-1919	1919-29	1929-39	1939-49	1949-59
Changes in full-time[a] earnings of males (dollars)	685	878	328	561	562
Changes in full-time[b] earnings of females (dollars)	386	504	252	585	576
Changes in family[c] earning power (dollars)	1,071	1,382	580	1,146	1,138
Expected changes in labor force rates	+2.2	+3.2	+2.1	+6.0	+5.7
Actual changes[d] in labor force rates	+4.4	+2.7	+2.1	+7.8	+8.4
Expected as per cent of actual changes	50%	119%	100%	77%	68%

[a] In 1949 prices. SOURCE: Long, *The Labor Force*, Table 17, p. 118; and *Survey of Current Business*.

[b] In 1949 prices. SOURCE: Long, *The Labor Force*, Table C-8, p. 356.

[c] Sum of first and second lines.

[d] SOURCE: Long, *The Labor Force*, Table A-6, p. 297.

whole United States population, rather than white urban families for which equation 6 was estimated. The historical trend for the latter is steeper than for the aggregate. On the other hand, secular improvements in the census reporting system, urbanization, and decline in homework for pay which was easily overlooked by interviewers and respondents, lend an opposite bias to the census data. The latter bias is probably strongest in the earliest period, for which the relative

LABOR FORCE PARTICIPATION

discrepancy between actual and estimated is largest (1889-1919 in Table 10). The "fit" since 1919, which is on the whole surprisingly good, shows an interesting trend: the early decade is "overexplained" by equation 6, and the per cent of actual changes "accounted for" by equation 6 declines over time. Implicit in this finding is a suggestion that the negative income elasticity has been decreasing over time,[39] or that the positive wage rate elasticity has been growing over time. Both developments are consistent with the theory underlying the analysis in this paper: they are to be expected, if the degree of substitutability between home production and wage goods has been historically increasing.[40]

This historical change can also be viewed as an omission in equation 6 of a set of relative prices, which are fixed in cross sections. These are relative prices of commercial performance of household tasks. A secular decline in such prices relative to other consumer prices means that the secular increase in opportunity costs of work at home is *underestimated* by equation 6.

On the other hand, it cannot be assumed that productivity in the home remained constant while productivity in the market increased over time. To the extent that productivity in the home increased with the growth of productivity in the market, the female wage rate *overestimates* the increase in the relative price of female labor among its alternative uses. However, in the face of a small family income elasticity of demand for home production and with secularly rising incomes, the growing productivity at home meant a decline of hours of work at home. This, in turn, was likely to mean a shift toward market activities.[41] Thus, to the extent that the increase in w over time overestimates the change in relative prices, a positive effect toward market work is exerted (in a residual fashion) via income effects on home production and leisure.

[39] This is consistent with an observed secular flattening of gross income-labor force slopes in cross sections.

[40] See discussion under Work Choices.

[41] To take an extreme illustrative example, if growth of productivity was as rapid in the home as in the market, and the income elasticity of demand for home production close to zero, w would measure nothing else but the decline of hours of work at home. In other words, the income elasticity of hours of work at home would be -1. Since the negative income elasticity of total hours of work is surely less than unity, a shift toward market work is clearly implied.

OF MARRIED WOMEN

The evaluation of the relative importance of these factors in bringing about the results shown in Table 10 is not undertaken here.[42] It requires a fuller theoretical development and empirical specification of the model presented in this paper.

SECULAR AND CYCLICAL EFFECTS OF TRANSITORY COMPONENTS

The consideration of labor force responses to actual or expected "transitory" changes may have some relevance to historical changes. Educational and occupational trends may put more young married women into the labor market while their husbands acquire formal training or experience on the job and family income is temporarily low. The trends toward early marriages and greater longevity generate prospects of long-lasting reduction in homework after the children are grown. Such expectations may motivate women toward more education and training and induce higher labor force rates throughout the life cycle. The spread of contractual commitments (insurance, installment buying, etc.) to lower income groups may make the adjustment of money income to expenditures more compelling than the adjustment of expenditures to money income.

Analysis of cyclical changes in labor force participation of married women requires an assessment of the effect of transitory changes in income as well as of cyclical change in the female wage rate. The first effect is negative: a decline in employment of head, hence in family income, induces (or temporarily prolongs) labor force activities of wives. On the other hand, cyclical changes in female wage rates or of employment opportunities favor the shifting of market activities to periods of prosperity. The income factor is stressed by the proponents of the "added worker" hypothesis. The employment opportunity is stressed by its opponents. Empirical data do not show any definite cyclical patterns in labor force behavior.

If, for the analysis of work choices of wives, we define the wage rate somewhat more broadly to include employment opportunities, it can be shown that the estimated parameters in equation 3 indeed predict an almost complete cancellation of the two opposing tendencies, hence the absence of pronounced cyclical patterns. Define the wage

[42] But see the very interesting data and hypotheses presented by Long, *The Labor Force*, Ch. 7.

LABOR FORCE PARTICIPATION

rate as an expected magnitude, that is, a product of the actual wage rate and the probability of being employed. If employment in the community drops by p per cent and actual wage rates remain unchanged, the expected wage rate drops by p per cent. Since the loss of family income is due to the loss of employment, its decline is also p per cent on the average. But with the same per cent decline in w and x (ex ante family income), the net outcome depends, according to equation 3, on the comparative strengths of the negative transitory income elasticity (β_t) and the positive wage rate elasticity (a). According to our empirical estimate ($a = + 1.5$ in Table 1, $\beta_t = -1.4$ in the modal group, Table 5) the net effect is negligible. Even if a slight margin in favor of the wage rate is likely, the difference is not clear enough to yield discernible patterns.

While the parameter estimates predict no clear-cut cyclical patterns of labor force participation of married women in the aggregate, they point to differential patterns of subgroups depending on employment experience of husbands. In families whose heads have become unemployed, the relative decline in family income is much stronger than the relative decline in the "expected" wage rate of the wife. In such families, therefore, labor force rates of wives are likely to increase in recessions. In all other families, incomes are relatively stable but wage-rate expectations decline somewhat. The likely result in these families is a slight decrease in labor force rates of wives.

These conclusions are confirmed by a recent study[43] of the 1958 recession experience, based on a subsample of the Census Current Population Survey. According to this study, 21.6 per cent of the wives of unemployed husbands increased their labor force participation during the recession period, 16.8 per cent decreased it, and 61.6 per cent did not change. At the same time, 11.1 per cent of the wives of employed husbands increased their labor force participation, 16.6 per cent decreased it, and 72.3 per cent did not change.

[43] Arnold Katz, "Cyclical Unemployment and the Secondary Family Worker," Board of Governors, Federal Reserve System. The paper was presented at the meeting of the Econometric Society, December 1960, in St. Louis, Missouri.

In his paper, Katz presents additional evidence in favor of our hypothesis that families may maintain consumption levels through labor force adjustments to transitory income changes, and that for married women the response to such income changes is quite pronounced. He shows, for example, that a wife's labor force adjustment to her husband's unemployment is more extensive when this idleness is less anticipated.

OF MARRIED WOMEN

FAMILY INCOME DISTRIBUTION AND CONSUMPTION[44]

Analysis of economic factors influencing labor force behavior of married women carries a direct implication that family income composition and distribution, consumption behavior, and labor supply are intimately related problems. Decisions of family members about work are related to family income in an ex ante sense and are reflected in the ex post total money income of the family. The labor supply function here presented is an analytical bridge between the distribution of personal income (of family heads, for example) and the distribution of total money income of the family. The income effect on market labor supply, both in its long-run and transitory senses, implies a reduction in income inequality when moving from personal incomes (of heads) to family incomes. The wage-rate effect implies an increase in inequality, since incomes of husbands and market earning powers of wives are positively related. For particular population groups observed, the more prevalent the transitory components in heads' incomes, and the weaker the association between the wage rates of the family members, the greater the equalizing effect of labor supply on family income distribution—and conversely.

With respect to consumption behavior, it is clear that the analysis of economic adjustments to changes in family income must include adjustments in the composition of consumption, particularly between the "visible" items (money expenditures) and the "invisible" ones such as leisure and home production. This is an apparent adjustment, on the money income side, of the money income–money expenditures equation, and is an alternative to adjustment on the expenditure side or in asset position, or both. The three alternatives have distinct implications for a money economy.

Finally, in studying factors affecting family consumption, it is not sufficient to look at sociodemographic characteristics of the family head in order to add explanatory variables to income or to gauge the permanent income of the family. For short-period observations the knowledge of employment status and labor force behavior of family members is of primary importance.[45]

[44] For a more detailed discussion and empirical evidence, see my paper "Labor Supply, Family Income, and Consumption," *American Economic Review*, May 1960, pp. 574-583.

[45] A time-series consumption function based on such data is presented by the author in "Employment and Consumption," *Review of Economics and Statistics*, February 1960, pp. 20-26.

COMMENT

CLARENCE D. LONG, The Johns Hopkins University

During the last half-century, there has been an enormous increase in the labor force participation of married women. Even now, however, at any given time two of three wives are at home, in school, in institutions, or playing bingo with other wives, and are therefore unwilling or unable to work. Whether various economic and social forces will bring more of these wives into the labor force is an absorbing economic question, especially since wives are the majority of adult women and form the largest source of additional gainful labor. The economic forces that have aroused most attention have been those centering around income or wages. Real incomes have been rising in most western nations. Do these rising incomes have the effect of bringing more wives into the labor force or of driving out some of those now working?

On this question there has been a confusion of evidence, especially as between moment-of-time and over-time relationships. Moment-of-time studies have been of two sorts: One sort, among different localities such as cities or metropolitan areas, have usually shown that the higher a locality's per capita income, adjusted to adult-male equivalents, the lower the labor force participation rates of its females, including those in ages in which most women are married. The other sort, among different income groups in the same locality, have shown even more uniform tendency for husbands in higher income groups to have smaller proportions of wives in the labor force.

On the basis of these moment-of-time relationships, one might expect that a great rise of real incomes over time would have resulted in a notable decline in the tendency of wives to work. On the contrary, the labor force participation of wives has not only failed to decline, it has risen enormously—perhaps sixfold from 1890 to 1960.

What has been the cause of this apparent contradiction between the inverse behavior at a moment of time, and the positive behavior over time? Various studies, including my own,[1] have attributed it to the difference between static factors at a moment of time and dynamic factors over time, the latter including (1) declining burden of house-

[1] Clarence D. Long, *The Labor Force under Changing Income and Employment*, Princeton University Press for National Bureau of Economic Research, 1958, pp. 97-140.

OF MARRIED WOMEN

work due to fewer children, better appliances, more outside services for the home; (2) declining hours of work in office and factory jobs, so that more women could perform a dual function of wage earner and wife or mother; and (3) the opening up of new job opportunities for women. Other dynamic forces were also explored: rising wages and improved education of females, relative to males; and the push and pull of young and older males who were, on net balance, leaving the labor force.

My study even attempted some simple statistical illustrations of how these various dynamic factors may have contributed to the inflow of wives into the labor force. But it did not attempt to set up a rigorous analytical model, because the factors seemed too numerous, the relationships among them too complex and changing, and their statistical measurement too inadequate to permit us to fit them into any mathematical framework. Thus, the contradiction between the over-time positive relation and moment-of-time inverse relation was not fully or precisely reconciled.

This gap Jacob Mincer now undertakes to fill by demonstrating that the same model can explain both moment-of-time and over-time relationships.

Most recent investigations into the relation of labor force participation to wages recognize that wages exert both income and price effects on willingness to work. Under the income effect, higher wages should, other things equal, cause the worker to take some of the higher income in the form of more leisure and therefore less labor force participation. Under the price effect, the same wage rise also raises the price or cost of leisure to the worker; his enjoyment of leisure is marred by the thought of how much earnings he is foregoing, so that he is tempted to work more rather than less.

Which effect triumphs? Ever since Lionel Robbins wrote his article on the elasticity of demand for income in terms of effort,[2] economists have recognized that the outcome cannot be predicted on theoretical or a priori grounds, but depends on the relative preferences of individuals as between real income and leisure and thus can only be determined by empirical investigation. Most empirical investigations of moment-of-time relationships do, however, indicate that the income effect has triumphed over the price or substitution effect, and that

[2] "On the Elasticity of Demand for Income in Terms of Effort," *Economica*, June 1930, pp. 123-129.

99

LABOR FORCE PARTICIPATION

higher earnings have been associated with lower labor force participation.

Mincer's model adds two novel features to the analysis of the relationship between income and labor force participation.

First, he points out that the choice is not a mere two-way choice between leisure and paid work, but a three-way choice between leisure, paid work, and unpaid housework or family chores. The outcome of this three-way choice will be a family decision. And this family decision will depend on husband's income, wife's earnings, relative desires for market goods, home goods, and leisure; substitutability of market goods for home goods (as whether a wife can buy a washing machine or pay a commercial laundry to take over that part of housework). Mincer simplifies this problem by setting up a model, in which the labor force participation of wives depends on incomes of husbands, earnings of wives, and other factors or tastes.

Second, he makes use of Milton Friedman's consumption theory, namely, that people adjust their consumption expenditures, not to their current incomes (the absolute-income hypothesis) but to their permanent incomes. A family whose head normally earns $10,000 a year tends to spend on consumption, say, $8,000 a year. If the regular income of the family head should drop temporarily to $5,000, the family will continue to spend $8,000 because it has geared its spending and living habits to what it regards as its long-run income and is unwilling to adjust its scale of living to temporary fluctuations in income. But where does it get the wherewithal to pay for the $3,000 excess of consumer spending? It may make up this excess in two broad ways: either by drawing on past savings or future credit—assets of various kinds; or by having some member of the family enter the labor force. Young and poorly educated families may not have much savings or credit; for these, the only alternative may be increased labor force participation of son, daughter, or wife. Mincer's hypothesis is that the labor force participation of the wife may be greater, the smaller the permanent income of the husband, and the smaller the current income in relation to the permanent income.

Having set up his hypothesis, Mincer tests it against a variety of moment-of-time data.

1. Cross-section data, from a number of standard metropolitan areas.

2. Newly available data of the Bureau of Labor Statistics' Survey of Consumer Expenditures in 1950, in which the labor force participation

OF MARRIED WOMEN

of wives was classified by age, education, and income of family head, and by wife's earnings, with separate labor force participation rates given for wives whose husbands earned currently much less than when fully employed.

3. Census sample data for March 1957, in which the labor force rates of wives were classified by education of wives (as broadly reflecting their earning power), stratified by husbands' income groups in 1956.

4. Census sample data on long-run work experience for wives (since marriage), by income group of husband in 1955, and short-run labor force rates by the same income groups.

The results of these moment-of-time studies are as follows:

First, he finds, as others have, that wives' labor force participation rates respond negatively to husband's incomes: the more husbands earn, the less wives work. But he finds, in addition, that wives' labor force participation rates respond positively to wives' earning power: the more the wife is capable of earning, the more likely she is to work. Moreover, the wives' positive elasticity with respect to wives' earnings is about double their negative elasticity with respect to husbands' income.

Second, his findings support his hypothesis that wives are more apt to work if husbands' current earnings were below permanent earnings; and that the response of wives' labor force to so-called transitory income is stronger than to permanent income—in fact more than double. Given a period long enough for transitory elements to disappear, the inverse relationship seemed to disappear also, because the strong positive elasticity with respect to wives' earnings more than offset the remaining weak negative elasticity with respect to permanent income of husbands.

Third, the response of labor force to income, both permanent and transitory, is weaker the higher the educational level of family heads over 35—presumably because better educated family heads have other assets which make it unnecessary for wives to work if income is low. Higher-income husbands tend to have higher-earning wives, but the relationship is a weak one.

Mincer, having tested his econometric model against moment-of-time data, is now ready to use it to explain why the labor force participation of wives has grown enormously with income since 1890. For this purpose he uses changes from one census year to the next in full-time

LABOR FORCE PARTICIPATION

earnings of males, in full-time earnings of females, and in family earnings (the sum of the male and female earnings). Full-time and not current earnings are used, because over long periods the problem of transitory incomes is supposed to be not relevant. Inserting these earnings changes into his equation derived from moment-of-time data, he estimates what the change in labor force rates of wives will be from one decade to the next and then compares this predicted change with the actual change recorded from the census data.

The results are noteworthy. For each interdecennial comparison, his model predicts increases in wives' labor force participation. Thus, Mincer observes, there is no apparent contradiction between the findings of the labor force behavior of married women in cross-section and time series. The impression of a contradiction derives from the way the cross-section has been looked at, in terms of gross relations between income of husbands and labor force participation of wives. The gross inverse relation at a moment of time is due largely to two factors: (1) the existence of transitory components in income—without them the cross-sectional negative relationship will hardly be noticeable; and (2) the weak covariation of wives' earning power with husbands' income, a weakness which nullifies the strong tendency of wives' labor force rates to be positively associated with their own earnings. Over long periods of time, the transitory component is largely absent and the female earnings rise as much as male earnings (if not more). This combination, of a big rise in female earnings, and a strong positive relationship between wives' labor force participation and their own earnings, more than offsets the weak income relation with husbands' permanent income.

So much for the description of what Mincer has undertaken to do. Now for an appraisal of his success.

As to moment-of-time relationships, Mincer has proved his case fairly well. I find reasonably convincing his evidence that: (1) transitory-income influences are stronger than permanent-income influences in explaining labor force participation; (2) wives' labor force participation is positively related to wives' own potential earnings, and is stronger than the negative income elasticity; and (3) the wives' earnings, while varying with husbands' earnings, do not vary nearly as much, so that in moment-of-time data the positive wage-rate elasticity of wives is largely cancelled out, leaving the negative income effect triumphant. The evidence that he has amassed rests on data

102

OF MARRIED WOMEN

that are independent enough in source and rich enough in classification
to establish his hypothesis rather convincingly.

As to his studies over time, he has made something of a case: that
the rise of labor force participation of wives has been due to the
greater upward pull of their own rising earnings over the downward
pull of their families' rising incomes, especially since full-time wages
of females have gone up faster than those of males.

A number of features of the study suggest, however, that more is
needed than two variables—earnings of husbands and of wives—to
explain the labor force behavior of wives in the long-run periods.

For one thing, the equation does not predict the over-all changes
fully but only four-fifths of the rise. This underprediction need not be
very disturbing; on the contrary, it would be suspicious if Mincer
could fully explain the entire rise in labor force of wives for 70 years
by only two variables. In view of the many other factors which could
help explain this rise, it is perhaps a virtue of his equation that it leaves
some room for their impact.

For another thing, the equation does not predict decade movements
very accurately. For the three-decade changes between 1890 and 1920,
it is far off indeed. (However, since the census labor force data were
slightly undercounted in 1890 and 1920 and greatly overcounted in
1910, Mincer was doubtless justified in bypassing the decade-to-decade
movements in the first 30 years and merely studying the whole change
from 1890 to 1920. But even that change is twice as great as his equation predicts.) For the next decade, 1919-29, the equation overpredicts
the actual change by a fifth. For 1939-40 and 1949-59, it underpredicts
the actual changes by wide margins. Only in 1929-39, a decade of
depression—when, incidentally, transitory income, ignored in this equation, might have been expected to operate—was the prediction exactly
right.

Next, the study does not take account of one of the most interesting
developments of those decades—the behavior of the labor force of
Negro women. Yet, Negro wives show the same inverse labor force
income relationship as white wives at a moment of time, and the wages
of Negro women have probably risen not only more rapidly than those
of Negro men, but also more rapidly than those of white women. I
have the impression that employment opportunities for Negro women
have also improved relatively. Yet the labor force participation rate

LABOR FORCE PARTICIPATION

of Negro females has declined since 1900 and especially since 1930.
The case of Negro women provides a severe challenge to an econometric model which attempts to unify the explanation of moment-of-
time and over-time behavior. A model which purports to explain dynamic increases also carries the obligation of explaining dynamic
decreases. I think the data are available for such a study, at least since
1940. In any event, the case of Negro wives calls for discussion.

In addition, although Mincer indicates that the possession of young
children makes the labor force–income relationship at a moment of
time more steeply inverse, his model over time makes no allowance for
the decline of young children relative to the number of wives. This
would presumably help explain why his model does not predict the
full rise in labor force participation of wives.

Finally, the study does not take advantage of the existence of recent
annual data to test the year-to-year changes in labor force participation
of wives against the year-to-year changes in husbands' incomes and
wives' earnings, and using, of course, both permanent and temporary
incomes. If Mincer does not feel that the annual statistics of labor
force and earnings are adequate for such a test, his discussions should
at least point out the statistical and analytical difficulties.

On the whole, this paper impresses me as first-rate. The ideas are
fertile, the analysis stimulating, the empirical applications resourceful,
especially with regard to the cross-sectional data. I do not regard the
case as proven. Before Mincer can be said to have fully demonstrated
the usefulness of his model in resolving the apparent contradiction
between inverse cross-sectional behavior and positive dynamic behavior, he will have to carry out further empirical investigation: First,
separate investigation of the labor force behavior of Negro wives
both at a moment of time and over time. Second, further cross-sectional
analysis of wives' behavior before 1950. Third, an analysis of wives'
labor force behavior in detailed localities, for example rural and urban
areas or individual cities of the United States and of other countries.
Fourth, an analysis of wives' labor force behavior over time, by age,
education, and number of children, or presence and absence of children. Fifth, an analysis of labor force behavior from one year to the
next, to test the flexibility of the model, especially the functional relationship of the labor force to transitory income.

Until these further studies are made, however, this study must remain
as I find it now: not really an empirical explanation of the dynamic

OF MARRIED WOMEN

behavior of the labor force participation of wives, but an idea for such future investigation. On the basis of this idea, a scholar with an appetite for hard work would be justified in launching an extensive inquiry into the dynamic behavior of labor force of wives. I hope it will be Mincer who does it. In any event, we should be grateful to him for a careful and imaginative piece of work.

[12]

Economica, 47, 51–72

Married Women's Participation and Hours

By R. LAYARD, M. BARTON and A. ZABALZA

London School of Economics

INTRODUCTION

Since 1950 the proportion of wives under 60 who work has risen from 25 to 60 per cent. Although this is one of the major transformations of our time, its causes are little understood. Many people, if asked, would attribute the change to the falling birth rate. Yet, as Figure 1 shows, the fertility rate rose during much of the period when female participation also rose. And participation rose sharply among women aged 25–34 as well as among older women.[1] Another possible explanation is the rising real wage of husbands and wives. While one might expect

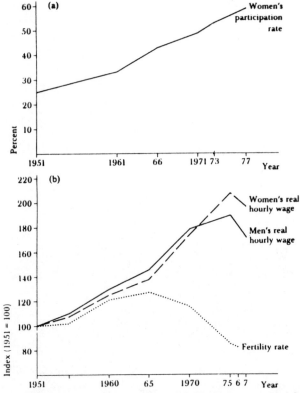

FIGURE 1   (a) Participation rate of married women (20–59); (b) Some possible influences. The participation rates in (a) are those shown in footnote 1. Real hourly earnings are defined for full-time manual workers (18 and over for women, 21 and over for men) in all industries, excluding extra pay for overtime hours. The fertility rate is defined as total births per 1,000 women aged 15–44 in Great Britain. (Sources: *Annual Abstract of Statistics 1976*, *British Labour Statistics Historical Abstract 1886–1968*, *British Labour Statistics Yearbook 1975*, *1976* and *1977*, and Department of Employment *Gazette*.)

the income effect of these improvements to discourage work, the positive substitution effect of better opportunities for women is likely to outweigh any negative cross-substitution effect of the husband's wage increase. So one asks whether wage changes, among other things, can help to explain the transformation in the working role of women.

This question is intrinsically interesting but is also important for two practical reasons. First, one wants to be able to forecast the future size of the labour force, possibly as a step towards predicting unemployment. Second, one wants to know the strength of labour supply responses in order to evaluate the efficiency cost of various tax and social security policies. It is commonly believed that women's labour supply response is more elastic than men's and may thus be an important possible source of welfare cost.

To explain the evolution of participation using only time series data is clearly going to be very difficult, for husbands' and wives' wages are highly collinear. Cross-sectional evidence is crucial, and we use data on 3,877 families from the 1974 General Household Survey. This means that the study has also a third motivation—to explain which women work and how long they work.

After surveying the theory of participation and hours, we present in Section II logit estimates of the factors influencing the participation decision. These suggest that the probability of participating responds with an elasticity of about 0·5 to the wife's own wage, and with a negative elasticity of $-0·3$ to the husband's wage. The estimated income effect is very low. These elasticities explain about a third of the growth of participation up to 1973. However, they may explain most of the growth from 1973 to 1977, since husbands' real wages fell somewhat over that period while wives' real wages rose substantially. But the elasticities we have quoted are about a half of those found in the United States, suggesting a smaller responsiveness here to monetary incentives and a smaller welfare cost of distortions. However, the estimates are necessarily tentative.

The age of the youngest child is another fundamental influence on participation, and the recent fall in family size helps to explain the recent increase in the participation of younger, but not of older, women. Regional differences in participation rates are, other things equal, small. If a wife's husband is unemployed she is much less likely to be found working, but it is difficult to be sure how far this is due to the disincentive effects of the social security system and how far it reflects local labour market conditions.

In Sections III and IV we use ordinary least squares (OLS) to analyse the hours of work of those women who do work and the hours of participants and non-participants taken together. The hours of participants appear to be weakly related to wages of husband or wife, and the effect of wages on overall hours (of participants and non-participants) seems to come mainly through their effects on participation. In Section V we impose the Tobit framework on the analysis, in order to explain participation and hours by the same fundamental supply relation. This leads to very similar estimates of the effects on overall hours to those got by OLS, but with a more even split between effects via participation and via hours of workers.

Even though the influences we are able to measure account for only a part of the long-term rise in women's participation, we believe they can be used to improve forecasting methods. And they also help us in evaluating the welfare cost of tax and social security policies.

I. THEORY

First, some theory. We assume that each woman faces a given wage rate at which she can choose to work any number of hours, or none. Suppose she is unwilling to work at all for less than some wage W^*. If W rises above W^*, the hours that the woman works will, at least initially, rise as W rises, provided the utility function is strictly quasi-concave and twice differentiable.[2] We shall assume the supply function is linear. Thus for $H > 0$ the supply function is

$$(1) \qquad H = a_0 + a_1 X + \varepsilon$$

where H is annual hours, X is a vector of measured variables, including wages, which affect work effort, and ε is a random variable independent of X and with mean zero.

Let us use $\hat{H}$ to describe $(a_0 + a_1 X)$, recognizing that $\hat{H}$ may well be negative for someone whose measured characteristics do not dispose them to work:

$$\hat{H} = a_0 + a_1 X.$$

So actual hours are $(\hat{H} + \varepsilon)$ *provided* $(\hat{H} + \varepsilon)$ is positive. If $(\hat{H} + \varepsilon)$ is negative, the person does not work:

$$H = \hat{H} + \varepsilon \qquad \text{if } \hat{H} + \varepsilon > 0$$

$$H = 0 \qquad\qquad \text{if } \hat{H} + \varepsilon \leqslant 0.$$

The participation decision

It follows that for a person with given $\hat{H}$, the probability of working is

$$P = \text{Pr}\,(\hat{H} + \varepsilon > 0)$$

$$= \text{Pr}\,(\varepsilon > -\hat{H})$$

$$= 1 - F(-\hat{H})$$

where F is the cumulative distribution function of ε. Figure 2 illustrates this. If $\hat{H}$ was, for example, 500 hours a year, the probability that the person would participate is the shaded area $(1 - F(-500))$. If the distribution is symmetrical, as we shall assume, this is also equal to $F(\hat{H})$:

$$P = F(\hat{H}).$$

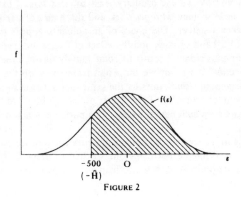

FIGURE 2

The higher $\hat{H}$, the higher the probability of participating. Or, in terms of participation rates, if we compare groups with different values of $\hat{H}$, their expected participation rates will be measured by $F(\hat{H})$. In our particular study we use individual data on participation. We assume that F is the logistic distribution and thus use logit to explain the participation decision.[3]

Hours of participants

Let us look now at the hours of work of those who are working. Can we estimate a_1 by ordinary least squares regressions for those who participate? Unfortunately not. For participants are a self-selected group and their errors are not a random drawing from the population at large. In fact the expected value of ε for a given participant is clearly related to her $\hat{H}$, thus:[4]

$$E(H|H > 0) = E(\hat{H} + \varepsilon|\varepsilon > -\hat{H})$$

$$= \hat{H} + E(\varepsilon|\varepsilon > -\hat{H})$$

$$= \hat{H} + \frac{1}{1 - F(-\hat{H})} \int_{-\hat{H}}^{\infty} \varepsilon f(\varepsilon)\, d\varepsilon$$

$$= \hat{H} + \frac{f(-\hat{H})}{1 - F(-\hat{H})} \quad \text{(if } \varepsilon \text{ is normal).}$$

Clearly the expected error $E(\varepsilon|\varepsilon > -\hat{H})$ rises steadily as $(-\hat{H})$ rises, and by the same token it falls steadily as $\hat{H}$ rises. Suppose we compare two people, one of whom has measured characteristics (X) that make her less likely to work than the other. Then, if *both* of them are working, it follows that the person with the lower $\hat{H}$ is likely to have a more hard-working nature as indicated by the expected value of her unmeasurable ε.

This is shown in Figure 3. For simplicity of exposition we assume for the moment that the distribution of ε is rectangular. The line *EBF* shows the $\hat{H}$-function $(\hat{H} = a_0 + a_1 X)$, while the two lines parallel to it show the range of possible values of H that could be observed with any particular X (treated as a scalar). The diagram implies that no woman for whom X is less than OA will participate, and all of those for whom X is more than OG will participate.[5] The locus of expected hours for participants is $ACBF$. The mean ε for participants is as follows:

If $X =$	$E(\varepsilon\|H > 0) =$
OA	ε_{max}
OE	$\frac{1}{2}\varepsilon_{max}$
OG	0

The expected value of ε among participants falls monotonically with X.

It follows that if one tried to estimate (1) by an ordinary least squares regression run on a sample of participants, the estimate of a_1 would be biased down owing to the negative correlation between X and ε. We therefore estimate equation (1) not only by a (biased) OLS regression run on participants, but also by an unbiased Tobit analysis which we shall explain shortly.

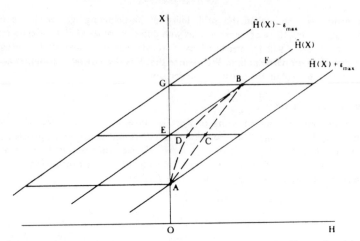

FIGURE 3. The $\hat{H}$ function ($\hat{H} = a_0 + a_1 X$) is given by $OEBF$. The predicted hours of participants are given by $ACBF$. The predicted hours of all the sample are given by $OADBF$.

Hours of all women

Finally, we may be interested in predicting how the average number of hours worked by participants *and* non-participants will vary with X. This unconditional expectation of hours is given by the expected hours of participants times the probability of participation:

$$E(H) = E(H \mid H > 0) . \Pr(H > 0)$$

$$= \left\{ \hat{H} + \frac{1}{1 - F(-\hat{H})} \int_{\hat{H}}^{\infty} \varepsilon f(\varepsilon) \, d\varepsilon \right\} F(\hat{H})$$

$$= \left\{ \hat{H} + \frac{f(-\hat{H})}{1 - F(-\hat{H})} \right\} F(\hat{H})$$

Hours at $X = OE$ are measured by ED ($= \frac{1}{2}\varepsilon_{\max} \cdot \frac{1}{2}$). Thus, the locus of unconditional expected hours is the nonlinear locus $OADBF$. Note that the elasticity of expected hours with respect to X is simply the sum of the separate elasticities for participation and for hours of participants:

$$\frac{d \log E(H)}{d \log X} = \frac{d \log \Pr(H > 0)}{d \log X} + \frac{d \log E(H/H > 0)}{d \log X}.$$

To estimate the expected hours function for all women, one could use an OLS regression of H on X. But this would involve forcing a linear pattern on a relationship that is nonlinear owing to the fact that H cannot be less than zero. Once again a better approach is via the Tobit method, though we also show the OLS results.

Tobit analysis

Tobin's problem (1958) was to estimate the demand (or supply) function for a good, from a sample of individuals some of whom did not demand (or supply) any of it. In our case we are concerned with the supply of hours, which cannot be negative. The aim is to estimate the parameters of the $\hat{H}$-function:

$$\hat{H} = a_0 + a_1 X$$

using both the data on hours supplied by participants and the information about those individuals who choose not to participate. To derive the likelihood function, let us first consider non-participants. The likelihood that individual i is not participating is $\Pr(\hat{H}_i + \varepsilon_i < 0)$ which equals $F(-\hat{H}_i)$. The likelihood that individual j is supplying positive hours H_j is $\Pr(\hat{H}_j + \varepsilon_j = H_j)$ which equals $f(H_j - \hat{H}_j)$. Thus, if there are I non-participants and J participants, the likelihood of observing our set of sample values is

$$L = \prod_{i=1}^{I} F(-\hat{H}_i) \prod_{j=1}^{J} f(H_j - \hat{H}_j)$$

$$= \prod_{i=1}^{I} F(-a_0 - a_1 X_i) \prod_{j=1}^{J} f(H_j - a_0 - a_1 X_j).$$

Parameter estimates are obtained by maximizing this likelihood function with respect to the parameters; these estimates are unbiased as the problem of negative correlation between X and ε has been avoided.

We are now ready to look in turn at[6]

(a) participation (logit and OLS estimates);
(b) hours of participants (OLS estimates);
(c) hours of participants and non-participants (OLS estimates);
(d) Tobit estimates of (a) − (c).

II. PARTICIPATION

The analysis is based on the 1974 General Household Survey, using data on 3,877 married women aged 60 or under (OPCS, 1974). The variables (X) that we use to explain participation are as follows.[7]

(1) *Predicted log gross hourly earnings of wife*. We must use the predicted gross hourly earnings of the wife since for women who do not work we do not know what wage they would be paid. Thus we assume that

$$\ln W = b_0 + b_1 S + u$$

where W is hourly earnings[8] and S is a vector of characteristics relevant to productivity. We estimate this equation using observations for participants only. There are some problems with this since participants are a self-selected group and an individual's u may affect whether she works. For example, an individual with an unfavourable S may work only if she has a positive u. Thus among participants u will not be independent of S. Heckman (1977) has proposed a method of dealing with this problem, but his own work showed that the wage equation estimated on participants only was not seriously biased. The estimated wage equation is shown in the Appendix, Table 1.

We use the predicted *log* gross hourly earnings since the appropriate earnings function is in the logs and it is econometrically preferable to use the predicted value from the estimated equation rather than to transform it to its antilog, unless there is a behavioural presumption that it is the natural value that affects hours. There is no obvious presumption that this is so. We shall often for simplicity of speech refer to a person's hourly earnings as her wage.

(2) *Gross hourly earnings of husband.* We use actual recorded hourly earnings except when the husband is unemployed or self-employed, where we use the hourly earnings predicted from an equation run on employed men. We catch the effect of husband's unemployment through a separate dummy variable (see below), but even where the husband is temporarily unemployed, we expect the husband's wage (if in work) to affect the wife's current labour supply.[9] To examine whether the hybrid variable used for men was causing problems, we also ran all estimations using predicted wages throughout. The results were very similar.

(3) *Net annual unearned income.* This is rent, dividends and interest multiplied by 0·67 (to allow for tax) and multiplied by 2·36 (to allow for the average level of under reporting), *plus* family allowance net of tax, *plus* owner–occupier's imputed rent *minus* net mortgage interest.[10] Since over 95 per cent of families in the sample were paying the standard rate of tax, little bias is introduced by taking the standard tax rate as exogenous and as applying to the whole range of income from rent, dividends, interest and Family Allowance. Any alternative approach would be enormously more complicated. Note that the alternative of using gross unearned income is not open, unless imputed rent and rent, interest and dividends are entered separately, since imputed rent is not taxable.

(4) *Age of youngest child* (7 dummies). These dummies, along with the total number of children, have more explanatory power as judged by $\bar{R}^2$ than the numbers of children in each of the age groups shown. The omitted category is "No child".

(5)–(10) *Number of children; Ethnic background* (3 dummies); *Has long-standing illness* (dummy); *Age* (4 dummies); *Region* (10 dummies); *Husband currently unemployed* (dummy).

Results

The first column of Table 1 shows the results of the logit analysis. The statistic shown is the effect of each variable on participation evaluated at the mean of P (i.e., $\gamma a_1 (0·54) (0·46)$).[11] For continuous variables or for dummy variables having only small effects, there is no difficulty in interpreting the statistic; but for dummy variables with large coefficients, the effect, as we shall show, requires some further computation. The second column of the table gives the corresponding OLS estimates. The results of the two exercises are similar, and we shall comment only on the logit results. The elasticities are in Table 2.

Wage and income effects

The own wage elasticity is 0·49 and the husband's wage elasticity −0·28. The income elasticity is very low, −0·04. These wage elasticities are rather lower than those typically found from individual data in the United States, but the low income elasticity is echoed there. The equation implies that a simultaneous doubling of husbands' and wives' real wages from their 1951 levels while holding other factors constant would increase the participation rate of wives by 11 percentage points. Between 1951 and 1973 both husbands' and wives' wages roughly doubled, and income rose by rather less. Yet the participation rate of married women under 60 rose by 29 percentage points. So our estimates of income and wage effects explain

TABLE 1

ANALYSES TO EXPLAIN PARTICIPATION, HOURS OF PARTICIPANTS AND HOURS OF PARTICIPANTS AND NON-PARTICIPANTS

	Participation		Hours of participants		Hours of participants and non-participants	The "Tobit line"
	Logit (1)	OLS (2)	Net wage (3)	Gross wage (4)	Gross wage (5)	Gross wage (6)
Own log wage	0·26	0·20	74	99	315	576
(predicted £ per hr)	(0·04)	(0·04)	(72)	(65)	(58)	(90)
Husband's wage (£ per hr)	−0·13	−0·10	−116	−121	−179	−335
	(0·02)	(0·01)	(31)	(31)	(23)	(42)
Net unearned income	−0·12	−0·09		−27	−84	−271
(£'000 p.a.)	(0·03)	(0·02)		(47)	(35)	(69)
Intercept (£'000 p.a.)			−13			
			(46)			
Unemployed husband	−0·34	−0·27	76	77	−301	−748
	(0·05)	(0·04)	(92)	(92)	(62)	(121)
Youngest child 0–2	−0·81	−0·67	−1053	−1036	−1306	−2393
	(0·03)	(0·03)	(74)	(71)	(49)	(66)
3–5	−0·49	−0·41	−793	−779	−1003	−1515
	(0·03)	(0·03)	(66)	(65)	(52)	(64)
6–10	−0·24	−0·19	−522	−513	−600	−840
	(0·03)	(0·03)	(57)	(57)	(49)	(60)
11–13	−0·13	−0·10	−327	−321	−338	−509
	(0·04)	(0·03)	(60)	(60)	(54)	(81)
14–15	0·04	0·02	−250	−243	−142	−132
	(0·05)	(0·04)	(61)	(61)	(59)	(95)
16–17	0·01	−0·02	−238	−237	−232	−162
	(0·09)	(0·07)	(114)	(114)	(109)	(182)
18+	−0·06	−0·07	−314	−310	−335	−341
	(0·12)	(0·10)	(170)	(170)	(148)	(256)
No. of children	0·04	0·03	−3	−2	26	86
	(0·01)	(0·01)	(20)	(20)	(15)	(28)
Coloured, West Indies	0·24	0·19	438	426	527	725
	(0·13)	(0·09)	(143)	(143)	(143)	(235)
Other coloured	−0·08	−0·06	327	316	79	52
	(0·08)	(0·06)	(125)	(125)	(99)	(179)
Irish-born	0·14	0·11	−2	−5	115	252
	(0·06)	(0·05)	(78)	(78)	(71)	(125)
Long-standing illness	−0·07	−0·06	−54	−51	−124	−174
	(0·02)	(0·02)	(35)	(35)	(30)	(52)
Age: under 25	0·05	0·03	105	100	100	148
	(0·03)	(0·03)	(54)	(54)	(46)	(67)
25–34	0·04	0·03	58	54	77	118
	(0·02)	(0·02)	(38)	(38)	(34)	(46)
45–54	−0·12	−0·09	−131	−126	−244	−314
	(0·02)	(0·02)	(40)	(40)	(37)	(52)
55–60	−0·24	−0·21	−266	−256	−514	−668
	(0·03)	(0·03)	(59)	(59)	(52)	(79)
North	−0·01	0·01	12	12	13	−15
	(0·03)	(0·03)	(63)	(63)	(54)	(78)
Yorkshire and Humberside	−0·06	−0·05	−82	−83	−83	−173
	(0·03)	(0·03)	(60)	(60)	(51)	(73)

Continued overleaf

TABLE 1—*(cont.)*

North West	0·04	0·03	82	83	88	141
	(0·03)	(0·03)	(54)	(54)	(47)	(62)
East Midlands	−0·04	−0·03	63	64	−18	−62
	(0·04)	(0·03)	(65)	(65)	(54)	(6)
West Midlands	0·07	0·06	86	87	111	181
	(0·03)	(0·03)	(55)	(55)	(49)	(67)
East Anglia	−0·05	−0·04	−95	−95	−115	−165
	(0·05)	(0·04)	(82)	(82)	(69)	(112)
South East (excl. GLC)	0·03	0·03	−79	−79	−13	4
	(0·03)	(0·03)	(49)	(49)	(43)	(59)
South West	0·01	0·01	−55	−54	−45	−29
	(0·04)	(0·04)	(64)	(64)	(55)	(88)
Wales	−0·11	−0·08	142	142	−46	−187
	(0·04)	(0·04)	(72)	(71)	(58)	(98)
Scotland	−0·01	−0·002	101	100	48	35
	(0·04)	(0·03)	(58)	(58)	(49)	(7)
Constant	0·60	0·99	1,820	1.812	1,668	1,820
		(0·05)				
R^2		0·20	0·23	0·23	0·27	
Log likelihood	−2,200					−18,287

Notes
(a) The logit coefficients shown are $\partial P/\partial X = \gamma a_1 P(1 - P)$ evaluated at the mean of P.
(b) Standard errors are in parentheses.
(c) The Tobit values have been rescaled by the estimated value for $1/\sigma$ of 0·000903.
(d) The omitted region is GLC area. The net wage and intercept variables are defined in Section III.

TABLE 2

ELASTICITIES

	Independent variable		
Dependent variables	Own wage*	Husband's wage	Income
Participation			
Logit	0·49	−0·28	−0·04
OLS	0·37	−0·21	−0·03
Hours of participants			
OLS	0·08	−0·10	−0·003
Hours of participants and non-participants			
OLS	0·44	−0·28	−0·02
Tobit	0·49	−0·32	−0·04

* All own wage elasticities are calculated on the basis of gross wages.

less than half of the long-term rise in women's labour force participation. This is consistent with some US analyses of individual data which do not suggest that much of the growth of women's participation can be explained by the growth of real wages and real income (Schultz, 1976).

Turning to the more recent past, between 1973 and 1977, the real weekly wages of women rose by about 10 per cent while the gross real wages of men fell by nearly as much, and real unearned income (including the real value of tax allowances) fell substantially. Statistically this explains most of the increase in women's participation since 1973, though in fact our elasticities should not really be applied slavishly to short-run changes since other long-run forces must also have been at work in the recent past. An additional explanation must be the much greater uncertainty affecting all families, which would make them feel poorer even if their average income had not changed. It can hardly be a coincidence that in this recession both personal savings *and* wives' work have increased markedly.[12]

However at this point we should enter a caveat. Our results depend heavily on the functional form used: linear in the log of wife's wage and in the natural value of the husband's wage. We adopted this form because it fitted slightly better than the function where both wages were entered in log form. In the latter case the difference between wife's and husband's wage elasticity was somewhat less, but more important is the fact that a projection of the function back through time would account for a much smaller part of the growth in women's participation.[13] We therefore regard our findings in this section as fairly tentative.

Effect of young children

We can now look at other influences on participation. The most important of these is of course the family responsibilities of the wife.[14] Suppose we take a woman who has average own and husband's wage and average income, a working husband, and is white, not born in Ireland, in good health, aged 25–34, and living in Greater London. If she has one child and that child is under three, she has a probability of participation that is about 65 percentage points less than someone with the same characteristics but no children.[15] If her youngest child is between three and six, her probability of participation is about 41 percentage points less, and if the youngest child is between six and ten, only 16 percentage points less. If the child is above fourteen, its effect on participation is either measured as positive or is insignificant. On top of this, the number of children has a positive effect on participation. Since larger families have lower real income than smaller families with the same wage and income opportunities, the mother may be driven out to work.

Since only children under six have any major effect on participation, changes in family size cannot have a very large direct effect on participation. For example, if children are born three years apart and every women decides to have two children in her lifetime instead of three, then within six years the participation rate of women under 60 (assuming the same number of women in each group from 20 to 60) will have risen by 5 per cent.[16] This change will be concentrated among women aged 25–34. But as an earlier footnote shows, the increased participation has been spread across all ages. Moreover, all ages were increasing their participation during the period 1951–1966 when the fertility rate rose by about a quarter.[17] Since 1966 the fertility rate has fallen by over a third,[18] yet the rate of labour force participation has been growing at a slightly lower rate of growth. So, while fertility levels must be having an effect, it is difficult to suppose that this effect is the main force at work.

Ethnic background, health and age

Wives born in the West Indies or in Ireland are more likely to go out to work. If the woman is ill, she is somewhat less likely to work. The older a woman is (holding family responsibilities constant), the less likely she is to work. It is unfortunately not possible to say from one year's cross-section to what extent this is an effect of age and to what extent it reflects different lifetime behaviour patterns by different cohorts.

Regional differences

The literature on participation has often pointed to the differences between regions. However, when other things are held constant, the differences are less than is sometimes supposed. Taking Greater London as the standard, the main differences are that participation is some 7 percentage points higher in the West Midlands and 3 points higher in the rest of the South East; while it is 11 percentage points lower in Wales, 6 points lower in Yorkshire and Humberside, and 5 points lower in East Anglia.[19]

Clearly these differences in part reflect differences in the degree of urbanization between regions.[20] Unfortunately the 1974 GHS tapes do not allow one to identify the type of urban or rural area in which each household was situated. The 1971 tapes did separate individual households into those in conurbations, other urban areas, semi-rural areas and rural areas. Greenhalgh (1977a) then did an OLS regression of participation on this variable and also on the set of regional dummies. The coefficients on the locational dummies for the individual household were:

Conurbation	Other urban	Semi-rural	Rural
+0·031	—	−0·033	−0·160

The coefficients on the regional dummies were jointly insignificant at the 95 per cent level. We can now take the estimated effects of household location and see to what extent they explain the estimated regional effect in Table 1. Taking Greater London as the standard and using Census data on the residential structure in each region, we find the predicted differences shown in Column (1) below. Next to these we list the differences estimated in Table 1. Residential structure goes a long way to explaining the low participation rate in Wales, Yorkshire and Humberside, East Anglia, and East Midlands, though it does not explain the high rates in the West Midlands and the South East.

	Predicted from residential structure (1)	From Table 1 (2)
North	−0·039	−0·006
Yorkshire and Humberside	−0·027	−0·063
North West	−0·017	0·041
East Midlands	−0·040	−0·041
West Midlands	−0·026	0·069
East Anglia	−0·067	−0·045
South East (excluding GLC)	−0·064	0·034
South West	−0·054	0·006
Wales	−0·060	−0·111
Scotland	−0·046	−0·007

Unemployed husband

Wives with unemployed husbands are 31 percentage points less likely to work than otherwise similar wives with husbands at work.[21] This is a striking finding. The gross difference has often been observed, but we have now confirmed that it exists holding other things constant.

What does it mean? One possibility is that it reflects the working of the Supplementary Benefit system. About half of the families of unemployed men receive Supplementary Benefit, which, after the disregards, is reduced pound for pound for any earnings of the wife. This creates an incentive for wives to stop work when their husbands become unemployed, and cases have been observed where this happens. However, a wife presumably would do this only if she expected her husband to remain unemployed for some time, as it is not always easy to go back to work the moment you want to do so. As the average expected duration of unemployment among men becoming unemployed was under 20 weeks, many wives might consider it a bit risky to stop work for such a comparatively short period of time.

On another interpretation, wives who have unemployed husbands are less likely to participate than others because they live in local areas where there is less work for husbands as well as wives. In time series analysis it has been found in Britain (Corry and Roberts, 1974) and the United States (Mincer, 1966) that female participation typically falls when employment opportunities deteriorate, the substitution (discouraged worker) effect outweighing the income (added worker) effect of husbands losing their jobs.[22] If so, the same phenomenon could explain differences between local (rather than regional) areas in participation. Unfortunately the data do not enable us to separate the "area" from the "person" effect, and one must suppose that our result reflects a mixture of both of these.

III. Hours Worked by Participants

We now turn to the hours worked by those who participate. This raises a problem we have not so far needed to face; for the wage that determines whether a woman works at all is the net wage she would be paid on her first few hours of work. And in Britain that wage is her gross wage.[23] However, once tax comes into the picture, a wife's hours are determined by her marginal *net* wage (which determines the relevant slope of the budget line) and by the location of the budget line. Ignoring for the moment the husband's wages and unearned income, the wife's budget line is as shown in Figure 4.[24] Y^0 is the wife's earned income allowance. As long as $H < Y^0/W$, the wife can increase Y at the rate W for each hour worked. After that point has been reached income can be increased only at a rate $W(1 - t^0)$, where t^0 is the standard rate of tax. Thus the first segment of the budget line has the equation

$$Y = WH \qquad H < Y^0/W$$

and the second segment has the equation

$$Y = WH - t^0(WH - Y^0)$$
$$= W(1 - t^0)H + t^0 Y^0 \qquad H > Y^0/W.$$

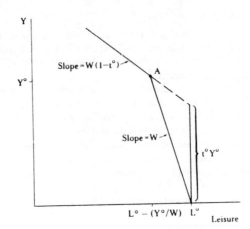

FIGURE 4

Or, more generally, we can write the budget constraint as

$$Y = W(1 - t)H + tY^0$$

where $t = 0$ $H < Y^0/W$

$t = t^0$ $H > Y^0/W.$

Individuals may choose one of four general alternatives:

(a) do not work (corner solution);
(b) work $H < Y^0/W$ (interior solution);
(c) work $H = Y^0/W$ (corner solution);
(d) work $H > Y^0/W$ (interior solution).

Inspection of the data reveal that few individuals work $H = Y^0/W$. In Britain in 1974 Y^0 was £625 per year, and the distribution of women's annual earnings was as shown in the Appendix, Table 2. The density is somewhat higher in the neighbourhood of £625 than elsewhere, and the fact that few people earn exactly £625 must presumably be due to the fact that individuals cannot choose their hours with the necessary precision. One could of course assume that people with hours within $\pm \alpha$ hours of Y^0/W were in fact at corner solutions and use maximum likelihood methods to estimate the structure of the utility function. However, in the present paper we simply assume that all individuals were at interior solutions.[25]

There remains however one serious problem: the tax rate is endogenous.[26] For the complete model is as follows:

$$(2) \qquad H = a_0 + a_1 \ln \{W(1 - t)\} + a_2(tY^0 + I) + a_3 Z + \varepsilon$$

$$(3) \qquad \begin{cases} t = 0 & H < Y^0/W \\ t = t^0 & H > Y^0/W \end{cases}$$

where I is net unearned income and Z is a vector of other relevant variables. The more hard-working people (with higher ε) are more likely to be taxpayers. Thus, if (2) were estimated by ordinary least squares, the coefficient on $W(1 - t)$ would be biased down and the coefficient on tY^0 would be biased up. To deal with this problem we use two-stage least squares.[27] In the first stage we regress a dummy variable t, where $t = t^0$ for taxpayers and $t = 0$ for non-taxpayers, on $\ln W$, I and Z. Then we estimate (2), using predicted t instead of actual t. We continue to measure $\ln W$ by the predicted log wage, even though we know the actual wage of every participant. The reason is that wage is measured by annual earnings divided by (weeks times usual weekly hours). If hours are mis-measured, this introduces a spurious element of negative correlation between W and H. The dependent variable is annual hours, which have generally been found a more appropriate variable than weekly hours, given that married women's weeks vary largely owing to voluntary choice. The results are given in Table 1, column (3).

Wage and income effects

The own wage effect is estimated to be very small and not significantly different from zero, but we have already explained that it is biased down relative to the slope of the true supply function (2). The result is similar to US results (Schultz, 1976). The estimate of the net wage elasticity is 0·06. The husband's wage elasticity is −0·10 and the income elasticity negligible. Thus a simultaneous equi-proportional increase in husband's and wife's wage would lead to little change in hours. This may or may not help to explain why the number of part-time women workers in the labour force has grown so sharply since 1961, while the number of full-time women workers has slightly fallen.[28]

In case we are suffering from some econometric bias associated with the use of $\hat{t}$, we also estimate the reduced form of equations (2) and (3) imposing on it the incorrect linear form

(4) $H = b_0 + b_1 \ln W + b_2 I + b_3 Z + v.$

The true shape is illustrated in Figure 5. The line AB represents equation (2) given $t = 0$. The line CD represents equation (2) given that $t = t^0$. (Remember that $b_1 > 0$ and probably $b_2 < 0$.) The individual participates if $\ln W$ exceeds OE. As the

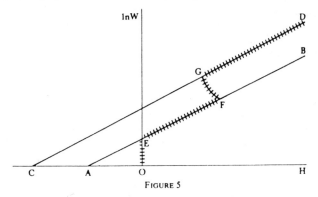

FIGURE 5

wage increases she expands her labour supply along EB. But when she reaches point F, $HW = Y^0$. If the wage rises further, she will for a while continue to earn the same income by working less and her labour supply will fall along the line FG. Throughout this range she is at a corner solution like that at point A in Figure 4.

(with the corner moving horizontally to the right). Once G is reached, the individual is again at an interior solution and, as the wage increases, she moves out along GD. Thus the true supply function consists of the locus $OEFGD$ (as hatched). Though this function is nonlinear, it is still interesting to examine the results of forcing a line through the points from E onwards. One would expect that, relative to the net wage supply function, the gross wage function would be biased to have a steeper slope (i.e. a lower $dH/d \ln W$). In fact there is no significant difference.

Other effects

Very young children affect the hours of participants much as they do the participation decision. People with a young child under three will work 1,000 hours a year less than those without children. But even if their children are older, mothers will still tend to work rather less. The number of children seems to have little effect on hours.

If they go out to work, coloured women are likely to work longer. Older women are more likely to work part-time, but this effect is not as strong as one might expect. The only significant regional difference in hours is in Wales, where working women spend about 140 more hours a year at work than in Greater London.

IV. HOURS WORKED BY PARTICIPANTS AND NON-PARTICIPANTS

We can next look at hours worked including all the zero hours worked by non-participants. If we can explain this, we can explain the total labour input from married women. We give in column (5) our OLS estimate, even though a linear estimate is incorrect since the relationship between expected hours and X is nonlinear. We use wife's gross wage and net unearned income, the same variables as in the participation equation.[29]

The own wage elasticity is 0.44, which is about equal to the sum of the OLS wage elasticity of participation plus the wage elasticity of hours for participants. The husband's wage elasticity is -0.28, which is also roughly consistent with the estimates from the participation and hours equation. Once again the income elasticity is small. The other effects are consistent with the estimates we have already obtained.

V. THE TOBIT ANALYSIS

Finally we come to our Tobit results. Again we use the wife's gross wage, since the gross wage is also the marginal wage for three-quarters of all women and using the predicted marginal tax rate would not correctly represent the structure of the participation decision.[30] Column (6) shows the coefficients of the "Tobit line":

$$\hat{H} = a_0 + a_1 X.$$

These are not of course the coefficients of an expected hours equation for participants, since, as Figure 1 shows, this is also affected by the average positive error term for participants and its joint distribution with the X variables. Nor are they the coefficients of an expected hours equation for participants and non-participants, which is affected not only by the errors among participants but also by the implied probabilities of participation.

TABLE 3

TOBIT ESTIMATES: EFFECTS OF VARYING WIFE'S PREDICTED LOG WAGE

Wife's predicted log wage	$\hat{H}$ (1)	Predicted participation rate (2)	Average hours of participants (3)	Average hours of participants and non-participants (4) = (2).(3)
($\mu = -0.46$)				
($\sigma = 0.22$)				
−0.7	94.8	0.534	918.1	490.3
−0.5	210.1	0.595	965.1	554.9
−0.3	325.4	0.616	1012.1	623.5
−0.1	440.7	0.655	1064.6	697.3
+0.1	555.9	0.692	1119.2	774.5

Notes
(a) $\hat{H} = 498.3 + 576.4 \ln \hat{W}$ where the constant has been corrected to include the sum of the means of all excluded variables times their coefficients.
(b) The predicted participation rate equals $F(H/\sigma)$ where $\sigma = 1107.4$ and where F is the cumulative of the standard normal distribution.
(c) The average hours of participants and non-participants are given by the Tobit expected value locus, $E(H|\hat{H}) = \{\hat{H} F(\hat{H}/\sigma) + \sigma f(\hat{H}/\sigma)\}$.

The meaning and power of the Tobit approach can be brought out by taking the main variables of interest and constructing for each of them tables like Table 3. In this table all variables except own predicted log wage are set at their mean and we now trace out the effect of varying own wage upon

(a) $\hat{H}$;
(b) the probability of participation;
(c) the expected hours of participants;
(d) the expected hours of participants and non-participants.

As the wife's wage rises, both the probability of participating and the expected hours if working rise. The overall effect is to raise unconditional expected hours. The estimated elasticity (0.49) is very similar to that obtained by OLS.[31] We can also do the same exercise for the other variables and the results are shown in Table 2. For participants, the elasticities along the Tobit line are of course much greater than those we have quoted, and they provide the proper basis for calculating the welfare costs of distortions among participants.[32]

VI. CONCLUDING COMMENTS

We have explained a good deal of the differences in labour supply among the women of today. We have also obtained estimates of wage and income effects which explain between a third and a half of the postwar increase in participation. More work is needed to explain the time series. For example, there may have been a reduction in job rationing (especially of part-time jobs), which requires the simultaneous estimation of a model of supply and demand for female labour on which we are now embarking. But the effects we have measured (assuming they are correct) can already help to improve forecasting, by proceeding as follows:

(a) Use our estimates to isolate the "unexplained growth" in participation, and make assumptions about the future course of this "unexplained growth".

(b) Forecast the value of those variables whose effects we do measure, and use our estimates to predict the consequential changes in participation.

(c) Adding (a) and (b) will give a forecast total change in participation.

This should be better than crude extrapolation of trends.

ACKNOWLEDGMENTS

This paper arises from work done jointly with Tony Cornford who constructed the basic computer files with great efficiency. We are grateful to O. Ashenfelter, C. Greenhalgh, J. Heckman, D. Metcalf and S. Nickell for hours of instructive discussion on this topic, to OPCS for providing the GHS data, and to the Department of Employment and the Social Science Research Council for financing the study.

APPENDIX

TABLE 1

REGRESSION TO PREDICT WIFE'S LOG HOURLY EARNINGS

		Experience (years)	
Constant	−1·07		
Left full-time education at		Under 5	0·09
15	0·05		(0·03)
	(0·03)	5–9	0·01
16	0·14		(0·01)
	(0·03)	10–19	−0·01
17	0·22		(0·00)
	(0·05)	20–29	0·00
18	0·33		(0·00)
	(0·06)	30–39	−0·00
19+	0·75		(0·00)
	(0·04)	40+	−0·02
			(0·01)
Father's occupation*			
Professional and managerial	0·16	Coloured, West Indies	0·04
	(0·04)		(0·10)
Other manual	0·08	Other coloured	−0·12
	(0·04)		(0·09)
Skilled	0·06	Irish-born	−0·00
	(0·04)		(0·05)
Semi-skilled	−0·03	Long-standing illness	−0·02
	(0·04)		(0·02)
Non-professional self-employed	0·05	R^2	0·22
	(0·05)	N	2206
Other	0·11		
	(0·06)		

* Father's occupation is classified according to the Registrar-General's Socioeconomic Groups as follows:

Professional and managerial	1–6	Unskilled	14
Other non-manual	7–9	Non-professional self-employed	15–17
Skilled manual	11–12	Others	19, Y
Semi-skilled	10, 13, 18		

The omitted category is unskilled.

TABLE 2

ANNUAL EARNINGS OF MARRIED WOMEN UNDER 60

Earnings (£ p.a.)	Percentage
Under 12	41·1
12–112	3·9
112–212	4·5
212–312	3·8
312–412	4·1
412–512	4·2
512–537	1·1
537–562	1·3
562–587	0·9 } 4·5
587–612	1·2
612–637	1·1
637–662	1·3
662–687	1·1 } 4·7
687–712	1·2
712–812	3·4
812–912	3·1
912–1,012	3·1
1,012–1,112	2·4
1,112–1,212	3·0
1,212–1,312	2·2
1,312–1,412	2·1
1,412–1,512	1·3
1,512–1,612	1·5
1,612 and above	6·0
All	100·0
N (=100·0%)	4,321

TABLE 3

MEANS AND STANDARD DEVIATIONS OF ALL VARIABLES
(excluding wives of unemployed husbands)

	Participants and non-participants		Participants	
	Mean	S.D.	Mean	S.D.
Participation	0·56	0·50	NA	NA
Annual hours	739	817	1317	655
Own log wage (predicted) (gross) (log £ per hr)	-0·46	0·22	-0·45	0·23
Own log wage (predicted) (net) (log £ per hr)	-0·66	0·21	-0·68	0·21
Husband's wage (£ per hr)	1·13	0·56	1·10	0·48
Net unearned income (£ p.a.)	157	305	146	273
Intercept (£ p.a.)	269	314	272	279
Youngest child: 0–2	0·20	0·40	0·07	0·26
3–5	0·15	0·35	0·12	0·32
6–10	0·17	0·37	0·19	0·40
11–13	0·07	0·26	0·09	0·28
14–15	0·05	0·21	0·06	0·25
16–17	0·01	0·11	0·01	0·12
18+	0·01	0·08	0·01	0·08
No. of children	1·29	1·24	1·11	1·24
Coloured, West Indies	0·01	0·08	0·01	0·09
Other coloured	0·01	0·11	0·01	0·10
Irish-born	0·03	0·16	0·03	0·17
Long-standing illness	0·18	0·39	0·17	0·38
Age: under 25	0·12	0·33	0·10	0·30
25–34	0·32	0·47	0·27	0·44
45–54	0·24	0·43	0·27	0·45
55–60	0·08	0·27	0·08	0·27

TABLE 4

CORRELATIONS

	Participation	Annual hours	Own log wage (predicted) (gross)	Own log wage (predicted) (net)	Husband's wage	Net unearned income	Intercept	Unemployed husband
Participants and non-participants								
Participation	—							
Annual hours	0·02	—						
Own log wage (predicted) (gross)		0·02	—					
Own log wage (predicted) (net)		-0·17	0·93	—				
Husband's wage	0·07	-0·09	0·38	0·35	—			
Net unearned income	-0·06	-0·06	0·24	0·19	0·33	—		
Intercept		-0·00	0·25	0·17	0·33	0·99	—	
Unemployed husband	-0·09	-0·06	-0·04	-0·03	-0·09	0·00	-0·00	—
Participants								
Annual hours		—						
Own log wage (predicted) (gross)		0·01	—					
Own log wage (predicted) (net)		-0·15	0·93	—				
Husband's wage		-0·09	0·40	0·38	—			
Net unearned income		-0·04	0·20	0·18	0·28	—		
Intercept		0·03	0·24	0·17	0·29	0·99	—	
Unemployed husband		0·04	0·00	0·00	-0·07	0·01	0·01	—

NOTES

[1] The participation rates by age were:

	20–24	25–34	35–44	45–54	55–59	All aged 20–59
1951	36·6	24·4	25·7	23·7	15·6	25·0
1961	41·4	29·5	36·4	35·3	26·0	33·7
1966	43·9	34·3	48·6	49·8	38·4	43·5
1971	46·7	38·4	54·5	57·0	45·5	49·0
1973	51·3	43·6	60·1	62·6	47·6	53·9
1977	54·9	48·8	68·0	68·1	50·8	59·4

See Department of Employment *Gazette*.

[2] For an illustration of this using the Stone–Geary utility function, see Barzel and McDonald (1973).

[3] Thus we assume that the probability (P) of participation is given by

$$P = \frac{1}{1 + e^{-\gamma H}} = \frac{1}{1 + e^{-\gamma(a_0 + a_1 X)}}.$$

Maximizing the likelihood of the observed decisions, given the Xs, yields estimates of γa_0 and γa_1, from which we derive the estimated effects of the X's shown in Table 1, column (1). We also used OLS and obtained very similar results, as did Schultz (1976) for the United States. (If $F(.)$ followed the cumulative normal distribution we should instead use probit analysis, but in fact the logistic and the cumulative normal distributions have very similar shapes.)

[4] For the normal distribution

$$\int_{-\hat{H}}^{\infty} \varepsilon f(\varepsilon)\, d\varepsilon = f(-\hat{H}),$$

since, if z is the standard normal variable,

$$\frac{d}{dz} f(z) = \frac{d}{dz} \frac{1}{\sqrt{2\pi}} e^{-\frac{1}{2}z^2} = -z f(z)$$

and hence

$$\int_{z^0}^{\infty} f(z)\, dz = f(z^0).$$

[5] Using the rectangular distribution one can easily see the relationship between the participation response and the hours response (a_1). For X between OA and OG, $dP/dX = 1/AG = a_1/2\varepsilon_{max}$. Thus the response is greater the greater a_1 and the smaller the spread of individual tastes. (All elasticities are greater the less the spread of tastes.)

[6] For an analysis of US data on similar lines see Schultz (1976).

[7] The small number of self employed women are treated as nonparticipants since for the subsequent analysis we do not know their annual weeks worked. This did not affect our results on participation.

[8] Hourly earnings equal annual earnings divided by annual weeks times weekly hours. The same measure is used for husbands.

[9] We also ran all our regressions excluding families where the husband was unemployed. The results were very similar to those reported below.

[10] For the figure of 2·36, see Layard *et al.* (1978), Appendix 4, Table 1. Imputed rent is measured by gross value since, for tenants, average rent $\simeq$ average gross value, and the elasticity of rent with respect to gross value is approximately unity. Net mortgage interest is based on gross payment to building societies times 0·67 times the fraction of the payment that is interest, predicted by the husband's age.

[11] Since

$$P = \frac{1}{1 + e^{-\gamma(a_0 + a_1 X)}}.$$

$$\frac{\partial P}{\partial X} = \gamma \frac{e^{-\gamma(a_0 + a_1 X)}}{\{1 + e^{-\gamma(a_0 + a_1 X)}\}^2} a_1$$

$$= \gamma a_1 P(1 - P).$$

[12] As we point out later on, one might have expected participation to fall in the current recession, so powerful forces must have been at work to increase it.

[13] The values were

	R^2	Own wage elasticity	Husband's wage elasticity
(a) Function using husband's absolute wage	0·219	0·37	−0·21
(b) Function using log husband's wage	0·213	0·32	−0·21

Using formulation (a) the *de facto* husband's wage elasticity has been more or less constant over time since participation and husbands' wages have risen at about the same rate. Using formulation (b) the *de facto* husband's wage elasticity was much larger in absolute size in the past, since

$$\varepsilon_H \text{ (evaluated at 1950)} = \varepsilon_H \text{ (evaluated at 1974)} \frac{P_{74}}{P_{50}}$$

where ε_H is the husband's elasticity, and P_{74} and P_{50} are the participation rates in 1974 and 1950 respectively.

[14] One could of course argue that these are affected by the earning opportunities of the wife, high wages leading to fewer children. If this were so, the estimates of Table 1 would underestimate the total effects of wage changes on participation. However, if Table 1 is estimated without the children variables, the wage and income effects are practically unaffected.

[15] To obtain this number, one computes

$$P = \frac{1}{1 + e^{-\gamma_{01} x}}$$

for the two relevant X vectors. The result is very similar to the figure of $(−0·67 + 0·03)$ read off the OLS analysis.

[16] This is $0·65 \, (3/40) = 0·05$. Suppose we call the age at which a woman i has her first child T_i. Then initially all women aged between T_i and $T_i + 9$ have youngest child aged under three (assuming one child born every three years and three children per completed family). In addition all women aged $T_i + 9$ to $T_i + 12$ have youngest child aged between three and five. If instead the completed family size is two, then in the new steady state (reached after six years) all women aged T_i to $T_i + 6$ have youngest child aged under three and all aged $T_i + 6$ to $T_i + 9$ have youngest child aged between three and five. So the net effect is to "free" three cohorts of mothers from having youngest child under three. This raises participation by 0·65 over a three-year period. If this effect is averaged over the 40 years for which we are calculating the aggregate participation rate, this aggregate rate rises by $0·65 \, (3/40)$. During the transition the effect is of course less. For example, after three years all women aged T_i to $T_i + 6$ have youngest child under three and all women aged $T_i + 6$ to $T_i + 12$ have youngest child aged between three and five. The example is artificial because reductions in the size of completed family may be accompanied by a greater spacing between children. If so, this reduces the effect on participation.

[17] Central Statistical Office, *Social Trends* (1976), p. 64.

[18] From 2·77 to 1·77: *OPCS* (1977), p. 44.

[19] The hypothesis that all the regional coefficients are simultaneously zero can be rejected at the 5 per cent level, though it is just acceptable at the 2 per cent level.

[20] Unemployment does not show up as a clearly important influence. The correlation between the set of dummy coefficients and the unemployment rate is 0·28 (t-statistic $= 0·8$); the result is the same whether the total unemployment rate is taken or the unemployment rate for females.

[21] −0·31 differs from −0·34 shown in Table 1, column (1), owing to the logit formulation.

[22] In the present recession women's participation has not fallen, presumably owing to the factors discussed above.

[23] In 1974, the tax (if any) paid by a family not paying higher rate tax or investment income surcharge was

    0·33   (husband's income − husband's allowances)
    +0·33 (wife's earnings − wife's allowance);

if the latter term were positive, and if the latter term were negative, it was

    0·33   (husband's income − husband's allowances).

So the marginal tax rate on the wife's earnings was zero if she earned less than her allowance, and in a few families it was zero for even higher levels of earnings, when the husband had not exhausted his allowances.

72   ECONOMICA

[24] Figure 4 ignores higher rates of tax and the effect of means-tested benefits.

[25] In similar works, Greenhalgh (1977b) has found that omitting individuals with earnings within £50 of the allowance makes little difference to the estimated coefficients.

[26] Approximately half the women who work pay tax on their earnings.

[27] Unfortunately the structure of the model is not linear since t is a function of HW, rather than a weighted sum of H and W. It is not clear how much this matters.

[28] *Social Trends* (1976), p. 96; *Department of Employment Gazette* (November 1973). Note that one cannot infer from the conditional supply function for an individual how average aggregate hours of workers will change in response to a wage change. For example, let us suppose that the Tobit model is correct and that a simultaneous doubling of husband's and wife's wages would lead to an increase in the individual probability of participation *and* in conditional expected hours. Even so, a doubling of all husband's and wife's wages in the population could lead to a fall in average hours worked by participants if it induced large numbers of people to participate who were almost indifferent between working and not working and so had small conditional expected hours. It all depends on how the independent variables are distributed in the population.

[29] We also did the analysis with wife's net wages and intercept, with almost identical results.

[30] A forthcoming paper will give a full maximum-likelihood analysis in which choices between all parts of the budget constraint are treated symmetrically.

[31] A similar result was obtained by Schultz (1976) for the United States. For participation, our elasticities are rather less than those from the logit analysis, and for hours of participants our elasticities are higher than those from the OLS exercise.

[32] Calculating the welfare costs of distortions affecting participation is somewhat more complicated. For the essential tools see Ashenfelter (1977, Appendix).

REFERENCES

ASHENFELTER, O. (1977). The labour supply response of wage earners in the rural negative income tax experiment. LSE Centre for Labour Economics, Discussion Paper No. 17.

BARZEL, Y. and McDONALD, R. J. (1973). Assets, subsistence and the supply curve of labour. *American Economic Review*, 63, 621–633.

CORRY, B. A. and ROBERTS, J. A. (1974). Activity rates and unemployment: the UK experience: some further results. *Applied Economics*, 6, 1–21.

GREENHALGH, C. (1977a). Participation and hours of work for married women in Great Britain. LSE Centre for Labour Economics, Discussion Paper No. 25.

—— (1977b). Estimating labour supply functions with progressive taxation of earnings. LSE Centre for Labour Economics, Discussion Paper No. 13.

HECKMAN, J. J. (1977). Sample selection bias as a specification error. University of Chicago, mimeo.

LAYARD, R., PIACHAUD, D. and STEWART, M. (1978). *The Causes of Poverty*, Background Paper No. 5, Royal Commission on the Distribution of Income and Wealth, London: HMSO.

MINCER, J. (1962). Labour force participation of married women. In *Aspects of Labour Economics* (H. G. Lewis, ed.). Washington, DC: National Bureau of Economic Research.

—— (1966). Labour force participation and unemployment. In *Prosperity and Unemployment* (R. A. Gordon and M. S. Gordon, eds) New York: John Wiley.

OPCS (Office of Population Censuses and Surveys) (1974). *General Household Survey 1974*. London: HMSO.

—— (1977). *Population Trends*, No. 9. London: HMSO.

SCHULTZ, T. P. (1976). Estimation of labour supply of married women. Rand, mimeo.

TOBIN, J. (1958). Estimation of relationships for limited dependent variables. *Econometrica*, 26, 24–36.

[13]

Why Are More Women Working in Britain?

Heather E. Joshi, *London School of Hygiene and Tropical Medicine*

Richard Layard, *London School of Economics*

Susan J. Owen, *University of Cardiff*

In Britain, female labor force participation rose steadily from the Second World War to 1977. To explain this, we estimate a pooled time-series, cross-section supply function for single-year age groups of women. The life-cycle pattern is explained quite well by the presence of children. At a second stage we try to explain the rising level of the cohort intercepts estimated at the first stage. Real wage growth may be an explanatory factor, as cross-section evidence suggests it should be. Finally, we point to the 15% rise in the relative pay of women in the mid-1970s caused by the Equal Pay Act. This did not cause the expected decline in the relative demand for female employees.

This paper is a shortened version of a longer paper (Joshi, Layard, and Owen 1983), which itself draws on another paper (Joshi et al. 1981). For further analysis of various demographic aspects see also Joshi and Owen (1981). The data used in our computing have been deposited in the ESRC Data Archive at Essex University under the title *Female Fertility and Employment by Cohort*. We are very grateful to Y. Deshpande and A. Tripathy for their computing and to L. Llorens, S. Rodriguez, and Z. Tzannatos for research assistance. We are also grateful for advice and comments to many colleagues in our respective centers. We should like to thank the Economic and Social Research Council, the Department of Employment, and the Leverhulme Trust Fund for financial support.

[*Journal of Labor Economics*, 1985, vol. 3, no. 1, pt. 2]

1. Introduction and Summary

The increasing number of women at work is one of the most striking phenomena in the history of postwar Britain. In 1931 only 32% of women aged 20–64 were in the labor force; by 1981 the proportion had risen to 58%. Why is this? There is clearly a demand side as well as a supply side to the story. After laying out the facts in Section II of this paper, we concentrate on a supply model in Section III and conclude in Section IV with some reflections on the largely unresolved problems relating to the demand side.

Female participation rose steadily from the Second World War until 1977, from which time it has been static. Until the 1970s the main increase was among married women aged over 35. Most of the extra workers have been part time.

To explain the increase in labor supply we estimate a pooled time-series, cross-section supply function for single-year age groups of women from 1950 to 1974. This function is estimated in two steps, for reasons to do with the pattern of serial correlation. In the first step, the proportion of women working in each age group is explained by the number of children they have of different ages, by age itself, by the state of the business cycle, and by a dummy for each individual birth cohort. As one might expect, the cohort dummies pick up most of the secular increase in participation, while the children and age variables map out the life-cycle pattern of participation. To understand the secular rise in participation we need to explain the coefficients on the cohort dummies, the second stage of the estimation process. We do this by various measures of early work experience, as well as by time and by the real wage levels prevailing at certain stages of life.

A key issue is the role of real wages. It is impossible to separate the influence of male and female wages, since the relativity between them was almost constant from 1950 to 1974. But we can examine the effect of the general wage level. We concentrate on the level of wages when the cohort was aged 35. If this variable is included but the time trend is excluded, the implied elasticity of participation with respect to the real wage level is about .4, while if the time trend is included the elasticity falls to .3, with a *t*-statistic of 2.4. However, we do not want to claim too much for this estimate, given some of the other less satisfactory experiments reported below.

It is interesting to compare these elasticities with those obtained from cross-section estimates on individual data relating to married women. These are based mostly on the General Household Survey (GHS) (a continuous survey of households in Great Britain published annually by the Office of Population Censuses and Surveys) and they differ according to which year's data set is used and which model. The GHS estimates

Gender and Economics

of the effect of an equiproportional rise in all wages and incomes range from .34 to zero (see App.).

So what does explain the postwar rise in participation? It is certainly not explained by demographic trends, since up to the end of the 1960s the number of young children at home was growing. It could be the growth in real wages, but the evidence here is suggestive rather than conclusive.

One would like to have an explanation that accounted also for the earlier trends in women's work. From the mid-nineteenth century up till the Second World War there was no trend at all. At the same time there was a fairly steady rise in real wages and from the 1880s a fairly steady fall in the number of young children at home. There was also increased schooling keeping children out of the home. It is hard to see why these influences did not produce an increase in women's paid work over that period.

Three possible explanations suggest themselves. First, job rationing in the interwar period may have discouraged female labor supply. In particular, employers may have had little incentive to provide part-time jobs, which have proved particularly attractive to women in the postwar period. One can well imagine that even with no change in hourly wages many women would be willing to take part-time jobs if these became available, even if they were not willing to take the equivalent full-time job.[1]

Second, the postwar period witnessed two major developments, which we have not documented and which affected the supply side. First were dramatic falls in the real prices of domestic appliances (especially of refrigerators, gas and electric cookers, noncoal heating appliances, vacuum cleaners, and washing machines) and the prices of processed foods and easy-care fabrics. This drastically reduced the time required to feed a family to a given standard, to keep a house clean, and to wash the clothes and linen. Theory does not enable one to sign the effect of such price changes, but on balance one would expect them to reduce the supply of housework. Second was a major fall in the morbidity of children, which made it much easier for women to offer a reliable supply of labor outside the home.

Finally, we offer the tentative thought that changes in women's labor supply may not be easy to explain in terms of recent values of any variable. Rather they may reflect long-term changes in the roles women see for themselves in life. The basic exogenous change here could be the reduction in the late nineteenth and early twentieth centuries in the mortality of children and young adults. This lowered the number of

---

[1] This proposition depends simply on the quasi-concavity of the utility function.

children needed in order to generate a given number of adult survivors. Again, theory does not predict the effect on fertility, but what actually happens is that people choose to have fewer children. At the same time the life expectancy of adult women rises, so that the fraction of her adult life a woman spends rearing children falls dramatically. This releases the woman for other roles. But it could easily take decades for labor supply behavior to react fully to this opportunity.

In Section IV we turn to the demand side. The puzzle here is that the relative hourly earnings of women (compared with men) rose by 15% from 1973 to 1976 because of the Equal Pay Act, but apparently with no effect on relative employment. Indeed, in the typical private-sector industry the employment of women relative to men increased sharply. What can explain this? One possible explanation is the Sex Discrimination Act, which outlawed discrimination in employment (rather than in pay). But most observers believe this law to have been too weak to account for what happened. The alternative explanation is simply that employers began to realize the true worth of female labor.

II. Trends in Women's Work, Pay, and Fertility

The growth in women's work is a relatively modern phenomenon. The proportion of adult women who were economically active remained at around one-third from the mid-nineteenth century until the Second World War (see table 1). Except briefly during the First World War things began to change only after the Second World War. Between 1931 and 1981 the economic activity rate of women aged 20–64 rose from 32% to 60%.

Until the 1970s the main increase was among women over 35. This shows clearly in table 2. Until the 1970s there was little increase among women in their childbearing twenties. But in the early 1970s, when the birthrate was falling, this group participated much more, while for women in mid-life the trend continued strongly upward. However, from around 1977 both trends stopped dead in their tracks, despite the economic recovery in 1978–79.

The main growth has been among married women (see table 3). Between 1951 and 1981 their participation rate more than doubled, and for mothers of dependent children the rise was proportionately more.[2] However, at the same time, the proportion of women who were married rose sharply, so that the overall participation rate of women rose less than it otherwise would have done.

Remarkably, there has been no growth at all in the propensity to

---

[2] Nowadays nearly all women return to work at some point after childbearing—a practice that was formerly rare. For data on work histories see Martin and Roberts (1984).

Table 1
Activity Rates: Women Aged 20–64 (%)

	All	Married	Single, Widowed, and Divorced
Census years:			
1851	34.5	n.a.	n.a.
1861	35.2	n.a.	n.a.
1871	34.5	n.a.	n.a.
1881	33.1	n.a.	n.a.
1891	33.5	n.a.	n.a.
1901	33.9	13.0	65.6
1911	32.5	10.5	66.4
1921	30.6	9.4	65.2
1931	31.6	10.9	66.7
1941	n.a.	n.a.	n.a.
1951	36.3	23.2	70.0
1961	41.0	31.6	73.3
1966	48.3	41.8	72.0
1971	51.5	45.9	72.7
1981	57.7	54.0	68.9
Recent years:			
1971	52.0	46.8	72.9
1972	52.7	47.6	72.4
1973	55.6	51.4	72.3
1974	57.3	53.4	72.5
1975	57.4	54.0	72.2
1976	58.6	55.3	71.7
1977	60.0	57.0	71.4
1978	59.9	56.7	71.7
1979	59.8	56.5	72.4
1980	59.7	56.2	72.0
1981	59.9	56.5	72.2

SOURCES.—Census years: Original census reports. Data for 1861–1931, England and Wales only: otherwise Great Britain; 1851–71 are obtained as follows. The census in 1871 and earlier uses a different concept of the occupied population from the census of 1881 and after. But a consistent series of the occupied population has been estimated in Department of Employment and Productivity (1971), table 102. We compute the ratio of this to the population ages 20–64 in 1851–81. For 1851–71 we divide this ratio by the ratio of its value in 1881 to the actual proportion of women ages 20–64 occupied in 1881. Recent years: *DE Gazette* (April 1981) adjusted to exclude students from numerator and denominator. The Department of Employment series is based on a variety of sources, especially the *Labour Force Survey*.

work full time. The whole growth has been in part-time work (see table 4).[3]

As table 5 shows, there has been a big increase in female unemployment (using survey definitions). In the early postwar years, unemployment was low, about the same for women and men. Since the early 1970s it has risen sharply, but rather less for women than men.

[3] Trends in part-time work during the 1970s differ according to the data source. Details available on request.

Table 2
Age-specific Activity Rates (%)

			Age			
	20–24	25–34	35–44	45–54	55–64	20–64
Census years:						
1851	59.1	41.3	35.5	36.8	37.0	42.1
1861	. . .	. . .	. . .	. . .	. . .	. . .
1871	60.0	40.4	36.3	38.4	39.5	42.5
1881	55.9		29.0		26.1	33.1
1891	58.1	33.0	25.1	25.4	24.4	33.5
1901	56.5	31.5	25.8	28.2	29.2	33.9
1911	62.0	33.8	24.1	23.0	20.4	32.5
1921	62.2	33.5	22.9	21.0	19.3	30.6
1931	65.1	36.3	24.5	21.1	17.8	31.6
1941	. . .	. . .	. . .	. . .	. . .	. . .
1951	65.4	40.5 33.5	35.2	34.4	27.6 15.0	36.3
1961	62.3	39.5 36.6	42.4	43.3	36.9 20.4	41.0
1966	61.6	40.4 41.5	52.7	54.8	46.3 27.0	48.3
1971	60.2	43.1 45.0	57.2	60.4	51.0 28.0	51.5
1981	69.2	55.4 53.4	65.5	66.0	52.3 22.4	57.7

			Age			
	20–24	25–34	35–44	45–54	55–59	60–64	20–64
Recent years:							
1971	64.1	44.0	57.4	60.6	51.1	28.2	52.0
1972	65.6	44.9	58.0	61.2	51.3	28.2	52.7
1973	66.8	48.7	62.3	65.2	52.6	28.2	55.6
1974	68.4	51.2	65.3	66.1	53.3	28.2	57.3
1975	68.8	52.0	65.9	66.3	53.3	28.2	57.4
1976	70.9	53.8	67.5	66.9	55.0	26.8	58.6
1977	72.4	56.5	68.7	67.1	57.3	25.0	60.0
1978	73.4	56.2	69.0	67.2	56.0	22.8	59.9
1979	73.3	56.2	68.5	67.5	54.9	21.3	59.8
1980	73.8	56.3	68.3	67.8	54.9	20.5	59.7
1981	73.2	56.2	68.2	68.4	54.6	19.2	59.9

SOURCES.—See table 1. In table 2 there is a break in the series between 1871 and 1881 for which we have not attempted to adjust, whereas we did attempt an adjustment in table 1.

Wages

We can now look at two main variables that might explain the trends in female labor supply: real wages and fertility. Real wages of women and men have been rising ever since the eighteenth century, and though the rate of growth has been most rapid since the Second World War, the proportional increase from, say, 1850 to 1950 was greater than that since 1950. As figures 1 and 2 and table 6 show, women's wages rose relative to men's during the Second World War, and the relativity rose again sharply between 1973 and 1975, by around 15%. This 15% rise happened both for manual workers, shown in the table, and for nonmanual workers. It was due to the Equal Pay Act of 1970, which outlawed the use of separate rates of pay for men and women from

Table 3
Activity Rates by Marital Status and Age: Marriage Rates, Female Nonstudents, Great Britain (%)

Marital Status	Year	Age									All Ages	20–59
		Under 20	20–24	25–34	35–44	45–54	55–59	60–64	65–69	70 and Over		
Single	1951	94.9	92.4	87.1	79.8	74.5	66.4	35.0	21.6	6.8	76.4	76.7
	1961	94.3	91.9	89.5	85.1	81.7	75.1	39.2	19.6	6.3	76.1	86.1
	1971	90.3	93.6	85.8	85.1	82.6	76.4	33.3	16.6	4.4	71.1	87.5
Married	1951	38.3	37.1	24.5	24.9	23.4	15.6	6.7	3.6	1.5	21.5	24.2
	1961	41.8	41.8	29.5	36.4	33.9	26.0	12.7	5.2	1.5	29.4	33.7
	1971	41.5	45.8	38.4	54.2	56.8	45.1	24.8	10.0	2.6	42.0	48.8
	1981	45.7	55.1	48.6	64.0	64.4	49.7	22.3	6.9	2.0	47.3	57.2
Widowed and divorced	1951	100.0	64.4	67.6	66.2	53.9	38.1	18.4	10.1	2.9	20.9	52.4
	1961	75.0	62.7	68.4	71.7	67.7	51.8	28.2	13.4	3.0	22.9	62.3
	1971	38.9	52.4	60.2	70.9	73.9	62.2	33.7	15.0	2.8	23.1	66.8
All	1951	92.0	66.7	37.1	34.7	34.0	27.7	14.4	9.0	3.2	35.0	42.4
	1961	91.8	63.9	39.5	36.6	42.0	36.9	20.4	10.3	3.1	38.3	43.4
	1971	88.3	63.6	44.0	57.1	60.6	50.9	28.0	12.7	3.0	43.9	54.6
	1981	91.8	74.5	54.9	65.7	66.1	52.3	22.4	7.6	2.0	47.4	62.3
Percentage of women never married	1951	95.7	52.7	18.8	13.9	15.6	15.9	15.9	16.8	16.6	24.5	26.6
	1961	93.7	43.0	13.5	10.0	11.3	14.2	14.8	15.3	16.0	20.8	15.5
	1971	82.8	36.7	10.7	7.4	8.4	10.0	11.8	13.9	15.4	17.5	12.6

SOURCES.—Census reports on occupation, economic activity, and education. In the adjustment to exclude students all students were assumed to be single (approximately true in 1971).

Table 4
Full- and Part-Time Work among Women Aged 20–64 (%)

	Full-Time Workers	Part-Time Workers	Unemployed	All Active
1951	30.3	5.2	0.8	36.3
1961	29.8	10.2	1.0	41.0
1966	31.7	15.2	1.4	48.3
1971	29.0	20.2	2.3	51.5
1981	31.6	22.4	3.7	57.7

SOURCE.—Census reports, for Great Britain. In 1951, 13 out of 15 of self-employed were assumed full time. The percentages of all women aged 20–64 who were self-employed in the 5 years were 1.5, 1.7, 1.9, 2.0, and 2.6
NOTE.—Full time means worked more than 30 hours normally (or 24 for teachers).

January 1976 onward.[4] Two main pieces of evidence are sufficient to establish this causality. First there is the timing: the rise corresponds exactly to the last possible moment allowed by the law, and the relativity has remained fairly stable ever since. Second, if one looks at wage rates negotiated in national collective bargaining agreements, the rates of women relative to men moved in almost exactly the same pattern as for earnings—though, as one would expect, relative earnings rose slightly less.[5]

There is little reason to think that human capital accounts for the recent narrowing of the male-female wage gap. The educational attainment of women relative to men was constant or declining for cohorts entering the labor force up to the 1960s, as attested by the *Education Tables* of the 1961 census and the *Qualified Manpower Tables* of the 1971 census. It is true that since then women have increased their educational activity rather more rapidly than men, but the quantitative effect of this on the human capital in the labor force has been small.[6] Moreover, most of the newly educated are still quite young, and for young adults extra education directly raises earnings but also indirectly reduces earnings by reducing work experience.[7]

[4] In addition to requiring equal pay for equal work (i.e., the same work), it insisted that where job evaluation was in force there should be equal pay for work of equal value. However, the general principle of equal pay for work of equal value was only being introduced in 1983.
[5] *DE Gazette* (see App. B). The data relate to manual workers. The question how women's pay is determined is examined at length in Zabalza and Tzannatos (1983), who show that conventional demand-side factors explain very little of the rise. They also show that among workers covered by collective bargaining agreements, the relative rise occurred entirely through changes within bargaining groups with no change in men's relative pay between groups.
[6] See the various reports of the General Household Survey (GHS) published by the Office of Population Censuses and Surveys (OPCS).
[7] At older ages this would not matter so much if the effect of experience on earnings is concave. Note that the available evidence does not enable one to calculate trends in the work experience of women currently working. The work

Table 5
Unemployment Rates (%)

	Census Data (Survey Definition)		Department of Employment (Registered Unemployment Rate)	
	Women	Men	Women	Men
Census years:				
1951	1.9	2.2	0.9	0.9
1961	2.5	3.0	0.9	1.3
1966	3.2	2.8	0.6	1.4
1971	4.8	5.4	1.2	4.2
1981	7.4	11.4	7.7	13.3
	General Household Survey (Survey Definition)		Department of Employment (Registered Unemployment Rate)	
Recent years:				
1971	3.6	3.3	1.2	4.2
1972			1.4	4.6
1973	3.3	3.2	1.0	3.3
1974	2.0	3.2	0.8	3.2
1975	3.2	4.3	1.6	4.9
1976	3.6	5.6	3.3	6.9
1977	4.8	5.4	4.0	7.2
1978	4.4	5.1	4.2	6.9
1979	4.7	5.4	4.1	6.3
1980	6.2	6.7	5.2	7.8
1981	9.4	11.1	7.7	13.3
1982	9.4	12.4	8.9	15.2

SOURCES.—Census reports, data for Great Britain. Registered unemployment, annual average: *DE Gazette.*
NOTE.—Covers all ages, except for General Household Survey, which relates to women under 60 and men under 65.

Fertility

Fertility fell from around the 1880s, when the total period fertility rate was about 4.5, until the 1930s when it was under 2 (see fig. 3 and table 7). It rose briefly after each world war, but there was a sustained rise from the mid-1950s to the mid-1960s. From the late 1960s there was a precipitate fall until 1978, when a slight recovery began. Thus fertility, unlike wages, has been anything but trended.

---

of Zabalza and Arrufat (1983) argues that human capital explains most of the female-male wage gap in the late 1970s. Whereas the actual hourly earnings of married women were 62% of males' earnings, they would have been between 67% and 73% if they had been determined by the male rather than the female earnings function. On this issue see also Stewart and Greenhalgh (1984).

Joshi et al.

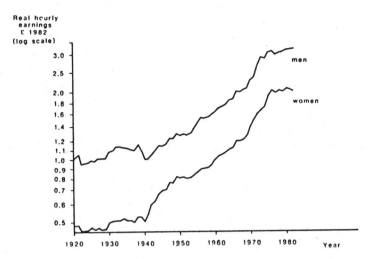

FIG. 1.—Real hourly earnings of men and women, Great Britain, 1920–82

III. The Supply Model

We turn now to the problem of explanation. For this purpose we use as dependent variable the proportion of women of each age who worked as employees in each year from 1950 to 1974.[8] There are clearly two main features to be explained: the life-cycle pattern of participation and the difference in pattern between the different cohorts.

These two features are illustrated in figure 4. This shows the work history of six selected cohorts of women over the period 1950–74. Each cohort is labeled by the date at which it was age 20. Thus for the cohort age 20 in 1962 we see an early fall in participation, followed by the beginning of a return to work. For those age 20 in 1954, we see more of this pattern of reentry. Indeed, we can see how steep it is and how misleading it would be to infer life-cycle behavior from the evidence of the cross section. The cross section of work in 1974 can be obtained by joining up the loose ends of each cohort profile. This suggests that participation is falling between ages 48 and 56, whereas the profile for the 1938 cohort rose over those ages. The apparent drop is due to differences in the behavior of the different cohorts, rather than an effect of aging. Figure 4 also makes it clear that the main increase in women's

[8] There is no annual series on labor force participation. The employment series we use is based on a survey of one-half of 1% of all employees covered by National Insurance. This was discontinued in 1975 and no subsequent time-series data exist on age-specific employment (except from surveys with large sampling error).

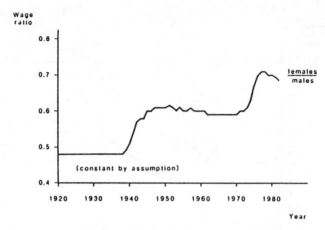

Fɪɢ. 2.—Ratio of female to male hourly earnings, Great Britain, 1920–82

work has been in midlife. However, the graph does not bring out the full increase in participation at younger ages that happened in the 1970s.

The age-specific employment rates are explained by three kinds of variables:

i) those whose values change from year to year and are age specific (e.g., number of children under 5)—we call these life-cycle variables;

ii) those whose values change from year to year but affect all ages

Fɪɢ. 3.—Total period fertility rate, England and Wales, 1920–82

Table 6
Average Hourly Real Earnings of Adult Full-Time Manual Workers
(1982 Prices in £'s = 1)

Year	Women over 18	Men over 21	Women as Proportion of Men	Year	Women over 18	Men over 21	Women as Proportion of Men
1920	.47	1.01	.47	1950	.79	1.29	.61
1921	.48	1.05	.47	1951	.80	1.30	.62
1922	.43	.95	.47	1952	.78	1.28	.61
1923	.44	.96	.47	1953	.79	1.31	.60
1924	.45	.96	.47	1954	.84	1.37	.61
1925	.47	.99	.47	1955	.86	1.44	.60
1926	.46	.97	.47	1956	.89	1.50	.60
1927	.47	1.01	.47	1957	.90	1.48	.61
1928	.46	1.01	.47	1958	.92	1.52	.60
1929	.46	1.01	.47	1959	.94	1.58	.60
1930	.50	1.09	.47	1960	.99	1.66	.60
1931	.51	1.10	.47	1961	1.04	1.73	.60
1932	.51	1.13	.47	1962	1.05	1.77	.59
1933	.51	1.13	.47	1963	1.07	1.80	.59
1934	.52	1.12	.47	1964	1.11	1.88	.59
1935	.51	1.12	.47	1965	1.13	1.92	.59
1936	.51	1.11	.47	1966	1.20	2.03	.59
1937	.50	1.10	.47	1967	1.20	2.03	.59
1938	.53	1.15	.47	1968	1.22	2.10	.58
1939	.53	1.09	.49	1969	1.29	2.20	.59
1940	.51	1.00	.51	1970	1.41	2.38	.59
1941	.55	1.01	.54	1971	1.48	2.46	.60
1942	.60	1.06	.57	1972	1.60	2.65	.60
1943	.64	1.10	.58	1973	1.69	2.78	.61
1944	.67	1.15	.58	1974	1.74	2.76	.63
1945	.69	1.15	.60	1975	1.95	2.92	.67
1946	.70	1.17	.60	1976	2.06	2.94	.70
1947	.76	1.25	.61	1977	1.97	2.77	.71
1948	.76	1.25	.61	1978	2.05	2.87	.71
1949	.80	1.31	.61	1979	2.02	2.90	.70
				1980	2.10	3.00	.70
				1981	2.07	3.01	.69
				1982	2.05	3.02	.68

SOURCES.—Data relate to April. Wages (£): 1938–82; U.K. Department of Employment and Productivity (1971), tables 46–48; and comparable *DE Gazette* thereafter ("April survey" grafted backward onto New Earnings Survey). Earlier: The *Abstract* gives data for male/female weekly wage ratios in 1935. It also gives data on average hourly wages (for men and women combined) back to 1920. We assumed that the male/female ratio for 1920–35 was constant. Prices: *Abstract* Tables 89–93 and *Department of Employment Gazette* thereafter (1982 prices = 1).
NOTE.—Weekly earnings of women relative to men did not change between 1886 and the interwar period (Department of Employment and Productivity 1971).

equally (e.g., the state of the economy)—we call these calendar-time variables; and

iii) those that differ between cohorts but do not change over the life cycle (e.g., year of birth)—we call these cohort variables.

If t denotes date and j denotes cohort, we can refer to these three sets of variables as L_{tj}, B_t, and C_j respectively. Hence if E_{tj} is the proportion of nonstudent women at work as employees, $E_{tj} = f(L_{tj}, B_t, C_j)$. The particular variables we consider are (i) life-cycle variables: children of

Table 7
Total Period Fertility Rate

Year	Total Period Fertility Rate	Year	Total Period Fertility Rate
1841–45	4.59	1951	2.14
1851–55	4.62	1952	2.16
1860–65	4.66	1953	2.21
1871–75	4.81	1954	2.20
1881–85	4.58	1955	2.22
1891–95	4.01	1956	2.35
1901–05	3.46	1957	2.45
1911–15	2.83	1958	2.51
1916–20	2.42	1959	2.53
1921–25	2.39	1960	2.66
1926–30	2.00	1961	2.77
1930	1.94	1962	2.84
1931	1.89	1963	2.88
1932	1.82	1964	2.94
1933	1.72	1965	2.84
1934	1.75	1966	2.76
1935	1.75	1967	2.66
1936	1.77	1968	2.58
1937	1.79	1969	2.48
1938	1.83	1970	2.41
1939	1.83	1971	2.38
1940	1.74	1972	2.19
1941	1.71	1973	2.02
1942	1.92	1974	1.90
1943	2.02	1975	1.79
1944	2.24	1976	1.73
1945	2.04	1977	1.68
1946	2.46	1978	1.75
1947	2.69	1979	1.86
1948	2.38	1980	1.90
1949	2.26	1981	1.82
1950	2.18	1982	1.77

SOURCES.—Office of Population Censuses and Surveys, *Birth Statistics* (1980), table 1.4., and *Population Trends* (Spring 1983).
NOTE.—Fertility rate $= \sum_i (B_i/P_i)$, where i is age $15 \leqslant i \geqslant 44$, B is births, and P is female population.

different ages, wages, and age; (ii) calendar time variables: business cycle (vacancies); and (iii) cohort variables: completed family size, male and female wages at specified ages, education, unemployment experience early in working life, experience of wartime working, and trend.[9]

Our aim is to estimate a supply function for female labor (in terms of numbers of workers rather than woman-hours). There is an obvious problem of identification, since for data reasons the dependent variable has to be age-specific employment, not labor force.[10] However, there is

[9] For exact definitions of variables see Joshi et al. (1981), annexes A, C; or Joshi and Owen (1981), annexes A, B.
[10] The National Insurance Card data also give, separately by age, data on those not employed but receiving "credits." But these exclude unregistered unemployed and include the sick.

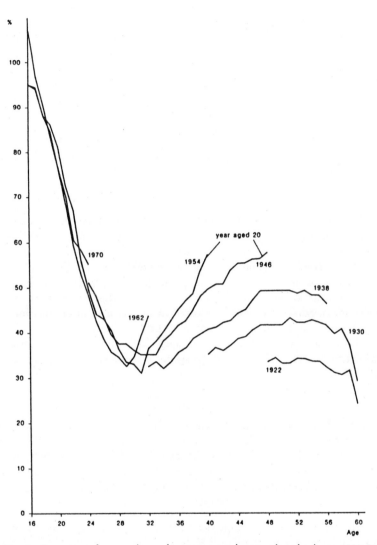

FIG. 4.—Percentage of women in employment as employees: selected cohorts, 1950-74

a relationship among employment (E), labor supply (S), and vacancies (V) given by the U/V curve: $E = S + \gamma V + \text{constant}$. There is also a supply relation, in which supply may respond to vacancies as well as to other variables (Z): $S = Z\beta + \alpha V + \text{constant}$. Hence, eliminating S, $E = Z\beta + (\alpha + \gamma)V + \text{constant}$. This means that all is well, provided we include vacancies in our equation.

Our estimation proceeds in two steps. First, in equation (1), we estimate the effect of all variables that are not purely cohort variables. We estimate their effect simultaneously with a vector of coefficients (a) on the vector of cohort dummies (D_j). Thus we estimate

$$E_{ij} = L_{ij}b + B_t c + D_j a + u_{ij}. \tag{1}$$

Then as a second stage we estimate the effects of the cohort variables by regressing the $\hat{a}_j s$ estimated in equation (1) on the purely cohort variables (C_j):

$$\hat{a}_j = C_j c + v_j. \tag{2}$$

This two-stage approach is necessary if we are to handle problems of autocorrelation in a satisfactory manner.[11] There are two dimensions in which we found important serial correlation. One is serial correlation in the unexplained behavior of a given cohort over its life cycle (i.e., between adjacent ages for the same people). This is captured in the error terms of equation (1).[12] The second is serial correlation in the unexplained behavior of adjacent cohorts, captured in the error term of equation (2). For both equations, ρ was estimated by grid search.

The equations are estimated for ages 20–59 for the 43 cohorts on which there were at least 10 observations at these ages during the period 1951–74.[13]

Results

Table 8 shows estimates of equation (1) and table 9 shows estimates of equation (2). Let us look at these one by one. Table 8 enables us to look at the effect of the life-cycle and calendar-time variables, while table 9 turns to the cohort variables. As we go through the variables, we shall first describe them and then document their effects.

[11] As an estimation strategy, this is a standard procedure for pooled time series. It resembles the procedure adopted by Heckman and MaCurdy (1980) for their micro-panel data: they specify fixed effects, to capture "permanent" variables among individuals, analogous to our a_j.

[12] Once cohort dummies were included there was little serial correlation in the error terms of adjacent time periods holding age constant, or adjacent age groups holding time constant. (ρ was .16 and .20, respectively, in regression 1 of table 9.)

[13] We restrict our analysis to ages 20–59 to avoid specific questions associated with women's retirement age and educational enrollment. There was some doubt about the National Insurance data on teenage employment, but data for ages below 20 are used where necessary to allow for lags.

Table 8
Estimates of Equation (1)

Explanatory Variables (other than Cohort Dummies)	Regression Coefficients (with *t*-Statistics)			
	1	2	3	4
Age	−.0052	−.0058	−.0047	−.0064
	(19.98)	(13.86)	(12.38)	(8.45)
$(\text{Age} - 39.5)^2$	−.00013	−.000079	−.00013	−.000089
	(7.29)	(2.53)	(7.34)	(3.24)
Children ages 0–4 per woman	−.346	−.339	−.350	−.336
	(38.17)	(34.65)	(37.75)	(31.64)
Children ages 5–10 per woman	−.141	−.134	−.140	−.128
	(28.72)	(22.37)	(28.68)	(14.39)
Children ages 11–14 per woman	−.072	−.0707	−.0735	−.066
	(8.78)	(8.62)	(8.94)	(7.47)
(Children ages 11–14 per woman) × (cohort birth year − 1925)	.0030	.0032	.0032	.0031
	(4.47)	(4.71)	(4.67)	(4.57)
Vacancies × 10^{-6} × dummy (age 20–39)	.058	.0578	.0615	.0579
	(12.07)	(11.89)	(12.07)	(11.92)
Vacancies × 10^{-6} × dummy (age 40–59)	.040	.0412	.0434	.0412
	(8.36)	(8.49)	(8.53)	(8.54)
Age-specific wage ratio males to females, 1968		.0306		
		(1.81)		
Current real wage of women			−.00045	
			(1.82)	
(Cohort birth year − 1000) × age spline*				.0000023
				(1.73)
Dependent variable: proportion of nonstudent women employed				
$\hat{\rho}$	.6	.6	.6	.6
DW	2.13	2.13	2.14	2.15
$\bar{R}^2$	.997	.997	.997	.997
SSE	.07415	.07385	.07383	.07388
df	799	798	798	798
N	850	850	850	850

* Age spline = (age − 30) × dummy (30–59) − (age − 50) × dummy (50–59). For full definition of variables see Joshi et al. (1981), annex C.

Life-Cycle and Calendar-Time Variables

Children. Children are not exogenous if chosen jointly with work decisions. Thus a reduced-form supply function of work would have in it the cost of children rather than their number. However, we can eliminate the cost variable by substituting in from the demand function for children, to get a relationship between work and children.[14] This is the only practicable procedure if we want to trace out the life-cycle pattern of work.

Cross-sectional work on micro data makes it clear that the effect of children is best measured by the presence of any child, interacted with

[14] We are assuming that between cohorts those with a high "taste" for work have on average a normal "taste" for children.

Table 9
Estimates of Equation (2)

Explanatory variables	Regression Coefficients (with t-Statistics)							
	1	2	3	4	5	6	7	8
Cohort birth year	.0057 (8.50)		.0011 (.51)	.0023 (1.22)	.0013 (.68)	.0052 (10.73)	.0084 (4.59)	.0082 (6.14)
Years at ages 20–29 during World War II	.0031 (1.46)	.0040 (2.00)	.0038 (1.87)	.0048 (3.13)	.0041 (2.77)	.0036 (2.62)	.000024 (.0079)	.00040 (.68)
Average unemployment rate at age 15–24 (%)	-.0046 (1.97)	-.0080 (4.38)	-.0072 (2.95)	-.0042 (1.91)	-.0012 (.40)	.0028 (1.11)	-.0045 (1.66)	.0043 (1.73)
Log average real wages of men and women at age 35		.166 (9.40)	.138 (2.39)	.153 (2.90)	.119 (2.25)			
Log male wage – log female wage at age 35				.190 (2.37)				
Log average real wages of men and women at age 20					-.309 (2.37)	-.395 (3.18)		-.134 (2.34)
Log male wage – log female wage at age 20							-.120 (1.76)	-.480 (3.91)
Constant	-2.221 (7.4)	.121 (3.33)	-.314 (.37)	-1.379 (1.23)	-.425 (.40)	-3.046 (7.74)	-2.601 (4.36)	-4.806 (5.73)
(Dependent variable: cohort coefficient $\hat{d}_i$)								
$\hat{\rho}$	.5	.5	.5	.3	.3	.2	.6	.2
DW	2.28	2.29	2.32	2.28	2.14	1.98	2.40	2.03
R^2	.887	.902	.899	.952	.952	.959	.836	.964
SSE	.00809	.00706	.00701	.00640	.00639	.00725	.00753	.00629
df	38	38	37	36	36	37	37	36
N	42	42	42	42	42	42	42	42

NOTE.—For full definition of variables, see Joshi et al. (1981), annex C.

Table 10
Hypothetical Effect on Female Employment of Changes in the Child
Population, 1951-81, Great Britain (1,000s)

Children	Change in Population			Effect on Employment		
	1951-61	1961-71	1971-81	1951-61	1961-71	1971-81
0-4 years	−76	238	−1044	26	−82	361
5-10 years	212	998	−964	−30	−141	134
11-14 years	801	−112	215	−58*	5*	−3*
Total	937	1124	−1793	−62	−218	492
Actual change in employment of women aged 20-59				564	1,149	687

SOURCE.—Census reports.
NOTES.—Estimated effect on employment calculated using coefficients from table 8, equation (1).
* Change in population of ages 11-14 times the coefficient on children 11-14 at end year (reflecting effect of the interaction with cohort).

the age of the youngest child.[15] However, no time series evidence is available for this. Instead we use three variables: (i) children under age 5 (preschool) per woman, (ii) children 5-10 (primary school age) per woman, and (iii) children 11-14 per woman (15 being the minimum school-leaving age till 1973). Each variable measures the number of children (born to the cohort) per woman (married and unmarried) in the cohort.[16]

Turning to the results, the final column of table 8 shows our preferred equation. Each preschool child lowers participation by 35%, each primary school child by 14%, and each secondary school child by 7% (for the cohort age 20 in 1945).

It is interesting to see how children affect the fraction of a woman's life that she works as an employee. Each child reduces the years a mother works by about 2.9, so that if mothers averaged 2.5 children they would work about 7 fewer years than childless women. Put another way, these average mothers would work 44% of the years between ages 20 and 59, while the average childless woman would work 62% of that time.

We can next examine how far fertility changes explain the evolution of postwar female employment. Table 10 shows on the left-hand side the changes in the number of children over each decade and on the

[15] The number of children also has a minor, nonlinear effect (Joshi and Owen 1981, sec. 4(i)).
[16] The numbers are derived from data on births and therefore ignore mortality and migration. Joshi and Owen also experimented with other variables such as marital status and the existence of any child, some of which marginally improved the fit.

right-hand side the predicted effect of these changes on female employment. The changes in the number of children between 1951 and 1971
seem to have depressed female activity to a relatively small extent,
whereas the sharp decline in the number of young children between
1971 and 1981 would produce, given these coefficients, a marked rise
(of almost half a million workers). Thus, of the actual intercensal changes
in female employment (shown at the bottom of the right-hand panel),
the increases observed between 1951 and 1971 occur *despite* increased
numbers of children and must be explained by other factors. On the
other hand, most of the estimated increase between 1971 and 1981 *is*
attributable to falling numbers of children.

One puzzle is why participation has increased more over time at older
rather than at younger ages. We have in part picked this up by finding that the deterrent effect of secondary school children declined
over time.[17]

Real wages. We do not have time-series data on age-specific wages.
Instead we use data on age-specific wages for 1 year and on aggregate
wages for all years. The former could explain a part of the life-cycle
pattern of participation (see Smith 1973; Becker and Ghez 1975), while
the latter could explain time-series variation. We take them in that order.

The cross-sectional ratio of hourly earnings of women relative to men
in 1968 was as follows:

Age					
18–20	21–24	25–29	30–39	40–49	50–59
.81	.73	.70	.62	.58	.63

Source.—*New Earnings Survey,* 1968 (described in App. B), table 40B.

The relative earnings of women are highest early in life, which may help
to explain why they participate most then; but the data do not suggest
that there is any relative wage incentive for women to return to work
in midlife. It is therefore not surprising that the variable attracts the
wrong sign (in col. 2 of table 8).

Turning to the time-series wage variables for men and women (hourly
earnings of adult full-time manual workers), these are almost perfectly
collinear, since there was no appreciable change in the male/female wage
ratio between 1950 and 1974. We therefore included only the female
real wage. This too attracted the wrong sign (see col. 3 of table 8). Note
that this result is obtained in the presence of a vector of cohort dummies
that are picking up the positive trend in participation.

Age. Age itself could have an effect in two ways. The waning of

---

[17] There is no evidence for a changing deterrent effect of younger children.

vitality later in life, particularly if anticipated, suggests that work should be done earlier rather than later. But even apart from this, it will make sense to concentrate work earlier in life if the return to savings sufficiently compensates for the postponed enjoyment of consumption and time at home.[18] This pattern will be further reinforced if retirement and pension arrangements lead to higher consumption in old age than would be freely chosen. The sample is restricted to ages below 60 to exclude any impact of the formal retirement age.

We include as variables not only age but age squared. It appears that age leads to a decline in participation at an increasing rate, so that between 20 and 59 it reduces participation by 20 percentage points. In order to try to allow for the fact that the main growth in participation is at older ages, we included an interaction term between cohort birth year and an age spline (col. 4). This had a positive but very small effect and was not highly significant.[19]

Vacancies.   Vacancies (for men and women) registered at employment exchanges are more or less untrended between 1950 and 1974. We tried them, as well as two other indices of the business cycle—the male unemployment rate and a Wharton index of excess capacity—both of which yielded less stable estimates. We had reason to expect a differential impact of demand on the employment of women at different ages (Joshi 1981), and after experimentation discovered a different effect above and below 40. However, the vacancy effects are rather low.

To conclude our analysis of equation (1), various tests suggested that results were extremely similar when the sample was confined to cohorts having a full 25 observations, or to ages over 30. Splitting the sample over calendar time (into three equal periods) significantly improved the fit, but not strongly so ($F_{90/709} = 2.12$), the main differences from the overall estimates being rather minor ones during the period 1951–58. If the equation was estimated separately for the age group 20–29, it became somewhat less stable.

In a separate analysis we investigated whether it is better to specify equation (1) only with an autoregressive error, as above, or also with a lagged dependent variable (which might reflect state dependence in work behavior). We concluded that the choice makes little difference to any of our other results and that it is intrinsically difficult to determine the issue.

[18] If the interest rate exceeds the pure rate of time preference, individuals will consume more later in life, and hence, if the price of home time in terms of goods is constant, they will also consume more home time later in life. For models of life-cycle planning see Smith (1973) and Heckman and MaCurdy (1980).
[19] The effect of age per se disappears at ages below 40 when family structure is specified in more detail (see Joshi and Owen 1981).

Differences between Cohorts

The coefficients on the cohort dummies generated by the preferred version of equation (1) $(\hat{a}_i)$ show a fairly linear trend up to the cohort at age 20 in 1955. After that the trend flattens off, though one should note that for these later cohorts most of our data are on participation in their twenties only.[20] If these cohorts should in fact conform to the rising trend only when they reach mid-life, we would not have enough evidence to detect this from participation early in life.

Table 9 shows the results of fitting equation (2) to explain the cohort coefficients. Before discussing the results, we shall review all the variables considered for the analysis, some of which were eventually rejected.

Completed family size. We have already allowed for the influence of children at the time when they are at home. However, we also want to know whether family size has an effect at times other than when the children are young. For example, if a woman has been out of the labor force for a long time with children, she may be less likely to work when they are grown up. She may also be less likely to work before she has a family if she expects to have a large one (though this could go the other way if the need to accumulate savings was strong enough). We therefore look at the effect of *completed* family size as proxied by numbers of children born by age 36. This grew steadily from the cohort aged 20 in 1928 to that aged 20 in 1958. We also experimented with the proportion of women who ever had children by age 36. This also grew very sharply: comparing the 1928 and 1958 cohorts, we have the following approximate changes: fertility (cumulated to age 36), +60%; percentage who ever had children (by age 36), +20%; children per mother (by age 36), +30%. However, as our data come from a period dominated by an upswing in fertility, it is not surprising that completed fertility attracted a perverse sign in our regressions, and we therefore rejected it as an explanatory variable.

Education. Another factor possibly affecting women's work is education, which may act directly as well as through its effect on wage levels. If we look at the crude differences in participation between different educational groups we see the joint effect of these forces. Table 11 shows how in 1961 better-educated women were more likely to work than less-educated women, holding age constant. However, the difference between the different groups is so small that, even if all women had moved from the lowest to the highest educational group, it would only

---

[20] The coefficients for cohorts aged 20 in 1922 to 1964 were .64, .67, .67, .66, .70, .70, .71, .73, .72, .74, .74, .77, .75, .78, .78, .78, .79, .79, .83, .81, .82, .82, .84, .84, .85, .87, .88, .89, .89, .88, .90, .89, .91, .94, .92, .93, .92, .92, .91, .93, .93, .93, .92.

Table 11
Female Economic Activity Rates by Terminal Education Age, 1961 (%)

Age	Terminal Education Age				
	Under 15	15	16	17–19	20 and Over
15–19	(83)	93	95	94	. . .
20–24	(57)	59	78	78	87
25–44	40	39	42	43	56
45 and over	26	29	31	29	46
All	31	56	49	45	56

SOURCES.—Data for Great Britain constructed from census of England and Wales, 1961, *Education Tables*, and census of Scotland, 1961, *Terminal Education Age Tables*.
NOTE.—Parentheses indicate small base numbers.

account for a fraction of the actual increase in women's participation since World War II.

To isolate the direct effect of education on women's work (rather than its effects via wages), we included in our regressions a variable that reflected the minimum compulsory school-leaving age for the cohort in question. We also included as an alternative the proportion of the cohort with A-level standard qualifications or above (higher secondary) (from the *Qualified Manpower Tables* of the 1971 census). Both were highly correlated with the trend, and it proved impossible to detect a distinct education effect.

Early unemployment and wartime work experience. Past job rationing may influence present activity. If a cohort experiences severe job rationing early in life, it fails to acquire human capital in a way that our wage series (which are not age specific) fail to identify. In addition, the cohort's perception of job opportunities may be permanently affected, even if actual job opportunities are not. We therefore include as a variable the average percentage unemployment rate during the years when the cohort was age 15–24.

The Second World War enormously increased women's participation in all kinds of work. Female employment rose by about 45% between 1938 and 1943, and then after the war returned to about halfway between its prewar and wartime levels. The experience of warwork led many women (especially in their twenties) to acquire skills they would not otherwise have acquired. This must have made many of them more willing to work later. We therefore include as a cohort variable the number of wartime years experienced by cohorts when they were between 20 and 29.

Real wages. The variables mentioned so far are not going to do very much to explain the strong trend in the coefficients on the cohort dummies. An obvious candidate for this job is real wages. From cross-sectional work we have some a priori expectations about the effects of wage changes. If the man's wage increases, the wife's labor supply will fall. But if the wife's wage increases, her labor supply will increase, and this effect is usually found to be sufficiently strong to ensure that an equiproportional increase in husband's and wife's wage will lead to a net increase in the wife's labor supply. It may of course be the case that labor supply depends in part at least on individual wages relative to the general average. If this is so, the cross-section estimates of wage effects will exceed in absolute magnitude the time-series effects.

In time series, men's wages and women's wages are highly correlated (for 1950–74, r = .99, and each is nearly as highly correlated with time). Thus it is not easy to distinguish their separate effects, although one may still be able to estimate the net effect of a rise in the *general* level of real wages.

In our regressions we experimented with earnings when the cohorts were age 20 and again when they were 35. We also included the level of men's pay relative to women's at both ages.

Trend.   Finally there may be omitted trended variables that help to explain the upward tendency in participation (e.g., social attitudes, better health). The natural way to allow for this is to include a time trend: the date of birth of the cohort. There are many other variables we would have liked to include that may or may not be adequately proxied by a time trend. Notable among these are child-care facilities and the prevalence of family breakup, both of which involve several elements that are not systematically recorded.[21]

Results of Analysis of Cohort Dummies

We can now turn to table 9, which is estimated with an autoregressive error. Column 1 shows a simple time trend, plus the effects of the war and of early unemployment, which are as expected. The time trend is .57% per year. Column 2 drops the time trend and replaces it by the wage level when the cohort was 35. This highly trended series implies a wage elasticity (at average participation) of .36, which compares with the cross-sectional elasticity computed by Layard, Barton, and Zabalza (1980) of .21 for an equiproportional increase in husband's and wife's wages. Thus one might say that the cross-sectional estimate "explains"

---

[21] For broken families we only know the proportion of women *currently* divorced or widowed. The former was still quite small in 1974, reaching a maximum of 3.8% in the 32–36 age bracket. The number of widows has been falling and in 1974 was 5% at 48 years and 12% at 56. There are no good time series on the proportion of lone women with children, but in any case they are a small proportion of all mothers (7% in the 1975 General Household Survey). If they were to be adequately treated, we should also have to bring in their income maintenance opportunities (see Horton 1979).

roughly half the time series changes. The next step, however, is to see whether the time series can yield their own estimate of wage elasticities when some reasonable allowance has been made for the effect of other trended variables. Thus in column 3 we include both a time trend and the wage variable and let them fight it out. The result is that the wage effect falls by about one-fifth of itself, and the time trend is correspondingly about one-fifth of .57% per year. However, we do not want to put too much weight on these results, given the high correlation of this wage variable and the trend.

In the rest of the table we explore other variants. Column 4 adds the wage of men relative to women at age 35—with significant effects of a perverse sign. However, the wage ratio at age 20—reflecting the big differences between the wage ratio for cohorts beginning work before and after World War II—does yield a negative sign, shown in column 5. This variable is highly correlated with the unemployment level in early life and greatly reduces the measured impact of the latter. The *t*-value is higher on the wage ratio at 20, but one cannot be very confident about which variable is playing the greater role. The remaining columns of the table show perverse signs on the level of the wage at 20.

IV. Some Demand-Side Issues

We turn now to the demand side. There is a major puzzle here for economic theory, which we feel is worth airing. As a result of the Equal Pay Act, between 1973 and 1976 the relative wage of women rose by 15% and stayed there. Most economists would have predicted that in the private sector at least this would reduce the relative employment of women. But no such result occurred. Why was this?[22]

A possible explanation is that two acts were passed in 1970: the Equal Pay Act and the Sex Discrimination Act. The latter outlawed any discrimination in employment practices (especially hiring and firing) on grounds of sex or marital status. If there had formerly been massive discrimination in employment, which was suddenly reduced in 1976 when the Sex Discrimination Act became operative, this could have offset the effect of the Equal Pay Act, as it was intended to. However, the impact of the Sex Discrimination Act is not generally believed to have been large, and the number of cases brought to tribunals has been quite small.[23] The number of cases under the Equal Pay Act has also

[22] For a further discussion of this issue see Zabalza and Tzannatos (1983).

[23] On average, the annual number of applications has been around 200, the number of cases actually heard around 80, and the number of cases upheld around 15. For this reason we reject the approach of Landes (1968), which argues that if employers are faced with a cost if they discriminate against women this will raise their demand price for women.

Table 12
The Composition of Employment (Employees Only)

| | Whole Economy | | | | Private Sector | |
| | Female Hours Male Hours (1) | Demand Index (2) | Proportion of Women in Private Sector (3) | Proportion of Men in Private Sector (4) | Female Hours Male Hours (5) | Demand Index (6) |
Year						
1950	.412	.377	.762	.688	.457	.408
1951	.413	.379	.763	.691	.456	.408
1952	.405	.375	.757	.687	.446	.402
1953	.409	.378	.760	.689	.452	.405
1954	.409	.379	.761	.692	.450	.404
1955	.404	.377	.762	.698	.441	.399
1956	.403	.378	.757	.698	.437	.398
1957	.400	.383	.754	.703	.428	.401
1958	.396	.383	.747	.698	.424	.401
1959	.393	.387	.743	.701	.416	.403
1960	.393	.388	.745	.711	.412	.400
1961	.392	.390	.739	.712	.407	.399
1962	.392	.394	.734	.711	.405	.402
1963	.388	.397	.728	.710	.398	.403
1964	.386	.399	.728	.717	.392	.402
1965	.388	.401	.723	.719	.390	.400
1966	.398	.404	.715	.720	.395	.400
1967	.398	.405	.699	.712	.391	.398
1968	.403	.410	.700	.713	.395	.399
1969	.405	.412	.691	.712	.393	.398
1970	.415	.415	.682	.712	.397	.397
1971	.412	.420	.667	.713	.398	.394
1972	.432	.428	.668	.710	.406	.401
1973	.435	.427	.662	.713	.404	.397
1974	.449	.420	.686	.725	.425	.396
1975	.469	.428	.642	.699	.431	.393
1976	.470	.445	.618	.700	.415	.407
1977	.476	.444	.619	.704	.419	.406
1978	.482	.450	.622	.704	.426	.413
1979	.492	.451	.619	.699	.435	.414
1980	.505	.456	.612	.688	.443	.418

SOURCES.—Column 1: total employment: *DE Gazette*. Percentage part-time, census year 1951: census; 1961–66: Department of Employment and Productivity (1971); 1971: census, assuming those with hours not stated are self-employed; and 1981: census; intercensal years to 1971: linear interpolation; *General Household Survey* used to interpolate between 1971 and 1981. Hours per person, to 1970, April survey of manual workers grafted onto *New Earnings Survey* (1970–81) manual workers. Column 2: $\sum (F_i/M_i)_{70}(M_u/M_i)$, where M_i is male employment in the ith industry, and F_i is female employment, the resulting measure being standardized to equal col. 1 in 1970. Columns 3 and 4: *DE Gazette*, employment by industry tables (private sector = agriculture, manufacturing, construction, distributive trades, insurance, etc., and miscellaneous services). Column 5: cols. 1, 3, and 4. Column 6: as col. 2 but for the restricted range of industries.

been fairly small,[24] but then one should bear in mind that collectively bargained pay is more visible and any one case will affect more people.

To investigate these issues, we first calculate the relative employment of women and men in man-hours (see table 12). The results of this

[24] In the first year (1976), there were 1,742 applications, 709 cases heard, and 213 upheld; in 1982 these numbers had fallen to 39, 13, and 2, respectively.

exercise will surprise many people. They indicate that the proportion of hours contributed by women fell somewhat from 1951 to the mid-1960s and rose sharply only during the 1970s when the rise was continuous (see table 12, col. 1). The reason is that the number of full-time women workers fell slightly, while the number of male workers rose sharply and more than enough to offset the rise in part-time workers.

Turning to the explanation of labor demand, the most obvious influence to examine first is the effect of changes in the pattern of employment between more and less female-intensive industries. We do this by means of an index in which the female/male ratio in each industry (assumed constant) is weighted by the (changing) fraction of all males working in that industry.[25] This index is shown in table 12, column 2. There was a steady rise in the female intensity of the structure of the economy, but at a much more rapid pace in the 1970s than earlier. During the 1970s the index rose by 4.5 percentage points, reflecting the vast expansion of service industries. But the actual ratio of woman-hours to man-hours rose twice as much as this, by nine points. Thus there were also sharp increases in the proportion of women workers within each industry, in spite of the sharp rises in women's pay.

One might not perhaps be surprised by this if it happened in the public sector. So let us see what happened in the private sector (cols. 5, 6). The structure of demand index for the private sector rose very little, reflecting only a mild shift toward private rather than public services. But the actual ratio of female to male employment rose quite sharply. So our puzzle holds even when we confine our gaze to the private sector.

To see whether we could resolve the puzzle we did some very crude regressions for the private sector, shown in table 13. In the first of these we regressed the employment ratio on the structure of demand, vacancies, time, and the wage ratio. The coefficient on the wage ratio was highly significant but of the wrong sign. This confirmed the results of earlier work in which it proved possible to estimate a sensible demand system for labor in manufacturing up to 1969 (Layard 1982) but impossible to extend the work into the 1970s. The only way to save the situation is to introduce dummies to represent the effect of the Sex Discrimination Act. This is done in column 2. The dummy allows for anticipatory effects and takes the value $\frac{1}{6}$, $\frac{2}{6}$, $\frac{3}{6}$, $\frac{4}{6}$, $\frac{5}{6}$, and 1, respectively, in each year from 1971 to 1976, and 1 thereafter. The result is that the wage becomes significantly negative, but a huge and implausible effect has been attributed to the Sex Discrimination Act.

[25] The index is thus $\sum_i (F_{it}/M_i)_0 (M_{it}/M_t)$. The rationale is as follows. Suppose the demand function in each sector is $(F_{it}/M_{it}) = a_i f(R_t)$, where R_t is relative wages. Hence $(F_{it}/M_{it}) = (f(R_t)/f(R_0))(F_{it}/M_i)_0$ and $(F_t/M_t) = \sum (F_{it}/M_{it})(M_{it}/M_t) = (f(R_t)/f(R_0)) \sum (F_i/M_i)_0 (M_{it}/M_t)$.

Table 13
Regressions to Explain Log Female/Male
Employment Ratio in Private Sector

	1	2
Constant	.59	−.29
	(1.41)	(.92)
Log demand structure index	.63	.49
	(1.25)	(1.46)
Log vacancies	.04	−.01
	(1.93)	(.60)
Time	−.01	−.01
	(5.16)	(9.09)
Log female/male hourly earnings	.80	−.76
	(4.59)	(2.62)
Dummy for Sex Discrimination Act		.28
		(5.85)
$\bar{R}^2$	.70	.87
DW	.66	1.32

NOTE.—t-statistics in parentheses. Vacancies are vacancies/employment, where vacancies have been adjusted from 1974 onward using the Confederation of British Industry series on labor shortages. The dummy is described in the text. Dependent variable is log of table 12, col. 5.

Appendix A
Cross-sectional Supply Responses

Table A1 shows the main elasticities that have been estimated on British data for married women. In addition Joshi (1984) estimated for nonmarried women that the net supply response is .32 (.40 − .08). This may be biased upward since the imputed wage is based on work experience.

To obtain a net supply response for all women (married and nonmarried) one should note that about one fifth of women ages 20–59 are nonmarried.

The work of Blundell and Walker (1982) does not use data on nonparticipants and is not therefore quoted.

Appendix B
Sources of U.K. Official Statistics

For the most part we have used material which refers to that part of the United Kingdom known as Great Britain, namely, England, Wales, and Scotland but not including Northern Ireland. A source frequently cited is the *Gazette* of the Department of Employment (DE) and its predecessors. The monthly publication has been known as the *Employment Gazette* since 1971, *Employment and Productivity Gazette* from 1964 to 1970, and the *Ministry of Labour Gazette* before that. We refer to it in all these incarnations as *DE Gazette*. The Department of Employment and its predecessors also produce, annually, another series which we

Table A1
Elasticities of Participation of Married Women

	Source	Own Wage	Husband's Wage/Earnings	Unearned Income	Net Effect
1. Layard et al. (1980)	1974 GHS	.49	−.28	−.04	.17
2. Arrufat and Zabalza (1983)	1974 GHS	1.41	−.93	−.14	.34
3. Zabalza (1980)	1975 GHS		⎱ −0.35		.06
4. Greenhalgh (1980)	1971 GHS	0.36	⎰		.01
5. Greenhalgh (1977)	1971 census	1.35	−.88	−.23	.24
6. Joshi (1984)	1980 Women and Employment Survey	0.87	−.28		.59

NOTE.—Models:
1. Logit model of participation.
2. Maximum likelihood on hours of work (including zero). This supercedes Zabalza (1983).
3. OLS model of participation.
4. OLS model of participation.
5. OLS on participation rates.
6. OLS on activity (0/1 dummy). The wage was imputed on basis of actual work experience, which may impart upward bias to wage elasticity.

have quoted by the year when its data were collected (in April), the *New Earnings Survey*.

We have also made extensive use of a large number of census reports from successive decennial censuses of population, 1851–1981; there was also one midterm census in 1966 for a 10% sample. The organization currently (i.e., since the census of 1971) responsible for conducting the population census in England and Wales is the Office of Population Censuses and Surveys (OPCS). They produce the published *Tables for England and Wales and for Great Britain* (incorporating material collected in Scotland by the General Register Office, Scotland). These tables are published in a number of volumes for each census by HMSO in London. We have principally used those tables concerning occupation, and latterly, economic activity. Where necessary, we have consulted tables published by HMSO in Edinburgh to collect information from the Scottish census to amalgamate with data published separately for England and Wales. The OPCS was preceded as the "author" of the census of England and Wales by an organization known as the General Register Office. The author of censuses from 1861 to 1921 appears as Census of England and Wales, and for 1951 as Census of Great Britain.

HMSO also publishes for the OPCS series which we have cited: *General Household Survey* and *Birth Statistics* (annually), and *Population Trends* (quarterly).

References

Arrufat, J. L., and Zabalza, A. "Female Labour Supply with Taxation, Random Preferences and Optimization Errors." Discussion Paper no. 174. London: London School of Economics, Centre for Labour Economics, 1983.

Becker, G., and Ghez, G. *The Allocation of Goods and Time over the Life Cycle*. New York: Columbia University Press (for NBER), 1975.

Blundell, R., and Walker, I. "Modelling the Joint Determination of Household Labour Supplies and Commodity Demands." *Economic Journal* 92 (1982): 351–64.

Greenhalgh, C. "A Labour Supply Function for Married Women in Great Britain." *Economica* 44 (August 1977): 249–65.

———. "Participation and Hours of Work for Married Women in Great Britain." *Oxford Economic Papers* 32 (July 1980): 296–318.

Heckman, J., and MaCurdy, T. "A Life-Cycle Model of Female Labour Supply." *Review of Economic Studies* 47 (January 1980): 47–74.

Horton, R. "Work and the Single Parent." Working Paper no. 131. London: London School of Economics, Centre for Labour Economics, 1979.

Joshi, H. "Secondary Workers in the Employment Cycle, Great Britain 1961–74." *Economica* 48 (February 1981): 29–44.

———. *Women's Participation in Paid Work*. Department of Employment Research Paper no. 45. London: Department of Employment, 1984.

Joshi, H.; Layard, R.; and Owen, S. "Female Labour Supply in Post-War Britain: A Cohort Approach." Discussion Paper no. 79. London: London School of Economics, Centre for Labour Economics, 1981.
———. "Why Are More Women Working in Britain?" Discussion Paper no. 162. London: London School of Economics, Centre for Labour Economics, 1983.
Joshi, H., and Owen, S. "Demographic Predictors of Women's Work Participation in Post-War Britain." Discussion Paper no. 81-3. London: London School of Hygiene and Tropical Medicine, Centre for Population Studies, 1981.
Landes, W. M. "The Economics of Fair Employment Laws." *Journal of Political Economy* 76 (July/August, 1968): 507–22.
Layard, R. "Youth Unemployment in Britain and the United States Compared." In *The Youth Labor Market Problem*, edited by R. Freeman and D. Wise. Chicago: University of Chicago Press (for NBER), 1982.
Layard, R.; Barton, M.; and Zabalza, A. "Married Women's Participation and Hours." *Economica* 47 (February, 1980): 51–72,
Martin, J., and Roberts, C. M. *Women and Employment: A Lifetime Perspective.* London: HMSO, 1984.
Smith, J. P. "Family Decision-Making over the Life-Cycle." R-1121-EDA. Santa Monica, Calif.: Rand Corporation, 1973.
Stewart, M., and Greenhalgh, C. "Work History Patterns and Occupational Attainment of Women." *Economic Journal* 94, no. 375 (September 1984): in press.
U.K. Department of Employment and Productivity. *British Labour Statistics: Historical Abstract 1886–1968.* London: HMSO, 1971.
Zabalza, A. "The 1974/75 GHS comparison exercise." Working Paper no. 203. London: London School of Economics, Centre for Labour Economics, 1980.
———. "The CES Utility Function, Non-linear Budget Constraints and Labour Supply: Results on Female Participation and Hours." *Economic Journal* 93 (June 1983): 312–30.
Zabalza, A., and Arrufat, J. L. "Wage Differentials between Married Men and Women in Great Britain: The Depreciation Effect of Non-Participation." Discussion Paper no. 151. London: London School of Economics, Centre for Labour Economics, 1983. (Forthcoming in *Review of Economic Studies.*)
Zabalza, A., and Tzannatos, Z. "The Effect of Britain's Anti-discriminatory Legislation on Relative Pay and Employment." Discussion Paper no. 155. London: London School of Economics, Centre for Labour Economics, 1983. (Forthcoming in *Economic Journal.*)

C
Gender Differences in Occupations and Earnings

[14]

Occupational Segregation, Wages and Profits When Employers Discriminate by Race or Sex*

BARBARA R. BERGMANN†

There are two phenomena associated with employment discrimination against blacks: (1) blacks are distributed among occupations differently from whites, even after differences in education are accounted for; and (2) within occupations, whites earn more than blacks do. The same two phenomena are observed as between men and women. It has been customary to analyze the occupational and wage aspects of discrimination as if they were logically separate and their effects additive.[1] In this paper the two aspects are treated in a unified way, through the development of a model which marries the wage differential approach of Becker [1] to the approach emphasizing the "crowding" effects of occupational segregation originally noticed by Edgeworth [3] and developed by Bergmann [2]. The result allows a clearer view of the distributive effects of employment discrimination.

The Connection Between Wage Differentials and Distribution by Occupation

We shall conduct the analysis initially in terms of a labor market in which there are two occupations and in which all workers have the same degree of skill. Another assumption, which will not significantly affect the results but will make the exposition simpler, is that the marginal productivity of labor in each occupation in each firm is a linear function of the number of workers employed in that occupation and is independent of the number of workers employed in the other occupation. We shall also assume that, although employers in certain situations will hire blacks on some jobs only on condition that they accept a lower wage than the employer would be willing to pay to whites, employers will still arrange matters so as to set the marginal productivity of each man equal to his wage. This amounts to saying that once an employer allows the low wages of Negroes to overcome his aversion to hiring them for a given occupation,[2] he will not deny

* Work for this paper was done in part while the author held a Ford Faculty Research Fellowship in Economics and in part under a grant from the U.S. Office for Economic Opportunity now administered by the U.S. Department of Labor. I would like to thank Martin C. McGuire, Lloyd C. Atkinson and Christopher Clague for suggestions.

† Professor of Economics at the University of Maryland.

[1] A leading example is Thurow, [6, Chapter VII].

[2] The aversion to hiring blacks we cite here may be the result of racial prejudice or, as will be brought out below, may arise out of a loyalty to the employers' group which may be making a good thing financially out of discrimination.

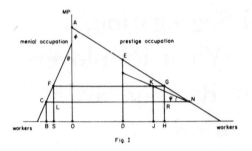

Fig. I

himself the extra profit he can get by utilizing the labor-intensive methods their low wages make sensible.[3]

Let us start by assuming that there is perfect segregation by occupation. In Figure I, *AE* is the marginal productivity curve in one of the occupations, which is assumed initially to be closed to blacks. All of the whites (*OD*) work in this occupation, and their marginal productivity, and hence their wage is *DE*. Similarly, all blacks (*OB*) work in the other occupation, which has marginal productivity curve *FC* and they have marginal productivity and wage *CB*. The result of the segregation of these occupations, given the positions of the marginal productivity curves and the numbers of blacks and white workers (whose supply of labor we have assumed to be perfectly inelastic) is that the black occupation is overcrowded, in the sense that the marginal productivity of labor is lower in that occupation, and total output could be increased by lowering employment in the black occupation and shifting some of the labor to the other occupation.

Following Becker, we shall assume that there is some crucial differential between white and black wages in each occupation which will make employers indifferent as be-

tween white and black workers. For our current purposes it is simplest initially to specify this crucial differential as a fixed money amount which does not differ from one employer to another, although it does differ for each occupation. We would expect it to be high for occupations to which for some reason prestige attaches and low and possibly zero or negative for occupations considered menial.

Segregation of the two occupations is stable if

$d_m \leq$ (prestige marginal productivity)
      $-$ (menial marginal productivity) $\leq d_p$

where d_m and d_p are the crucial differentials in the menial and prestige occupations respectively. If the difference in the marginal productivities becomes greater than d_p, we would expect some black workers to be able to move to the prestige occupation as shown in Figure I. We may think of certain firms switching from white to black crews in the prestige occupation so as to employ the $BS = JH = KG$ black workers whom we have assumed to have moved over from the menial occupation. As a result of the reduced concentration of blacks in the menial occupation, productivity and the wage level there has risen to *SF*, and this is the wage we would expect black workers to earn in the prestige occupation, since it is their opportunity cost when leaving the menial occupation.[4]

We may generalize this point by drawing a "supply curve" (line *NK*) of black workers to the prestige occupation. It is convenient to draw this curve so that the quantity of black workers supplied to the prestige occupation at each wage is measured leftward from the marginal productivity curve of the prestige occupation. The position of this supply curve

---

[3]This assumption is counter to the one usually made by Becker and most other writers, but it makes the exposition simpler and is probably more realistic. It probably contains the implication of occupational segregation (real or faked by contrived differences in job titles) within firms.

[4]We are assuming here, of course, that blacks will not be willing to sacrifice income in order to enter the prestige occupation. In the next section, the assumption that whites would not sacrifice income to avoid a move into the menial occupation is made.

(which is linear) depends on the positions of the marginal productivity curves in the two occupations and on the total number of blacks in the labor market. The wage at point N is that wage below which no black workers will come to work in the prestige occupation and is, of course, that wage which blacks can earn if all of them are crowded into the menial occupation. The slope of the supply curve through N depends on the slopes of the two marginal productivity curves.[5]

How does this assumed move of black workers to the prestige occupation affect white wages? In order to answer this question, we must recall that the marginal productivity curve in any occupation is derived by lateral summation from the marginal productivity curves of each of the firms for this kind of labor. If certain firms swing over to hiring black labor for the prestige occupation, then the new demand curve for white labor in that occupation will be lateral summation of the marginal productivity curves of the remaining firms. In Figure II this new demand curve has been drawn as AK, on the assumption that KG black workers have entered the prestige occupation and all firms have linear marginal productivity curves which cross the axis at A for the prestige occupation. In this case, the wage rate of white workers must fall from DE to DM. Figure II displays the range of possibilities when d_p is allowed to vary between zero and plus infinity and d_m is assumed to be zero. As before, the supply curve of Negroes to the prestige occupation is NK, which crosses the total supply curve of white workers at P. This point on the supply curve will be realized if d_p is zero. In that case, wages of white workers and black workers in both occupations will be DP, and the segregation of black workers in the menial occupation will presumably have no further rationale.

[5] $\cot \psi = (JH + RN)/GR = BS/FL + RN/GR = \tan \theta + \tan \phi$, where ψ, θ and ϕ are the angles indicated in Figure 1.

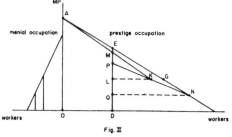
Fig. II

The other extreme is, of course, the realization of point N, which we have already discussed and which occurs when $d_p \geq EQ$. A movement from N to an intermediate position, such as K, means a lowering in d_p from some indeterminably large amount (bounded from below by EQ) to an amount equal to LM. This is accomplished through a rise in the wages of all black workers by an amount QL, and a fall in the wages of white workers by EM.

As we have drawn the curves, the fall in the wages of white workers is smaller in absolute value than the rise in the wages of blacks, but this is clearly not the only possibility. The situation in our diagrams is drawn to represent roughly the racial situation in the United States, where the number of black workers is small relative to the number of whites, and where whites are assigned to a relatively broad range of occupations and blacks to a relatively narrow range, (i.e., where there are many occupations where the d's are positive and large, and few occupations where they are zero). In a country like South Africa, where the discriminated-against races constitute more than 60 per cent of the urban population, and where whites thus have reserved for them a relatively narrower range of occupations, a reduction in the 5-to-1 white to non-white income ratio might cause greater wage reduction for whites than wage rise for non-whites.[6] Similarly if we consider sex discrimination in the United States, where occupa-

[6] See Hutt [4].

tional segregation by sex is extreme and the gap in wages between white women and white men is greater than the gap between white men and black men, a reduction in discrimination entailing a desegregation of occupations might very well result in a wage level reduction for men of a larger magnitude than the rise in wage levels for women. This is particularly true if the already large female labor force were to be augmented to any large degree by women who had previously been kept out of the labor market because of discarded notions about women's proper role and because of the low pay and tedious nature of the jobs previously open to women.

We may remark at this point that there may exist crucial differentials which are not expressed in the data for any particular period. For example, where the desegregated occupation has zero crucial differential, whites and blacks will have the same wage in the entire economy, despite the fact that there is a segregated occupation in which whites may be greatly preferred. Obviously a change in the racial composition of the population or a change in the marginal productivity curves may in such a case create a wage gap between blacks and whites where none existed before without any change in the degree of racism.[7] This consideration would tend to argue that the changes in the distribution of races and the sexes among occupations (correcting for educational differences) is at least as important an indicator of genuine progress towards a color-blind and unisex economy as changes in the black-white or the male-female income gap.

Occupational Segregation

The analysis of the last section can be summarized by a simple algorithm for determining the distribution of whites and blacks be-

---

[7] A similar point was made by Becker, *op. cit.* This phenomenon may have occurred in Great Britain.

tween the two occupations, given the marginal productivity schedules, the numbers of white and black workers and the value of the crucial differential for each occupation: Initially put all whites into the occupation in which the crucial differential is most in their favor and blacks into the other occupation. We then observe the difference in the marginal productivity of whites and blacks, and depending on what that difference is we redistribute workers as suggested in Figure III.

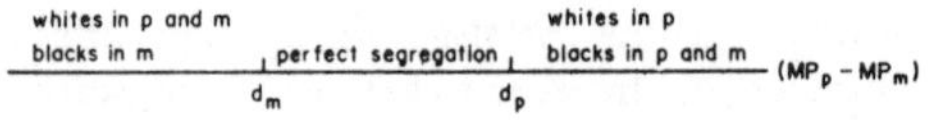

whites in p and m   whites in p
blacks in m   perfect segregation   blacks in p and m
        d_m d_p $(MP_p - MP_m)$

Fig. III

If desegregation takes place, the movement of workers will be sufficient to bring the difference in the marginal productivities and the wage rates of the two races into equality with the crucial differential in the desegregated occupation.

In the real world of more than two occupations, there are many occupations which are quite rigidly restricted to one race-sex group, but there will generally be more than one integrated occupation in a typical local labor market. Some occupations will have identical crucial differentials attached to them. Another reason for the multiplication of integrated occupations is that educational and training differences among workers and differing production processes among employers make for a series of labor markets rather than a single market in which everybody is a substitute for everyone else in every respect but race and sex. Of course, a factor which cuts the other way is that workers may be forced by discrimination (i.e., by very high d values) out of the market for which they are fitted by education and into a market which includes workers of a lower educational level. Negro high school graduates working as laborers and maids and female college graduates working as typists are the examples which come to mind.

Another reason for occupational integration is the existence of individuals who are highly specialized to particular occupations. Of particular interest is the white person whose talents are such that his natural niche in the economy is in the menial occupations, in which the preference for white workers is nil or small. Paradoxically, such a white is injured by high preference for whites in the occupations for which he is unfit. Such preferences increase the number of blacks in the market to which the low-talented white is restricted and hence lowers both his wage rate and productivity along with theirs. Blacks or women who are very highly specialized to occupations of high prestige (by preference rather than by inability to do anything else) have to put up with lower income than they might make in the lower prestige occupations within which they would face little or no discrimination against them. In any case, specialization to occupations will tend to increase the degree of integration.

It may be remarked here that the disadvantage suffered by the specialized because of discrimination is not restricted to those who cannot escape the occupations to which they are specialized. An interesting case is that of men who by preference and talent would be fitted to do hospital work of a professional or technical nature below the level of physician. Here the field has largely been pre-empted by female nurses, whose number has undoubtedly been swelled by the exclusion of women of energy and intelligence from most managerial posts.

An economy with a high degree of racial or sexual prejudice and a high degree of occupational integration must be one in which each occupation's differentials are distributed over a range and the distributions for many occupations overlap. It is probably correct to throw out the single-value-of-d assumption in occupations where a black clientele is served separately from the white clientele or where

some employers are black (teachers, preachers, morticians, etc.). For most other cases, we would argue that employers' ideas concerning the proper occupational spheres for blacks and women (and the financial incentive needed to make employers go against their notions of propriety) are probably not inborn and unalterable. If such attitudes *were* "biological" in this sense, we might expect considerable variation from one employer to another. What is much more likely is that attitudes concerning which occupations are "proper" for women and blacks are part of the social system and are learned, and most employers have learned pretty much the same thing.

Measuring the degree of occupational segregation is fraught with difficulties. When we leave the theoretical realm of the simple two-occupation model, the slippery and inexact nature of the concept of "occupation" begins to give trouble. The measured degree of segregation we find empirically will obviously depend on how we group jobs into occupations and establishments into labor markets. This means that it is more sensible to compare two situations based on comparable occupational classification than to make absolute judgments about the degree of segregation in one place at one time. But even comparisons may be suspect and only the obvious importance of occupational classification in the phenomenon of discrimination makes them worthwhile.

Discrimination and Profits

Most previous discussions of discrimination have been in terms of employers who won't hire members of the discriminated-against group. This has meant a general emphasis on the unprofitability of discrimination to the discriminator. The most prejudiced discriminator was pictured as precisely the one who was thought to be missing out on the cheapness of a group of laborers, a cheapness which he was creating by his own behavior. If any employers gained it was thought to be the least prejudiced. Putting the focus on occupational segregation highlights the fact that the discriminating employer does hire black men as janitors and white women in clerical capacities, while his wife hires black women as domestic servants. In fact, one characteristic of the occupations white men have chosen as "fit" for blacks and white women is that their use is not narrowly restricted to one group of employers. Whatever the profits or losses to employers from discrimination, they are fairly general throughout the system.

As the previous sections will have made clear, when employers discriminate against blacks they lower the wages of blacks and raise the wages of whites. When they discriminate against women they lower the wages of women and raise the wages of men. As a result, employers may on balance gain or lose financially. If gains are possible to employers who discriminate, all sorts of interesting possibilities are raised. For one, the inclination of employers to restrict blacks and women to jobs for which they are "fit" may have nothing at all to do with a "taste for discrimination."[8] It may instead be adherence to an easily policed gentlemen's agreement on the part of employers whose purpose is the raising of profits. (Note that it is much easier to watch out for and put pressure on violators of "Thou shalt hire them only as janitors" than violators of "Thou shalt pay them 80¢ an hour less than whites.") The crucial differential may measure the bribe required to provoke disloyalty to the employers' group on the part of those employers who integrate a prestige occupation

rather than the payment for loss of utility from working with blacks or women.[9]

Under what condition will discrimination make for larger profits? As we have seen, discrimination by occupational segregation generally entails differing marginal productivities by occupation. Assuming there are two occupations, and that within each labor will be paid its marginal productivity (this time with no difference in productivity or wages permitted within an occupation by race), profits (Π) depend on the production function (f) and its partial derivatives (f_1, f_2) and on the distribution of the fixed labor force between the two occupations (L_1, L_2):

(1) $\Pi = f(L_1, L_2) - L_1 f_1(L_1, L_2)$
$$- L_2 f_2(L_1, L_2).$$

Then remembering that

$$\frac{dL_1}{dL_2} = -1,$$

a first-order condition for profit maximization is

(2) $\dfrac{d\Pi}{dL_1} = -L_1(f_{11} - f_{12})$
$$- L_2(f_{21} - f_{22}) = 0$$

Now, the marginal productivities do not appear in this condition, so that satisfaction of the condition will not necessarily be consistent with equality of the marginal productivity of labor in both uses.[10]

It must also be noted that each of the two "occupations" may be a cluster of occupations grouped together, and it is employers who do the grouping. They may be able to do it in such a way as to improve their profits.

---

[8] Many readers of *The Economics of Discrimination* have been repelled from Becker's formally correct analysis because of his Chicagoesque use of the non-pejorative word "taste" to characterize the propensity of discriminators to act in the way they do.

[9] Compare Thurow, *loc. cit.*

[10] It turns out that if the production function is homogeneous to any degree, profit maximization and equality of the marginal productivities of the two types of labor are consistent with each other, but this is obviously not the general case.

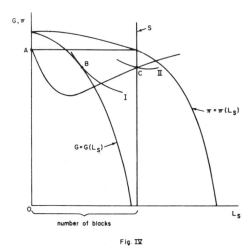

Fig. IV

Another source of profits to discriminators would lie in racial or sexual differences in the elasticity of the supply of labor. If employers have monopsonistic power, Joan Robinson's [5] classic discussion of price discrimination would apply. Occupational segregation need not be enforced, but the difficulty of paying people in the same occupation in the same shop different wages may dictate some occupational segregation when employers play this game.

Occupational segregation affects relative prices as well as relative wages and the following model demonstrates that even where segregation lowers profits it may at the same time raise the real income of profit-takers. Consider an economy in which there are only two occupations (aside from profit-taking entrepreneur): labor can be employed in manufacturing goods or it can be employed in the form of household servants in the households of the profit takers. Profits from manufacturing can be expressed as

(3) $\Pi = f(L_g) - L_g f'(L_g),$

where Π, f and L_g are profits, the production function for manufactured goods and the

amount of labor in manufacturing, respectively. The amount of labor is assumed fixed at

$$L = L_g + L_s.$$

where L_s is the amount of labor in domestic service. It is easy to rewrite (3) so as to make Π a function of L_s. In Figure IV the $\Pi(L_g)$ curve has been graphed, with profits measured on the "goods" axis. If profit-takers draw their servants from the labor market in the usual competitive way, they must pay them in goods an amount equivalent to the goods value of the marginal productivity of labor in manufacturing. Profit-takers will be able to consume goods (G) equal to profits less wages for servants:

(4) $G = f(L_g) - L_g f'(L_g) - L_s f'(L_g)$

Equation (4) can also be rewritten so as to make G a function of L_s, and graphed in Figure IV, where it lies inside the Π locus, which it meets at the goods axis where all profits are consumed as goods. The place on the G locus which will be selected under a regime of nondiscrimination depends on the rate of preference substitution between goods and servants; Figure IV shows indifference curve I tangent to the G curve at point B.

The result is different if employers all refrain from hiring some distinguishable portion of the labor force (blacks, women, Catholics) for manufacturing jobs. The supply curve of labor to the domestic service occupation becomes inelastic; we show it in the diagram as vertical line S, whose position depends on the size of the excluded group, here assumed to be blacks. The intersection of this supply curve with the profits curve gives the amount of goods which profit-takers will receive from the manufacturing operation (OA in the diagram). The intersection of the offer curve $O(L_s)$ from point A with the supply curve of servants determines the position of profit-takers under a regime of occupational segregation. In Figure IV this is point C, which may very well be on a higher indifference curve (curve II) than the nondiscriminatory position at B.

The superiority from the point of view of the profit-takers of the discriminatory situation over the nondiscriminatory situation depends on which group the profit-takers has chosen to discriminate against. Consideration of Figure IV shows that picking on too large a group or too small a group as the target for exclusion will mean a failure to improve the position of the profit-takers over the position they could achieve in a nondiscriminatory system. If discrimination had no motive other than increasing the material welfare of the group which sets hiring policy, then whether discrimination in the form of occupational segregation appeared or not would depend on the availability of a well-defined "target" group of the right size. The fact that the target groups vary greatly throughout the world in the proportion of the labor force which they constitute would argue that a de-

sire to maintain a social system which subordinates women and members of certain racial and religious groups is of more importance in the decision processes which control hiring than a desire for economic advantage.

REFERENCES

[1] Becker, G. S. *The Economics of Discrimination.* Chicago: The University of Chicago Press, 1957.
[2] Bergmann, B. R. "The Effect on White Incomes of Discrimination in Employment," *Journal of Political Economy,* March/April, 1971.
[3] Edgeworth, F. Y. "Equal Pay to Men and Women," *Economic Journal,* December, 1922.
[4] Hutt, W. H. *The Economics of the Colour Bar.* London: Andre Deutsch, 1964.
[5] Robinson, J. *The Economics of Imperfect Competition.* London: MacMillan & Co., 1950.
[6] Thurow, L. C. *Poverty and Discrimination.* Washington: The Brookings Institution, 1969.

317-49 (1974) 8510 J24 8242 J31 J16 U.S.

[15]

Family Investments in Human Capital: Earnings of Women

Jacob Mincer

Columbia University and National Bureau of Economic Research

Solomon Polachek

University of North Carolina

I. Introduction

It has long been recognized that consumption behavior represents mainly joint household or family decisions rather than separate decisions of family members. Accordingly, the observational units in consumption surveys are "consumer units," that is, households in which income is largely pooled and consumption largely shared.

More recent is the recognition that an individual's use of time, and particularly the allocation of time between market and nonmarket activities, is also best understood within the context of the family as a matter of interdependence with needs, activities, and characteristics of other family members. More generally, the family is viewed as an economic unit which shares consumption and allocates production at home and in the market as well as the investments in physical and human capital of its members. In this view, the behavior of the family unit implies a division of labor within it. Broadly speaking, this division of labor or "differentiation of roles" emerges because the attempts to promote family life are necessarily constrained by complementarity and substitution relations in the household production process and by comparative

Research here reported is part of a continuing study of the distribution of income, conducted by the National Bureau of Economic Research and funded by the National Science Foundation and the Office of Economic Opportunity. This report has not undergone the usual NBER review. We are grateful to Otis Dudley Duncan, James Heckman, Melvin Reder, T. W. Schultz, and Robert Willis for useful comments, and to George Borjas for skillful research assistance.

advantages due to differential skills and earning powers with which family members are endowed.

Though the levels and distribution of these endowments can be taken as given in the short run, this is not true in a more complete perspective. Even if each individual's endowment were genetically determined, purposive marital selection would make its distribution in the family endogenous, along the lines suggested by Becker in this volume. Of course, individual endowments are not merely genetic; they can be augmented by processes of investment in human capital and reduced by depreciation. Indeed, a major function of the family as a social institution is the building of human capital of children—a lengthy "gestation" process made even longer by growing demands of technology.

Optimal investment in human capital of any family member requires attention not only to the human and financial capacities in the family, but also to the prospective utilization of the capital which is being accumulated. Expectations of future family and market activities of individuals are, therefore, important determinants of levels and forms of investment in human capital. Thus, family investments and time allocation are linked: while the current distribution of human capital influences the current allocation of time within the family, the prospective allocation of time influences current investments in human capital.

That the differential allocation of time and of investments in human capital is generally sex linked and subject to technological and cultural changes is a matter of fact which is outside the scope of our analysis. Given the sex linkage, we focus on the relation within the family between time allocation and investments in human capital which give rise to the observed market earnings of women. Whether these earnings, or the investments underlying them, are also influenced or reinforced by discriminatory attitudes of employers and fellow workers toward women in the labor market is a question we do not explore directly, though we briefly analyze the male-female wage differential. Our major purposes are to ascertain and to estimate the effects of human-capital accumulation on market earnings and wage rates of women, to infer the magnitudes and course of such investments over the life histories of women, and to interpret these histories in the context of past expectations and of current and prospective family life.

The data we study, the 1967 National Longitudinal Survey of Work Experience (NLS), afford a heretofore unavailable opportunity to relate family and work histories of women to their current market earning power. Accumulation of human capital is a lifetime process. In the post-school stage of the life cycle much of the continued accumulation of earning power takes place on the job. Where past work experience of men can be measured without much error in numbers of years elapsed since leaving school, such a measure of "potential work experience" is

S78   JOURNAL OF POLITICAL ECONOMY

clearly inadequate for members of the labor force among whom the length and continuity of work experience varies a great deal. Direct information on work histories of women is, therefore, a basic requirement for the analysis of their earnings. To our knowledge, the NLS is the only data set which provides this information, albeit on a retrospective basis. Eventually, the NLS panel surveys will provide the information on a current basis, showing developments as they unfold.[1]

II. The Human-Capital Earnings Function

To the extent that earnings in the labor market are a function of the human-capital stock accumulated by individuals, a sequence of positive net investments gives rise to growing earning power over the life cycle. When net investment is negative, that is, when market skills are eroded by depreciation, earning power declines. This relation between the sequence of capital accumulation and the resulting growth in earnings has been formalized in the "human-capital earnings function." A simple specification of this function fits the life cycle "earnings profile" of men rather well. The approach to distribution of earnings among male workers (in the United States and elsewhere) as a distribution of individual earnings profiles appears to be promising.[2]

For the purpose of this paper, a brief development of the earnings function may suffice:

Let C_{t-1} be the dollar amount of net investment in period $t-1$, while (gross) earnings in that period, before the investment expenditures are subtracted, are E_{t-1}. Let r be the average rate of return to the individual's human-capital investment, and assume that r is the same in each period. Then

$$E_t = E_{t-1} + rC_{t-1}. \tag{1}$$

Let $k_t = C_t/E_t$, the ratio of investment expenditures to gross earnings, which may be viewed as investment in time-equivalent units. Then

$$E_t = E_{t-1}(1 + rk_{t-1}). \tag{2}$$

[1] For a description of the NLS survey of women's work histories, see Parnes, Shea, Spitz, and Zeller (1970). For an analysis of earnings of men, using "potential" work-experience measures, see Mincer (1974). Though less appropriate, the same proxy variable was used in several recent studies of female earnings. Direct information from the NLS Survey was first used by Suter and Miller (1971). The human-capital approach was first applied to these data by Polachek in his Columbia Ph.D. thesis, "Work Experience and the Difference between Male and Female Wages" (1973). This paper reports a fuller development of the analysis in that thesis.

[2] See, for instance, Rahm (1971), Chiswick and Mincer (1972), Chiswick (1973), Mincer (1974), and a series of unpublished research papers by George E. Johnson and Frank P. Stafford on earnings of Ph.D.'s in various fields.

By recursion $E_t = E_0(1 + rk_0)(1 + rk_1) \ldots (1 + rk_{t-1})$. The term rk is a small fraction. Hence a logarithmic approximation of $\ln(1 + rk) \simeq rk$ yields

$$\ln E_t = \ln E_0 + r \sum_{i=0}^{t-1} k_i. \tag{3}$$

Since earnings net of investment expenditures, $Y_t = E_t(1 - k_t)$, we have also

$$\ln Y_t = \ln E_0 + r \sum_{i=0}^{t-1} k_i + \ln(1 - k_t). \tag{4}$$

Some investments are in the form of schooling; others take the form of formal and informal job training. If only these two categories of investment are analyzed, that is, schooling and postschool experience,[3] the k terms can be separated, and

$$\ln E_t = \ln E_0 + r \sum_{i=0}^{s-1} k_i + r \sum_{j=s}^{t-1} k_j \tag{5}$$

where the k_i are investment ratios during the schooling period and the k_j thereafter. With tuition added to opportunity costs and student earnings and scholarships subtracted from them, the rough assumption $k_i = 1$ may be used.[4] Hence,

$$\ln E_t = \ln E_0 + rs + r \sum_{j=s}^{t-1} k_j. \tag{6}$$

The postschool investment ratios k_j are expected to decline continuously if work experience is expected to be continuous and the purpose of investment is acquisition and maintenance of market earning power. This conclusion emerges from models of optimal distribution of investment expenditures C_t over the life cycle (see Becker 1967 and Ben-Porath 1967). A sufficient rationale for our purposes is that as t increases, the remaining working life $(T - t)$ shortens. Since $(T - t)$ is the length of the payoff period on investments in t, the incentives to invest and the magnitudes of investment decline over the (continuous) working life. This is true for C_t and a fortiori for k_t, since with positive C_t, E_t rises, and k_t is the ratio of C_t to E_t.

In analyses of male earnings, a linearly (or geometrically) declining approximation of the working-life profile of investment ratios k_t appears to be a satisfactory statistical hypothesis.

---

[3] The inclusion of other categories in the earnings function is an important research need, since human capital is acquired in many other ways: in the home environment, in investments in health, by mobility, information, and so forth.

[4] According to T. W. Schultz, this assumption overstates k, especially at higher education levels, leading to an understatement of r.

It will be useful for our purpose of studying earnings of women to decompose net investments explicitly into gross investments and depreciation. Let C^*_{t-1} be the dollar amount of gross investment in period $t-1$, δ_{t-1} the depreciation rate of the stock of human capital, hence of earnings E_{t-1} during that period, and $k^*_t = C^*_t/E_t$, the gross investment ratio. Hence

and

$$E_t = E_{t-1} + rC^*_{t-1} - \delta_{t-1}E_{t-1}$$

$$\frac{E_t}{E_{t-1}} = 1 + rk^*_{t-1} - \delta_{t-1} = 1 + rk_{t-1}, \quad \text{by equation (2)}, \quad (1a)$$

thus

$$rk_t = rk^*_t - \delta_t. \tag{2a}$$

The earnings function (3) can, therefore, be written as

$$\ln E_t = \ln E_0 + \sum_{i=0}^{t-1} (rk^*_i - \delta_i). \tag{3a}$$

In transferring the analysis to women, we face two basic facts: (1) After marriage, women spend less than half of their lifetime in the labor market, on average. Of course, this "lifetime participation rate" varies by marital status, number of children, and other circumstances, and it has been growing secularly. (2) The lesser market work of married women is not only a matter of fewer years during a lifetime, and fewer weeks per year, or a shorter work week. An important aspect is discontinuity of work experience, for most of the married women surveyed in 1967 reported several entries into and exits from the labor force after leaving school.

The implications of these facts for the volume and the life-cycle distribution of human-capital investments can be stated briefly:[5]

1. Since job-related investment in human capital commands a return which is received at work,[6] the shorter the expected and actual duration of work experience, the weaker the incentives to augment job skills over the life cycle. With labor-force attachment of married women lasting, on average, about one-half that of men, labor-market activities of women are less likely to contain skill training and learning components as a result both of women's own decisions and decisions of employers, who may be expected to invest in worker skills to some extent.

2. Given discontinuity of work experience, the conclusion of optimization analysis to the effect that human-capital investments decline

---

[5] For a mathematical statement of the optimization analysis applied to discontinuous work experience, see Polachek (1973, chap. 3).

[6] For the sake of brevity, the term "work" refers to work in the job market. We do not imply that women occupied in the household do not work.

TABLE 1

LABOR-FORCE PARTICIPATION OF MOTHERS: PROPORTION WORKING,
WHITE MARRIED WOMEN WITH CHILDREN, SPOUSE PRESENT

	PROPORTION WORKING (%)			
AGE	In 1966	After First Child	Ever	SAMPLE SIZE
30–34	43	64	82	925
S < 12	46	71	75	294
S = 12	43	63	84	446
S > 12	40	59	88	185
35–39	47	67	87	945
S < 12	45	66	82	336
S = 12	49	68	88	422
S > 12	47	67	92	187
40–44	53	70	88	1,078
S < 12	52	72	78	465
S = 12	54	70	91	446
S > 12	51	68	93	167

SOURCE.— NLS, 1967 survey.
NOTE.—S = years of schooling.

continuously over the successive years of life after leaving school is no longer valid. Even a continuous decline over the years spent in the job market cannot be hypothesized if several intervals of work experience rather than one stretch represent the norm.

3. The more continuous the participation, the larger the investments on initial job experience relative to those in later jobs.

Women without children and without husbands may be expected to engage in continuous job experience. But labor-force participation of married women, especially of mothers, varies over the life cycle, depending on the demands on their time in the household as well as on their skills and preferences relative to those of other family members. The average pattern of labor-force experience is apparent in tables 1–3, which are based on the NLS data reported by women who were 30–44 years of age at the time of the survey. According to the data:

1. Though less than 50 percent of the mothers worked in 1966, close to 90 percent worked sometime after they left school, and two-thirds returned to the labor market after the birth of the first child (table 1). Lifetime labor-force participation of women without children or without husbands is, of course, greater.

2. Never-married women spent 90 percent of their years after they left school in the labor market, while married women with children spent less than 50 percent of their time in it. In each age group, childless women, those with children but without husbands (widowed, divorced, or separated), and those who married more than once spent less time in the market than never-married women, but more than mothers married once, spouse present (table 2).

TABLE 2

WORK HISTORIES OF WOMEN AGED 30–44 BY MARITAL STATUS (AVERAGE NUMBER OF YEARS)

Group	h_1	e_1	h_2	e_2	h_3	e_3	Σe	Σh	S	N_c	Sample Size
White, with children:											
Married once, spouse present	0.57	3.55	6.71	1.14	1.22	1.69	6.4	10.4	11.8	3.16	2,398
Remarried, spouse present	0.54	2.43	7.85	2.60	2.02	2.00	7.1	10.3	10.6	3.28	341
Widowed	1.11	4.25	9.37	1.51	1.44	2.56	8.4	11.9	12.0	2.44	45
Divorced	0.94	2.96	6.54	4.24	2.38	2.92	10.1	9.8	10.8	2.98	133
Separated	0.74	3.97	7.81	2.71	1.14	2.08	8.7	9.6	10.1	2.86	65
White, childless:											
Married once, spouse present	1.01	5.18	...	4.39	3.35	4.90	14.5	3.3	11.7	...	147
Never married	...	7.08	...	...	1.46	7.48	14.5	1.5	12.9	...	153
Black, with children:											
Married once, spouse present	1.12	3.00	7.12	2.95	2.14	3.26	9.1	10.3	10.0	4.59	563
Remarried, spouse present	0.96	2.44	7.43	4.93	2.05	3.36	10.7	11.7	9.6	4.22	170
Widowed and divorced	1.19	2.23	7.67	4.36	1.90	3.68	10.3	10.8	9.8	4.20	149
Separated	1.28	2.86	6.24	5.57	2.38	2.81	11.2	9.8	9.4	4.22	191
Black, childless:											
Married once, spouse present	2.33	4.75	...	3.83	4.58	4.77	13.4	6.9	10.9	...	71
Never married	...	7.15	...	...	4.74	6.45	13.6	4.7	10.9	...	47

NOTE.—h_1 = years not worked between school and first marriage; e_1 = years worked between school and first marriage (for never-marrieds, = years worked prior to current job); h_2 = interval of nonparticipation following birth of first child; e_2 = years worked after h_2 prior to current job; h_3 = interval of nonparticipation just prior to current job; e_3 = years on current job; Σe = years worked since school; Σh = years of nonparticipation since school; S = years of schooling; N_c = no. of children.

3. Table 3 shows the characteristic work histories of mothers,[7] spouse present (MSP), who represented over two-thirds of the women in the sample. We show chronologically the length of nonparticipation (h_1) during the interval between leaving school and marriage; the years of market work between school and the birth of the first child (e_1); an uninterrupted period of nonparticipation, h_2, starting just before the first child was born, followed by e_2 and h_3, which sum intermittent participation and nonparticipation, respectively; and finally e_3, the present job tenure of women working at the time of the survey.

It is clear from the tabulations that, after their schooling, the life cycle of married women features several stages which differ in the nature and degree of labor-market and home involvement. There is usually continuous market work prior to the birth of the first child. The second stage is a period of nonparticipation related to childbearing and child care, lasting between 5 and 10 years, followed by intermittent participation before the youngest child reaches school age. The third stage is a more permanent return to the labor force for some, though it may remain intermittent for others. In our data, which were obtained from women who were less than 45 years old, only the beginning of the third stage is visible.

The following conjectures about investment behavior in each of these stages are plausible in view of the described patterns which are to some extent anticipated by the women.

1. Prospective discontinuity may well influence many young women during their prematernal employment (e_1) to acquire less job training than men with comparable education, unless they do not expect to marry or have an overriding commitment to a work career.

2. During the period of childbearing and child care, prolonged nonparticipation may cause the skills acquired at school and at work to depreciate. Some revisions of expectations and of commitments may also take place.[8] Little investment, if any, can be expected during the episodic employment period e_2.

3. There is likely to be a stronger expectation of prospective continuity of employment after the children reach school age. To the extent that the current job (e_3) is more likely to represent this more-permanent return to the labor force than e_2 does, strong incentives to resume investments in job-related skills should reappear.

---

[7] The six intervals shown in table 3 are aggregated from eight available ones. Both sets are described in the Appendix.

[8] We are reminded by T. W. Schultz that erosion of market skills during periods of nonparticipation is likely to be associated with growth in nonmarket productivity. If so, the longer the time spent out of the labor force the greater the excess of the reservation or "shadow" price over the market wage, hence the smaller the probability of subsequent labor-force participation.

TABLE 3

WORK HISTORIES OF MARRIED WOMEN BY AGE, EDUCATION, AND CURRENT WORK STATUS

Age and Category	Variable									Sample Size
	h_1	e_1	h_2	e_2	h_3	e_3	Σe	Σh	N_c	
30–34:										
Worked in 1966:										
$S < 12$	1.93	2.37	5.80	3.18	2.20	1.90	7.45	9.93	3.42	135
$S = 12$–15	0.90	2.84	5.41	2.21	1.39	2.31	7.36	7.70	2.89	233
$S \geq 16$	0.37	2.57	2.65	2.22	1.22	2.00	6.79	4.24	2.39	35
Did not work in 1966, but worked since birth of first child:										
$S < 12$	1.67	2.23	6.29	1.31	5.09	...	3.54	13.05	3.50	68
$S = 12$–15	0.81	2.90	4.65	1.23	4.75	...	4.13	10.21	3.49	93
$S \geq 16$	0.50	1.85	3.57	1.71	3.57	...	3.56	7.64	3.00	14
Has not worked since birth of first child:										
$S < 12$	4.54	1.42	9.64	...	...	...	1.42	14.18	3.24	85
$S = 12$–15	2.28	3.21	7.93	...	...	...	3.21	10.21	3.03	211
$S \geq 16$	1.95	1.11	7.20	...	...	...	1.11	9.15	3.14	34
35–39:										
Worked in 1966:										
$S < 12$	1.94	2.78	7.98	3.47	2.78	3.40	9.65	12.70	3.37	152
$S = 12$–15	0.98	3.42	6.85	3.09	2.01	3.70	10.21	9.84	2.99	250
$S \geq 16$	1.01	2.95	4.72	2.04	1.25	5.46	10.45	6.98	2.72	43
Did not work in 1966, but worked since birth of first child:										
$S < 12$	2.15	2.96	9.00	1.80	6.40	...	4.76	17.55	3.70	65
$S = 12$–15	1.20	3.74	7.42	1.18	5.94	...	4.92	14.56	3.51	101
$S \geq 16$	0.38	5.75	6.50	1.15	2.62	...	6.90	9.50	2.87	8
Has not worked since birth of first child:										
$S < 12$	4.23	3.54	13.53	...	...	...	3.54	17.76	3.58	113
$S = 12$–15	2.97	3.85	11.62	...	...	...	3.85	14.59	3.16	170
$S \geq 16$	1.88	2.65	10.15	...	...	...	2.65	12.03	3.50	26

Continued overleaf

TABLE 3 (*Continued*)

40–44:										
Worked in 1966:										
S < 12	2.41	3.29	10.38	3.94	2.95	4.93	12.16	15.74	3.18	240
S = 12–15	1.55	4.16	8.74	3.57	2.63	4.43	12.16	12.92	2.72	297
S ≥ 16	0.93	3.20	6.89	3.06	1.86	4.89	11.15	9.68	3.65	29
Did not work in 1966, but worked since birth of first child:										
S < 12	2.35	3.31	12.95	1.51	6.89	...	4.82	22.19	3.41	89
S = 12–15	1.39	3.68	10.43	1.24	8.23	...	4.92	20.05	3.36	82
S ≥ 16	3.19	1.19	9.80	1.34	4.80	...	2.53	17.79	3.59	5
Has not worked since birth of first child:										
S < 12	6.23	2.63	17.66	...	...	...	2.63	23.89	3.93	130
S = 12–15	3.36	4.88	15.12	...	...	...	4.88	18.48	3.12	141
S ≥ 16	3.03	2.67	13.35	...	...	...	2.67	16.38	2.96	31

NOTE.—See notes to table 2 for explanation of variables.

These conjectures imply that the investment profile of married women is not monotonic. There is a gap which is likely to show negative values (net depreciation) during the childbearing period and two peaks before and after. The levels of these peaks are likely to be correlated for the same woman, and their comparative size is likely to depend on the degree of continuity of work experience. The whole profile can be visualized in comparison with the investment profiles of men and of single women. For never-married women, stage 1 (e_1) extends over their whole working life, and the investment profile declines as it does for men. To the extent, however, that expectation of marriage and of childbearing are stronger at younger ages and diminish with age, investment of never-married women is likely to be initially lower than that of men. At the same time, given lesser expectations of marriage on the part of the never-married, their initial on-the-job investments exceed those of the women who eventually marry, while the profile of the latter shows two peaks.

The implications for comparative-earnings profiles are clear: Greater investment ratios imply a steeper growth of earnings, while declining investment profiles imply concavity of earnings profiles. Hence, earnings profiles of men are steepest and concave, those of childless women less so, and those of mothers are double peaked with least overall growth.

III. Women's Wage Equation

To adapt the earnings function to persons with intermittent work experience we break up the postschool investment term in equation (6) into successive segments of participation and nonparticipation as they occur chronologically. In the general case with n segments we may express the investment ratio $k_i = a_i + b_i t$, $i = 1, 2, \ldots, n$, and

$$\ln E_t = \ln E_0 + rs + r \sum_{i=1}^{n} \int_{ti}^{t_{i+1}} (a_i + b_i t)\, dt. \qquad (7)$$

Here a_i is the initial investment ratio, b_i is the rate of change of the investment ratio during the ith segment: $(t_{i+1} - t_i) = e_i =$ duration of the ith segment. Note that in (7) the initial investment ratio refers to its projected value at $t_1 = 0$, the start of working life. In a work interval m which occurs in later life there is likely to be less investment than in an earlier interval j, though more than would be observed if j continued at its gradient through the years covered by m. In this case, a_m in equation (7) will exceed a_j.

Alternatively, a_j and a_m can be compared directly in the formulation

$$\ln E_t = \ln E_0 + rs + r \sum_{i=1}^{n} \int_{0}^{e_i} (a_i + b_i t)\, dt, \qquad (8)$$

since a_i is the investment ratio at the beginning of the particular segment i.

While the rate of change in investment b_i is likely to be negative in longer intervals, it may not be significant in shorter ones. Since the segments we observe in the histories of women before age 45 are relatively short, a simplified scheme is to assume a constant rate of net investment throughout a given segment, though differing among segments. The earnings function simplifies to

$$\ln E_t = \ln E_0 + rs + r \sum_i a_i e_i. \tag{9}$$

Whereas $(ra_i) > 0$ denotes positive net investment (ratios), $(ra_i) < 0$ represents net depreciation rates, likely in periods of nonparticipation.

The question whether the annual investment or depreciation rates vary with the length of the interval is ultimately an empirical one. Even if each woman were to invest diminishing amounts over a segment of work experience, those women who stay longer in the labor market are likely to invest more per unit of time, so that a_i is likely to be a positive function of the length of the interval in the cross section.

Thus, even if $k_{ij} = a_{ij} - b_{ij}t$ for a given woman j, if $a_{ij} = \alpha_j + \beta_j t$ across women, on substitution, the coefficient b of t may become negligible or even positive in the cross section. On integrating, and using three segments of working life as an example, earnings functions (7), (8), and (9) become:

$$\begin{aligned} \ln E_t = a_0 &+ rs + r[a_1 t_1 + \tfrac{1}{2}b_1 t_1^2 + a_2(t_2 - t_1) \\ &+ \tfrac{1}{2}b_2(t_2^2 - t_1^2) + a_3(t - t_2) + \tfrac{1}{2}b_3(t^2 - t_2^2)], \end{aligned} \tag{7a}$$

$$\begin{aligned} \ln E_t = a_0 &+ rs + r(a_1 e_1 + \tfrac{1}{2}b_1 e_1^2 + a_2 e_2 \\ &+ \tfrac{1}{2}b_2 e_2^2 + a_3 e_3 + \tfrac{1}{2}b_3 e_3^2), \end{aligned} \tag{8a}$$

$$\ln E_t = a_0 + rs + r(a_1 e_1 + a_2 e_2 + a_3 e_3). \tag{9a}$$

In this example, t is within the last (third) segment, and the middle segment, $e_2 = h$, is a period of nonparticipation or "home time." The signs of b_i are ambiguous in the cross section, as already indicated; the coefficients of e_1 and of e_3 are expected to be positive, but those of e_2 (or h) negative, most clearly in (9a).

The equations for observed earnings ($\ln Y_t$) differ from the equations shown above by a term $\ln (1 - k_t)$—as was shown in the comparison of equations (3) and (4). With k_t relatively small, only the intercept a_0 is affected, so the same form holds for $\ln Y_t$ as for $\ln E_t$.

It will help our understanding of the estimates of depreciation rates to express earnings function (9a) in terms of gross-investment rates and depreciation rates:

$$\begin{aligned} \ln E_t = \ln E_0 &+ \sum_i (rk_i^* - \delta_i) \\ = \ln E_0 &+ (rs - \delta_s) + (rk_1^* - \delta_1)e_1 \\ &+ (rk_h^* - \delta_h)h + (rk_3^* - \delta_3)e_3. \end{aligned} \tag{9b}$$

This formulation suggests that depreciation of earning power may occur not only in periods of nonparticipation (h), but at other times as well. On the other hand, market-oriented investment, such as informal study and job search, may take place during home time, so that $k_h^* > 0$. Positive coefficients of e_1 and e_3 would reflect positive net investment, while a negative coefficient of h is an estimate of net depreciation. If $k_h^* > 0$, the absolute value of the depreciation rate δ_h is underestimated.

IV. Empirical Findings

Tables 4–8 show results of regression analyses which apply our earnings function to analyze wage rates of women who worked in 1966, the year preceding the survey. The general specification is $\ln w = f(S, e, h, x) + u$, where w is the hourly wage rate; S is the years of schooling; e is a vector of work-experience segments; h is a vector of home-time segments and x is a vector of other variables, such as indexes of job training, mobility, health, number of children, and current weeks and hours of work; u is the statistical residual.

The findings described here are based on ordinary least-squares (OLS) regressions. The tables show shorter and longer lists of variables without covering all the intermediate lists. In view of a plausible simultaneity problem we attempted also a two-stage least-squares (2SLS) estimation procedure, which we describe in the next section. Since the 2SLS estimates do not appear to contradict the findings based on OLS, we describe them first below.

1. Work History Detail and Equation Form

When life histories are segmented into five intervals (eight is the maximum possible in the data), three of which are periods of work experience and two of nonmarket activity,[9] both nonlinear formulations (equation forms [7] and [8]) are less informative than the linear specification (9). Rates of change in investment (coefficient b) are probably not substantial within a short interval, and the intercorrelation of the linear and quadratic terms hinders the estimation. Dropping the square terms reduces the explanatory power of the regression slightly but increases the visibility of the life-cycle investment profile. Conversely, when the segments are aggregated, the quadratic term becomes negative but does not quite acquire statistical significance by conventional standards. The quadratic term for current work experience is negative and significant. In the case

[9] Tables 2 and 3 show six intervals, including a very short nonparticipation interval h_1 between school and marriage. This interval is aggregated in other home time in the regressions.

of never-married women, one segment of work experience usually covers most of the potential working life. Here the nonlinear formulation over the interval is as natural and informative as it is for men.

2. *Investment Rates*

Table 4 compares earnings functions of women by marital status and presence of children, tables 5 and 6 by level of schooling, and table 7 by lifetime work experience. In each table we can compare groups of women with differential labor-force attachment. According to human-capital theory, higher investment levels should be observed in groups with stronger labor-force attachment.

We can infer these differences in investment by looking at the co-efficients of experience segments, e_1 (prematernal), e_2 (intermittent, after the first child), and e_3 (current). These increase systematically from married women with children to married women without children to single women in table 4, and from women who worked less than half to those who worked more than half of their lifetime in table 7. An exception is the coefficient of e_3 which appears to be somewhat higher for the group who worked less (see table 7). Note, however, that these coefficients are investment ratios (to gross wage rates), not dollar volumes. Since wage rates are higher in the groups with more work experience, the conclusions about increasing investment hold for dollar magnitudes, a fortiori, and the anomaly in table 7 disappears.[10]

Classifications by schooling show mixed results. In table 5, where schooling is stratified by <12, 12–15, and 16+, investment ratios (co-efficients of e_i) are lower at higher levels of schooling (with the exception of the coefficient of e_1). Translated into dollar terms,[11] no clear pattern emerges. At the same time in table 6, where the schooling strata are ≤ 8, 9–12, and 13+, a positive relation between investment volumes and levels of schooling is somewhat better indicated. Note that the sample size for the highest-schooling groups (10+) is quite small in table 5, as is that for the lowest-schooling groups (≤ 8) in table 6.

3. *Investment Profiles*

Another implication of the human-capital theory refers to the shape of the investment profile: it is monotonically declining in groups with continuous participation, hence earnings are parabolic in aggregated

---

[10] The coefficient of e_3, calculated as $\partial \ln W/\partial e$, is 15 percent higher in the right-hand group. However, the wage rate of this group is about 25 percent lower.

[11] Wage rates are roughly 30 percent higher in successive schooling groups.

TABLE 4
EARNINGS FUNCTIONS, WHITE WOMEN

With Children

Var.	b (1)	t	Var.	b (2)	t
C	.38	...	C	.21	...
S	.076	11.5	S	.063	10.5
(A-S-6)	.014	3.8	e	.012	1.6
(A-S-6)²	-.001	-4.2	e²	-.0002	-0.5
R²	.16		e3	.021	2.8
			h	-.0008	-1.9
			h²	-.007	-1.5
				.000	0.2
			R²	.25	

Var.	b (3)	t	No Children b (4)	t	Never Married b (5)	t
C	.09	...	-.42	...	.55	4.9
S	.064	12.0	.081	4.4	.077	1.5
e₁	.008	2.8	.014	1.6	.026*	1.6
e₂	.001	0.3	.011	1.3	-.0007†	-1.1
e₃	.012	2.7	.015	2.2	.009	1.5
h₁	-.012	-2.5	-.005†	-1.5	-.009‡	-0.6
h₂	-.003	-0.7	.0028§	0.7	...	...
etr	.0002	1.5	.0003	2.4	.0003	1.7
ect	.010	3.2	-.003	-1.2	-.011	-1.8
hlt	-.0003	-1.3	-.002	-1.3	-.0008	-1.2
res	.001	1.2	.006	1.7	-.012	-2.2
loc	.044	2.7	-.021	-0.4	-.02	-0.3
ln Hr	-.11	-3.7	-.15	-1.6	-.43	-4.4
ln Wk	.03	1.6	.25	2.2	.21	1.4
N_c	-.008	-1.0	...	...	...	...
R²	.28		.39		.41	
N	993		147		138	

NOTE.—Var. = variable; C = intercept; S = years of schooling; A = age; e = total years of work; e_1 = years of work before first child; e_2 = years of work after first child; e_3 = years of work after first child; h = total home time; h_1 = home time after first child; h_2 = other home time; etr = experience × training (months); ect = experience × certificate (dummy); hlt = duration of illness (months); res = years of residence in county; loc = size of place of residence at age 15; ln Hr = (log of) hours of work per week on current job; ln Wks = (log of) weeks per year on current job; N_c = no. of children; R^2 = coefficient of determination; t = t-ratio; b = regression coefficient; N = sample size.

* Total work experience, e.
† e^2.
‡ Total home time, h.
§ h^2.

S90

TABLE 5

EARNINGS FUNCTIONS OF WMSP, BY SCHOOLING

VAR.	S < 12				S = 12–15				S = 16+			
	b	t	b	t	b	t	b	t	b	t	b	t
C	−.095	…	−.98	…	−.61	…	−.03	…	.86	…	.36	…
S	.046	4.7	.039	3.8	.105	5.1	.086	4.0	.038	0.4	.107	1.1
e_1	.016	3.1	.015	2.2	.012	1.7	.008	1.3	.023	1.5	.010	0.5
e_2	.014	2.8	.012	1.8	.006	1.2	0	0	−.013	−2.3	−.016	−3.0
e_3	.021	4.7	.019	3.2	.015	3.7	.011	1.9	.002	1.6	.004	2.4
h_1	−.002	−0.6	.001	0.2	−.013	−3.4	−.018	−2.8	−.023	−2.2	−.012	−1.7
h_2	.002	0.5	.003	0.5	−.001	−0.2	−.006	−1.0	.006	0.4	.002	1.0
etr	…	…	.0004	1.2	…	…	.0004	2.0	…	…	.0007	0.5
ect	…	…	.016	2.4	…	…	.008	1.9	…	…	.032	2.1
hlt	…	…	−.0006	−1.7	…	…	0	0	…	…	0	0
res	…	…	.001	0.5	…	…	.002	1.3	…	…	.008	1.2
loc	…	…	.06	2.4	…	…	.036	1.6	…	…	.05	0.8
ln Hrs	…	…	−.044	−0.9	…	…	−.11	−3.9	…	…	−.16	−3.4
ln Wks	…	…	.045	1.5	…	…	.031	1.2	…	…	.05	0.7
N_e	…	…	−.004	−0.4	…	…	−.002	−0.2	…	…	−.05	−1.5
R^2	.17	…	.22	…	.14	…	.18	…	.16	…	.39	…
N	435	…	…	…	622	…	…	…	83	…	…	…

NOTE.—WMSP = white married women, spouse present. See table 4 for key to symbols.

TABLE 6

EARNINGS FUNCTIONS OF WMSP (WITH CHILDREN), BY SCHOOLING

VAR.	$S \leq 8$				$S = 9\text{-}12$				$S = 13+$			
	b	t	b	t	b	t	b	t	b	t	b	t
S	.049	1.6	.044	1.3	.051	3.2	.055	3.4	.068	2.8	.079	2.7
e_1	.007	0.4	-.002	-0.4	.013	1.7	.012	1.5	.021	1.4	.018	1.2
e_2	-.004	-2.1	-.028	-1.8	.009	1.6	.003	0.6	-.020	-1.5	-.020	-1.4
e_3	-.002	-0.3	-.008	-0.5	.013	0.7	.009	0.5	.009	2.0	.011	2.2
h_1	-.011	-1.5	-.007	-1.2	-.014	-1.8	-.010	-1.6	-.043	-3.1	-.031	-2.8
h_2	-.006	-0.4	-.003	-0.2	-.002	-0.4	-.002	-0.4	-.005	-0.4	-.004	-0.3
hlt.	...	...	-.0007	-0.7	...	...	-.0011	-2.3	...	...	-.009	-0.6
ln *Hrs*	...	...	-.050	-0.7	...	...	-.090	-1.8	...	...	-.130	-1.1
ln *Wks*	...	...	-.070	-0.6	...	...	.060	1.6	...	...	.090	1.2
N_c	...	...	-.008	-0.2	...	...	-.019	-0.4	...	...	-.010	-2.0
R^2	.26		.32		.21		.26		.27		.33	
N	182		...		593		...		218		...	

NOTE.—WMSP = white married women, spouse present. See table 4 for key to symbols.

TABLE 7
EARNINGS FUNCTIONS OF WMSP BY LIFETIME WORK EXPERIENCE

VAR.	WORKED MORE THAN HALF OF YEARS			WORKED LESS THAN HALF OF YEARS		
	b	t	M	b	t	M
C	−.28	...	...	−.10	...	...
S	.073	9.4	11.8	.059	7.9	11.0
e_1	.009	2.1	4.9	.003	0.4	2.2
e_2	.006	1.4	5.6	−.005	−0.6	1.5
e_3	.017	2.0	4.9	.022	3.8	1.6
e_3^2	−.0002	−0.7	...	−.001	−1.5	...
h_1	−.014	−2.3	2.2	−.010	−2.6	10.7
h_2	.011	1.7	2.1	−.004	−0.9	4.7
hlt	−.0008	−2.1	10.8	−.0001	−0.3	13.7
res	.002	1.1	12.1	.002	1.0	11.8
loc	.064	2.8	0.97	.024	1.0	0.90
ln *Hrs*	−.08	−2.0	3.52	−.13	−4.4	3.40
ln *Wks*	.07	1.9	3.71	.023	1.0	3.29
N_c	−.015	−1.4	2.21	−.001	−0.2	3.18
R^2	.22	...	...	.21	...	...
N	536	...	...	604	...	...

NOTE.—WMSP = white married women, spouse present. See table 4 for key to symbols.

experience for men and never-married women.[12] In the groups with discontinuous participation, the profiles are not expected to be monotonic.

We can summarize the implicit profiles schematically, in terms of the coefficients of e_1, length of work experience before the first child, h_1, uninterrupted nonparticipation after the first child, and e_3, the current work interval. We find (table 4, col. 3) that white married women with children (with spouse present) have current investment (ratio which exceeds the investment (ratio) incurred in experience before the first child.[13] Presumably, current participation in the labor force, which takes place when most of the children have reached school age, is expected to last longer than the previous periods of work experience. This is certainly true of women over age 35, and it holds in regressions with or without standardization for age.

Looking at regressions within three education levels (tables 5–6), we find that coefficient of prematernal experience (e_1) exceeds the coefficient of current work experience (e_3) at the highest level of schooling (in the short equations, though not in the long ones), and the opposite is true at lower levels. For women without children the coefficient of prematernal work experience equals that of current work experience. The investment profile of never-married women has a downward slope. Comparable

[12] In the earnings regressions, the quadratic term of aggregated experience is often negative, but not significant statistically.

[13] All statements about differences in coefficients refer to point estimates. The differences are mentioned because they are suggestive, though they would not pass strict tests of statistical significance within a given equation.

early segments of their post school job experience contain higher investment ratios—indeed, the fit implies a linear decline of such ratios over the life cycle. Evidently, women who intend to spend more time in the labor force invest more initially. This is true, presumably, even if their plans are later changed following marriage and childbearing.

4. Depreciation Rates

The coefficient of home time is negative, indicating a net depreciation of earning power. During the home-time interval (h_1), associated with marriage or the birth of the first child, this net depreciation amounts to, on average, 1.5 percent per year. In table 5 the depreciation rate is small $(-0.2$ percent) and insignificant for women with less than high school education, larger $(-1.3$ percent) for those with 12–15 years of schooling, and largest $(-2.3$ percent) for those with $16+$ years of schooling. In table 6, the net depreciation rate is -1.1 percent for women with elementary schooling or less, -1.4 percent for women with some high school, and -4.3 percent for women with at least some college. Sampling differences probably account for the different estimates in the two tables. The depreciation rate also appears higher in the group who worked more than half the years (table 7).

It would seem that the depreciation rate is higher when the accumulated stock of human capital is larger. An exception appears in the comparison of women without children (married and single) with women with children. The former have a lower depreciation rate. Of course, these women spend much less time out of market work, and some of this time might be job-oriented (e.g., job search).

It is useful to return to the formulation (9b) of the earnings function for a closer analysis of the depreciation rates: $\ln E_t = \ln E_0 + (rs - \delta_s) + (rk_1^* - \delta_1)e_1 + (rk_h^* - \delta_h)h + (rk_3^* - \delta_3)e_3$. Our coefficient of home time measures the depreciation rate only if market-oriented investment k_h^* is negligible. This is likely to be true for the period of child caring, the period defined as h_1 in the regression (h_2 in the tabulations).

An interesting question is whether the depreciation rate (δ_h) during nonparticipation is different from the depreciation that occurs at work as well. The question is whether depreciation due to nonuse of the human capital stock (atrophy?) exceeds the depreciation due to use (strain?) or to aging (?). We are inclined to believe that depreciation through nonuse ("getting rusty") is by far more important, particularly in groups of the relatively young (below age 45). Moreover, the atrophy aspect suggest that depreciation due to nonparticipation is strongest for the market-oriented components of human capital acquired on the job, and weakest for the inborn, initial, or general components of the human-capital stock. If so, a fixed rate of "home-time depreciation" applicable to on-the-job accumulation of human capital would appear as a varying rate in the earnings function: given the volume of other human capital, the larger the on-the-job accumulated component of human capital, the higher the observed (applied to the total earning power) depreciation rate.[14]

This may be an explanation of the observed higher depreciation rates at higher schooling and experience levels of mothers. In particular, there is a positive relation between the coefficients of h_1 (in absolute value) and of e_1 across schooling groups (table 6), experience groups (table 7), and race groups (compare tables 4 and 8).

5. *Effect of Family Size*

Do family size and number of children currently present affect the accumulation of earning power beyond the effect on work experience? The answer is largely negative: when numbers of children and some measures of their age are added to work histories in the equations, the children variables are negative but usually not significant statistically. Their inclusion reduces the absolute values of the coefficients of experience and of home time and does not add perceptibly to the explanatory power of the regression. Note, however, that the children variable does approach significance in the relatively small groups of highly educated women (tables 5–6), and more generally among women with stronger labor-force attachment (table 7). Possibly, shorter hours or lesser intensity of work are, to some extent, the preferred alternatives to job discontinuity.

6. *Formal Postschool Training*

The coefficients of experience, a_i, represent estimates of rk_i, where k_i is the average investment ratio across women over the segment and r is the average rate of return. Individual variation in k_i is not available to us. We have some individual information, however, on months of formal job training received after completion of schooling as well as on possession of professional certificates by, among others, registered nurses, teachers, and beauticians. If the length of training and possession of a certificate are positive indexes of k, we may represent $a_i = a_0 + \beta \cdot tr$, where tr is the length of training. The term $a \cdot e$ in that equation becomes

$$(a_0 + \beta tr) \cdot e = a_0 \cdot e + \beta(tr \cdot e).$$

Thus, an interaction term $(tr \cdot e)$ can be added to the equation, and if the hypothesis is correct, the coefficient β should be positive. This is indeed

[14] Where δ is the observed depreciation rate, δ_J the rate applicable to job-accumulated capital H_J, and H_0 the volume of other human capital, $\delta = (\delta_J H_J)/(H_J + H_0) = \delta_J/[1 + (H_0/H_J)]$. With a fixed rate δ_J for all individuals, the larger H_J the larger δ.

the case in most of our equations, confirming the training interpretation of the experience coefficients in the earnings function. Both interactions with months of job training and with possession of a certificate are significant for married women. The training interaction variable is also positive in the earnings function of single women, but the certificate variable is negative. Whereas the negative coefficient of the certification-experience variable implies less than average investment behavior among persons who work continuously, the corresponding positive coefficient for intermittent workers implies more than average investment behavior.

7. *Effects of Mobility*

Research in mobility has shown that, so long as mobility is not involuntary—resulting from layoffs—it is associated with a gain in earnings. However, geographic labor mobility of married women is often exogenous, due to job changes of the husband. In that case, it may militate against continuity of experience and slow the accumulation of earning power. We used the information on the length of current residence in a county or a Standard Metropolitan Statistical Area (SMSA) as an inverse measure of mobility. This variable has a small positive effect on wage rates of white MSP women and a significant negative effect for single women. To the extent that mobility is job oriented for single women and exogenous for married women, the differential signs provide a consistent interpretation.

8. *Hours and Weeks in Current Job*

When (logs of) weeks and hours worked in the survey year are included in the regression, a negative sign appears for the weekly-hours coefficient and a positive but less significant one for the weeks-worked coefficient. The hours' coefficients are smaller for married women than for single women and smaller for white than for black women. The negative sign of weekly hours may be partly or wholly spurious since some pay periods indicated by respondents were weeks or months and the hourly wage rate was obtained by division through hours. Of course, the direction of causality is suspect: it is more likely that women with lower wage rates work longer hours than the converse. Deletion of the variables, however, has a minimal effect on the equations.

9. *Other Variables*

Three other variables were included in the equations:

1. Twenty percent of the married women who worked in 1966 dropped out of work in 1967. We used a dummy variable with value 1 if persons

TABLE 8
EARNINGS FUNCTIONS OF BLACK WOMEN

MSP WITH CHILDREN			NEVER MARRIED		
Var.	b	t	Var.	b	t
C	$-.02$	...	C	$-.48$	...
S	.095	11.2	S	.110	3.7
e_1	.005	0.8	e	.004	0.1
e_2	.001	0.3	e^2	$-.0003$	-0.2
e_3	.006	1.4	e_3	.001	0.2
h_1	$-.006$	-1.2	h	$-.02$	$-.05$
h_2	$-.005$	-0.9	h^2	.001	1.1
etr	.0005	1.3	etr	.0006	1.4
ect	.008	1.9	ect	.003	0.4
hlt	$-.0002$	-0.5	hlt	$-.001$	-1.8
res	.002	0.9	res	.001	0.2
loc	.11	4.0	loc	.23	2.7
ln Hrs	$-.30$	-7.4	ln Hrs	$-.13$	-0.7
ln Wks	.08	2.2	ln Wks	.03	0.2
N_c	.005	0.6	N_c	...	...
R^2	.39	...	R^2	.46	...
N	550	...	N	70	...

NOTE.—MSP = white married women, spouse present. See table 4 for key to symbols.

working in 1966 stopped working in 1967, and 0 otherwise.[15] This variable had a negative sign, since it indicated a shorter current job experience compared with the prospective work interval of others who continued to work in 1967—the completed interval of those dropping out was not longer than the interval of stayers. In effect, women who dropped out of the labor force in 1967 had wage rates about 5 percent lower than women who continued working, given the same characteristics and histories.[16] The proportion of dropouts is somewhat larger at lower education levels.

2. The size of community in which the respondent lived at age 15 had a positive effect on earning power of married women but no effect on that of single women.

3. Duration of current health problem in months was used as a measure of health levels. It is an imperfect measure for retrospective purposes and shows a very small negative effect on the wage rate.

10. Black Women

The regressions for black MSP (table 8) show experience coefficients about half the size of the corresponding white population. Home time or depreciation coefficients are not significant; neither are the children

[15] Not shown in the tables.
[16] Without standardization, women who had dropped out had wage rates about 10 percent lower than women who continued working.

variables. The implication is that there is less investment on the job, even though black women spent more time than white women in the labor market. They had more and younger children, on average. The other variables behave comparably with those in the white regressions except that hours of current work and location at age 15 show stronger effects. In contrast to white women, the size of community of residence at age 15 has a positive effect for never-married women as well. Again, the experience coefficients are smaller for black single women than for whites. Perhaps contrary to expectations, neither health problems nor rates of withdrawal from the labor force in 1966 differ for black as compared to white married women with children, spouse present. Rates of return to schooling appear, if anything, to be higher for black women.

V. Lifetime Participation and the Simultaneity Problem

The earnings function, as we estimate it, relates wages of women to investments in schooling and on-the-job training and to a number of additional variables already discussed.

The interpretation of some of the independent variables as factors affecting earning power may be challenged on the grounds that they may just as well be viewed as effects rather than causes of earning power. Presumably, women with greater earning power have stronger job aspirations and work commitments than other women throughout their lifetimes. Hence, what we interpret as an earnings function may well be read with causality running in the opposite direction—as a labor-supply function. This argument is most telling for concurrent variables, such as last year's hours and weeks worked in relation to last year's wage rate. But these variables are of only marginal importance in the wage equation of married women. All other independent variables temporally precede the dependent variable (current wage rate), which makes the earnings function interpretation less vulnerable, though not entirely so for there is a serial correlation between current and past work experience and current and past earning power. Since lifetime work experience depends, in part, on prior wage levels and expectations, our experience variables are, in part, *determined* as well as *determining*. If so, the residual in our wage equations is correlated with the experience variables, and the estimates of coefficients which we interpreted as investment ratios are biased.

How serious this problem is for our analysis depends on the strength of individual correlations between current and past levels and expectations of earning power and on the strength of effect of these prior levels on subsequent work histories of individuals. Of course, when the data are grouped these correlations and effects are likely to be strong. Better-educated women tend to have higher wage rates than less educated women throughout their working lives, (see, for instance, Fuchs 1967) and as our table 3 shows, they spend a larger fraction of their lives in the

labor force. Table 3 also shows that married mothers who currently do
not work, spent, on average, less of their lifetime working than those who
currently work.

One econometric approach to an estimation of the earnings function in
the presence of endogeneity of "independent" variables is the two-stage
least-squares (2SLS) approach. We estimate work experience as a variable
dependent on exogenous variables, some of which are in the earnings
function and others outside of it. In effect, we estimate a "lifetime labor-
supply function." The second step is to replace the work-experience
variables (e) in the earnings function by the estimated work experience$(\hat{e})$
from the labor-supply function. Parameter estimates in this revised
earnings function are theoretically superior to the original, simple least-
squares estimates.[17]

Our application of a 2SLS procedure is far from thorough, for two
reasons:

1. It is difficult to implement it on the segmented function, since each
of the segments would have to be estimated by exogenous variables. For
this purpose we aggregate years of work experience and compare the
reestimated earnings function with the original, using aggregated experience.

2. One of the variables in our lifetime labor-supply function is the
number of children, which is not exogenous. In principle, we should
expand the equation system to three to include the earnings function, the
labor-supply function, and the fertility function. At this exploratory level
we prefer not to do it, particularly since the fertility function would be
estimated by the same variables as the labor-supply function.

The supply function obtained for all white MSP women was

$$\frac{e}{e_p} = \begin{array}{ccc} .514 + & .020\ S_F - & .0064\ S_M - & .062\ N_c, \\ & (5.1) & (1.8) & (12.0) \end{array}$$

where e is total years of work, e_p is "potential job experience," that is,
years since school, S_F is education of wife, S_M is education of husband,
and N_c is number of children. The addition of earnings of husband
reduced the coefficient of S_M to insignificance without changing the
coefficient of determination, which was $R^2 = .14$.

Estimated values of the numerator $(\hat{e})$ are used to reestimate the earnings function. A comparison of 2SLS and OLS estimates of the earnings
function is shown in table 9. If anything, the reestimated function shows
larger positive coefficients for (total) experience and stronger negative
coefficients for home time. The children variable becomes even less
significant (in terms of t-values) than before. The reestimation leaves our
conclusions, based on the OLS regressions, largely intact.

---

[17] Since $\hat{e}$ is a function of exogenous variables, it is not correlated with the stochastic
term in the reestimated earnings function.

S100

TABLE 9
EARNINGS FUNCTION, WMSP WOMEN, OLS AND 2SLS

VAR.	OLS		2SLS		OLS		2SLS	
	b	t	b	t	b	t	b	t
C	−.20	...	−.06	...	.19	...	.26	...
S	.069	12.8	.063	12.0	.053	9.4	.048	8.5
e	.010	3.2	.012	2.7	.008	2.8	.010	1.9
h_1	−.008	−3.0	−.015	−7.7	−.007	−1.9	−.013	−5.5
h_2	.0006	0.2	−.006	−2.3	.001	0.5	−.006	−1.9
e_3	.009	3.2	.009	3.5	.009	3.4	.010	3.7
tr	...	...	...	...	.005	2.2	.006	2.2
$cert$	...	...	...	...	.18	5.1	.18	5.1
hlt	...	...	...	...	−.0003	−1.3	−.0003	−1.4
res	...	...	...	...	.001	1.3	.021	1.4
loc	...	...	...	...	.044	2.8	.042	2.5
ln Hrs	...	...	...	...	−.11	−5.0	−.11	−4.9
ln Wks	...	...	...	...	.03	1.5	.03	1.6
N_e	...	...	...	...	−.010	−1.3	.003	0.3

NOTE.—WMSP = white married women, spouse present; tr = months of training; $cert$ = certification (dummy); see table 4 for key to other symbols.

VI. Prediction

A test of the predictive power of the earnings function was performed on a small sample of women who did not work in 1966 but were found in the same first NLS survey to have returned to work in 1967. They were not included in our analyses, but their life histories and 1967 wage rates are available. The latter were predicted with several variants of the earnings function and compared to the reported wage rates. On average, the prediction is quite close, and the mean-square error is even smaller—relative to the variance of the observed wage rates—than the residual variance in the regressions.[18] In other words, the predictive power outside the data utilized for the regressions is no smaller than within the regressions. The test, however, is weak, because the sample is so small (45 observations). Similar tests will be performed on larger samples of women who return to the labor market in subsequent surveys.

VII. Earnings Inequality and the Explanatory Power of Earnings Functions

As table 10 indicates, the earnings function is capable of explaining 25–30 percent of the relative (logarithmic) dispersion in wage rates of white married women and about 40 percent of the inequality in the rather small sample of wage rates of single women in the 30–44 age group who worked in 1966. The earnings function is thus no less useful in understanding the structure of women's wages than it is in the analysis of wages of males.

[18] The (squared) correlation between predicted and actual wage rates was .37. The mean of actual rates was 5.196, with $\sigma = .335$; the mean of predicted wages was 5.187, with $\sigma = .204$.

EARNINGS OF WOMEN   S101

TABLE 10

EARNINGS INEQUALITY AND EXPLANATORY POWER OF WAGE FUNCTIONS, 1966

Group	$\sigma^2 (\ln W)$	R_W^2	$\sigma^2 (\ln Y)$	R_Y^2	$\sigma^2 (\ln H)$	N
Married women by education (yrs):						
< 12	.17	.21	.81	.76	.64	435
12–15	.18	.17	.92	.78	.74	622
+ 16	.17	.16	.77	.74	.60	83
Total.........	.22	.28	.97	.78	.75	1,140
Single women	.30	.41	.62	.66	.32	138
Married men	.32	.30	.43	.50	.11	3,230

NOTE.—$\sigma^2 (\ln W)$ = variance of (log) wages; $\sigma^2 (\ln Y)$ = variance of (log) annual earnings; $\sigma^2 (\ln H)$ = variance of (log) annual hours of work; R_W^2 = coefficient of determination in wage rate function; R_Y^2 = coefficient of determination in annual earnings function.

The dispersion of hours worked during the survey year is much greater among married women, $\sigma^2 (\ln H) = .75$, than among men, $\sigma^2 (\ln H) = .11$. The (relative) dispersion in annual earnings of women is, therefore, dominated by the dispersion of hours worked. This factor is also important in the inequality of annual earnings of single women and of men of comparable ages, but much less so. It is not surprising, therefore, that the inclusion of hours worked in the earnings function raises the coefficient of determination from 28 percent in the hourly-wage equation to 78 percent in the annual-earnings equation of married women, from 41 percent to 66 percent for that of single women, and from 32 to 50 percent for that of men.

The lesser inequality in the wage-rate structure of working married women than in the structure of male wages is probably due to lesser average, and correspondingly lesser variation in, job investments among individuals. At the same time, the huge variation in hours, reflecting intermittency and part-time work as forms of labor-supply adjustments, creates an annual earnings inequality among women which exceeds that of men. However, the meaning of that inequality, both in a causal and in a welfare sense, must be seen in the family context. As was shown elsewhere (Mincer 1974), the inclusion of female earnings as a component of family income narrows the relative inequality of family incomes compared with that of incomes of male family-earners.

VIII. Some Applications

1. *The Wage Gap*

To compare wage rates of women with wage rates of men, we analyzed earnings of men from the Survey of Economic Opportunity (SEO) for the same year (1966). We find that the average wage rate of white married men, aged 30–44, was $3.18, compared with $2.09 for white married women and $2.73 for white single women in our NLS data.

TABLE 11
EXPERIENCE AND DEPRECIATION COEFFICIENTS, 1966, AGES 30–44

VAR.	MARRIED WOMEN		SINGLE WOMEN		MARRIED MEN	
	b	M	b	M	b	M
S	.063	11.3	.077	12.5	.071	11.6
$\hat{e}$	.012	9.6	...	...	...	...
e	...	...	.026	15.6	.034	19.4
e^2	...	...	−.0006	258	−.0006	409
e_3	.009	3.2	.009	8.0	...	...
h_c	−.015	6.7	...	...	...	...
h_0	−.006	3.5	...	...	...	...

SOURCES.—Women: NLS, 1967; men: SEO, 1967.
NOTE.— S = years of schooling; h_c = home time following birth of first child; h_0 = other home time; e = years of work experience since completion of schooling; e_3 = current job tenure; $\hat{e}$ = 2SLS estimate of total work experience; b = regression coefficient; M = means.

TABLE 12
EFFECTS OF WORK EXPERIENCE ON WAGE RATES

	RELATIVE CONTRIBUTION OF		PERCENT OF WAGE GAP EXPLAINED	
	Actual Experience (1)	Men's Experience (2)	(3)	(4)
Married women	+.02	+.26	45	42
Single women	+.32	+.33	7	40
Married men	+.42	...	...	...

We inquired to what extent the larger wage ratio (152 percent) of married men to married women and the smaller one (116 percent) of married men to single women can be explained by differences in work histories and by differences in job investment and depreciation. For this purpose we estimated a single earnings function of men, aged 30–44, in SEO. The coefficients and means of the variables for these men are shown in table 11, which also gives the NLS estimates for both married and single women.

Note that married men and married working women have just about the same average schooling, while never-married women are somewhat better educated (by 1 year, on average). The coefficients of schooling are somewhat lower for married women but higher for single women. The big differences are in years of work experience since completion of schooling. These are 19.4 for men, 15.6 for single women, and 9.6 for married women. The coefficients of initial experience are .034 for men, .026 for single women, and about half as much for married women.

Multiplying the coefficients by the variables (table 11) and summing yields contributions of postschool investments to the (log of) wage rates as shown in table 12. These differences, roughly 40 percent between husbands and wives and 10 percent between married men and single women, are about 70 percent of the observed difference in wage rates between married men and married women and a half of the difference between married men and single women.

If one prefers to be agnostic about the human-capital approach, one can treat the earnings function simply as a statistical relation and the regression coefficients as average "effects" of work experience and of nonparticipation on wages, without reading magnitudes of investment or depreciation into them. In that case we may ask how much the sex differential in wage rates would narrow if work experience of women were as long as that of men, but the female coefficients remained as they are. A multiplication of the female coefficients by the male variables in table 11 yields the following answers: for married women, 45 percent of the gap would be erased; for single women, only 7 percent of the much smaller gap (table 12, col. 3). The answer is similar for married women if the converse procedure is used, that is when the work experience of women is multiplied by the male coefficients (table 12, col. 4). For single women, the reduction of the gap is larger than in the first procedure.

We believe, however, that the weight of the empirical analysis of female earnings supports the view that the association of lower coefficients with lesser work experience is not fortuitous: a smaller fraction of time and energy is devoted to job advancement (training, learning, getting ahead) per unit of time by persons whose work attachment is lower. Hence, the 45 percent figure in the explanation of the gap by duration-of-work experience alone may be viewed as an understatment.

Indeed, comparing the annual earnings of year-round working women and men in the 30–40 age groups, Suter and Miller found a female-to-male earnings ratio of 46.7 percent. However, the ratio rose to 74 percent for women in this group who worked all their adult lives. The same comparison for high school educated persons yielded 40.5 as against 74.9 percent. Thus lifelong work experience reduces the wage gap by 51 or 58 percent, respectively.[19]

At this stage of research we cannot conclude that the remaining (unexplained) part of the wage gap is attributable to discrimination, nor, for that matter, that the "explained" part is not affected by discrimination. More precisely, we should distinguish between the concepts of direct and indirect effects of discrimination. Direct market discrimination occurs when different rental prices (wage rates) are paid by employers for the same unit of human capital owned by different persons (groups). In this sense, the wage-gap residual is an upper limit of the direct effects of market discrimination. Indirect effects occur in that the existence of

[19] Suter and Miller (1971, table 1). Their figures are not quite comparable with ours: their male data come from the Current Population Survey (CPS), and ours from SEO. They compare full-time earnings rather than wage rates, and they compare men and women without regard to marital status.

market discrimination discourages the degree of market orientation in the expected allocation of time and diminishes incentives to investment in market-oriented human capital. Hence, the lesser job investments and greater depreciation of female market earning power may to some extent be affected by expectations of discrimination.

Of course, if division of labor in the family is equated with discrimination, all of the gap is by definition a symptom of discrimination. Otherwise, the analyses of existing wage gaps and of their changes over time remain meaningful, not tautological.

Our data on work histories show some interesting trends which suggest a prospective narrowing of the wage differential. Table 3 shows that the uninterrupted period of nonparticipation which starts just prior to the birth of the first child has been shrinking when older women are compared with younger ones. Women aged 40–44 who had their first child in the late 1940s stayed out of the labor force about 5 years longer than women aged 30–34 whose first child was born in the late 1950s. Family size is about the same for both groups, but higher for the middle group (35–39) whose fertility marked the peak of the baby boom. Still, the home-time interval in that group is shorter (by about 2 years) than in the older group and longer than in the younger. Thus, the trend in labor-force participation of young mothers was persistent. If, by the time the 30–34-year-old women get to be 40–44 (i.e., in 1977), they will have had 4 years of work experience more than the older cohort, and their wage rates will rise by 6 percent on account of lesser depreciation and by another 2–4 percent due to longer work experience. Thus, the total observed wage gap between men and women aged 40–44 should narrow by about one-fifth, while the gap due to work experience should be reduced by one-quarter.[20]

2.   *The Price of Time and the Opportunity Costs of Children*

The loss or reduction of market earnings of mothers due to demands on their time in child rearing represents a measure of family investment in the human capital of their children. This investment cost has been measured by valuing the reduction of market time at the observed wage rate. As pointed out by Michael and Lazear (1971), this valuation is incomplete for two reasons. First, if job investments take place at work, the observed wage rate understates the true foregone wage (gross or capacity wage) by the amount usually invested during the period when

[20] Two opposing biases mar this conjecture: The shorter home-time interval for younger women is an average duration for those who already returned to work. It will lengthen with the passage of time as additional women return to the labor force. It can be shown, however, that the apparent trend is genuine. At the same time, the assumption of unchanged job-investment behavior leads to an understatement.

earnings are foregone. Second, as is clear from earnings-function analysis, the reduction of market time in turn reduces future wage rates because of a depreciation in earning power during the period of nonparticipation. The present value of future earnings lost through depreciation is a component of the opportunity cost of time, hence of children.[21]

The data and the estimated wage functions permit a tentative, perhaps only an illustrative, empirical assessment of the opportunity cost of women's time and of children. Specifically, the marginal opportunity cost per hour of a year spent at home—rather than in the market— consists of (1) the gross wage rate (W_g), that is the observed but foregone wage (W) augmented by currently foregone investment costs, and (2) the present value of the reduction of the future gross wage through current depreciation:[22]

1. We can estimate W_g since $W = W_g(1 - k)$, and rk is estimated in the earnings function by a_1, the coefficient of work experience (e_1) preceding the interruption $k = a_1/r$, where r is the rate of return.

2. The present value of the reduction in W_g due to depreciation, using r as the discount rate, is $d/r \cdot W_g$, where d is the (depreciation) coefficient of home time in our wage equations.[23]

The estimates of marginal opportunity costs of a year (in dollars per hour) are shown in panel I of table 13 for three education groups of white mothers, aged 35–39. In panel II we calculate total opportunity expenditures incurred during the nonparticipation period following the birth of the first child. This is the period for which the earnings functions show significant depreciation coefficients. The length of the period depends, in part, on the number of children. Though interpreting all of the foregone earnings this period as an opportunity expenditure on children may be an overstatement, we impose an opposite bias by ignoring subsequent periods of non participation[24] which may also be child induced. Figures in panel II are the marginal costs per hour (per year) multiplied by h, the duration of home time. Figures in panel III are average opportunity expenditures per child (N_c) in each group. Since h is in years, the dollar figures in panels II and III should be multiplied by annual hours of work. For example, with 1,500 hours of work per year, the opportunity investment expenditures per child range from about $8,000 spent in 8.8 years by mothers with less than high school education to $17,000 spent in 5.2 years by mothers with college education or more.

---

[21] As Robert Willis suggested to us, this is strictly correct for the excess of depreciation during home time over the depreciation at other times. As we stated earlier, we believe that the latter is negligible in our age groups.

[22] Note that we are looking at household productivity as the return, the purpose of reducing market work, not as a negative element in costs.

[23] A 10 percent discount rate was used in these calculations.

[24] Inclusion would lead to a 20–25 percent increase in expenditures for the age group.

TABLE 13

MARGINAL PRICE OF TIME AND OPPORTUNITY COSTS OF CHILDREN, 1966, WORKING WHITE MOTHERS (AGED 35–39)—BY YEARS OF SCHOOLING ($)

	PRICE OF TIME PER HOUR			TOTAL OPPORTUNITY EXPENDITURES ON CHILDREN			OPPORTUNITY EXPENDITURES PER CHILD		
	<12	12–15 (I)	16+	<12	12–15 (II)	16+	<12	12–15 (III)	16+
1. Observed wage	1.66	2.25	3.54	14.60	16.33	18.51	4.23	5.52	6.60
2. Capacity wage	1.96	2.59	4.60	17.25	18.87	24.05	5.00	6.41	8.57
3. Depreciation	0.05	0.30	1.40	0.44	2.18	7.32	0.13	0.73	2.63
Sum (2 + 3)	2.01	2.89	6.00	17.69	21.05	31.37	5.13	7.14	11.20
Assuming 1,500 hr work per year									
h_c	...	...	...	8.80	7.26	...	7,740	10,710	16,800
N_c	...	...	...	3.45	2.96	5.23	...	...	...
h_c/N_c	...	...	...	2.55	2.45	2.81	...	...	...

NOTE.—h_c = duration of home time; N_c = no. of children.

Only panel I represents the marginal price of time. Note that the observed wage rate[25] represents 80 percent of the marginal price of an hour below college levels and only 60 percent at higher levels. The same proportions hold in the other two panels. However, figures in these panels are not prices but expenditures which depend on both the price of time and the number of children and the average home-time interval per child. Both of these variables can be viewed as responses to the marginal price of time. As the table indicates, observed wage rates and, even more so, marginal prices of time (panel I) increase with education. Lesser fertility and closer spacing of children are the responses:[26] both numbers of children and interval of home time per child diminish. Consequently, the differences in total expenditures by education level are reduced. While the marginal price of time of the highest education group is three times as high as that of the lowest, the expenditures per child are a little over twice as high, and total expenditures are only 70 percent higher.

Since the opportunity costs of labor-force withdrawal ("home time") are not quite the same thing as the opportunity costs of children, we again caution the reader to view the estimates of table 13 as largely illustrative. They clearly illustrate the point which the title of this paper intends to convey: foregone market-oriented human capital of mothers is a part of the price of acquiring human capital in children, and more generally, a price exacted by family life. Of course, the greater market specialization, longer hours, and greater intensity of work and of job training on the part of husbands and fathers can be viewed as a "price exacted by family life" in exactly the same sense.

Implicitly, families balance such prices against perceptions of received benefits.[27] Of course, both perceptions of net benefits and prices change. While perceptions are matters of individual psychology and of cultural climate, the marginal opportunity cost of time has risen secularly with the rise in real wages and with the growth of human capital. It is natural for economists to connect to this basic fact both upward trends in labor-force participation of women and downward trends in fertility,[28] changes in the family, and even some of the rhetoric which accompanies these developments.

[25] In principle, wage rates just before the period h are required. The wage at ages 35–39 represents, on average, a small overstatement: wage profiles of married women with children are relatively flat in the age span 25–39 within education groups.

[26] Direct evidence on closer spacing at higher levels of education is shown in research for a Columbia Ph.D. dissertation by Sue Ross (1973). In the NLS data, there is a strong correlation between the length of home time and the birth interval from oldest to youngest child.

[27] Some of these benefits are analyzed in the papers of Lee Benham and Arleen Leibowitz in this volume.

[28] For economic analyses which bear on the upward secular trends in labor-force participation of married women, see Mincer (1962) and Cain (1966). For analyses bearing on fertility trends, see "New Economic Approaches to Fertility," *J.P.E.*, vol. 81, no. 2, suppl. (March/April 1973).

Appendix

Note on the Construction of Work-Experience Intervals

The 1967 NLS survey of women aged 30–44 permits a division of time elapsed since leaving school into, at most, eight intervals. The following information was used in constructing these intervals: (*a*) Dates were available for school leaving (S), first marriage (M), birth of first child (C), start of first job, return to labor force after birth of first child, start of current job, and end of last job, if currently not working. (*b*) Number of years during which the woman worked at least 6 months between: (1) school leaving and first marriage, (2) marriage and birth of first child, (3) return to labor force after the first child, and (4) the start of current job.

On this basis, we describe the intervals in the order of their chronological placement: interval h_1 (on average, half a year) is the interval between school and first job; e_1 is the number of years of work between school and marriage. The placement and continuity of this interval checks rather closely with the data, though direct statements are absent; e_2 is years worked (similarly defined) between first marriage and birth of first child; h_2 is the residual home time, given information on the length of interval between first marriage and birth of first child. The assumption of continuity and order of placement of e_2 and h_2 are somewhat arbitrary. They are justified by evidence of frequent identity of job e_1 and e_2 and the plausibility of h_2 starting during pregnancy. Indeed, h_2 is a fraction of a year, on average; h_3 is the uninterrupted interval of home time following the birth of the first child. It is placed by direct information; e_3 is years of work and h_4 the residual amount of time in the interval between returning to the labor force at the end of h_3 and start of current job. However, neither e_3 nor h_4 needs to be continuous. The succession of h_4 after e_3 is more plausible than the converse. Also $(e_3 + h_4)$ is, on average, about 3 years altogether; e_4 is clearly defined and placed as the current job interval.

In tables 2 and 3 we aggregate $(e_1 + e_2)$ and call it e_1, $(h_2 + h_3)$ is h_2, and the other intervals are correspondingly renamed.

In the regressions we added h_1 to h_3 to get h_2 other home time. Separately, or together, these intervals are quite short and show little effect in our analysis.

[16]

350 - 71
(1982)

OCCUPATIONAL SEGREGATION
BY SEX: DETERMINANTS
AND CHANGES*

ANDREA H. BELLER

ABSTRACT

The human capital and discrimination explanations of occupational segregation are tested in this paper. The empirical evidence is mixed on the supply-oriented human capital explanation, but it supports the demand-oriented discrimination explanation. The enforcement of federal equal employment opportunity (EEO) programs measures discrimination indirectly. Findings show that between 1967 and 1974, both Title VII of the Civil Rights Act of 1964 and the federal contract compliance program increased a working woman's probability of being employed in a male occupation relative to a man's probability. This success of EEO laws suggests that discrimination was a determinant of occupational segregation originally.

The link between sex differences in occupations and in earnings has been documented empirically in a number of studies (Fuchs [7] and Oaxaca [10],

The author is Assistant Professor, Department of Family and Consumer Economics, University of Illinois at Urbana-Champaign.

* The research described in this paper was supported by funds from the Mary Ingraham Bunting Institute of Radcliffe College and by Grant No. 91-25-78-04 from the Employment and Training Administration, U.S. Department of Labor. Initial support came from funds granted to the Institute for Research on Poverty, University of Wisconsin-Madison, by the Department of Health, Education, and Welfare. The author wishes to thank Gary Chamberlain and Richard Freeman for their helpful comments and suggestions, David Marion and Evan Shouten for able research assistance, and the late Gerald Somers for his special encouragement. This paper also benefited from presentation at the Labor Seminars at Harvard University and the University of Illinois at Urbana-Champaign and from helpful comments from the editors of this journal. Since grantees conducting research and development projects under government sponsorship are encouraged to express their own judgment freely, this research does not necessarily represent the official opinion or policy of the Departments of Labor or of Health, Education, and Welfare. The grantee is solely responsible for the contents of this paper. [Manuscript received April 1980; accepted November 1980.]

The Journal of Human Resources   •   XVII   •   3

0022-166X/82/0003-0371 $01.50/0

for example.)[1] If more than half the population is denied access to 60 percent of the occupations, being crowded into a few at lower earnings, equality of opportunity does not exist. But if women freely choose to enter only a third of all occupations and those occupations pay less, then women's lower earnings may not be a fundamental social problem. The major issue is whether the dramatic differences in the occupational distributions of the sexes result from different choices made by each, given equal opportunities, or from unequal opportunities to make similar choices.

Within an economic framework, the determinants of an individual woman's probability of entering a given occupation include her labor market choices, employer choices, and premarket conditions. We will consider the first two only.[2] Polachek [11] developed a human capital explanation for women's *labor market choices,* based on sex-role differentiation. According to this approach, women choose to enter occupations for which earnings losses from anticipated absences from the labor force over the life cycle will be the smallest. Because they plan to leave the labor force during the child-bearing and rearing years, women find occupations attractive in which skills deteriorate the least with absences from the labor force, and they enter them disproportionately. Bergmann developed a discrimination explanation of *employer choices.* According to this approach, because women face barriers to entry into certain occupations, they tend to become crowded into a small number of occupations without barriers. Increasing the supply of labor reduces earnings in these other occupations, and limiting the supply of labor raises earnings in the occupations that become male (Bergmann [4]).

Despite the importance of the problem and the persuasiveness of these explanations, little empirical evidence exists on the relative explanatory power of these two approaches. Accordingly, we test these explanations against one another by examining, for working women and men, the determinants of the probability of being employed in a male occupation and of changes in that probability since equal employment opportunity (EEO) laws went into effect. While Polachek's human capital approach can be tested directly by examining coefficients on labor supply variables, Bergmann's discrimination approach can be tested only indirectly. This is done by examining the effects of EEO

---

1 Occupational segregation continues to be extreme. As recently as 1973, more than 40 percent of all employed women were found in only ten occupations: secretary, retail trade, sales worker, elementary school teacher, waitress, typist, cashier, sewer and stitcher, and registered nurse. Moreover, ranking occupations by women's median annual earnings, only three of the ten largest women's occupations—elementary school teacher, registered nurse, and secretary—fell in the top half of the earnings distribution and none in the top decile (Sommers [14]).

2. Premarket conditions include tangible and intangible influences on women's decision-making, such as discrimination in education via admissions and tracking, sex-role socialization, and perceptions about the labor market.

laws over time. Should the findings indicate that EEO laws increase a working woman's probability, relative to a man's, of being employed in a nontraditional occupation, that would be strong evidence that discriminatory barriers to entry contributed to women's occupational distribution in the first place.

Section I establishes a working definition of male occupations and statistically describes the dimensions of occupational segregation. In Section II, the determinants of occupational segregation are developed using these human capital and discrimination approaches. The empirical model is developed in Section III, and the empirical results are presented in Section IV. Section V is the conclusion.

I. A DEFINITION OF MALE OCCUPATIONS

Since the definition is relative and somewhat arbitrary, we start by defining a "male" occupation. If choice were totally free and men and women had the same preferences and resources, we would expect to find the sexes distributed equally among all occupations, with minor random differences. Then, the expected proportion of jobs held by men in each occupation would be equal to their proportion of the labor force. We choose to allow up to five percentage points for random deviation and define a "male" (or, alternatively, "male-dominated" or "nontraditional") occupation as one in which the men's share of employment exceeds their share of the experienced civilian labor force by five or more percentage points. An "integrated" occupation is defined as one in which men hold between five points higher and five points lower than their share of the labor force.

Occupational segregation is both extreme and persistent. Its extensive nature is illustrated by the data in Table 1 where each 3-digit Census occupation's sex label is defined relative to the male share of employment in 1960, .672, or 1970, .619.[3] Its persistence is revealed by the finding that between 1960 and 1970, only eight out of the 267 largest occupations and 16 out of all 440 detailed occupations changed label, or around 3 or 4 percent; in the next four years, only five out of the 267 largest occupations, or 2 percent, changed label. Thus, a majority of occupations are male-dominated and very few are integrated; women are found clustered in less than one-third of all occupations.

In the subsequent statistical analyses, the detailed occupation's 1960 sex label is used to examine entry into a fixed set of occupations over time. A male occupation is defined as one in which men hold .722 or more of the jobs, and an integrated occupation is one in which men hold between .623

---

3 To perform these computations, we had to use special tabulations to reconcile the new 1970 with the 1960 3-digit Census occupation codes (Priebe [12]). The figures in this table treat each occupation as a single unit.

TABLE 1

STABILITY IN THE SEX LABELS

OF DETAILED OCCUPATIONS, 1960–1974

Sex Label	Fixed Sex Labels All Occupations		Variable Sex Labels[a] Large Occupations		
	1960 (1)	1970 (2)	1960 (3)	1970 (4)	1974 (5)
Male	289	305	162	168	163
Integrated	27	25	17	19	19
Female	124	110	88	80	85
Total	440	440	267	267	267
			Percent		
Male	65.7	69.3	60.1	62.9	61.0
Integrated	6.1	5.7	6.4	7.1	7.1
Female	28.2	25.0	33.0	30.0	31.8
Total	100.0	100.0	100.0	100.0	100.0

Source: U.S. Bureau of the Census, *U.S. Census of Population: 1960,* Final Report PC(2)-7A, Subject Reports, Occupational Characteristics (Washington: U.S. Government Printing Office, 1963), Table 1; U.S. Bureau of the Census, *U.S. Census of Population: 1970,* Final Report PC(2)-7A, Subject Reports, Occupational Characteristics (Washington: U.S. Government Printing Office, 1973), Table 1; 1975 Current Population Survey, Annual Demographic File, computer tapes.

Note: Some statistics in Tables 1 and 2 are based upon the 267 largest occupations in 1974 selected from among 440 detailed (3-digit) 1970 Census occupations. We selected 25 persons as a minimum in a detailed occupation in the 1974 CPS in order to compute the male proportion. This criterion threw out occupations with roughly fewer than 40,000 individuals in 1974.

a Fixed sex labels are ones determined relative to the male share of the labor force in 1960, .672, while variable sex labels are determined relative to the male share in 1960 or in 1970, .619.

and .721 of the jobs.[4] The proportions of males and of females employed in male occupations in 1967, 1971, and 1974 are shown in Table 2.

This extreme degree of occupational segregation is serious because, on the average, male occupations are more desirable in pecuniary terms for both sexes. Table 3 shows the gross and net differential in weekly earnings between persons employed in male occupations and in other occupations, by sex. In 1967, women employed in male occupations earned one-third more than

4   We chose this definition of a male occupation because it has been used previously in the literature (cf. Jusenius [9]). To check the robustness of the conclusions with respect to this arbitrary choice, we also performed the statistical analysis for two more restrictive definitions, 10 and 20 percentage points more male than the labor force as a whole.

TABLE 2

PROPORTION OF WORKING MEN AND WOMEN EMPLOYED
IN MALE OCCUPATIONS FOR 1967, 1971, AND 1974

	1967	1971	1974
Men	.604	.807	.805
Women	.087	.137	.153

Source: U.S. Bureau of the Census, *U.S. Census of Population: 1960,* Final Report
PC(2)-7A, Subject Reports, Occupational Characteristics (Washington: U.S. Government Printing Office, 1963), Table 1; Current Population Survey, Annual Demographic File, 1968, 1972, and 1975.
Note: In going from 1967 to 1971 and 1974, we move from the 1960 Census occupation
codes to the 1970 codes. Priebe [12] enabled us to make this transition; however, the
break in the figures in this table, and consequently in the dependent variable in the
statistical analyses, may reflect an imperfect reconciliation with the increased number
of occupational categories. For all three years, the sex label is determined by the
occupation's male proportion in 1960.

TABLE 3

GROSS AND NET PERCENTAGE DIFFERENTIAL IN WEEKLY EARNINGS
BETWEEN MALE AND OTHER OCCUPATIONS, BY SEX, 1967 AND 1974

Between Male and Other Occupations[a]	Women		Men	
	1967	1974	1967	1974
Gross differential	.330	.295	.497	.294
Net differential	.123	.119	.140	.097

Source: Current Population Survey computer tapes, Annual Demographic File, 1968
and 1975.
a The gross differential in weekly earnings is simply the percentage difference between
   the average earnings of women (or men) in male occupations and women (or men)
   in other occupations. The net differential is the coefficient on a dummy variable
   computed with earnings in logarithms controlling for education, experience, weeks
   worked, part-time work, region, SMSA, number of children, marital status, local
   unemployment rate, government, home specialization, and race interactions. The
   male equation also includes variables for veteran status and health. All figures in
   this table are significant at better than the .01 level.

women employed in other occupations, and men earned a full 50 percent
more. Despite this earnings advantage, only 8.7 percent of working women,
contrasted to 60.4 percent of working men, were employed in these occupations.
This gross differential could reflect various factors, such as greater human
capital among persons in male-dominated occupations or greater labor effort

(hours or weeks worked). Controlling for such human capital and labor supply differences reduces these earnings differentials by about two-thirds; nevertheless, a significant net differential between male and other occupations of about 12 percent remains. Despite a substantial decline in the gross differential between 1967 and 1974, that net differential remained unchanged for women while falling for men; in 1974, even though the earnings advantage of male occupations was larger for women than for men, only 15.3 percent of working women, contrasted to 80.5 percent of men, were employed in them.

If the earnings advantage to being in male occupations is as great for women, why don't they enter them as readily as do men? To answer this question, we turn to an analysis of the determinants of an individual's entry into nontraditional occupations.

II. THE DETERMINANTS OF ENTRY INTO NONTRADITIONAL OCCUPATIONS

What are the determinants of the probability that an individual woman works in a nontraditional occupation? Have these determinants shifted over time with the implementation and enforcement of equal employment opportunity laws, changing attitudes toward women's role, and the women's liberation movement? The two possible explanations that we consider here are a human capital approach and a discrimination approach.

A Human Capital Approach

Under a theory of occupational choice, individuals weigh their expected returns from entering an occupation, potential lifetime earnings plus a monetary value for their like or dislike of a particular type of job, and their costs of entry into that occupation, primarily training costs plus earnings forgone during training. Because returns and costs vary among individuals due to differences in native ability, tastes and preferences, and access to resources to finance training, individuals differ in their probability of entering any particular occupation (Boskin [6]). If women and men were alike in all of these respects, and there were no barriers to entry for one sex, the occupational distributions of men and women would be similar—that is, all occupations would be integrated.

By incorporating the effects of sex-role differentiation into this model, Polachek [11] develops an explanation for the different occupational choices of men and women. Men, especially husbands, allocate more time to work in the market over the life cycle than do women, especially wives. Differences in potential labor supply can generate differences in potential lifetime earnings across occupations if occupations differ in the extent to which continuous and full-time participation is necessary to maintain and improve skills and productivity. Women choose to enter those occupations with the smallest earnings losses from anticipated absences from the labor force and thus become segregated into occupations characterized by the relatively slow rate at which skills deteriorate from disuse.[5] If occupations do differ in the extent to which absences from the labor force are penalized, then returns among occupations will differ systematically according to sex, and men and women will choose to work in different occupations. Sex differences in occupational earnings will generate sex differences in the types and amounts of education and training acquired.

According to this approach, the probability that a woman is employed in a nontraditional occupation should be negatively related to variables indicating a weaker attachment to the labor force over the life cycle. Thus, we should expect to find married, spouse-present women less likely to be employed in nontraditional occupations than other marital-status groups, and the greater the number of children, the lower the probability that a woman is employed in a nontraditional occupation. More weeks worked should be associated with a higher probability and part-time work with a lower probability.

A Discrimination Approach

Under this approach, occupational segregation is caused by employers discriminating against women in their hiring practices in certain occupations. Their practices set up a barrier to the entry of women, reducing the demand for women relative to men. In these occupations, which become male-dominated, the earnings of women relative to men are reduced, and restrictions on employment increase earnings in this male sector. These entry restrictions also force women to become crowded into occupations in which employers do not discriminate against them, and crowding lowers earnings in this nonmale sector.

Removing these barriers to entry into male occupations that women face should reverse these effects by increasing the employment ratio of women to men in male-dominated occupations, by increasing the relative earnings of

---

5   This theory assumes that occupations are in fact inherently different with respect to the loss of skills during absences from the labor force, but this has not been proven. Although Polachek estimated rates at which skills deteriorate for each of the broad 2-digit Census occupations, he did so using data on women's earnings. Differences in earnings losses among occupations for women would only be uncontaminated estimates of productivity losses if discrimination against women in the labor market were constant across all occupations. If it differed among occupations, then earnings losses could differ systematically with discrimination and Polachek's estimates would not measure productivity losses alone. Male earnings data would be required to provide uncontaminated estimates of differential productivity losses with absences from occupations. (This point was made by Michael Boskin in conversation.)

378 | THE JOURNAL OF HUMAN RESOURCES

TABLE 4

GROSS AND NET PERCENTAGE DIFFERENTIAL IN WEEKLY EARNINGS
BETWEEN WOMEN AND MEN, BY SEX LABEL OF OCCUPATION,
1967 AND 1974

Between Women and Men[a]	Male Occupations		Other Occupations	
	1967	1974	1967	1974
Gross differential	−0.644	−0.638	−0.478	−0.539
Net differential	−1.470	−0.863	−0.910	−0.735

Source: Same as Table 3.

a The gross differential in weekly earnings between women and men is the percentage difference between the average earnings of women and men in male occupations or in other occupations. The net differential is the difference in the intercepts from separate regressions for each sex which are computed with earnings in logarithms controlling for education, experience, weeks worked, part-time work, region, SMSA, number of children, marital status, local unemployment rate, government, home specialization, and race interactions. The male equation also includes variables for veteran status and health. All figures in this table are significant at better than the .01 level.

women in these occupations, and by reducing the earnings differential between male-dominated and other occupations. If we observe the economic effects of discrimination being reversed, then we can argue that discrimination has been reduced; to have been reduced, it must have existed initially. This is admittedly an indirect test of a difficult-to-identify concept, that of discrimination.

Some preliminary evidence is already available. From Table 3 we observe a decrease between 1967 and 1974 in the net earnings advantage to entering the male occupations for men (line 2). Since the vast majority of incumbents are men, male earnings can be taken to represent labor earnings, and this decline to indicate a narrowing earnings differential between the male and nonmale sectors. Between 1967 and 1974, the net earnings advantage for women increased relative to that of men.[6] Further, the ratio of the proportion of women working in the male occupations to the proportion of men increased from .144 in 1967 to .188 in 1974. Of course, it is possible that these changes reflect trends, such as a shift in demand toward the more female-intensive among male occupations.

---

6 In the most narrowly defined male occupations, .872 or more male, the net earnings advantage of women increased not only relative to that of men, but also absolutely from 1.0 percent in 1967 to 9.2 percent in 1974. Over this same period, the net advantage of men remained virtually unchanged at 6.0 percent.

Table 4 shows that the gross sex differential in earnings in male occupations barely declined, in contrast with the significant increase in the sex differential in other occupations. But most striking is the decline in the net sex differential in earnings in male occupations computed after controlling for schooling and labor supply differences. The observed increase in the relative employment and earnings of women in the male occupations and the decline in the earnings differential between male-dominated and other occupations are all effects that would result from a decline in discrimination. Their occurrence strongly suggests that discrimination against women in the male occupations decreased during the late sixties and early seventies.

An EEO Variant

Further evidence of discrimination's impact on occupational segregation would be furnished if equal employment opportunity (EEO) laws were found to increase women's entry into the nontraditional occupations.[7] The employment provision of these laws increases the demand for women relative to men, which can, in turn, increase relative wages. Although the long-run effects may be perverse (Heckman and Wolpin [8]), federal EEO laws seem better suited to eliminating discrimination in employment than in wages (Beller [2]). Two laws govern concurrently: Title VII of the Civil Rights Act of 1964, as amended by the Equal Employment Opportunity Act of 1972, and Executive Order 11246 as amended, the federal contract compliance program. The former prohibits discrimination by private employers of 15 or more employees and by state and local governments and educational institutions. Its scope is much broader than that of the latter. Directed specifically at current and potential holders of federal contracts, the contract compliance program nevertheless contains a stronger sanction than does Title VII—the power to withhold millions of dollars in federal contracts. Moreover, affirmative action plans which grew out of this program are fairly widespread (Beller [3]).

The expected costs of violating Title VII vary across states and were altered by the 1972 amendments. Two variables are constructed for the pre- and post-1972 periods to estimate expected costs: the probability of apprehension for violating Title VII, and the probability of paying a penalty if found in violation. The probability of apprehension is estimated by the ratio

---

7   It can be argued that EEO laws could have this effect regardless of the existence of discrimination. Considering how actively companies resist settlements under Title VII legislation, however, we believe that in this case the law would be ineffective. In fact, its effectiveness can be taken to mean that, at least in the interpretation of the courts, discrimination exists. The contract compliance program is more subject to this qualification because the voluntary affirmative action plans under it may make male occupations more attractive to women regardless of whether discrimination existed initially.

of the number of investigations of sex discrimination charges completed by the Equal Employment Opportunity Commission (EEOC)—or by a state or local commission to which a charge had been deferred—to the number of women in each state group and of each class of worker employed in 1970. The probability of paying a penalty is estimated by the ratio of successful (voluntary) settlements of sex discrimination charges (successful conciliations plus successful predecision settlements) to attempted (voluntary) settlements.[8] These variables are defined for each of the 23 state groups identified in the Current Population Survey (CPS), separately for the private sector and for government.

The 1972 amendments to Title VII strengthened the law and extended its coverage. By granting the EEOC the right to sue private-sector respondents, the amendments increased the likelihood that an unsuccessful outcome in the voluntary conciliation process would lead to a court case. Thus, after 1972, voluntary settlements should be more common and effective. The amendments also expanded coverage to bring under the law governmental units, educational institutions, and employers of 15–24 employees (the previous minimum was 25). Thus, after 1972, the deterrent effect of investigations had a potentially larger impact. To allow for these differences in the effects of pre- and postamendment enforcement, we constructed these variables separately for the periods January 1968–March 1972 and April 1972–December 1974.

Affirmative action should be more successful in industries selling a large proportion of their total output to the federal government than in industries selling only a small share to the government (Smith and Welch [13]). The effect of the federal contract compliance program is measured by a single variable, the federal share of industry product, estimated by the ratio of purchases by the federal government to value-added originating in each of 50 industry groups.

---

8   Some clarification of these variables and the data used to construct them may be helpful. First, the EEOC determines whether a settlement is "successful" or "unsuccessful." Second, not all investigations or settlements have the same potential impact. About 30 percent of discrimination charges have been processed as systemic, while the other 70 percent have been processed as limited scope. Those on systemic discrimination, defined by the EEOC as "employment 'systems' which perpetuate discriminatory effects of past discrimination (even after the original discriminatory acts have ceased) as opposed to overt 'acts' of discrimination" (EEOC [15], p. 35), should have a greater impact. Because we cannot identify these types separately, all charges must be treated alike for purposes of this study. Finally, there is some possibility of variation in the choice by the EEOC of which complaints to settle. We ignore this possibility in defining the variables because all investigated complaints in which there is a finding of cause should be followed by an attempted settlement, and this should be determined by the order in which the complaints are received. The settlement variable is thus defined over cases where discrimination appears to exist. Cases where discrimination does not seem to exist drop out between the two measures.

III. THE EMPIRICAL MODEL

We test these two competing hypotheses on the causes of occupational segregation using a linear probability model. The probability of a working woman
or man being employed in a male occupation, $p(mo)$, is estimated as a function
of measures of schooling, experience, labor supply, and EEO programs. We
adapt the human capital earnings function to our purpose of estimating $p(mo)$
by replacing the usual dependent variable, earnings, with a binary variable
indicating whether a person is employed in a nontraditional occupation or in
other occupations. We control for schooling and experience along with other
variables traditionally included in the human capital earnings function. Evidence on the human capital explanation for occupational segregation presented
above is provided by estimates of the labor supply parameters. Coefficient
differences on the EEO variables estimate the success of EEO laws in reducing
the barriers to entry of women into nontraditional occupations.

Once enforcement occurs, variation across states in Title VII's enforcement and across industries in affirmative action should be positively related
to the probability of a working woman being employed in a male occupation.
A positive coefficient in a postenforcement cross-section is evidence of the
success of EEO laws as long as no relationship exists between these variables
before enforcement takes place. Should a prior relationship exist, estimates
from a postenforcement cross-section alone would not provide such evidence.
In this case we must subtract coefficients estimated from a preenforcement
cross-section from the comparable postenforcement coefficients. Thus, the
effect of enforcement is actually measured by a difference over time in coefficients from two comparable cross-sections rather than by a coefficient estimate
from a single postenforcement cross-section. Since most men are employed
in male occupations, changes across states or industries in the occupational
structure between male and other occupations should be picked up by EEO
coefficients estimated on male data. Hence, our methodology involves estimating and comparing pre- and postenforcement cross-sections for both males
and females. The full model consists of equations with preenforcement data
from 1967 or 1971 and postenforcement data from 1974.

The model may be written as follows:

(1) $p_{i,t}^S = b_t^S + E_i\beta_t^S + X_{i,t}^S\gamma_t^S + Z_{i,t}^S\delta_t^S + u_t^S$

and

(2) $p_{i,t-1}^S = b_{t-1}^S + E_i\beta_{t-1}^S + X_{i,t-1}^S\gamma_{t-1}^S + Z_{i,t-1}^S\delta_{t-1}^S + u_{t-1}^S$

where p_i = the probability that the ith individual working woman or man
will be employed in a male occupation, E_i = a vector of (j) EEO variables,
j = 1, 2, ..., 5, assigned to each individual by geographic area and type
of employer for Title VII and by industry of employment for federal contract
compliance; X_i = a vector of human capital and labor supply variables; Z_i =

a vector of control variables; β, γ, δ = vectors of parameters on the EEO, human capital and labor supply, and control variables, respectively; u = a disturbance term with expected value equal to zero; and S = sex, where F = female and M = male.

The estimated effect of each EEO measure on the probability of a working woman or man being employed in a male occupation is equal to $(\hat{\beta}^S_{j,t} - \hat{\beta}^S_{j,t-1})$. The estimated effect of each measure on the sex differential in these probabilities, $p^M - p^F$, is equal to $[(\hat{\beta}^M_{j,t} - \hat{\beta}^M_{j,t-1}) - (\hat{\beta}^F_{j,t} - \hat{\beta}^F_{j,t-1})]$.

Data on the 3-digit Census occupations of men and women and on their economic and demographic characteristics are taken from the U.S. Census Bureau's Annual Demographic File of the 1975, 1972, and 1968 Current Population Survey (CPS). All men and women who worked in the previous years, except the self-employed, are included in the samples. Data on Title VII's enforcement come from the compliance files of the EEOC. Data on federal contract compliance were supplied by Smith and Welch.

IV. EMPIRICAL RESULTS

Polachek's human capital explanation predicts differences in labor supply characteristics between individuals in male and in other occupations. By comparing the means of selected variables for persons in male occupations and other occupations, we can ascertain the magnitude of these differences and how they changed between 1967 and 1974.[9]

On average, labor supply and other demographic differences distinguishing the population of working women in nontraditional occupations from those in other occupations diminished over time. In 1967, on average, women in male occupations worked 3.5 more weeks per year, had 0.65 years more education, and had 2.2 years more experience (defined as age – education – 6), and 6.4 percent fewer of them worked part time compared to women in other occupations. Among men, these differences were even larger. Most of these differences among women had narrowed or even disappeared by 1974; only the difference in the proportion working part time was larger. These changes made women in nontraditional occupations more representative of all working women than previously.[10]

How do these characteristics affect the probability that a working woman is employed in a male occupation, and have these parameters, like the average

---

9 Sample means for women and men appear in Appendix Table A-1, available from the author on request.

10 The youngest cohorts of women and black women entered nontraditional occupations at an increasing rate during this period, with the most dramatic change occurring among black women. Their proportion in the nontraditional occupations increased from only 7.9 percent in 1967 to 11 percent in 1974, equal to their percent of other occupations.

values themselves, changed over time? Table 5 presents OLS estimates of the coefficients on labor supply and EEO variables from equations on the probability of being employed in a male occupation for females, and Table 6 presents the same for males.[11]

Are the estimated regression coefficients on the labor supply variables in the direction predicted by the sex-role-differentiation, human capital approach to occupational segregation? The results are mixed. As predicted, women who work part time are between 3.8 and 4.4 times less likely to be employed in male occupations than women who work full time. Women who stated that their main reason for part-year work was "home," taken to represent a greater commitment to work in the home than to work in the market, are 2.8 percent less likely than other women to be employed in nontraditional jobs. But single women are only slightly more likely (around 1.0 percent) than married, spouse-present women to be employed in nontraditional occupations, while other marital status groups are not more likely. Contrary to predictions, the probability that a working woman is employed in a nontraditional occupation increases as the number of children increases, by 0.4 percent per child.

We predicted a positive relationship between weeks worked and the probability of being employed in a nontraditional occupation; $p(mo)^F$ turns out to be a cubic function of weeks worked.[12] For 1974, the probability declines up to 22.7 weeks worked, nearly half a year, rises to 48.9 weeks worked, and then falls again. What the last part of the curve may be telling us is simply that female occupations have shorter vacations than male occupations. Over the range of the curve where most women work, the sign is consistent with the prediction; however, why the probability falls as weeks worked increases to half a year is unclear.[13]

---

11 Logit estimates of the 1974 equation for white females only are presented in Appendix Table A-2, available from the author on request. The results do not differ to any great degree. These estimates were run on the sample of white women only in order to eliminate the race interactions. Nevertheless, the statistical significance of the logit coefficients is in each case virtually identical with that of the OLS coefficients. For this reason we feel confident in emphasizing the significance of the OLS estimates.

12 The predictive ability of the linear probability model can be improved by estimating it as a nonlinear function of some of the variables. We fit the equation on the 1974 female sample and applied the final specification to the other year-sex groups. Only "weeks worked" fit differently than in the usual human capital specification.

13 Since the relationship disappears when we control for broad occupational categories, it may be that the farm labor occupations which are highly male with few weeks worked are causing the negative relationship initially. By broad occupational categories, these results are consistent with Polachek's: differences in weeks worked among women are related to differences in their distribution across the broad occupational categories. But the same relationship does not hold within occupational categories for women, nor does it hold generally for men.

TABLE 5
PROBABILITY OF BEING IN A "MALE" OCCUPATION FOR EMPLOYED
FEMALES IN 1967, 1971, AND 1974, FOR THE UNITED STATES
(*t*-values in parentheses)

Independent Variables[a]	Coefficients		
	1967	1971	1974
Constant	−.010	.297	.400
	(0.36)	(9.01)	(11.44)
Labor supply			
Weeks worked (*WW*)	−.003	−.006	−.009
	(1.06)	(2.13)	(2.91)
WW^2	$.08 \times 10^{-3}$	$.16 \times 10^{-3}$	$.27 \times 10^{-3}$
	(0.80)	(1.38)	(2.18)
WW^3	$-.55 \times 10^{-6}$	$-.14 \times 10^{-5}$	$-.25 \times 10^{-5}$
	(0.50)	(1.00)	(1.81)
Part-time	.0005	−.038	−.044
	(0.10)	(7.05)	(8.03)
Single	−.001	.012	.010
	(0.15)	(1.76)	(1.36)
Other married	.008	−.012	.003
	(1.54)	(1.92)	(0.53)
Number of children	.0002	.001	.004
	(0.11)	(0.68)	(1.60)
Home specialization	−.011	−.009	−.028
	(1.83)	(1.19)	(3.60)
Contract compliance			
Federal share of industry product	.171	.306	.241
	(14.58)	(18.19)	(14.00)
Black*federal share	.110	.006	.103
	(3.40)	(0.15)	(2.29)
Title VII			
Incidence of investigations			
Jan. 1968–March 1972	−.011	−.007	−.008
	(0.51)	(0.27)	(0.27)
April 1972–Dec. 1974	—	−.001	.022
		(0.08)	(2.13)
Probability of successful settlement			
Jan. 1968–March 1972	.012	.016	.033
	(1.26)	(1.36)	(2.79)
April 1972–Dec. 1974	—	−.014	.034
		(1.12)	(2.73)
Number of observations	24,963	24,662	24,925
Mean of dependent variable	.087	.137	.153
R^2	.029	.025	.028

Continued overleaf

TABLE 5 (*Continued*)

Source: Current Population Survey, Annual Demographic File, 1968, 1972, and 1975.
a The equations also include education measured by a spline function and experience
   defined as age – education – 6; dummies for race = black, region, live in an SMSA,
   work for the government; a continuous measure for the local unemployment rate
   in an SMSA or the rest of the state; and interactions between race and most
   variables. The labor supply variables, presented above, are defined as follows: weeks
   worked and number of children are measured continuously and dummy variables
   are used for part-time, single (never married), other marital status groups excluding
   married spouse present, and home specialization, defined as 1 for a woman who
   cites the "main reason for part-year work" as "home." The male equations exclude
   number of children and home and include veteran status and health, defined as 1
   for a man who cites the "main reason for part-year work" as "health." The EEO
   variables are defined in the text. The complete equations are available from the
   author on request.

We observe some sex differences in the determinants of $p(mo)$. As predicted, marital status for men works in a direction opposite to that for women.
Single women, but married men, have the greatest commitment to the labor
force and are most likely to be employed in male-dominated occupations.
Compared to women, men who work part time are a little less likely to be
in male occupations. In 1971 and 1974, men's probability of being in a male
occupation is independent of weeks worked; in 1967 the relationship is opposite
to that of women in 1974—first increasing, then decreasing, then increasing
again.

Does the human capital model explain well who enters the male occupations? The answer would have to be that it does not. First, the logit estimates
on the probability of a white woman being employed in a male occupation
in 1974 indicate virtually no difference in the significance of individual coefficients over the OLS estimates. The human capital model does not distinguish
well the ones from the zeros, especially given the large number of observations,
22,161, and the fair proportion of ones, .1535. Second, even if women have
the same labor supply characteristics as men, their probability of being in a
male occupation would be only slightly higher than it actually is. Attributing
to females the male values of the labor supply characteristics, but assuming
that the female parameters still hold, increases a woman's probability of
being in a male occupation by only 0.4 percent in 1967, 0.8 percent in 1971,
and 1.1 percent in 1974, according to the OLS estimates. According to the
logit estimates, it increases a white woman's probability of being in a male
occupation by 1.6 percent in 1974. Most of these increases come from the
sex differences in the percent working part time and the percent citing "home"
as the main reason for part-year work. Thus, even as women's labor market

TABLE 6

PROBABILITY OF BEING IN A "MALE" OCCUPATION FOR EMPLOYED
MALES IN 1967, 1971, AND 1974, FOR THE UNITED STATES
(*t*-values in parentheses)

Independent Variables[a]	Coefficients		
	1967	1971	1974
Constant	.094	.913	.865
	(2.23)	(26.34)	(24.00)
Labor supply			
Weeks worked (*WW*)	.019	−.003	$.31 \times 10^{-3}$
	(4.37)	(0.62)	(0.08)
WW²	$-.64 \times 10^{-3}$	44×10^{-5}	$-.54 \times 10^{-4}$
	(3.67)	(0.03)	(0.37)
WW³	$.71 \times 10^{-5}$	$-.37 \times 10^{-6}$	$.89 \times 10^{-6}$
	(3.60)	(0.24)	(0.55)
Part-time	−.071	−.058	−.085
	(7.28)	(7.39)	(10.74)
Single	−.111	−.059	−.070
	(12.55)	(8.03)	(9.50)
Other married	−.045	−.012	−.033
	(3.94)	(1.26)	(3.59)
Health	.001	.023	.014
	(0.07)	(1.81)	(1.06)
Contract compliance			
Federal share of industry product	.140	.144	.135
	(10.78)	(12.07)	(10.52)
Black*federal share	−.019	.051	−.005
	(0.44)	(1.32)	(0.13)
Title VII			
Incidence of investigations			
Jan. 1968–March 1972	.018	.018	−.002
	(0.64)	(0.68)	(0.08)
April 1972–Dec. 1974	—	.028	.037
		(2.90)	(3.76)
Probability of successful settlement			
Jan. 1968–March 1972	.027	.038	.025
	(2.02)	(3.24)	(2.11)
April 1972–Dec. 1974	—	.021	−.012
		(1.56)	(0.92)
Number of observations	35,230	33,664	31,881
Mean of dependent variable	.604	.807	.805
R^2	.106	.052	.060

Source: Same as Table 5
a Same as Table 5.

behavior approaches that of men, it is expected to increase their entry into male occupations very little. From these results we conclude that the answer to the occupational segregation problem must lie elsewhere.

EEO Laws and the Discrimination Hypothesis

We argued above that if EEO laws increased the entry of women into non-traditional occupations, this would suggest initial discrimination. According to the empirical estimates, both Title VII of the Civil Rights Act and the federal contract compliance program increased working women's chances of being employed in a male occupation between 1967 and 1974. The effects of Title VII are stronger after the law was amended in 1972, while, conversely, the affirmative action aspects of contract compliance, strong initially, eroded somewhat after 1971.

The enforcement variables in preenforcement cross sections were unrelated to the probability of women being employed in male occupations: the Title VII coefficients are insignificant in the 1967 and 1971 cross-sections in Table 5. Were this true in the male equations as well, the effect of Title VII's subsequent enforcement could be measured by the coefficients from postenforcement cross-sections alone. But, as seen in Table 6, the preamendment probability of successful settlement and the postamendment incidence of investigations are both postively related to the likelihood of males being employed in male occupations, which can be taken to indicate a more male occupational structure. Thus, in order to compute the effect of enforcement net of these preexisting differences in the occupational structure, we present coefficient differences on the four Title VII variables in Table 7.

According to Table 7, all of the coefficient differences are positive for females, and three out of the four are negative for males. Moreover, all Title VII measures narrowed the sex differential in the probability of being employed in a male occupation ($p^M - p^F$).[14] An increase of one investigation per 1000 employed women before the 1972 amendments narrowed the sex differential in the probability of being employed in a nontraditional occupation in 1974 by 2.3 percent, and after the amendments by 1.4 percent. An increase in the probability of successful settlement from 0 to 1 narrowed the sex differential by 2.4 percent for preamendment enforcement and by 8.0 percent for post-

---

14   Controlling for broad 2-digit Census occupation enables us to estimate the effect of Title VII on changes in the rate of entry into male occupations within broad occupational categories. The remainder of the overall effect is due to movement across categories, say from clerical to managerial, or from operative to crafts occupations. Controlling for broad occupation reduces three of the four positive effects for females, but alters none of the effects for males. Thus, much of Title VII's effect on women is through transfers across broad occupational groups. Significantly though, Title VII reduces the likelihood that men are employed in male occupations not by forcing them out of their major occupational group, but by moving them into less male 3-digit occupations within their broad occupational category.

TABLE 7

ESTIMATED EFFECT OF TITLE VII ON THE PROBABILITY
OF BEING IN A MALE OCCUPATION, BY SEX, 1967–1974

| | Sex | | Sex Differential |
	Females (1)	Males (2)	(2) – (1)
Preamendment enforcement			
Investigations/1000			
employed women	+.0025	−.0202	−.0227
Settlements	+.0216	−.0025	−.0241
Postamendment enforcement			
Investigations	+.0225	+.0089	−.0136
Settlements	+.0474	−.0324	−.0798

Source: Same as Table 5

Note: The numbers in this table are coefficient differences on the Title VII enforcement variables between 1967 and 1974 for preamendment enforcement, and between 1971 and 1974 for postamendment enforcement and are computed from the estimates shown in Tables 5 and 6.

amendment enforcement. This latter effect is the largest and probably the most significant estimated: where the EEOC had successfully conciliated charges of sex discrimination between April 1972 and December 1974, the sex differential in the probability of being in a male occupation was 8.0 percent smaller in 1974.[15] Summing across all four Title VII measures, evaluating change at the mean of each enforcement measure, we find that between 1967 and 1974, on the average, Title VII narrowed by 6.2 percent the sex differential in the probability of being employed in a male occupation.[16] (The

---

15 Stronger postamendment effects were predicted and are found for settlements but not for investigations. Since the investigations variable may be more influenced by changes in women's attitudes as well as by the effects of the legislation per se, the strong results for postamendment settlements thus appear to provide some support for the hypothesis. Since the effects of legislative changes are expected to occur with at least some lag, the results might be greater if we had a longer time period available since the amendments took effect.

16 We also performed these estimates and computations for equations in which the dependent variable measured continuously the proportion male in the individual's 3-digit Census occupation. In this formulation, the coefficient differences on the Title VII variables are smaller and less significant, but are basically in the same direction. The dichotomous specification is probably better, especially for females, since their earnings first increase and then decrease as the "maleness" of male occupations increases. Thus, based on earnings variation, treating male occupations as a single unit to compare with other occupations seems appropriate. Moreover, a frequency distribution on the 1960 proportion male in occupations reveals a dichotomous clustering around very low and very high male proportions. And, finally, we

TABLE 8
ESTIMATED EFFECT OF FEDERAL CONTRACT COMPLIANCE
ON THE PROBABILITY OF BEING IN A MALE OCCUPATION,
BY SEX AND RACE, 1967–1974

	Sex				Sex Differential	
	Females		Males			
Race	1967–1971	1967–1974	1967–1971	1967–1974	1967–1971	1967–1974
White	+.135	+.070	+.005	−.005	−.130	−.075
Black	+.031	+.063	+.074	+.009	+.044	−.055
Race differential	+.104	+.007	−.069	−.014	—	—

Source: Same as Table 5.

mean enforcement measures are multiplied by the figures in column 3 to obtain this result.)

The federal contract compliance program also significantly increased the probability that a working woman would be employed in a male-dominated occupation. Table 8 presents estimated coefficient differences on the contract compliance variable, with the effects separated by race. Multiplying these differences by a one standard deviation change in the output an industry sells to the federal government, or by 0.15, narrows the sex differential in the probability of being employed in a male occupation by 2 percent among whites (.15 × −.130) but expands it by 0.6 percent among blacks (.15 × .044) between 1967 and 1971 (Table 8, column 5). Since the probability remains virtually unchanged for white males (column 3), we know that these estimates capture the effects of affirmative action and not merely a structural change toward the male occupations from which women benefited coincidentally. From this estimate, it would appear that affirmative action broke down barriers to the entry of women into nontraditional occupations. However, the remainder of these estimates present a much less optimistic picture.

By 1974, nearly half of the gains white woman had made compared to white men in 1971 are eroded; instead of being 2 percent more likely than in 1967, they are only 1 percent more likely to be employed in a male occupation in an industry that sells an additional 0.15 of its output to the federal government. By contrast, black women appear to have increased their gains, especially relative to black men, but this only brings them closer to a

do not expect EEO laws to affect entry into nonmale occupations relative to one another, nor to have a larger effect the more male the male occupation is. Rather, we expect the law to treat segregated-male occupations as one unit differently from other occupations.

par with the gains of white women. One can speculate that the recession eroded the gains from affirmative action, once again confirming the "last hired, first fired" scenario.[17]

Adding the effect of the contract compliance program to that of Title VII, evaluated at their respective means, yields a total estimated effect of EEO laws: between 1967 and 1974, they narrowed by 6.6 percent the sex differential in the probability of being employed in a male occupation. Economy-wide, affirmative action adds only 0.4 percent to the total effect because few individuals are employed in industries that are widely affected by the program. (Alternatively, it is possible that our measure of the program is a poor indicator for the economy as a whole.) The mean federal share is only 6 percent for women and 9 percent for men. While the effect of the program would be quite large among industries that are heavy contractors, only a limited number of women can benefit since most are employed in other industries. Despite these limitations, the contract compliance program, along with Title VII, did increase women's entry into nontraditional occupations, suggesting that these programs are working.

We argued above, with qualifications, that the success of EEO laws in increasing women's entry into male occupations would be convincing evidence that discrimination had originally been a cause of occupational segregation. By analogy, if a law reverses the effects caused by discrimination, then discrimination probably existed. EEO laws narrowed the sex differential in the probability of being employed in a male occupation by about 6.6 percent. This figure suggests that EEO laws lowered barriers to the entry of women into male occupations and also that discrimination against women in the male occupations was a significant determinant of occupational segregation. EEO laws moved the distribution slightly closer to equality. By contrast, the human capital approach had very little to contribute to explaining occupational segregation empirically. At the outside, even if women behaved as men do with respect to the labor market, the sex differential in the probability of being employed in a male occupation would be narrowed by only 1.1 percent.

V. CONCLUSION

Although occupational segregation of the sexes is extreme, we find evidence

---

17 Controlling for broad occupation, we find that in 1971 slightly less than half of the narrowing in the sex differential in probabilities ($p^M - p^F$) caused by the contract compliance program occurred within broad occupational groups and slightly more than half by movement across groups. By 1974, all of the gains within occupational groups had been lost, and only the improvements across groups remained. Whether or not a connection should be made, we simply note that the across-broad-occupation changes must be reported on EEO-1 employer reports that employers over a certain size are required to file annually with the EEOC, but changes within occupational groups are not reported.

that it began to diminish during the 1970s and that the decline is associated with the successful enforcement of EEO laws against sex discrimination in employment. Both Title VII of the Civil Rights Act of 1964 and the federal contract compliance program were found to have increased a working woman's probability of being employed in a male occupation compared to a man's probability. The success of EEO laws suggests that discrimination was a determinant of occupational segregation originally, as argued by Bergmann.

We found mixed evidence on Polachek's human capital explanation of occupational segregation. We saw, however, that differences in both labor supply and other human capital characteristics between women in male and in other occupations have narrowed, suggesting that, in any case, the importance of labor supply differences as a determinant of occupational segregation is declining.

REFERENCES

1. Orley Ashenfelter and James Heckman. "Measuring the Effect of an Antidiscrimination Program." In *Evaluating the Labor Market Effects of Social Programs,* eds. Orley Ashenfelter and James Blum. Princeton, N.J.: Industrial Relations Section, Princeton University, 1976.
2. Andrea H. Beller. "The Economics of Enforcement of an Antidiscrimination Law: Title VII of the Civil Rights Act of 1964." *Journal of Law and Economics* 21 (October 1978): 359–80.
3. ————. "The Impact of Equal Employment Opportunity Laws on the Male/Female Earnings Differential." In *Women in the Labor Market,* ed. Cynthia B. Lloyd. New York: Columbia University Press, 1979.
4. Barbara Bergmann. "Occupational Segregation, Wages and Profits When Employers Discriminate by Race or Sex." *Eastern Economic Journal* 1 (April-July 1974): 103–10.
5. Francine D. Blau and Carol L. Jusenius. "Economists' Approaches to Sex Segregation in the Labor Market: An Appraisal." *Signs* 1 (Spring 1976:2): 181–200.
6. Michael J. Boskin. "A Conditional Logit Model of Occupational Choice." *Journal of Political Economy* 82 (March/April 1974): 389–98.
7. Victor R. Fuchs. "Differences in Hourly Earnings Between Men and Women." *Monthly Labor Review* 94 (May 1971): 9–15.
8. James J. Heckman and Kenneth I. Wolpin. "Does the Contract Compliance Program Work: An Analysis of Chicago Data." *Industrial and Labor Relations Review* 29 (July 1976): 544–64.
9. Carol L. Jusenius. "The Influence of Work Experience, Skill Requirement, and Occupational Segregation on Women's Earnings." *Journal of Economics and Business* 29 (Winter 1977): 107–15.
10. Ronald Oaxaca. "Male-Female Wage Differentials in Urban Labor Markets." *International Economic Review* 14 (October 1973): 693–709.
11. Solomon W. Polachek. "Occupational Segregation Among Women: Theory, Evi-

dence, and a Prognosis." In *Women in the Labor Market,* ed. Cynthia B. Lloyd. New York: Columbia University Press, 1979.

12. John A. Priebe. "1970 Occupation and Industry Classification Systems in Terms of Their 1960 Occupation and Industry Elements." U.S. Bureau of the Census, Technical Papers No. 26, 1972.

13. James P. Smith and Finis R. Welch. "Black/White Male Earnings and Employment: 1960–1970." R-1666-DOL. Santa Monica, Calif.: Rand Corporation, June 1975.

14. Dixie Sommers. "Occupational Rankings for Men and Women by Earnings." *Monthly Labor Review* 97 (August 1974): 34–51.

15. U.S. Equal Employment Opportunity Commission. *Ninth Annual Report.* Washington: U.S. Government Printing Office, 1975.

16. Harriet Zellner. "Discrimination Against Women, Occupational Segregation and the Relative Wage." *American Economic Review* 62 (May 1972): 157–60.

[17]

THE FAILURE OF HUMAN CAPITAL THEORY TO EXPLAIN OCCUPATIONAL SEX SEGREGATION*

PAULA ENGLAND

ABSTRACT

Predictions from Polachek's theory explaining occupational sex segregation are tested and found to be false. The NLS data do not show that women are penalized less for time spent out of the labor force if they choose predominantly female occupations than if they choose occupations more typical for males. Thus, there is no evidence that plans for intermittent employment make women's choice of traditionally female occupations economically rational. It is not surprising, then, that NLS women with more continuous employment histories are no more apt to be in predominantly male occupations than women who have been employed less continuously. I conclude that human capital theory has not generated an explanation of occupational sex segregation that fits the evidence.

I. INTRODUCTION

A striking characteristic of workplaces is the segregation of women and men into different occupations. In several recent papers Polachek argues that human capital theory can provide an explanation for occupational sex segregation [15, 16, 18]. In this paper I show that the propositions derived from Polachek's theory conflict with empirical evidence and conclude that human capital theory cannot explain the bulk of occupational sex segregation.[1]

The author is Associate Professor of Sociology and Political Economy, University of Texas at Dallas.

* This paper was prepared for the 1980 meetings of the Southwest Economics Association, Houston, Tex. The research was supported by NIMH grant 5T 32 MH 14670 03 while the author was a postdoctoral fellow at Duke University. Discussions with the following people have helped me clarify the arguments presented here: E.M. Beck, Tabitha Doescher, Carol Jusenius, Peter Lewin, Solomon Polachek, Barbara Reagan, and Mary Beth Walker. My thanks to each of them. [Manuscript received March 1980; accepted July 1980.]

1 Polachek and Mincer [12, 13, 14, 17] also use human capital theory to develop an explanation of the gap between men's and women's earnings. This paper addresses the adequacy of the explanation offered by human capital theory for segregation, but does not discuss whether their explanation of sex differences in earnings is valid.

The Journal of Human Resources • XVII • 3

0022-166X/82/0003-358 $01.50/0

Polachek's segregation theory starts from the fact that women's employment is intermittent because of domestic responsibilities. (The fact that women rather than men take responsibility for childbearing and housework, as well as the fact that these tasks are performed outside of what we usually call markets, must be explained outside of the model he proposes.) While women are out of the labor force, their job skills are usually depreciating rather than appreciating as they would be in any job that involved training. It is economically rational for women who plan to spend a lot of time out of the labor force to choose jobs with low penalties for intermittent employment. Thus, even in the absence of discrimination by employers, maximizing choices made by the suppliers of labor will lead to occupational sex segregation, according to Polachek. He states: "If life cycle labor force participation differs across individuals, and if the costs of these varying degrees of labor force intermittency vary across occupations, then individuals will choose those occupations with the smallest penalty for their desired lifetime participation" [15, p. 144].

In Polachek's model the lower current wages of those who have spent more time out of the labor force result from both depreciation and forgone appreciation.[2] An occupation's rate of depreciation for a woman is revealed by the extent that her real wages upon returning to the occupation after time at home are lower than they were when she resigned her job to take up full-time homemaking. Thus, Polachek's hypothesis is that women who plan intermittent employment will prefer occupations with lower penalties for depreciation, whereas men or women who plan continuous employment will have no reason to avoid jobs with high depreciation risks.

It is less obvious why Polachek thinks women will choose occupations with low rewards for experience (that is, low appreciation). For even if one plans only intermittent employment, greater lifetime earnings accrue in an occupation that rewards what little experience one does accumulate. Indeed, even if occupations with high appreciation also have higher depreciation, it pays women to choose such occupations if the higher rate of appreciation while they are employed more than compensates for the high rate of depreciation they suffer while at home [4, note 6]. Why, then, does Polachek regard a high rate of appreciation as indicative of a high *penalty* for intermittency? His reasoning presumably stems from the neoclassical assumption that occupations with lower appreciation offer higher starting wages [23], and, conversely, that occupations with high appreciation can offer lower starting wages.

---

2   Polachek's metaphoric use of the term "atrophy" suggests that only depreciation rates of occupations are relevant for explaining sex segregation. However, he has confirmed in private conversation (January 1980) that he believes both depreciation and appreciation rates to be relevant, and that he views jobs with high appreciation rates as posing a "penalty" to those planning intermittence because of the lower starting wages that he presumes go along with them.

For women who are employed only a short time, the higher starting wages that jobs with low appreciation are reputed to offer may make them attractive, despite the low rates of appreciation. This point is standard in the human capital literature, but has not been made explicit in Polachek's writing.

We may conclude that high appreciation indexes an occupation's penalty for intermittence only when (1) the rate of appreciation is not high enough to make up for the rate of depreciation in the occupation, and (2) the starting wages in the occupation are low enough that they more than offset the effect of appreciation on the projected lifetime earnings of women planning intermittent employment. Showing that predominantly male occupations offer women higher appreciation would not be sufficient as confirmation of Polachek's theory without empirical tests of these two conditions.

Both appreciation and depreciation can be explained from either a neoclassical or an institutionalist perspective. Human capital theory explains appreciation in terms of the greater productivity of experienced workers, along with the assumption that labor is paid according to its marginal productivity. Similarly, neoclassical proponents of human capital theory see depreciation as a result of one's skill getting either rusty or obsolete. In contrast, institutionalists see some of the relationship between employment continuity and earnings as a result of legal, contractual, or traditional agreements in the workplace which have little to do with productivity. For example, seniority clauses in union contracts are often explained as institutionalized appreciation. Either theory could lead to sex segregation through the incentives they create for women to choose certain jobs, though Polachek favors the neoclassical view.

The empirical analysis presented in this paper refutes two predictions generated from Polachek's theory of segregation. First, I show that the earnings of women in predominantly female occupations do not show lower rates of either depreciation or appreciation than do the earnings of women in occupations containing more males. Second, I will show that women who have spent more of their postschool years out of the labor force are no more apt to be in predominantly female occupations than are women who have been employed more continuously. The analysis makes use of the sample of women 30 to 44 years of age from the 1967 National Longitudinal Survey (NLS). (See [21] for a description of the data.)

II. SPECIFYING A MODEL TO ESTIMATE OCCUPATION-SPECIFIC PENALTIES FOR INTERMITTENT EMPLOYMENT

Estimating Appreciation and Depreciation

Polachek [15, 16] assesses penalties for intermittence by estimating the following two wage functions for women, ages 30 to 44, in each of nine (or five) occupations:

$$(1) \qquad W = a_1 + b_1S + b_2Y + b_3H + e_1$$
$$(2) \qquad W = a_2 + b_4S + b_5P + e_2$$

where W = hourly earnings (ln used by Polachek); S = years of school; Y = years of labor force exposure, that is age ($= A$) minus S minus 6; H = postschool years spent out of the labor force at home;[3] P = percent of postschool years spent at home ($= H/(A - S - 6)$); and e = error term representing all other determinants of earnings.

Polachek takes the coefficient on percent hometime to reveal the effect on current earnings of the combination of depreciation and forgone appreciation. Having spent a higher proportion of one's postschool years at home indicates less time for possible appreciation as well as more time in which job skills could depreciate. The coefficient on years of hometime is interpreted by Polachek as a measure of depreciation that does not include any effects of forgone appreciation. That is, he sees the coefficient on H as measuring the effects on earnings of the erosion of skills rather than of the failure to increase skills during hometime (see [15, note 17] and [14, pp. 105–107]). While it is true that the coefficient on hometime is less affected by appreciation than is the coefficient on percent hometime, Polachek fails to realize that the former also picks up some of the effect of appreciation; it is not a net measure of depreciation. If years of labor force exposure is held constant, women who differ on years of time spent at home will, by definition, differ by the same number of years in employment experience. Thus, the coefficient on years of hometime in equation (1) will pick up some of the effect of experience on earnings.

The specification below shows a rearrangement of terms in equation (1) to provide distinct estimates of both depreciation during hometime and appreciation through experience:

$$(3) \qquad W = a_3 + b_6S + b_7H + b_8E + e$$

where all notation is as above and E = years of labor force experience ($= A - S - 6 - H$). Clearly, $b_2 = b_8$ and $b_3 = b_7 - b_8$. Since I have argued above that occupations' rates of depreciation more clearly constitute *penalties* for intermittence than do their rates of appreciation, it is desirable to have a measure of depreciation which is as uncontaminated as possible by

---

3 The available measures of hometime and experience differ slightly between the data sets used by Polachek, the NLS (described in [16]) and the PSID (described in [12]). In the NLS the respondents were asked in how many of their postschool years they had been employed for at least six months. The PSID asked women in how many years they had worked for pay since they were age 18.

TABLE 1

POLACHEK'S FEMALE PENALTY RATES FOR OCCUPATIONAL GROUPS

Occupational Group	NLS Data[a] Percent Hometime[c]	PSID Data[b] Percent Hometime[d]	PSID Data[b] Years Hometime[c]	Average % Female of Detailed Occupations in the Groups[e]
Professionals	—	−.27	−.004	65
Teachers	−.13[f]	—	—	71
Other	−.19	—	—	62
Managers	−.59	−.42	−.024	17
Clerical and sales	—	−.24	−.004	74
Clerical	−.40	—	—	80
Sales	−.17	—	—	47
Craft	−.64	—	—	19
Operative	−.06	−.18	−.014	52
Unskilled	—	−.15	+.007	84
Household	+.56	—	—	97
Service	−.21	—	—	80

Sources: NLS rates from Polachek [16]. PSID rates from Polachek [15]. Sex composition of occupation groups from NLS data.

a   NLS data described in [21]. Respondents are females aged 30–44 in 1967.
b   PSID data described in [9]. Polachek limited his analyses to white women 30–50 years of age in 1976.
c   Regression coefficient on H in equation (2). See text.
d   Regression coefficient on P in equation (1). See text.
e   Computed by taking the mean of the percent female of the 1967 or most recent Census across respondents in this broad occupational group.
f   Negative sign on penalty rate indicates a loss associated with hometime. Polachek's papers reverse the signs.

effects of forgone appreciation. Specification (3) shows this directly. In the analyses that follow, I present estimates of penalty rates from each of the equations (1), (2), and (3) above.

Choosing Occupational Categories

Polachek contends that variation in occupations' penalties creates different optimal occupational choices for those anticipating continuous employment than for those planning more intermittent employment. Thus, he collapses the Census major occupational groups into five categories in one analysis and into nine in another (see Table 1 for his categories). *My analysis differs from Polachek's primarily in categorizing occupations by their sex composition so that we can test whether occupations with relatively low penalties*

TABLE 2

PENALTY RATES FOR WHITE FEMALES' EMPLOYMENT INTERMITTENCE
BY OCCUPATIONAL SEX COMPOSITION

Occupational Group	Betas Measuring Effects on 1967 Hourly Earnings in $				N
	Equation (1)	Equation (2)	Equation (3)		
	Hometime	Hometime	Employment Experience	Hometime	
Sex composition of respondent's detailed Census occupation:					
0–20% female	−.06*	−.13*	−.03*	−.02	137
20.1–40% female	−.02*	−.51*	.01	−.02	256
40.1–60% female	−.04*	−.75*	.02	−.02	245
60.1–80% female	−.03*	−.59*	.01	−.02	394
80.1–100% female	−.04*	−.75*	.03*	−.01	845

Source: 1967 NLS data described in [21].

Notes: For specifications of equations (1), (2), and (3), see text. For 28 respondents number of postschool years in which she was employed was recorded as larger than total number of postschool years. These 28 cases were dropped from all analyses reported in Tables 2 and 3.

* The regression coefficient is significant at the .01 level.

for intermittency are those in which females are most heavily concentrated.

My sample, like Polachek's, is restricted to females, which avoids confounding penalty rates with wage discrimination. In addition, Polachek's theory proposes that *women* are penalized less for intermittence in female than in male occupations. Polachek [16] used the sample of women aged 30 to 44 in 1967 provided by the National Longitudinal Survey (NLS, described in [21]). I have used these same data for my analysis. Polachek has also tested his model on a female subsample from the Panel Study of Income Dynamics (PSID, described in [9]).

A first approach collapses the (more than 300) detailed Census occupational categories into five groups according to their sex composition. Each of the three earnings functions discussed above is estimated on each of the five groups: those containing 0–20 percent female, 20.1–40 percent female, etc. These results, which will be discussed later, are in Table 2.

A second approach also tests the hypothesis that the coefficients on hometime and employment vary according to occupations' percent female, but it pools all the occupations into one regression rather than fitting a separate regression for each occupational group. The percent female (= F)

of respondents' detailed Census occupation is an additive variable that is added to equations (1), (2), and (3), and F is interacted with H, P, and E in each equation, respectively (see Table 3, which will be discussed later). If the penalty rates that are indicated by the coefficients on H, P, or E are lower in predominantly female occupations, then FH and FP should have positive effects and FE should have a negative effect. In this pooled specification the sample size is much larger, although a common error-variance is assumed.

Polachek's theory refers to occupational choices made early in one's adult life on the basis of plans for employment intermittence, but a woman's *current* occupation may not coincide with this choice. Indeed, Polachek justifies using only five (or nine) broad occupational categories because this "minimizes the amount of occupational mobility within the data, so that lifetime occupational choices can be dealt with explicitly" [15, p. 145]. It turns out that my categories of occupational groups, based on the percent female, show about the same amount of occupational mobility between the respondents' first and current (1967) occupation as do Polachek's categories.[4] And, as I have argued above, using the percent female to categorize occupations is more relevant for testing the theory he proposes.

Alternate Specifications

Following Polachek's later paper [15], I present results on white women only. This removes any spurious effects of race discrimination from the coefficients of interest. Unlike Polachek, I use the arithmetic rather than logarithmic values of wages. However, the regression results reported in Tables 2 and 3 are similar substantively whether arithmetic or logarithmic wages is the dependent variable, whether black women are included or excluded, and whether

---

4   To see how minimal the movement between Polachek's broad occupational categories is, I have rank-ordered his categories (from [15] and [16]) according to the average percent female each contains. After giving this theoretically relevant ordinal dimension to Polachek's occupational categorization, I have computed the Pearson correlation between the rank of NLS respondents' first and 1967 occupational category. Over his five-occupation categorization, the correlation is .40; over his nine-occupation categorization it is .35. The two categorizations I have chosen for occupations yields similar correlations: .39 between the percent female of respondents' first and 1967 detailed Census occupation, and .36 when first and 1967 occupations are divided into five categories on the basis of their sex composition. The fact that the correlations between first and 1967 job are as high across my occupational categorization as across Polachek's categories demonstrates that grouping occupations by sex composition is as well suited for capturing lifetime choices as are the categories employed by Polachek.

Polachek considers occupation to be a nonordinal variable [15]. But if differences in penalty rates are to explain segregation, these differences must correlate with the ordinal dimension of occupational sex composition. Numerous of Polachek's comments suggest (without evidence) that penalty rates are correlated with the ordinal dimension of skill and training requirements, but this assertion is not logically necessary to his theory. For evidence that the skill demands of female occupations compare quite favorably with those in male occupations, see [8].

control variables for hours worked and number of children are added or not. Thus, the tests of Polachek's theory that are reported below seem quite robust.

III. PENALTIES FOR INTERMITTENCE IN MALE AND FEMALE OCCUPATIONS: EMPIRICAL FINDINGS

Table 1 collects Polachek's empirical findings on the penalty rates of various occupations. We see that occupations which employ a higher proportion of females do not consistently show lower penalties, as Polachek's theory predicts. In the NLS data, clericals suffer higher penalties for percent hometime than either nonteaching professionals or operatives, and service workers have higher rates than operatives. In the PSID data (described in [9]), operatives experience less penalty for percent hometime than do those in clerical and sales work, and penalties to years of hometime are the same for professionals as for clerical and sales workers. There are enough discrepancies from the prediction of Polachek's theory to cast doubt on its validity. Particularly serious is the failure of clerical and sales occupations to show consistently lower penalties than occupations with more males, since about 40 percent of employed women do clerical or sales work. A supply-side theory of segregation that cannot explain women's choices of these jobs is hardly convincing. However, in fairness to Polachek's thesis, one should note that the prediction that predominantly female occupations have lower penalties for intermittence hardly receives a fair test with the occupational groups he used; the categories of professional, sales, operative, and service each contain some detailed occupational categories that are segregated enclaves for *each* gender.

To improve on Polachek's occupational categorization by making categories nonoverlapping on the theoretically relevant dimension of sex composition, I have divided detailed Census occupational categories into five groups (containing 0–20 percent female, 20.1–40 percent female, etc.). Estimates of the penalty rates for intermittence suffered by NLS women are presented in Table 2 for each of the five occupational groups. The results do not show the predicted monotonic relationship between occupations' sex composition and either depreciation or appreciation. In equation (2) the coefficients on percent hometime, which measure a combination of depreciation and forgone appreciation, are significantly larger for women in occupations with more than 40 percent female than for those in occupations with less than 40 percent female.[5] The effects of hometime in equation (1) (which tap both depreciation and forgone appreciation) show no monotonic relationship to occupations' sex composition, which we also see in the reparameterization of

---

5 I have assumed a *t*-distribution for the standard error of the difference between the two regression coefficients.

366 | THE JOURNAL OF HUMAN RESOURCES

TABLE 3

REGRESSIONS ON WHITE FEMALES' HOURLY EARNINGS

	Equation (4)	Equation (5)	Equation (6)	Equation (7)
Constant ($/hour)	.46	.99	.48	.41
Regression coefficients (on $/Hour)				
S: Schooling (years)	.15*	.14*	.15*	.15*
Y: Years since school	.02*	b	b	b
H: Hometime (years)	−.04*	b	−.02	−.02*
P: % hometime (10% = unit)[a]	b	−.09*	b	b
E: Employment experience (years)	b	b	.02	.02*
F: Occupation's % female (10% = unit)[a]	−.03*	−.04*	−.03	−.02*
H × F[a]	(+).00	b	(+).00	b
P × F[a]	b	.03	b	b
E × F[a]	b	b	(+).00	b
R^2	.16	.16	.16	.16
N	1877	1877	1877	1877
Mean hourly earnings	2.07	2.07	2.07	2.07

Source: 1967 NLS data described in [21].

a Regression coefficients for percent female in respondent's detailed 1960 occupational category and percent hometime are expressed in metric of 10% = 1 unit.

b Variable not entered in this equation.

* Regression coefficient is statistically significant at the .05 level, two-tailed test.

the estimates of the net effects of appreciation and depreciation in equation (3). This categorization of occupations by sex composition provides no evidence that predominantly female occupations offer women lower rates of either depreciation or forgone appreciation.

The estimates from the pooled-occupation specifications appear in Table 3. If the effects of experience and hometime vary by occupations' sex composition, then the interaction terms in regressions (4), (5), and (6) should be significant, but none of them is. This means that there is no significant tendency for predominantly female occupations to offer women lower rates of depreciation or forgone appreciation. Since there is no evidence that choosing a predominantly female occupation promises optimization of lifetime earnings for women planning intermittence, there is no economic incentive for women to segregate themselves voluntarily into traditionally female occupations. In fact, equation (7) in Table 3 shows that net of education, hometime, and experience, women have lower wages if they are in predominantly female occupations. Women do not maximize lifetime earnings by working in traditionally female occupations; on the contrary, they earn less in such occupations at every level of experience.

IV. EMPLOYMENT INTERMITTENCY AND TRADITIONAL OCCUPATIONAL CHOICES: EMPIRICAL FINDINGS

If Polachek's explanation of segregation is correct, we should also find that women whose employment is more continuous have occupational distributions more like those of men. Yet there is very little evidence to support this notion.

Zellner [23] tested the hypothesis indirectly. She reasoned that if women expecting more constant employment choose male occupations more frequently, there should be a correlation between variables known to influence women's employment stability, such as the number of children, and the sex composition of their occupations. Contrary to this prediction, she found that, among married employed women, neither having more children nor younger children increased the probability of a woman being employed in a predominantly female occupation in 1970.

With the same rationale, I have used the NLS data to compare the sex composition of the occupations for married and single employed women. Presumably single women anticipate more constant employment, but those NLS white women who had never been married and had no children were no less apt to be in predominantly female occupations than were other white women. The mean percent female of the women's occupations was 68 for both groups.

Polachek has presented data to support the notion that women planning intermittent employment are more apt to choose female occupations; however, in my view the data he presents do not support his contention. He has shown that those male and female college students expecting the most years of employment tend to major in business, engineering, education, or biology, while those who expect fewer years of employment tend to major in the humanities, physical sciences (other than biology), or social sciences [18]. Yet education students are disproportionately female and physical scientists are usually male; in neither of these cases is the prediction of his theory upheld.

Polachek has also predicted how women's occupational distribution would change if they were employed continuously [15, Table 9.7]. He projects that more women would be professionals, managers, and operatives, and fewer would be in clerical, sales, or unskilled (service or labor) jobs. The projection into such broad occupational groups tells us very little about what women's

TABLE 4

RELATIONSHIP OF PROPORTION OF POSTSCHOOL YEARS SPENT
EMPLOYED TO SEX COMPOSITION
OF WHITE WOMEN'S MOST RECENT OCCUPATION

Percent Female in Detailed Census Occupational Category of Women's Most Recent Job	Average Proportion of Years Between Completion of Schooling and 1967 in Which Women Were in the Labor Force at Least 6 Months	N
0–9.9	.43	58
10–19.9	.52	204
20–29.9	.53	115
30–39.9	.44	336
40–49.9	.42	369
50–59.9	.46	146
60–69.9	.43	616
70–79.9	.40	214
80–89.9	.44	706
90–100	.48	990
All occupations	.45	3754

Source: 1967 NLS data described in [21].

continuous employment would do to sex segregation since the categories of professionals, sales, operatives, and unskilled workers each contain both male and female occupations.

Wolf and Rosenfeld [22] lend weak support to Polachek's theory. They found that either men or women who had been out of the labor force in 1965 were slightly more likely to be in female occupations in 1970 than those whose had been employed in both 1965 and 1970, and those who were employed in both years were slightly more apt to be in predominantly male occupations than those who were out of the labor force in 1965. (Census detailed occupation categories containing 70 to 100 percent female were labeled "female"; categories with 0 to 25 percent female were called "male.")

However, a direct test of the hypothesis that women whose employment is more continuous are more apt to choose male occupations is possible with the NLS since it records the number of postschool years in which women have been in the labor force for at least six months. Whether the sample consists of all women or white women, the simple correlation between the proportion of postschool years spent employed and the sex composition of women's most recent detailed occupational category is not statistically significant (see Table 4). Nor is there a significant correlation between the percent female of one's first job and the proportion of postschool years eventually spent in the labor force.

In summary, the bulk of evidence does not confirm that women with more continuous employment plans or histories are more apt to be in occupations containing more males.

V. CONCLUSION

Polachek's explanation of occupational segregation, based on human capital theory, is not supported regarding two major predictions. First, the NLS data do not show that women are penalized less for time spent out of the labor force if they choose female occupations. Thus, there is no evidence that plans for intermittent employment make women's choice of a traditionally female occupation economically rational. Indeed, holding schooling, hometime, and experience constant, women have higher wages if they are employed in an occupation containing more males. Second, NLS women with more continuous employment histories are no less apt than other women to be in predominantly female occupations. We must tentatively conclude that human capital theory has not generated an explanation of occupational sex segregation that fits the evidence.

These negative findings have two implications for future research. A powerful replication of the above tests would make use of the longitudinal aspects of either the NLS or PSID data. Since the same respondents were surveyed in several different years, the analysis could ascertain how experience and hometime change women's real earnings over time, and whether these relationships vary with the sex composition of one's occupation. If, as I suspect, such a replication does not confirm the explanation of segregation generated by human capital theory, empirical attention should be given to explanations generated by other theoretical perspectives (for a review, see [7]). Bearing in mind that supply- and demand-side explanations are not mutually exclusive, social scientists need to investigate the complementary relationships between sex role socialization and market discrimination.

REFERENCES

1. Gary Becker. *Human Capital,* 2nd ed. New York: Columbia University Press, 1975.
2. Mark Blaug. "The Empirical Status of Human Capital Theory: A Slightly Jaundiced Survey." *Journal of Economic Literature* 14 (September 1976): 827–55.
3. Martha Blaxall and Barbara Reagan, eds. *Women and the Workplace: The Implications of Occupational Segregation.* Chicago: University of Chicago Press, 1976.
4. Patricia Brito and Carol Jusenius. "Career Aspirations of Young Women: Factors Underlying Choice of a Typically Male or Typically Female Occupation." Paper presented at the American Statistical Association meetings, San Diego, 1978.

370 | THE JOURNAL OF HUMAN RESOURCES

5. College Placement Council. "A Study of 1973–74 Beginning Offers." Final Report. Bethlehem, Pa.: College Placement Council, July 1974.
6. Paula England. "Assessing Trends in Occupational Sex Segregation, 1900–1976." In *Sociological Perspectives on Labor Markets,* ed. Ivar Berg. New York: Academic Press, 1981. Pp. 273–95.
7. ————. "Explanations of Occupational Sex Segregation: An Interdisciplinary Review." 1980, unpublished.
8. Paula England, Marilyn Chassie, and Linda McCormack. "Skill Demands and Earnings in Female and Male Occupations." *Sociology and Social Research,* 66 (1982): 147–68.
9. Institute for Social Research. *A Panel Study of Income Dynamics.* Ann Arbor: Institute for Social Research, University of Michigan, 1975.
10. Richard Levinson. "Sex Discrimination and Employment Practices: An Experiment with Unconventional Job Inquiries." *Social Problems* 22 (1975): 533–43.
11. Janice Madden. *The Economics of Sex Discrimination.* Lexington, Mass.: D.C. Heath, 1973.
12. Jacob Mincer and Solomon Polachek. "Family Investments in Human Capital: Earnings of Women." *Journal of Political Economy* 82 (2:March/April 1974):S76–S108.
13. ————. "Women's Earnings Reexamined." *Journal of Human Resources* 13 (Winter 1978): 118–34.
14. Solomon Polachek. "Discontinuous Labor Force Participation and Its Effects on Women's Market Earnings." In *Sex, Discrimination, and the Division of Labor,* ed. Cynthia Lloyd. New York: Columbia University Press, 1975. Pp. 90–122.
15. ————. "Occupational Segregation Among Women: Theory, Evidence, and a Prognosis." In *Women in the Labor Market,* eds. Cynthia Lloyd, Emily Andrews, and Curtis Gilroy. New York: Columbia University Press, 1979. Pp. 137–57.
16. ————. "Occupational Segregation: An Alternative Hypothesis." *Journal of Contemporary Business* 5 (1976): 1–12.
17. ————. "Potential Biases in Measuring Male-Female Discrimination." *Journal of Human Resources* 10 (Spring 1975): 205–29.
18. ————. "Sex Differences in College Major." *Industrial and Labor Relations Review* 31 (July 1978): 498–508.
19. Steven Sandell and David Shapiro. "The Theory of Human Capital and the Earnings of Women: A Reexamination of the Evidence." *Journal of Human Resources* 13 (Winter 1978): 103–17.
20. Paula Stephan and Sharon Levin. "Some Determinants of Occupational Clustering by Sex: The Ph.D. Fields." Paper presented at the Conference on Occupational Careers Analysis sponsored by Social Science Research Council and National Institute on Aging, Greensboro, N.C., 1976.
21. U.S. Department of Labor. *Dual Careers.* Vol. 1, Manpower Research Monograph No. 21. Washington: U.S. Government Printing Office, 1970.
22. Wendy Wolf and Rachel Rosenfeld. "Sex Structure of Occupations and Job Mobility." *Social Forces* 56 (1978): 823–44.
23. Harriet Zellner. "The Determinants of Occupational Segregation." In *Sex, Discrimination, and the Division of Labor,* ed. Cynthia Lloyd. New York: Columbia University Press, 1975. Pp. 125–45.

[18]

385 – 89

[1968]

J 71

Gary S, Becker

DISCRIMINATION, ECONOMIC

As a general and somewhat loose statement, economic discrimination can be said to occur against members of a group whenever their earnings fall short of the amount "warranted" by their abilities. Public interest has usually been centered on groups that are either numerical minorities (such as Negroes in the United States, Untouchables in India, Jews in the Soviet Union, Laplanders in Sweden, and Chinese in Indonesia) or are political, social, or economic minorities (such as the Blacks in South Africa, immigrants from Africa in Israel, and women in most countries). Until recent years, economic discrimination was generally seen as evidence of exploitation of minorities by majorities. This interpretation is clearest in writings with Marxist sympathies (Aptheker 1946), although it is also found in weaker form in much of the literature (Allport 1954, p. 210).

In the past, economists tended to neglect the study of discrimination against minorities, primarily because they were reluctant to interpret any appreciable economic phenomena in terms of "exploitation," which stems from what is technically called monopsony power [see MONOPOLY]. The growing interest of economists in discrimination during the last decade has been stimulated by an approach that is not based as much on exploitation as on considerations that may involve even a sharper break with traditional economic theory. In this approach, members of a group earn less than their abilities warrant if other persons are willing to "pay" (that is, give up resources) in order to avoid employing, working with, lending to, training, or educating these members.

Discrimination in the market place. Further discussion is facilitated by distinguishing discrimination affecting the talents that are brought to the market place from discrimination in the market place itself. Since the latter is taken to mean that less is earned than is warranted by productivity, such discrimination would not exist *if all persons maximized money incomes* and if all markets were competitive. For, under these circumstances, the increased money incomes of employers, employees, or consumers, resulting from associating with members of a group receiving less than their productivity, would stimulate a demand for such members that would continue until their earnings rose sufficiently to cover their productivity.

Accordingly, discrimination in competitive markets is said to occur because some participants have *tastes for discrimination*, more loosely called "prejudice." Because of these tastes, they are willing to forfeit money income or other resources in order to avoid employing, working with, or buying from members of a particular group. Indeed, the intensity of their prejudice is measured by how much they are willing to forfeit (Becker 1957, chapter 1). The measuring rod of money provides an operational and quantifiable concept of prejudice that is consistent with the economist's concept of tastes and the statistician's concept of subjective probabilities (Savage 1954). Objections to such a behavioristic concept of prejudice and hatred might be tempered upon reflecting that a hatred cannot be very strong, in any meaningful sense, if there is a reluctance to satisfy it by parting with some resources. This approach to discrimination not only incorporates common notions about prejudice much more fully than does one based on exploitation, but also is more consistent with the general prevalence of workably competitive markets.

Although the extent of market discrimination depends, of course, on the intensity of the average taste for discrimination, it by no means depends on this alone. Also very relevant are any differences among participants in the desire to discriminate, the relative number and occupational distribution of minority members, the extent of competition in product markets, and the degree of substitution between different groups (Becker 1957). For example, consider discrimination by employers against a group working in a competitive industry. Even if the employers' average taste for discrimination were large, market discrimination could be negligible if the group were a small fraction of the total labor force in the industry and if some employers' tastes for discrimination were weak (or even negative). For then, members of the group could be fully employed by these employers. An increase in the size of the group or a decline in the fraction of employers with weak tastes for discrimination would tend to increase market discrimination, perhaps substantially, because members could no longer be fully employed by these employers, and some members would have to find employment among those employers with stronger tastes for discrimination. However, the latter would employ these members only if the cost of discriminating were sufficiently large—that is, the earnings of members sufficiently low—to offset their tastes.

Even the market form in which the discrimination manifests itself can be very important. If the result were simply lower hourly earnings, discriminators would have to balance the gain from discriminating—satisfying their prejudice—against the cost of discriminating—their loss in income from not associating with persons receiving less than their productivity. If, however, because of market imperfections, trade union behavior, or minimum wage or "equal pay" legislation (Alchian & Kessel 1962), hourly earnings of minorities were prevented from falling, the cost of discrimination would be eliminated because no resources would be forfeited by not hiring minorities; and discriminators would be encouraged to discriminate still more. The result would be greater unemployment of minorities, and discrimination would take the market form of, say, lower annual earnings rather than lower hourly earnings.

Quantitative evidence on the extent of market discrimination against different minorities is surprisingly limited; the most extensive evidence relates to Negroes in the United States. Significant market discrimination against them is suggested by the much lower earnings of urban male Negroes than of urban male whites of the same age, years of schooling, and region, and the somewhat greater unemployment of Negro males, even when occupation is held constant. The absolute occupational position of Negroes has risen substantially in both the North and South during the last hundred years. Since, however, the position of whites has risen at about the same rate, the relative position of Negroes has changed surprisingly little, the greatest change (a rise) coming after 1940. One of the most striking findings is that market discrimination is apparently relatively slight against young new entrants into the labor force, but it increases significantly with age. This finding is presumably explained by a combination of inadequate preparation of Negroes for occupational advance and greater market prejudice against more advanced Negroes. Similar findings would probably apply to other minority groups in the world. (For evidence on the economic position of Negroes, see Becker 1957, chapters 7–10;

Dewey 1952; Gilman 1963; and Ginzberg et al. 1956.)

Deficiencies brought to the market place.   Perhaps more than half the total difference between the earnings and abilities of Negroes in the United States results from deficiencies brought to the market place, rather than from market discrimination itself; again, a similar relation would probably be found for other minorities. These deficiencies include poor health, low morale and motivation, and limited information about opportunities. The most pervasive force, however, is insufficient and inferior education and training. For example, in 1960, Negro males aged 25–64 averaged less than 8 years of schooling, while whites averaged more than 10.5 years; and Negro schooling has clearly been inferior in quality.

An important cause of deficiencies in education and training are the limitations imposed by poverty itself, especially when combined with the usual difficulties in financing large expenditures. Of course, poverty may in part result from either past discrimination, as exemplified by Negro slavery, or current discrimination, thus leading to the so-called vicious circle of discrimination (Myrdal 1944). Discrimination by governments and private institutions in charge of education and training facilities has been common, as illustrated by the government restrictions on the education of Blacks in South Africa and (at least in the past) Jews in eastern Europe, the quotas applied by certain private universities in the United States, or the racial (and even religious) restrictions on admission to apprenticeship and other training programs administered by trade unions in many countries.

Role of government.   Undoubtedly, some of the worst economic discrimination, as well as other kinds, is directly traceable to government action. One need only note the restrictions placed on the economic advance of Blacks in South Africa, the harassment of the Chinese in Indonesia and other parts of Asia, or the virtual confiscation of some of the property of Japanese Americans in the United States during World War II. On the other hand, government action is often a force in widening opportunities and thus breaking down economic discrimination: of greatest influence is the enforcement of equality before the law, although the provision of free or subsidized education has also been important. Legislation of the "fair employment" kind, prohibiting racial, ethnic, religious, and other forms of discrimination in employment, can have some effect too. Very little scholarly analysis has been made of the economic effects resulting from

210

this kind of legislation. In the United States, the evidence provided by the states with such legislation suggests that it somewhat increases both the earnings and unemployment of minorities (Landes 1966).

A few of the more extreme nineteenth-century advocates of a competitive market economy believed that eventually its extension and development would eliminate most economic discrimination and hatred. Unfortunately, this has not yet taken place; discrimination exists, and at times even flourishes, in competitive economies, the position of Negroes in the United States being a clear example. At the same time, one must realize that the pressures of competition, the emphasis on material goods, the impersonality of and the cost accounting in a market economy often help mitigate, and sometimes even eliminate, the effects of prejudice. Indeed, in desperation, market participants in the United States, South Africa, Great Britain, Indonesia, and elsewhere have (successfully) appealed to their governments for protection from the "unfair" competition of various minorities.

In spite of the widespread public interest in economic discrimination throughout the world, relatively little is known about its quantitative importance and socioeconomic determinants. Much greater understanding of the formation of prejudice is necessary, although economists are unlikely to be of great value here. Their comparative advantage lies in analyzing how prejudices combine with various institutional arrangements to produce actual discrimination. It has already been mentioned that the degree of competition, the size of minority groups, and many other factors as yet insufficiently studied also affect the amount of market discrimination.

Likewise, the effect of prejudice, by the electorate, trade union members, or directors of educational institutions, on the extent of nonmarket discrimination is determined by whether different political issues are effectively tied together, whether the costs of discriminating or the gains from not discriminating are hidden, and on many other institutional arrangements (Becker 1957, chapter 5; 1959). Consider, for example, the election by majority rule of representatives to decide on two issues, one dealing with discrimination against a minority. Assume that the minority is more concerned about discrimination while the majority, although more concerned about the other issue, does not agree on how to resolve it. A successful campaign could be conducted by promising to satisfy the minority on discrimination and a segment of the majority on the other issue. The decision on

discrimination could, therefore, be more favorable to the minority than if each issue were decided separately (by, say, referendum), or if the majority were less split on the other issue, or if the majority attached greater importance to discrimination. Considerably more study of institutional arrangements is required in order to know more about the factors determining the talents that minorities are permitted to bring to the market place.

GARY S. BECKER

BIBLIOGRAPHY

ALCHIAN, ARMEN A.; and KESSEL, REUBEN A. 1962 Competition, Monopoly, and the Pursuit of Pecuniary Gain. Pages 156–183 in Universities–National Bureau Committee for Economic Research Conference, Princeton, N.J., 1960, *Aspects of Labor Economics*. Princeton Univ. Press. → Includes a discussion by Gary S. Becker and Martin Bronfenbrenner.

ALLPORT, GORDON W. 1954 *The Nature of Prejudice*. Reading, Mass.: Addison-Wesley. → An abridged paperback edition was published in 1958 by Doubleday.

APTHEKER, HERBERT 1946 *The Negro People in America: A Critique of Gunnar Myrdal's* An American Dilemma. New York: International Publishers.

BECKER, GARY S. 1957 *The Economics of Discrimination*. Univ. of Chicago Press.

BECKER, GARY S. 1959 Union Restrictions on Entry. Pages 209–224 in Philip D. Bradley (editor), *The Public Stake in Union Power*. Charlottesville: Univ. of Virginia Press.

DEWEY, DONALD J. 1952 Negro Employment in Southern Industry. *Journal of Political Economy* 60:279–293.

GILMAN, HARRY J. 1963 The White/Non-white Unemployment Differential. Pages 75–113 in Mark Perlman (editor), *Human Resources in the Urban Economy*. Washington: Resources for the Future.

GINZBERG, ELI et al. 1956 *The Negro Potential*. New York: Columbia Univ. Press. → A paperback edition was published in 1963.

LANDES, WILLIAM 1966 An Economic Analysis of Fair Employment Practice Laws. Ph.D. dissertation, Columbia Univ.

MYRDAL, GUNNAR (1944) 1962 *An American Dilemma: The Negro Problem and Modern Democracy*. New York: Harper. → A paperback edition was published in 1964 by McGraw-Hill.

SAVAGE, LEONARD J. 1954 *The Foundations of Statistics*. New York: Wiley.

[19]

PAY DIFFERENCES BETWEEN MEN AND WOMEN

HENRY SANBORN

THIS article describes pay differences between men and women in America in 1949, then considers the extent and nature of pay discrimination against women.

SUMMARY OF PAY DIFFERENCES

Table 1 shows that in 1949 the median wage and salary income of employed women was 58 percent of that of men. Within given detailed Census occupations, however, women on the average earned 64 to 66 percent as much as men. Thus, part of the reason for the low sex-income ratio, .58, is that men tend to be in higher-paying occupations than women. The estimate under "F wts" is the ratio of (1) the mean of the median occupational incomes for women, weighted by the numbers of women in

each occupation, divided by (2) the mean of the occupational incomes of men, also weighted by the numbers of women in each occupation.[1]

When account is taken that in 1949 men worked longer hours than women, the sex-income ratio increases to .74–.76. Differences in education within each occupation tended to *lower* the ratio slightly because on the whole working women have more education than men. The fact that employed men are older (and presumably have worked longer) than employed women accounts for a small part of the sex-income differences, raising the female-male income ratio to .76. Differences in place of residence, measured by urban-rural status within each occupation, had a small negative effect on the sex-income ratio, while differences in racial composition of employed persons within each occupation had virtually no effect.

This study examines the extent and nature of pay discrimination against women in the United States in 1949. Using 1950 Census and other data, the author adjusts for such factors as productivity differences, quit and absence differences, differences in work experience, and the like. The results of these adjustments lead the author to conclude that, whereas sex-discrimination on the part of consumers and fellow employees is compatible with his evidence, a strong degree of employer discrimination against women appears unlikely.

Henry Sanborn teaches economics at The City College of The City University of New York. His article is based on a thesis completed at the University of Chicago. The author wishes to express his gratitude for the suggestions of his thesis advisors, Professors H. Lewis, A. Rees, and G. Shultz, none of whom, however, reviewed or necessarily agrees with this article.—EDITOR

---

[1] This study covers 262 detailed Census occupations with 79 percent of all male and 84 percent of all female wage and salary workers in 1949. The sex-income ratio under "F wts" is $(\Sigma Q_F Y_F)/(\Sigma Q_F Y_M)$, and under "M wts" it is $(\Sigma Q_M Y_F)/(\Sigma Q_M Y_M)$, with the summations over the 262 occupations. Only Census occupations with at least 30 incomes recorded for each sex were used. If the sex-income ratios were not weighted by employment, some occupations with very few employees would have the same influence on the economy-wide measure of pay differences as occupations like teachers with many employees. More details of the Census adjustment procedures are in the appendix.

PAY DIFFERENCES BETWEEN MEN AND WOMEN   535

Table 1. Ratio of Female to Male Wage and Salary Income in 1949, Unadjusted and after Adjustments for Selected Variables.

Adjustment	Ratio of Female to Male Income		Percent Rise in Ratio from Each Adjustment	
	F wts*	M wts*	F wts	M wts
Unadjusted......................	.58			
Occupational distribution...................	.64	.66	10.3	13.8
Hours of work...........................	.74	.76	15.9	14.9
Education...............................	.74	.75	−0.4	−1.8
Age.....................................	.76	.76	2.5	1.7
Urbanness, race †........................	.75	.76	−0.2	−0.5
BLS data...............................	.81	.82	6.8	8.0

Sources of the tables are in most cases too numerous to list explicitly. The main Census source is U.S. Bureau of the Census, *Census of Population 1950. Occupational Characteristics, No. P-E 1B*, 1956. The BLS data are indicated in n. 4 below.

*The ratio in each case incorporates adjustments for variables above it in the table. Percentage changes were computed before rounding. In this and subsequent tables, the headings "F wts" and "M wts" designate Paasche and Laspeyres indexes, respectively (see n. 1).

†All of the difference is attributable to urbanness, since the race adjustment was negligible.

Even with these corrections many Census occupations are too broad for confidence that men and women are doing similar work. Therefore, where possible, sex-earnings data by more narrowly defined occupations have been analyzed, mainly those compiled by the Bureau of Labor Statistics on operatives and clerical workers. As among Census occupations, so among BLS occupations, women are disproportionately in the lower-paying occupations. Within these narrower occupations, the ratios of female to male earnings were significantly higher than in the corresponding Census occupations. The increase in the Census-adjusted sex-income ratio to .81–.82 represents an application of the BLS ratios only to those Census occupations covered to some extent by the BLS data.

Adjustments (described below) for male-female differences in turnover, absenteeism, and work experience of people of the same age raise the over-all sex-income ratio to an estimated .87–.88. This leaves unexplained a still signifi-

cant sex-income difference of 13 percent, but certainly much less than the initial difference of 42 percentage points.[2] In conclusion, we ask whether the remaining differences imply discrimination against women. The only discrimination considered here is lower pay to women than to men for the same work. Another form of discrimination, not dealt with here, might be the refusal to give women equal opportunities for advancement.

1950 CENSUS FINDINGS

Let us look more closely at the findings from the 1950 Census. Table 2 shows the sex-income ratios by major occupation before and after adjustments. The

[2]Sex-income ratios were also computed by detailed occupation from the 1940 Census. Both before and after adjustments, these ratios were generally similar to those of 1950. See H. Sanborn, "Income Differences between Men and Women in the United States," unpublished Ph.D. thesis, University of Chicago, 1960, pp. 28–34. A study of sex-income differences from the 1960 Census cannot be made from data yet available.

Table 2. Unadjusted and Adjusted Ratios of Female to Male Wage and Salary
Income in 1949, by Major Occupation.

Occupation	Unadjusted	Adjusted (Census)*		Adjusted (BLS and Other)*	
		F wts-M wts	% change†	F wts-M wts	% change†
All occupations...............	.58	.75–.76	30	.81–.82	7–8
Professional..................	.61	.86–.82	42–32	.89–.83	4–1
Managerial...................	.55	.67–.69	22–25	.67–.69	none
Clerical......................	.69	.82–.77	19–12	.94–.79	14–3
Sales........................	.41	.68–.69	66–67	.68–.69	none
Craft........................	.64	.68–.73	6–15	.69–.74	1
Operatives...................	.60	.71–.78	18–29	.76–.82	7–6
dur. gds. mfg...............	.67	.77–.78	14–16	.85–.86	11
nondr. gds. mfg............	.60	.68–.72	13–20	.73–.80	8–11
Pvt. household wkrs...........	.48	.62–.64	30–34	.62–.64	none
Service......................	.47	.64–.77	37–63	.65–.78	1–2
Farm laborers................	.39	.76	97	.76	none
Laborers.....................	.73	.75–.82	3–13	.81–.88	9–7

The Census adjustments are for sex-differences in occupational distribution, hours worked, education, age, urban-rural status, and race. The BLS and other changes are discussed below.

†The "% change" for Census adjustments is from the unadjusted figures, while that under BLS and other data is the change from the Census-adjusted figures.

highest adjusted ratios, before consideration of the BLS data, are slightly above .8 in professional and clerical occupations. The lowest are between .62 and .69 in a number of major occupations.

A summary picture of the values of individual adjustments is seen in Tables 3 and 4. Not only did the adjustments raise the sex-income ratios, but they reduced considerably the dispersion of

their distribution. The largest adjustments raising sex-income ratios tended to occur in those occupations with the lowest unadjusted ratios, and conversely.

Only the hours corrections were consistently greater than unity. Men worked longer hours than women in all but ten of the 262 occupations and in most cases over 10 percent more than women. Even though many individual age and educa-

Table 3. Distribution of Sex-Income Ratios in 262 Detailed Occupations, Unadjusted and
Adjusted for Hours, Education, Age, Urbanness, and Race, 1949.

Value of Ratio	Number of Ratios		Value of Ratio	Number of Ratios	
	Unadjusted	Adjusted		Unadjusted	Adjusted
.20–.29	6	–	.80– .89	19	57
.30–.39	7	1	.90– .99	8	14
.40–.49	20	8	1.00–1.09	3	1
.50–.59	49	14	1.10–1.19	1	1
.60–.69	83	66	1.20–1.29	–	–
.70–.79	63	100	1.30–1.39	3	–

PAY DIFFERENCES BETWEEN MEN AND WOMEN 537

Table 4. Values of Adjustment Factors in 262 Occupations by Type of Adjustment.*

	Hours	Education	Age	Urbanness	Race
Mean value of adjustment factor.	1.165	.99	1.01	1.00	1.00
Range of values...............	.61–1.99	.83–1.26	.46–1.52†	.99–1.13	.98–1.04
Number below .95.............	5	28	20	5	none
Number 1.05 or more..........	240	8	38	7	none

*An adjustment factor is the number by which the female income in an occupation was multiplied to correct for male-female differences with respect to a characteristic, such as hours, education, etc.

†The age adjustment factor, .46, was for newsboys; the second lowest was .77.

tion corrections differed considerably from unity (see Table 4), their net effect (shown in Table 1) was small, because corrections above and below unity tended to offset each other. Greater education of working women than men tended to occur more in the lower-paying than in the higher-paying occupations. In fact, among sales and managerial workers, men had more education than women. In the professional occupations, women were relatively concentrated in occupations where they had more education than men—nurses, social workers, technicians, and musicians and music teachers, while men had more education where they were relatively more concentrated—accountants and auditors, clergymen, civil engineers, and dentists.

The adjustments for age differences between employed men and women are intended to correct for differences in labor force experience, since work experience contributes to market productivity and to income. If an occupation had two people in it, a man aged 45 and a woman aged 35, the age correction would (in principle) raise the woman's income by the percentage by which the man's rose because of his labor force experience between ages 35 and 45. As such, this correction fails to account for an additional labor force experience difference between these two people, namely that the

man when aged 35 probably had more labor force experience than the woman at age 35. An adjustment for this "experience-given-age" difference is described below.

The age adjustments increased the income of women by an average of 1.7 percent to 2.5 percent. There was a decided tendency for men to be older than women in the higher-paying occupations and for women to be older in the lower paying. Since many women leave the labor force for marriage and childbirth, one might expect men to be older than women in nearly all occupations, but men in lower-paying occupations move up occupationally more than do women,[3] and perhaps women who reenter the labor force after some years of absence tend to enter the lower-paying occupations more available to inexperienced workers.

The variations in income among urban-rural and among racial classes within given occupations were estimated to be much smaller than for all occupations combined. Therefore, significant urban-rural or race adjustments occurred only in the presence of overwhelming distribution differences between men and women, and these were infrequent. For example, among paperhangers and among bus drivers, women's incomes

[3]Ibid., pp. 63–64.

were raised by only 13 percent, although over 70 percent of men, but under a third of women, were urban dwellers. For elevator operators, where the indicated ratio of nonwhite to white income was .89, the race adjustment factor was only 1.03, even though nonwhites constituted 42 percent of the women against 20 percent of the men.

BLS DATA—NARROWER OCCUPATIONS

The adjustments based on Census data leave unaccounted for a 24 percent income difference between men and women. Where possible, other data, mostly BLS, have been examined to see whether finer occupational breakdowns will reduce this difference.[4]

After BLS occupations were classified into their corresponding Census occupations, weighted sex-earnings ratios were computed in each group of suboccupations, using only those data and suboccupations with earnings for *both* men and women. These ratios show earnings comparisons between men and women who are doing more comparable work and they abstract from the tendency for men to be in the relatively higher-paying suboccupations within the Census occupations. Also computed from the BLS data were unstandardized ratios using all suboccupations within a given Census occupation, whether or not

[4]See *ibid.* for the detailed findings from and procedures used with the BLS data. Most of the BLS data used came from the Wage Structure series covering mainly production workers and from Occupational Wage Surveys, covering mainly office workers. These sources give average hourly earnings in narrowly defined occupations by industry and/or by city. Nearly all of the Wage Structure surveys published between 1945 and 1955 were analyzed, though most useful information comes from the years 1945–1948, when the surveys gave earnings by sex in many more occupations.

earnings for both sexes were reported. These ratios compare in concept and most of them resemble in value the hours-corrected Census sex-income ratios.

From surveys of 30 separate industries where BLS occupations come under the Census occupation, operatives (nec) of the given industry, the standardized BLS ratios were .85 or higher in 16 of the 30, and above .80 in all but four. In two of these four the ratios were .77 and .78, leaving only two which were below .7. This represents a substantial rise from the hours-corrected Census ratios, which for operatives averaged about .76.[5] Among production occupations other than operatives (nec), BLS ratios were also much higher than the corresponding Census ratios for operatives and laborers,

[5]As an example, in the Census occupation, operatives (nec), glass and glass products, the hours-corrected sex-income ratio was .71. From a 1947 BLS survey, the unstandardized sex-earnings ratio within this Census occupation was .68, while the standardized ratio, based only on BLS occupations with both men and women, was .85. U.S. Bureau of Labor Statistics, *Glassware*, Wage Structure No. 53, 1947.

Where the results from BLS data were incorporated into the Census findings (Table 2), the replacement of Census ratios by BLS ratios was done conservatively by whichever of the following two methods gave the lower sex-income ratio: (1) the standardized BLS ratio was substituted directly for the Census ratio; or (2) the Census ratio was multiplied by the ratio of standardized to unstandardized BLS ratio. Thus for glassworkers, .85 was substituted for .71. But if the unstandardized BLS ratio had been, say, .80 instead of .68, the Census ratio, .71, would have been raised to .71 times .85/.80.

Less conservatively, it saved computational work to assume the education, age, urban-rural and race corrections would still apply to these BLS ratios, although sex-differences with respect to these variables are probably smaller within the BLS occupations than within the Census occupations. This convenience did not affect the general results because of the small and generally offsetting magnitudes of these four adjustments.

but less consistently higher among several craft occupations.

The two exceptionally low BLS ratios were .67 and .66 for operatives (nec) in the manufacture of shoes and of apparel and accessories, respectively. Since these ratios are based on 27 and 28 different suboccupations, their values cannot be attributed to small sample size. An attempt was made to see if some further standardization could account for part of these large earnings differences. Standardization by other variables, such as plant size or unionization, published in the Wage Structure surveys, did not yield significant results.

The Chicago office of the BLS allowed me to compute sex-earnings ratios in the footwear industry by individual plant.[6] The survey for which these plant data were gathered gives a standardized sex-earnings ratio of .69, about the same as the .67 from earlier footwear surveys. For the combined Great Lakes-Midwest region, this ratio was .79, and when standardized by individual plant, the ratio rose to .88. Thus, within the Great Lakes and Midwest regions, a tendency for women to be in relatively low-paying plants accounted for about half of the 21 percent difference in the earnings of men and women within given occupations. The important conclusion from this is that further breakdowns to eliminate incomparabilities between men and women, other than sex, would reduce further much of the reported earnings differences between men and women.

This conclusion is supported by one BLS survey which specifically analyzes earnings differences between men and women in seven operative occupations in

machinery industries:[7] assemblers (classes B and C), inspectors (classes B and C), and three machine-operator occupations. The sex-earnings ratios in these seven occupations, based only on plants employing both sexes, ranged from .95 to .99 for time paid workers and from .88 to .99 for incentive paid workers, with an unweighted average ratio of .96. The Census ratios in the corresponding occupations, operatives (nec) in miscellaneous machinery and in electrical machinery, were .80 and .74. From BLS wage structure surveys, the standardized ratios (using only occupations with earnings for both sexes) were .92 and .89, based on 44 and 36 such occupations, respectively. Taking these seven occupations alone from the wage structure surveys, we find an average sex-earnings ratio of .89, in contrast to the average ratio standardized by individual plant, .96. Thus even where the BLS survey increased the Census results substantially (here from .80 and .74 to .92 and .89), further consideration *by plant* brings the ratio yet closer to unity.

We shall next consider clerical and then sales and managerial employees. The Occupational Wage Surveys give earnings and hours per week in clerical occupations by sex and major industry. Each survey covers a separate city or metropolitan area. The results of the standardization by city, industry, and suboccupation were as follows:[8]

---

[6]These data were published, though not by individual plant, in U.S. Bureau of Labor Statistics, *Footwear*, BLS Report 133, April 1957.

[7]U.S. Bureau of Labor Statistics, *Women Production Workers in Machinery Industries*, BLS Report 98, 1956.

[8]These data are based on 1949 surveys of 16 large cities and represent all areas of the country (U.S. Bureau of Labor Statistics, *Salaries of Office Workers in Large Cities in 1949*, BLS Bulletin 960–1 to 4, 1949). Bookkeepers were subdivided into two occupations, while office machine operators and stenographers, typists, and secretaries each had five subdivisions. Earnings in each occupation were given separately in up to seven industries.

540   INDUSTRIAL AND LABOR RELATIONS REVIEW

	Hours-Adjusted Census Sex-Income Ratio	BLS Sex-Earnings Ratio	
		F wts	M wts
Bookkeepers..........	.81	.83	.83
Office machine operators..........	.82	.94	.94
Office boys...........	.93	1.00	.99
Stenos, typists, and secretaries..........	.75	.95	.93

Substantial increases are shown in three of the four occupations.

The Wage Structure surveys provide earnings by sex of retail sales workers. In department stores in 1945, based on seven occupations with both sexes, distinguished by goods sold, female and male weighted sex-earnings ratios were .63 and .60, compared with the hours-corrected Census ratio for retail sales workers (nec), .68.[9] However, in a 1950 survey of department and women's ready-to-wear stores, with weekly earnings given by city and sex, but not for the country as a whole and without numbers of persons, the average ratio of female to male weekly earnings, weighted by the number of cities covered in each occupation, was .77.[10] Thus, it is not clear whether any change in the Census ratio is appropriate. This Census occupation contains 92.5 percent of the female sales workers covered in this study; therefore, a sizeable change in the ratio, .68, would significantly affect the overall picture of male-female income differences.

Sex-earnings ratios of sales workers, largely in retailing, were also calculated from biennial reports of the Texas

State BLS for 1948 and 1950. These are based on a much wider variety of industries than the BLS surveys cited above, including bakeries, cleaners, garages, hotels, cinemas, and candy, clothing, dairy, hardware, and grocery stores (all listed separately). Female and male weighted sex-earnings ratios, based on data with earnings for both sexes, were .66 and .70 in 1947–1948 and .57 and .52 in 1949–1950.[11] These findings tend to confirm those from the Wage Structure surveys that within narrow sales occupations men earn substantially more per hour than women.

These surveys by the Texas BLS provide the only non-Census data I have found on managerial workers. In these reports, hours and weekly earnings by sex are given in several classes of managerial occupations—managers, assistant managers, supervisors, and superintendents—by industrial breakdowns somewhat narrower than those of the Census. Most of the companies surveyed were in service industries or retailing. The standardized ratios of female to male hourly earnings were .70 and .71 in 1947–1948 and .67 and .63 in 1949–1950. These ratios tend to confirm a conclusion from the Census data that in managerial occupations women are paid significantly less than men.[12]

Another Census occupation which was further adjusted is teachers (nec). This was corrected for the fact that relatively

---

[9] U.S. Bureau of Labor Statistics, *Department and Clothing Stores*, Wage Structure No. 26, 1946.

[10] U.S. Bureau of Labor Statistics, *Department and Women's Ready-To-Wear Stores*, Wage Structure No. 78, 1950.

[11] State of Texas, Bureau of Labor Statistics, *Twentieth and Twenty-first Biennial Reports, 1947–1948, 1949–1950*, Texas, 1948, 1950. No indication is given of how companies were surveyed nor the portion of establishments in the state covered. Employment in sales occupations with both sexes was: 1947–1948, 8663 women and 5107 men; 1949–1950, 3047 women and 792 men.

[12] Employment in managerial occupations with both sexes was: 1947–1948, 976 women and 3110 men; 1949–1950, 283 women and 832 men.

PAY DIFFERENCES BETWEEN MEN AND WOMEN 541

more women than men teach in elementary grades where incomes are lower.[13] These facts, together with the hours-corrected Census sex-income ratio, .90, imply that for a given level of school the sex-income ratio is .96.[14] The Census occupation, teachers (nec), also includes principals and superintendents, both higher paying than class teachers and comprised of relatively more men than women. This might account for the remaining 4 percent income difference between men and women teachers.[15]

---

[13]Employment and incomes by grades in 1949–1950 were:

	Number of Teachers (000)		Median Salary
	Females	Males	
Elementary	607	58	$3185
Secondary	208	159	3672

The numbers are from U.S. Office of Education, *Biennial Survey of Education in the U.S., 1948–1950: Statistical Summary of Education, 1949–1950*, 1950, Table 7, p. 9. The salaries are from p. 22 of G. J. Stigler, *Employment and Compensation in Education*, Occasional Paper 33, National Bureau of Economic Research, New York, 1950, and were in turn derived by Stigler from the April 1949 *Research Bulletin* of the NEA. These salaries refer to full-time teachers and do not include nonteaching income.

[14]This is reasoned as follows: If m_1 and f_1 represent male and female salaries of elementary school teachers and m_2 and f_2 are the salaries of secondary school teachers, equations (1) and (2) state that for given school grades the salary of both sexes combined is the weighted average of the salary of each sex:

(1) $3185 = (58m_1 + 607f_1)/665$;
(2) $3672 = (159m_2 + 208f_2)/367$.

Equation (3) says the sex-income ratio is .90, the Census figure:

$$(3) \quad \frac{(607f_1 + 208f_2)/815}{(58m_1 + 159m_2)/217} = .90.$$

If we let x be the sex-income ratio common to both levels of teaching, then

$$x = \frac{f_1}{m_1} = \frac{f_2}{m_2}.$$

Substituting and solving for x, we find x = .96.

[15]If men and women *both* earned the salaries of footnote 13, and if there were no sex-income differences in this occupation, the distribution differences shown in footnote 13 would imply a sex-income ratio for the combined levels of

The Census ratios have been adjusted on the basis of this supplementary information, as summarized in Table 2. No change seemed justified for sales and managerial workers and none was made for private household workers or farm laborers, since no further data covered them. Among professional, clerical, craft, and service workers, only the few occupations on which data were found were adjusted. For laborers and durable goods operatives (nec), the entire groups were adjusted by weighted composites of the BLS data, even though the BLS data did not cover each detailed Census occupation. The same was done with nondurable operatives (nec), except for operatives in apparel and accessories, whose Census ratio was not changed. It seems certain that further information eliminating non-sex differences between employed people would bring the ratios much closer to unity.

The highest sex-income ratios in Table 2, averaging about .85, are found among professional and clerical workers, durable goods operatives, and laborers. Next, averaging slightly below .8 are nondurable and other operatives, farm laborers, and some service occupations. Sex-income ratios in craft occupations average barely above .7, while the lowest ratios, between .6 and .7, are in managerial, sales, and domestic service occupations.

PRODUCTIVITY DIFFERENCES

The information I have found on productivity differences between men and women is limited to BLS surveys of operatives in the shoe and furniture industries. Since these data were collected to study the effect of age on productivity, special care was taken to insure that all those in a given plant and occupation

---

teaching equal to .92, quite close to the adjusted Census ratio, .90.

were performing the same work at the same rate of pay. The Washington BLS office permitted me to record, by individual plant, earnings by sex and occupation of all workers paid on a piece basis. Any male-female difference in earnings would thus represent a difference in physical output. The female and male weighted sex-earnings ratios in the furniture industry were both .87 and in the shoe industry were .90 and .93, respectively. For the combined industries, these ratios were .89 and .90.[16] From the Census data, after all adjustments, the sex-income ratios of operatives (nec) in the furniture and footwear industries were .84 and .73, respectively. Within BLS occupations with both sexes, these respective ratios were .87 and .68. Thus, in the furniture industry, the 13 percent productivity difference between men and women equals the within-occupation earnings difference found in earlier BLS surveys. In the footwear industry, the productivity difference seems to be about 10 percent. This in turn about equals the 12 percent–13 percent sex-earnings difference found in the Great Lakes and Midwest regions, after standardization by individual plant.

It would be foolhardy to infer from this scanty information that productivity and distribution differences together account for all the reported sex-income differences in operative occupa-

tions and even more unjustified to extend such a conclusion to nonoperative occupations. But these data do caution against attributing the unexplained income differences to discrimination.

QUIT AND ABSENCE DIFFERENCES

If the employment of women imposes costs upon the employer which could have been avoided by the employment of men, then in the absence of discrimination women will receive less than men who are otherwise the same in market productivity. Higher rates of quit and absence are two frequently cited causes of such costs. Unfortunately, their impact on sex-income differences cannot be measured accurately from available data. If the quit-rate difference between men and women is 5.1 percent per year and the cost to the employer per instance of quit lies between $100 and $500, then the expected cost of this differential quit rate is ½¢ to 2½¢ per hour of women's employment.[17] If we take $200 as the

---

[16]These figures are based on the following numbers of men and women doing the same work at the same piece rates:

	No. of plants	Employment Men	Women
Furniture	6	226	113
Shoes	10	461	375

In one-fourth of the occupations in individual plants, the average earnings of women exceeded those of men. I am grateful for the cooperation of Mr. Jerome Mark, author of the BLS study, *Comparative Job Performance by Age*, BLS Bulletin 1223, 1957; also BLS Bulletin 1203, 1956.

[17]The expected cost per hour of the differential quit rate is the differential yearly quit rate times the cost per quit, divided by the hours per year. In 1950 annual quit rates in manufacturing, compiled by the BLS, were 19.5 percent for men and 24.6 percent for women (S. Goldstein, "An Economic Appraisal of Aggregate Labor Turnover in Manufacturing," unpublished Ph.D. thesis, American University, 1957, p. 131). The International Harvester Company, in "The Cost of Labor Turnover," 1951, estimates the average cost of turnover in 1951 as $557 per separation, with $126 the cost for common laborers and much larger amounts for college-trained people. The Merchants and Manufacturers Association of Los Angeles, in a 1948 survey of 49 companies, found an average cost of $191.65 ("Employment Turnover Cost," Survey Analysis No. 28, Oct. 25, 1948). A 1944 study by F. M. Disney gave estimates of $36 for maintenance and labor, $145 for clerical employees, and $301 for administrative and professional, cited in Goldstein, *op. cit.*, pp. 287ff. Hours per year are based on 1950 Census data (*Occupational Characteristics, op. cit*).

PAY DIFFERENCES BETWEEN MEN AND WOMEN 543

maximum quit cost of persons earning $1.00 an hour, $400 for $1.50, and $500 for $2.00, the maximum sex-earnings differential "justified" by quit differences between men and women appears to be less than 1.3 percent.

For both sexes, quit rates are higher among the younger, less skilled, and unmarried workers.[18] Since these characteristics are associated somewhat with particular occupations, it is plausible that within detailed Census occupations the differential quit rate is less than 5.1 percent. This adds to the expectation that 1.3 percent is an exaggeration of the quit-associated sex-earnings difference.[19]

Information on the incidence and costs of absenteeism is even less adequate than on turnover. In a 1949 survey, covering 16,508 men and 1309 women in manufacturing industries, absence rates—mandays lost per hundred workdays scheduled—were 3.2 percent and 6.5 percent for men and women, respectively.[20] Within given age groups, the differences between men and women were generally less than 3.3 percent. A 1954 survey of absence rates for one month in 219 Los Angeles firms revealed lower absence rates and differentials between men and women of only about 1 percent.[21]

Lacking satisfactory cost data, one can only conjecture about the impact of

absenteeism on male-female income differences. On the one hand, absences of key personnel could seriously affect the productivity of complementary human and nonhuman inputs who are paid their usual value produced. On the other hand, companies may reduce the effects of absenteeism on the productivity of complementary inputs by hiring substitutes, adding to the work of inputs not absent, and increasing the absentee's work when he returns. Where such measures nearly eliminate the costs of absenteeism, significant sex-income differences will not arise from absence differences. Where absence costs are high and unavoidable, there may develop not only pay differences but also reduced opportunities for advancement for women. As a guess, it would not be surprising if an absence differential of 2 percent would cause men to receive at least 1 percent more per hour than women doing the same work.[22]

WORK EXPERIENCE DIFFERENCES FOR GIVEN AGE

As noted earlier, the age adjustments do not correct for the fact that employed men of a given age have greater labor force experience than employed women of the same age. While data showing actual years of labor force experience by age and sex are unavailable, Table 5 does indicate that, unlike men, many women do enter and leave the labor force at early ages and reenter at later ages. For the cohort who were 20–24 in 1940 and 30–34 in 1950, the number of men

---

[18]See Goldstein, *op. cit.*, pp. 121–144 and 264–271; also Sanborn, *op. cit.*, pp. 44–45.

[19]In apparel manufacturing, where within-occupation earnings differences between men and women are exceptionally large, the female quit rate was 11.1 percentage points higher than that of men; but this quit difference still explains less than a 2 percent sex-earnings difference for operatives (nec) in this industry.

[20]M. D. Kossoris, "Absenteeism and Injury Experience of Older Workers," *Monthly Labor Review*, Vol. 67, July 1948, pp. 16–19.

[21]Merchants and Manufacturers Association of Los Angeles, Survey Analysis No. 38, Sept. 24, 1954.

[22]A given sex-difference in absence rates could cost considerably more than the same sex-difference in quit rates. A quit rate of 1 percent means once a year 1 percent of the work force quits (though probably not all at the same time), while an absence rate of 1 percent means that 1 percent of the scheduled man-days are lost *all year* (though not likely at a constant rate).

Table 5. Ratio of Experienced Workers in the Labor Force in 1950 to 1940 for Various Cohorts by Sex.

Age 1940:	15–19	20–24	25–34	35–44	45–54	55–64
Age 1950:	25–29	30–34	35–44	45–54	55–64	65–74
Men............	2.60	1.11	1.02	.94	.79	.48
Women..........	1.89	.73	1.09	1.20	.98	.57

Source: U.S. Bureau of the Census, *Census of Population 1940. The Labor Force, Part I, U.S. Summary,* 1943, Table 65, and 1950 Census, *Occupational Characteristics, op. cit.,* Table 4.

in the labor force rose 11 percent while the number of women dropped 27 percent over the ten years. Yet between these years, among the cohort aged 35–44 in 1940 and 45–54 in 1950, males in the labor force declined 6 percent, while women gained 20 percent. Similar contrasts obtain for other cohorts, except the first.[23] Data by age and sex showing years of employment covered by old-age insurance and other data showing years on the current job confirm that above age 25 to 30 men of a given age have worked longer than women of that age.[24]

Based on these data, three sets of assumptions have been made of the years by which men exceed women of the same age in labor force experience:

To evaluate the significance of these experience differences on male-female pay differences, a rough estimate has been made of the average rise in income associated with a year's labor force experience. This income rise was 1.1 percent per year for 1949.[25] Multiplied by 1.1 percent, the three estimated experience-given-age differences (2.8, 4.1, and 6.0 years) imply income differences between men and women of 3.1 percent, 4.5 percent, and 6.6 percent. If over time the labor force participation of *older* women is rising as compared with that of women below 45, and that of men constant, the average experience-given-age difference between men and women will rise.

Years Difference between Men and Women in Labor Force Experience.

Age:	under 25	25–29	30–34	35–39	40–49	50+	all ages*
Small:............	0	0	1	3	5	7	2.8
Medium:..........	0	1	2	4	7	10	4.1
Large:............	0	1	3	6	10	15	6.0
F ept, %:.........	25.3	12.9	11.1	11.6	20.3	18.9	100

*Weighted by employment at each age.

---

[23]These figures surely understate the contrast in that, with dropouts, the number of working women 45–54 in 1950 who were not in the labor force in 1940 probably exceeds 20 percent of the 1950 female labor force ages 45–54, and many women employed both dates were in and out between them. On the other hand, most men aged 45–54 in 1950 were undoubtedly in the labor force ten years earlier and continuously so between 1940 and 1950.

[24]These data are shown in Sanborn, *op. cit.,* pp. 60–62.

[25]This 1.1 percent is based on hours-corrected male age-income data, assumes a continuous uniform income rise from age 25–29 to the peak at ages 45–54, and was computed by weighting the income rises with age of three education classes by female employment by education. The annual income rises for no, some, and four years of college were 0.9 percent, 1.6 percent, and 2.7 percent, respectively.

OCCUPATIONS WITH THE LARGEST PAY DIFFERENCES

After adjustments based on Census and BLS data, the average within-occupation ratio of female to male income is .81–.82. It seems conservative to expect that within-occupation differences in quit and absence rates together account for an additional 1.5 percent income difference and that the experience-given-age difference explains another 4.5 percent. This brings the adjusted sex-income ratio to .87–.88.[26] With this addition of 6 percentage points, there would be many detailed occupations with ratios close to unity. But there would also be many with large sex-income differences remaining. Let us look at the occupations with the lower sex-income ratios.

There are 31 detailed Census occupations which together account for 94 percent of the female employment in occupations with adjusted ratios below .7. All but two of these occupations[27] fall into at least one of these four categories: (1) those with unusually broad titles[28]— we have seen that in a wide variety of occupations (clerical, craft, operative, labor, and teaching) men are employed disproportionately in higher-paying suboccupations and that within these suboccupations female-male pay differences are much less than indicated by the adjusted Census sex-income ratios; (2) operatives (nec) by specific industries, for which BLS surveys were not available to enable further adjustments; (3) managerial, sales (including waiters), and craft occupations, where, as argued below discrimination seems most plausible; and (4) occupations involving work which resembles that done by housewives.[29]

The low sex-income ratios in domestic-like occupations may result wholly or in part from differences between men and women in tastes for domestic-like employment. Suppose men have a strong dislike for working in these occupations relative to employment in other occupations, and women have, if not a preference, at least less dislike. And assume that, for either sex, in any given occupation some people are more productive than others and that people rank differently in their productivity from one occupation to another. Men will enter domestic-work occupations only if they have a productivity advantage in these occupations compared with other occupations which more than offsets their distaste for domestic-like employment.

---

[26]An extension to other occupations of the male-female productivity differences found among shoe and furniture operatives cannot be added to these figures, .87–.88. This is because the age and experience-given-age adjustments are themselves alternative estimates of at least part of these productivity differences.

[27]The two exceptions are cashiers and elevator operators, which together contain 4.4 percent of the women in the 31 occupations. The low sex-income ratio for cashiers may stem from the presence of higher-paid male bettakers at race tracks. The low ratio of elevator operators is unexplained. In this occupation, women had much more education than men (adjustment factor .91) and a much larger portion of women than men were nonwhites.

[28]For example: musicians and music teachers; managers and officials (nec) mfg.; salesmen, retail (nec); salesmen, mfg. (nec); foremen (nec), other nondurable; and attendants, professional and personal service (nec).

[29]With adjusted ratios ranging from .42 to .67, there are three private household occupations; also laundry and dry-cleaning operatives; practical nurses; charwomen and cleaners; housekeepers and stewards, ex pvt hse; cooks, ex pvt hse; apparel operatives (where the principle duties are operating sewing, stitching, and basting machines); tailors and tailoresses; and milliners. There were three domestic-like occupations with adjusted ratios above .7: dressmakers and seamstresses, ex factory (.75); pvt household workers, living in (.76); and janitors and sextons (.77), and from BLS data (.93). (This footnote includes some occupations not in the 31 referred to in the text.)

But women will not require so large a productivity advantage and, if they prefer these occupations, may enter them even though they are more productive in other occupations. As a result, the average productivity of men in these occupations will exceed that of women and the sex-income ratio will be less than unity.[30] This reasoning, of course, does not determine the magnitude of the implied sex-income differential.

PAY DISCRIMINATION AGAINST WOMEN

BY EMPLOYERS

The final possible cause of income differences to be considered is discrimination against women, which in this context will mean paying women less than men for the same quantity and quality of work, with allowance for employment costs, as from absenteeism.[31] From the evidence presented in this article, including that on turnover, absenteeism, and work experience, it is clear that within a wide range of occupations, market discrimination against women, if it exists

---

[30]This assumes (1) that the men whose productivity in domestic-work occupations is higher than in other occupations would not have had *lower* than average productivity in other occupations and/or (2) that the women with relatively high productivity in domestic-work occupations would not have had *above* average productivity in other occupations.

[31]To repeat, we consider here only pay differences, not discrimination in promotion. Strong promotional discrimination could reduce the supply curve of women's labor and raise the equilibrium wage in an occupation for both sexes. It could not cause a pay difference in favor of women in the lower jobs if men and women are perfect substitutes, though it could lead to pay differences against women in the higher jobs, if some women in effect overcome the promotional discrimination by offering to work for less. Yet the regression cited below shows no tendency for pay differences to correlate with income level.

at all, is under 10 percent.[32] It does not seem plausible that the same employer would *not* discriminate at all in some occupations and at the same time *would* discriminate by 25 percent or more—meaning he hires men to do what women could be hired to do at 25 percent less—unless there were significant differences in the relationships between employer and employees, differences which distinguish areas where he does and does not discriminate. Similarly, because of the profits which could be made by those who discriminate only slightly or not at all, it does not seem likely that there could be large areas of employment where employer discrimination causes differentials of 25 percent or more, while at the same time there could be large areas where employer discrimination (by different employers) causes differentials of under 10 percent, unless, again, there are significant differences in employer-employee relationships distinguishing the two groups of occupations.

The fact is, however, that occupations with low sex-income ratios do not appear to differ consistently with the others in employer-employee contacts. Where employer-employee relationships are close, we find both high sex-income ratios (professional and clerical) and low ratios (managerial and domestic work) and where employer-employee relationships are more impersonal we find both high ratios (laborers and some operatives) and low ratios (sales, craft, some service, and some operatives). Nor was there any tendency for the ratio of female to male

---

[32]Some employers may be willing to discriminate by more than 10 percent, i.e., to pay more than a 10 percent premium to men to avoid hiring women, and others may be inclined to discriminate by less, while at the same time, the discrimination in the market is 10 percent. See G. S. Becker, *The Economics of Discrimination,* Chicago, 1956.

income, after adjustments, to be any different in high-paying occupations from that in low-paying occupations.[33] Therefore, it seems unlikely that discrimination by employers accounts for the large income differentials between men and women still unexplained.

BY CONSUMERS

Let us consider the possibilities of discrimination against women first by consumers and then by fellow workers. From the high sex-income ratios in operative and laborer occupations, it does not appear that consumers discriminate on the basis of which sex made a product. It likewise seems unlikely that consumer discrimination accounts for much of the sex-income differentials in managerial and craft occupations, since most of the employees in these occupations do not deal directly with consumers either— though the contacts here are greater than by operatives or laborers. The differentials in sales and service occupations *are*, however, compatible with discrimination on the basis of the sex of the employee who sells the product or renders direct service to consumers—which is where one would expect to find consumer discrimination, if it exists. For example, suppose all consumers would pay a 2 percent premium to have a particular product sold by a man rather than by a woman and the salesman's wage is

10 percent of the price of the product. The marginal value of the salesman's labor is 10 percent of the value of the product. But if the product price must be reduced 2 percent when sold by a woman, the *saleswoman* adds only 8 percent of the value of the product. The sex-income differential would, therefore, be 20 percent. If the *salesman's* wage were 5 percent of the sales price, the same consumer discrimination, 2 percent of the product price, would cause a female-male wage differential of 40 percent. Thus, a small amount of discrimination by consumers could account for the large wage differences in sales occupations and also in several service occupations: waiters and waitresses (.62),[34] counter and fountain workers (.69), and bartenders (.66). This argument does not apply to domestic servants and related occupations, since in these the employee renders a large portion of the value of the service paid for by the consumer and a much greater discrimination is needed to account for the large sex-income differentials found in these occupations.

BY FELLOW WORKERS

Discrimination against women by fellow employees may occur when employees object to having women employed in a particular capacity. This objection could be evinced by complaints, slow-downs, strikes, dissension among employees, and quitting. The employer could react by not hiring women in this capacity or by replacing the discriminators, possibly employing all women and no men in what was formerly an all-male occupation. These reactions would not show up as earnings differences between men and women within any given occupation and company. Another reaction,

---

[33] A regression between the logs of (Census) adjusted female and male incomes over the 262 occupations had a slope of 1.028 (or 1.009 with the omission of the maverick occupation "newsboys"). In his study of nonwhite-white income differences, Morton Zeman found the nonwhite-white income ratio to be lower the higher the income level. His regression equation (based on logs of incomes) had a slope of .750, M. Zeman, "A Quantitative Analysis of White-Nonwhite Income Differences in the United States in 1939," unpublished Ph.D. thesis, University of Chicago, 1955.

---

[34] Adjusted Census ratios are in parentheses.

however, might be to buy the acceptance of women by paying the objectors more than they would earn otherwise. This becomes, to the employer, an added cost of hiring women. If the employer could as well have hired men, then he will incur this cost only if it can be paid from the women's productivity. The larger the number of workers (possibly women as well as men) who must be paid to accept a given number of women, the greater the resulting sex-income difference. As with consumer discrimination, a small degree of discrimination may result in a large pay difference. For example, if 100 men require a bonus of 2 percent (per time worked) to accept 10 women in some occupation, there will be a sex-earnings difference of 22 percent from this discrimination.[35]

It is sometimes said that workers who would not object to working with women or to supervising them would at the same time object to being supervised by women. Such discrimination may account for the low sex-income ratios in managerial and foreman occupations, where the ratio of possible discriminators to women hired is high. Of course this discrimination, like that of customers, need not be expressed consciously or explicitly as X percent of one's wage or of a product price; and yet from experience the nondiscriminating employer could find such an arrangement the cheapest way to retain his discriminating employees or customers.[36]

Another form of coworker discrimination which could result in male-female income differences is the exclusion of women from labor unions. If predominantly male unions succeed in obtaining wages above those which exist in the same occupations in nonunion employment, differentials in favor of men will appear in Census occupations. It is consistent with both theoretical expectations and empirical evidence that craft unions achieve the greatest gains for their workers.[37] Thus, we would expect the exclusion of women from labor unions, as a way of rationing available jobs, to have its greatest effect on male-female income differences among craft workers, next among operatives, and least among laborers (of the three major occupations most widely unionized). In the absence of union membership data by sex and of more evidence on the effectiveness of unions, this exclusion of women from unions can only be conjectured as a possible partial explanation of the relatively low sex-income ratios in craft occupations.

In conclusion, then, it appears that, if discrimination is an important cause of male-female income differences, it is not discrimination by employers but by consumers and fellow employees that is effective, and that discrimination by consumers lowers female wages primarily in sales and waitress occupations, whereas discrimination by coworkers affects sex-income ratios mainly in managerial and craft occupations. It is not claimed here that such discrimination exists or is important, because these are the Census occupations where further occupational distribution differences also seem likely.

[35] Men would receive 2 percent more than without discrimination and women 20 percent less, so the sex-income ratio would be .8/1.02 or .784.

[36] Among managerial occupations in government service, where civil service regulations and political pressure may dampen the effects of fellow-employee discrimination, sex-income ratios are much higher than in other managerial occupations. In fact, sex-income ratios in nearly all predominantly government occupations—managerial and other—are relatively high; see Sanborn, *op. cit.*, pp. 77–78.

[37] For a summary of the theory and evidence, see A. Rees, *The Economics of Trade Unions*, Chicago, 1962, chap. 4.

Such discrimination, however, is entirely compatible with the evidence presented in this study, while a strong degree of employer discrimination against women does not seem plausible from this evidence.

Appendix

Methods of Adjusting 1950 Census Data

The 1950 Census classifies all wage and salary workers into 402 detailed occupational titles. Of these only 262 were used in this study. Occupations were omitted on two grounds: (1) they were too broad for one to expect men and women would be doing comparable work; and (2) the median incomes were based on fewer than 30 observations for at least one sex.

The estimated hours worked in 1949 by sex and detailed occupation were derived from the product of the mean hours worked in the Census week (April 1950) by sex and occupation times the mean weeks worked in 1949.[38] For each occupation, the female income was multiplied by an "hours adjustment factor" consisting of the ratio of hours worked by men to hours worked by women. Then, with these adjusted female incomes, new weighted averages of female income were computed which, divided by the male average incomes, give the ratios .74 and .76 in Table 1.

With the next four adjustments—education, age, urban-rural status, and race—a common problem arose: the Census gives distributions of persons by sex and detailed occupation and by each of these four variables, but there is no information showing how income changes with these variables within *detailed* occupations. Suppose in occupation A men and women are distributed as follows by education classes and the income of men in *all* occupations by education is as indicated:

Yrs. school:	under 8	8	9–11	12	13–15	16+	Total
Men..............	10	20	40	15	10	5	100
Women...........	15	25	50	5	3	2	100
Male income........	$500	1000	1500	2000	3000	5000	

We find the mean income men would have earned in the occupation, if, in each education category, these men earned the incomes earned by men of that education in *all* occupations. This mean is $1700. Then find the same for women (assuming they, too, earned the male in-

comes) giving a mean of $1365. These means differ from each other because of educational distributional differences between men and women in the occupation. The ratio of these means, 1700/1365 = 1.245, is the "education adjustment factor" for that occupation. The female income in the occupation, already corrected for hours, would be multiplied by this to "correct" for educational dif-

---

[38]Occupational Characteristics, *op. cit.*, Tables 15 and 17. These products were adjusted upward because there is a positive correlation between hours and weeks worked.

550   INDUSTRIAL AND LABOR RELATIONS REVIEW

ferences between men and women. A similar procedure was followed with each occupation to adjust for within-occupation differences in education, age, urbanness, and race.[39]

Before the age-adjustment factors were

computed, the age-income data were adjusted to eliminate the effects on them of the way hours worked per year differ with age. These corrections flattened the age-income curve and hence reduce the magnitude of the age adjustments.[40]

Since the place of residence and race adjustments were of negligible significance to the study of sex-income differences, their details will be omitted. In both cases, the *all*-occupation income relationships were adjusted to estimate *within*-occupation income differences (discussed in Sanborn, *op. cit.*, pp. 110–120).

---

[39]Analysis of unpublished age-income and education-income patterns by *major* occupation (for 1946) suggests that the *all*-occupation income patterns by age and education were not much steeper than income changes by age and education within *detailed* occupations. Therefore, the adjustment factors were probably not made unduly large by the use of all-occupation income data. I am grateful to Mr. Brunsman of the Census Bureau for these figures. They are analyzed in Sanborn, *op. cit.*, pp. 137–142.

[40]If the hours worked at age 30–34 equal 100, the reciprocals of the hours worked at other age groups are:

Age	14–17	18–19	20–24	25–29	30–34	35–44	45–54	55–64	65–74	75+
Reciprocals of hours, index............	239	149	116	105	100	99	101	105	112	126

Source: Occupational Characteristics, *op. cit.*, Tables 13 and 14 and see Sanborn, *op. cit.*, pp. 109–110.

[20]

MANAGERIAL DISCRIMINATION IN LARGE FIRMS

William G. Shepherd and Sharon G. Levin *

RECENT research on employment discrimination against blacks and women suggests that no single determinant — education, location, growth, or others — is primary. Yet the belief persists (see Alchian and Kessel, 1962; Arrow, 1971; Ashenfelter, 1969; Becker, 1957; Bergmann, 1971; Comanor, 1971; Shepherd, 1969; Thurow, 1969) that the employers' power to choose may be important, via their managerial preferences and discretionary resources. These influences would be visible in large industrial firms which possess market power.

In this paper we test whether the industrial structure and performance of large firms have in fact been related to their employment of blacks and women. The analysis covers about 200 of the largest United States industrial enterprises, using employment data for 1966 and 1970. The focus is on white-collar employment patterns. Being more directly subject to upper management control than is blue-collar employment, the white-collar patterns may provide a sensitive test of whatever role is played by "enterprise policy" under varying conditions and constraints.

First we discuss the basic hypotheses to be tested in section I. Section II explains the variables and the basic models which are to be analyzed. Section III presents the empirical results. And finally, the findings are summarized in section IV.

I Hypotheses

Discrimination in employment is the inclusion of the extraneous racial, ethnic or sex characteristics as elements in hiring and promotion decisions (Arrow, 1971; Becker, 1957; Bergmann, 1971). Its presence may be strongly influenced by the degree of market power held by the firm. On the whole, competitive discipline would enforce decisions which are neutral (that is, not more or less discriminatory than the surrounding society). And, if black and female wage rates are at relatively low levels because of general discrimination, blacks and women would tend to be substituted at the margin for white male employees with equal qualifications. Even horizontal discrimination enforced by fellow workers, which may be endemic in blue-collar and craft jobs, would not persist under perfect competition, for a nondiscriminatory firm would have costs lower than the rest. Therefore, it would thrive, expand, and ultimately impose its behavior on the others. In any event, white-collar employment patterns — at the upper levels of the firm — provide a relatively direct test of whatever role may be played by management, or "enterprise policy." They would be expected to be neutral to race and sex under competition, even in firms whose employment of blue-collar workers may reflect discrimination.

By contrast, the result under market power is not determinate. Profit-maximizing being at least partially voluntary (Alchian and Kessel, 1962; Leibenstein, 1966; Williamson, 1967), those who run a firm with market power may maximize managerial preference functions which include negative racial or sex elements. To this extent, an analysis of maximizing behavior predicts that negative discrimination, rather than neutrality, will normally occur under market power.

Yet, instead, upper-level managers may exercise their discretion "affirmatively" toward neutrality or even "positive" discrimination. That has been a major tenet of recent federal policies. Or, in many cases, the conflicting tendencies within a firm may, at the least, yield a stand-off between these alternative tendencies of hiring policy.

Or indeed, ultimately there may be no structure-discrimination relationships at all. Differences in minority participation may arise primarily from local preferences and variations in supply, or from managers' preferences unrelated to market power, possibly because all firms of any size possess some discretion, and

Received for publication May 12, 1972. Revision accepted for publication February 21, 1973.

* The authors wish to thank Lester Taylor and William S. Comanor for their helpful advice on a number of points. The research was supported by a grant from the Office of Economic Opportunity, Executive Office of the President, Washington, D.C. The interpretations herein are the authors' alone, not necessarily those of any United States government agency.

[412]

MANAGERIAL DISCRIMINATION IN LARGE FIRMS   413

upper-level discrimination in a few choice jobs need not impose large economic costs on the entire firm. Like other researchers, we will try to filter out certain local supply factors, but even so the demand patterns may still fail to emerge. Such an absence of observed statistical relationships, if it occurs, could reflect either (1) counterpoised positive and negative discrimination by various powerful firms, (2) a simple lack of accurate data for testing, or (3) a strict irrelevance of market power to minority employment.

II Variables and Models

Our analysis covers individual firms, rather than the industry-wide averages used in (Ashenfelter, 1969; Becker, 1957; Bergmann, 1971; Comanor, 1971; Shepherd, 1969; Thurow, 1969). This permits finer detail, and it uses a recent model of market power (Shepherd, 1972) which includes the main structural elements and has shown consistent statistical properties. The variables are listed in table 1.

These main elements of market power are the firm's average market share (M), its asset size (S), and its advertising-intensity (A); the last two may be elements in barriers against new entry (Bain, 1967; Shepherd, 1972). In the basic model, fitted to data from 1960–1969 for 231 of the largest United States industrial corporations, M emerges as the primary element in firms' market power. But we also include the other elements for completeness in the present study, in order not to prejudice the analysis.

These variables may show a positive or negative relation to minority employment, *ceteris paribus*. There have been indications that the negative discrimination hypothesis holds (Ashenfelter, 1969; Becker, 1957; Shepherd, 1969), but these have not been conclusive. Therefore, the data provide an unconstrained test between contrary hypotheses.

Minority employment is represented by the participation rates of male blacks (MB) and females (F), as a per cent of all employees in the upper white-collar jobs. We focus on the three top job categories: (1) Officials and Managers, (2) Professionals, and (3) Technicians. The first category (which we designate as $MB1$ and $F1$) is the acid test of opportunity

TABLE 1. — BASIC VARIABLES FOR ANALYSIS

Dependent Variables	
$MB1$, $F1$	Male blacks, or females, as a per cent of all male Officials and Managers
$MB3$, $F3$	Male blacks, or females, as a per cent of all male Officials and Managers, Professionals, and Technicians
$\Delta MB1$, $\Delta MB3$, $\Delta F1$, $\Delta F3$	Change during 1966 to 1970 in participation rates
Independent Variables: Company Attributes	
M	Average market share of the firm in its primary markets
S	Natural logarithm of total net asset size of the firm
A	Advertising expenditure as a per cent of sales
E	Percentage growth of firm sales, 1961 to 1968
PD	Dummy variable = 1 if firm sells mainly producers' goods
W	Dummy variable = 1 if firm sells mainly women's goods
R	Regional dummy variable; $R1$ = primarily southern, $R2$ = middle states, $R3$ = northern non-metropolitan areas, others = not specific
IM, IF	Incidence = firm-wide male black or female participation rate
RE	Residual employment for 1966 (= actual participation rate minus fitted participation rate)
Independent Variables: SMSA Attributes	
POP	Natural logarithm SMSA population, 1966
ΔPOP	SMSA percentage population growth, 1960 to 1966
U	SMSA unemployment rate
NWP	Blacks as per cent of SMSA
$PM1$, $PM3$, $PF1$, $PF3$	SMSA minority participation rates at various job levels
IM, IF	Incidence = local firm male black or female total participation rate

for upward mobility. Actually all three categories in aggregate $(MB3$ and $F3)$ do represent the relatively attractive jobs, with much more "opportunity" than the lesser white-collar jobs and, of course, blue-collar jobs.

We present analyses on both bases. However, even category 1 is broad. Thus, many blacks and women in Officials and Managers jobs, for example, are concentrated down in the very lower ranges of that category, and black foremen and women clerical supervisors are remote from the upper executive offices which the phrase "Officials and Managers" implies (Ashenfelter, 1969; U.S. Equal Employment Opportunity Commission, 1969). Participation rates, therefore, probably overstate the degree of genuine management involvement and opportunity for minorities. But properly interpreted, participation rates may offer a reasonably reliable indication of differences in the *relative* degree of minority access.

So, although white-collar participation rates are not a comprehensive or wholly trustworthy measure of employment opportunity and company policy, we regard them as a useful, available first approximation for research purposes. The upper 3 categories are reasonably distinct from the other 2 white-collar job types (clerks and salesworkers), and they avoid some of the qualitative inter-industry differences which those 2 categories involve.

Our working hypothesis is that when the supply of minority workers is very elastic, then the micro-economic effect of discrimination by any individual employer will appear primarily in the quantity hired in the "best" jobs, rather than the relative wage of those hired. This justifies focusing on the quantity effect as shown by participation rates in upper jobs, because supply is highly elastic to any one firm in a labor pool (such as a metropolitan area or the entire country). This is especially so for white-collar jobs in large cities, where each employing unit usually takes a very small share. But we are not dogmatic about supply being perfectly elastic. And we will control, whenever possible, for variations in local supply conditions.

In analyzing company-wide patterns of minority white-collar job participation, we include several industry-specific demand attributes, in addition to the main structural elements discussed above. The industry-specific variables are the regional focus of the company [1] (if any), the company's growth rate, the company's product type (producers' or women's goods), and the total incidence of minority participation in the company (at all job levels). The last two require some explanation. First, for product type, we suspect that firms who sell mainly producer-durable goods to other firms may be free to discriminate

against minorities. But, on the other hand, firms who deal extensively with "women's" goods (in our panel these are soaps, drugs, toiletry, and publishing companies) [2] may have strong private incentives to employ women in decision-making positions. These "women's" industries would be distinct from the common run of manufacturing industries. Secondly, we suspect that blacks and women tend to be put in supervisory positions primarily over other blacks and women. This too would reflect private incentives for specific minority hiring. Therefore, to test the degree of such possible unity in firm hiring at the blue-collar and white-collar levels, a global measure of "incidence" is included in the model. [3] Furthermore, we also include an incidence-squared term to test for nonlinearity in this relationship. The question is whether extensive minority hiring in lower jobs leads to proportional hiring of minority supervisors, or more or less. The squared term tests for nonproportionality on either side.

A company-wide analysis of minority white-collar participation, however, may mask the variation among the local plants in hiring practices. Is it the company's market structure and industry-specific characteristics that determine "enterprise" policy, or is it simply the local market conditions that dictate most or all of the end result? To evaluate this question as fully as the data permit, we conduct a disaggregated city-based analysis which includes (besides the company-wide determinants) data for city size, growth, unemployment rates, and city-wide minority participation rates at white-collar levels. [4] In addition, we substitute the company's aggregate minority "incidence" rates in the local area for its averages over all locations.

[1] The regional distribution of company plants was evaluated using Fortune listings (1966). Since these data are imperfect, it was possible only to assign firms to broad categories, which are noted in table 1, under variable *R*. Although the groupings are not precise, they may represent regional emphases adequately to detect broad associations with employment patterns.

[2] This group includes 25 of the 174 industrial firms in the 1970 company-wide analysis. For these 25 firms, $F1 = 6.47$ and $F3 = 15.11$ compared to $F1 = 2.26$ and $F3 = 5.95$ for all 174 firms.

[3] The MB and F variables are not significantly collinear with I because the upper white-collar jobs are a very small share of total employment.

[4] The SMSA's are Atlanta, Baltimore, Birmingham, Boston, Chicago, Detroit, Houston, Los Angeles, Minneapolis-St. Paul, New Orleans, New York, Philadelphia, Pittsburgh, St. Louis and San Francisco. They are selected to provide both a full range of regional types and to cover the more important SMSA's. The firms and SMSA attributes are given in a technical appendix which is available on request from the authors.

MANAGERIAL DISCRIMINATION IN LARGE FIRMS   415

Finally, the determinants of *changes* in minority white-collar employment for the period 1966–1970 are also examined. Here another explanatory variable is introduced, residual employment, to test a "catch-up" hypothesis. The plausible expectation is that firms whose relative deficit in minority participation in 1966 was the greatest would have the largest rises during 1966–1970. They would, in short, tend toward the levels appropriate to their market position. The minority deficits are measured by a firm's residual (actual minus fitted) $MB3$ and $F3$ participation rates in a structural analysis of 1966 data in the presence of the other possible determinants. Thus significant negative coefficients relating these variables to 1966–1970 changes would indicate, holding other things constant, that, on the average, the most discriminatory performers in 1966 were catching up to the better performers. If, instead, the coefficients are positive, there would appear to be a relatively erratic process of absorbing minorities into large firms.

The influences of the explanatory variables are assumed to be primarily additive and linear [5] over the range of observations. That seems as logical as any alternative forms for the relationships. The estimation technique used is ordinary least-squares. The coverage of firms is based on the 231-firm study of large industrials (Leibenstein, 1966), which provides the basic market-structure data. The firms are

[5] Asset size and population of the SMSA are linear in their natural logarithms. But I^2 is used as an explanatory variable to pick up any nonlinearities.

primarily nonconglomerate corporations drawn from the largest 250 manufacturing firms.

III Findings

General Patterns

Totals for the large-firm panels are shown in table 2. Consider blacks first. At the 3 upper white-collar levels, the large firms were in 1966 at only about two-thirds of the national averages, even though their total male black participation rate was, at 8.7 per cent, slightly above the national average. If these firms had matched general patterns throughout the economy, *national* levels of black managerial hiring ($MB3$) would have been higher by 7 per cent on average. The 10 best individual large-firm performers (which were in fact widely spread among industry types) had $MB1$ values averaging 1.8 per cent. If all the included large firms had reached this target level, they would have raised *national* $MB1$ rates by no less than 33 per cent. In short, the potential impact of managerial policies toward blacks is large.

The actual levels of black participation ($MB1$ and $MB3$) rose during 1966–1970, nearly tripling the 1966 shares in each job group. This was more rapid than the rise in the national averages, so that by 1970 the large industrials were nearly in line with national performance levels. By 1970 almost every one of the firms had at least one male black in each job category, whereas in 1966 scores of firms had none at all in all of the upper three job groups. Yet the gap between performance and

TABLE 2. — PARTICIPATION RATES OF MALE BLACKS AND FEMALES, IN LARGE INDUSTIAL FIRMS, 1966 AND 1970

		Category 1: Officials and Managers	Category 2: Professionals	Category 3: Technicians	Categories 1, 2 and 3 Combined	Total Company Employment, All 9 Job Categories
LARGE INDUSTRIAL FIRMS						
Male Blacks as per cent of All	1966	.51	.49	1.45	.71	8.70
Male Employees	1970	1.47	1.42	3.08	1.78	10.52
Females as per cent of Total	1966	1.51	2.23	7.38	3.26	17.09
Employees	1970	1.42	4.53	7.49	3.82	17.72
NATIONAL AVERAGES						
Male Blacks as per cent of All	1966	.75	.88	2.29	1.08	8.17
Male Employees	1970	1.30	1.40	3.40	1.71	9.20
Females as per cent of Total	1966	9.20	13.20	27.80	15.86	33.96
Employees	1970	10.03	23.10	25.01	13.74	33.92

Sources: U.S. Equal Employment, Opportunity Commission, various compilations.

potential remained large in 1970. Achievement of the 10-best performance level by the whole industrial group would still have raised national $MB1$ levels sharply in 1970, by 42.4 per cent. As the large firms progressed, so had the rest of the economy.

In female participation rates, the large industrial firms had $F1$ and $F3$ averages which were only about one-sixth to one-fourth of the national averages. The potential national impact from neutral performance by these firms in hiring women was therefore larger than in the case of blacks.

For women, the 1966–1970 rise in participation was much less than for male blacks, both in the large firms and in the whole economy. Only in Professional jobs did female participation rise by much. Female participation in Officials and Managers, and Technicians, jobs did not rise significantly. Especially in the best jobs (categories 1 and 2), women lost ground in the large firms during 1966–1970 compared to trends in the whole economy.

The gap between average and the 10 best performing industrial firms is especially large for females. Women participate only marginally more than do black males in upper white-collar jobs, and at recent rates of change they would soon participate less. This despite their far higher participation in the total labor force and their relatively high levels of training. If the whole panel discriminates so strongly against women, this is likely to override any inter-company differences *within* the sample that may emerge under the following analysis.

Regression Results

Table 3 presents the analysis of minority white-collar employment in 1970. Looking at male black employment first, we find that the individual elements of market structure (M,S, and A) show only weak associations with white-collar hirings. They suggest that market power, perhaps as it may inhere in absolute size and the degree of advertising intensity, may yield slightly higher minority participation rates. Growth of the company is at most a weak positive factor fostering male black managerial employment; while it is apparent, as hypothesized, that producer-durable firms are significantly more exclusionary than other

TABLE 3. — ANALYSIS OF MINORITY WHITE-COLLAR EMPLOYMENT IN 174 LARGE INDUSTRIAL FIRMS, 1970

Equation Number	Dependent Variable	Constant	Market Share (M)	Size (S)	Advertising Intensity (A)	Growth (E)	Incidence (I)	Incidence Squared (I^2)	Producer-durable Dummy Variable (Pd)	Women's Industry Dummy Variable (W)	South (R1)	Middle States (R2)	Northern Non-Metropolitan (R3)	R^2	F ratio
(1)	$MB1$	−.633[a] (1.83)	.001 (.11)	.088[a] (1.76)	.002 (.17)	.112 (1.46)	21.440[b] (7.81)	−40.025[b] (4.04)	−.481[b] (3.52)		−.822[b] (2.64)	.086 (.71)	.141 (.53)	.512	17.102[b]
(2)	$MB3$	.116 (.31)	.002 (.35)	.098[a] (1.83)	.034[b] (2.76)	.140[a] (1.70)	19.470[b] (6.62)	−48.015[b] (4.53)	−.632[b] (4.32)		−.314 (.94)	.146 (1.12)	−.676[b] (2.35)	.482	15.167[b]
(3)	$F1$	1.315 (1.10)	.022 (1.25)	.017 (.09)	−.140[b] (2.79)	.174 (.62)	−6.826 (1.31)	31.290[b] (3.78)	−1.162[b] (2.22)	3.905[b] (4.90)				.491	19.896[b]
(4)	$F3$	1.497 (.85)	.039[a] (1.67)	.044 (.17)	−.018 (.27)	−.270 (.71)	12.403[a] (1.75)	9.938[a] (.89)	−1.376[b] (1.94)	7.098[b] (6.58)				.627	34.670[b]

t ratios are in parentheses.
[a] indicates statistic significant at $\alpha = .10$.
[b] indicates statistic significant at $\alpha = .05$.

firms. There is a fairly strong direct association between blacks' total and managerial participation rates. However, this tapers off as aggregate incidence increases. Evidently, lower-level minority hiring is not fully reflected in managerial opportunity for black males. The regional differences are as expected for blacks. In the South and non-metropolitan North, black participation rates are less than for nationally spread firms. Overall the relationships for male black employment are significant, and they explain approximately 50 per cent of the variation in upper-level participation rates.

For women (equations (3) and (4) in table 3) the results are roughly similar to those for black men. However, size is no longer significant (although market shares (M) now is), and female white-collar participation appears to be just linearly related to aggregate incidence.[6] Again we find that producer-durable goods firms hire and promote minority workers at a significantly lower rate than other firms. Furthermore, it seems that women's opportunity in the upper-level jobs is confined mainly to a distinct subset of firms in traditional "women's" industries. On the average, *ceteris paribus*, we find that female participation in the top three job categories ($F3$) is 7 per cent higher in "women's" industries than it is in nonproducer-durable goods industries. An effect of this magnitude must be regarded as quite large.

Which of the significant variables are the "strongest" determinants of minority white-collar participation rates can be roughly indicated by comparing their standardized regression coefficients or "beta" coefficients. The beta coefficient shows on the average how many standard deviations the dependent variable changes due to a unit standard deviation change in the independent variable. Thus, by transforming equations (2) and (4) in table 3 into standardized form (respectively, equations (2′) and (4′) below) and ignoring the in-

significant factors, we find that for blacks the strongest regressors are the incidence variables, while the women's industry dummy variable is the most powerful factor in explaining female white-collar participation.

$$M\tilde{B}3 = .12\tilde{S} + .19\tilde{A} + .10\tilde{E} + 1.16\tilde{I} - \quad (2')$$
$$.82\tilde{I}^2 + .30\tilde{PD} - .15\tilde{R}3$$

$$\tilde{F}3 = .09\tilde{M} + .31\tilde{I} - .12\tilde{PD} + .42\tilde{W} \quad (4')$$

If hiring practices are determined solely by local market conditions, then the company-wide analysis presented in table 3 might turn out to be spurious. The validity of the company-wide results can be appraised by analyzing minority white-collar participation rates for a disaggregated cross section of cities and company plants. In 1966, the large-firm sample had about 2,000 plants in the 15 Standard Metropolitan Statistical Areas (SMSA's) which make up our stratified sample of cities. These were consolidated into one observation per firm per city, numbering 1,132 altogether. Most of these 1,132 are small plants, with too few white-collar workers to give meaningful patterns. We focus our analysis on the firm-city cases whose total employment in the upper three white-collar job categories was 25 or more; there were 431 such cases.[7]

Unfortunately, the 1966 data are generally less reliable than the 1970 data. The reporting system was new and some errors in reporting and storage occurred. Also some firms in the 1966 panel are missing from the 1970 panel because of mergers. Therefore we may encounter difficulty in separating our evaluation of the role of local versus company-wide influences on enterprise policy from the data problems in the samples. Both panels need to be used, each with its relative strengths; a single pooled analysis would not be as illuminating.

Table 4 presents the results of the city-based analysis for black males. Equations (1) and (4) in table 4 examine the importance of local conditions alone in explaining white-collar

---

[6] Without I^2 in equation (3) of table 3, the regression loses little explanatory power, while I becomes significantly greater than zero. This new regression is

$$F1 = -.282C + .012M - .158A^{**} + .160E - .010S$$
$$\quad\quad (.22) \quad\quad (.68) \quad\quad (3.05) \quad\quad (.54) \quad\quad (.05)$$
$$+ 11.899I^{**} + 3.980W^{**} - 1.004PD^*$$
$$\quad (6.91) \quad\quad (4.81) \quad\quad (1.854)$$
$$\quad\quad\quad\quad\quad\quad R^2 = .447 \quad\quad\quad (3)^1$$

[7] The group is heterogeneous and weighted toward the very largest firms. In 192 of the 431 cases, there were in 1966 no male blacks in the upper three job levels; in 87 cases, there were no women at those levels. Mean values for 1966 were: $MB1 = 1.01$ per cent, $MB3 = 1.81$ per cent, $F1 = 2.69$ per cent, and $F3 = 6.39$ per cent.

TABLE 4. — ANALYSIS OF MALE BLACK EMPLOYMENT IN LARGE INDUSTRIAL FIRMS: CITY-BASED (SMSA) SAMPLE, 1966

Equation Number	Dependent Variable	Constant	SMSA Participation Rates (P3JB1 or PMB3)	Log of Population (LPOP)	Per Cent Change in Population (ΔPOP)	Log of Per Cent of Nonwhite Population (LNWP)	Unemployment Rate (U)	Incidence (I)	Incidence Squared (I^2)	Market Share (M)	Size (S)	Advertising Intensity (A)	Growth (E)	Producer-durable Dummy Variable (PD)	South (R1)	Middle States (R2)	Northern Non-Metropolitan (R3)	R^2	F ratio
			Independent Variables												Regional Dummy Variables				
(1)	MB1	−5.759 (.92)	.011 (.01)	1.000[a] (1.79)	−.050 (.95)	.444 (.51)	−1.077[b] (2.79)	7.143[b] (2.44)	−2.478 (1.11)									.060	3.861[b]
(2)	MB1	2.365 (1.62)	.011 (.01)							−.001 (.50)	−.116 (.57)	.106 (1.60)	−.029 (.09)	−.672 (1.05)	−1.146 (.73)	−.721 (1.22)	−1.671 (.63)	.025	1.353
(3)	MB1	−4.137 (.63)	.011 (.01)	.843 (1.49)	−.058 (1.11)	.463 (.53)	−1.079[b] (2.80)	8.181[b] (2.62)	−2.871 (1.21)	−.001 (.45)	−.072 (.36)	.148[b] (2.25)	.252 (.81)	−.276 (.44)	−.999 (.62)	−.938 (1.61)	−1.481 (.57)	.087	2.636[b]
(4)	MB3	−3.622 (.91)	.840 (1.25)	.748[b] (2.00)	−.013 (.36)	.074 (.15)	−.795[b] (3.11)	8.136[b] (4.06)	−3.423[b] (2.24)									.115	7.853[b]
(5)	MB3	2.086[b] (2.03)								−.001 (.63)	−.002 (.01)	.031 (.68)	.366[a] (1.70)	−.946[b] (2.11)	−1.764 (1.59)	−.031 (.07)	−1.279 (.69)	.034	1.857[a]
(6)	MB3	−4.798 (1.14)	.687 (1.03)	.775[b] (2.07)	−.016 (.44)	.122 (.25)	−.776[b] (3.07)	9.269[b] (4.38)	−3.638[a] (2.26)	−.001 (.51)	.067 (.48)	.068 (1.53)	.659[b] (3.13)	−.512 (1.19)	−1.695 (1.55)	−.222 (.56)	−1.137 (.65)	.157	5.157[b]

t ratios are in parentheses.

[a] indicates statistic significant at $\alpha = .10$.

[b] indicates statistic significant at $\alpha = .05$.

participation rates. Although both relationships are significant, they explain less than 10 per cent of the variation in top-level employment rates. However certain local market conditions do exert their expected influence. White-collar male black participation is higher in larger cities, having smaller unemployment rates, and having higher total incidences of black males in their firms. Just as in the company-wide analysis, upper-level male black employment in the top three job categories rises with total incidence, but tapers off as incidence increases.

In trying to determine what role company-wide policy may play in influencing minority white-collar participation rates, we will evaluate the significance of the company-wide factors (M, S, A, E, Product type, and Regional focus) taken as a group. This is done with an F test of the "explained" sum of squares gained by including the company-wide variables, together with the local market variables in equations (3) and (6) in table 4.[8]

For $MB3$, but not for $MB1$,[9] we can reject, with a 95 per cent degree of confidence, the null hypothesis that company-wide policy is *not* a significant determinant of top-level participation rates.[10] However, out of all the possible company-wide factors, only advertising intensity and growth of the company are statistically significant. This contrasts with the result in table 3 where for $MB3$ product type and asset size were also significantly different from zero. This difference can in part be attributed to differences in the composition and coverage of the two data sets. But particularly in the case of product type, it appears that local market conditions override its importance. (Compare equations (5) and (6) in table 4.) Furthermore, although A and E are significant, their contributions are small compared to the strength of the local incidence factor in explaining $MB1$ and $MB3$.[11]

For women (table 5), none of the local factors is significant except for aggregate incidence in the company's own local plants. This is not surprising, but it does mean that local conditions of growth, employment rates, size, etc., will not be specific sources of additional opportunity for women in the future. The role of incidence also contrasts sharply with that found for black males. Managerial participation rates for females decline with I, but increase with I^2. Therefore, once again, women's opportunities appear to be centered in the relatively few industries which hire women clerks and operatives in high proportions.[12] As I rises to high levels, the I^2 term predominates, raising $F1$ and $F3$ sharply. But for low or moderate levels of I, there is little or no such effect.

We can reject, on statistical tests, the hypothesis that the group of company-wide structural and industry-specific characteristics is *not* a significant determinant of female white-collar employment levels.[13] Yet here the only company-wide explanatory variable that is consistently significant is product type. As we have observed earlier, producer-durable goods firms discriminate strongly against women. Again the incidence terms proved to be the strongest regressors in the relationships explaining female top-level participation rates.[14]

$$\tilde{M}B1 = -.15\tilde{U} \quad\quad + .26\tilde{I} + .13\tilde{A}$$

$$\tilde{M}B3 = \ .16LP\tilde{O}P + .16\tilde{E} - .16\tilde{U} + .41\tilde{I} - .21\tilde{I}^2.$$

[13] This requires further explanation. It seems that the women's industry dummy variable and incidence are closely related because elimination of W from equation (3) primarily affects the magnitudes of I and I^2 without the loss of much explanatory power. This new regression without W is:

$$F1 = -.588C - .0003M - .232S - .006A + .048E$$
$$\quad\quad (.12) \quad\quad (.19) \quad\quad (.91) \quad\quad (.07) \quad\quad (.13)$$
$$\quad - 2.112PD** + .047PF1 + .467LPOP$$
$$\quad\quad (2.68) \quad\quad\quad (.42) \quad\quad (.90)$$
$$\quad + .027\Delta POP - .329U - 22.437I** + 57.082I^2**$$
$$\quad\quad (.47) \quad\quad (.61) \quad\quad (4.71) \quad\quad (9.55)$$
$$\quad\quad\quad\quad\quad\quad\quad\quad\quad\quad\quad R^2 = .414.$$

[13] The F test statistic for $F1 = 2.23 > F$ critical $.05,6,418 = 2.12$. Therefore for $F1$ we reject H_0 with a 95 per cent degree of confidence. The F test statistic for $F3 = 2.06$ exceeds the critical F value with a degree of confidence $\geqq 90$ per cent.

[14] The standardized regressions for $F1$ and $F3$ ignoring the insignificant factors are:

$$\tilde{F}1 = -.53\tilde{I} + 1.06\tilde{I}^2 - .12P\tilde{D}$$
$$\tilde{F}3 = -.40\tilde{I} + 1.09\tilde{I}^2 - .10P\tilde{D}.$$

---

[8] A complete description of this F test is given by Johnston (1963, pp. 123–125).

[9] Since in all cases except $MB1$ we were able to reject the null hypothesis for company-wide policy, we attribute the null finding for $MB1$ to measurement errors in the data. The F test statistic for $MB1 = 1.505 < F$ critical $.05,8,415 \doteq 1.94$. Therefore, we accept H_0.

[10] The F test statistic for $MB3 = 2.581 > F$ critical $.05,8,415 \doteq 1.94$. Therefore we reject H_0.

[11] The standardized regressions for $MB1$ and $MB3$, ignoring the insignificant factors, are:

TABLE 5. — ANALYSIS OF FEMALE EMPLOYMENT IN LARGE INDUSTRIAL FIRMS: CITY-BASED (SMSA) SAMPLE, 1966

Equation Number	Dependent Variable	Constant	SMSA Participation Rates (PPI or PF3)	Log of Population (LPOP)	Per Cent Change in Population (ΔPOP)	Unemployment Rate (U)	Incidence (I)	Incidence Squared (I²)	Market Share (M)	Size (S)	Advertising Intensity (A)	Growth (E)	Producer-durable Dummy Variable (PD)	Women's Industry Dummy Variable (W)	R^2	F ratio
(1)	$F1$	−5.001 (1.21)	.042 (.37)	.616 (1.19)	.027 (.47)	.373 (.69)	−21.656[b] (4.57)	57.334[b] (9.62)							.398	46.720[b]
(2)	$F1$	8.109[b] (3.68)	.061 (.54)	.471 (.91)	.028 (.48)	.273 (.51)			−.002 (1.06)	−.479 (1.55)	−.275[b] (2.27)	.104 (.24)	−3.558[b] (3.65)	6.206[b] (3.37)	.083	6.396[b]
(3)	$F1$	−.817 (.17)	.010 (.08)	.545 (.94)	.015 (.21)	−.215 (.39)	−22.066[b] (4.63)	56.128[b] (9.34)	−.001 (.41)	−.201 (.79)	−.085 (.86)	.035 (.10)	−2.037[b] (2.58)	2.122 (1.41)	.417	24.916[b]
(4)	$F3$	−.498 (.09)					−20.056[b] (3.97)	72.745[b] (11.43)							.566	92.167[b]
(5)	$F3$	12.907[b] (4.63)							.002 (.82)	−.504 (1.29)	−.242 (1.58)	−.371 (.67)	−4.364[b] (3.54)	6.400[b] (2.75)	.074	5.647[b]
(6)	$F3$	2.563 (.43)	.024 (.18)	.408 (.70)	.017 (.25)	−.239 (.44)	−20.562[b] (4.04)	72.307[b] (11.25)	−.0001 (.05)	−.026 (.10)	.036 (.34)	−.492 (1.30)	−2.017[b] (2.38)	.203 (.13)	.578	47.713[b]

Independent Variables

t ratios are in parentheses.
[a] indicates statistic significant at $\alpha = .10$.
[b] indicates statistic significant at $\alpha = .05$.

TABLE 6. — ANALYSIS OF CHANGES IN MINORITY WHITE-COLLAR EMPLOYMENT IN LARGE INDUSTRIAL FIRMS, 1966–1970

Equation Number	Dependent Variable	Constant	Change in Incidence (ΔI)	Residual Employment (RE)	Market Share (M)	Size (S)	Advertising Intensity (A)	Growth (E)	Producer-durable Dummy Variable (PD)	Women's Industry Dummy Variable (W)	South (R1)	Middle States (R2)	Northern Non-metropolitan (R3)	R^2	F ratio
(1)	$\Delta MB3$	.690[b] (2.25)	4.166[b] (2.27)		-.004 (.90)	.075 (1.51)	.020[a] (1.83)	-.026 (.35)	-.274[b] (2.12)		-.019 (.08)	-.061 (.51)	-.964[b] (4.05)	.207	4.235[b]
(2)	$\Delta MB3$	.702[b] (2.28)	4.331[b] (2.33)	6.759 (.63)	-.004 (.87)	.074 (1.48)	.019[a] (1.72)	-.026 (.35)	-.281[b] (2.16)		-.039 (.16)	-.062 (.51)	-.969[b] (4.06)	.209	3.831[b]
(3)	$\Delta F3$	1.399 (1.23)	-.631 (.46)		-.004 (.19)	-.090 (.45)	.133[b] (2.86)	-.338 (1.09)	.020 (.04)	-.394 (.54)				.077	1.764[a]
(4)	$\Delta F3$	1.919[a] (1.77)	-2.667[a] (1.92)	-23.882[b] (4.38)	-.006 (.36)	-.200 (1.06)	.154[b] (3.50)	-.418 (1.43)	.320 (.63)	-.029 (.04)				.183	4.116[b]

f ratios are in parentheses.
a indicates statistic significant at α = .10.
b indicates statistic significant at α = .05.

Table 6 presents our analysis of the *changes* in minority participation rates over the period 1966–1970. For blacks, the catching-up hypothesis is not confirmed. Deficits in minority hiring, as measured by residual employment in 1966, are not significantly related to rises in black participation $\Delta MB3$. On the positive side, changes in company-wide incidence (*I*) and market power (as reflected in advertising-intensity) have led to significant gains in black participation rates. But, on the other hand, producer-durable goods firms and firms located in the non-metropolitan North absorbed blacks at significantly lower rates than the rest. These suggest that there are specific limits to further rises in black participation.

For women, almost every result is different. The catching-up hypothesis appears to be operative; firms with the largest deficits in 1966 scored the largest gains in female participation levels during 1966–1970. However the prospects for women do not appear as favorable as they do for male blacks. A swelling in the total incidence of females does not lead, *ceteris paribus*, to increases in their share of white-collar positions. Therefore, that potential source of women's opportunity appears absent.

One implication is that resistance to upper-level female participation is more deeply entrenched than it is against black males. This had been suggested by other findings in our study. Alternatively, black participation rates may simply have not yet reached the 4–7 per cent range that women have reached in some upper-level jobs. Once black participation begins to rise above the sprinkling implied by a 1.8 per cent rate, then perhaps it too will encounter increasingly strong resistance. Or finally, the seeming contrasts in prospects for male blacks and women might merely reflect the coming of the age of the "black" movement by 1970, while the "women's" movement is still in its infancy (or, conceivably, has already exhausted its potential).

IV Summary

Our data base has been extensive but imperfect, and there are likely to be cross-currents in the relationship under study. Therefore, it is not surprising that we have found few strong statistical correlates of managerial hiring of minorities. An added reason may be that the big differences are between large firms as a group and all other smaller firms as a group, rather than among large firms.

Taking the group of large firms altogether in 1966 and 1970, both male blacks and women are essentially at token levels in managerial jobs, even after a sharp rise for male blacks. By contrast, women's managerial participation in large firms has not been rising, even though the supply of qualified women is presumably relatively abundant at most skill levels. Except for a few "women's" industries, the management of large corporations is in fact a distinctively white male preserve.

Minority participation does vary among the large firms, but our analysis has identified only a few possible determinants of the variation. Neither the company-wide nor the local factors appeared to be strong. For blacks, only incidence and location came through strongly and consistently. And the positive effect of incidence appears to taper off; as black production workers are added, the rise in black managers is not proportional. For women, the basic influence appears to be the type of industry. In producers-goods firms, women are distinctly scarcer; while their main opportunities lie in a narrow subset of "women's" industries. As for market power, it appears to be neither a positive nor a negative determinant. Whether this is a stand-off between counter-influences we cannot yet say. It does appear that variations among the firms are less important than differences between these firms and all others.

Local determinants appear as expected for male blacks, though they are not powerful. For women, local factors play little apparent role at all.

Our research appears to have narrowed down the probable influences on minority employment at managerial levels. But type 2 error may be lurking in our results, for our data may be faulty and the panel of large firms is slight. Our analysis leaves only a few analytical determinants which would underlie further rises in minority participation. In short, the known sources of further opportunity are few and weak.

REFERENCES

Alchian, A. A., and R. A. Kessel, "Competition, Monopoly, and the Pursuit of Pecuniary Gain," in *Aspects of Labor Economics* (Princeton: National Bureau of Economic Research, 1962).

Arrow, K. J., "Some Models of Racial Discrimination in the Labor Market," RAND document no. RM–6253–RC, Santa Monica, Feb., 1971.

Ashenfelter, O., *Minority Employment Patterns, 1966*, mimeographed, 1969.

Bain, J. S., *Industrial Organization*, rev. ed. (New York: John Wiley and Sons, 1967).

Becker, G. S., *The Economics of Discrimination* (Chicago: University of Chicago Press, 1957).

Bergmann, B., "The Effect on White Incomes of Discrimination in Employment," *Journal of Political Economy* (1971), 294–313.

Comanor, W. S., "Racial Discrimination in American Industry," 1971 (mimeo).

Fortune magazine, *Plant and Product Directory of the 1,000 Largest U.S. Industrial Corporations, 1965–66*, New York, 1966.

Johnston, J., *Econometric Methods* (New York: McGraw-Hill Book Company, 1963).

Leibenstein, H., " 'Allocative Efficiency' and 'X-efficiency,' " *American Economic Review*, 1966, 392–415.

Shepherd, W. G., "The Elements of Market Structure," this REVIEW (Feb. 1972), 25–37.

———, "Market Power and Racial Discrimination in White-Collar Employment," *Antitrust Bulletin*, 1969, 141–161.

Thurow, L., *Poverty and Discrimination* (Washington, D.C.: Brookings Institution, 1969).

U. S. Equal Employment Opportunity Commission, Report no. 1, *Job Patterns for Minorities and Women in Private Industry, 1966*, parts I, II and III, Washington, D.C., 1969.

Williamson, O. E., *The Economics of Discretionary Behavior: Managerial Objectives in a Theory of the Firm*, Markham, 1967.

[21]

STATISTICAL THEORIES OF DISCRIMINATION

IN LABOR MARKETS

DENNIS J. AIGNER and GLEN G. CAIN

Economic discrimination has been difficult to explain by means of standard neoclassical economic models that assume pervasive competition. Why, after all, should two groups of workers who have the same productivity receive different remuneration? The challenge to explain this phenomenon is posed most sharply by the marked differentials in wages and earnings between blacks and whites and between men and women—differentials that remain substantial despite diligent efforts to control for supply-side productivity traits.

This paper examines that issue from a perspective suggested by Kenneth Arrow, John J. McCall, Edmund S. Phelps, Melvin W. Reder, and A. Michael Spence, all of whom focused on certain implications of employer uncertainty about the productivity of racial (or sex) groups of workers, particularly in the context of hiring and placement decisions.[1] This paper offers several models that clarify the meaning of economic "statistical discrimination," simplify the theory, and yield plausible empirical implications. On the other hand, the paper also identifies several shortcomings of "statistical discrimination" models; shows that the often-cited Phelps model does not constitute economic discrimina-

Economic discrimination in labor markets is conventionally defined as the presence of different pay for workers of the same ability. This paper analyzes that problem with the aid of a simple stochastic model in which employers hire, place, and pay workers on the basis of imperfect information about their abilities. The available information consists of both group membership (black, white; male, female) and information about individual performance on some fallible indicator of ability (e.g., a test). Several types of economic discrimination within the context of competitive market assumptions are examined by means of several models, and the empirical plausibility and implications of these models are discussed. The authors conclude that the statistical theories are unlikely to provide an important explanation of labor market discrimination under conventional neoclassical assumptions.

Dennis J. Aigner and Glen G. Cain are both Professors of Economics at the University of Wisconsin. They express their gratitude for the extensive comments of Arthur S. Goldberger. This research was supported in part by funds granted to the Institute for Research on Poverty at the University of Wisconsin-Madison by the Office of Economic Opportunity pursuant to the Economic Opportunity Act of 1964 (GGC), and by NSF grant GS-30005 (DJA). The opinions expressed here are those of the authors.—EDITOR

[1] Kenneth Arrow, "Models of Job Discrimination" and "Some Mathematical Models of Race in the Labor Market," in Anthony H. Pascal, ed., *Racial Discrimination in Economic Life* (Lexington, Mass.: Lexington Books, D. C. Heath and Co., 1972), pp. 83–102 and 187–204; and "The Theory of Discrimination," in Orley Ashenfelter and Albert Rees, eds., *Discrimination in Labor Markets* (Princeton, N. J.: Princeton University Press, 1973), pp. 3–33; John J. McCall, *Income Mobility, Racial Discrimination, and Economic Growth* (Lexington, Mass.: Lexington Books, D. C. Heath and Co., 1972); and "The Simple Mathematics of Information, Job Search, and Prejudices," in Anthony H. Pascal, ed., *Racial Discrimination in Economic Life* (Lexington, Mass.: Lexington Books, D. C. Heath and Co., 1972), pp. 205–44; Edmund S. Phelps, "The Statistical Theory of Racism and Sexism," *American Economic Review*, Vol. 62, No. 4 (September 1972), pp. 659–61; Melvin W. Reder, "Human Capital and Economic Discrimination," in Ivar Berg, ed., *Human Resources and Economic Welfare; Essays in Honor of Eli Ginzberg* (New York: Columbia University Press, 1972), pp. 71–88; and A. Michael Spence, "Job Market Signaling," *Quarterly Journal of Economics*, Vol. 87, No. 3 (August 1973), pp. 355–74 and *Market Signaling* (Cambridge, Mass.: Harvard University Press, 1974).

tion, statistical or otherwise; and concludes that these models probably do not explain most labor market discrimination.

The Basic Model

We introduce the statistical model of discrimination with the version by Phelps, contained in an article with the imposing title, "The Statistical Theory of Racism and Sexism."[2] The essential features are as follows. In the hiring and placement of workers, employers base their decisions on some indicator of skill, y, (such as a performance test) that measures the true skill level, q. The terms "ability," "productivity," and "skill" will be used interchangeably herein. In practice, y would undoubtedly involve a number of measures, but the assumption here will be that a single test score is all that is measured by y. The measurement equation is

$$(1) \qquad y = q + u,$$

where u is a normally distributed error term, independent of q, with zero mean and constant variance; q is also assumed to be normally distributed with a mean equal to α and with a constant variance.

Employers can observe the test score, y, but they are interested in this only insofar as it gives them information about the unobservable variable, q. Thus, the immediate interest of the employer is the expected or predicted value of q, which we shall label $\hat{q}$.

The expected value of q, given y ($E(q|y)$) is:

$$(2) \qquad \hat{q} = E(q|y) = (1 - \gamma)\alpha + \gamma y,$$

where α is the group mean of q (and y) and

$$(3) \qquad \gamma = \frac{Var(q)}{Var(q) + Var(u)} = \frac{Cov(q,y)}{Var(y)}$$

$$= \left[\frac{Cov(q,y)^2}{Var(q)Var(y)} = r^2 \right],$$

where r^2 is the squared coefficient of correlation between q and y. In classical test score theory, γ is the reliability of a test score, y, as a measure of the true score, q. Clearly, $0 < \gamma < 1$.

By normal distribution theory, Equation 2 is the least squares regression, expressing q in terms of a group effect $[(1-\gamma)\alpha]$ and an individual effect (γy). It is useful to think of Equation 2 as a conditional expectation from a linear population regression function:

$$(4) \qquad q = (1 - \gamma)\alpha + \gamma y + u'$$

where u' is the usual well-behaved error term. In principle, the regression is operational, because employers could measure the actual q of a worker on the basis of a *post hoc* evaluation of the worker's performance.

Now, consider two differentiated groups of workers, say whites and blacks, with possibly different means, α^W and α^B, and possibly different variances of q and u. (Although we use whites and blacks throughout, our discussion is equally applicable to males and females.) The employer is assumed to pay a worker an amount, $\hat{q}$, based on the specific information available for each group and individual (see Equation 2):

$$(5a) \qquad \hat{q}^W = (1 - \gamma^W)\alpha^W + \gamma^W y^W$$

$$(5b) \qquad \hat{q}^B = (1 - \gamma^B)\alpha^B + \gamma^B y^B.$$

The slope, γ, will generally differ for the two groups if the variances of q and u differ, as shown by Equation 3.[3]

The nature of the hiring and placement process requires that the employer make a subjective assessment of a worker's skill. We assume that this *assessment* of q, given y, will equal the *expectation* of q, conditional on y. This assumption is in keeping with wage-maximizing behavior by work-

---

[2]*American Economic Review* (September 1972).

[3]Any random error in y as a measure of q is represented by u. A *systematic* error in y as a measure of q for one or the other racial groups could also be introduced, but this would not add substantively to our analysis. For example, if blacks scored below whites by some constant amount for any q value, a negative intercept term could be added to Equation 1. However, a simple transformation in which this intercept difference was added to q^B would restore comparability in the q values for both groups according to a new set of equations like Equations 5a and 5b. This type of bias in the test instrument would not, by itself, affect the reliability of the instrument and is, therefore, inconsequential. The unreliability of y as a measure of q, however, is another matter, as we demonstrate later.

ers and profit-maximizing behavior by employers, since a job market function of employers is to assess (or predict) factor productivity, given the costs of available information, and to pay the factors of production accordingly. Employers who are inefficient in this function will tend to be weeded out by the "market mechanism" of competition. As Spence concludes in considering a similar model of employer behavior, "In an equilibrium the subjective distribution and the one implied in the market mechanism are identical," assuming that neither group of workers is completely isolated from employers.[4]

To anticipate a possible source of confusion, we should emphasize that the assumed correspondence between the employers' subjective conditional expectation of q and the conditional expectation of realized q in the market implies that the group means (the αs) are estimated without bias. In particular, employers will not persist in believing that $\alpha^W > \alpha^B$ if, in fact, $\alpha^W = \alpha^B$. If employers mistakenly believe $\alpha^W > \alpha^B$, then they will mistakenly overpay whites relative to blacks, and we may doubt that such mistaken behavior will persist in competitive markets. Indeed, as an explanation of discrimination against blacks, a theory of discrimination based on employers' mistakes is even harder to accept than the explanation based on employers' "tastes for discrimination," because the "tastes" are at least presumed to provide a source of "psychic gain" (utility) to the discriminator.[5] To

interpret the "statistical theory of discrimination" as a theory of "erroneous" or "mistaken" behavior by employers, as have some economists,[6] is therefore without foundation. Furthermore, Andrew I. Kohen errs by claiming that, "Phelps [1972] demonstrates that irrespective of the validity of using sex" as a proxy variable for productivity characteristics of the job applicant, "discrimination is the outcome."[7] Phelps demonstrates no such result.

Definitions of Economic Discrimination

Economic discrimination is said to exist when workers do not receive pay or remuneration commensurate with their productivity—when, in short, equal productivity is not rewarded with equal pay. Our focus is on labor market discrimination, which means that we will generally assume that the worker's pre–labor market investments and endowments are given. We adopt the prevailing convention of defining productivity in terms of physical output or actual job performance, acknowledging, however, that this definition can be ambiguous. As others have pointed out, discrimination against a particular group of workers can always be explained away by attaching a cost to some characteristic of the group that is not directly related to their work abilities.

It is necessary to distinguish group discrimination from individual discrimination that is independent of group mem-

---

[4]Spence, "Job Market Signaling," pp. 360–61.

[5]It is more precise to say that the wage policy of employers whose subjective assessment of q persistently differs from the expected value of actual q would not be viable unless all current and potential employers made the same error. Otherwise, the forces of competition would lead to an expansion of output by employers who erred the least (or not at all) at the expense of those who erred the most. Thus, imposing a wedge between the subjective expectation of q and the actual expected value of q is analytically equivalent to imposing employers' "tastes for discrimination" as a wedge between the employers' subjective evaluation of the worth (or productivity) of a worker and his actual worth. As both Gary S. Becker and Arrow have made clear, variance in tastes for discrimination among employers will lead to a situation in which relatively non-

discriminating employers drive the discriminating employers out of business in the long-run competitive equilibrium. See Gary S. Becker, *The Economics of Discrimination* (Chicago: University of Chicago Press, 1971), 2d ed.; and Arrow, "Models of Job Discrimination" and "The Theory of Discrimination."

[6]Cynthia B. Lloyd, "The Division of Labor Between the Sexes: A Review," in Cynthia B. Lloyd, ed., *Sex, Discrimination, and the Division of Labor* (New York: Columbia University Press, 1975), pp. 1–24 and Harriet Zellner, "Discrimination Against Women, Occupational Segregation, and the Relative Wage," *American Economic Review*, Vol. 62, No. 2 (May 1972), pp. 157–60.

[7]Andrew I. Kohen, section entitled "Differentiation in the Market," (pp. 1256–62) in Hilda Kahne, "Economic Perspectives of the Roles of Women in the American Economy," *Journal of Economic Literature*, Vol. 13, No. 4 (December 1975), pp. 1249–92.

bership. Race or sex discrimination is a consequence of group discrimination; discrimination among individuals within a group, on the other hand, carries no presumption of group discrimination nor, therefore, of race or sex discrimination. Group discrimination in labor markets is evident when the average wage of a group is not proportional to its average productivity. On this basis, our findings reveal that even nondiscriminatory practices by employers may yield a discriminatory outcome: groups that have the same average ability may receive different average pay.

Within-group or individual discrimination is inevitable. The fact that within a group, all individual workers with the same true ability will not receive the same pay is clearly shown in Equation 4, in which *q* is not exactly predicted by *y*. To illustrate that this does not necessarily involve group discrimination, consider a case in which all college graduates are offered one wage, equal to their average productivity and higher than the wage offered to all high-school graduates. Although individual discrimination occurs within each schooling group (except in the unrealistic case of zero variance in ability within each group), no presumption of between-group discrimination is warranted. The distinction between these two types of discrimination has not always been clear in the literature.[8]

Perhaps not so obvious is the fact that group discrimination may be absent even though the wages, $\hat{q}$, of blacks and whites with the *same* ability, q_0, are not generally equal. Generally, $E(\hat{q}^B | q_0) \neq E(\hat{q}^W | q_0)$—expressions obtained by taking expectations conditional on *q* in Equation 2. Thus: $E(\hat{q} | q) = (1 - \gamma)\alpha + \gamma E(y | q)$. But $E(y | q) = q$; so

$$(6) \qquad E(\hat{q} | q) = (1 - \gamma)\alpha + \gamma q,$$

and γ and α may differ for blacks and whites. However, there need not be any average difference in compensation between groups, because the individual inequalities of the above expectation over the range of *q* may be offsetting between whites and blacks. These points are demonstrated and clarified in our analysis of particular models.

A Phelps Model

The implications of Phelps's model, outlined previously, depend on assumptions about the average abilities, the variances of ability, and the variances of measurement error for the two groups—blacks and whites. Phelps makes three assumptions, each of which we question at some point in our discussion. In most of his paper he assumes, first, that u^W and u^B have the same variances; second, that the variance of q^W is less than the variance of q^B; and, third, the the average ability of blacks is lower than that of whites.[9]

[8]For one example, see Francine B. Blau and Carol L. Jusenius, "Economists' Approaches to Sex Segregation in the Labor Market: An Appraisal," in Martha Blaxall and Barbara Reagan, eds., *Women and the Workplace* (Chicago: University of Chicago Press), pp. 181–99. In discussing sex discrimination, Blau and Jusenius claim that "stereotyping, the treatment of each individual member of a group as if he/she possessed the average characteristics of the group" is "appropriately defined as a form of discrimination even if the employers' perceptions of the average [group] . . . differential are correct" (p. 194). In another source Michael J. Piore, in discussing race discrimination, labels as statistical discrimination a situation in which job candidates are rejected because they do not possess traits that "tend to be statistically correlated with job performance" (p. 56). See Michael J. Piore, "Jobs and Training," in Samuel H. Beer and Richard E. Barringer, eds., *The State and the Poor* (Cambridge, Mass.: Winthrop Press, 1970), pp. 53–83. If the decision rules *are* correct on average, however, then Piore's assertion that the employer is "discrimina-

tory" says no more than that the decision maker, like the rest of us in our decisions, lacks perfect knowledge! Finally, consider the following quotation by Lester C. Thurow in *Generating Inequality* (New York: Basic Books, Inc., 1975):

[Statistical discrimination] occurs whenever an individual is judged on the basis of the average characteristics of the group, or groups, to which he or she belongs rather than upon his or her own characteristics (p. 172).

The statement is meaningless unless the following questions are answered: Are the group characteristics correctly judged on average? Is a person's age or test score, for example, an "own" characteristic, or does it also refer to the group (population) with that particular value or score? Is statistical discrimination averted only when *all* relevant "own" characteristics are known?

[9]The lower mean value of q^B is represented in Phelps's paper by a dummy variable for race (1 if black) with a negative coefficient, but the presenta-

It is disconcerting that Phelps assumed a difference in average abilities at the outset, because discrimination is defined as differences in pay for workers of the same ability, or, equivalently, a difference in pay that is not related to a difference in ability. Sometimes, of course, the assumption of equal ability is facilitated by narrowing the race (or sex) comparisons to subgroups of workers of the same age, schooling, or experience. For expository reasons, we will initially assume equal average abilities for the two groups: $\alpha^B = \alpha^W = \alpha$. The case of unequal average abilities will be examined later.

The other two assumptions in the basic Phelps model, $Var(u^B) = Var(u^W)$ and $Var(q^B) > Var(q^W)$, dictate that the slope, γ, of the q-on-y regression in Equations 2 or 4 is steeper for blacks than for whites. This is clear from Equation 3. It means that the test score, y, is a more reliable predictor of q for blacks than for whites. Accepting this unusual result for the moment, let us examine its consequences.

As Phelps noted, "at some high test score and higher ones the black applicant is predicted by the employer to excel over any white applicant with the same or lower test scores."[10] Figure 1A shows this—as well as the corollary proposition that at low test scores the white worker is predicted to excel over a black worker with the same test score. Low-scoring whites being paid more than low-scoring blacks is offset by high-scoring whites being paid less than high-scoring blacks. In what sense, then, does this picture depict racial economic discrimination? Each worker is paid in accordance with his expected productivity, based on an unbiased predictor. Moreover, the two groups, which have (by assumption) the same mean ability, receive the same mean wages.

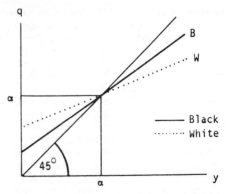

Figure 1A. Predictions of Productivity (q) by Race and Test Score (y), Assuming a Steeper Slope for Blacks.

The apparent definition of economic discrimination revealed by Figure 1A, and which we must ascribe to Phelps, is "different pay for the same y scores." But since y scores are intended only to indicate expected productivity, it is discrimination with respect to q and not y that is economically relevant.[11] Even a legal requirement that payments be equal for equal y scores would contribute nothing to the overall improvement of the status of blacks, since, as is clear in Figure 1A, what blacks would win at the lowest q values (relative to whites) they would lose at the highest q values.

In any event, the assumption that $\gamma^B > \gamma^W$—or that the y score is a more reliable indicator of q for blacks than whites—is

---

tion is not entirely clear. His equation (5') would appear to represent a single regression model for workers of both races, in which z is an additive term that is equivalent to a dummy variable (0 if white). However, the additivity of z gives the wrong impression, because the all-worker regression requires a zy interaction to capture Phelps's assumption that the slope of y on q is different for the two races.

[10] Phelps, "The Statistical Theory of Racism and Sexism," p. 661.

[11] Recall that the definition of economic discrimination as wage differences among workers with the same productivity implies pervasive *within*-group discrimination, given the conditional variance in q. Thus, some whites with a given test score, y_0, who are hired at a wage commensurate with $E(q|y_0)$, will have an actual q that is greater than $E(q|y_0)$; others will turn out to have an actual q that is less than the expected value. We could fairly say that the former (positive residuals) are discriminated against and the latter (negative residuals) receive preferential treatment. Presumably, there is more of this sort of discrimination at the time of initial hirings than after the elapse of time, when the experience of workers and employers will narrow the conditional variance of q, given what will then be an augmented y. But, as stated earlier, a within-group conditional variance does not imply discrimination between groups.

unappealing. The Scholastic Aptitude Test has been found, for example, to be a *less* reliable indicator of college grades for blacks than for whites.[12] At the same time, we see no reason to assume the variance in true ability differs for the two races, although arguments can be made for a difference in either direction.[13] Moreover, an implication of the hypothesis that $\gamma^B > \gamma^W$ is that the white-black differential in pay—reflecting a differential in expected q—narrows (and eventually becomes negative) as the y indicator increases. The bulk of the empirical evidence points, however, to the opposite result: if y is measured by years of school completed or by years of experience—two of the most important and commonly used indicators of productivity—the empirical relation between y and earnings (or wages) shows blacks faring worse relative to whites as y increases.[14]

A model that reflects this evidence and assumes that the testing process is less reliable for blacks is shown in Figure 1B. We will examine implications of this specification below, but the point here is that economic discrimination is no more evident in Figure 1B than it is in 1A. As be-

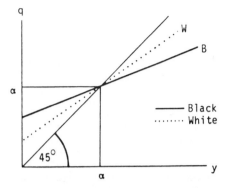

Figure 1B. Predictions of Productivity (q) by Race and Test Score (y), Assuming a Steeper Slope for Whites.

fore, each worker is paid according to his expected productivity, resulting in equal average wages for the two racial groups. The only difference shown by 1B is that whites with y scores above the mean receive higher wages than blacks, and the reverse is true for y scores below the mean.

An Alternative Model

Up to this point we have assumed explicitly that the employers know $E(q|y)$ and implicitly that the dispersion of $q|y$ is costless. This is equivalent to assuming that q enters the profit function linearly, or that the employer is risk-neutral with respect to q. It is more realistic to permit q to enter the profit function (or the "utility of profit" function) nonlinearly, which would allow the correct decision rule for hiring labor to involve higher moments of q. In the simple model adopted below, only the conditional variance of q, written $Var(q|y) = Var(q)(1-\gamma)$, is required to reflect risk aversion and to yield a theoretical explanation for economic discrimination.[15]

---

[12]Robert L. Linn, "Fair Test Use in Selection," *Review of Educational Research*, Vol. 43, No. 2 (1973), pp. 139–61.

[13]Blacks confront environmental restrictions on fulfilling their capacities, and this may lead to a smaller variance of q^B. On the other hand, perhaps whites face a more homogeneous set of environmental determinants of q, which would make the variance of q^W smaller. Any number of possibilities suggest themselves.

[14]For example, Finis Welch in "Education and Racial Discrimination," in Orley Ashenfelter and Albert Rees, eds., *Discrimination in Labor Markets* (Princeton, N.J.: Princeton University Press, 1973), pp. 43–81, remarks: "It is well known that, on balance, the ability of schooling to boost Negro earnings has been less than for whites, at least for males" (p. 43). Weiss supports this finding and also finds that "scholastic achievement" (as measured by test scores) was a better predictor of earnings for white males than for black males. See Randall D. Weiss, "The Effect of Education on the Earnings of Blacks and Whites," *Review of Economic Statistics*, Vol. 52, No. 2 (May 1970), pp. 150–59. Finally, a flatter age (experience)/wage profile is shown for black males and women than for white males in Robert E. Hall, "Why Is the Unemployment Rate So High at Full Employment?" *Brookings Papers on Economic Activity*, No. 3 (Washington, D.C.: The Brookings Institution, 1970), p. 394.

[15]The expression for the conditional variance of q is derived from normal distribution theory. It is an analogue of the expression for the residual variance in a simple linear regression as: $(1 - r^2) Var$ (dependent variable). Thus, in the population regression, Equation 4, we have $Var(q|y) = Var(u') = Var(q) -$

$\gamma^2 Var(y) = Var(q) - \left[\dfrac{Var(q)}{Var(y)}\right]^2 Var(y)$, using

an expression for γ from Equation 3; so $Var(q|y) = Var(q)(1 - \gamma)$.

STATISTICAL THEORIES OF DISCRIMINATION   181

To simplify the problem, assume that labor is the only factor of production, that output is fixed, and that prices and wage rates are exogenously determined. Thus, profits, Π, are solely a function of labor services. Given the number of workers required to maximize the utility-of-profits function, $U(\Pi)$, the employer need only choose the type of labor—here the assumed equally productive B or W groups—to maximize $U(q)$.

Several well-known utility functions result in a decision rule that depends on the variance of the argument. We adopt a function used by Michael Parkin,[16] which for our purposes may be written:

(7) $U(q) = a - be^{-cq}$ $b, c > 0,$

whence

(8) $E[U(q|y)] =$
$$a - be^{-c\,E(q|y)+c^2/2\,Var(q|y)},[17]$$

where a, b, and c are parameters of the utility function and e is the base of the natural logarithm.

It is easily seen that maximizing $E[U(q|y)]$ is equivalent to maximizing its logarithm, which in turn is equivalent to maximizing $[E(q|y) - k\,Var(q|y)]$, where $k = c/2$. Let $R = k\,Var(q|y)$, which may be interpreted as a risk factor.

It follows that an employer with this utility function will attempt to hire from the group of workers that maximizes expected productivity, q, discounted for risk. This risk can arise from differing variances in the distribution of q, or u, or both. Substantively, the risk costs of variance in worker abilities may stem from variance in output within homogeneous jobs or from the costs of mistakes in assigning workers to heterogeneous job slots. For the sake of convenience we have adopted a conditional variance that does not depend on the level of y, so that the risk factor is constant over the range of test scores (see footnote 15).

The empirical question of whether the conditional variance in q, given y, is larger or smaller for black or white workers is, therefore, crucial in determining the direction of discrimination. Assuming racial equality in $Var(q)$, this question hinges on the reliability of y as a predictor of q, namely γ, and we have already suggested that the tests are less reliable for blacks. Thus, $\gamma^B < \gamma^W$ (as depicted in Figure 1B) follows from the assumption that $Var(u^B) > Var(u^W)$.[18]

Figure 2 shows the new y, q relationships incorporating the risk factors, R^B and R^W, and the assumptions, $\gamma^B < \gamma^W$ and $\alpha^B = \alpha^W = \alpha$. The lines W and B are from Equation 2 in conjunction with the assumption that $\alpha^W = \alpha^B$ and $\gamma^B < \gamma^W$. The parallel lines, W-R^W and B-R^B are the risk-discounted counterparts representing $E(q|y) - k\,Var(q|y)$ or $E(q|y) - R$. To see that the figure reveals economic discrimination against blacks in the sense that they receive lower pay on average for the same expected ability, simply note the lower black value of $(q$-$R)$, given $y = \alpha$. The expected value of q for both whites and blacks equals α for $y = \alpha$, and therefore the lower pay for blacks is entirely attributable to the larger R factor for blacks. In Figure 3, which graphs the conditional distribution of q for the point were $y = \alpha = E(y)$ and where $E(q) = \alpha$ for both races. The observed smaller conditional variance of q^W in Figure 3 (which would be the same at any value of y) is, of course, precisely the source of the larger size of γ^W, given that $Var(q^B) = Var(q^W)$.

The risk discount borne by black workers in the form of a lower relative wage could be interpreted in terms of the extra search costs employers would have to bear to reduce the conditional variance of q^B to

---

[16]Michael Parkin, "Discount House Portfolio and Debt Selection," *Review of Economic Studies*, Vol. 37, No. 4 (October 1970), pp. 469–98.

[17]Since q is normally distributed, e^{-cq} is lognormal, and its expected value is $e^{-cE(q)+(c^2/2)Var(q)}$.

[18]A lower slope for blacks would also result from the assumption that $Var(u^B) = Var(u^W)$ and $Var(q^B) < Var(q^W)$. Indeed, the risk discount, $Var(q|y)$, is symmetric with respect to $Var(u)$ and $Var(q)$ since, by manipulations of relations in Footnote 15, we see

$$Var(q|y) = \frac{Var(q)Var(u)}{Var(q) + Var(u)}.$$

In our comparisons between blacks and whites we cannot, however, interchange the terms "reliability" ($= \gamma = r^2$) and "risk-discount" [$= Var(q|y)$] unless we hold equal either $Var(q)$ or $Var(u)$ for the two groups.

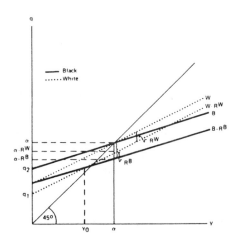

Figure 2. Predictions of Productivity (q) by Race and Test Score (y) with "Risk-Discounts" and Flatter Slope for Blacks.

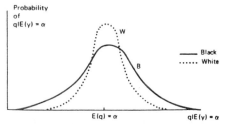

Figure 3. The Distribution of Productivity (q), Given the Test Score $y = E(y)$, by Race.

Note: $E(q|E(y)) = E(q) = E(q^B) = E(q^W) = E(y^B) = E(y^W)$.

equal $Var(q^w|y)$. However, the model does not require any ad hoc assumptions about the direct hiring costs being larger for blacks compared to whites, although cost differentials may exist. The geographic segregation of black workers away from white employers (firms), for example, may well impose extra search and informational costs upon black workers.[19]

Figure 2 represents a hypothetical model, of course, but it is consistent with our view of reality in two important respects. First, as a consequence of actual employer practices, economic discrimination against blacks, women, and other groups does exist, resulting in group differences in pay despite equal group abilities to perform on the job. However, if the definition of ability includes reliability in test-taking—on grounds, perhaps, that this aptitude conveys useful information to employers—then one could deny that *economic* discrimination exists. Our prefer-

ence is to retain the term "economic" in describing this type of discrimination, although such discrimination stems from inadequate test instruments rather than employers' acting upon their tastes for discriminating against black or female workers.

A second realistic feature is that the differential wage or income advantage of white male workers increases as the indicator variable increases. In Figure 2, however, the wages of B workers exceed those of W workers with the same y scores for $y < y_o$, and only if the risk penalty were as large as $q_2 - q_1$ would every W worker be paid more than every B worker for a given y score, over the whole range of y. We are not aware of any actual data revealing a smaller wage for Ws compared to Bs for low scores of productivity indicators. Furthermore, although we have not expressed the units in dollars, the empirical magnitudes of the differential $(R^B - R^W)$ borne by black workers—perhaps 10 to 30 percent for the same number of years of schooling completed—seem too large to be rationalized by risk aversion.

Indeed, three reasons are suggested for skepticism about the size of R.[20] First, large firms have some capacity to self-insure against risks of output variability or mistaken job assignments. In perfect capital markets, even small firms could "purchase" such insurance through various pooling devices. Second, dispersion in risk

[19]For an analysis of this particular disadvantage to black workers, see McCall, "The Simple Mathematics of Information, Job Search, and Prejudices," and John F. Kain, "Housing Segregation, Black Employment, and Metropolitan Decentralization: A Retrospective View," in George M. von Furstenberg, Bennett Harrison, and Ann R. Horowitz, eds., *Patterns of Racial Discrimination, Vol. I: Housing* (Lexington, Mass.: Lexington Books, D. C. Heath and Co., 1974), pp. 5–20.

[20]We are grateful to Orley Ashenfelter, H. Gregg Lewis, Donald A. Nichols, and Melvin W. Reder for helpful suggestions about this section.

STATISTICAL THEORIES OF DISCRIMINATION

aversion among employers leads to a situation in which those with the least aversion reduce the R discount by "bidding up" the wages of black workers, in the same manner as employers with the lowest "tastes for discrimination" serve to equalize the wages of black and white workers of the same productivity. Finally, a large R factor should activate a market for "test instruments" that are tailored to the separate groups to achieve more nearly equal reliability. (For example, just as tests in their native language have been prepared for foreign workers, so test developers could devise ways to communicate more clearly with members of minority groups.) The wage differential should not exceed the "signaling cost"—to use Spence's suggestive term.[21]

Other Models of Discrimination

A second model that attempts to explain the wage differential comes from A. Michael Spence.[22] He provides a dynamic equilibrium analysis in which group differences in wages persist in competitive labor markets. In his model employers are uncertain about the workers' q values and base their wage offers (qs) on the workers' y scores—which, like our y scores, do not represent productivity skills, per se. Workers attain y scores by investing their time and resources, and the Spence model assumes that the cost of y is negatively correlated with q. This assumption drives the wage system, under plausible conditions, to an equilibrium in which q is positively correlated with y, so that the employers' expectations are self-confirming and the workers' signaling behavior reproduces itself.[23]

In the Spence model, however, the level of y (call this y^*) that distinguishes high- from low-ability workers (to use his simple case of just two levels of productivity) is arbitrary over a certain range. This leads

to multiple equilibria, and it then is a small step to show that there may be different equilibria for two distinguishable racial groups of workers, even though the two groups have identical productivity distributions and face the same signaling cost per unit of y. In particular, if the threshold level (y^*) is higher for blacks than whites, but still low enough so that it pays high-ability blacks to acquire the y^* signal, then high-ability white workers will obviously earn a higher net wage—the employer's wage offer minus the costs of attaining y^*.

The question is, however, whether this type of discriminatory situation is stable. If workers know their own productivity (or, equivalently, their costs of attaining y^*), then the high-ability black workers will know they are being underpaid (or, more accurately, overtaxed for y signals), relative to high-ability white workers. It is not difficult to construct examples of arrangements between individual high-ability black workers and employers, whereby the former agree (to the benefit of both parties) to accept lower wages in return for signaling with a lower y^*— eventually a y^* as low as that for white high-ability workers.[24] In equilibrium there would be common wage offers, y attainments, and, therefore, common net wages for similarly productive white and black

---

[24]A simple example of a breakdown in the Spence model of discrimination may be obtained from Glen G. Cain, Department of Economics, University of Wisconsin—handout entitled, "Criticisms and Counter-Examples of the Spence Model of 'Market Failures' in a World of Job Market Signaling," April 27, 1976. See also the suggestions of Stiglitz and Thurow about "trial-period" wage offers by workers as mechanisms by which a unique equilibrium (or, at least, a nondiscriminatory equilibrium) can be achieved. See Joseph E. Stiglitz, "Theories of Discrimination and Economic Policy," in George M. von Furstenberg, Ann R. Horowitz, and Bennett Harrison, eds., *Patterns of Racial Discrimination, Vol. II, Employment and Income* (Lexington, Mass.: Lexington Books, D. C. Heath and Co., 1974), pp. 5–26 and Thurow, *Generating Inequality*, p. 173. Still another source of possible attainment of a unique equilibrium—this time from actions initiated by employers—is suggested by Spence, *Market Signaling* in Appendix E (especially pp. 174–76), and this possibility is given credence and analyzed by John G. Riley, "Competitive Signaling," *Journal of Economic Theory*, Vol. 10 (April 1975), pp. 174–86.

---

[21]Spence, *Market Signaling*.

[22]Spence, *Market Signaling* and "Job Market Signaling."

[23]Indeed, the informational feedback loop that Spence describes provides an effective counterargument to the claim, mentioned earlier, that employers' "erroneous" or "mistaken" behavior will sustain discrimination.

workers—in other words there would be no economic discrimination.

Another model of economic discrimination is suggested by the work of the psychologist R. L. Thorndike (reported by Linn).[25] It incorporates reliability differences but without recourse to risk aversion. As we present it, this "selection-truncation model" contains one feature of Spence's model—namely, a lower-bound threshold value of y, below which all y scores signal what is, in effect, a single q value. Above the lower-bound threshold, the y, q relation is positive and continuous as it was previously in our models. As in the preceding case, black workers have equal average ability but receive a lower average wage; here, however, employers are not practicing racial discrimination.

The crucial assumption of the selection-truncation model is that the hiring or selection decision is confined to the upper end of the y distribution. Given their advantage in test reliability, whites tend to be preferred on the basis of expected values of q, given y, even though their q distribution is actually identical to that of blacks. The potential preference for blacks at the lower end of the y distribution is nullified because workers with low y scores are not hired. Clearly, a higher average value of $\hat{q}$ (or wage rate) for whites would emerge—evidence of economic discrimination in market outcomes—despite the fact that employers are not race-biased in their hiring process: that is, they hire workers solely on the basis of $E(q|y)$.

Figure 4 shows this result in an extreme form. Perfect reliability for Ws and zero reliability for Bs are assumed. The distribution of q is identical for Ws and Bs (as indicated on the vertical axis). Only values of $q > \alpha$ are eligible for hire. (Assume that α represents a comprehensive, legal minimum wage, here unrealistically set equal to the wage corresponding to the overall average value of productivity.) Given the costs of hiring and associated costs of making a mistake, all blacks, but only half the whites, would be unemployed or not in the labor force. The model has,

[25]Linn, "Fair Test Use in Selection."

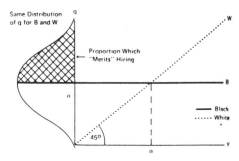

Figure 4. Predictions of Productivity (q) by Race and Test Score (y), Assuming Perfect and Zero Predictive Relations for Whites and Blacks, Respectively.

of course, greater relevance to, say, college admissions than to the labor market, but it may be at least suggestive of some economic situations. In fact, theories of the labor market that emphasize pervasive long-run wage rigidities, such as the "job competition" theory of Thurow, are fertile soil for the type of selection-truncation model of discrimination presented here.[26]

Unequal Average Abilities

We return now to the model in Phelps's paper in which the variances of q and u are equal for the two groups and the mean ability of blacks is less than the mean ability of whites. Here, the systematic effect of blackness, $\alpha^B < \alpha^W$, leads to a lower predicted value of q for blacks than whites, even if the y scores are equal, because y is, by assumption, a fallible indicator. Phelps remarks that $\alpha^B < \alpha^W$ might reflect "disadvantageous social factors."[27]

[26]Thurow, *Generating Inequality*, pp. 173-75.
[27]The three words in quotes are used by Phelps but are not written in a single phrase, although the expression fairly conveys his meaning. Without more information, however, the interpretation of this expression—and of $a^B < a^W$—could be ambiguous. Does the lower value of a^n reflect a real deficiency in skills, as would be the case if the social factors were less schooling, less training, and poorer health? Or does $a^B < a^W$ reflect merely a misconception or a false stereotype held by employers? In accordance with our earlier expressed preference for believing that employers will not persist in erroneous behavior, we assume the first interpretation.

The relevant y, q relation for Ws and Bs is shown in Figure 5. The B line is below and parallel to the W line; the equality of slopes is a consequence of the assumptions of equal variances of q, u, and, therefore, y. As noted earlier, competitive forces in the market lead employers to pay workers according to their expected productivity; thus, white workers will be preferred to (and get higher wages than) black workers with the same y score. Unlike Phelps, we do not believe that different pay for the same y score demonstrates economic discrimination. Indeed, were Bs to get paid the same as Ws when both had the same y scores, there would manifestly be discrimination against Ws, since by Phelps's assumption the latter are more productive (i.e., they have a higher average q).

One could argue, of course, that the very existence of different average ability, $\alpha^B < \alpha^W$, demonstrates a type of discrimination in which workers are not paid in accordance with their *innate* abilities, and we would agree. But we would generally view its source in premarket discrimination—discrimination in schooling or in the acquisition of other forms and amounts of human capital that workers possess when they enter the labor market. (In Spence's

terms, the discriminated groups are faced with higher costs of signaling.) Given these handicaps, however, the differential pay (or difference in employer demand) appears to be no more economically discriminatory than are the lower wages that would be paid to workers with less experience, other factors (like the y score) being equal. (Of course, "legal discrimination," or other definitions of discrimination, need not be bound by economic terms, nor are wage payments in accordance with expected productivity necessarily synonymous with good social policy.)

Finally, although Figure 5 demonstrates nondiscrimination by the "outcome" criterion of a proportional relation between average compensation for the groups and their respective average productivities, at every ability level a black will be paid less than his white counterpart. This is seen also in Equation 6, $E(\hat{q}|q) = (1-\gamma)\,\alpha + \gamma q$. For the same ability ($q$ value) and regression slope (γ) but lower black mean ability, $(1-\gamma)\alpha^B < (1-\gamma)\alpha^W$.

This apparent paradox is resolved simply by recalling that here we *assume* less average ability for blacks *and* imperfect information. Thus, blackness is *assumed* to provide information that $E[\hat{q}^B|y]$ ex ante is lower than $E[\hat{q}^W|y]$ ex ante for all y. But the employer's ex ante expectation that a black worker will be less productive than a white worker, given the same y scores, must result in a black worker with a given q ability receiving a lower wage than a white worker with that same q ability, *on average*, because $E(\hat{q}|q)$ and $E(\hat{q}|y)$ involve exactly the same parameters. In the presence of *perfect* information ($\gamma=1$), the systematic difference in $E(\hat{q}|y)$ or $E(\hat{q}|q)$ for the two racial groups disappears, of course, and the lines for both color groups coincide with the 45° line.

In light of known premarket discrimination against blacks, the assumption by employers of unequal average abilities is realistic, and so is the assumption of imperfect information. The systematic inequality in $E(\hat{q}|q)$ that results is, therefore, profoundly disturbing, and perhaps this inequality is what is referred to by the economists mentioned in footnote 8. One consolation is that this inequality should

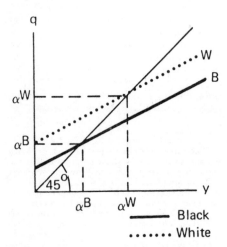

Figure 5. Prediction of Productivity (q), by Race and Test Score (y), Assuming the Slopes Are Equal.

decline as employers assimilate more knowledge over time, thereby reducing $Var(u)$ and raising γ.

We end this discussion with the cautionary remark that assuming $\alpha^B < \alpha^W$ along with $\gamma^B = \gamma^W$ may not be very realistic. If the "raw-labor" abilities of blacks and whites are equal, a higher average ability of white workers must reflect an advantage in human capital acquisitions. Under these conditions, there is no basis for assuming that white workers have the same variance in q, and, therefore, no presumption that the γ values for the two groups are equal.

Conclusions

Several economists have heretofore advanced statistical theories of discrimination in labor markets. Although the Phelps model does not, in our opinion, explain or describe racial or sex discrimination, it provides a useful point of departure for several models that do. The models focus on differential reliability in productivity indicators among identifiable groups of workers. On empirical grounds the differential is more plausibly introduced when blacks (or women) are assumed to have less reliable scores. When we combine this reliability differential with risk aversion by employers, our model depicts economic discrimination that is qualitatively consistent with empirical evidence. In another model the combination of lesser reliability for blacks (or women) on tests with truncation of lower-scoring applicants also reveals a kind of economic discrimination. Both examples call attention to the potential inequities that may stem from lower test reliabilities for minority groups.

We are reluctant, however, to claim too much for these models. In the model that uses risk aversion, there are grounds for questioning whether the size of the risk premium would be very large, and we know of no empirical support for a "crossover" point at the lower end of the indicator scale, where blacks earn more than whites for comparable indicator scores. Obviously, we have made no thorough attempt to test the model, or even to give more satisfactory empirical definitions of

the y variable. The $\hat{q}$ variable itself has been assumed to represent a wage rate throughout, implicitly relying on the proposition that wages measure productivity and that competition will, on average, match equal productive abilities with equal wages. Finally, one may argue that there is no discrimination when productivity is defined either to include the informational content of "signaling" or in terms of contributions to an employer's utility function that allows for risk aversion.

In Spence's model of market signaling, discrimination may result if the costs of signaling differ for different groups or if different groups have different initial signals. The former case represents a type of pre–labor market discrimination that results in the discriminated group having lower average abilities in the labor market. The latter case is not clearly indicative of sustained discrimination. A number of variations of the Spence model are currently being investigated by various economists, however, so final judgments should be withheld.

Other real world influences that affect economic discrimination have also been ignored. We have not dealt with monopoly or monopsony.[28] Tastes for discrimination by employers or their systematic subjective underevaluations of the abilities (q values) of the discriminated groups have been

---

[28]As the reader may know, however, the evidence for these anticompetitive sources for sustained economic discrimination is meager. Orley Ashenfelter produces evidence *against* a net antiblack discrimination effect of unions in "Racial Discrimination and Trade Unionism," *Journal of Political Economy*, Vol. 80, No. 3 (May/June 1972), pp. 435–64. Becker, *The Economics of Discrimination*, 2d ed., pp. 7–8, has disputed the claim made by Thurow, *Poverty and Discrimination* (Washington, D.C.: The Brookings Institution, 1969), that monopsony power by employers is an important explanation. And Armen A. Alchian and Reuben A. Kessel have argued that monopoly power in the product market is consistent with long-run economic discrimination only (or mainly) when there are constraints on the employers' ability to maximize money profits, as in regulated monopoly industries. (See "Competition, Monopoly, and the Pursuit of Pecuniary Gain," Universities-National Bureau Committee for Economic Research, *Aspects of Labor Ecomomics: A Conference of the Committee* (Princeton, N.J.: Princeton University Press, 1962), pp. 156–75.

downplayed. While neither of these latter modes of behavior, by itself, is consistent with long-run economic discrimination in a competitive model, introducing additional factors may provide consistency. It would take a more extensive discussion to deal with Arrow's list of additional considerations, which includes capital market imperfections, wage rate rigidities, discontinuities in hiring decisions, and self-fulfilling prophecies.[29] It is fair to say, however, that most of the explanations of discrimination that rely on noncompetitive, disequilibria, and "noneconomic" forces have been offered very tentatively and leave a number of unanswered questions.

---

[29] Arrow, "The Theory of Discrimination," pp. 26–32. See Stiglitz, "Theories of Discrimination and Economic Policy" for insightful and sometimes skeptical comments about these considerations.

[22]

THE SEX DIFFERENTIAL IN EARNINGS: A REAPPRAISAL

MARIANNE A. FERBER and HELEN M. LOWRY

I N 1972 "the median annual earnings of women 14 years old and over who did full-time year-round work were about 58 percent of that of full-time year-round male workers."[1] Since in 1956 this proportion was 63 percent, it has actually decreased somewhat in recent years.[2] A considerable literature has emerged, showing that some, much, or virtually all of this differential is caused by factors other than discrimination.[3] These studies have demonstrated a number of measurable differences between the male and female labor force and these differences have been used to explain women's lower earnings. However, three major problems common to most of this work

This study investigates the effect that the proportion of women in an occupation has on the level of earnings in the occupation. Using data from the 1970 U.S. Census, the authors find that most of the variance in the median earnings of workers in 260 occupations can be explained by the sex composition of the occupation, the median number of years of schooling of workers in the occupation, and the interaction of these two factors. The authors find, for example, that education has an important positive effect on earnings in all occupations, but a greater impact in those occupations that are predominantly male. Also, whereas men ordinarily benefit more from education than do women, they lose some of this advantage in those occupations with a high proportion of women. Their results lead the authors to conclude that discrimination is one of the likely causes of lower earnings in occupations with a high proportion of females. The authors also suggest that previous researchers who point to differences in the labor market behavior of females as primary sources of differences in earnings may be guilty of "circular reasoning" in that such differences in behavior may as likely be the result, as the cause, of sex differentials in earnings.

Marianne A. Ferber is Associate Professor of Economics, University of Illinois at Urbana-Champaign. Helen M. Lowry is a Project Coordinator at the Survey Research Center, Oregon State University. The authors would like to express their thanks to Robert Ferber and Joan Huber for their helpful suggestions.—EDITOR

---

[1] *The Economic Report of the President* (Washington, D.C.: G.P.O., 1974), p. 154.

[2] Testimony of Marina Whitman, U.S. Congress, Joint Economic Committee, 1973, "Midyear Review of the Economy," Hearing before the Joint Economic Committee, Congress of the United States, Ninety-third Congress, First Session, Part 1, p. 19.

[3] Henry Sanborn, "Pay Differences Between Men and Women," *Industrial and Labor Relations Review*, Vol. 17, No. 4 (July 1964), pp. 534–50; Donald J. McNulty, "Differences in Pay Between Men and Women Workers," *Monthly Labor Review*, Vol. 90, No. 12 (December 1967), pp. 40–43; Mary T. Hamilton, "A Study of Wage Discrimination by Sex: A Sample Survey in the Chicago Area," (Ph.D. dissertation, University of Pennsylvania, 1969); Victor R. Fuchs, "Differences in Hourly Earnings Between Men and Women," *Monthly Labor Review*, Vol. 94, No. 5 (May 1971), pp. 9-15; Solomon Polachek, "Work Experience and the Difference Between Male and Female Wages," (Ph.D. dissertation, Columbia University, 1973); *The Economic Report of the President* (1974); Burton Malkiel and Judith Malkiel, "Male-Female Pay Differentials in Professional Employment," *American Economic Review*, Vol. 63, No. 4 (September 1973), pp. 693–705; Ronald Oaxaca, "Male-Female Wage Differentials in Urban Labor Markets," *International Economic Review*, Vol. 14, No. 3 (October 1973), pp. 693–709.

378   INDUSTRIAL AND LABOR RELATIONS REVIEW

have so far received inadequate attention. (1) Do the existing differences between the male and female labor force explain as much of the gap as estimated? (2) To what extent are the existing differences themselves caused by discrimination? (3) Can it be reasonably argued that the explanations of the gap involve circular reasoning?

This paper addresses each of these issues in turn. Questions are raised with regard to the methods and conclusions of four of the most widely cited sources —Sanborn, Fuchs, Polachek[4] and the Council of Economic Advisers (CEA) — especially with regard to their estimates of the impact of the differences in occupational patterns of men and women. Second, statistical evidence is marshalled to support the proposition that the educational and occupational patterns of the female labor force are themselves most likely caused by discrimination. Discrimination in the narrow sense, which we call direct discrimination, exists when people equally qualified are not treated equally in the labor market, whether by employers, fellow workers, customers, or others.[5] To the extent that this discrimination leads to behavior that further handicaps the person discriminated against, there arises what we call cumulative or incremental discrimination. Last, it is argued that with regard to women working shorter hours, experiencing interrupted careers, possibly investing less in education and training, being less willing to move or commute in order to improve their employment opportunities, and reacting differently to differences in marital status, circular reasoning is clearly involved.[6]

Earnings and Occupational Distribution

The subject of women's earnings and occupational distribution has received a good deal of attention. Sanborn, using the detailed Bureau of Labor Statistics occupational categories, found that the median earnings of employed women increase from 58 percent of men's earnings to 81–82 percent when women are given the same occupational distribution as men.[7] Fuchs, after adjusting for marital status, class of worker, and length of trip to work, found that women earn 66 percent as much as men, arguing that virtually all of the remaining differential could be accounted for by differences in occupational distribution, if we had a sufficiently detailed breakdown of categories.[8] Marina Whitman, then a member of the CEA, stated that, "Department of Labor surveys have found that the differential almost disappears when men's and women's earnings are compared within detailed job classifications and within the same establishment."[9] One would thus conclude that if women had the same distribution by occupation and establishment as

---

[4]Polachek's work is important because, according to a letter from Herbert Stein, testimony by Marina Whitman was based on it. See U.S. Congress, Joint Economic Committee, Part 1, p. 36.

[5]We believe this definition to be preferable to that of Fuchs, who includes the attitudes of consumers and fellow employees under the heading of "role differentiation." Victor R. Fuchs, "Women's Earnings: Recent Trends and Long Run Prospects," *Monthly Labor Review*, Vol. 97, No. 5 (May 1974), p. 23. Malkiel and Malkiel ("Male-Female Pay Differentials," pp. 702-04) find that differences in male and female assignments by job level is one of the main forms of discrimination.

[6]Oaxaca ("Male-Female Wage Differentials," p. 708) briefly suggests the possibility that "feedback from labor market discrimination on male-female differences" may exist.

[7]Sanborn, "Pay Differences," p. 545.

[8]Fuchs, "Differences in Hourly Earnings," p. 14.

[9]Testimony of Whitman, U.S. Congress, Joint Economic Committee, Part 1, p. 21.

men, the wage differential would virtually disappear beyond that accounted for by differences in the male and female labor force. (But using very detailed categories leads to such a high degree of segregation that a large proportion of categories are almost entirely male or female. Discrimination at that level simply takes the form of men and women working largely in different categories.) At the opposite extreme we find Polachek, who concludes that women's earnings would increase by only 5 percent (or 3 percent of men's earnings) if the occupational distribution of women were the same as that of men,[10]

The studies by Sanborn and Fuchs use average earnings of all workers to estimate the gain women would experience if they shifted into occupations and establishments that are at present disproportionately male. They assume, for example, that when a women moves from an occupation with average earnings of $10,000 to one where average earnings are $15,000, her earnings would go up by 50 percent. This approach is bound to overestimate the real improvement in women's earnings. To the extent that men earn more than women within an occupation (the type of category used by the census as opposed to the Department of Labor surveys referred to by Whitman), the presence of a larger proportion of men itself raises the level of earnings of all workers in a more largely male occupation as compared to that in a more largely female one.

In order to investigate how the "maleness" of an occupation affects the earnings of women differently from the earn-

ings of men, we set up the following regression models:

(1) $\quad Y_{mi} = b_o + b_1 E_{mi} + b_2 M_i$

(2) $\quad Y_{fi} = b_o + b_1 E_{fi} + b_2 M_i,$

where Y_{mi} = median earnings of male workers in occupation i,

Y_{fi} = median earnings of female workers in occupation i,

E_{mi} = median number of years of schooling of male workers in occupation i,

E_{fi} = median number of years of schooling of female workers in occupation i,

M_i = proportion of workers who were male in occupation i.

Since the amount of education required to perform in an occupation is probably the strongest determinant of earnings in that occupation, we felt it was appropriate to look at the effect of "maleness" in the presence of the effect of education.

The coefficients in Equations 1 and 2 were estimated using 1969 data on 260 occupations (see Appendix). Each observation was weighted by the number of male or female workers in the occupation. All the estimated coefficients are significantly different from zero at the one percent level.

(1) $Y_m = -11194 + 1245E_m + 5008M,$
$\quad R^2 = .76$

(2) $Y_f = -6777 + 832E_f + 1438M,$
$\quad R^2 = .50$

The coefficients of E_m and E_f indicate that schooling is a better investment for men than it is for women. The coefficients of M in the two equations indicate the extent to which women and men profit differently from working in a dominantly male occupation.

[10]Polachek, "Work Experience and the Difference Between Male and Female Wages." (This conclusion was described in private correspondence from Herbert Stein to the authors.)

Polachek avoided the mistake of over-estimating women's gains by assuming that when women shift to other occupations, their earnings will equal those of women presently in that field.[11] Perhaps this approach introduced a spurious factor that biased his results downward, for his estimate of only a 5 percent increase in women's earnings—if women were occupationally distributed as men are—is surprisingly low. Polachek used data from the 1960 census, wherein women's earnings were not shown for occupations where the base number of responses was less than 1,000, many of these occupations being ones with high earnings. In fact, in those 214 detailed occupational categories for which the median earnings of women were not provided, the weighted average of the medians of men's earnings was $543 (or 10 percent) higher than the median of all men's earnings. These 214 occupations represented 17 percent of the male labor force.[12]

The Impact of Education

Another question must also be raised with regard to Polachek's conclusion. His study, like others concerned with an explanation of the gap between men's and women's earnings, did not seriously address the effect of variations in education between men and women. The fact that the mean number of years of schooling of men and women is now equal may explain the lack of concern with this issue. Nonetheless there are still differences that deserve attention.

It is clear from Equations 1 and 2 that additional education is of much less value to women than to men, perhaps because women tend to be relatively highly educated in occupations where additional schooling is not greatly rewarded and relatively less educated in occupations where education is greatly rewarded.[13] If this is the reason, women would earn more if their combined occupational and educational distribution resembled that of men.

To test this hypothesis we estimated the impact on women's earnings were they to duplicate the male occupational and educational distribution. In other words, if 5.7 percent of the total male labor force consists of craftsmen with nine to eleven years of schooling, we assume that 5.7 percent of the female labor force would also be in this category. Given the 12 major occupational categories and 6 educational categories of the 1970 census, there are seventy-two cells. If we fill each of these cells with the same percentage of the female labor force as were filled by the male labor force (the experienced labor force, 25–64 years old, working 50–52 weeks in 1969), and if we assume women's mean earnings would stay as they were in each cell, then we find that the grand mean of women's earnings would increase by $627 (or 12 percent).

Because women with higher levels of education are more likely than other women to work, women in the labor market have 0.1 year more schooling than men. Although the effect is minor,

---

[11]Ibid.

[12]Although the weighted average of medians is admittedly an unorthodox statistic, it seems the most descriptive one. Surely the median of median earnings would be less descriptive. U.S. Bureau of the Census, *Census of Population: 1960, Subject Reports, Occupational Characteristics*, Final Report PC (2)-7A, Table 30, pp. 396–415.

[13]Marianne A. Ferber and Helen Lowry, *The Economic Status of Women: Cross Cultural Comparisons*, Faculty Working Paper 189 (Urbana-Champaign, Illinois: Bureau of Economic and Business Research, College of Commerce and Business Administration, University of Illinois at Urbana-Champaign, June 20, 1974), Table 11, p. 25.

this fact should be taken into account. Based on Equation 2 above, we might estimate the value of the additional education to be $83, or 2 percent of the grand mean of women's earnings. Thus the adjustment, when women have the same occupational pattern as men and when the appropriate adjustment in educational distribution has been made, accounts for 7 percentage points of the differential between the earnings of women and men, not for 3 (Polachek's estimate).

Our calculations were based on only the 12 major occupational categories; but a finer breakdown should account for an even larger number of percentage points, because in order to achieve the same distribution as men in more detailed occupational categories, even more women would have to change jobs. Both nurses and doctors, for example, are included in the major category "Professional, Technical and Kindred Workers;" when subdivided into nurses and doctors, clearly more women fall into the first category and more men into the second. If as large a proportion of working women were doctors as the proportion of working men are, many women who now earn nurses' wages would earn doctors' fees instead.

One additional comment needs to be made about the various studies discussed here. All of them assume that the earnings of both men and women in various occupations will remain as they are, even as a large proportion of women move from one occupation to another. This assumption is unwarranted, for a sharp decrease in supply is likely to result in a higher wage rate and an increase in supply in a lower wage rate. Men's and women's earnings are not likely to be affected to the same extent, because predominantly male occupations would experience the greatest influx of workers, and, therefore, the greatest relative wage reductions. Estimates based on present earnings therefore do not reflect accurately what would happen if there were a major change in the occupational distribution of women.

Causes of Low Incomes

We have demonstrated that at least part of the income differential between men and women is explained by the occupational distribution of women. We shall argue that even a relatively small differential may well cause some of the differences in behavior that in turn cause women's earnings, in comparison to men's earnings, to decrease further. It is thus important to determine the possible causes of lower earnings in "women's" occupations.

To investigate further the effect of the proportion of women in an occupation on the level of earnings in the occupation, we used the same data with which Equations 1 and 2 were estimated. Each occupation provided two observations, one for the men in that occupation and one for the women, yielding 520 weighted observations for estimating the coefficients in the following model:

$$(3) \quad Y_{ij} = b_0 + b_1 F_i + b_2 E_{ij} + b_3 S_{ij} + b_4 (F_i \times E_{ij}) + b_5 (F_i \times S_{ij}) + b_6 (E_{ij} \times S_{ij}) + b_7 (F_i \times E_{ij} \times S_{ij})$$

where Y_{ij} = median earnings of workers in occupation i of sex j,

F_i = proportion of workers who are female in occupation i,
= $1 - M_i$,

E_{ij} = median number of years of schooling of workers in occupation i of sex j,

S_{ij} = sex (male = 1, female = 0) of workers in occupation i of sex j.

The reason for including education and sex as variables is obvious: they are known to be important determinants of earnings,[14] whether or not the differences in earnings are justified by differences in the characteristics of the male and female labor force. The interaction terms were added because it seemed plausible that they would be significant. Education would be expected to add more to the men's earnings; the proportion of women in an occupation might well have a different impact on men than on women and on more-educated than on less-educated workers.

The regression was estimated by means of a step-wise procedure. The estimates of the coefficients, in the order in which the variables entered, are shown in the Table.

Table. Estimates of Coefficients of Education, Sex, and Proportion of Females in Occupation.
(N = 520)

Variable	Final Unstandardized Regression Coefficient	Cumulative R^2
Constant	−1634	—
$E \times S$	826*	.59
E	527*	.77
$F \times E \times S$	−1416*	.84
$F \times E$	534***	.84
$F \times S$	13,792*	.84
S	−5877**	.84
F	−7949**	.84

* Significant at the .01 level.
** Significant at the .05 level.
*** Significant at the .10 level.

[14]This fact has been most recently confirmed in an article by Dixie Sommers, "Occupational Rankings for Men and Women by Earnings," *Monthly Labor Review*, Vol. 97, No. 8 (August 1974), pp. 34–51.

As expected, the level of education of workers in an occupation is important in determining the level of earnings, but, interestingly, the interaction between education and sex has an even greater positive effect than education alone, indicating once again that education is considerably more rewarding for men than for women. This may be partly explained by the fact that "from school onward the career orientation of women differs strikingly from that of men. Most women do not have as strong a vocational emphasis in their schooling."[15] However, when Whitman's explanation continues, "and for those who do, the preparation is usually for a stereotyped 'female' occupation," we are back to the question of why and to what extent earnings are lower in these occupations.

Another interesting result is that the most important impact of a large proportion of women in an occupation is a negative effect on the differential benefits of education to the men in that occupation. The only variable in which F appears that contributes more than one percent to R^2 is the interaction $F \times E \times S$, and the estimated coefficient of this variable is negative. In other words, whereas men ordinarily profit more from their educational training than do women, it appears that they lose some of this advantage in those occupations with a high proportion of women. It seems that men who attempt to keep women out of the professions for fear that their earnings may be unfavorably affected by the competition from women know what they are doing.[16]

[15]Testimony of Whitman, U.S. Congress, Joint Economic Committee, Part 1, p. 16.

[16]Incidentally, Fuchs uses the fact that men's earnings are lower in occupations with a larger proportion of women as proof that men do not object to women as fellow workers. If they did

THE SEX DIFFERENTIAL IN EARNINGS

The interaction of the proportion of women and education has a positive effect on women's earnings, but it does not add even one percent to the explanation of the variation in median earnings. The pure effect of the proportion of women is positive on men's earnings and negative on women's earnings, but again, the additional variance explained is close to zero. It is most significant that however small the pure effect of sex, that effect is negative.

If we consider Equation 3 separately for men $(S = 1)$ and women $(S = 0)$, and if we set $M = 1 - F$, we obtain results that can be readily compared to those from Equations 1 and 2.

(4) $Y_m = -1668 + 471E_m - 5843M + 882(E_m \times M)$, $R^2 = .84$

(5) $Y_f = -9583 + 1061E_f + 7949M - 534(E_f \times M)$, $R^2 = .84$

In the first place, the addition of the interaction term has increased the power to explain the variation in median earnings by 8 percentage points (76 to 84) for men and by an astonishing 34 percentage points (50 to 84) for women. Second, it can be seen that the pure effect of education is actually more positive for women than for men, but that the more "male" an occupation is, the less women in that occupation benefit

---

object, he argues, they would have to be paid a premium. There is an important flaw in this reasoning. If men were prejudiced against working with women, the result would be a decrease in the supply of men as women move into the occupation. Assuming that employers regard women as a reasonably close substitute—as is likely to be the case in an occupation experiencing a significant influx of women—such a shift would not result in an increase in men's earnings, but in a decrease in the number of men employed. This conclusion is supported by the fact that, as a rule, occupations that begin to admit women freely become "women's" occupations. Fuchs, "Differences in Hourly Earnings," p. 14.

from their education. Conversely, men reap their greatest benefits from education in highly "male" occupations. It should be noted that the pure effect of the proportion of men adds less than one percent to the explanatory power of the regression equation. Consequently, the negative coefficient of M in Equation 4 should not be viewed with too much surprise.

It is clear, therefore, that the lower earnings in occupations with a higher proportion of women cannot be ascribed solely to the lower productivity of women, unless, of course, one is prepared to believe that women's productivity is somehow adversely affected by the mere presence of men and that men become less productive when they work with women.

It might be argued that by happenstance women are better suited for the type of work less valued in the market place—they make good nurses and elementary school teachers while men, in general, are better equipped to become doctors and university professors, and that the minority of men who have "female" tastes or skills are subject to a similar unhappy coincidence. There is, however, a problem with this line of reasoning: what is regarded as a "male" or "female" occupation varies widely in different economies. We find, for example, that only about 7 percent of physicians, 12 percent of pharmacists, 2 percent of dentists, and 4 percent of craftsmen are women in the United States, whereas women constitute 65 percent of physicians in the USSR, 92 percent of pharmacists in Norway, 77 percent of dentists in Finland, and 41 percent of craftsmen in the Philippines. On the other hand, 44 percent of sales workers and 75 percent of clerical workers in the United States are female,

384   INDUSTRIAL AND LABOR RELATIONS REVIEW

while women constitute only one per-cent of sales workers in Algeria and one percent of clerical workers in Libya.[17] This evidence indicates that the concentration of women in particular occupations is influenced by factors other than the inherent affinity of women for those particular types of work, and that the scarcity of women in other occupations is not due to their inability to perform the required tasks.

The results of this study are quite consistent, however, with the hypothesis that the exclusion of women from many occupations creates a large supply of labor in those to which women are admitted and in which earnings are then correspondingly depressed. This hypothesis is also confirmed by evidence that in the United States an increase in the proportion of women in an occupation over time has had a negative effect on earnings in that occupation and vice versa. Using a simple correlation between the change in the proportion women constituted of the workers in each of 260 occupations between 1949 and 1969 and the change in men's median earnings in each occupation, we get a correlation coefficient of $-.308$. Similarly, using women's median earnings, we find a correlation coefficient of $-.330$. Both are significant at the one percent level.

All this evidence points rather clearly to discrimination as the cause of lower earnings in women's occupations. Such discrimination may take the form of arbitrarily excluding women from many occupations, thus maintaining high earnings in these fields and causing crowding and unduly low earnings in others. Or it may be widespread preju-dice that manifests itself directly by putting a lower valuation on "women's work," whether done by women or men.

Productivity and Earnings

Evidence that women spend less time at work and commuting, accumulate fewer years of work experience than men, and in many highly-paid professions have less education, is not in dispute. Nor is the negative effect of most of these factors on women's productivity, and hence on their earnings, in dispute.[18] Although no hard evidence has yet shown that women receive less on-the-job training or that they are less likely to make a decision to move or to refuse to move on the basis of their own career opportunities, both conjectures appear plausible.

The important question that needs to be raised is whether the differing behavior of men and women might not be rational adjustments to the fact that, *ceteris paribus,* women earn less than men. Assuming maximization of family income to be the goal, a wife as qualified as her husband should therefore undertake household duties at the expense of time spent on the job or on job-related activities, because her opportunity costs are lower. If a choice must be made, a

---

[17]Ferber and Lowry, *The Economic Status of Women*, Table 4, p. 11 and Table 5, p. 14.

[18]Some recent work, however, fails to find any effect of differences in mobility on men's or women's earnings. Gary Brown, "Male-Female Wage Differentials," (Ph.D. dissertation, University of Illinois at Urbana-Champaign, 1974). There is also some question as to whether the positive correlation between people's earnings and the distance they commute to work can be interpreted to mean that it is the willingness to commute farther that causes the higher earnings. It is possible that the causal connection is the other way around. It is reasonable to suppose that people with better paying jobs can afford to commute farther and are able to live in the more expensive suburbs, which are generally farther away from their places of work.

THE SEX DIFFERENTIAL IN EARNINGS 385

son, equally as qualified as a daughter, should get more education, because the pay-off is higher. Given the differences in allocation of household duties, an employer should expect to gain more by training male rather than female employees and should thus invest more in the former. Given all these handicaps for women, a family should decide whether or not to move largely on the basis of the husband's job opportunities.

To the extent that this view is valid, the existence of different behavior patterns of women in the labor market cannot be used to prove that discrimination does not exist, but rather to provide evidence that once there is direct discrimination, forces inevitably arise that cause many prophecies to become self-fulfilling. For example, a company refuses to promote a woman because she is likely to move when her husband chooses to change jobs. Since such a woman has little to lose, she is likely to quit her job when her husband gets a good offer elsewhere.

Some of these questions, as well as additional ones, also arise when differences in marital status are advanced as reasons for the gap between men's and women's earnings. It is frequently pointed out that while married women earn far less than married men, single women earn almost as much as single men. Again, these facts are not in dispute, but the conclusion that they prove the absence of discrimination is highly debatable.

The contention that a married man is more highly motivated to work and succeed, because he has a family to support, and that a married woman is less motivated, because her husband can support her, is a pertinent case of circular reasoning. A totally objective outsider—who might have to come from

Mars since the moon has already been contaminated by astronauts—might find it difficult to understand why in a family with two adults the man is usually the head of the household, while the woman is the dependent. It seems obvious to us that societal attitudes explain the different behavioral patterns of married men and women.

As long as these differences in societal attitudes exist, however, they seem to us to support the contention that, in the absence of discrimination in the labor market, single women should be expected to earn *more* than single men. For in our society it may be chiefly the strong, independent, career-oriented women who choose to remain single, or at any rate experience difficulty in finding acceptable marriage partners, since they are expected to marry men with qualifications equal or superior to theirs. On the other hand, it may often be the less aggressive, perhaps unsuccessful men who hesitate to undertake family responsibilities.

Conclusions

We have not just attempted to provide one more set of estimates of the contribution various factors make to the explanation of the differential earnings of men and women, although we have tried to evaluate certain aspects of some of the work done by others. Our main goal has been to determine whether any direct discrimination exists, and to question whether some of the differences in male and female behavior in the labor market may not result from cumulative discrimination. To the extent that this is so, such differences cannot then legitimately be used to explain that women's lower earnings are not caused by discrimination.

We found that occupational distribution accounts for part of the gap in earnings between men and women, particularly when the different educational pattern of women is also taken into account. We showed, furthermore, that attempts to explain the lower earnings in occupations with a larger proportion of women as a result of factors other than discrimination are unsatisfactory. We therefore conclude that women are rewarded less in the labor market than men, and that direct discrimination causes differential behavior between men and women that further increases the gap in earnings.

This shift of emphasis from previous work is important. While other authors are, or appear to be, interested only in measuring the facts as they are, they tend to imply that the large gap between men's and women's earnings must not be regarded as a result of discrimination and that the apparently immutable behavior patterns of women explain much of the earnings differential. Perhaps, these authors imply, the whole gap might be accounted for in this way if only the necessary data were available. We, too, have attempted to use existing statistical data and relationships to explain the earnings gap. However we conclude that differences in behavior can themselves be caused by differences in earnings and hence a relatively modest amount of direct discrimination may well result in a great deal of cumulative discrimination. Focusing on the narrow issue of direct discrimination is thus not particularly useful, and perhaps even misleading. For such an emphasis ignores the fact that, like a stone cast into water, discrimination introduced into the labor market is likely to produce effects considerably more far-reaching than the initial impact itself.

Appendix

The data used in this study were taken entirely from U.S. Bureau of the Census publications.

The occupations included are all those listed in the 1970 census that were determined, after careful examination, to have been defined identically in the 1950 census.[19] The resultant sample represents 58 percent of all the detailed occupations listed in the 1950 census and 42 percent of all those listed in the 1970 census. The sample also represents 46 percent of the experienced civilian labor force with earnings in 1949, and 40 percent of the experienced civilian labor force with earnings in 1969. All the major occupational categories are broadly represented in the sample chosen.

The earnings data for 1949 were taken from U.S. Bureau of the Census, *Census of Population: 1950, Subject Reports, Occupational Characteristics* (Washington, D.C.: G.P.O., 1956) Vol. IV, Part I, Chapter B, P-E No. 1-B, Table 19, pp. 183–98. Where median earnings were not given (because the base number of responses was fewer than 3,000), they were estimated from the fourteen earnings brackets provided in Table 19 in the following manner. With the necessary assumption that empty cells represented zeros, it was first determined into which bracket the median would fall. Then the estimated median earnings within that bracket was interpolated on a straight-line basis. For example, if the total number of workers in an occupation was 1,000, and 400 of them earned less than $2,000 and 600 of them earned less than $2,500, then the estimated median earnings were taken to be $2,250.

---

[19] A list of the occupations used may be obtained on request from the authors.

When this method was applied to occupations with no empty cells, the results agreed with the medians given by the Bureau of the Census.

The estimates obtained in the manner described above were assumed to lead to less bias than the omission of occupations from the study. In the 1950 census data, 6 of the chosen occupations had missing median earnings figures for men and 130 had missing median earnings figures for women. These occupations represented 8,910 men and 130,800 women. The weighted average of the medians of those men's earnings estimated by the authors was $518 less than the grand median of all men's earnings given by the Bureau of the Census. For the women, the estimated medians averaged $384 above the grand median. Hence it was decided that omitting from the study occupations for which the Bureau of the Census did not publish median earnings figures would lead to bias in estimating regression coefficients using the occupations as weighted observations.

The earnings and education data for 1969 were obtained from U.S. Bureau of the Census, *Census of Population:* *1970, Subject Reports, Occupational Characteristics,* Final Report PC (2) -7A, (Washington, D.C.: G.P.O., 1973), Tables 1, 5, and 16, pp. 1–11, 59–86, 284–311. Median earnings figures missing in Table 1 (because the base number of responses was less than 400) , were estimated from the thirteen earnings brackets shown in Table 16 and missing median school years completed figures were estimated from the eight educational brackets presented in Table 5, by means of the method described above for the 1949 earnings data. The method was again checked on some occupations for which the Bureau of the Census did provide medians. In the 1970 census data, the 2 occupations lacking men's median earnings accounted for 419 men for whom the weighted average of median earnings was $2,877 below the grand median for men and for whom the weighted average of median number of years of schooling was 1.3 years fewer than the grand median for men. For women the comparable figures were 27 occupations, 7,210 women, $944 above the grand median earnings for women and 1.7 fewer years of schooling than the grand median for women.

[23]

Journal of Economic Literature
Vol. XXVII (March 1989), pp. 46–72

Male-Female Wage Differentials and Policy Responses

By MORLEY GUNDERSON
University of Toronto

Without implicating them for any of the contents of the paper, I am grateful to the following for helpful discussions or comments: Andrea Beller (University of Illinois), David Bloom (Harvard and Columbia), Glen Cain (University of Wisconsin), Ron Ehrenberg (Cornell), Victor Fuchs (Stanford), Bob Gregory (Australian National University), Jonathan Leonard (University of California, Berkeley), Roberta Robb (Brock University), and Paul Weiler (Harvard). Financial support of the Humanities and Social Sciences Committee of the Research Board of the University of Toronto is gratefully acknowledged.

The single most important development in the labor market over the last 40 years has been the increase in the number of women, especially married women, at work for pay. There have been other periods (e.g., during the two world wars) when women constituted a large fraction of the labor force and assumed jobs once the prerogative of men, but these changes turned out to be largely temporary and after the wars most women gave up their paying jobs (Mark Aldrich and Robert Buchele 1986; Ray Marshall and Beth Paulin 1987). The influx of women into the labor market since the 1950s, however, is showing no signs of being a temporary phenomenon and it is broadly based across virtually all developed countries (Table 1). It is a change associated with equally dramatic shifts in marital patterns, family formation, the demand for child care and alternative work-time arrangements, the division of labor within the household, and the nature of household work itself.

As illustrated in Table 1, the increased participation of women in the labor market generally has been accompanied by an increase in their earnings relative to those of men, although a substantial gap remains. In the United States and Canada, the overall gap has remained roughly constant, but there is some evidence that it has narrowed slightly in more recent years[1] especially after controlling for the effects of changes in the skills and attributes of female and male workers.

[1] The earnings data of Table 1 relate to men and women with different skills and attributes. Recent entrants into the labor market have little accumulated experience and, insofar as women are disproportionately represented among the recent entrants, so their earnings will be disproportionately affected. It is important, therefore, to determine the extent to which the relative wages of men and women with the same characteristics have changed. Evidence of the declining earnings gap for persons of the same characteristics is provided in Francine Blau and Andrea Beller (1988), Francine Blau and Marianne Ferber (1987b), June O'Neill (1985), and James Smith and Michael Ward (1984) for the United States; and in Jac-Andre Boulet and Laval Lavallee (1984) for Canada.

TABLE 1

FEMALE PARTICIPATION RATES AND EARNINGS RATIOS,
VARIOUS INDUSTRIALIZED COUNTRIES, 1960 AND 1980

Country	Labor Force Participation Rates		Ratio of Women's to Men's Earnings	
	1960	1980	1960	1980
Australia	29.5	55.4	.59	.75
Britain	43.4	62.3	.61	.79
Canada	27.9	50.4	.59	.64
France	44.5	57.0	.64	.71
Germany	46.5	56.2	.65	.72
Italy	35.2	39.9	.73	.83
Japan	47.7	52.7	.46	.54
Sweden	51.0	76.9	.72	.90
United States	37.8	51.3	.66	.66
USSR	77.4	88.2	.70	.70

Source: Adapted from Jacob Mincer (1985, pp. S2, S6). Canadian figures have been added, based on the Labour Force Survey for participation rates and from the Census for earnings. Age groups, time periods, and the definition of earnings differ slightly from country to country.

With the majority of women now participating in the labor force, increased attention has focused on women's earnings and employment opportunities. This attention is reflected in numerous policies initiated since the 1960s designed to raise female earnings and employment opportunities. The rationale for these policies is to counteract the effect of discrimination and, according to some perspectives, to reduce flagrant inequalities in labor market outcomes even if they do not result from discrimination. The efficacy of these policy initiatives has been under considerable scrutiny in part because of the persistence of the overall male-female earnings gap. This has spawned considerable debate on the extent to which the earnings gap reflects discrimination and the extent to which the gap has been affected by various policies.

The purpose of this paper is to (1) discuss the methodological problems in computing the male-female earnings gap, (2) outline the procedures used to estimate the components of the male-female earnings gap giving emphasis to their implications for the potential role of alternative policies, (3) summarize the empirical evidence on the determinants of the gap, (4) outline the policy responses, and (5) discuss the empirical evidence on the impact of the policy initiatives.[2]

The emphasis throughout is on the labor market, while recognizing the importance of constraints, attitudes, and policy responses outside of the labor market.[3] The studies reviewed here pertain mainly to the United States, where most of the em-

---

[2] By focusing on policies designed to narrow the male-female wage gap, this review differs from a number of related reviews. The emphasis in Glen Cain (1986) is on the theory of discrimination and on the empirical issues pertaining to race and sex discrimination, but not on the effect of government policies. This is also the case with respect to reviews of sex discrimination by Janice Madden (1985), Blau and Ferber (1987b), and Francine Blau (1984), albeit the latter does discuss U.S. studies that attempted to estimate the impact of federal legislation. Cain (1985), in reviewing welfare analysis of policies toward women, focuses on the theoretical rationale for intervention, not on the empirical impact of the policy initiatives. Charles Brown (1982), in reviewing the empirical studies of the impact of policies, emphasizes U.S. studies on racial discrimination; as well, his review was completed prior to the publication of a number of recent studies that have provided new evidence on females. Jonathan Leonard (1986) reviews some of this recent evidence, but his analysis is restricted to U.S. studies, its focus is on blacks as well as females, and it does not relate the policies to the evidence on the male-female wage gap. Mincer (1985) provides an international review of female labor supply, fertility, and wages; he does not discuss the impact that alternative policy responses have had on the wage gap. Hilda Kahne (1975) provides a broad review of the economic role of women with respect to numerous interrelated dimensions such as labor force participation, fertility, earnings, occupational attainment, and household production. The policy initiatives she discusses focus largely on income tax legislation, social security legislation, and welfare assistance. Ronald Ehrenberg (1987) restricts his review to the empirical literature on the effects of comparable worth on wages and employment in the United States.

[3] The latter are emphasized in Frank Mott (1982) for younger females, Lois Banfill Shaw (1983) for middle-aged females, and Eileen Appelbaum (1981) for female reentrants to the labor market.

pirical work has been conducted. However, there is some discussion of Canada, Britain, and Australia—other countries where empirical studies exist but the government policies differ somewhat. This review also contains an expanded discussion of comparable worth, a policy receiving considerable attention today but involving procedures not always well understood. The review focuses only on those studies that *directly* examine the impact of legislation in this area. It does not deal with those studies that tangentially comment on the effectiveness of the legislation.[4]

I. Methodological Issues in Computing the Earnings Gap

A number of key questions must be addressed before determining what policies, if any, are justified. What is the magnitude of the female-male pay gap? How much of it can be attributed to discrimination as opposed to differences in productivity-related factors? To what extent may differences in the productivity-related factors reflect discrimination exercised prior to entry into the labor market? What is the relative importance of different components of the gap—wage discrimination for the same job, discriminatory occupational segregation, different human capital endowments?[5]

The appropriate measure of the earnings gap depends in part on the purpose of the analysis. If the purpose is to obtain a measure of the wage differential attributable to labor market discrimination (so as to determine an appropriate labor market policy response), then it is necessary to remove the effects of a wide range of wage-deter-

mining factors, including those that may reflect discrimination outside of the labor market. Such an array of factors includes age, education, training, labor market experience, job-specific seniority, race, union status, health, hours of work, city size, firm size, region, and absenteeism.

Some portion of the differences in productivity-related characteristics and job characteristics themselves may reflect discriminatory pressures from within and outside of the labor market or they may arise as a response on the part of women to wage discrimination and occupational segregation in the labor market.[6] This could be the case for such variables as education, training, general labor market experience, company seniority, absenteeism, and hours of work. For example, women may have higher turnover and absenteeism because they are assigned to low-wage, dead-end jobs or because they bear a disproportionate burden of household responsibility. Or women may not enroll in certain education programs, even if they have an aptitude for them, because they perceive that opportunities to use such training will be closed to them in the labor market (Solomon Polachek 1978). To the extent that these are discriminatory, then it would not be appropriate to control for, or "net out," the effect of such differences in arriving at a measure of the pay gap that reflect *all* such sources of discrimination, and hence that may be amenable to redress through a wide range of policies both within and outside the labor market.

Whether it is appropriate to control for the wage gap arising out of the allocation of men and women to different occupations also depends on the purpose of the analy-

---

[4] Such studies include Debra Barbezat (1987) Blau and Beller (1988), Dallas Cullen, Alice Nakamura, and Masao Nakamura (1986), Victor Fuchs (1986), Sharon Bernstein Megdal and Michael Ransom (1985), Smith and Ward (1984, p. xiii).

[5] The methodological issues associated with estimating discriminatory pay gaps are outlined in more detail in David Bloom and Mark Killingsworth (1982) and Cain (1986).

[6] On the importance of prelabor market discrimination and sex-role socialization, including a review of some of the literature, see Mary Corcoran and Paul Courant (1987). Reuben Gronau (1988) highlights how wage-determining factors like on-the-job training, turnover, and work intensity are affected by wages, which in turn are determined by these factors.

sis. If the focus is on unequal pay for the same work in the same narrowly defined occupation, then it is appropriate to control for differences in the distribution of males and females across narrowly defined occupations. (Such differences are beyond the scope of conventional equal pay legislation.) But if the purpose is to obtain a measure of the pay gap that reflects differences in the occupational distribution of females, then it is not appropriate to control for occupation differences.

Most data sets do not contain information on all relevant control variables, thereby giving rise to omitted variable bias when the omitted variables are partially correlated with pay and the included variables. To the extent that females have less general labor market experience, company-specific seniority, or labor market–oriented education than do males, not fully controlling for these differences could erroneously lead to attributing some of their effect to discrimination.

Other variables are measured imprecisely. For example, occupational control variables often include only indicators of broad occupations that mask considerable wage differences within occupations. In such circumstances differences in the broad occupational distribution may not account for much of the overall earnings gap because much of the gap may reflect differences *within* the broad occupations. Similarly, many of the data sets contain only crude controls for hours of work (e.g., full-time versus part-time). Some of the lower annual earnings of females may reflect fewer hours worked within such broad categories.

Some empirical studies (Jacob Mincer and Solomon Polachek (1974) for the United States; Walter Block (1982) and Roberta Robb (1978) for Canada) have restricted their analysis to never-married males and females whose household responsibilities are likely to be more similar than married individuals. In this way a sample is selected that minimizes some differences (e.g., responsibility for care of children) that are often unobserved to the researcher. However, this very selection procedure also introduces new differences that are also conventionally unobserved to the researcher. For example, never-married females may be highly motivated, career oriented, and possess a comparative advantage in labor market work. In such circumstances the wage gap based on never-marrieds may underestimate the wage gap for a random male and female with the same observed characteristics.

The same may also apply to the wage gap as it is conventionally estimated from labor force participants. Male and female participants may possess different attributes that are unobserved to the researcher but that nevertheless influence wages. Failure to control for such factors may lead to biased estimates of the discriminatory gap defined as wage differences for the same productivity-related factors, whether observed or unobserved by the researcher (Blau and Beller 1988; Paul Miller 1987).

II. Methods for Computing the Earnings Gap

In varying degrees, the following empirical procedures for computing the earnings gap deal with the previously discussed methodological issues.[7]

A. Narrowly Defined Occupations

One simple procedure to control for many of the variables that could influence the overall earnings gap is to compare male and female wages within narrow occupations, perhaps even within the same establishment. If the occupations are sufficiently

[7] Earlier studies, (e.g., Henry Sanborn 1964) are not reviewed here because they simply compared the average earnings of all males and females with the average of particular subgroups, such as those of the same age or education, without simultaneously controlling for the myriad of factors that affect the earnings gap.

narrowly defined, then they will be a surrogate for the human capital and other requirements of the job that otherwise have to be controlled for in the form of independent variables in multiple regression wage equations. In fact, using narrowly defined occupations may even control for some of the differences between men and women that may be important determinants of the earnings gap but that are unobserved by the researcher.

B. Regression Procedures and Wage Decomposition

The standard procedure[8] to analyze the determinants of the male-female earnings gap is to estimate earnings equations for samples of individual men and women separately. Specifically, the procedure is to fit equation (1) to a sample of male (m) workers and equation (2) to a sample of female (f) workers:

$$W_m = b_m X_m + u_m \qquad (1)$$

$$W_f = b_f X_f + u_f \qquad (2)$$

where W is wages or average hourly earnings, usually measured in logarithmic terms so that the estimated coefficients measure approximately the proportionate effect on wages of changes in the right-hand side variables. X is a vector of measured characteristics of the workers such as education, training, and experience, as well as control variables like race, marital status,

---

[8] This procedure, or some variant, has been used in a large number of empirical studies: Alan Blinder (1973), Corcoran and Gregory Duncan (1979), Burton Malkiel and Judith Malkiel (1973), Mincer and Polachek (1974, 1978), Ronald Oaxaca (1973), Steven Sandell and David Shapiro (1978) for the United States; Morley Gunderson (1979), R. A. Holmes (1976), Robb (1978) for Canada. This review does not contain a discussion of the results of studies based upon reverse regression whereby indices of labor quality are regressed on pay. Arthur Goldberger (1984) reviews this literature and concludes that reverse regression procedures are not appropriate, except in special circumstances which can be tested by a procedure he outlines.

and location. The vector of regression coefficients, b, reflects the return that the market yields to a unit change in endowments such as education and experience. The error term, u, reflects measurement error as well as the effect of factors unmeasured or unobserved by the researcher.

A property of ordinary least-squares regression analysis is that the regression lines pass through the mean values of the variables so that

$$\overline{W}_m = \hat{b}_m \overline{X}_m \qquad (3)$$

$$\overline{W}_f = \hat{b}_f \overline{X}_f. \qquad (4)$$

The hats denote ordinary least-squares estimated values. If females receive the same return as do males for their endowments of wage-determining characteristics (i.e., if females were given the male pay structure), then their average wage would be

$$\overline{W}_f^* = \hat{b}_m \overline{X}_f. \qquad (5)$$

This is often interpreted as the average female wage that would prevail in the absence of wage discrimination (where wage discrimination is defined as unequal pay for the same endowments of wage-determining characteristics). Subtracting (5) from (3) gives the difference between average male earnings and the average hypothetical female earnings that would prevail if females were paid according to the male pay structure: This difference reflects their different endowments of wage-generating characteristics, i.e.,

$$\overline{W}_m - \overline{W}_f^* = \hat{b}_m \overline{X}_m - \hat{b}_m \overline{X}_f =$$
$$\hat{b}_m(\overline{X}_m - \overline{X}_f). \qquad (6)$$

Subtracting (4) from (5) yields the difference between the hypothetical "nondiscriminatory" female wage and their actual wage. This difference reflects the different returns to the same wage-generating characteristics, i.e.,

$$\overline{W}_f^* - \overline{W}_f = \hat{b}_m \overline{X}_f - \hat{b}_f \overline{X}_f$$
$$= (\hat{b}_m - \hat{b}_f)\overline{X}_f. \qquad (7)$$

Gunderson: Male-Female Wage Differentials and Policy Responses 51

Adding (6) and (7) yields

$$\overline{W}_m - \overline{W}_f = \hat{b}_m(\overline{X}_m - \overline{X}_f)$$
$$+ (\hat{b}_m - \hat{b}_f)\overline{X}_f. \quad (8)$$

That is, the overall average male-female wage gap can be decomposed into two components: One is the portion attributable to differences in the endowments of wage-generating characteristics $(\overline{X}_m - \overline{X}_f)$ evaluated at the male returns $(\hat{b}_m)$; the other portion is attributable to differences in the returns $(\hat{b}_m - \hat{b}_f)$ that males and females get for the same endowment of wage-generating characteristics $(\overline{X}_f)$. This latter component is often taken as reflecting wage discrimination.[9]

III. Evidence on the Earnings Gap

The diversity of estimates of the male-female earnings gap and its components reflects differences in empirical procedures, data sets, proxy variables, and concepts of what is meant by wage discrimination or occupational segregation. Summaries of the empirical evidence are found in a number of reviews.[10] Donald

[9] An alternative decomposition of the earnings gap is derived by replacing equation (5) with the hypothetical wage that males could expect to earn if they were paid according to the female pay structure. Because both male and female wages are affected by discrimination, the male-female wage *gap* for workers of the same characteristics need not equal the wage *gain* that females would receive if they were paid the competitive wage, as opposed to the male wage. David Neumark (1988) shows how a weighted average of the male and female coefficients may approximate the competitive wage that would prevail in the absence of discrimination.

[10] Recent reviews include 21 U.S. studies in Cynthia Lloyd and Beth Neimi (1979, pp. 232–38); 14 U.S. studies in Donald Treiman and Heidi Hartmann (1981, pp. 20, 36); 20 U.S. studies in Janice Madden (1985); 30 U.S. studies in Steven Willborn (1986, pp. 13–15, 20–24); 21 U.S. studies in Cain (1986, pp. 750–52); 22 U.S. studies in Blau and Ferber (1987a); 12 Canadian studies in Gunderson (1985a, p. 229); 9 U.S. studies, 5 Canadian studies, and 4 British studies in Naresh Agarwal (1981, pp. 120–25).

Treiman and Heidi Hartmann (1981 p. 21) provide a comprehensive list of common control variables: education, age, race, training, labor market experience or its proxy, seniority with a particular employer, marital status, health, hours of work, city size, region, quality of schooling, absenteeism, and number of children.

From the various studies, the following generalizations emerge regarding sex differences in earnings.

1. The greater the number of variables used to control for differences in productivity-related factors, the smaller the productivity-adjusted wage gap relative to the unadjusted gap.

2. Even when they use extensive lists of control variables most studies do find *some* residual wage gap that they attribute to discrimination. When the gap is close to zero that usually results from the inclusion of control variables whose values themselves may reflect discrimination.

3. Factors originating from outside the labor market (e.g., differences in household responsibilities, *type* of education, career interruptions) are an important source of the overall earnings gap, highlighting the limited scope for policies that focus only on the labor market.

4. Differences in the occupational distribution of males and females account for a substantial portion of the overall earnings gap.[11] In contrast, pay differences for the same nar-

[11] Treiman and Hartmann (1981, p. 33) indicate that differences in the occupational distribution between men and women account for a much larger portion of the earnings gap when detailed, as opposed to broad, occupations are used. This explains why fairly small effects of differences in occupation distribution are found in studies like Oaxaca (1973), which use broad occupational groups that mask the effect of the segregation of women into the lower-wage jobs within such groups.

rowly defined occupation[12] within the same establishment do not account for much of the gap.[13] This finding suggests a greater potential role for equal employment opportunity policies (to break down occupational segregation both within and across firms) and comparable worth policies (to enable comparisons across occupations) than for conventional equal pay policies (which require comparisons within the same job and establishment).

5. Differences in pay across establishments also account for a substantial component of the earnings gap,[14] thereby limiting the scope of equal pay and comparable worth policies which require comparisons within the same establishment.

6. The productivity-adjusted earnings gap tends to be smaller in the public than private sector. In the private sector itself, the discriminatory gap tends to be smaller when product markets are competitive (Orley Ashenfelter and Timothy Hannan 1986).

7. Being married has a differential effect on the earnings of men versus women. The gap is widest between married men and married women,

suggesting that household responsibilities may have an important effect on the earnings gap.

8. Differences in labor market experience and the continuity of that experience, including the accumulation of company seniority, account for a substantial portion of the earnings gap. As women become more attached to the labor force and accumulate both general labor market experience and company-specific experience and seniority, the gap should diminish.[15]

9. While women have similar *levels* of education to men, the *type* of education women acquire is often not as oriented toward gaining skills that are rewarded in the labor market. In recent years, however, this has been changing, and this should help reduce the gap in the future.[16]

10. Differences in preferences for certain types of jobs account for a substantial portion of the earnings gap (Richard Butler 1982; Thomas Daymont and Paul Andrisani 1984; although it is difficult if not impossible to determine the extent to which these preferences are shaped by discrimination.

11. Both the male-female earnings gap[17]

---

[12] Ratios of female/male earnings of 0.80 and more are common: Alan Bayer and Helen Astin (1968), George Johnson and Frank Stafford (1974), Sanborn (1964) in the U.S.; Gunderson (1976, 1985b), Sylvia Ostry (1968), R. Robson and M. Lapointe (1971) in Canada.

[13] Ratios of female/male earnings of 0.90 and 0.95 and more are typical: Francine Blau (1977), John Buckley (1971), Nancy Gordon, Thomas Morton, and Ina Braden (1974), Malkiel and Malkiel (1973), Donald McNulty (1967) in the U.S.; Gunderson (1975), William Schranke (1977) in Canada; Brian Chiplin and Peter Sloane (1976) and William Siebert and Peter Sloane (1981) in Britain.

[14] Blau (1977), for example, found that more of the male-female wage differential within occupations came from across firms than within firms. Additional evidence on this is summarized in Barbara Reskin and Heidi Hartmann (1986, p. 12).

[15] The study with the most detailed measures of work history (Corcoran and Duncan 1979, p. 10) finds that 39 percent of the earnings gap can be attributed to differences in work histories between men and women. The most important factors are differences in company seniority prior to current job (12 percent of gap), training on current job (11 percent of gap), the proportion of working years that were full-time (8 percent of gap), and years out of the labor force since completing school (6 percent of the gap). Blau and Ferber (1986, p. 206) cite evidence of the substantial difference in the labor market experience of men and women and of the reduction of that difference in recent years.

[16] Evidence on this point and a citation of some related literature are given in Blau and Ferber (1986, p. 188).

[17] Evidence cited in Footnote 1.

and the extent of occupational segregation[18] appear to be declining during the 1970s and 1980s, especially when changes in the skills and attributes of the workers are accounted for.

IV. Policy Initiatives

The main policies to deal with the differential pay and employment opportunities of males and females are equal pay policies (including comparable worth), equal employment opportunity legislation (including affirmative action), and facilitating policies to assist in the adaptation of females to the labor market (e.g., day care, flexible hours, and education policies). Each of these areas is first discussed in general terms, followed by a discussion of the specific legislation in the equal pay and equal employment opportunity area.

A. Equal Pay and Comparable Worth

Equal pay policies generally require equal pay for the same (or substantially similar) work in the same establishment. Comparable worth (also termed *equal pay for work of equal value*, and *pay equity*) is the latest and strongest form of intervention in the equal pay front. Comparable worth basically differs from equal pay insofar as comparable worth allows comparisons across otherwise dissimilar occupations, usually based upon job evaluation procedures.

The comparable worth procedure typically involves four steps. First, predominantly female and predominantly male jobs within an establishment are compared with each other. The concept of gender predominance itself can differ, albeit an occu-

pation represented by 70 percent or more of one sex is a common cutoff.

Second, a group of "experts" assign job evaluation point scores to the various components (usually skill, effort, responsibility, and working conditions) involved in the job. The range of the points for each component can differ, which obviously affects the weights that are implied for each component. The point scores for each component are then simply summed to get a total point score for the job.

Third, the total point scores and wages for each of the predominantly male jobs are compared with the total point scores and wages of the predominantly female jobs. This can be done by running a simple regression of pay on total point scores first for the predominantly male jobs and then for predominantly female jobs. The slopes can differ to reflect the possibility that male- and female-dominated jobs may receive different returns to the job evaluation point score. The fourth step involves adjusting female wages to male wages when the job evaluation point scores indicate that the jobs are of equal value.

Typically, the female pay line averages about 80 to 90 percent of the height of the male pay line. Relative to the typical overall unadjusted earnings ratio of approximately 0.60, the job evaluation procedures can be thought of as yielding an adjusted ratio of approximately 0.80 to 0.90 when comparisons are made within the same organization for jobs of the same average productivity and working conditions as measured by job evaluation scores.[19]

The practical problem of job evaluation schemes applied to the comparable worth area have been discussed by both support-

---

[18] Andrea Beller (1984, 1985) indicates that the decline in occupational segregation has been most pronounced for new and recent labor market participants, and for managerial and professional jobs.

[19] Comparable worth cases have occurred in Washington State, Connecticut, Michigan, Minnesota, Iowa, and San Jose in the U.S., and the federal jurisdiction in Canada. These and other cases are discussed in Ronald Ehrenberg and Robert Smith (1987a, 1987b), Gunderson (1984), Robb (1987), and Robert Smith (1988).

ers and critics of comparable work (Donald Treiman 1979; Robert Livernash 1980). Gender bias can still prevail if, for example, a larger range of points is allocated for tasks that are performed more often in the predominantly male job, or if compensating points are awarded for dirty work conditions in the predominantly male jobs but not the predominantly female jobs.

Job evaluation systems were not designed for purposes of establishing comparable worth (Mark Killingsworth 1985; Donald Schwab 1980). They were designed to provide relative, ordinal rankings of jobs, not a cardinal number to which a dollar value would be assigned. Separate job evaluation systems were usually used for different occupational groupings (e.g., white-collar and blue-collar) in recognition of some fundamental incomparabilities across quite dissimilar jobs. Market forces were often implicitly considered in that the "worth" of certain benchmark jobs was given by the market wage, and the wages of the other jobs were set relative to these benchmark jobs. If the job evaluation suggested a wage adjustment that was out of line with market realities, then the evaluation system itself was often revised.

Numerous technical issues are associated with estimating pay lines and adjusting wages, but they have received scant discussion in the job evaluation literature. What is the appropriate functional form for the pay lines that relate point scores to pay? Should the separate point scores for each of the various job components be entered as separate regressors in a multiple regression equation relating pay (dependent variable) to the point scores of each component such as skill, effort, responsibility, and working conditions (separate independent variables)? Or should the scores be summed to get a total that is entered as a single regressor—a procedure that effectively constrains the slope coefficients on each

of the separate scores to be equal?[20] What is the appropriate adjustment procedure—the female payline to the male payline, the female payline to the average payline, each female observation to the male payline? Should extrapolation of the payline be allowed outside of the range over which there are no observations? There may otherwise be no predominantly male jobs to compare with the female jobs at the low end of the point scores. Such a procedure would effectively allow for proportionate pay for work of proportionate value and eliminate the requirement that comparisons be made only when the value of the jobs is the same.

A large number of program design features pertaining to the administration of equal value legislation have to be worked out, and they can have a significant influence on the scope and ultimate effect of the legislation. Such design features include the following: the definition of gender predominance (substantially larger numbers may be encompassed if one moves from a cutoff of 70 percent to 60 percent female-dominated); exclusions for small businesses (on the grounds that job evaluation procedures are not as common for them and that it will be difficult to find sufficient numbers for comparison groups); the use of a complaints-based approach versus a regulatory regime (the latter would require job evaluation to be in place whether or not a complaint was lodged); the definition of establishment and in particular whether comparisons can be made across different bargaining units or establishments of the same company; the question of phasing and retroactive settlements; and the allowable exceptions for such fac-

---

[20] Ehrenberg and Smith (1987b) suggest that these may not be problems because they find that comparable worth pay gaps are relatively insensitive to the functional form of the earnings equation and to the use of total scores or separate scores for each component.

tors as seniority, merit, training, and shortages.

The previous discussion referred to the practical problems associated with the administration of job evaluation procedures and comparable worth. Of more fundamental concern—at least to many economists—is that even if the practical problems can be worked out, the concept of comparable worth is viewed by many to be fundamentally flawed. It is an administrative concept of value that may bear little or no relationship to the economic concept of the value. Comparable worth is akin to the notion of "value-in-use" rather than "value-in-exchange." Just as water may have a high "value-in-use" but a low "value-in-exchange" because of its abundance (vice versa for diamonds, because of their scarcity), so some jobs may appear to have a high value-in-use because of the inputs of skill, effort, and responsibility required. However, such jobs need not command a high market wage if there is an abundance of people willing to do them. Value is determined at the *margin* according to basic principles of supply and demand, not according to a job evaluator's concept of the *average* value of the *inputs* required to do the job. The latter is akin to the search for a "just price," a concept that is at best elusive without reference to basic notions of what people are willing to pay to have a job done and what others are willing to accept to do the job.

Supporters of comparable worth can argue against these attacks. Job evaluation must have some useful information content, given its survival value in private industry. (However, as discussed previously, it is now being used for a different purpose than its original rationale.) Also, hedonic price equations have been used extensively to provide implicit evaluations in other areas—the value of life (from wage-risk trade-offs), value of education (from earnings equations), and the value of quality attributes (to correct for quality change in the consumer price index). The problem is not so much one of estimating relationships between wages and point scores, but of assigning point scores. This problem can be reduced in a number of ways: having a comprehensive list of factors that make up the job content; not summing point scores across components; having the evaluators simply specify the components (leaving it up to the market to determine the nondiscriminatory shadow prices). The last procedure—termed the *policy-capturing approach*—involves using regression analysis to estimate the shadow prices (regression coefficients) for job evaluation scores for the predominantly male occupations, then using these estimates as weights to apply to the scores in the female-dominated job.

There is likely to be considerable error in the assignment of point scores, but wouldn't one expect this error in job evaluations to be random across male and female jobs? Even if the lower pay in the female-dominated jobs reflects supply side choices and the willingness of people to enter the lower-paying female-dominated occupations, such "willingness" is often constrained by pressures elsewhere, and comparable worth may counteract some of those pressures. Supporters of comparable worth also argue that women should not have to leave female-dominated jobs to get higher pay, and this is especially important for older women whose mobility is likely to be severely constrained.

This debate over the pros and cons of comparable worth highlights the substantial conceptual divide between the *individual-oriented* pay gap analysis used by most economists and the *job-oriented* analysis used in comparable worth studies. Proponents of comparable worth argue that preferences for different types of work or decisions to acquire certain types of education should not give rise to pay differences across jobs of comparable worth. In short, supporters of comparable worth largely reject the notion that market forces should be the prime determinants of pay. Hence, they often have a normative conflict with economists who tend to emphasize the importance of market forces in reducing discrimination and who stress that individual preferences should be allowed to affect occupational choices providing there is an equality of *opportunity* both within and outside the labor market.

B. Legislation on Equal Pay and Comparable Worth

In the United States, equal pay legislation was first introduced through the federal Equal Pay Act of 1963 as an amendment to the Fair Labor Standards Act.[21] The Equal Pay Act requires equal pay for work of equal skill, effort, responsibility, and working conditions. It does not allow comparisons across jobs of different content, and hence it does not entail the comparable worth concept. Compliance is through both complaints and routine investigation.

The principle of equal pay is also a component of Title VII of the Civil Rights Act of 1964. Known as the Equal Employment Opportunity (EEO) provisions, that legislation forbids wage and employment discrimination on the basis of race, color, religion, national origin, and sex. In *Gunther vs. County of Washington* (1981) the U.S. Supreme Court determined that comparable worth comparisons were not precluded under Title VII; however, the court did not endorse the principle or indicate how it should be applied.

In addition to the federal Equal Pay Act

and Title VII, most states have equal pay laws, applying mainly to their public sector employees. As of 1984, 25 states had legislation relating to comparable worth. Of these, 10 had actually implemented or were about to implement comparable worth for their public sector employees, even though in some cases state legislation did not require implementation (Ehrenberg and Smith, 1987b, Table 1).

As pointed out by Cook (1985, p. 4), most comparable worth policies have not been implemented through the courts or legislation. In the case of legislation, numerous states have laws that require comparable worth in both the public and private sectors. However, the legislation has been enforced or implemented, not on the basis of comparable worth, but on conventional equal pay. Only in Minnesota, Iowa, and to a lesser extent the state of Washington has there been a serious attempt to legislate *and* implement comparable worth, and it has been confined to the public sector.

In Canada, where labor matters are largely under provincial jurisdiction, all jurisdictions have a form of equal pay legislation, following the initiative of Ontario in 1951. Canada appears to have gone further than the United States in legislating comparable worth. Such legislation has been in place in Quebec since 1976, in the federal jurisdiction since 1978 (covering approximately 10 percent of the Canadian work force), in Manitoba for its civil servants since 1985, and in Ontario since 1987.[22] The amount of litigation in the area

---

[21] Discussions of the legislation and jurisprudence—its evolution, interpretation through the courts, and implementation—is discussed in Aldrich and Buchele (1986), Blau and Ferber (1986), Alice Cook (1985), and Ehrenberg and Smith (1987b) for the United States; Gunderson (1985a) for Canada; and Jennie Farley (1985), Cynthia Goodwin (1984), Eve Landau (1985), and Willborn (1986) for international comparisons.

[22] In June 1987, the government of Ontario passed the Pay Equity Act, legislating equal pay for work of equal value for *both* private and public sector employers. The legislation is to be phased in, with wage adjustments in the public sector beginning no later than January 1990 and in the private sector beginning no later than January 1991. Rather than relying only on the usual complaints-based system, the Ontario legislation is based upon a "proactive, system-wide" application of comparable worth. This approach requires all employers in the public sector and employers of 100 or more employees in the private sector

has been scant, however, in part because of the reliance upon a complaints-based system in the federal jurisdiction and Quebec.

In Britain, equal pay for equal work was passed in 1970 but its implementation was delayed until the end of 1975 to allow an adjustment period. Britain is also part of the European Economic Community, and as such it is subject to the Treaty of Rome, which adopted the concept of equal value in 1976. In spite of this formal adoption of the principle of equal value in the EEC, its enforcement has been minimal.

Australia is often singled out in the equal value area because federal and state tribunals establish wages by decree for the vast majority of the Australian work force.[23] That system led to the *official* fixing or "markdown" of female wages at 54 percent of male wages for the same job up until 1949 when the ratio was officially raised to 75 percent. In 1969 (to be fully operative by 1972) the principle of equal pay for equal work was adopted in that the official markdown was to be eliminated between males and females in the same job. In 1972 (to be fully operative by 1975) the principle of equal pay for work of equal value was adopted in that the official markdown between predominantly male and female occupations was also eliminated. While this policy has been termed one of comparable worth, it is not comparable worth in the American sense of the awards being based upon a system of formal job evaluation (albeit "work value assessments" can be used by the Australian tribunals in their award decisions).

C. Equal Employment Opportunity and Affirmative Action Legislation

Equal employment opportunity legislation is designed to create an equality of opportunity in the various phases of the employment decision such as recruiting, hiring, training, transfers, promotions, and terminations. Affirmative action is concerned with *results* more than opportunities. It involves actions such as the aggressive hiring of females or preferences to females when candidates are otherwise equal.

Affirmative action is designed to compensate for the cumulative effects of a history of inequality and systemic discrimination. The term *systemic* (not to be confused with *systematic*) describes discrimination that results as an unintended by-product; in legal parlance it results when an action has a "disparate impact" even if there was not "disparate treatment." For example, it can occur when firms have job requirements that effectively exclude certain groups or that unintentionally place people into positions based upon stereotypes.

Affirmative action programs generally involve the following procedures. First, a data base is established comparing the sex composition of the organization with that of the surrounding *relevant* labor market. Second, targets are set to achieve a representation of the internal female work force that is similar to its representation in the surrounding labor market. Third, a plan and timetable are established for achieving the targets.

In the United States, equal employment opportunity legislation (like equal pay legislation) is a component of Title VII (the EEO provision) of the Civil Rights Act of 1964. All Canadian jurisdictions have similar laws. Affirmative action plans in the U.S. are part of Executive Order 11246 for employers involved in federal contracts (hence the phrase "contract-compliance

---

to utilize bona fide job comparison or evaluation procedures and to make the required wage adjustments. If it turns out to be rigidly enforced, this legislation will be the first major use of comparable worth in the private sector.

[23] The Australian situation is discussed in R. Gregory and R. Duncan (1981). It is contrasted with the situation in the United States in R. Gregory and V. Ho (1985) and with the situation in Britain in R. Gregory, A. Daly, and V. Ho (undated).

legislation").[24] In Canada, it was not until 1986 that the federal government initiated affirmative action in the federal jurisdiction (only about 10 percent of the Canadian work force) as well as for federal contractors.

D. Facilitating Policy

Equal pay and equal employment opportunity legislation have been the main thrust of policy initiatives to deal with sex discrimination, but other initiatives have been followed, generally to facilitate the adaptation of women into the labor market in a manner that would improve their pay and employment opportunities.

Day care policies and flexible work arrangements can be important because women spend a disproportionately large amount of time on household work, even when both spouses work in the labor market (Fuchs 1986; Gronau 1986). Policies to facilitate divorce, support payments, and the more equitable division of family assets upon divorce have been advocated not only on their own right but because they may enable the labor market decisions of women, especially those related to location and hours, to be less dependent upon the decision of their husband. And to the extent that they lead to more dissolved marriages, the policies may encourage women to invest in skills that are more valuable in the labor market than the increasingly unstable marriage market. Education[25] and training policies can enhance the wages and employment opportunities of women, but it is important that they be free of sex-role stereotyping. Otherwise they may simply

lead to women acquiring skills that are not highly valued in the labor market.[26]

V. Expected Impact of Policies

In response to equal pay (including comparable worth) legislation, firms should increase female wages so as to avoid the expected penalty associated with not complying.[27] Even firms that do not discriminate may raise female wages so as to reduce the probability of erroneous litigation. As with any wage-fixing legislation, an adverse employment effect is likely to occur as firms substitute other factors of production for the more expensive female labor (substitution effect)[28] and as they reduce their scale of operations as the cost increase leads to a price increase and hence a reduction in the firm's output (scale effect).

The effect of equal pay laws on the wages of *males* is theoretically indeterminant. On the one hand, employers may seek to comply by lowering male wages, or at least the rate of increase of male wages. On the

---

[24] A brief chronology of the major legislative initiatives in the United States is given in Finis Welch (1981).

[25] Title IX (educational amendments to the Civil Rights Act of 1964), passed in 1972, prohibits discrimination on the basis of sex in education programs receiving federal assistance.

[26] Evidence of changes in education, training, day care, and flexible work arrangements to facilitate the adaptation of women into the labor market is discussed in Blau and Ferber (1986, pp. 185–89) and Reskin and Hartmann (1986, pp. 99–122).

[27] This section focuses on the expected impact of antidiscrimination policies on the wages and employment of covered and noncovered workers. Broader welfare issues are discussed in Cain (1985), and the efficiency aspects of eliminating statistical discrimination are discussed in Stewart Schwab (1986) and references cited therein. Broader general equilibrium effects are outlined in Perry Beider et al. (1988) while Welch (1976) and George Johnson and Welch (1976) illustrate how the potential impact of an economy-wide affirmative action program depends upon such factors as the extent to which quotas are properly set, and the extent to which firms "bump" minority workers into jobs for which they are not qualified, or engage in reverse wage discrimination.

[28] Some of this substitution may also occur *within* the female work force as employers may substitute females who are less likely to be covered by equal pay. They may also try to increase qualifications, effectively substituting more qualified for less qualified females.

other hand, the employment and wages of males may increase as they are substituted (perhaps subtly) for the higher-priced female labor; the opposite would occur where they are complements in production.

In response to equal pay legislation in the covered sector, wages in the *noncovered* sector could rise or fall depending upon the relative importance of induced supply and demand changes. The supply influx of disemployed workers from the covered sector could depress wages in the noncovered sector. Demand in the noncovered sector could increase or decrease (with corresponding effects on wages) depending upon the complementarity or substitutability with covered workers.

In contrast to equal pay legislation which fixes wages, equal employment opportunity legislation (including affirmative action) increases the demand for female labor at all phases of the employment decision. This should serve to increase *both* wages and employment. Equal employment opportunity policies, however, may do little to assist women who do not want to change jobs to enhance their earnings.

VI. Evidence on Impact of Policies

While the focus of most of the U.S. studies on the impact of legislation has been on the impact on black workers, many studies provided separate estimates by sex and so can be used to provide evidence on the effect on female workers.[29] The prototype model in most of these studies is of the form

$$Y = bX + aL + u \qquad (9)$$

where Y is a measure of labor market success of females (e.g., earnings, employments, probability of entering a male-dom-

[29] Studies that focused exclusively on blacks are not reviewed here; many are reviewed in Brown (1982).

inated occupation), X is a vector of control variables, L is a measure of the legislative initiative, b and a are parameters reflecting, respectively, the impact of the control variables and the legislation and u is the error term. As discussed subsequently, the legislative initiative is usually captured by a variable indicating the time period or jurisdiction where the legislation is in place, or by variables indicating enforcement activity under the legislation. It is also possible to test for whether the legislative initiative itself is endogenous by estimating an equation of the form

$$L = cZ + dY_{-1} + e \qquad (10)$$

where Z is a vector of control variables, Y_{-1} is the measure of labor market success of females in previous periods, and e is an error term. The two studies using such a procedure—James Heckman and Kenneth Wolpin (1976) and Leonard (1984c)—do not find evidence of any significant effect of the previous labor market experience of females (i.e., d is insignificantly different from zero), at least under the affirmative action initiatives of the federal contract compliance program. Whether this conclusion also holds for other legislative initiatives is unknown.

A. Equal Employment Opportunity Legislation in the United States

As noted earlier, Title VII EEO legislation was designed to combat both wage and employment discrimination. Its effects on female earnings, therefore, should be positive, while the effects on employment may be positive (resulting from the equal employment opportunity aspects) or negative (emanating from the equal pay aspects).

Table 2 summarizes the results of the various studies of the effect of Title VII. Beller (1976) constructs separate enforcement variables reflecting the probability of an investigation (ratio of investigations to

Journal of Economic Literature, Vol. XXVII (March 1989)

TABLE 2
IMPACT OF EQUAL EMPLOYMENT OPPORTUNITY LEGISLATION (TITLE VII
OF THE CIVIL RIGHTS ACT OF 1964), UNITED STATES

Study	Data	Dependent Variable	Impact
Beller (1976)	CPS 1967, 1974	Earnings	Increased female earnings by 4.7 percent over 1967–74 Effect larger after enforcement amendments Increasing probability of an investigation more effective than increasing the probability of a settlement
Beller (1979)	CPS 1967, 1974	Earnings	Reduced gender earnings gap of .68 by .07 between 1967–74 .01 from increased female earnings and .06 from reduced male earnings But statistically insignificant More pronounced in private sector Stricter enforcement leads to larger effects
Beller (1980)	CPS 1968–75	Earnings	Reduced gender gap by .096 between 1968–74 .057 from increased female earnings and .039 from reduced male earnings Enforcement more effective in expanding economy
Beller (1982a)	CPS 1967, 1974	Probability of female entering male-dominated occupation	Reduced sex differential in the probability of being employed in a male-dominated job by .062 between 1967–74 Did so by increasing female probability and reducing male probability Effect larger after enforcement amendments Increasing the probability of a settlement more effective than increasing the probability of an investigation
Leonard (1984a)	EEOC Reports 1966, 1978	Change in employment share	Sometimes negative, generally insignificant
Oaxaca (1977)	Census 1960, 1970	Earnings	No significant change in the discrimination component of the earnings gap between 1960 and 1970 Widened for whites but narrowed for blacks
Oaxaca (1977)	Current Population Reports 1955–71	Earnings	Reduced earnings gap in postlegislative period but statistically insignificant and quantitatively small

number of women) and the probability of a settlement conditional upon an investigation (ratio of successful settlements to attempted settlements) based on data from the compliance files of the EEOC. These enforcement variables are included as regressors in typical earnings equations estimated to a sample of approximately 24,000 individuals from the Public Use Tapes of the Current Population Survey (CPS). A separate equation is estimated for each of 1967 and 1974, years that come before and after the 1972 amendment of Title VII, which provided more effective enforcement by expanding coverage and giving the EEOC the right to sue a respondent. Beller includes the enforcement measures in what she terms the "pre-enforcement cross section" of 1967 to capture the effect of unobserved factors that may be correlated with the enforcement measures. This enables the estimation of a purer enforcement effect by subtracting the enforcement coefficients of the 1967 preamendment cross section equation from the 1974 postamendment equation.[30]

The impact of Title VII has been quantified at more aggregate levels. Leonard (1984a) uses 555 state-by-2-digit-SIC (Standard Industry Classification) industry cells within manufacturing, and regresses the change (between 1966 and 1978) in the percentage of workers who are female on the number of Title VII class action suits per employer as a measure of compliance. Time series regressions have been used to see whether there was a shift in the underlying time pattern after controlling for the effect of the business cycle and any time trend (Oaxaca 1977).[31] The decomposition procedure, as discussed earlier, has been applied in years prior to and subsequent to the implementation of legislative initiatives, to see whether the portion of the earnings gap attributable to discrimination has dissipated in the postlegislative period (Oaxaca 1977).

As the last column of Table 2 indicates, the empirical results on the effect of Title VII are somewhat inconclusive. There is

[30] Beller's subsequent studies largely expand upon that methodology in a number of ways: estimates on the effect on male earnings as well as female earnings, and on the government and private sectors separately (Beller 1979); estimates of the effect on the probability of entering a male-dominated occupation (Beller 1982a); estimates for each year between 1968 and 1975 to see whether the effectiveness of enforcement depends upon the state of the economy (Beller 1980); and separate estimates in the periods before and after the passage of Title IX of the Education Amendments in 1972, to determine the additional effect of those amendments (Beller 1982b).

[31] Specifically, the male-female median earnings gap for year-round full-time workers for the years 1955–71 was regressed on a time trend, a measure of the business cycle, and a dummy variable shift parameter for the years 1966–71, when the legislative initiatives should have had sufficient time to have their effect.

some evidence that it has increased female earnings and reduced the earnings gap (Beller 1976, 1979, 1980). However, much of the reduction in the earnings gap occurs because EEO initiatives actually led to a reduction in male earnings (Beller 1979, 1980). Insignificant effects are found in other data sets, based on other methodologies (Oaxaca 1977). The legislation seems to have had some effect on reducing occupational segregation (Beller 1982a), but its effect on female employment has been negative or insignificant (Leonard 1984a). Stricter enforcement procedures led to a larger impact (Beller 1976, 1979, 1980, 1982a). In order to reduce the wage gap, ensuring a successful settlement was less effective than increasing the probability of an investigation (Beller 1976). The opposite was the case for reducing occupational segregation (Beller 1982a).

Clearly, the evidence does *not* unambiguously indicate that the EEO initiatives of Title VII were a resounding success, although there is some evidence of a positive effect on the earnings and occupational position of women. There is also some evidence that the legislation is more effective when it is strictly enforced and when the economy is expanding.

B. Affirmative Action Contract Compliance in the United States

A number of empirical studies (Table 3) have examined the effect of affirmative action under the federal contract compliance program based on Executive Order 11246 in the United States. Most of the studies focused on black earnings relative to white earnings, but they were often applied separately by sex and hence shed some light on the effects on females relative to males.

As in the prototype equation (9), the studies typically regress a measure of success (e.g., the proportion of the establish-

TABLE 3

IMPACT OF AFFIRMATIVE ACTION UNDER THE U.S. FEDERAL CONTRACT COMPLIANCE PROGRAM
OF EXECUTIVE ORDER 11246

Study	Data	Dependent Variable	Impact
Goldstein and Smith (1976)	EEO reports on 74,563 establishments, 1970, 1972	Change in wage and employment shares of females	Insignificant increase in wages and employment for black females Significant decrease in wages and employment for white females Overall, females, especially white females, were net losers and males, especially black males, were net gainers
Heckman and Wolpin (1976)	EEO reports on 3,677 establishments, Chicago, 1970–73	Employment	Significant negative effect on employment of females, especially white females, with gains for black males
Beller (1982a)	CPS 1967, 1974	Probability of female entering male-dominated occupation	Large significant positive effect
Osterman (1982)	1,718 females from Panel Study of Income Dynamics, 1978, 1979	Whether female quit job	Large significant effect on reducing quits Compliance reviews increased effectiveness
Smith and Welch (1984)	EEO reports on over 100,000 establishments in each of 1960, 1970, 1974, 1978, and 1980	Employment	Positive effect on employment was small for white females but large for blacks, especially black females
Leonard (1984b)	EEO reports on 13,936 matched establishments, 1974, 1980	Index of occupational advance	Significant positive effect Compliance reviews increased effectiveness
Leonard (1984c)	EEO reports on 68,690 matched establishments, 1974, 1980	Change in employment share	Large significant positive effect on female employment growth, especially in growing establishments Compliance reviews did not enhance effectiveness for females but did for other minorities
Leonard (1985)	3,091 establishments that completed a compliance review in 1974 or 1975	Change in employment share	Targets established by the regulatory agency had an independent effect in enhancing female employment growth

ment's employment that is female) on a number of control variables as well as measures of the policy initiative (e.g., whether the firm has a government contract and hence is subject to contract compliance, and whether the firm underwent a compliance review). The studies often involve establishment data from the EEO reports.[32]

The earlier studies of Morris Goldstein and Robert Smith (1976) and Heckman and Wolpin (1976) found that females, especially white females, were net losers and that males, especially black males, were net gainers. This reflects the early emphasis on race and not sex discrimination. When the emphasis was broadened to sex discrimination, around 1974, the federal contract compliance program seemed to benefit females in several ways: reduced occupational segregation (Beller 1982a; Leonard 1984b), reduced quits (Paul Osterman 1982), and increased employment (Smith and Welch 1984; Leonard 1984c). For example, Leonard (1984c) found that, over the period 1974 to 1980, affirmative action increased the growth of employment by 2.8 percent for white females and 12.3 percent for black females. Aggressive enforcement through increased compliance review (Osterman 1982; Leonard 1984b) or through more stringent targets (Leonard 1985), generally enhanced the effectiveness of the legislation. The legislation appeared to be more effective in expanding firms (Leonard 1984c).

Smith and Welch (1984) find that between 1970 and 1980, most minority groups increased their share of employment disproportionately in federal contractor establishments, especially in the higher level managerial and professional occupations. This effect was substantial for blacks, especially black females, but not for white females. However, Smith and Welch indi-

cate that because of data problems[33] with the EEO-1 files used in most of the studies, caution should be exercised before concluding that affirmative action initiatives have been successful.

Smith and Ward (1984, p. xiii) also caution against attributing minority wage gains to affirmative action programs. They emphasize the importance of controlling for the substantial changes in the composition, education, and experience of the female work force occurring at the same time. For example, the rapid rise in the ratio of female to male wages from 0.60 in 1980 to 0.64 in 1983 cannot be attributed to affirmative action legislation because the legislation was introduced much earlier (1964), and enforcement actually declined between 1980 and 1983. They argue that the increase in the ratio of female to male wages can be attributed to the increase in the education and labor market experience of females relative to males.

In summary, affirmative action under the federal contract compliance program appears to have improved the labor market position of those groups to which it is directed, with stricter enforcement enhancing effectiveness. The negative effect on female wages and employment found in the earlier studies can be discounted because these results pertained to a period before the affirmative action program was directed toward females. The more recent studies generally find a positive effect in establishments subject to affirmative action (e.g., enhancing employment growth by 2.8 percent for white females and 12.3 percent for black females over a six year period). However, this does not translate into large effects for the economy as a whole because few firms are subject to affirmative action. Also, data problems and difficulties in dis-

---

[32] The data are described in detail in the data appendix of Leonard (1984c) and critically assessed in Smith and Welch (1984).

[33] Employers apparently reclassified some employees to give the appearance of expanded minority employment, and they undercounted minorities in the early years when race identification was not common in personnel records.

entangling the pure legislative effect from the myriad of other factors that have changed in the labor market for females over the same period suggests that these estimates should be used with caution.

C. Comparable Worth in the United States

As indicated previously, in situations where it has been applied, comparable worth adjustments typically involved raising wages in the predominantly female jobs by 10 to 20 percent to bring them in line with wages of the predominantly male jobs of the same job evaluation point score. While this indicates what happened in those particular jobs in those particular situations, it does not indicate the extent to which a comprehensive application of comparable worth would close the overall male-female wage gap. The overall gap depends upon factors beyond the purview of comparable worth: wage differences that reflect differences in skill, effort, responsibility, and working conditions; wage differences within predominantly male or female occupations; wage differences across mixed occupations; or wage differences across establishments or industries.

Johnson and Gary Solon (1986) estimate the *potential* effect of a comprehensive comparable worth program. They use the May 1978 Current Population Survey data to estimate earnings equations of the form

$$W_m = a_m F_m + b_m Z_m + u_m \qquad (11)$$

$$W_f = a_f F_f + b_f Z_f + u_f \qquad (12)$$

where W denotes (the logarithm of) hourly earnings, F denotes the proportion of the occupation that is female,[34] Z denotes control variables, u denotes the error terms, a and b are parameters and m and f denote males and females respectively. The control variables are designed to capture ele-

ments that job evaluators might consider in assigning point scores and to remove the effect of factors that are allowed to determine wages under a comparable worth system.

Johnson and Solon estimate the wage gap as

$$\overline{W}_m - \overline{W}_f = \hat{a}_m \overline{F}_m - \hat{a}_f \overline{F}_f$$
$$+ \hat{b}_m \overline{Z}_m - \hat{b}_f \overline{Z}_f \qquad (13)$$

where overbars ($-$) denote the mean value and the hats ($\cdot$) denote ordinary least-squares estimates of the parameters. They argue that comparable worth would eliminate the relationship between wages and the sex composition of the occupation, after controlling for the effect of other factors (e.g., proxies for job evaluation points and interestablishment wage differentials as reflected in the Zs). Logically, this would be captured by setting $a = 0$ and recomputing the earnings gap after removing such an effect of comparable worth (i.e., by subtracting $\hat{a}_m \overline{F}_m - \hat{a}_f \overline{F}_f$ from equation 13); but that implies that males would receive a larger comparable worth adjustment because their estimates indicate that $a_m > a_f$. Therefore, they constrain the adjustment of males and females to be equal (i.e., $\hat{a}_m = \hat{a}_f$) and they "bound" the impact of comparable worth by alternatively using a_f and a_m as weights to calculate, respectively, $\hat{a}_f(\overline{F}_m - \overline{F}_f) = 0.034$, and $\hat{a}_m (\overline{F}_m - \overline{F}_f) = 0.080$. The former term reflects the contribution to the wage gap of gender differences in the proportion of the occupation that is female, weighted by the return that females receive for the "femaleness" of their occupations; the latter term reflects the same concept, weighted by the male return. Assuming that comparable worth would eliminate this effect of femaleness of the occupation implies that comparable worth would reduce the average gap of ($\overline{W}_m - \overline{W}_f$) = 0.41 by an amount ranging from 0.034 to 0.080 (depending upon whether male or female weights are used) which is

---

[34] Studies that use the proportion of the occupation that is female as an explanatory variable in earnings equation are discussed in Treiman and Hartmann (1981, pp. 28–32).

respectively 8 to 20 percent of the overall earnings gap. Johnson and Solon suggest that realistic coverage would reduce this adjustment by about half and they indicate that the effect of comparable worth is restricted mainly because it cannot address wage differentials arising across establishments and industries.

Their analysis likely underestimates the effect that comparable worth would have on the wage gap because comparable worth would eliminate the gap arising from *intraestablishment* differences in pay for the same job evaluation point scores (i.e., it would raise b_f to b_m for the Zs representing job evaluation scores in equation 13. Based on work by Blau (1977) and others, Johnson and Solon argue that *intraestablishment* differences in pay are likely to be small for *people* within the same narrowly defined occupation. However, the comparable worth adjustments in fact are designed to make wage comparisons across female-dominated and male-dominated *jobs* (as long as job evaluation scores are the same); and these wage differences could be more substantial within establishments.

These small, economy-wide estimates of the impact of comparable worth are consistent with the fact that comparable worth adjustments *within a given organization* would typically raise wages in female-dominated jobs by 10 to 20 percent.[35] Because comparable worth comparisons cannot be made across organizations, their economy-

wide impact is severely restricted. Furthermore, as pointed out by Johnson and Solon (1986, p. 1123), the particular case studies of comparable worth may have involved unusually large adjustments because they were in the public sector and in the forefront of the comparable worth movement.

Obviously, any policy initiative that would raise the wages of a particular group by 10 to 20 percent potentially could engender an adverse employment effect for that group. Ehrenberg and Smith (1987a, 1987b) simulate that a typical comparable worth wage adjustment of 20 percent would lead to only a 2 to 3 percent reduction of employment in those female-dominated jobs. This small adverse employment effect arises becaue they estimated small demand elasticities in the public sector. Using a similar methodology, Aldrich and Buchele (1986) simulated slightly larger adverse employment effects for the private sector, with comparable worth wage increases of 10 to 15 percent leading to a female employment reduction of about 3 percent. Such elasticities have been estimated on the basis of incremental wage adjustments; whether they would hold for more substantial wage changes of 10 to 20 percent remains an open question.

D. Equal Pay Legislation in Canada

Gunderson (1975) estimates the impact of Ontario's equal pay legislation by comparing the male-female wage differential in the same establishments and in the same narrowly defined occupations, in the years before and after the legislation was to be effectively enforced. The legislative effect was captured by a dummy variable for the postlegislative period, in a cross-section regression, based on the years immediately before and after the legislative change. The use of narrowly defined occupations is important because it reduces the need to control for observable or unobservable wage-determining characteristics and it is also

[35] Elaine Sorenson (1986, 1987) estimates a male payline by regressing the wages from male-dominated jobs on their job evaluation point scores based on data from comparable worth cases in Washington, Minnesota, Iowa, and Michigan. The average job evaluation score in the female-dominated jobs is then weighted by the male regression coefficient to estimate the hypothetical pay that females would receive if paid according to the nondiscriminatory male pay structure; that is, if they received the same value as did males for their job evaluation scores. This comparable worth wage adjustment would have raised wages in female-dominated jobs by an average of 17 percent, closing almost one-half of the average unadjusted male-female wage gap, at a cost of about 8 percent of payroll.

the level of aggregation where equal pay comparisons are allowed. Comparisons within the same establishment minimize the need to control for regional or local labor market differences and it is the level of aggregation where equal pay comparisons are allowed. The legislation had no impact on narrowing the male-female wage gap.

It is also possible that the legislation may not show its effect after only one year following its implementation. However, in time series regressions based upon a number of narrowly defined occupations the 1969 legislative change again was found to have no impact in narrowing the male-female wage differential after controlling for the trend and cyclical changes in the gap.[36]

E. British Equal Pay Initiatives

In Britain, the ratio of female to male hourly earnings had been roughly constant throughout the 1950s and 1960s. It increased from 0.58 in 1970 (the year of passage of the Equal Pay Act) to 0.66 in 1975 (the year of implementation) and thereafter remained roughly stable (A. Zabalza and Z. Tzannatos 1985a, 1985b). This increase of 0.08 was generally uniform within occupations, industries, and age groups, suggesting that it was not attributable to compositional changes in the female work force. Zabalza and Tzannatos attribute the substantial increase in female pay largely to the legislation, not to factors such as autonomous shifts in female labor supply, changes in industrial structure, or wage controls. The legislation in large part had its effect through the channels of collective bargaining which cover slightly over 60 percent of the work force. The ratios of

[36] This is the case whether the legislative initiative was tested for by the use of a simple dummy variable shift parameter at the time of the legislated change (Gunderson 1976, based upon the years 1946–71) or by a spline function to allow for the legislation to have a transitional effect over a longer time period (Gunderson 1985b, based upon the years 1946–79).

female to male job rates (minimum wages specified in the collective agreement for different jobs), which had been relatively stable at around 0.08 to 0.83 from 1950 to 1970, increased to unity by 1976 (Z. Tzannatos and A. Zabalza 1984).[37]

Based upon a time series regression, over a period 1949–75, B. Chiplin, M. Curran, and C. Parsley (1980) also find the postlegislative period to be associated with a statistically significant 8 percentage point increase in the ratio of female to male hourly earnings, after controlling for the effect of the trend and business cycle. They indicate that it is difficult to disentangle the effect of the Equal Pay legislation, introduced in 1970, from the wage controls, introduced in 1973. They provide some crude calculations of the magnitude of the flat rate increases allowed under the controls and estimate that these increases (which were equal for males and females) accounted for most of the increase in the ratio of female to male wages in the post Equal Pay period. However, it is not appropriate to subtract the full amount of this flat increase under the wage controls because the decision to allow such flat rate increases (which would disproportionately benefit females) may have been made to accommodate the equal pay initiatives.

F. Australian Equal Pay Initiatives

The impact of the Australian initiatives in the equal pay area is particularly noteworthy because of the dramatic legislated wage changes. Gregory and Duncan (1981) estimate the employment effect of the Aus-

[37] Zabalza and Tzannatos (1985a, 1985b) also find that the antidiscrimination initiatives did not have any adverse employment effects for females. However, in 1975 when the Equal Pay Act was implemented, the Sex Discrimination Act requiring equal employment opportunity also became law. Their analysis does not permit disentangling the separate effects of the two laws to determine whether the increases arising from the Equal Pay Act would have reduced employment were it not for the possible employment-enhancing effect of the Sex Discrimination Act.

tralian legislation by estimating an equation relating the ratio of female to male employment to their relative wages (as affected by the legislation), to a time trend and to the unemployment rate over the period 1948 to 1978. Their analysis indicates the following: (1) by 1977, the ratio of female to male award wages was 0.933, up to 21 percent from the ratio of 0.774 at the time of the equal value awards of 1972, and up 30 percent from the ratio of 0.720 at the time of the equal pay awards of 1969; (2) the relative wage increases awarded by the arbitration tribunals were not offset by the small market wage adjustments that can occur above the award wages; (3) the increase in the wage ratio (arising from the legislation) was associated with a statistically significant reduction in the growth of female employment relative to male employment; (4) after the legislative change, the average annual growth of female employment was still 3 percentage points greater than male employment; it would have been 4.5 percentage points greater were it not for the relative wage changes associated with the legislation; (5) the reduction in female employment growth was largest in manufacturing, and next largest in the service sector, with no reduction in the public sector; (6) most of the reduction occurred because of a reduction in the growth of female-dominated industries, not because of a direct substitution of males or capital within each industry; (7) the substantial female wage gains and moderate reduction in their employment growth led to a substantial increase in their income share.[38]

The analyses and interpretation given by Gregory and Duncan have been challenged

[38]Gregory and Duncan (1983) provide some updated time series plots to substantiate their earlier conclusions. They indicate that female earnings had maintained their 30 percent improvement since the legislated initiatives and yet female employment growth was faster than male employment growth. Furthermore, female unemployment continued to fall relative to male unemployment.

by P. A. McGavin (1983) and Killingsworth (1985), who indicate that there is stronger evidence of an adverse effect on *hours* of work of females and that the absence of a substantial *aggregate* adverse employment effect for females can be attributed in part to the sustained growth of female employment in the government sector.

Clearly the Australian experience has led to different interpretations of the behavioral responses to what are indisputably dramatic wage gains on the part of females. Perhaps a balanced conclusion is that there was *some* adverse employment effect but not a substantial one, given the dramatic increase in female relative earnings. Whether this reflects a conscious policy to sustain female overall employment by increasing their employment in the public sector remains unresolved. So does the relevance of the Australian experience, given the peculiar policy of wage fixing through legislative tribunals. A competitive market response may not have occurred because market forces may have only a minimal effect in such a labor market in the first place.

VII. Overall Assessment

It is not possible to attach a precise magnitude to the relative importance of each and every factor that affects the differences in wages and employment opportunities between males and females. Nevertheless, the empirical evidence provides some guide for the potential role of different policies, specifically: (1) at least some of the differences in wages and the occupational distribution of males and females reflect discrimination in the labor market, suggesting a potential rationale for policy initiatives for that reason (as well as to redress an inequality of outcomes); (2) occupational segregation accounts for more of the earnings gap than does discriminatory pay differentials within the same job and establishment, implying a larger potential role for equal employment opportunity (including affirmative action) and comparable worth as opposed to conventional equal pay policies; (3) because differences in pay across establishments and industries account for a substantial portion of the gap, this severely restricts the scope of policies like equal pay and comparable worth, both of which are limited to comparisons within the same establishment; (4) a substantial portion of the earnings gap reflects decisions made outside the labor market, thereby limiting the scope of labor market policies.

The empirical studies of the effects of the various policies suggest the following conclusions: (1) equal employment opportunity policies and affirmative action policies tend to improve the position of the groups to which they are targeted; (2) stricter enforcement tends to enhance effectiveness; (3) comparable worth, where applied, has raised the wages of females relative to males by 10 to 20 percent, although its economy-wide effect is likely to be severely limited by the fact that it does not enable comparisons across establishments and industries; (4) equal pay legislation is not likely to have an effect if it is limited to a complaints-based system dealing with pay differentials within the same job and establishment, although it can have a substantial effect if it works through the mechanism of collective bargaining (Britain) or wage-fixing tribunals (Australia); (5) although there is not a consensus, the substantial wage increases resulting from many of the policy initiatives do not appear to have led to large adverse employment effects, especially in the public sector.

What are the unresolved and important issues that should constitute the research agenda for the future? First, more evidence is needed on the relative importance of interestablishment, as opposed to intra-establishment, wage differentials as determinants of the earnings gap because equal pay and equal value policies are restricted

to comparisons within the same establishment. Second, it is important to get a better picture of the extent to which the earnings gap reflects a compensating wage differential for cost differences associated with differences in such factors as absenteeism, turnover, and pensions—control variables that are often omitted in conventional data sets. Third, new and updated information is needed on the earnings patterns for the more recent cohorts of women who likely have a more permanent attachment to the labor force and who may be entering the new sectors that do not have a legacy of segregation and discriminatory practices.

Finally, given the importance of comparable worth as the likely "wave of the future," more effort—especially on the part of economists—will have to be placed on the technical issues and program design and implementation features so as to help attain the objectives of the legislation with a minimum of adverse consequences. Economists tend to shy away from program design and implementation issues because these are administrative and not economic matters. Yet they are issues that can benefit from an economist's perspective, especially pertaining to allocative efficiency, distributive equity, and—in the comparable worth area—the econometric estimation of the relationship between pay and job evaluation points. Policy design, like nature, abhors a vacuum. If economists are not involved in the policy design issues, that vacuum will be filled by others, with the likely result that even the most basic principles of economics will be ignored.

REFERENCES

AGARWAL, NARESH. "Pay Discrimination: Evidence, Policies and Issues," in *Equal employment issues: Race and sex discrimination in the United States, Canada and Britain.* Eds.: HARISH JAIN AND PETER SLOANE. NY: Praeger Pub., 1981, pp. 118–43.
ALDRICH, MARK AND BUCHELE, ROBERT. *The economics of comparable worth.* Cambridge, MA: Ballinger Pub. Co., 1986.
APPELBAUM, EILEEN. *Back to work: Determinants of*

Gunderson: Male-Female Wage Differentials and Policy Responses 69

women's successful re-entry. Boston: Auburn House Pub. Co., 1981.

ASHENFELTER, ORLEY AND HANNAN, TIMOTHY. "Sex Discrimination and Product Market Competition: The Case of the Banking Industry," *Quart. J. Econ.*, Feb. 1986, *101*(1), pp. 149–73.

BARBEZAT, DEBRA. "Salary Differentials by Sex in the Academic Labor Market," *J. Human Res.*, Summer 1987, *22*(3), pp. 422–28.

BAYER, ALAN AND ASTIN, HELEN. "Sex Differences in Academic Rank and Salary Among Science Doctorates in Teaching," *J. Human Res.*, Spring 1968, *3*(2), pp. 191–200.

BEIDER, PERRY ET AL. "Comparable Worth in a General Equilibrium Model of the U.S. Economy," *Research in Labor Economics*, 1988, 9, pp. 1–52.

BELLER, ANDREA. "EEO Laws and the Earnings of Women," *Industrial Relations Research Association Proceedings.* Madison: U. of Wisconsin, 1976, pp. 190–98.

————. "The Impact of Equal Employment Opportunity Laws on the Male-Female Earnings Differential," in *Women in the labor market.* Eds.: CYNTHIA LLOYD, EMILY ANDREWS, AND CURTIS GILROY. NY: Columbia U. Press, 1979, pp. 304–30.

————. "The Effect of Economic Conditions on the Success of Equal Employment Opportunity Laws: An Application to the Sex Differential in Earnings," *Rev. Econ. Statist.*, Aug. 1980, *62*(3), pp. 370–87.

————. "Occupational Segregation by Sex: Determinants and Changes," *J. Human Res.*, Summer 1982a, *17*(3), pp. 371–92.

————. "The Impact of Equal Opportunity Policy on Sex Differentials in Earnings and Occupations," *Amer. Econ. Rev.*, May 1982b, *72*(2), pp. 171–75.

————. "Trends in Occupational Segregation by Sex and Race, 1960–1981," in *Sex segregation in the workplace.* Ed.: BARBARA RESKIN. Washington, DC: National Academy Press, 1984, pp. 11–26.

————. "Changes in the Sex Composition of U.S. Occupations, 1960–1981," *J. Human Res.*, Spring 1985, *20*(2), pp. 235–50.

BLAU, FRANCINE. *Equal pay in the office.* Lexington, MA: Lexington Books, 1977.

————. "Discrimination Against Women: Theory and Evidence," in *Labor economics: Modern views.* Ed.: WILLIAM DARITY, JR. Boston: Kluwer-Nijhoff, 1984, pp. 53–89.

BLAU, FRANCINE AND BELLER ANDREA. "Trends in Earnings Differentials by Gender, 1971–1981," *Ind. Lab. Relat. Rev.*, July 1988, *41*(4), pp. 513–29.

BLAU, FRANCINE AND FERBER, MARIANNE. *The economics of women, men and work.* Englewood Cliffs, NJ: Prentice-Hall, 1986.

————. "Discrimination: Empirical Evidence from the United States," *Amer. Econ. Rev.*, May 1987a 77(2), pp. 316–20.

————. "Occupations and Earnings of Women Workers," in *Working women: Past, present and future.* Eds.: KAREN KOZIANA, MICHAEL MOSKOW, AND LUCRETIA TANNER. Washington, DC: Bureau of National Affairs, 1987b, pp. 37–68.

BLINDER, ALAN. "Wage Discrimination: Reduced Form and Structural Estimates," *J. Human Res.*, Fall 1973, *8*(4), pp. 436–55.

BLOCK, WALTER. "Economic Intervention, Discrimination, and Unforeseen Circumstances," in *Discrimination, affirmative action and equal opportunity.* Eds.: WALTER BLOCK AND MICHAEL WALKER. Vancouver: Fraser Institute, 1982, pp. 103–25.

BLOOM, DAVID AND KILLINGSWORTH, MARK. "Pay Discrimination Research and Litigation: The Use of Regression," *Ind. Relat.*, Fall 1982, *21*(3), pp. 318–39.

BOULET, JAC-ANDRE AND LAVALLEE, LAVAL. *The changing economic status of women.* Ottawa: Economic Council of Canada, 1984.

BROWN, CHARLES. "The Federal Attack on Labor Market Discrimination: The Mouse That Roared?" *Research in Labor Economics*, 1982, 5, pp. 33–68.

BUCKLEY, JOHN. "Pay Differences Between Men and Women in the Same Job," *Mon. Lab. Rev.*, Nov. 1971, *94*(11), pp. 36–39.

BUTLER, RICHARD. "Estimating Wage Discrimination in the Labor Market," *J. Human Res.*, Fall 1982, *17*(4), pp. 606–21.

CAIN, GLEN. "Welfare Economics of Policies Towards Women," *J. Lab. Econ.*, Jan. 1985, *3*(1, Part 2), pp. S375–96.

————. "The Economic Analysis of Labour Market Discrimination: A Survey," in *Handbook of labour economics, Volume 1.* Eds.: ORLEY ASHENFELTER AND RICHARD LAYARD. Amsterdam: Elsevier Science Publishers, 1986, pp. 693–785.

CHIPLIN, BRIAN; CURRAN, M. AND PARSLEY, C. "Relative Female Earnings in Great Britain and Impact of Legislation," in *Women and low pay.* Ed.: PETER SLOANE. London: Macmillan, 1980, pp. 57–126.

CHIPLIN, BRIAN AND SLOANE, PETER. "Personal Characteristics and Sex Differentials in Professional Employment," *Econ. J.*, Dec. 1976, *86*(344), pp. 729–45.

COOK, ALICE. *Comparable worth: A case book of experiences in states and localities.* Hawaii: Industrial Relations Center, U. of Hawaii at Manoa, 1985.

CORCORAN, MARY AND COURANT, PAUL. "Sex-Role Socialization and Occupational Segregation: An Exploratory Investigation," *J. Post Keynesian Econ.*, Spring 1987, *9*(3), pp. 330–46.

CORCORAN, MARY AND DUNCAN, GREG. "Work History, Labour Force Attachment, and Earnings Differences between the Races and Sexes," *J. Human Res.*, Winter 1979, *14*(1), pp. 3–20.

CULLEN, DALLAS; NAKAMURA, ALICE AND NAKAMURA, MASAO. "Have Equal Opportunity/Affirmative Action Programs Had Any Impact on the Occupational Segregation of U.S. Women?" Paper presented at the American Economic Association Meetings, Dec. 1986.

DAYMONT, THOMAS AND ANDRISANI, PAUL. "Job Preferences, College Major, and the Gender Gap in Earnings," *J. Human Res.*, Summer 1984, *19*(3), 408–28.

EHRENBERG, RONALD. "Econometric Analyses of the

Empirical Consequences of Comparable Worth: What Have We Learned?" Revised version of paper presented at the Colloquium on Comparable Worth, Rutgers U., Oct. 1987.

EHRENBERG, RONALD AND SMITH, ROBERT. "Comparable-Worth Wage Adjustments and Female Employment in the State and Local Sector," *J. Lab. Econ.*, Jan. 1987a, 5(1), pp. 43–62.

———. "Comparable Worth in the Public Sector," in *Public sector payrolls*. Ed.: DAVID WISE. Chicago: U. of Chicago Press, 1987b, pp. 243–88.

FARLEY, JENNIE, ed. *Women workers in fifteen countries*. Ithaca, NY: ILR Press, 1985.

FILER, RANDALL. "Sexual Differences in Earnings: The Role of Individual Personalities and Tastes," *J. Human Res.*, Winter 1983, 18(1), pp. 82–99.

———. "Male-Female Wage Differences: The Importance of Compensating Differentials," *Ind. Lab. Relat. Rev.*, Apr. 1985, 38(3), pp. 426–37.

———. "The Role of Personality and Tastes in Determining Occupational Structure," *Ind. Lab. Relat. Rev.*, Apr. 1986, 39(3), pp. 412–24.

FUCHS, VICTOR. "His and Hers: Gender Differences in Work and Income, 1959–1979," *J. Lab. Econ.*, July 1986, 4(3, pt. 2), pp. S245–72.

GOLDBERGER, ARTHUR. "Reverse Regression and Salary Discrimination," *J. Human Res.*, Summer 1984, 19(3), pp. 293–318.

GOLDSTEIN, MORRIS AND SMITH, ROBERT. "The Estimated Impact of the Antidiscrimination Program Aimed at Federal Contractors," *Ind. Lab. Relat. Rev.*, July 1976, 29(4), pp. 523–43.

GOODWIN, CYNTHIA. *Equal pay legislation and implementation: Selected countries*. Ottawa: Labour Canada, 1984.

GORDON, NANCY; MORTON, THOMAS AND BRADEN, INA. "Faculty Salaries: Is There Discrimination by Sex, Race, and Discipline," *Amer. Econ. Rev.*, June 1974, 64(3), pp. 419–27.

GREGORY, R. G.; DALY, A. AND HO, V. "A Tale of Two Countries: Equal Pay for Women in Australia and Britain." Mimeo. Australia National U., undated.

GREGORY, R. G. AND DUNCAN, R. C. "Segmented Labor Market Theories and the Australian Experience of Equal Pay for Women," *J. Post Keynesian Econ.*, Spring 1981, 3(3), pp. 403–28.

———. "Equal Pay for Women: A Reply," *Australia Econ. Pap.*, June 1983, 22(40), pp. 60–67.

GREGORY, R. AND HO, V. "Equal Pay and Comparable Worth: What Can the U.S. Learn from the Australian Experience?" Discussion Paper No. 123, Centre for Economic Policy Research, Australian National U., July 1985.

GRONAU, REUBEN. "Home Production—A Survey," in *Handbook of labour economics, Volume 1*. Eds.: ORLEY ASHENFELTER AND RICHARD LAYARD. Amsterdam: Elsevier Science Publishers, 1986, pp. 273–304.

———. "Sex-related Wage Differentials and Women's Interrupted Labor Careers—the Chicken or the Egg," *J. Lab. Econ.*, July 1988, 6(3), pp. 277–301.

GUNDERSON, MORLEY. "Male-Female Wage Differentials and the Impact of Equal Pay Legislation," *Rev. Econ. Statist.*, Nov. 1975, 57(4), pp. 462–69.

———. "Time Pattern of Male-Female Wage Differentials," *Relations Industrielles*, Nov. 1976, 31(1), pp. 57–71.

———. "Decomposition of the Male/Female Earnings Differential: Canada 1970," *Can. J. Econ.*, Aug. 1979, 12(3), pp. 479–85.

———. *Costing equal value legislation in Ontario*. Toronto: Ontario Ministry of Labour, 1984.

———. "Discrimination, Equal Pay, and Equal Opportunities in the Labour Market," in *Work and pay; the Canadian labour market*. Ed.: CRAIG RIDDELL. Toronto: U. of Toronto Press, 1985a, pp. 219–65.

———. "Spline Function Estimates of the Impact of Equal Pay Legislation: The Ontario Experience," *Relations Industrielles*, 1985b, 40(4), pp. 775–91.

HECKMAN, JAMES AND WOLPIN, KENNETH. "Does the Contract Compliance Program Work?" *Ind. Lab. Relat. Rev.*, July 1976, 29(4), pp. 544–64.

HOLMES, R. A. "Male-Female Earnings Differentials in Canada," *J. Human Res.*, Winter 1976, 11(1), pp. 109–17.

JOHNSON, GEORGE AND SOLON, GARY. "Estimates of the Direct Effects of Comparable Worth Policy," *Amer. Econ. Rev.*, Dec. 1986, 76(5), pp. 1117–25.

JOHNSON, GEORGE AND STAFFORD, FRANK. "The Earnings and Promotion of Women Faculty," *Amer. Econ. Rev.*, Dec. 1974, 69(5), pp. 888–903.

JOHNSON, GEORGE AND WELCH, FINIS. "The Labor Market Implications of an Economywide Affirmative Action Program," *Ind. Lab. Rel. Rev.*, July 1976, 29(4), pp. 508–22.

KAHNE, HILDA. "Economic Perspectives on the Roles of Women in the American Economy," *J. Econ. Lit.*, Dec. 1975, 13(4), pp. 1249–92.

KILLINGSWORTH, MARK. "The Economics of Comparable Worth: Analytical, Empirical, and Policy Questions," in *Comparable worth: New directions for research*. Ed.: HEIDI HARTMANN. Washington, DC: National Academy Press, 1985, pp. 86–115.

LANDAU, EVE C. *The rights of working women in the European community*. Luxembourg: Commission of the European Communities, 1985.

LEONARD, JONATHAN. "Antidiscrimination or Reverse Discrimination: The Impact of Changing Demographics, Title VII, and Affirmative Action on Productivity," *J. Human Res.*, Spring 1984a, 19(2), pp. 145–74.

———. "Employment and Occupational Advance Under Affirmative Action," *Rev. Econ. Statist.*, Aug. 1984b, 66(3), pp. 377–85.

———. "The Impact of Affirmative Action on Employment," *J. Lab. Econ.*, Oct. 1984c, 2(4), pp. 439–63.

———. "Affirmative Action as Earnings Redistribution: The Targeting of Compliance Reviews," *J. Lab. Econ.*, July 1985, 3(3), pp. 363–84.

_____. "The Effectiveness of Equal Employment Opportunity Law and Affirmative Action Regulation," *Research in Labor Economics*. Vol. 8, Part B. Ed.: RONALD EHRENBERG. Greenwich, CT: JAI Press, 1986, pp. 319–50.

LIVERNASH, E. ROBERT, ed. *Comparable worth: Issues and alternatives*. Washington, DC: Equal Employment Advisory Council, 1980.

LLOYD, CYNTHIA AND NEIMI, BETH. *The economics of sex differentials*. NY: Columbia U. Press, 1979.

MADDEN, JANICE. "The Persistence of Pay Differentials: The Economics of Sex Discrimination," in *Women and work: An annual review*. Eds.: LAURIE LARWOOD, ANN STROMBERG, AND BARBARA GUTEK. Beverly Hills, CA: Sage, 1985, pp. 76–114.

MALKIEL, BURTON AND MALKIEL, JUDITH. "Male-Female Pay Differentials in Professional Employment," *Amer. Econ. Rev.*, Sept. 1973, 63(4), pp. 693–705.

MARSHALL, RAY AND PAULIN, BETH. "Employment and Earnings of Women: Historical Perspective," in *Working women: Past, present, and future*. Eds.: KAREN KOZIARA, MICHAEL MOSKOW, AND LUCRETIA TANNER. Washington, DC: Bureau of National Affairs, 1987, pp. 1–36.

McGAVIN, P. A. "Equal Pay for Women: A Re-Assessment of the Australian Experience," *Australian Econ. Pap.*, June 1983, 22(40), pp. 48–59.

McNULTY, DONALD. "Differences in Pay Between Men and Women Workers," *Mon. Lab. Rev.*, Dec. 1967, 12(12), pp. 40–43.

MEGDAL, SHARON BERRSTEIN AND RANSOM, MICHAEL R. "Longitudinal Changes in Salary at a Large Public University: What Response to Equal Pay Legislation?" *Amer. Econ. Rev.*, May 1985, 75(2), pp. 271–74.

MILLER, PAUL. "Gender Differences in Observed and Offered Wages in Canada, 1980," *Can. J. Econ.*, May 1987, 20(2), pp. 225–44.

MINCER, JACOB. "Intercountry Comparisons of Labor Force Trends and of Related Developments: An Overview." *J. Lab. Econ.*, Jan. 1985, 3(1, pt. 2), pp. S1–S32.

MINCER, JACOB AND POLACHEK, SOLOMON. "Family Investment in Human Capital: Earnings of Women," *J. Polit. Econ.*, Mar./Apr. 1974, 82(2, p. 2), pp. S76–S108.

_____. "Women's Earnings Reexamined," *J. Human Res.*, Winter 1978, 13(1), pp. 118–34.

MOTT, FRANK, ed. *The employment revolution: Young American women in the 1970s*. Cambridge, MA: MIT Press, 1982.

NEUMARK, DAVID. "Employers' Discriminatory Behavior and the Estimation of Wage Discrimination," *J. Human Res.*, Summer 1988, 23(3), pp. 279–95.

OAXACA, RONALD. "Male-Female Wage Differentials in Urban Labor Markets," *Int. Econ. Rev.*, Oct. 1973, 14(3), pp. 693–709.

_____. "The Persistence of Male-Female Earnings Differentials," in *The distribution of economic well-being*. Ed.: F. THOMAS JUSTER. Cambridge, MA: Ballinger Co., 1977, pp. 303–54.

O'NEILL, JUNE. "The Trend in the Male-Female Wage Gap in the United States," *J. Lab. Econ.*, Jan. 1985, 3(1, pt. 2), pp. S91–S116.

OSTERMAN, PAUL. "Affirmative Action and Opportunity: A Study of Female Quit Rates," *Rev. Econ. Statist.*, Nov. 1982, 64(4), pp. 604–12.

OSTRY, SYLVIA. *The female worker in Canada*. Ottawa: Queen's Printer, 1968.

POLACHEK, SOLOMON. "Sex Differences in College Major," *Ind. Lab. Relat. Rev.*, July 1978, 31(4), pp. 498–508.

RESKIN, BARBARA F. AND HARTMANN, HEIDI I., eds. *Women's work, men's work*. Washington, DC: National Academy Press, 1986.

ROBB, ROBERTA. "Earnings Differentials between Males and Females in Ontario, 1971," *Can. J. Econ.*, May 1978, 11(2), pp. 350–59.

_____. "Equal Pay for Work of Equal Value: Issues and Policies," *Can. Public Policy*, Dec. 1987, 13(4), pp. 445–61.

ROBSON, R. AND LAPOINTE, M. *A comparison of men's and women's salaries and employment fringe benefits in the academic profession*. Ottawa: Information Canada, 1971.

SANBORN, HENRY. "Pay Differences Between Men and Women," *Ind. Lab. Relat. Rev.*, July 1964, 17(4), pp. 534–50.

SANDELL, STEVEN AND SHAPIRO, DAVID. "An Exchange: The Theory of Human Capital and the Earnings of Women: A Reexamination of the Evidence," *J. Human Res.*, Winter 1978, 13(1), pp. 103–17.

SCHRANK, WILLIAM. "Sex Discrimination in Faculty Salaries; A Case Study." *Can. J. Econ.*, Aug. 1977, 10(3), pp. 411–33.

SCHWAB, DONALD. "Job Evaluation and Pay Setting: Concepts and Practices," in *Comparable worth: Issues and alternatives*. Ed.: ROBERT LIVERNASH. Washington, DC: Equal Employment Advisory Council, 1980, pp. 49–77.

SCHWAB, STEWART. "Is Statistical Discrimination Efficient?" *Amer. Econ. Rev.*, Mar. 1986, 76(1), pp. 228–34.

SHAW, LOIS BANFILL, ed. *Unplanned careers: The working lives of middle-aged women*. Lexington, MA: D.C. Heath and Company, 1983.

SIEBERT, WILLIAM AND SLOANE, PETER. "The Measurement of Sex and Marital Status Discrimination at the Workplace," *Economica*, May 1981, 48(190), pp. 125–42.

SMITH, JAMES AND WARD, MICHAEL. *Women's wages and work in the twentieth century*. Santa Monica, CA: Rand, 1984.

SMITH, JAMES AND WELCH, FINIS. "Affirmative Action and Labor Markets," *J. Lab. Econ.*, Apr. 1984, 2(2), pp. 269–301.

SMITH, ROBERT. Comparable Worth: Limited Coverage and the Exacerbation of Inequality," *Ind. Lab. Rel. Rev.*, Jan. 1988, 41(2), pp. 227–39.

SORENSEN, ELAINE. "Implementing Comparable Worth: A Survey of Recent Job Evaluation Studies," *Amer. Econ. Rev.*, May 1986, 76(2), pp. 364–67.

_____. "Effect of Comparable Worth Policies on

72			*Journal of Economic Literature, Vol. XXVII (March 1989)*

Earnings," *Ind. Relat.*, Fall 1987, 26(3), pp. 227–39.

TREIMAN, DONALD. *Job evaluation: An analytic review.* Washington, DC: National Academy of Sciences, 1979.

TREIMAN, DONALD AND HARTMANN, HEIDI, eds. *Women, work and wages: Equal pay for jobs of equal value.* Washington: DC: National Academy Press, 1981.

TZANNATOS, ZAFIRIS AND ZABALZA, ANTON. "The Anatomy of the Rise of British Female Relative Wages in the 1970's: Evidence from the New Earnings Survey," *Brit. J. Ind. Relat.*, July 1984, 22(2), pp. 177–94.

WELCH, FINIS. "Employment Quotes for Minorities," *J. Polit. Econ.*, Aug. 1976, 84(4, Part 2), pp. S105–39.

_____. "Affirmative Action and Its Enforcement," *Amer. Econ. Rev.*, May 1981, 71(2), pp. 127–33.

WILLBORN, STEVEN. *A comparable worth primer.* Lexington, MA: D. C. Heath and Co., 1986.

ZABALZA, ANTON AND TZANNATOS, ZAFIRIS. "The Effect of Britain's Anti-discriminatory Legislation on Relative Pay and Employment," *Econ. J.*, Sept. 1985a, 95(379), pp. 679–99.

_____. *Women and equal pay: The effects of legislation on female employment and wages in Britain.* Cambridge, Eng.: Cambridge U. Press, 1985b.

[24]

The Economic Journal, 101 (*May* 1991), 508–522

Printed in Great Britain

GENDER DISCRIMINATION IN THE BRITISH LABOUR MARKET: A REASSESSMENT*

Robert E. Wright and John F. Ermisch

It is clear that women's wages, on average, are much lower than men's wages in Great Britain. In the recent past, considerable attention has been directed towards estimating the proportion of the male-female wage differential due to 'gender discrimination' (see Chiplin and Sloane, 1976; Dolton and Makepeace, 1986; Greenhalgh, 1980; Joshi and Newell, 1987; Miller, 1987; Siebert and Sloane, 1981; Zabalza and Arrufat, 1985).[1] These studies support two conclusions. The first is that gender discrimination appears to exist, but the empirical estimates of its extent vary considerably. The second is that the equal opportunities legislation introduced in the 1970s, such as the *Equal Pay Act* (1970), *Sex Discrimination Act* (1975) and *Employment Protection Act* (1975), contributed significantly to reducing discrimination in the British labour market.

The purpose of this paper is to provide new estimates of gender discrimination using better data, collected in the *1980 Women and Employment Survey* (WES). The WES is the first British survey to collect detailed work histories and earnings data for a nationally representative sample of British women. Therefore, for the first time, estimates of discrimination based on real work experience data are presented.

A number of the earlier studies use data from the *General Household Survey*, which does not collect actual work experience data. They have been forced to use 'potential work experience' or 'imputed experience' in their wage equations. This paper compares estimates based on potential or imputed experience with those based on actual experience using WES data. Our analysis finds that estimates of the parameters of a women's earnings function and a summary measure of gender discrimination using a measure of imputed experience differ little from those based on actual experience. Indeed, our estimates of gender discrimination are very robust to estimation method and only slightly higher than Miller's (1987) estimate for 1980. These estimates indicate that the oft-quoted and influential study by Zabalza and Arrufat (1982, 1985), which pioneered the use of imputed experience, severely underestimated the level of gender discrimination and exaggerated the impact

* The authors wish to thank Andrew Hinde, Stephen Jenkins, Heather Joshi, Cheryl Raabe and two anonymous referees for their helpful comments. The usual caveat applies. This research was supported by a grant from the Economic and Social Research Council: 'Income Inequality, Gender and Demographic Differentials'.

[1] These conventional estimates of 'discrimination' associate it with differences between men and women in regression coefficients relating their human capital attributes to their earnings. This is taken as a measure of what is sometimes labelled 'direct discrimination' (Mincer and Polachek, 1974). This approach ignores the effect of expected discrimination on the accumulation of human capital (e.g. education, on-the-job training), or what is called 'indirect' discrimination. As shown in the next section, its reliability as a measure of 'direct discrimination' is also questionable.

of the anti-discriminatory legislation of the 1970s, but it is still unclear why their results are so different.

The paper consists of five sections. In the first, the implications of human capital theory for men's and women's earnings functions and the measurement of gender discrimination are discussed. This provides the foundation for the critical review of previous studies in the second section. In the third and fourth sections, the degree of gender discrimination in pay in 1980 is estimated. Conclusions are presented in the fifth section.

I. HUMAN CAPITAL THEORY AND GENDER DISCRIMINATION

An important foundation for the estimates of gender discrimination is the extension, by Mincer and Polachek (1974), of the human capital model of earnings to workers with interruptions in their employment history. They show that, in these circumstances, optimal life cycle investment plans have no clear implications about whether human capital investments increase or decrease with experience in paid employment or even with the duration of a particular employment spell. A reasonable approximation, particularly for short spells in and out of employment, is the following wage offer function:

$$\log w_t = \log Y_0 + \log(1 - k_n) + rk_s S + r \sum_{i-1}^{n} k_i e_i, \qquad (1)$$

where: w_t is hourly earnings *net* of on-the-job investment in human capital in period t; Y_0 is gross earnings before human capital investment; k_i is the ratio of *net* investment to gross earnings in segment i of a person's work history; k_s is the ratio while in full-time education; e_i is the duration of segment i; S is the duration of education; and r is the rate of return to human capital. Note that $1 - k_n$ is the proportion of working time in the current work history segment *not* devoted to human capital investment; as k_n is relatively small, $\log(1 - k_n)$ is small relative to $\log Y_0$, and as a close approximation, it can be absorbed into the intercept of the equation.

In order to facilitate gender comparisons, a much simpler specification of the women's earnings function has usually been estimated (e.g. Miller, 1987; Zabalza and Arrufat, 1985). It groups the segments of a woman's work history into periods of employment ('work experience') and periods out of employment ('home time'), and it assumes that the *net investment ratios* differ between these types of segment, but assumes that they are the same for each segment of a given type:

$$\log w_t = \log Y_0 + \log(1 - k_n) + rk_s S + rk_W \sum_W e_i + rk_N \sum_N e_i, \qquad (2)$$

where W and N designate whether a work history segment is a period in or not in employment respectively and $\sum_j e_i$ indicates summation over all segments of type j ($j = W$ and N). Furthermore, it also assumes that the net investment ratios vary with the total time in each type of segment:

$$k_j = a_j + b_j \sum_j e_i, \quad j = W, N. \qquad (3)$$

It follows from equations (2) and (3) that wage offers are quadratic in experience and home time.

Equations (2) and (3) lead to the following two *wage offer* equations:

$$\log w_i = \beta_i \mathbf{X}_i + \alpha_i \mathbf{H}_i + \epsilon_i, \quad i = M, F \quad \text{and} \quad \mathbf{H}_M = 0, \tag{4}$$

where: w is the hourly wage rate; $\mathbf{X}$ is a K by 1 vector of human capital attributes other than 'home time'; β is a 1 by K vector of parameters representing the impact of these attributes on pay; $\mathbf{H}$ is a 2 by 1 vector of home-time and its square; α is a 1 by 2 parameter vector capturing the effect that the time women spent out of employment has on their wages; and ϵ is an error term. The subscripts M and F denote male and female respectively.

We cannot, however, observe the *wage offer* functions directly. Only persons that accept an offer will have their wage offer observed. We use Heckman's (1979) well-known technique to correct for any bias arising from this sample selection. Thus, $\sigma_{\epsilon u} \lambda$ is added to the right-hand side of equation (4) for women, where λ is the inverse of Mills' ratio, a consistent estimate of which is computed from the estimates of an employment participation equation, and $\sigma_{\epsilon u}$ is the covariance between ϵ_F and the error term in the participation equation.

'Direct discrimination' is usually defined as a different return to the same unit of human capital (Mincer and Polachek, 1974). In terms of equation (2), this would mean that r is lower for women than men. In previous studies, discrimination has been measured as differences between β_M and β_F, weighted by the average human capital attributes of women, $\bar{\mathbf{X}}_F$: $(\beta_M - \beta_F) \bar{\mathbf{X}}_F$. But it is clear from (2) that differences between β_M and β_F may reflect gender differences in human capital investment (different k_W and k_s) or in rates of return to human capital (r). Only the latter differences should be considered as 'direct discrimination'. It is not possible, however, to identify gender differences in r; thus we must rely on this conventional measure of gender discrimination.

If women's employment interruptions are exogenous, then $(\hat{\beta}_M - \hat{\beta}_F) \bar{\mathbf{X}}_F$ represents an upper bound on the degree of *direct* discrimination, because the *expected* interruption reduces women's investment in human capital *before the interruption*, both in education and on-the-job. As a consequence, the coefficients associated with education and work experience would be lower for women even if they earn the same returns on human capital as men, because of lower k_s and k_W. But, as Weiss and Gronau (1981) show, when the length (and existence) of work interruptions is endogenous, discrimination in pay induces longer labour force withdrawals (less work experience, more home time), creating a tendency for $(\hat{\beta}_M - \hat{\beta}_F) \bar{\mathbf{X}}_F$ to understate the full effect of discrimination on earnings differences. This measure cannot, therefore, be classified as either an upper or lower bound on gender discrimination.

Using a method similar to that suggested by Oaxaca (1973), it follows from equation (4) that the difference in the means of the logarithmic wages between men and women may be decomposed into four components using the following formula:

$$\overline{\log w}_M - \overline{\log w}_F = \hat{\beta}_M (\bar{\mathbf{X}}_M - \bar{\mathbf{X}}_F) + (\hat{\beta}_M - \hat{\beta}_F) \bar{\mathbf{X}}_F - \hat{\alpha} \bar{\mathbf{H}} - \hat{\sigma}_{\epsilon u} \bar{\lambda}, \tag{5}$$

where the left-hand side of (5) approximates the percentage wage differential between men and women. A bar represents a mean value, and the symbol '^' represents the estimate of the respective parameter(s). The first term on the right-hand side is the contribution to the wage difference arising from differences in average measured attributes between men and women. This term can be thought of as the wage gap that would persist if women's attributes were remunerated as men's. The second term reflects differentials in remuneration of measured attributes, and it is the imperfect measure of 'discrimination'. Following Zabalza and Arrufat (1985) and Miller (1987), the third term is the component of the wage differential attributable to time spent out of the labour force, which only applies to women. The last term is the contribution of sample selection bias to the observed wage differential. It is clear from equation (4) that subtraction of this last term from equation (5) yields the difference in average wage offers.

A summary index of the 'extent' or 'level' of discrimination implied by (5) is:

$$D_F = \{\exp\left[(\hat{\boldsymbol{\beta}}_M - \hat{\boldsymbol{\beta}}_F)\,\bar{\mathbf{X}}_F\right] - 1\} \times 100. \tag{6}$$

Therefore, D_F may be interpreted as the percentage increase in the hourly wage rate that women would receive, given their attributes, if they were remunerated like men (i.e. if there was no 'direct discrimination').[2] But for the reasons discussed earlier, caution should be exercised in interpreting this estimate of discrimination.

II. PREVIOUS ESTIMATES

Greenhalgh (1980), Miller (1987) and Zabalza and Arrufat (1982, 1985) present estimates of gender discrimination based on data collected in the *General Household Survey* (GHS). As the GHS does not contain detailed work histories, cumulative measures of work experience and home time are not available. In order to minimise the problems associated with using potential experience (age minus age at leaving school), Greenhalgh (1980) concentrates her analysis on the difference in wages between single men and women.[3] On the other hand, Miller (1987) and Zabalza and Arrufat (1982, 1985) use a measure of imputed work experience. In brief, they estimate a participation equation which 'predicts' the probability that a women is working in a particular year based on a set of assumed exogenous factors.[4] Cumulative measures of work experience and home time are then constructed by integrating this backwards projection.

Greenhalgh (1980) finds that the discrimination index, D_F, for single men

---

[2] An alternative summary index uses the male human capital attributes as the standardising factor. This index was not reported here as it leads to the same conclusions.

[3] Mincer and Polachek (1974) have shown that estimating a women's wage equation with potential experience leads to an underestimate of the rate of return to work experience.

[4] Beggs and Chapman (1988) adjust potential experience by a common multiplication factor based on the 'average' employment rate of women. However, as the authors point out, this adjustment is based on 'a set of restrictive assumptions' (p. 120).

and women was 24% in 1971 and 10% in 1975 — a sizable decline which she attributes to the anti-discrimination legislation introduced in the early 1970s. Indirectly, she estimates that the D_F for married men and women in 1975 was about 33%. However, Zabalza and Arrufat's (1982, 1985) estimate for married men and women in 1975 is much lower. They find that over 70% of the wage differential is due to the 'depreciation effect' of home time. They conclude that in the absence of discrimination the hourly wage rate of women would only be slightly higher (around 6%). Such a finding contrasts sharply with Miller's (1987) estimate for 1980. He finds that only 40% of the wage differential between married men and women can be attributed to the depreciation effect of home time. His analysis indicates that women's wages would be about 15% higher in the absence of discrimination.

Dolton and Makepeace (1986), using cohort data (including actual work experience) on a sample of 1970 college graduates interviewed in 1977, find that earnings of females would be about 20% higher if there was no discrimination. Likewise, Joshi and Newell (1946), using data on a cohort of individuals born in 1946, find that at ages 26 and 32 (i.e. in 1972 and 1977), women's wages would be 51% and 27% higher respectively in the absence of discrimination.

The estimates of Zabalza and Arrufat (1982, 1985) are troubling for a variety of reasons. First, they are in sharp disagreement with what Joshi and Newell (1987) found using nationally representative cohort data. Second, compared to the findings of Dolton and Makepeace (1986), their estimates imply that discrimination is higher among college graduates than it is in the married population as a whole. Third, their estimates are lower than those of Chiplin and Sloane (1976) and Siebert and Sloane (1981) for some professional workers. Fourth, they suggest that the level of gender discrimination in Great Britain is much lower than in, for example, the United States and Canada (Kuhn, 1987). Fifth, Miller's (1987) 'bottom line' estimate of discrimination is much higher, even though he uses the same imputation method. Finally, their estimates are very sensitive to Heckman's correction for sample selection bias.

III. EMPIRICAL SPECIFICATION

Equations (4) are estimated using data collected in the *1980 Women and Employment Survey* (WES). This survey was a nationally representative sample of British women between the ages of 16 and 59.[5] These data are well suited to examining the issues raised in this paper because detailed work histories were collected from women by recall. Therefore, direct measures of cumulative work experience and time spent out of employment are available. Although distinguished in the work histories, equal weights have been given to full-time and part-time employment experience in order to facilitate comparisons with the imputed experience measure and previous studies. In addition, socio-

[5] For a detailed discussion of the WES survey design, methodology and data quality see, Martin and Roberts (1984a, b).

economic information and wage data were also collected for the husbands of
women married at the time of the survey. As data on the actual work
experience for males are not available we have followed conventional practice
and used potential experience (i.e. home time is zero for men). Therefore, it is
possible to compare married women with married men, which provides a link
to the analyses performed by Zabalza and Arrufat (1982, 1985) and Miller
(1987).

The dependent variable in the analysis is the logarithm of hourly earnings.
Hourly pay has been calculated by dividing usual gross weekly earnings
(excluding overtime) by the usual number of hours worked (excluding
overtime and meal breaks). Accounting for missing information, the samples
consist of 3,636 married women of whom 2,094 are employed (full-time or part-
time).[6] The mean hourly earnings of married males and females are £2.52 and
£1.69, respectively, or an observed logarithmic wage gap of 0·398 (i.e.
0·925–0·527). This is a differential of 49% of average women's wages.[7]

Education consists of series of binary variables representing the highest level
of formal qualifications. The categories are: 'Higher'; 'A-level(s)'; 'O-levels';
'CSE's'; 'other qualifications' and 'no formal qualifications beyond basic
school leaving'. The reference category is the no qualifications group. A series
of regional binary variables, aimed at proxying differences across labour
markets, are also in included. The reference category is 'residing in Greater
London'. The means and standard deviations of these variables are given in
the Appendix Table.

Our imputation of work experience follows the general approach of Zabalza
and Arrufat, and Miller. It is based on a cross-section employment participation
equation and an adjustment for trends in participation across cohorts, and is
explained in detail in Wright and Ermisch (1990). While the means of actual
and imputed experience are almost identical in the full sample, which includes
women not employed, the variance in imputed experience is, of course, smaller.
At the individual level, the correlation coefficient between imputed and actual
work experience is quite high at 0·78.

We have purposefully kept our empirical specification simple in order to
concentrate our analysis on differences in the coefficients on work experience
and education and to facilitate comparability with earlier studies. It is often the
case that these wage equations are augmented with variables capturing
differences in occupations. However, as Miller (1987) points out, such an
approach assumes that differences in occupational attainment are 'justified',
but in fact they may be in part an outcome of discrimination. In other words,

---

[6] In the WES, 4,079 married women were interviewed. 79 women who were permanently sick and 19 who
were full-time students were excluded from the sample. A further 345 cases were dropped because
information was missing on at least one of the regression variables. Analysis in Joshi (1986) and Martin and
Roberts (1984*b*) indicate that it is unlikely that these 345 women form a non-random sub-sample.

[7] Dolton and Makepeace (1985) suggest that summary measures of discrimination should be calculated
using the complete distributions of male and female earnings. However, a recent paper by Jenkins (1989*g*)
indicates that this is not a straightforward task and implementation is clearly beyond the scope of this paper.
Nevertheless, as expected, the female–male wage ratio differs across the distribution. For example, at the
lower quartile, female wages are: 69·4% of male wages; at the median, 64·4%; and at the upper quartile,
only 62·9%. (See Appendix Table.)

occupational attainment may be endogenous in the model. As our model is a very simple 'human capital' specification of the wage equation, we focus on what may be termed the 'equal pay for equal human capital attributes' interpretation of discrimination (subject to the qualifications mentioned earlier).

IV. RESULTS

The specification of the model for the probability that a woman was employed at the time of the survey (i.e. the sample selection equation) is very similar to the model estimated by Joshi (1986) using data from the WES. 'Hausman-Wu tests' are used to test for the endogeneity-exogeneity of work experience in the wage determination and employment participation equations (Hausman, 1978; Wu, 1973). A likelihood ratio test provides strong evidence ($p < 0.001$) that work experience and home time are not exogenous in the labour force participation decision. Therefore, only the orthogonal component of work experience and home time (i.e. the instruments for these) are henceforth included in the selection equation.[8]

In contrast, an F-test allows us to accept the hypothesis that work experience is exogenous in the wage offer equation ($p < 0.1$). This result is robust to models in which sample selection bias was corrected for using Heckman's procedure. Interestingly, Heckman (1980) came to the same conclusion using American data, and he also found work experience to be endogenous in the participation equation.

Table 1 presents the parameter estimates of the wage offer equations. Columns 1–6 show the estimates for various specifications of the women's wage equation. Column 7 presents the parameter estimates of the men's wage equation. The results of the decomposition, based on equation (5), along with the estimates of the index of discrimination, D_F, are shown in Table 2.

Column 1 shows the model incorporating potential experience. As this specification implicitly assumes a continuous work history for women, the estimated rates of return to work experience are much lower than for men (cf. Column 7). Furthermore, as expected, this specification leaves a large percentage of the wage gap unexplained (i.e. 88·2%), supporting a high D_F estimate of 42·1%. Column 2 shows the same specification corrected for sample selection bias using Heckman's method. The coefficient of λ is statistically significant and *negative*, suggesting that married women who were employed at the time of the survey are not a random sample of all married women.[9] Because

[8] The details of the endogeneity tests and estimates of the participation equations are given in Wright and Ermisch (1990). Like Heckman (1980), Miller (1987) and Zabalza and Arrufat (1982, 1985), we assume that fertility is an exogenous factor. For evidence in support of this assumption see Joshi and Wright (1987). The variables included in the participation equations are: wife's age and its square, wife's education, region of residence, housing tenure, number and age of children, local unemployment rate, husband's employment status and non-labour income. The additional instruments used in the endogeneity tests for work experience/home time in the participation equation are: husband's age and its square, husband's education and social class and wife's age at marriage. In the wage equation test, all the above variables were included as instruments.

[9] This suggests that parameter estimates are likely to be biased in the studies that have used potential experience but have not corrected for sample selection bias (Greenhalgh, 1980).

of this self-selection of lower paid women into employment, the difference in *wage offers* is smaller than the observed gap in hourly pay (see Table 2).

Column 3 reports the parameters for the model that includes actual work experience and home time. Column 4 shows the same specification corrected for sample selection bias. The coefficient of λ is again statistically significant and negative. Dolton and Makepeace (1987a) also found that women possessing unmeasured attributes which enhance their earnings are less likely to be employed at the time of the survey. At first glance, this may appear counter-intuitive. But, in the context of an influential model of labour supply (Heckman, 1974), Ermisch and Wright (1989) show that a negative coefficient on λ is very plausible when a woman's reservation wage and her wage offer exhibit a relatively high positive correlation, and this is likely because women who are more productive in jobs also tend to be more productive in home activities. They also show that a negative coefficient on λ implies that, for given measured human capital attributes, wage offers exhibit less dispersion than reservation wages, which is likely (see also, Dolton and Makepeace, 1987b).

Our results, and those of Dolton and Makepeace (1987a), contrast with Zabalza and Arrufat's (1985) finding that women with unmeasured attributes that enhance their earnings are more likely to be employed. The size and direction of the selectivity effect depend on the measured attributes included in the employment participation (selection) equation. The correction for sample selection does not change the coefficients for work experience and home time. The parameter estimates suggest that (around the sample means) each additional year of work experience raises a woman's wage by about 0·7% and a year of home time lowers her wage by about 1·3%. It is important to note that these estimates are much smaller than those estimated by Zabalza and Arrufat (their estimates are 2–3 times larger), and also smaller than Miller's (1987) estimates, which are 1·5 and 1·8% respectively. Furthermore, like Dolton and Makepeace (1986), our estimates appear not to be sensitive to the correction for sample selection bias.

Finally, Columns 5 and 6 show the estimates using imputed work experience and home time. Evaluated at the means of actual work experience and home time, the parameters indicate that an additional year of work experience raises wages by 0·5% while an additional year of home time lowers wages by about 1·0%. Although somewhat lower, these rates of return are surprisingly close to the rates based on actual work experience and home time. In other words, it appears that the imputed measures are likely to be acceptable substitutes for actual values in empirical work.

The decomposition of the wage gap, reported in Table 2, suggests that about 17% of the observed wage differential may be attributed to differences in attributes. The contribution to the differential of home time is only about 25–30%, which is approximately one-third of that found by Zabalza and Arrufat, and also smaller than Miller's estimate of 43%. Most importantly, the component attributed to discrimination is about 50% per cent of the gap in wage offers. This entails a D_F estimate of about 20–25% – four to five times higher than the highest estimate of Zabalza and Arrufat (1985), and also

Table 1

Parameters estimates of male–female wage equations: Great Britain, 1980

Reg. no.	Females						Males
	(1)	(2)	(3)	(4)	(5)	(6)	(7)
method	OLS	Heckman	OLS	Heckman	OLS	Heckman	OLS
Potential Experience	0·044	0·028	(a)	(a)	(a)	(a)	0·246
(÷10)	[1·52]	[0·96]					[6·56]
Potential Exp. sq.	−0·898	−0·599	(a)	(a)	(a)	(a)	−0·465
(÷1000)	[1·58]	[1·05]					[6·29]
Actual Experience	(a)	(a)	0·203	0·187	(a)	(a)	(a)
(÷10)			[6·50]	[5·94]			
Actual Exp. sq.	(a)	(a)	−0·395	−0·358	(a)	(a)	(a)
(÷1000)			[5·21]	[4·70]			
Actual Hometime	(a)	(a)	−0·185	−0·180	(a)	(a)	(a)
(÷10)			[6·30]	[6·24]			
Actual Hometime sq.	(a)	(a)	0·363	0·358	(a)	(a)	(a)
(÷1000)			[2·94]	[2·92]			
Imputed Experience	(a)	(a)	(a)	(a)	0·249	0·217	(a)
(÷10)					[4·49]	[3·82]	
Imputed Exp. sq.	(a)	(a)	(a)	(a)	−0·591	−0·511	(a)
(÷1000)					[3·55]	[3·01]	
Imputed Hometime	(a)	(a)	(a)	(a)	−0·146	−0·133	(a)
(÷10)					[3·49]	[3·16]	
Imputed Hometime sq.	(a)	(a)	(a)	(a)	0·256	0·236	(a)
(÷1000)					[1·64]	[1·42]	
Education:							
Other	0·062	0·071	0·057	0·065	0·076	0·079	0·099
	[0·58]	[1·03]	[0·84]	[0·97]	[1·19]	[1·15]	[1·60]
CSE's	0·083	0·075	0·074	0·068	0·057	0·055	0·101
	[3·66]	[3·29]	[3·34]	[3·06]	[2·50]	[2·41]	[3·84]
O-level(s)	0·116	0·110	0·108	0·104	0·099	0·098	0·203
	[5·28]	[5·04]	[5·05]	[4·87]	[4·65]	[4·47]	[8·23]
A-level(s)	0·210	0·203	0·191	0·187	0·174	0·174	0·316
	[4·74]	[4·62]	[4·46]	[4·39]	[3·48]	[3·97]	[7·96]
Higher	0·508	0·495	0·492	0·482	0·465	0·463	0·509
	[21·63]	[20·98]	[21·53]	[21·04]	[15·99]	[19·13]	[21·01]
Region:							
North	−0·175	−0·172	−0·166	−0·163	−0·177	−0·175	−0·124
	[4·87]	[4·81]	[4·73]	[4·68]	[4·83]	[4·93]	[2·89]
York/Humberside	−0·168	−0·166	−0·166	−0·163	−0·164	−0·164	−0·106
	[5·20]	[5·18]	[5·29]	[5·27]	[4·87]	[5·15]	[2·67]
North West	−0·141	−0·140	−0·144	−0·143	−0·133	−0·133	−0·094
	[4·60]	[4·58]	[4·84]	[4·83]	[3·96]	[4·40]	[2·49]
East Midlands	−0·210	−0·207	−0·212	−0·210	−0·214	−0·213	−0·243
	[6·03]	[6·00]	[6·27]	[6·25]	[6·16]	[6·19]	[5·76]
West Midlands	−0·129	−0·128	−0·145	−0·144	−0·125	−0·125	−0·047
	[3·97]	[3·99]	[4·60]	[4·61]	[3·81]	[3·90]	[1·18]
East Anglia	−0·274	−0·256	−0·292	−0·278	−0·280	−0·272	−0·137
	[5·28]	[4·97]	[5·80]	[5·53]	[5·12]	[5·28]	[2·52]
South East	−0·149	−0·145	−0·144	−0·141	−0·146	−0·144	−0·082
	[5·30]	[5·21]	[5·29]	[5·22]	[4·66]	[5·22]	[2·49]
South West	−0·172	−0·168	−0·159	−0·155	−0·168	−0·166	−0·198
	[4·91]	[4·82]	[4·65]	[4·59]	[4·54]	[4·79]	[4·87]
Wales	−0·161	−0·144	−0·138	−0·124	−0·160	−0·152	−0·180
	[3·73]	[3·35]	[3·29]	[2·97]	[4·04]	[3·54]	[3·80]

Continued overleaf

Table 1 *(cont.)*

Reg. no. method	Females						Males
	(1) OLS	(2) Heckman	(3) OLS	(4) Heckman	(5) OLS	(6) Heckman	(7) OLS
Scotland	−0·158 [4·63]	−0·156 [4·62]	−0·152 [4·58]	−0·150 [4·57]	−0·159 [4·52]	−0·158 [4·70]	−0·167 [4·20]
Constant	0·521 [14·43]	0·585 [12·95]	0·473 [13·04]	0·523 [13·29]	0·477 [10·74]	0·514 [10·67]	0·595 [11·70]
λ	(a)	−0·087 [3·70]	(a)	−0·073 [3·17]	(a)	−0·042 [1·69]	(a)
R^2	0·224	0·229	0·269	0·272	0·238	0·238	0·249
F	35·2	34·2	40·1	38·8	34·0	32·5	36·0
N	2,094	2,094	2,094	2,094	2,094	2,094	1,868
SE	0·337	0·339	0·327	0·328	0·334	0·333	0·370
$\bar{\lambda}$	(a)	0·522	(a)	0·521	(a)	0·521	(a)

Notes:
    * The omitted categories are no formal educational qualifications and residing in Greater London. Absolute values of t-statistics in brackets.
    (a) = variable not included in regression.

Table 2

Decomposition of male–female wage differential: married persons, Great Britain, 1980

Components	Decomposition based on Table 1, equation no.					
	(1)	(2)	(3)	(4)	(5)	(6)
Hometime	(a)	(a)	0·102 [25·6%]	0·100 [25·1%]	0·112 [28·1%]	0·102 [27·1%]
Attributes	0·047 [11·8%]	0·047 [11·8%]	0·068 [17·0%]	0·068 [17·0%]	0·074 [18·6%]	0·074 [17·0%]
Discrimination	0·351 [88·2%]	0·306 [76·8]	0·229 [57·4%]	0·193 [48·4%]	0·212 [53·3%]	0·200 [50·2%]
Sample Selection	(a)	0·045 [11·4%]	(a)	0·038 [10·6%]	(a)	0·022 [5·5%]
Wage Offer Gap	0·398	0·353	0·398	0·360	0·398	0·376
D_F	42·1%	35·8%	25·7%	21·2%	23·6%	22·1%

Notes:
    Percentage of observed log wage gap contributed by component is in brackets.

higher than Miller's, which may be inflated by his failure to allow for sample selection effects.[10]

What is striking about our findings, is that the decomposition does not change significantly with different methods of estimating the women's wage

[10] Note that our estimates of D_F are higher when we do not control for sample selection bias. In their examination of gender and race earnings differences in the United States, Berger and Glenn (1988) also found that failure to control for sample selection bias leads to over-estimation of the extent of discrimination.

equation. The analysis suggests that the hourly wage rate of married women would be approximately one-fifth higher in the absence of discrimination.

Taken at face value, our finding that work experience is exogenous suggests that women's work interruptions are exogenous. Thus, our estimates suggest that direct discrimination is probably less than 21%. But our test of the exogeneity of work experience is conditional on childbearing being exogenous. While Joshi and Wright (1987) produce evidence supporting this assumption, it is open to some doubt.[11] We are, therefore, somewhat reluctant to interpret our estimates as an upper bound on direct discrimination.

Weiss and Gronau's (1981) analysis of the interaction between earnings and employment interruptions suggests that better estimates of discrimination can be obtained from gender comparisons rather late in the life cycle (see also, Gronau, 1988). As noted at the outset, expected interruptions in employment affect human capital investment ratios (k_s and k_W in equation (2)), and as a consequence, comparison of the coefficients of earnings functions confound gender differences in human capital investment with differences in rates of return. But Weiss and Gronau (1981) identify models in which differences in earnings growth reflect differences in labour force participation plans. Their analysis implies that if we observe two groups with a similar earnings growth rate, we can obtain a lower bound estimate of pay discrimination, and an exact estimate if withdrawals from the labour force are exogenous.[12]

Because earnings growth is more likely to be similar for men and women aged 40–59, we estimate earnings functions for this age group. Our estimates of the coefficients on work experience indeed show small changes in earnings with work experience at these ages for both men and women. The resulting gender discrimination coefficient (D_F) of 44% for this age group (40%, when not controlling for sample selection) should, therefore, be a lower bound estimate of discrimination. But this strictly only applies to generations born during 1921–40. As their lives were well advanced before the equal opportunities legislation of the 1970s, they have probably been less affected by it. This may explain the rather high lower bound estimate of discrimination, and it is why we have focused on the estimates for the entire population of married men and women in 1980.

[11] The evidence from Joshi and Wright (1987) applies to only one cohort. Exogeneity may be easier to accept in these circumstances because of limited variation in childbearing patterns within a cohort. There will be much more variation in childbearing patterns among cohorts. Furthermore, there is evidence from the same (WES) data that childbearing patterns are affected by potential earning power (Cigno and Ermisch, 1989; Ermisch, 1989).

[12] Like most of the previous analyses, our empirical analysis omits tenure in current job from the earnings equations. In our case, this is because we cannot measure it for men. Even in the absence of delayed payment contracts (Lazear, 1981), human capital theory suggests that it influences wages because of the effect of job-specific human capital on productivity. Because work experience and job tenure exhibit a positive correlation, its omission tends to bias the measured impact of work experience upward among both men and women. The bias increases with the impact of job tenure on earnings. In that delayed payment contracts are characterised by a stronger impact of job tenure on earnings, the bias will be larger for the group of workers with such contracts.

V. CONCLUSIONS

In summary, our analysis supports the following conclusions:

(i) Our estimates of gender pay discrimination in 1980, based on the Oaxaca decomposition technique, is that women's pay would be about 20% higher in the absence of discrimination. This estimate is four times the 'highest' 1975 estimate of Zabalza and Arrufat (1982, 1985) and slightly larger than the highest 1980 estimate by Miller (1987) of 18·5%.

(ii) Our estimate of discrimination is somewhat lower than the 1977/8 estimate by Joshi and Newell (1987) for persons from the 1946 birth cohort, but because our estimate comes from data including younger generations, we expect it to be smaller. Also as expected, it may be slightly higher than what was found for university graduates (Dolton and Makepeace, 1986) and professional workers (Chiplin and Sloane, 1976; Siebert and Sloane, 1981). Furthermore, it is in line with estimates for other industrialised nations.

(iii) With regard to methodology, our analysis indicates that measures of work experience that are imputed by a backward-projection from a cross-section employment participation equation are highly correlated with actual experience, and these measures produce estimates of women's earnings functions and of discrimination that are similar to those based on actual experience. The success of these imputed measures appears to arise because of the strong predictive power of childbearing patterns for women's work experience. We have also confirmed the importance of controlling for sample selection bias when estimating women's wage equations. Finally, our evidence supports the hypothesis that work experience is endogenous in women's labour force participation decisions, but is exogenous in the determination of women's wages.

(iv) In the absence of data on women's actual work experience, use of such an imputed measure in the estimation of pay discrimination appears to be the best solution. It is undoubtedly better than using a measure of potential experience, and it is likely to be preferable to using a sample of only single men and women, because of the sample selection bias suggested by the economic analysis of marriage (see, for example, Becker (1981), Chapter 4, and Lam, 1988). For instance, as a consequence of the gains from the division of labour within marriage, we would expect that women with higher earning potential would marry later, and evidence from the WES supports this hypothesis. In contrast, men with higher earnings would be more likely to marry earlier. Thus, a sample of singles would tend to bias downwards the measure of discrimination. Furthermore the vast majority of the population eventually marry, and labour force participation plans would affect the coefficients of single women's earnings equations as much as they affect those of married women's.

(v) Taking Joshi and Newell's 1972 D_F value of 51% as a 'baseline' estimate of the level of discrimination prevailing at the time of the introduction of the anti-discriminatory legislation, their 1977 estimate of 32%, along with our

1980 estimate of 21 %, suggests that discrimination declined in the 1970s, but it is far from being eliminated.

Birkbeck College

National Institute of Economic and Social Research

Date of receipt of final typescript: August 1990

REFERENCES

Becker, G. S. (1981). *A Treatise on the Family*. London: Harvard University Press.
Beggs, J. J. and Chapman, B. J. (1988). 'Labor turnover bias in estimating wages.' *Review of Economics and Statistics*, vol. 70, pp. 117-23.
Berger, M. C. and Glenn, D. E. (1986). 'Selectivity bias and earnings differences by gender and race.' *Economic Letters*, vol. 21, pp. 291-6.
Brown, R., Moon, M. and Zoloth, B. S. (1980). 'Incorporating occupational attainment in studies of male-female earning differentials.' *Journal of Human Resources*, vol. 15, pp. 3-28.
Carmichael, L. (1983). 'Firm specific human capital and promotion ladders.' *Bell Journal of Economics*, vol. 14, pp. 251-8.
Chiplin, B. and Sloane, P. J. (1976). 'Personal characteristics and sex differentials in professional employment.' ECONOMIC JOURNAL, vol. 86, pp. 729-45.
Cigno, A. and Ermisch, J. F. (1989). 'A microeconomic analysis of the timing of births.' *European Economic Review*, vol. 33, pp. 737-60.
Dolton, P. J. and Makepeace, G. H. (1985). 'The statistical measurement of discrimination.' *Economic Letters*, vol. 18, pp. 391-5.
—— and —— (1986). 'Sample selection and male-female earnings differentials in the graduate labour market.' *Oxford Economic Papers*, vol. 38, pp. 317-41.
—— and —— (1987a). 'Marital status, child rearing and earnings differentials in the graduate labour market.' ECONOMIC JOURNAL, vol. 97, pp. 897-922.
—— and —— (1987b). 'Interpreting sample selection effects.' *Economic Letters*, vol. 24, pp. 373-9.
Ermisch, J. F. (1989). 'Purchased child care, optimal family size and mother's employment.' *Journal of Population Economics*, vol. 2, pp. 79-102.
—— and Wright, R. E. (1989). 'Interpretation of negative sample selection effects in wage offer equations.' Mimeo. Department of Economics, Birkbeck College.
Gronau, R. (1988). 'Sex-related wage differentials and women's interrupted work careers – the chicken or the egg?' *Journal of Labor Economics*, vol. 6, pp. 277-301.
Greenhalgh, C. A. (1980). 'Male-female wage differentials in Great Britain: Is marriage an equal opportunity?' ECONOMIC JOURNAL, vol. 90, pp. 751-75.
Hausman, J. A. (1978). 'Specification tests in econometrics.' *Econometrica*, vol. 46, pp. 1251-72.
Heckman, J. J. (1974). 'Shadow prices, market wages, and labor supply.' *Econometrica*, vol. 47, pp. 679-94.
—— (1979). 'Sample selection bias as a specification error.' *Econometrica*, vol. 47, pp. 143-61.
—— (1980). 'Sample selection bias as a specification error with an application to the estimation of labor supply functions.' In *Female Labor Supply* (J. P. Smith, ed.), pp. 206-48. Princeton: Princeton University Press.
Hutchens, R. (1986). 'Delayed payment contracts and a firm's propensity to hire older workers.' *Journal of Labour Economics*, vol. 4, pp. 439-57.
Jenkins, S. P. (1989). 'Measurement of earnings discrimination using complete distributions of differentials.' Mimeo. Centre for Fiscal Studies, University of Bath.
Joshi, H. E. (1986). 'Participation in paid work: evidence from the Women and Employment Survey.' In *Unemployment, Search and Labour Supply* (R. Blundell and I. Walker, eds.), pp. 217-42. Cambridge: Cambridge University Press.
—— and Newell, M. (1987). 'Pay differences between men and women: longitudinal evidence from the 1946 birth cohort. Centre for Economic Policy Research, Discussion Paper no. 156.
—— and Wright, R. E. (1987). 'The endogeneity of work experience and parenthood in female earning functions.' Mimeo. Department of Economics.
Kuhn, P. (1987). 'Sex discrimination in labour markets: The role of statistical evidence.' *American Economic Review*, vol. 77, pp. 567-83.

Lam, D. (1988). 'Marriage markets and assortative mating with household public goods,' *Journal of Human Resources*, vol. 23, pp. 462–87.

Lazear, E. (1981). 'Agency, earnings profiles, productivity, and hours restrictions.' *American Economic Review*, vol. 71, pp. 606–20.

Martin, J. and Roberts, C. (1984 a). *Women and Employment: A Lifetime Perspective*. London: Department of Employment.

—— and —— (1984 b). *Women and Employment: Technical Report*. London: Department of Employment.

Miller, P. W. (1987). 'The wage effect of the occupational segregation of women in Britain.' ECONOMIC JOURNAL, vol. 97, pp. 885–96.

Mincer, J. and Polachek, S. (1974). 'Family investments in human capital: Earnings of women.' *Journal of Political Economy*, vol. 82 (supplement), pp. S76–108.

Oaxaca, R. (1973). 'Male–female wage differentials in urban labour markets.' *International Economic Review*, vol. 14, pp. 693–709.

Siebert, W. S. and Sloane, P. J. (1981). 'The measurement of sex and marital status discrimination at the workplace.' *Economica*, vol. 48, pp. 125–41.

Weiss, Y. and Gronau, R. (1981). 'Expected interruptions in labour force participation and sex-related differences in earnings growth.' *Review of Economic Studies*, vol. 48, pp. 607–19.

Wright, R. E. and Ermisch, J. F. (1990). *Male–Female Wage Differentials in Great Britain*. Department of Economics. Birkbeck College, Discussion Paper.

Wu, D.-M. (1973). 'Alternative tests of independence between stochastic regressors and disturbances.' *Econometrica*, vol. 41, pp. 733–50.

Zabalza, A. and Arrufat, J. L. (1982). Wage differentials between married men and women in Great Britain: the depreciation effect of non-participation. Centre for Labour Economics, LSE, Working Paper no. 382.

—— and —— (1985). 'The extent of sex discrimination in Great Britain.' In *Women and Equal Pay: The Effects of Legislation on Female Employment and Wages in Britain* (A. Zabalza and Z. Tzannatos, eds.), pp. 70 96. Cambridge: Cambridge University Press.

[25]

International Labour Review, Vol. 124, No. 3, May-June 1985

Labour market segmentation and women's employment: A case-study from the United Kingdom

Christine CRAIG, Elizabeth GARNSEY and Jill RUBERY *

I. Introduction

This article draws on evidence obtained from a study of women's pay and employment in the United Kingdom[1] to suggest that pay inequalities are rooted in the system of industrial organisation and in the system of social reproduction of the labour force. Neoclassical economists' explanations of such inequalities as being due to differences in workers' productivity or the result of institutional imperfections in the labour market are found wanting. Differences in the productivity of jobs in various firms and industries are greater than differences in the productivity of workers, while institutional and social forces cannot be dismissed as imperfections when their influence can be clearly identified throughout the structure of labour markets. Labour market segmentation theory has provided the most effective recent challenge to orthodox theory, providing a "demand-side" explanation of inequality according to which different types of firms and industries adopt different employment practices. Some firms operate internal labour markets in which wages, job hierarchies and labour allocation are determined by internal rules and by custom and practice rather than by external market forces. The development of these internal labour markets has been ascribed to the nature of the product market and technological conditions in which firms in the primary sector of the economy operate (Doeringer and Piore, 1971). It has also been ascribed to management attempts to forestall effective worker organisation by dividing the labour force (Gordon et al., 1982).

Important though these "demand-side" explanations have been, our previous research and analysis found them to be inadequate on two main counts (Craig et al., 1982). First, they assumed that labour supply factors played no direct role in shaping the pattern of employment organisation and

* University of Cambridge. The research project on which this article is based was funded by the Department of Employment, but the views expressed are those of the authors only.

of inequality. Labour supply was assumed to adapt to predetermined divisions in the labour market created by the demand for labour. Secondly, these theories in practice presented only a partial challenge to orthodox economic theory since they took it for granted that, unlike the primary sector, the secondary sector was characterised by competitive labour markets corresponding to the conventional model.[2] Where firms had no interest in creating internal labour markets it was thought that wages and conditions were determined by competitive forces.

The project described in this article was designed to evaluate critically, through an analysis of women's employment, these two assumptions of LMS theory: that the secondary sector conformed to a competitive labour market model and that the division of jobs into primary and secondary categories (or "good" jobs and "bad" jobs) was determined by demand-side factors and was therefore independent of the characteristics of the workers who were employed. To carry out this investigation we needed to look at a range of demand-side and supply-side factors that could be expected to influence pay structures. The main demand-side factors identified in segmentation theory are the size of firms, their control over their markets and the type of technology employed. Supply-side factors include institutional constraints on managerial discretion, as exerted by trade union organisation or legal controls, as well as broader social forces that structure the labour supply. By comparing male and female employment it was possible to investigate the influence of social and family status on the organisation of work and employment conditions. Because we investigated these factors across a wide range of firms we could compare their influence with those of the firms' product, technological and organisational characteristics and with the influence of other labour supply influences such as union organisation (Rubery, 1978) and education and training systems.

II. The research project

The research project involved semi-structured interviews with nearly 150 employers in six industries, concentrated in three local labour markets in the United Kingdom.

To facilitate comparisons of different conditions it was decided to study six industries offering a wide range of employment, product market, technological and institutional characteristics. Four manufacturing and two service industries were chosen where there were many different types of female and male employment in the lower clerical and manual occupations, to which we limited the scope of the project. Women dominated these jobs in the two service industries – retail pharmacy and building societies; they accounted for around half the labour force in footwear and electronics, and constituted a significant minority in plastics processing and printing. Although we did not investigate any industries with a predominantly male labour force, we did include some firms which had only male production workers. The product market and technological characteristics of the industries selected also varied widely. The service industries had relatively protected markets, but the footwear industry was facing a major collapse in demand, largely as a result of import competition, which was also undermining the mass production markets for electronics and printing. Prospects for firms producing high-quality and specialised products were brighter in these last two industries, while plastics processing had been forced to make major cutbacks in component manufacture owing to the domestic recession but had fared better in other markets such as packaging, materials and some end-product markets. The footwear industry was still mainly using traditional technology to make largely unchanged products while the electronics industry was employing a range of technologies, including some low-technology processes to produce high-technology products. Printing was undergoing a rapid change from traditional to new technology. The pace of technical change in plastics processing had been relatively slow. There was also a wide variety of institutional controls and forms of trade union and collective bargaining machinery in the six industries chosen. There was a strong collective bargaining presence at the industry level in footwear, and also in printing, where, however, there had been a recent growth of non-unionised firms. In large electronics firms, large building societies and some large plastics firms there was local firm-level bargaining but small firms were largely unregulated. Retail pharmacy was an almost completely non-unionised industry, which nevertheless had an industry-level collective bargaining system for determining minimum wage rates.

Our prime objective in the survey was to interview firms with fewer than 100 employees, including a large proportion with fewer than 50, since it was in the smaller-firm sector that least evidence was available on the formation of payment structures. However, we took in a few larger firms, including the main employer in the industry in each region, for purposes of comparison. In the two service industries these large firms were organised on a small-establishment basis, but in manufacturing the large firms also had large concentrations of employment.

The most striking finding from our research was that at the time of the survey, 1980-81, most women in lower white-collar and manual jobs in the sample firms in all six industries were paid less than 200 pence per hour, and most men were paid more. This finding corresponds by and large to national data which show that, in 1981, 40 per cent of full-time and 71 per cent of part-time women workers earned less than 200 pence per hour as against under 10 per cent of male full-time workers (Department of Employment, 1981). Our survey sample enabled us to look at a number of factors at the firm level that may explain the observed national data differences in male and female pay; these include the role of job segregation within and between firms and industries, training and experience, working hours, technology and product market conditions, and the institutional regulation of pay, employment conditions and labour allocation. Let us first summarise our findings on how these factors affected the employment position of women in the survey firms before going on to consider their implications for labour market segmentation theory.

III. Findings of the survey of women's pay and employment

Job segregation

Job segregation between men and women is often put forward as an explanation of women's low pay (see, for example, Martin and Roberts, 1984). However, segregation can affect pay in different ways. It can result in low pay because women are excluded from jobs requiring skills or from jobs in high-productivity industries. Alternatively, it can lead to the payment of low wages in "feminised" jobs, not because these jobs require little skill or are unproductive but because only women are employed in them. Our research showed that while both conditions existed, the feminisation effect predominated over the exclusion effect. We found a general tendency among firms to classify feminised jobs as low-skilled and assign them to low pay grades largely irrespective of job content and the workers' skills. Segregation of women's employment both within and between firms facilitated these pay policies and also pointed up the inadequacies of explanations based on job content. There tended to be little direct overlap within individual firms in the types of jobs performed by men and women. The main exceptions were jobs in which men were employed as trainees alongside female workers (who were permanently confined to lower-grade jobs) and also jobs for which male employees were drawn from relatively disadvantaged labour force groups (the young, the old, workers in ill-health, ethnic minorities) and paid at essentially "women's" wage rates. Men were also occasionally employed on supervisory or machine-setting jobs which they carried out in addition to the operating jobs also assigned to women, and even more occasionally women were employed in predominantly male occupations. In the cases where women had gained access to these jobs by acquiring formal qualifications or via the standard promotion route for both men and women, they were usually paid the same rates as men. However, where women had acceded to predominantly male jobs without formal qualifications in firms where payment structures were not strictly based on job characteristics, they were often paid lower wages for work similar to that performed by men. Unequal pay for exactly the same work as men in the same firm was relatively uncommon even within firms using informal payment systems.[3]

Although there was little overlap between men's and women's work within individual firms there was overlap at the industry level because firms within the industry applied different employment and pay policies. The following were the most notable examples of such overlap.

1. In the printing industry there had been a rapid growth in the 1970s of small and largely non-unionised firms employing female typists as typesetters on the new-technology equipment. These women were usually paid well below the average for craft workers in the industry. In unionised plants the craft workers (mainly men) who were retrained as typesetters to use the new technology were paid a premium above the average craft rates.

2. In electronics some firms employed relatively well-paid male workers with or without apprenticeship qualifications, while others used mainly low-paid women as production workers and testers, and sometimes a small number of young men who were also on low wages. These different employment policies involved some differences in work organisation; for example, where unskilled women were used on testing work their main tasks were identification of faults and not diagnosis or repair. However, in other cases there were no such differences in job content. Some firms said they used skilled men as they were expected to interpret blueprints, but other firms expected the same skills of their experienced female employees.

3. In plastics processing a major factor influencing the allocation of machine-operating work between men and women was working time. On machines which needed to be kept running for long periods to reduce costs, it was common to employ men, who were then expected to work overtime or shifts, but in some firms continuous working was achieved through a system of four-hour shifts which women were willing to work, or by employing women on day work and staffing the night shifts with men, who in practice were often drawn from disadvantaged groups. The result was that women and men were assigned to different types of machines according to the work organisation of the firm in which they were employed. The grading of machine operator jobs by type of machine varied between firms, but men's jobs were almost always more highly paid than women's jobs within the same firm. The male operators were more often trained to set their machines (and paid accordingly) – an example of the impact of women's exclusion from parts of the production process on their pay and employment position. While women were trained to set machines in the minority of firms that used mainly female labour, they were paid only a small differential in compensation for the additional skill.

4. In building societies which had no internal management training systems women constituted almost the entire clerical and administrative workforce. Comparisons with building societies which did operate management training systems revealed a widening of pay differentials between clerical and cashiering work and tasks with a higher administrative and supervisory content. In addition, women tended to be confined to clerical work and excluded from these more senior tasks, which were often upgraded from clerical to managerial work. This pattern is clearly illustrated by comparing the operation of cash collection offices (sub-branches set up solely to take in and pay out money). In building societies without internal

Gender and Economics

management training schemes, these offices were operated by senior female cashiers receiving relatively low pay; where such training schemes existed, the offices were operated largely by men in junior management positions at a correspondingly higher salary.

Retail pharmacy and footwear do not provide any major examples of overlap between male and female jobs at the industry level, in the first case because of the predominance of women in all non-professional jobs and in the latter case because of the persistence of a traditional pattern of segregation, with women being found mainly in the closing rooms (stitching the uppers together) and in polishing and packing, and men being employed in cutting the leather and attaching the uppers to the sole. These two industries, however, provide the clearest examples of how women's work attracts relatively low wages regardless of job content. In footwear, employers generally acknowledged that women closers were among the most skilled workers in the firm but their pay was consistently lower than that of men with equivalent skill or experience, especially when the workers were paid on time rates.[4] In retail pharmacy the job of dispensing assistant had become "feminised" since the Second World War because of a shortage of men with the requisite education who were prepared to work at the going wage rate. Dispensers were required to have a secondary education and two years' on-the-job experience, but were often paid rates close to those of ordinary shop assistants.

These examples show how widespread is the practice of paying women low wages, irrespective of job content, wherever they are employed in jobs that can be differentiated from those held by "prime" male workers. There was also a tendency to exclude women from higher-grade and potentially more interesting and demanding work in all types of firms. However, the significance of this factor is diminished when one compares women's employment across different types of firms. Employment on more skilled work is no guarantee of higher pay, particularly if it results in "feminisation" of this work at either the industry or the firm level in circumstances where firms are not subject to internal or external pressure to pay wages commensurate with the actual demands of the job. One of the paradoxes of women's employment appears to be that, once firms are compelled by external or internal forces to operate a "job-based" payment system (i.e. one reflecting job content), then the process of exclusion becomes more important as a factor perpetuating women's disadvantaged employment position. Thus in firms using informal payment systems women were likely to be employed on a wide range of tasks, and in firms using more formal payment systems they were likely to be confined to a narrower range of semi-skilled or unskilled tasks.

A similar paradox is to be found in the influence of established segregation between male and female jobs. In industries where job segregation was firmly entrenched and embodied in a formal payment system, women who entered "male" jobs usually did so at "male" wage rates. In our sample this applied primarily to women in footwear, a minority of whom were employed in "male" jobs at the corresponding pay levels, women in craft jobs in unionised printing firms, and women in management-level jobs in building societies. Where job structures were more fluid, women were more likely to be employed on a wide range of jobs, but here the pay and status of the jobs reflected the sex of the incumbent; thus the less rigid sex segregation in electronics and plastics processing did little to enhance the pay and status of women employees.

Training and experience

In both neoclassical and labour market segmentation theory it is implied that women's work is largely unskilled and casual; this was not an appropriate description of women's jobs in the six industries as revealed in our survey. A significant number of jobs that were not classed as skilled nevertheless required at least six months of on-the-job experience and often particular attributes and qualities, such as dexterity, sharp eyesight or acute hearing. A few employers spoke of problems of female labour turnover but many more stressed the importance to the firm of their stable and experienced female workforce. Indeed, among the reasons given by employers for preferring to employ women rather than men in many of the jobs surveyed was that they expected greater stability, more conscientious work and greater tolerance of repetitive but often exacting tasks from women employees. However, the acquisition of firm-specific skills through on-the-job experience did little to improve the pay of women workers. Firms that relied on a stable and experienced female workforce paid wages similar to those paid by firms that could get by with inexperienced casual workers.

While women were frequently employed in jobs requiring skills acquired through informal training, few women were found in occupations necessitating formal vocational training, such as apprenticeships. For some occupations in which women were employed the possibility was afforded of studying for a formal qualification (for example, dispensers in retail pharmacy or building society clerks could study for vocational/professional qualifications) but most women were employed without formal training, either because they themselves opted not to study or because the employer did not offer the opportunity. Employers appeared reluctant to finance vocational training: for example, the main attraction in employing women typists as typesetters was that the costs of retraining male craftsmen could thus be avoided. Women appeared more likely to be interested in taking up vocational training once they had become established in a firm or occupation; therefore trends such as that in building societies towards a separate managerial training system were likely to widen the division between female and male workers, with women being permanently confined to the clerical sector.

Working hours

The working hours requirements associated with different jobs were often cited by employers as an explanation for job segregation within the firm. However, comparisons between firms and industries revealed the limitations of this explanation. Custom and practice within the industry appeared to play a large part in determining the hours women were prepared to work. For example, while some firms claimed it was not possible to get women to work a full week, still less to do weekend work, the two industries that required regular Saturday working (building societies and retail pharmacy) were mainly staffed by women workers who were prepared to work on Saturdays.

In the footwear industry firms were able to employ semi-skilled and unskilled women on a full 40-hour week, but their skilled closers were almost always on a shorter working week because of established custom and practice. These women used their bargaining power as skilled workers to limit their working hours, whereas unskilled women had to adapt their domestic arrangements to the firms' production requirements. Job segregation in plastics was sometimes put down to women's unwillingness to work overtime or on a three-shift system, but firms that wished to operate a continuous working system and to employ women made alternative working arrangements, for example by using four-hour shifts.

While working hours could not fully explain the pattern of job segregation, they did have an influence on women's pay and promotion prospects. Part-time workers were more frequently found in low-paying firms and were usually excluded from promotion opportunities, which were fairly restricted even for full-time female staff. It was relatively uncommon to find women part-timers paid less than full-timers on the same job in the same firm. However, the opportunity to work part time was sometimes granted only to the more experienced or skilled workers.

Technological and market conditions

Women's pay was not found to be systematically linked to the technological or market conditions of the firms in which they were employed. However, although low pay for women was found in all types of firms and market conditions it held special significance for the competitive strategies of firms in particular contexts. In the plastics processing industry competition was largely based on labour costs. Where female labour was not available or not appropriate for certain operations, firms resorted to male labour drawn from disadvantaged groups. Similarly, non-unionised firms had been set up in printing to undercut unionised printing firms by employing female labour. Large electronics firms had often moved out of components manufacture to reap the benefits of purchasing from small firms with low overheads and low wage levels. The "ability to pay" could not, however, be plausibly advanced as an explanation for low wages in building societies with their relatively protected markets: women's pay in the finance sector in general, including building societies, had improved considerably in the 1970s and these wage increases had been fairly easily absorbed. In retail pharmacy too, though this was an industry based on low wage levels, the relatively high incomes of professionals and proprietors in the industry suggested that there was scope for female dispensers' and shop assistants' wages to be brought closer to the national average rates for women.

There was no simple relationship between the technology on which women were employed, the skills required of them, and the pay they received. When women used traditional, labour-intensive technology, requiring manual skills and judgement but producing low value added, their jobs were described by managers as labour-intensive or low-productivity work and classed as unskilled. When they were employed in jobs using more advanced technology that produced high value added, attention was focused on the simple nature of the tasks, and the limited amount of experience or judgement required was cited as grounds for giving the jobs a low skill grading. The printing industry provided a good example of the influence of workers' sex on skill grading and pay classifications. Where men were employed on the new technology it was thought reasonable by employers that they should receive an extra premium for the responsibility of operating the expensive machinery, which required accurate and efficient operation for profitability. Where women were employed, the "going rate" for typists was considered the appropriate rate of pay.

The institutional factors

Employment in a unionised firm was consistently the most important factor associated with higher wage levels for women, although only in a few instances were their minimum wage rates above 200 pence per hour. The wage levels for female unskilled and semi-skilled work in all types of firms were concentrated in the range of 140 to 200 pence per hour. Wage rates below that range were almost exclusively found in non-unionised firms, while rates above it were usually found only in unionised firms and a few non-unionised firms with formal payment structures. The collective bargaining system in the particular industry was important in determining the "industry norm"; for example, in 1981 the retail pharmacy Joint Industrial Council (JIC) agreement and the footwear industry collective agreement set relatively low minimum time rates of around 140 pence per hour with the result that time rates in both industries clustered around this level, whereas in printing the minimum rate established by the industry agreement was higher, at around 190 pence per hour, and resulted in a higher cluster of rates in both unionised and non-unionised firms. There was therefore some evidence that collective bargaining agreements had a general effect on the level of going wage rates within each industry. Nevertheless, there were significant differences in wage rates between unionised and non-unionised firms in the same industry. The influence of the type of payment system on wage levels was less clear-cut. Some large non-unionised firms used a formal and sometimes job-evaluated payment system, which bore a close relation to pay levels in unionised establishments. In industries where there was little chance of union-isation, such as retail pharmacy, large firms tended to formalise the payment system primarily for administrative convenience and their policies tended to concentrate pay around the JIC minimum levels for the industry as a whole.

A common feature observed in firms across the six industries was that, where there was no collective bargaining at the firm level and no formal job-based payment system, the range of differentials for production workers tended to be narrow, whereas the pay gap between workers with no formal skills on the one hand and craft or other key workers on the other tended to be rather wide. Firms with formal pay systems tended to have a continuous wage hierarchy with only small differentials between the top rate for one grade and the bottom rate for the next. Firms with informal pay systems tended also to have wider differentials between male and female workers, except when the men had been recruited from disadvantaged labour force groups. Women employed in firms with formal pay systems were still confined to lower grades but the top of their pay scale tended at least to equal or overlap the foot of the male workers' scale.

Firms which did not have formally graded payment structures and instead paid most of their women much the same rates, regardless of job content or experience, also often used an informal system of work organisa-tion. These workers tended to perform a wide range of tasks. Some supervisory tasks might also be shared out or concentrated among the more senior workers, but these responsibilities would not be reflected in either the average level or the structure of pay. For example, in building societies which had introduced a formal grading structure there was a senior cashier in charge of cashing-up the tills at the end of business, but in those societies still operating informal systems the cashing-up was often done in rotation by the cashiers for no extra pay. These homogeneous pay structures were almost always characterised by relatively low wages. Thus in practice there were two possibilities. Either women were employed in firms where they performed a wide range of tasks, including some which involved a high degree of responsibility, but were not compensated for the extra responsibility with higher pay; or they were employed in firms using a specialised division of labour in which the pay and job hierarchy excluded women workers from certain tasks, which were assigned a higher grading.

IV. Implications for labour market segmentation theory and for women's employment

Two main implications for segmentation theory follow from our research findings. Firstly, the pattern of employment organisation outside the formal, large-firm and unionised sector does not fit the hypothesis presented in the dual labour market model according to which such work is mainly unskilled and is carried out by interchangeable and casual workers. Secondly, labour supply factors can be identified as an independent cause of the development of structured or segmented labour markets.

Our findings to the effect that pay levels for production workers in firms using informal payment systems were relatively homogeneous might appear to provide some support for the dichotomy between structured primary labour markets and competitive secondary markets which is assumed in dual labour market theories. However, a closer examination revealed that this homogeneity in pay levels existed despite wide variations in the skills and experience of the workers and the demands of the jobs. Much attention has been focused on the creation of "artificial" hierarchies within formal payment structures; however, where there is no formal pay structure, the *absence* of additional payment to reward skill, experience, responsibility or the performance of unpleasant and demanding work is also important. Firms with informal pay structures often depend on a core of stable workers with a strong commitment to work, even under poor or difficult working conditions (see also Craig et al., 1982). Firm-specific skills make employers dependent on their workforce, but may do little to enhance external employment opportunities for their workers: high returns to employees from firm-specific skills can usually be achieved only through collective organisation at the workplace. If the labour supply is structured or segmented, firms do not have to operate a high-wage internal labour market system in order to obtain a stable labour force. This can be done, for example, by recruiting disadvantaged workers or changing the hours or location of work. The non-hierarchical payment structures found in "secondary-type" firms do not show that a competitive labour market system operates where everyone is paid according to his or her relative worth. They show that the labour supply is segmented and that it is therefore unnecessary for firms to reward workers on the basis of their productivity and contribution to output.

It is also important to note that the clustering of wage levels within a limited range in these firms does not indicate the existence of a market-clearing wage, as assumed in neoclassical theory. It was evident that in general there was an excess supply of women available, especially for part-time work at current wage levels, and that limited job opportunities constituted the main constraint on mobilisation of this labour supply. The factors that maintained wage levels within this range for the majority of firms even in the severe recession of 1980-81 included custom and practice within the firm, the general and specific level of industry collective wage agreements and wages council orders.[5] Expectations formed within the community also had some influence. Some firms did pay wages below conventionally "acceptable" levels, but they constituted a minority; this may seem surprising considering the absence of any legal or trade union controls over employment practices in a large number of the firms in our study, the excess supply of labour and the severity of the recession. These findings suggest that custom and practice, expectations and institutional and social controls are important in determining wage levels in both sectors. Thus primary-type and secondary-type employment conditions emerge not because there are institutionalised systems of wage determination in some firms while competitive wage determination prevails in others, but because institutional and social forces interacting with economic pressures result in relatively high wages in some firms and relatively low wages in others.[6]

Labour supply was found to be a central determinant of job and pay structures but these supply-side factors complemented and did not replace the industrial and technological factors identified in earlier segmentation models (Craig et al., 1985). Labour supply conditions interact with product market and technical conditions in the formation of a segmented employment structure. The survey showed that in some industries the survival of certain firms depended on the employment of workers at low wages relative to their productivity (as in the case of non-unionised printing firms and some electronics components firms); in other industries the character of competitive market conditions reflected the widespread use of low-wage labour (as in plastics processing). One of the main weaknesses of demand-side theories of segmentation is the assumption that market conditions are determined independently of firms' strategies both in the product market and in the labour market. In fact, these strategies collectively influence the conditions in an industry. Low wages are not necessarily a reflection of low productivity; they may simply reveal the absence of widespread trade union organisation. This can be demonstrated by examples from all countries of the passage, over time, of some industries from the secondary (low-wage) to the primary (high-wage) sector (for example, Kahn, 1975; Lawson, 1981).

Demand-side processes which generate a segmented structure of jobs are not separable from the supply-side processes which generate a segmented labour supply to fill these jobs. Firstly, market conditions are not independent of employment practices and, secondly, whatever their location in the industrial structure, jobs take on the characteristics of secondary jobs if they are filled by "secondary-type" workers. The latter proposition can be demonstrated from our survey results: women's employment conditions were relatively poor whatever the industrial context in which they were employed. Our survey also indicated that the most important factor associated with more favourable employment conditions for comparable workers and occupations was unionisation or the likelihood of unionisation. Size of firm, formalisation of payment structures, strong product market position, use of modern technology or reliance on workers' skill and experience were all factors which were frequently associated with higher pay; nevertheless, these factors did not guarantee higher pay without the influence of effective union organisation. However, the development of unionisation itself requires explanation, and evidence suggests that it is linked to favourable industrial conditions as well as to social and political conditions.

Union organisation cannot therefore be taken as an independent or sole explanation of relatively high pay. Nevertheless, in our survey high pay was seldom found in the absence of strong labour organisation.

It is notable that although unionisation affects relative pay for men and for women, it has not usually sufficed by itself to raise women's pay much above the level of unprotected male labour. Union organisation at the place of work is by no means the only social and institutional force underpinning wage hierarchies. While there is no doubt that union organisation and collective bargaining influence the pay and grading of jobs, our study indicates that other characteristics of the labour force, namely sex, race and formal qualifications, also influence the relative status and pay of a job. This happens even when the employers themselves do not expect these characteristics to affect actual or potential performance on the job.

Our research also suggests that more needs to be understood about the forces that generate a segmented or structured labour supply. Our survey of employers was supplemented by a small-scale survey of employees which indicated that workers' expectations were conditioned both by their perception of employment opportunities and by their position in the family, which determined their income needs and domestic responsibilities. This finding does not mean that opportunities and employment requirements are adequately matched in practice. Women were prepared to take low-paid and unrewarding jobs not because of weak attachment to work and limited income needs but because of the importance of their earnings to family living standards and the constraints on their choice of job. Indeed some of the women in our survey were the sole or main bread-winners and, because of the extent to which their households relied on their earnings, were particularly stable and conscientious employees. Mismatching between family income needs and employment opportunities is probably increasing, for both men and women, as a result of the contraction of employment. Women's position in the social and family structure and their relative job opportunities are subject to continual change. Nevertheless, our research shows that in the United Kingdom the single most important factor structuring the system of pay and employment is still the division between male and female employees.

Notes

[1] The project formed part of the programme of research by the Labour Studies Group at the Department of Applied Economics and we are grateful to our colleagues Roger Tarling and Frank Wilkinson for their help in this research.

[2] Labour market segmentation literature has introduced the terms "primary sector" and "secondary sector" to denote sectors of the labour market where markedly different terms and conditions of employment obtain. The primary sector offers high pay, secure employment prospects and good conditions of employment; the secondary sector offers low pay, unstable job prospects and poor conditions of employment (Doeringer and Piore, 1971). Some authors

identify subsectors within the main primary-secondary sector dichotomy. For an introduction to the theory of structured labour markets and workforce divisions see Garnsey et al. (1985).

[3] *Informal* payment systems are usually either ad hoc systems, where pay is determined on an individual basis between employer and worker, or systems which establish a common wage rate for most workers without providing differential rewards for skills, experience or additional responsibilities. *Formal* payment structures result from a systematic method of grading jobs and workers and of calculating related earnings levels. They are usually made explicit in a written statement of pay and employment policy.

[4] Where the piece-rate system was applied a few exceptional women closers earned more than men.

[5] Wages councils have fixed legal minimum wages for specific industries: there is no national minimum wage and industry agreements are no longer legally enforceable.

[6] See Stretton (1983) for another example of a case where wages are controlled by institutional and social forces under apparently "competitive" market conditions.

References

Craig, C.; Garnsey, E.; Rubery, J. 1985. *Payment structures in smaller firms: Women's employment in segmented labour markets*. London, Department of Employment Research Paper No. 48.

Craig, C.; Rubery, J.; Tarling, R.; and Wilkinson, F. 1982. *Labour market structure, industrial organisation and low pay*. Cambridge, Cambridge University Press.

—. 1985. "Economic, social and political factors in the operation of the labour market", in B. Roberts, R. Finnegan and D. Gallie (eds.): *New approaches to economic life: Economic restructuring, unemployment and the social division of labour*. Manchester, Manchester University Press.

Department of Employment. 1981. *New earnings survey 1981*. London, HM Stationery Office.

Doeringer, P., and Piore, M. 1971. *Internal labor markets and manpower analysis*. Lexington, Massachusetts, D. C. Heath.

Garnsey, E.; Rubery, J.; and Wilkinson, F. 1985. "Labour market structure and workforce divisions", in R. Deem and G. Salaman (eds.): *Work and society*. London, Open University Press.

Gordon, D. M.; Edwards, R.; and Reich, M. 1982. *Segmented work, divided workers: The historical transformation of labour in the United States*. Cambridge, Cambridge University Press.

Kahn, L. 1975. *Unions and labor market segmentation*. Ph.D. dissertation. Berkeley, University of California.

Lawson, T. 1981. "Paternalism and labour market segmentation theory", in F. Wilkinson (ed.): *The dynamics of labour market segmentation*. London, Academic Press.

Martin, J., and Roberts, C. 1984. *Women and employment. A lifetime perspective*. Report of the 1980 Department of Employment/Office of Population Censuses and Surveys Women and Employment Survey. London, HM Stationery Office.

Rubery, J. 1978. "Structured labour markets, worker organisation and low pay", in *Cambridge Journal of Economics* (London), Mar.

Stretton, A. 1983. "Circular migration, segmented labour markets and efficiency: The building industry in Manila and Port Moresby", in *International Labour Review*, Sep.-Oct.

[26]

Social welfare policies

Sex-role socialization and occupational segregation: an exploratory investigation

MARY E. CORCORAN and PAUL N. COURANT

Considerable research suggests that sex-based differences in such qualifications as years of schooling, the timing and duration of work experience, and labor force attachment do not explain the bulk either of the sex-based wage gap or of sex-based occupational segregation (see, for example, England and McCreary, 1986; Duncan and Corcoran, 1984; Corcoran, Duncan, and Ponza, 1984; England, 1982, 1984; Bielby and Baron, 1986; Treiman and Hartmann, 1981; Oaxaca. 1973). This presents a puzzle for many neoclassical economists who predict that group wage differences which are not due to group skill differences ought to be eroded over time by competitive forces (Arrow, 1972a, 1972b; Corcoran and Courant, 1985; Lewin and England,

Mary E. Corcoran is in the Department of Political Science and Institute of Public Policy Studies at the University of Michigan, and Paul N. Courant is in the Department of Economics and Institute of Public Policy Studies at the University of Michigan.

The project was funded by the Rockefeller Foundation and by the Institute for Research on Poverty Small Grant Program supported by the U.S. Department of Health and Human Services. The authors are especially grateful to Deborah Laren for handling the computer work on this study, for helpful suggestions about the analysis plan, and for editing advice. They also want to thank Martha Hill and Michael Ponza for giving them a copy of the Hill–Ponza parent–child datafile from the Panel Study of Income Dynamics, for allowing them to use their computer programs, and for providing considerable advice. Helpful comments from Gary Solon, from Sara McLanahan, and from participants in the University of Michigan American Institutions, Institute for Public Policy Studies, and Public Finance Seminars are gratefully acknowledged. Thanks are also due the participants of a joint U.S.-France conference on social welfare policy. None of the above individuals or institutions is responsible for any opinions expressed in this paper.

1986). Some researchers argue that the solution to this puzzle lies in events that occur prior to labor market entrance and that extending economic models of women's wages and occupational choices to include early sex-role socialization and pre–labor market discrimination may help explain the persistence of male/female differences in labor market outcomes (Killingsworth, 1985; Corcoran and Courant, 1985, 1986; and England and McCreary, 1986).

Certainly, the psychological literature suggests that boys and girls are raised in ways that tend to foster consistency with traditional sex roles. Eccles and Hoffman (1984) and Marini and Brinton (1984) claim that early sex-role socialization might influence boys' and girls' later economic behavior in two distinct ways. First, boys and girls are encouraged to develop different skills and personality traits. Girls, for example, are encouraged to be more passive, more people-oriented, and less mathematical than are boys. It could be that such sex differences in skills and personality traits mean that young men and women are differentially prepared for different kinds of jobs. Eccles and Hoffman (1984) also argue that socialization affects girls' and boys' preferences for performing particular tasks, with each sex tending to prefer sex-appropriate activities. This could lead to a situation where, on average, boys and girls have different incentives for choosing a particular job, even when there are no sex differences in abilities to perform that job.

At least three sets of researchers have attempted to bring sex-role socialization into economic models of women's labor market behavior. Killingsworth (1985) notes that "systematic differences in sex preferences rather than employer discrimination may account for at least some of the negative association . . . between overall average pay . . . and the proportion female in different jobs." Corcoran and Courant (1985; 1986) posit a model based on the statistical discrimination and screening literatures. In this model, sex differences in tastes, skills, and economic outcomes at one point influence employers' subjective evaluations of men and women workers; as a result, employers treat men and women differently, and these sex-based differences in treatment feed back into the next generation's sex-role socialization process. England and McCreary (1986) also argue that the labor markets feed into the sex-role socialization process and further argue that sex-role socialization may lead men to devalue women's attributes and so produce the motivation for future discrimination.

While there is considerable debate about how sex-role socialization might influence individual economic behavior, there is virtually no empirical evidence that links family sex-role socialization with actual labor market outcomes for a nationally representative sample of adult men and women. In this paper we report on three empirical exercises, all of which tend to confirm the idea that men and women have different tastes and talents (on average) when they get to the labor market and that these differences are in part due to socialization and training of boys and girls that is oriented toward maintenance of traditional sex roles.

The ideal way to explore how sex-role socialization influences economic behaviors would involve following a panel of children over time and examining how their family environments and their school environments affected their sex-role attitudes and aspirations; how families, schools, attitudes, and aspirations influenced decisions about investment in education and training; and how families, schools, attitudes, aspirations, and human capital affected job choice and wages. At key decision points—choice of college major, first job, and so on—we would need to ask detailed questions about the factors that influenced those decisions, particularly about paths not taken. We know of no data that would allow us to take this approach.[1]

We can, however, use currently available data to take a preliminary look at whether socialization might be important. At this stage we are looking for evidence of three types of relevant phenomena: (1) different tratment of boys and girls that will tend to provide boys with an advantage in the labor market; (2) direct links between the sex-role relevant labor market behavior of parents and that of their children's adult labor market behavior; and (3) labor market behavior on the part of adults that can be best explained as arising from the fact that men and women value traditional sex roles. None of these types of evidence would be as convincing as that which might be developed with the ideal data set discussed in the preceding paragraph, but it is worth noting that all three types of phenomena are quite different from each other, and finding examples of all three would suggest that socialization can have powerful effects on the adult labor market outcomes of men and women.

For the first two types of phenomena, we use a sample of young adults aged 25–30 years in 1981 to see if family factors that have been shown to influence sex differentiation in attitudes and aspirations also

---

[1] And even here we would not have examined the operation of the labor market itself.

affect education and occupational choice. For the third, we look at an unusual sample of couples—couples for whom wives' predicted hourly earnings exceed the husbands' predicted hourly earnings. If couples try to maximize income when making decisions about labor market work and family time, then these couples ought, on average, to have a nontraditional division of labor within the household and the wives' actual wages ought to exceed the husbands' actual wages.

Family socialization, education, and sex-typicality of jobs

A key assumption of socialization-based explanations of male–female wage differences is that sex-role patterns learned in childhood will affect adult economic behavior. Psychological studies of children's socialization have identified the following family factors which tend to reduce sex-role differentiation on psychological dimensions such as attitudes or aspirations: being raised in a female-headed household, being raised in a family with children of one sex, and having nontraditional parents (see Eccles and Hoffman, 1984, and Marini and Brinton, 1984, for summaries of this research). But no studies have yet established a link between early family socialization and women's actual labor market behaviors for a nationally representative sample of women.

We use a subset of young adults from the Panel Study of Income Dynamics (PSID) of the University of Michigan to test for such a link. PSID provides 14 years (1968–1981) of data for a nationally representative sample of 1,480 individuals aged 12–17 in 1968. These individuals were 25–30 years old in 1981.[2] All were children in their parents' homes in 1968 and had established their own homes by 1981. About 800 are women. For each of these young adults PSID provides measures of parental and family characteristics reported by the parents during the years the young adults lived in their parental homes and labor market information reported by the young adults after they had left home.

This PSID sample has both advantages and disadvantages for our purposes. Its strongest advantage is the richness of data on parents. Most important, PSID provides measures of the nature, timing, and duration of mothers' labor market behaviors as reported by the moth-

[2]This age range was chosen to ensure representativeness. Most children remain living with parents until age 17, and most have left home by age 25 years. See Hill et al. (1983) for a more extensive description of this sample.

ers. Psychological theories of sex-role socialization strongly emphasize the importance of identification with and role modeling of the
same-sex parent. PSID permits a direct test of whether girls emulate
mothers' work behaviors.

Two disadvantages are the relative youth of the PSID sample and the
lack of any direct measure of sex-role attitudes. At ages 25–30 years,
many young adults are still launching their careers, and so this sample
is not well suited for examining wages and wage growth. Therefore, we
concentrate on examining only education and the sex-typicality of occupations for these young adults. By age 25–30 years, most young adults
will have completed their schooling. And family socialization effects
on the choice of sex-appropriate occupations should be strongest early
in workers' careers, when young adults are leaving their parental family to establish their own households. The lack of a good measure of
sex-role attitudes means that we cannot directly test a key prediction of
socialization models—that is, that women who value traditional roles
will be more likely to choose "female" jobs. Instead, we test whether
family characteristics that have been shown to affect sex-role attitudes
also affect education and the choice of a "female" job. This is a much
weaker test.

Table 1 defines the variables we used in our analyses.[3] Two outcome
measures are examined for young women: educational attainment and
sex-typicality of jobs held since leaving home. Education equations are
also estimated for young men to see if families exert similar effects on
boys' and girls' schooling. All equations will be estimated separately
by race, since it has been argued that different processes may govern
both educational attainment and sex-role socialization for blacks and
whites (Barnett and Baruch, 1978; Dorr and Lesser, 1980; Datcher,
1981; Eccles and Hoffman, 1984).

We regress our outcome measures on three sets of predictor variables. First, we include as controls the following conventional background measures: family income, father's education, mother's education, father's occupation, and number of siblings. With the exception
of parental schooling, these should have similar effects on boys' and

---

[3]There are relatively little missing data on the predictor variables used in these analyses, since parents provided contemporaneous reports of their attributes. We deal
with missing data on predictor variables by using pair-wise deletion when creating
matrices for ordinary least square (OLS) regression. There are also relatively little
missing data on outcome measures. Any cases with missing data on outcomes are
dropped from analysis runs.

girls' attainments. If children emulate the same-sex parents, then father's education should be a more powerful predictor for men's schooling, and mother's education should be a more powerful predictor for women's schooling.

The second set of predictor variables includes three measures of mothers' work behavior: proportion of family income earned by mother, proportion of time worked by mother while the child was at home, and sex-typicality of mother's work experience. (See Table 1 for definitions of these variables.) These first two variables are included to pick up the extent of mothers' labor market commitment, following past research that indicates that girls whose mothers have worked extensively have more realistic work expectations, plan to work more in the future, and have more knowledge of occupations than other girls (see Marini and Brinton, 1984, pp. 210–211, for a summary of this research). However, extensive maternal work need not mean that mothers are transmitting aspirations for nontraditional market work to daughters, since most mothers, like most women, are employed in "female" jobs. An additional complication is that families in which mothers work a lot and contribute a large proportion of family income are likely to have less time and fewer resources than do families with similar levels of incomes in which mothers do not work. This ought to dampen achievement outcomes for both sons and daughters. Probably the cleanest measure of mothers' sex-role-relevant labor market behavior is the sex-typicality of jobs held by the mother.[4] Since "female" jobs are not characterized by low education, the sex-typicality of mothers' jobs likely will not affect daughters' schooling choices, but ought to affect their job choices.

The third set of variables includes four family composition variables: whether the child had a sibling of the opposite sex, an interaction between whether the child had a sibling of the opposite sex and family income, whether the child ever lived in a mother-only family, and years lived in a mother-only family. Eccles and Hoffman (1984) argue that there may be less sex-role stereotyping of daughters in families without sons. Girls may do better when they are not compared to—or do not compare themselves to—brothers, and parents may have higher aspirations for daughters when they have no sons. The opposite-sex sibling measure will test for this. Eccles and Hoffman also argue that parents may be less likely to differentiate between brothers and sisters in

[4]This could arise from tastes or "steering" into sex-typical jobs. In either case, it is readily observable by both researchers and daughters.

Table 1

Family background measures and child's outcome measures

Variable	Definition
Conventional background measures	
Family income	Annual family income (in thousands of 1980 dollars) averaged over the years child lived at home
Father's education	Years of schooling attained by father as reported by the father[a]
Mother's education	Years of schooling attained by mother as reported by the mother[a]
Father's occupation	Duncan scores of father's one-digit census occupations averaged over the years child lived at home[b]
Number of siblings	Number of child's brothers and sisters
Measures of mother's work behavior	
Proportion of family income earned by mother	Labor income earned by mother during the years child lived at home divided by total family income during that period
Mother's proportion time worked	Total time worked by mother during years while child lived at home divided by the product of the number of years child lived at home and 2,000
Sex typicality of mother's work experience	The percentage female in mother's occupation–industry categories averaged over the 14-year sample period.[c] Women who *never* worked during this time were assigned the sample mean.[d]
Family composition measures	
Mother-only household	= 1 if child ever lived in a mother-only household before leaving home[e] = 0 otherwise
Duration in mother-only household	Number of years child lived in a mother-only household[e]
Opposite-sex sibling	= 1 if an opposite-sex child aged 0–17 years lived in child's parental home in 1968 = 0 otherwise
Opposite-sex sibling × family income	Family income if there is an opposite-sex sibling = 0 otherwise
Outcome measures	
Child's education	Years of schooling completed by child
Sex-typicality of child's work experience	The percentage female in child's occupation–industry categories averaged over the period after which the child had left home. (This is coded in the same way as is sex-typicality of mother's work experience.)

families with abundant resources. We include the interaction term to
see if there is more differentiation between brothers and sisters in low-
income families. Theorists have also argued that there should be less
sex-role differentiation among children, particularly boys, raised in
female-headed households, since there is no "male" role model for
boys and since women who head households often must take on
nontraditional roles—for example, provider or disciplinarian. However, as McLanahan (1983) points out, absence of the father could also
affect children by reducing economic resources and parental time available to children within the family. Thus, the measures of father absence
may influence outcomes through several very different processes, and
the net effect could go either way.

Table 2 gives the results for educational attainment. There is one
major sex difference across the equations for nonblacks. Young
nonblack women with brothers acquire significantly less education than
do young nonblack women without brothers. This effect diminishes
with income.[5] There is no such effect for nonblack men. Nonblack men
with sisters do not acquire more education than do nonblack men
without sisters. Since we control for number of siblings in these analyses, this does not occur as a result of nonblack girls with brothers
coming from larger families. A second possibility may be that the
presence of brothers reduces education for both young nonblack men
and young nonblack women. To test for this, we added a same-sex

------

Notes to Table 1

[a]The child's report of parental education was used for cases with missing data on these
variables.
[b]The child's report of father's occupation was used for cases with missing data on this
variable.
[c]Industry is coded into two-digit categories for 1971 to 1981. Occupation is coded into one-
digit categories for the years 1971–74 and into two-digit categories for all the years thereafter.
For each occupation–industry subgroup, we calculated a measure of percentage female. (See
Corcoran, Duncan, and Ponza, 1983, for a more complete description of this procedure.)
[d]A dummy variable indicating whether the mother never worked is included to control for
possible measurement error.
[e]We were unable to obtain information on these two measures for children whose fathers reported being in their second marriage in 1968—about 15 percent of the sample. We included a
dummy variable for second marriages to control for possible measurement problems in all
analyses using these measures.

[5]Taking the regression results literally, the effect vanishes at the 74th percentile of
the income distribution. That is, the net effect of opposite-sex sibling and opposite-
sex sibling × income is negative for 74.2 percent of nonblack women with
brothers.

Table 2

Regression for young adults' education by race and sex (young adults aged 25–30 in 1981 who were living with parents in 1968 and who had left home by 1981)

Variable[a]	Nonblack women	Nonblack men	Black women	Black men
Family income	.0028 (.0096)	.0114 (.0116)	−.0467† (.0234)	.1082‡ (.0305)
Father's occupation	.0285‡ (.0066)	.0010 (.0067)	.0212‡ (.0075)	.0140 (.0099)
Father's education	.0781† (.0379)	.1708‡ (.0403)	.0321 (.0299)	.0641 (.0396)
Mother's educaton	.1260‡ (.0392)	.1296‡ (.0483)	.0184 (.0419)	−.0344 (.0416)
Proportion of family income earned by mother	−.0714 (1.0574)	1.6856 (1.3249)	.5874 (.9020)	3.3597‡ (1.2331)
Mother's proportion of time worked	.2126 (.5095)	−.3337 (.5853)	.2945 (.5921)	−2.1838‡ (.7562)
Sex-typicality of mother's work experience	−.1279 (.4820)	.5564 (.4822)	−.2455 (.4341)	.2950 (.6043)
Whether lived in mother-only household	−.3767 (.3327)	−.6309 (.4233)	−1.1052‡ (.3009)	−.9597‡ (.3561)
Duration in mother-only household	.0378 (.0355)	.0086 (.0497	.0520† (.0242)	.0516† (.0247)
Opposite-sex sibling	−.7955† (.3868)	.0007 (.4678)	−1.5537† (.4387)	1.0374* (.5394)
Opposite-sex sibling × income	.0210† (.0102)	.0019 (.0130)	.0900‡ (.0229)	−.0683† (.0310)
Number of siblings	−.0948† (.0414)	−.1155† (.0504)	.0013 (.0399)	−.1013† (.0429)
N	453	405	326	282
R²	.364	.268	.304	.251

Note: Standard errors are shown in parentheses below the coefficients.
*Significant at the 10 percent level.
†Significant at the 5 percent level.
‡Significant at the 1 percent level.
[a]Controls are also added for mothers who never worked outside the home and fathers who were in their second marriage in 1968.

sibling measure and an interaction term between same-sex sibling and income to the nonblack men's education equations. Results show no effect of brothers on nonblack men's schooling (not shown in table).

Sex differences for blacks in the effects of an opposite-sex sibling on schooling differed somewhat from those of nonblacks. Like nonblack women, black women with brothers acquire less schooling than do black women without brothers, and this effect is larger at lower levels of income.[6] However, while having sisters had no effect on nonblack men's education, black men with sisters were actually at an educational advantage—relative to black men without sisters—and this effect decreased as income increased.

We also tested to see whether having brothers hurt black men's schooling by adding a same-sex sibling measure and an interaction between same-sex sibling and income to the black men's education regression. The presence of brothers had no direct effect on black men's schooling, but the interaction term was negative and significant, suggesting that, at higher levels of family income, having a brother did reduce black men's schooling (not shown in table).

Other results are about as expected. Family status variables have generally positive effects on education—though the parental schooling measures are not significantly related to schooling for young blacks. Father's education also has a much larger effect on men's schooling that on women's schooling for nonblacks, but this difference is not statistically significant. The measures of mother's work behavior have no consistent effects on educational attainment for either blacks or nonblacks. There are, however, large effects on black men's schooling; black men's schooling goes up with the proportion of family income earned by their mothers and drops with mother's time spent working. This absence of consistent effects of mothers' work behavior on children's schooling is not surprising given that most of these variables may be picking up effects of omitted social class, available parental time, and trauma due to family breakup. Finally, living in a mother-only home lowered schooling for both black women and black men, and these effects diminished with the time spent in a mother-only home.

Table 3 reports the results of estimating the sex-typicality of young women's work experience after leaving home. Here, results are quite consistent with predictions of sex-role socialization theories. Women whose mothers worked in female-dominated fields tend also to work in such fields. Effects are sizeable and significant for both black and nonblack women, and effects for black women are 75 percent higher than those for nonblack women. There are few consistent or significant effects of the other maternal work variables, suggesting that the kinds of jobs mothers hold are more important than how much or whether or

[6]Here, again taking the specification literally, the net effect was negative for the lower income 70 percent of black women with brothers.

Table 3

Regression for sex-typicality of young women's work experience by race (young women aged 25–30 in 1981 who were living with parents in 1968 and who had left home by 1981)

Variable[a]	Nonblack women	Black women
Family income	−.0002 (.0010)	−.0002 (.0022)
Father's occupation	−.0011 (.0007)	.0018† (.0007)
Father's education	−.0001 (.0040)	−.0021 (.0029)
Mother's education	.0013 (.0042)	−.0053 (.0039)
Proportion of family income earned by mother	−.0946 (.1114)	−.0392 (.0863)
Mother's proportion of time worked	.0485 (.0539)	.0879 (.0574)
Sex-typicality of mother's work experience	.1355‡ (.0509)	.2522‡ (.0418)
Whether lived in mother-only household	−.0501 (.0351)	−.0744‡ (.0283)
Duration in mother-only household	.0071* (.0038)	.0054† (.0023)
Opposite-sex sibling	−.0090 (.0410)	−.0227 (.0420)
Opposite-sex sibling × income	−.0002 (.0011)	.0022 (.0022)
Number of siblings	.0007 (.0044)	−.0003 (.0037)
Education	−.0083* (.0050)	−.0070 (.0055)
N	445	317
R²	.063	.168

Note: Standard errors are shown in parentheses below the coefficients.
*Significant at the 10 percent level.
†Significant at the 5 percent level.
‡Significant at the 1 percent level.
[a]Controls are also added for mothers who never worked outside the home and fathers who were in their second marriage in 1968.

not they work. It may be that the maternal work variables affect other aspects of economic attainment such as labor force participation or wages. The conventional background and family composition measures are always insignificant for nonblack women and often insignificant for black women, suggesting that social class and family structure have few effects on young women's taste for sex-appropriate work.

Division of labor in potentially nontraditional households

Another way to investigate sex-role socialization is to examine the wages and work behavior of husbands and wives in couples where the wives' predicted earnings exceed the husbands' predicted earnings. In such families, wives have an absolute earnings advantage. According to Becker's (1974) production theory of marriage, the spouse with the higher wage rate ought to specialize in the market while the other spouse (the husband) ought to specialize in home production. Thus, if only economics matters, in most of these families the wives' actual wages should exceed husbands' actual wages and husbands should spend relatively more time than wives in home production.[7]

We used a sample of 3,066 pairs of married male household heads and wives in 1982 taken from PSID to investigate this issue. Couples were excluded if either spouse was over 64 years old, a student, retired, or disabled. For each husband–wife pair, we constructed measures of predicted hourly wages for both husband and wife. The earnings functions used to construct these predicted wage measures estimated hourly wages as a function of education, age, age squared, whether they lived in the South, and city size. The sample used for the men's equations was: all employed men under 65 years who were not students, retired, or disabled. The sample for the women's equation was: all employed women under 65 years who were not students, retired, or disabled and *who had worked continuously since leaving school*.[8] We restricted the sample to women who had continuous employment in order to estimate women's expected wage given that women do not stay at home for family responsibilities. We mean this to measure a woman's labor market opportunities upon completion of schooling.

Wives' expected hourly earnings exceeded husbands' expected hourly earnings for only 133 of the 3,066 husband–wife pairs (4.3 percent). These were very unusual couples: wives averaged about four years more schooling than did their husbands (12.8 versus 8.7). Wives' actual earnings exceeded husbands' actual earnings for only 33 of these 133 pairs (25 percent). This is far fewer than one would expect if families are solely income maximizers.

[7] This assumes husbands and wives are equally talented at home production.

[8] We also ran the equation for all women employed in the most recent year. The conclusions from that formulation are essentially the same as those reported in the text.

As a next step, we estimated the following equation for the 133 husband–wife pairs in which the wives had higher expected earnings than did their husbands.

$$p = a_0 + B_1 \, ed_h + B_2 \, exp_h$$

$$+ \, B_3 \, exp_h{}^2 + B_4 \, ten_h$$

$$+ \, a_1 \, ed_w + a_2 \, exp_w + a_3 \, exp_w{}^2$$

$$+ \, a_4 \, ten_w$$

where

p = 1 if wife's actual wage was larger than husband's wage;
    = 0 otherwise;
ed = years of school completed;
exp = work experience prior to current employer;
ten = years employed with current employer;
h = husband;
w = wife.

Here the dependent variable is a dummy variable that takes on a value of 1 when the wife's wage exceeds the husband's wage. The predictor variables are measures of the husband's and wife's education, work experience, and job tenure.

Table 4 reports the results when the equation is estimated using ordinary least squares.[9] The results are no surprise. Only two of the eight predictor variables have significant coefficients: wife's and husband's job tenure. The higher the wife's job tenure, the more likely her wage will exceed her husband's wage. The higher the husband's job tenure, the less likely his wife's wage will exceed his wage.

Since job tenure of both spouses seems to be a key factor in predicting which spouse will have higher wages, we regressed job tenure on potential experience (age − education − 6) and on number of children under age 14 years, separately for husbands and wives. Table 5 reports

---

[9]The same pattern of results is obtained when this model is estimated using probit analysis.

Table 4

Regression for dummy variable measuring whether wife's wage is greater than husband's wage (in all husband–wife pairs, wife's predicted wage exceeded husband's predicted wage)

Variable	
Husband's education	.0166 (.0288)
Wife's education	−.0134 (.0246)
Husband's experience prior to current job	.0038 (.0127)
Husband's experience squared	−.0002 (.0003)
Wife's experience prior to current job	.0137 (.0178)
Wife's experience squared	−.0002 (.0008)
Husband's job tenure	−.0243* (.0082)
Wife's job tenure	.0603* (.0130)
R^2	.219

Note: Standard errors are shown in parentheses below the coefficients.
*Significant at the 1 percent level.

Table 5

Regression for job tenure of each spouse

Variable	Husbands	Wives
Potential experience	.2303* (.0333)	.0862* (.0227)
Number of children younger than 14	−.0791 (.3901)	−.5849* (.2007)
R^2	.271	.159

Note: Standard errors are shown in parentheses below the coefficients.
*Significant at the 1 percent level.

the results. For wives, number of children strongly predicts job tenure. For each child under age 14, a wife's job tenure drops by .58 years. There is no effect of children on husband's job tenure. Thus, even in families in which wives have higher predicted earnings than do husbands, children reduce the wife's job tenure, but have no effect on the husband's job tenure. This, in turn, reduces the chances that wives will actually attain higher earnings than their husbands. This behavior, of course, is completely consistent with the proposition that one partner (or both) values traditional sex roles. Indeed, in this case, there is a clear monetary value placed on traditionality.

Conclusions

These empirical results tend to confirm the idea that pre-labor market differences between boys and girls may be important. The result concerning the effect of brothers on the schooling of nonblack girls indicates that families treat boys and girls differently in a way that advantages boys once they enter the labor market. If families do this in one way, it is plausible that they do it in other ways as well. Indeed, our results are especially interesting in light of the well-known fact that the typical courses of study undertaken by boys and girls are quite different from each other. Earlier in this paper, we suggested that unmeasured human capital differences might arise from sex-role socialization—girls might value behaviors that were relatively unprofitable in the labor market. It may also be the case that what girls study in school has effects on what they are able to do as women. If so, the fact that families treat boys and girls differently as regards schooling may be doubly important. The obvious research implication of this is to find out whether course of study has effects on pay and occupation (Project TALENT of the American Institutes for Research, and the Survey of Income and Program Participation, carried out by the Census Bureau, may provide some help here). While as a general matter we do not believe that further exploration of human capital explanations of pay differentials will be very informative in distinguishing between discrimination and socialization, the human capital approach could be very instructive in determining whether differences in the content of boys' and girls' schooling matter in the labor market.

That the sex-typicality of mothers' occupations influences that of daughters' also tends to indicate that sex-role socialization matters in the labor market behavior of women. Again, we find this result to be suggestive of a process at work rather than a description of the process or a good measure of its power. With better measures of the ways in which the upbringing of boys differs from that of girls, we would expect to see more of an effect, rather than less.

Finally, the finding that consistency with traditional sex roles regarding child rearing versus market work seems to be more important in determining household division of labor than is income maximization also supports the idea that, at the level of the labor market, different tastes (presumably arising from socialization) account for some of the differences between the behavior of men and that of women. In a way, the result is not surprising—it is universally known that women do most of the child rearing. Yet it is hard to account for either the finding or its plausibility unless one believes that there are powerful forces at work leading members of both sexes to perform traditional roles. That the outcome of these forces is readily observable in this case suggests that they may also be at work in other cases that are relevant to differences in pay between men and women.

We began by arguing that socialization might be an important part of an explanation of male–female pay differentials. Our findings here suggest that this indeed may be the case, although, in order to find out how the process works and how important it is, a great deal of work remains to be done.

REFERENCES

Arrow, K. "Models of Job Discrimination." In *Racial Discrimination in Economic Life*. Ed. by A. H. Pascal. Lexington, MA: D.C. Heath and Co., 1972a, pp. 83-102.

————. "Some Mathematical Models of Race in the Labor Market." In *Racial Discrimination in Economic Life*. Ed. by A. H. Pascal. Lexington, MA: D.C. Heath and Co., 1972b, pp. 187-204.

Barnett, R. C., and Baruch, G. K. *The Competent Woman*. New York: Halstead Press, 1978.

Becker, G. "A Theory of Marriage." In *Economics of the Family: Marriage, Children, and Human Capital*. Ed. by T. W. Schultz. Chicago: University of Chicago Press, 1974, pp. 299-344.

Bielby, W. T., and Baron, J. N. "Men and Women at Work: Sex Segregation and Statistical Discrimination." *American Journal of Sociology*, 1986.

Corcoran, M., and Courant, P. "Sex-Role Socialization and Labor Market Outcomes." *American Economic Review*, May 1985, *75* (2), 275-278.

————. Sex-Role Socialization, Statistical Discrimination and Women's Work: A Reformulation of Neoclassical and Structural Models of Wage Discrimination and Job Segregation. Manuscript, 1986.

Corcoran, M., and Duncan, G. "Work History, Labor Force Attachment, and Earnings Differences Between the Races and Sexes." *Journal of Human Resources*, Winter 1979, *14* (1), 3-20.

Corcoran, M.; Duncan, G.; and Ponza, M. "Work Experience and Wage Growth of Women Workers." In *Five Thousand American Families—Patterns of Economic Progress*. Ed. by G. Duncan and J. Morgan. Vol. 10. Ann Arbor, MI: Institute for Social Research, University of Michigan, 1983, pp. 249-323.

————. "Work Experience, Job Segregation, and Wages." In *Sex Segregation in the*

Workplace: Trends, Explanations, Remedies. Ed. by B. F. Reskin. Washington, D.C.: National Academy Press, 1984, pp. 171–191.

Datcher, L. P. "Race/Sex Differences in the Effects of Background on Achievement." In *Five Thousand American Families—Patterns of Economic Progress.* Ed. by M. S. Hill, D. H. Hill, and J. N. Morgan. Vol. 9. Ann Arbor, MI: Institute for Social Research, University of Michigan, 1981, pp. 359–390.

Dorr, A., and Lesser, G. S. "Career Awareness in Young Children." In *Women, Communication and Careers.* Ed. by M. Greene-Partsche and G. J. Robinson. Munich: K. G. Saur, 1980, pp. 36–75.

Duncan, G. J., and Corcoran, M. "Do Women 'Deserve' to Earn Less than Men?" In *Years of Poverty, Years of Plenty.* Ed. by Duncan et al. Ann Arbor, MI: Institute for Social Research, University of Michigan, 1984, pp. 153–172.

Eccles, J. P., and Hoffman, L. W. "Sex Differences in Preparation for Occupational Roles." In *Child Development and Social Policy.* Ed. by H. Stevenson and A. Siegel. Chicago: University of Chicago Press, 1984, pp. 367–420.

England, P. "The Failure of Human Capital Theory to Explain Occupational Sex Segregation." *Journal of Human Resources,* Summer 1982, *17* (3), 358–370.

————. "Wage Appreciation and Depreciation: A Test of Neoclassical Economic Explanations of Occupational Sex Segregation." *Social Forces,* 1984, *62,* 726–749.

England, P., and McCreary, L. "Gender Inequality in Paid Employment." In *Analyzing Gender.* Ed. by M. Feree and B. Hess. Beverly Hills, CA: Sage, 1986.

Hill, M. S., et al. "Final Report of the Project: Motivation and Economic Mobility of the Poor. Part 1: Intergenerational and Short-Run Dynamic Analyses." Ann Arbor, MI: Institute for Social Research, University of Michigan, August 1983.

Killingsworth, M. "The Case for and Economic Consequences of Comparable Worth." In *Comparable Worth: New Directions for Research.* Ed. by H. I. Hartmann. Washington, DC: National Academy Press, 1985.

Lewin, P., and England, P. Reconceptualizing Statistical Discrimination. Photocopy, 1986.

McLanahan, S. Family Structure and the Reproduction of Poverty. IRP Discussion Paper No. 720A-83. Madison, WI: Institute for Research on Poverty, University of Wisconsin, 1983.

Marini, M. M., and Brinton, M. C. "Sex Typing in Occupational Socialization." In *Sex Segregation in the Workplace: Trends, Explanations, Remedies.* Ed. by B. F. Reskin. Washington, DC: National Academy Press, 1984, pp. 192–232.

Oaxaca, R. "Male-Female Wage Differentials in Urban Labor Markets." *International Economic Review,* October 1973. *14* (3), 693–709.

Treiman, D. J., and Hartmann, H. I., eds. *Women, Work, and Wages: Equal Pay for Jobs of Equal Value.* Washington, DC: National Academy Press, 1981.

[27]

5l2 - 39
[1990]

Work, Employment & Society, Vol. 4, No. 2, pp. 189–216

June 1990

Abstract: A survey of a random sample of over 600 employed adults in the Northampton area is used to compare men's and women's perceptions of the content of their jobs and to construct an index of skill. Differences were found between men and women in perceptions of both the types of skills required in their jobs, with women emphasising personal and social skills, and in the level of skill involved. Men's jobs on average appeared to be higher skilled, but the main difference was found in fact not to be by gender but between full- and part-time jobs. Some of these differences may be related to differences in perceptions of skill. Women part-timers were much less likely than men to perceive their jobs as skilled, even when sharing similar perceptions of job content.

UK
J/6
J24

GENDER AND SKILLS

Sara Horrell, Jill Rubery and Brendan Burchell

Introduction[1]

Current debates over women's position in the labour market often centre on the question of how women's jobs compare in quality, job content and skill requirements to those of men's. Are women segregated into jobs which make different types of demands on employees than those that men occupy? Can women's low pay be explained by their concentration in lower skilled jobs than the average men's job, or is the problem one of low valuation of the skills used in women's jobs? Are there major differences by gender in job content or skills or are these differences more between full- and part-time jobs?

Sara Horrell is a research officer at the Dept. of Applied Economics, Cambridge University. She is completing her doctorate on women's labour market participation and household consumption patterns.

Jill Rubery is a lecturer in industrial relations in the School of Management at the University of Manchester Institute of Science and Technology. She has researched on a wide range of labour market issues. Recent projects include the Social Change and Economic Life Initiative, a study of working-time patterns for the Equal Opportunities Commission and editing a book on women and recession in several advanced industrial countries.

Brendan Burchell worked on the Social Change and Economic Life Initiative at the Dept. of Applied Economics, and is currently a lecturer in statistics and methods for the Social and Political Sciences Faculty, Cambridge University. He has published several articles concerned with the relationship between labour market experience and psychological health.

These questions cannot be answered without systematic investigation of the actual job content and skill requirements of the jobs occupied by men and women in the economy. Published data using occupational status for these job classifications will reflect the current labour market status of jobs, while the agenda for women's labour market research is to investigate whether this 'status' reflects job content and skill, or the 'status' of women as employees. Most useful research in this area has up to now involved case study techniques. One purpose of these studies has been to investigate whether women's jobs involve either attributes or skills not normally included in the assessment of jobs, or whether attributes usually associated with high skill are present in women's jobs but not recognised (Armstrong 1982; Coyle 1982; Crompton and Jones 1984; Craig et al. 1985). In practice both types of 'undervaluation' of women's jobs have been found, for example personal and caring skills are explicitly looked for by management in many female service jobs (Curran 1988; Craig et al. 1985) but these requirements do not serve to enhance the status and pay of women's jobs. In other cases women's jobs involve responsibilities or manual skills which are not reflected in their status or grading. In some cases these responsibilities are shared by all women in the job category so that responsibility pay is avoided and in others manual skills are more easily underestimated because of the use of informal instead of formal training systems. This under-valuation does not arise by chance but relates to women's low status in the labour market. To use Armstrong's famous quote: 'If it's only women it doesn't matter so much.' (1982: 27). How jobs come to be recognised as requiring skills or involving responsibilities is a social and not a technically-determined process (Rubery 1978; Wood 1982). If there are few pressures to reward women with higher pay or promotion, then there will also be limited pressure to examine the job content of women's jobs to legitimise an hierarchical structure. Women may find themselves concentrated in firms, industries or even processes (Bettio 1988) where the ability to pay is low because of low productivity. Many of these jobs will require high skill from the workers because of the use of less automated equipment but the pay will reflect the low productivity (Craig et al. 1982: ch. 6) and, as a consequence, these jobs may become associated with low skill. In practice individuals find it difficult to compare jobs in terms of content or skill because of inadequate knowledge and the complexities of such a multi-dimensional comparison, so that the pay level of a job may be taken as itself a proxy for skill or job content.

Although we now have quite a good understanding of how and why 'undervaluation' may occur at a case study level we do not know how far these case studies can be generalised to all women's jobs, or indeed whether there is not a perverse danger of focusing too much on the valuation of women's jobs and not on their confinement to low skilled employment. A more general study was required which would compare a representative sample of women's jobs to a representative sample of men's jobs but which would also build on the insights into the likely undervaluation of women's jobs from the case-study research. The Social Change and Economic Life Initiative presented such an opportunity. The survey in the Northampton labour market of 1000 individuals, including over 600 in employment, was used as a vehicle to explore gender difference in job content and skill of a random sample of adults aged 20 to 60. Questions were designed to look at jobs from a number of different dimensions, from the more conventional dimensions of education and training to the discretion allowed in a job, the actual job content and the various technical and social attributes that are required for doing a job well. This range of questions reflects the various academic literatures and debates on skill from the human capital school, to the Braverman 'deskilling' hypothesis (1974) and the feminist critique of conventional job categorisations. By extending the range of dimensions of job content we hoped to avoid the problems of underestimating job content, although the problem of how to measure and compare different dimensions of jobs, common to all job evaluation exercises, still remains. The use of subjective responses from individuals to investigate job content raises certain problems as we have no other observations on job require- ments[2] against which to compare the individual responses. However, the collection of data direct from individual job holders also has significant advantages. It increases the likelihood that the data will reflect the actual job content and labour requirements, rather than those specified in job descriptions and it reduces the likelihood that the data will simply reflect the actual position of the job in the pay hierarchy, as may be the case if similar information is collected from management representatives.

We first use the range of data available to build up a comparison of both the *level* of skill involved in men's and women's jobs and the *similarities and differences* in the components of men's and women's skill. This analysis of the various elements of skill is then used to construct an index of skill. This first section of the paper treats the respondents' answers to the survey as data on which a comparison of actual job content can be made. In the second section we relax this assumption and use the data to explore the neglected issue of whether there are any systematic differences in the way men and women perceive and evaluate the skills and responsibilities involved in their jobs.

The Survey Sample

The survey sample which we have used for the analysis consisted of 365 men and 333 women aged between 20 and 60, and either in employment or self-employed at the time of the survey in the summer of 1986.[3] The analyses have been carried out with a weighted sample to adjust for problems of under- and over-representation in the survey sample, in particular to adjust for any biases arising from using the Kish grid system for selection of respondents and for the over representation of women in the sample. Within the weighted sample males account for 59% and females for 41% of those in employment. Within the male weighted sample, employees accounted for 85% and the self-employed for 15%, but in the female weighted sample the proportions are 93.5% and 6.5% respectively. Only 4% of men in employment worked part-time, using self-definition of part-time work for employees and a cut off point of 30 hours for the self-employed, compared to 44% of females in employment. Men in part-time employment have been omitted from many of the analyses, except when whole samples are used, on the grounds of small sample numbers and the likelihood that part-time working for men cannot be equated in a labour market sense with part-time work for women. For most of the analyses we include both employees and the self-employed; however, one or two of the questions were not asked of the self-employed and we thus construct the skill index for employees only.

Comparing Men's and Women's Jobs: Towards an Index of Skill

To compare the skill level of men's and women's jobs requires the consideration of a wide range of factors to take into account both the different aspects of skill and job content and any differences in the nature of skills between men's and women's jobs. These factors are examined under three main headings. We start with the more conventional means of comparing skills, such as occupational scales and measures of training and qualifications. Secondly, we look in more detail at specific components of skill through questions designed to investigate the range of factors that might be important in doing a job well and the range of responsibilities a job may involve. Thirdly, we look at the degree of discretion or autonomy.[4] We conclude this section of the paper by attempting to bring together this disaggregated analysis into an index of skill which takes into account all the different facets of skill that we have analysed.

Skill Levels of Jobs: Some Conventional Classifications

The usual starting point for comparing the relative quality of jobs occupied by men and women is to turn to one or more of the now numerous occupational scales. The first section of table 1 uses the Registrar General's Social Class categories for 1980 to compare the distributions of male and female jobs for the whole sample, and also the distributions of male and female full-time workers and female part-time workers. These analyses reveal the widely-known fact that there are significant differences in the distribution of male and female jobs by social class category. Both men and

GENDER AND SKILLS

Table 1 Conventional Classifications of Skill (employees and self-employed)

		M	% F	MFT	% FFT	FPT[a]
(a)	*Social Class*					
1.	High professional	8	2	8	4	—
2.	Lower professional	29	29	28	35	21
3.1	Clerical	10	37	10	37	37
3.2	Skilled manual	34	7	34	9	5
4.	Semi-skilled manual	17	19	16	12	28
5.	Unskilled	3	5	3	2	8
		100	100	100	100	100
(b)	*Self-definition of skill*					
	See job as skilled	84	59	84	72	44
	Do not see job as skilled	16	41	16	28	56
(c)	*Qualifications required for current job*					
1.	Further education or A levels + training	25	18	26	25	10
2.	A levels or O levels + training	9	12	9	15	7
3.	O levels *or* training	31	25	31	25	25
4.	No qualifications	35	45	34	34	58
		100	100	100	100	100
(d)	*Training for current jobs*					
1.	2 years +	32	15	33	16	12
2.	6 months–2 years	9	11	10	16	5
3.	1–6 months	20	16	17	17	14
4.	None	39	59	40	51	70
		100	100	100	100	100
(e)	*Time taken to learn to do job well* (employees only)					
1.	2 years +	31	13	33	17	9
2.	6 months–2 years	23	17	23	25	9
3.	Up to 6 months	46	70	44	57	83
		100	100	100	100	100

	Analysis of Variance[b]		
	All	Full-timers	Women
Social class	G S	G S	FP S FP/S^3
Skill	G	G	FP
Qualifications required	[G^2]S	S	FP S
Training	G S	G^4 S	[FP] S
Learning time	G S	G^2 S	FP S^2

[a]M and F used in all tables for all men and all women in employment. MFT, FFT, FPT used for males in full-time jobs, females in full-time jobs; females in part-time jobs.

[b]G = gender, S = skill, FP = working time. Symbols are included if significant at 5% or less: significance is 1% unless otherwise indicated by superscript. Square brackets indicate a gender or working-time effect that was significant with a one way analysis of variance but not in the two way analysis of variance when 'skill' was controlled for.

Significant interaction terms are shown by both symbols separated by /.

women are concentrated in social class 3, but women are almost exclusively in the clerical category 3.1 and men in the skilled manual 3.2. Thus, although in principle social class and occupational scales are hierarchically organised, in practice in the middle range jobs are classified by type, i.e. manual or non-manual, without any direct attempt at assessing which clerical jobs should be considered 'higher quality' than which skilled manual jobs and vice versa. Thus it is necessary to look beyond these scales to determine relative job quality and skill. However the distributions by social class already reveal some interesting points to note about the nature of gender differences in jobs. Apart from the already mentioned differences in concentration within social class 3, women are found to be over represented in classes 4 and 5, the semi and unskilled manual classes and under represented in the professional classes 1 and 2. However, further disaggregation reveals that it is only female part-time workers who are over represented in classes 4 and 5 and under represented in classes 1 and 2, with female full-timers being slightly more likely that male full-timers to be found in the higher classes and slightly less likely to be found in the lower classes.

The problem we have identified with occupational scales is that in practice no direct comparisons of different types of jobs are made. The remaining four variables shown in table 1 do allow direct comparisons to be made. The first makes use of the respondents' own skill classification, that is the response to a question in the survey 'Do you consider your current job to be skilled?' No less than 84% of men considered their current job to be skilled compared to only 59% of women. Further disaggregation again reveals that much of this gender difference is associated with women's concentration in part-time jobs. Comparing only the full-time workers shows a much smaller gender difference, 84% to 72%, but only 44% of women in part-time jobs considered themselves to be in skilled jobs.

The final three variables are associated with the conventional means of comparing the skill levels of jobs, that is by comparing the 'investments in human capital' necessary to gain entry to the job or to learn to do the job well. Three aspects of training or learning are looked at. First the qualifications which the respondent considered would now be necessary for someone to get their kind of job, that is distinct from both the respondent's own qualifications and from what was required when the respondent first got the job. The detailed responses to this question have been collapsed into four categories: a further education qualification or a minimum combination of A levels plus some training; A levels or O levels plus some training; O levels or some training; no qualifications. The data show that men are significantly more likely to be employed in jobs with higher qualification entry requirements than are women. However, disaggregation so that only men and women in full-time jobs are compared this time not only reduces the gender differential but actually reverses it so that women are significantly more likely to be employed in jobs with higher entry requirements. In practice almost all of the difference revolves around the middle two categories, with women much more likely to require A levels or O levels plus training, and men more likely to require only O levels or training, including apprenticeships. Approximately one third of both male and female full-timers require no qualifications for their jobs and approximately one quarter of both groups require further education. These percentages compare to 58% of part-time jobs requiring no qualifications and 10% requiring further education.

Respondents were also asked whether they had received training for their current job and to estimate how long the training had lasted. This question on training was followed by a question on how long it had taken them after starting to do this type of work to learn to do it well, only asked of employees, not the self-employed. The purpose of asking both about training and learning time was to try to ensure that the more informal types of training and learning by doing were included but, in practice, the pattern of responses to the two questions is remarkably similar, with significantly longer training and learning periods reported for men compared to women. This time when the data were disaggregated into full-time jobs and part-time jobs the difference between men and women's jobs, taking only full-timers was reduced but remained significant in favour of men. However, the difference between the position of part-timers and that of full-timers, both male and female, is just as large as that for qualifications: 70% of part-timers said they had no training, and 83% said they had learnt to do their job well in under 6 months, compared to percentages for full-timers which varied from 40 to 51% for no training, and 44 to 57% for learning within 6 months.

One of the problems of analysing a whole set of variables associated with various aspects of skill for differences by gender and by working-time is that it is not clear whether one is uncovering the same set of gender or working-time differences because of the correlations between the different variables or differences which either further amplify or modify the differences previously uncovered. To overcome this problem, at least partially, we first analysed the three samples: the whole sample of those in work; all in full-time jobs; and all women in work, using a one-way analysis of variance to test for gender differences in the first two samples and differences by working-time among women[5]. We then also used a two-way analysis of variance, to test for gender or working-time differences in responses after taking into account differences in the shares of 'skilled' jobs held by men and women or by full-timers and part-timers. The variable that we used to control for the 'skill' of the job is the second variable analysed in table 1, namely the perception by the respondent of whether their job was skilled. In fact, throughout the text we refer to jobs as 'skilled', using inverted commas, when these jobs are distinguished from 'unskilled' jobs simply on the basis of respondents' perceptions of their jobs as 'skilled'. The adequacy of this variable as an 'objective' control for skill will be returned to in the last section of this paper. However, as the control variable may itself capture some sex bias, in the sense that women and part-timers may be less likely to evaluate their job as skilled after controlling for job content and quality (see below), the use of this variable as a control factor in fact provides a very strong test of whether there are further gender and working-time differences which exist over and above those accounted for in the response to the skill question.

The results of the two-way analyses of variance are presented in summary form at the bottom of table 1.[6] The results from the one-way analyses testing for either a gender effect (for the whole sample or the sample of full-timers) or a working-time effect (for the sample of women) are only presented and indicated in square brackets, whenever the gender or the working-time variable was not significant in the two-way analysis but was significant when 'skill' was not controlled for. These results show that for almost all the two-way analyses of variance gender and working-time were significant even after controlling for 'skill'. 'Skill' was positively related to social class for both full- and part-time women workers, but the difference between the social class levels of 'skilled' and 'unskilled' part-time women's jobs was much greater than was the case for full-time women's jobs.[7] However, in general, gender and working-time differences in job content do not seem to interact with the skill variable and are found to exist even after controlling for differences in shares of 'skilled' jobs.[8]

Components of Skill

So far we have been looking at a fairly standard range of variables which can be used as overall or global indicators of skill. An alternative approach, and one necessary to explore the issues associated with equal value claims, is to look for diversity in the types or components of skill between men's and women's jobs. Indeed, if the types of skills and the ways in which those skills are acquired and used differ markedly between men's and women's jobs then it is improbable that any fully satisfactory way of comparing levels of skills can be arrived at. Two batteries of questions were included in the team specific part of the Northampton area work attitudes survey to explore the extent of diversity in men's and women's jobs. The first asked respondents to say how important they considered each of six factors to be in doing their job well. These factors included two which were related to specific experience or knowledge (lengthy experience of this type of work, having professional, scientific, technical or business knowledge); one related to personal aptitude (having a particular knack or talent for this type of work); and three which were related to specific organisational knowledge or social skills (knowing your way round the organisation, good relations with people at work, good contacts with clients or customers). The potential importance of social and organisational skills has been increasingly stressed in the literature on internal labour markets where the skills necessary to function in a collective labour process may be more important than simple technical skills (Manwaring 1984). Moreover, personal and social skills may take on increasing importance with the sectoral shift towards service-based occupations (Curran 1988) where good relations with clients become critical for commercial success and analyses of skill which emphasise traditional manual and manufacturing type skills may underestimate the level of skills involved in the expanding job sectors.

The responses for each of these factors were scored from one, not important at all, to five, absolutely essential, and the average scores are shown in table 2. There are significant differences in the distributions of responses for all six factors between men and women but the direction of the sex difference varied by factor. Women were more likely to stress the importance of good contacts with clients and customers and good relations with people at work, while men scored higher on the other four factors. However, analysis of responses for only full-time workers still revealed a strong gender difference in the importance attached to good relations at work and contacts with clients and customers, but the only factor where men continued to score significantly higher than women was on lengthy experience of this type of work. There was very little difference in mean scores attached to the remaining three factors; knowing the organisation, having a particular knack or talent and, perhaps most surprisingly, having professional, scientific, technical or business knowledge. The increased similarity between men and women which emerges when only full-timers are considered is matched by a widening divergence between part-timers and full-timers. However, the two factors which women were found to stress, relations at work and contacts with clients, did not fall into this pattern as there was virtually no difference in the average scores for women working full-time or part-time. These factors are thus clearly related to all types of women's jobs, whereas on the other four factors there is a much clearer difference between full- and part-time jobs than by gender *per se*. These results are also associated with differences in the proportion of 'skilled' jobs held by part-timers. 'Skill' was associated with higher scores for all factors for the sample of women and, when the 'skill' variable is included in the analysis of variance, the part-time/full-time distinction is only significant for 'lengthy experience of this type of work' and for 'having a particular knack or talent'. The 'skill' variable is also significant for all factors for the whole sample, with the result that gender is not significant for having a knack or talent or having specialist knowledge. For full-timers the three factors already identified to have a gender effect remain significant by gender even when 'skill' is controlled for, while 'skill' is found to be significant for all factors except knowing your way round the organisation and good relations at work.

Table 2   Factors Important in Doing the Job Well (employees and
self-employed)

			Mean scores[a]		
	M	F	MFT	FFT	FPT
(i) Lengthy experience of this type of work	3.58	3.06	3.60	3.28	2.78
(ii) Knowing your way round the organisation	3.40	3.14	3.41	3.31	2.93
(iii) Good relations with people at work	3.57	3.85	3.56	3.86	3.83
(iv) Good contacts with clients or customers	3.69	3.90	3.68	3.94	3.85
(v) Having a particular knack or talent for this type of work	3.61	3.40	3.60	3.62	3.13
(vi) Having professional, scientific, technical or business knowledge	2.95	2.57	2.95	2.82	2.25
% saying essential or very important on:					
5 or 6 factors	25	20	26	25	13
3 or 4 factors	40	40	40	39	40
1 or 2 factors	28	32	28	31	33
0 factors	7	9	7	5	14

	Analysis of Variance		
	All	Full-timers	Women
(i)	G S	G S	FP S
(ii)	G S		[FP] S
(iii)	GS^2	G	S
(iv)	G S	G S	S
(v)	[G] S	S	FP S
(vi)	[G] S	S	[FP] S
no. of factors	[G^5] S	S	[FP] S

[a]Score 1 to 5, 5 = essential, 1 = not important at all.

Gender and working-time are thus clearly related to differences in
importance rating for particular factors, but while gender is associated with
differences in the factors emphasised by men and women (in particular
women stress more social skills) working-time is associated with part-
timers having lower scores on most factors than full-timers. Introduction of
the 'skill' variable tends to reduce the importance of the working-time
distinction and also some gender effects, mainly those where men appeared
to score higher before 'skill' was controlled for. Care must be taken with the
interpretation of these findings because of possible differences in the

propensities of men and women and full- and part-timers to consider their jobs to be skilled.

The purpose of including this question on different factors was essentially to explore diversity in types of skills. However, some jobs may involve a large number of these factors and for others only one or two may be relevant. The last section of table 2 shows the percentage of respondents who considered that no less than 5 or 6 of the factors to be either absolutely essential or very important for their job, compared for example to the percentage who did not think any of the factors to be essential or even very important. Most respondents in practice fell into the middle two categories, identifying between one and four factors as very important for their job, with these categories accounting for between 68 and 73% of the sample for each group. The main difference in distributions is again between the female part-time workers and all full-timers, with part-timers being much more likely to consider none of the factors to be very important and much less likely to consider 5 or more to be very important. Two-way analysis of variance, however, reveals that much of this difference is again accounted for by the 'skill' variable, with the working-time variable losing significance once 'skill' is controlled for.

The second battery of questions which we included to tap diversity of skills was one relating to responsibilities in the job. The association of responsibility with concepts of skill or job status has been well established. Analyses of the restructuring of employment following automation and 'deskilling' of manual work have pointed to the way responsibilities, for output, value-added or quantity, have been used to replace manual skill as a basis for job grading (Stieber 1959; Bettio 1988). Responsibility is also included as a key concept in most job evaluation schemes, but the types of responsibility cited in a scheme do not necessarily reflect the full range of possibilities. Our concern was to try to identify all the types of responsibility that respondents felt their job involved and not simply to concentrate on those normally included in a pay grading scheme. In addition to the question in the core part of the questionnaire on whether their job involved supervisory responsibilities,[9] respondents in Northampton were also asked to say if their job involved each or any of the following responsibilities: responsibility for health or safety of others; for checking work; for machines, materials or goods; for confidential information; for money; for maintaining output or services; and for meeting official or professional standards of quality or reliability. A point to note is the very high shares of respondents who consider their jobs to involve these responsibilities. With the exceptions of responsibility for money and responsibility for supervision, in each case over 50% of both men and women responded positively. Perhaps surprisingly the responsibility which attracted the highest response rate from both men and women, 80% and 66% respectively, was that for meeting official or professional standards, possibly indicating a widespread feeling of responsibility for standards and quality.

The list of responsibilities was designed to include some types of responsibilities thought to be associated with female jobs and others more often associated with male jobs, alongside others where we had no particular preconceptions of the likely outcomes. As with the analysis of importance factors, however, differences in response are not found to be simply related to gender but also to relate to 'skill' and to working-time. In fact the only responsibility which women were more likely to lay claim to was that for confidential information. Further disaggregation, revealed that this was more a responsibility associated with female full-time jobs than with all female jobs. With the exception of confidential information and money, males were found to be significantly more likely than women to

Table 3   Responsibilities Involved in the Job (employees and self-employed)

	M	% F	MFT	% FFT	FPT
% having responsibility for:					
(i) supervising others	48	31	48	43	15
(ii) safety or health of others	69	53	69	51	54
(iii) checking work	71	53	74	65	39
(iv) machines, materials or goods	76	54	76	56	53
(v) confidential information	57	63	57	71	52
(vi) money	44	48	44	47	49
(vii) maintaining output or services	71	59	71	64	52
(viii) meeting official or professional standards of quality and reliability	80	66	80	71	59
% who considered their job involved:					
6 to 8 responsibilities	44	32	45	41	20
3 to 5 responsibilities	44	44	44	40	50
0 to 2 responsibilities	12	24	12	19	31

	Analysis of Variance All	Full-timers	Women
(i)	G S	S	FP S
(ii)	[G] S^3	G S	
(iii)	G S	[G^5]S G/S^2	FP^2
(iv)	G	G	
(v)	G S	G S	FP^5 S
(vi)	S	S	S
(vii)	G^{2}S	S	[FP^3] S
(viii)	G^3 S	[G^2] S	S
no. of responsibilities	G S	S	[FP] S

claim they had each of the other responsibilities, a result which also held
true for comparisons of full-timers alone, except for responsibility for
maintaining output or standards and responsibility for supervising others.
However, controlling for 'skill' reduces the significance of gender particularly when comparing full-timers, such that the only cases where men are
found to be significantly more likely to claim responsibilities after controlling for 'skill' are for the safety or health of others and for machines,
material or goods. The skill variable is in fact found to be a significant
factor for the whole sample and full-timers on all items except machines,
materials or goods. This last responsibility in fact seems to be generally
related to male jobs irrespective of 'skill'. Women in part-time jobs are the
least likely to say they have responsibility in six out of the eight cases, but
there is only a significant difference in four cases: for confidential information, checking work,[10] maintaining output and, most marked of all, for
supervising others. Only 15% of part-timers had this type of responsibility
compared to over 40% for full-timers and this low percentage compares
with between 39 and 59% scores on all the other responsibility variables for
part-timers. Taking the female sample alone, 'skill' is found to be significantly associated with claiming responsibility for all items except safety and
health and machines, materials or goods.

To summarise then, the only responsibility clearly positively associated
with the female gender is confidential information and this in turn is found
only to be a characteristic of female full-time jobs. On most items, except
responsibility for money which is only related to 'skill', males tend to score
higher and part-timers lower, with female full-timers occupying a middle
position. Part-timers are particularly unlikely to have responsibility for
supervising others or for checking work. However, these relationships are
also closely related to 'skill' and the only item where men's higher score is
not related to being in a 'skilled' job is responsibility for machines,
materials or goods.

The last section of table 3 completes the analysis of this question by
summarising responses to all eight items. Men are significantly more likely
to have responded positively to a large number of items, both for the whole
sample and for full-timers only. Part-timers are much less likely to have
responded positively to a large number of items and more likely to have said
yes to two or fewer items. Again the number of responsibilities claimed is
positively related to being in a 'skilled' job so that when 'skill' is controlled
for gender is no longer found to be significant for full-timers, nor working-
time for the sample of women workers.

Discretion

The final aspect of jobs we explore as an indicator of skill is the degree of
discretion or control that men and women feel they have over the way they

do their work and the effort they put into their work. This accords with the Braverman (1974) notion of skill as the opportunity to exercise judgement and discretion within the job.

Three main questions were asked in the core survey which throw light on these issues. First, respondents were asked how much choice they felt they had over the way in which they did their job. Table 4 shows that there was very little difference in the responses to this question by men and women,

Table 4 Scope for Discretion or Choice at Work (employees and self-employed)

		M	% F	MFT	% FFT	FPT
(a)	*Amount of choice over the way that you do the job*					
	a great deal	60	55	60	59	51
	some	24	26	24	28	24
	hardly any	8	7	8	4	10
	no choice at all	8	12	8	9	14
(b)	*Closeness of supervision*					
	not supervised at all	41	31	41	27	34
	not at all closely supervised	32	37	32	37	36
	quite closely supervised	20	24	20	25	22
	very closely supervised	8	9	8	10	8
(c)	*Factors important in determining how hard you work*					
(i)	machine/assembly line	7	6	7	8	3
(ii)	clients/customers	32	47	31	47	45
(iii)	supervisor/boss	25	27	26	31	21
(iv)	fellow workers or colleagues	30	32	29	41	23
(v)	own discretion	66	66	67	67	63
(vii)	pay incentives	29	7	28	9	5
(vii)	reports/appraisals	18	13	18	18	8

	Analysis of Variance		
	All	Full-timers	Women
choice	S	S	[FP^5]
supervision	[G]	G^3	—
how hard you work:			
(i)			
(ii)	G	G	
(iii)			
(iv)		G^2	FP
(v)			
(vi)	G	G	
(vii)	S^2		FP^2S^4

60% of men and 55% of women felt they had a great deal of choice and 8% of men and 12% of women felt they had no choice at all. The pattern of responses was even more similar when full-timers only were compared and, although the usual differences between full- and part-time women workers were revealed, these were of a much smaller magnitude than most of the other data we have been analysing, with 51% of part-timers still feeling they had a great deal of choice. 'Skill' was found to be more important than gender in determining the degree of choice; it was not found to be significant for the sample of women workers alone, but its inclusion in the two-way analysis of variance did serve to reduce the significance of the working-time variable.

The second question relating to autonomy specifically asked about the closeness of supervision. Women were significantly more likely to have close supervision than men but the differences were in practice quite small, with 73% of men and 68% of women saying either that they were not supervised at all or that they were not supervised at all closely. For once a higher percentage of women in part-time jobs fell into the unsupervised category, 70% compared to 64% of women's full-time jobs, and also the 'skill' variable was found not to be significant. Thus, there seems to be little evidence of a gender, a working-time or a 'skill' factor in explaining the degree of supervision. The nature of the job and the actual possibilities for supervision may be in practice the critical variables which are not captured by this survey data.

The final question associated with the issue of autonomy and discretion asked respondents to say which factors were important in determining how hard they worked. These data thus enable us to explore the mechanisms of control, instead of the perceived level of choice or supervision. The most striking overall finding is that two thirds of the sample considered that their own discretion was important in determining how hard they worked and this proportion was remarkably similar for men and women, and for full- and part-timers. At the other end of the extreme very few respondents considered that a machine or assembly-line was important in determining how hard they worked. Only two factors were significantly related to gender. A much higher percentage of both full- and part-time women workers said that clients and customers were important in determining how hard they work than was the case for men. Conversely, pay incentives were much more frequently cited as a determinant of effort for men than for women. Women in full-time jobs were more likely to cite fellow workers and colleagues as important than were full-time men, but this did not appear as a general gender effect as part-time women workers were the least likely to mention fellow workers or colleagues. The only factor to show a major difference between full- and part-timers was report and appraisal systems, but this difference may have arisen primarily because such systems were not used in part-time jobs. In practice all the gender effects we have identified are likely to be primarily related to the actual nature of the job and not necessarily to differences in the way women and men respond to constraints and incentives. Unfortunately, however, we have no data to check the proportions of men and women in jobs with pay incentives or in jobs where there is direct customer contact. There is, however, indirect evidence to suggest that the system of control is not simply related to the status of the worker, but also to the intrinsic characteristics of the job. Unlike most of the other variables relating to job quality, the system of control was not related to whether or not the respondent perceived the job as 'skilled'. Clearly no attempt was made here to measure intensity of control or autonomy but nevertheless it is interesting that only reports and appraisals were significantly related to 'skill'.

All three variables relating to discretion and autonomy have failed to show very striking differences between the sexes, or between full- and part-time jobs. If discretion and autonomy are, as Braverman (1974) suggested, key indicators of skill, then either there is less difference between the skill level of men's and women's jobs than has been thought to be the case or women do not perceive the constraints imposed upon them. An alternative explanation may be that discretion and autonomy are much more widespread characteristics of jobs than the deskilling debate would have us believe, and thus they are not the key distinguishing characteristics separating out the 'skilled' from the 'unskilled'. This supports Blackburn and Mann's (1979) finding that the degree of autonomy was an important variable within the 'unskilled' or non-qualified male labour market. It also appears to be the case that the deskilling debate has focused attention too much on the technological and supervisory control systems associated with manufacturing, and too little attention has been paid to the more social forms of control, arising for example from direct contact with customers, which are potentially just as constraining as machine control.

Constructing an Index of Skill

To summarise our findings across the spectrum of factors associated with skill that the data has allowed us to analyse, we have constructed an index of skill. We have included seven factors in the index for employees. For the first five factors we have allowed a maximum score of 2, but for the last two, which both relate to discretion, we have only allowed a maximum score of 1. The discretion variables have already been found not to have a strong discriminatory effect between either types of jobs or labour supply categories. The maximum total score is thus twelve. The details of the factor scores are as follows:

   (i) qualifications required: higher education *2*; some but below higher *1*;
  (ii) length of training for current job: over 2 years *2*; 6 months to 2 years *1*;

(iii) length of time taken to learn to do job well: over 2 years *2*; 6 months to 2 years *1*;

(iv) importance attached to factors in doing job well: very important or essential on 5 or 6 factors *2*; on 3 or 4 factors *1*;

(v) number of responsibilities in the job: 6 to 8 responsibilities *2*; 3 to 5 responsibilities *1*;

(vi) the degree of choice over how the job is done: a great deal of choice *1*;

(vii) how closely the job is supervised: not supervised or not at all closely supervised *1*.

The main variables that we have analysed in the preceding sections but which are not included here are the social class of the job and the perception of the job as 'skilled'. The purpose of constructing the skill index is to some extent to provide an alternative way of grading the job than is offered by social class categories and thus inclusion of a social class score would be inappropriate. Similarly, we are attempting to summarise the factors that may influence whether or not a job might be considered to be skilled and it thus appeared more appropriate to compare the skill index to the direct question on whether the respondent considered the job to be skilled, than to include the latter in the construction of the index. Inclusion would have introduced an element of double counting as is borne out by the almost 100% correlation between those in the top band of the skill index (see table 6 below) and their perception of their job as 'skilled'. We also omitted the question on which factors determined how hard the respondent worked as these could not be readily converted to an hierarchical scale.

The cumulative frequency distributions of the skill index for male full-timers, female full-timers and female part-timers (figure 1) show clearly the pattern of divisions by skill implied by our analyses of the individual variables; male full-time jobs are distinctly less likely to fall into the lower skill categories than female full-time jobs, thereby providing evidence of a gender effect in the distribution of skilled jobs, but by far the largest difference in the distributions is between part-time jobs and full-time jobs, with a distinct concentration of part-time jobs in the low-skilled categories, 69% of part-time jobs coming into the bottom third of the scale for the skill index. Table 5 summarises these findings by showing the percentages of the distributions falling into three skill index bands: low skill from 0 to 4 points; medium skill from 5 to 8 points; and high skill from 9 and 12 points. This banding helps to reveal the main differences between the groups: both the male and the female full-time jobs are concentrated in the medium skill category, but women in full-time jobs are much more likely to fall into the low skill category than men in full-time jobs, 42% compared to 26%, and men are much more likely to be found in the high skill category, 25% compared to 15%. In contrast part-timers are very heavily concentrated in the low skill category although the share found in the high skill category, 9%, is not insignificant. The one way analysis of

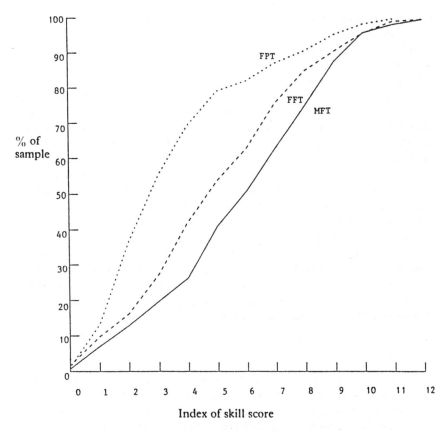

Figure 1 Cumulative frequency distributions by index of skill

Table 5 Index of Skill (employees)

	M	% F	MFT	% FFT	FPT
low (0–4)	27	55	26	42	69
medium (5–8)	49	33	49	43	21
high (9–12)	24	12	25	15	9

	Analysis of Variance		
	All	Full-timers	Women
whole index	G S	[G] S	FP⁵ S

variance showed a significant relationship between gender and the distribution across the skill index for the whole sample and for full-timers alone. Gender was no longer found to be significant for full-timers once the perception of the job as 'skilled' was entered into a two-way analysis of variance, but gender continued to be significant for the sample taken as a whole, indicating that for part-timers anyway the concentration in the lower skill band was not fully explained by their responses to the 'skill' question. This finding is confirmed by the fact that both the working-time variable and the 'skill' variable were significantly related to the score on the skill index for the sample of women.

Perhaps more significant than the differences in the distribution of jobs between men and women full-timers is the extensive overlap in the distributions, so that 75% of male full-time jobs and 85% of female full-time jobs fall into the first two thirds of the skill index scale. Thus, explanations of the low degree of overlap between male and female full-time workers pay which stress women's concentration in lower skilled jobs than men must be looked upon with scepticism (Horrell *et al.* 1989), although the argument for part-time work may be more sustainable, provided there is not a significant bias in the way part-timers perceive the demands of their job compared to full-timers.

Summary

Several points emerge fairly clearly from our analysis of the data on the skills involved in male and female jobs. The first is that there does seem to be a relatively systematic tendency for men to occupy more skilled jobs than those of women. The difference between the skill of men's and women's jobs declines if we compare only full-time jobs, but it is nevertheless apparent. The only factor on which women scored higher than men was the level of qualifications required to obtain the job. This is a very important indicator of the high quality of women's jobs but the weight of the evidence from all the other factors nevertheless suggests that men still have jobs with higher skill requirements. However, the more surprising aspect of this finding is the relative smallness of the differences in levels of skill between men's and women's full-time jobs, certainly when taken in comparison to the much greater differences between full- and part-time jobs. It is in this major growth area of employment that the main differences in job quality and skill are occurring, thereby worsening the pattern of distribution of skilled jobs for women taken as a whole.

The second finding is that there are significant differences in the types of skill required in men's and women's jobs. In particular, women tend to mention more social skills and social constraints, notably the role of direct contact with clients and customers, more frequently than do men. Too much of the debate on skills in the literature has concentrated on either the skills used by men or the skills used in manufacturing. There needs to be more research into the types of skills and the types of constraints found in women's jobs and in all service sector jobs. A third, related, finding is the lack of a strong systematic link between other aspects of skill and the degree of discretion or autonomy in a job. Partly this finding arises from trying to make comparisons across the whole range of jobs, including manual and non-manual, service and manufacturing, and while there may be a link between levels of skill and autonomy in any particular organisation or sector, differences in the nature of the job intervene to reduce the likelihood of finding such a relationship at the aggregate level. A further explanation may be that the reliance on workers' skill and discretion may be more pervasive than has been recognised because of the influence of the de-skilling debate. In particular, women may be used in low grade or supposedly low skill jobs in preference to men because they are considered to be more reliable in situations where even low grade workers still have considerable discretion and autonomy.

This issue brings us to the fourth finding, namely the relatively high scores from respondents on many of the questions about skill, suggesting that a large share of the employed population see their jobs as requiring a range of different and often quite demanding skills and responsibilities. The workforce as a whole does not appear convinced by either the deskilling argument or by the argument that the qualities and attributes of the worker makes little difference to the productivity of the job in the lower job grades. However, for this survey we have no other independent evidence on job demands against which to compare the descriptions the respondents provided of their jobs and thus the question of the actual pervasiveness of skill and discretion requirements cannot be further explored. This raises a related issue of how individuals perceive and describe their jobs. So far we have taken respondents' answers at face value as descriptions of jobs that can be aggregated and compared across individuals and the relatively systematic patterns across a range of variables that we have uncovered suggest that the data do reflect differences in the quality of jobs. However, to the extent that individuals, or indeed the sexes, differ in the way they perceive and describe their jobs, we may need to modify or qualify the above conclusions we have drawn on actual differences in jobs between labour force groups. It is to this issue of perceptions of skill by men and women that we now turn.

Perceptions of Skill

From our initial analyses we already know that the overwhelming majority of men consider themselves to be in a 'skilled' job, that a sizeable majority of women in full-time jobs consider their jobs to be 'skilled', but that only

44% of women in part-time jobs consider their jobs to be 'skilled'. We also know, from our analyses of variance, that many of the other job character-istics associated with skill are correlated with whether or not the res-pondent considered themselves to be in a 'skilled' job. There is thus good corroborating evidence to suggest that, in answering the question whether they considered their job to be 'skilled', the respondents were using as their frame of reference the set of factors which are generally recognised as contributing to skill: training, qualifications, responsibilities, special skills or qualities, etc. The evidence of consistent responses across a range of diverse questions throughout a long questionnaire also provides support for the view that the data can be taken to reveal genuine differences in jobs between respondents. However, there may still be important differences in the significance that a particular individual or type of worker will attach to a particular job characteristic. These differences may be especially likely to occur if there is a systematic tendency in the labour market for the skills and job content of particular groups to be undervalued, i.e. the pheno-menon that we are engaged in investigating here, for that undervaluation may even affect the employee's perception of their job.

These questions cannot be fully explored in this paper but we have considered this question from one perspective, by exploring whether there is any difference in the probability of men and women and full- and part-timers to describe their jobs as 'skilled' once one has controlled for other aspects of job content. The most general way of controlling for job content is to use our constructed index of skill. Table 6 shows that in the highest skill bracket there is an almost perfect tendency for individuals from all labour force groups to consider their job to be 'skilled', but in the medium and lower skill brackets, women in part-time jobs are much less likely than full-timers to consider their jobs to be 'skilled'. It must be stressed that these results come about even after controlling for job content and are thus independent of the very high concentration of part-timers in the low skilled bracket. No significant difference was found between male and female full-timers in their propensity to describe their jobs as 'skilled' after controlling for the index of skill. However, some gender differences between full-timers do appear in the rest of table 6 where we have undertaken a similar analysis for the main variables used to construct the index of skill and for social class and occupational segregation. These all also reveal a systematic tendency for part-timers to be much less likely to consider themselves to be 'skilled' after controlling for social class, quali-fications required, training time, learning time (although not a significant difference), number of factors considered essential or important to do the job well, and number of responsibilities involved in the job. Thus, part-timers appear to need to register a higher score on all of these factors than is the case for full-timers before they would consider their job to be 'skilled'.

Table 6   Perceptions of Job as Skilled, Controlling for Index of Skill, for Component Variables in the Index of Skill and for Social Class (employees and self-employed)

	Percentage who see their jobs as skilled:		
	MFT	FFT	FPT
Index of Skill (IS)			
(employees only)			
low skill	55	47	29
medium skill	90	87	66
high skill	97	100	100
Qualifications required for the job (QR)			
Further education or A levels + training	98	98	100
A levels or O levels + training	97	84	68
O levels *or* training	86	77	59
No qualifications	69	55	25
Training for current job (T)			
2 years +	97	100	100
6 months to 2 years	97	88	83
1 to 6 months	82	78	43
none	71	55	31
Time taken to learn to do the job well (L)			
(employees only)			
2 years +	96	91	89
6 months to 2 years	91	90	70
up to 6 months	76	60	37
Importance of factors in doing job well (F)			
Essential or very important on:			
5 to 6 factors	95	89	79
3 to 4 factors	89	81	50
1 to 2 factors	74	46	33
0 factors	48	73	20
Number of responsibilities in job (R)			
6 to 8 responsibilities	90	87	75
3 to 5 responsibilities	83	75	39
0 to 2 responsibilities	61	35	31
Social class (SC)			
1. Higher professional	97	100	—
2. Lower professional	92	84	82
3.1 Clerical	88	61	47
3.2 Skilled manual	87	77	71
4. Semi-skilled manual	66	60	13
5. Unskilled manual	36	33	10

	Full-timers	Analysis of Variance	Women
Index of skill IS	IS		FPIS
Qualifications required QR	GQR		FPQR
Training T	GT		FPT
Learning time L	G^4L		L
Importance of factors F	GF G/F		FPF
No. of responsibilities R	GR		FPR FP/R^4
Social class	SC		G^2SC

Female full-timers were also significantly less likely to consider their job to be 'skilled' than male full-timers when controlling for each of the aspects of skill and social class. However, closer examination of the data reveals that much of this difference occurs in the lowest skill bands. Thus women who have no qualifications, have received no training, are able to learn their job in 6 months and have less than three responsibilities in their job are all much less likely to consider their job to be 'skilled' than men who gave the same responses, while the proportions who say their jobs are 'skilled' in the middle ranges of job content are much more similar between men and women. The data on importance of factors in doing the job well appear to contradict this trend as a high percentage of women with no scores of essential or important consider their job to be 'skilled', but only 8 full-time women fell into this category so the high share only relates to 6 observations. Much of the difference in perceptions of 'skill' that thus emerges between men and women is more related to men's tendency to say they are in a 'skilled' job even when their job scores low points on any measure of job content. However, there is also a further significant and even more striking tendency for women in part-time jobs to do the opposite and maintain that their job is not 'skilled' even when scoring medium points on job content or quality. Only in the top parts of the job content scales are part-time women as likely as full-time women to say that their job is 'skilled'. These findings of a tendency by women and part-timers to downgrade the skill level of their jobs may also apply to their assessment of other aspects of job content. For example women or part-timers may be less likely to recognise that they have responsibilities in a job or to stress the importance of various factors and qualities. If there is a systematic downward bias in the other aspects of job quality then we would be underestimating the tendency for women and part-timers to downgrade their skill as each level of job content would represent a higher actual level of job content than was the case for men.

This evidence of differences in the tendency for men and women and, in particular, women in part-time jobs, to describe their jobs as 'skilled', encouraged us to explore this issue further by asking, in a follow-up survey based on a subset of the original survey sample, not only whether they considered their job to be 'skilled' but also why they said that they thought their job was 'skilled' or not. This follow-up survey sample only covered 184 of the original respondents. Using the same weighting as used for the main survey, this sample represented 168 respondents, of which 130 were in employment and only 79 were in the same job. Comparisons of the responses of those who were still in the same job to the question whether they considered their job to be 'skilled' in the 1986 main survey with their responses to an identical question in the 1988 follow-up survey revealed that of the respondents who initially thought their job was 'skilled' 94% still considered their job to be 'skilled' 2 years later. However, only 5 of the 12 who had said that they were not 'skilled' in the original survey and had remained in the same job still claimed to be 'unskilled' two years later. This upgrading of their perceptions of their jobs may be in part the result of completing extensive detailed surveys about their current job, which may have made them more conscious of what their job entailed. A further methodological issue is revealed by the follow-up survey. Although in principle the selection of respondents for the follow-up survey was random, in practice the achieved sample included a higher proportion of those who in the first survey had considered their job to be 'skilled'. Thus those in 'skilled' jobs appear to be more likely to be willing or available for re-interviewing. The consequence of this bias in selection was that in practice we only obtained a very limited number of responses to the question why they had said their job was not 'skilled' (20) compared to over a hundred responses to why they said they thought their job was 'skilled'. [11] The responses to the question why they considered their job to be 'skilled' are analysed in table 7.[12] The need for special training or qualifications was the most frequent response by both men and women. Men were, however, more likely to emphasise the nature of the job itself and any special expertise and knowledge required than were women. Other factors that were relatively frequently mentioned by women but not by men were the need for personal qualities such as patience and on-the-job experience. The differences between men and women in their responses were relatively small, but where differences can be detected they support the view that women emphasise social or personal skills and informal experience, and men, where they do not require special training, still tend to see the job they do as inherently skilled. This latter emphasis suggests that men tend to consider their own job as much more special and different from other jobs than do women, and could explain the tendency for men to consider their job to be 'skilled' even when scoring low on other aspects of job content as measured by the skill index.

The most frequent explanations of why both men and women considered their job not to be 'skilled' referred to the simple or repetitive nature of the job or to the fact that 'anyone can do it'. Some of the specific answers given, however, provide clues as to the reasons why women may tend to under-

Table 7 Why Respondents Consider their Jobs to be 'Skilled'
(number of responses: main reason only)

	Males	Females in:	
		Full-time jobs	Part-time jobs
Job requires:			
training, qualifications or apprenticeship	19	8	6
expertise, special knowledge	17	4	2
on-the-job experience	2	5	1
personal attributes (e.g. patience)	1	4	1
special abilities (not many can do it)	4	2	—
job itself is skilled	18	6	3
other	—	1	—
Total	61	30	13

Why Respondents Consider their Jobs Not to be 'Skilled'

	Males	Females in:	
		Full-time jobs	Part-time jobs
no training required	1		
anyone can do it	1	2	5
job itself not skilled	2		6
practice needed, not skill	1		
other		1	
Total	5	3	11

(*Source*: Welfare survey 1988, carried out by PAS on behalf of the Cambridge
SCELI team.)

estimate the skill level of their jobs. Some of their responses showed a
tendency to downgrade the status or skill of a job because it was associated
with female skills: 'anyone who knows how to sew could do it' or 'just
working with old people is not a skilled job' or 'just a shop assistant'. One
showed a clear tendency to equate skill with formal training only and to
discount qualities or attributes that may be acquired by other means: 'I
suppose I haven't actually trained – more a caring job than a skill'. Others
did not seem to count the training or experience they had acquired as
important: 'anyone can do it with a bit of training' or 'it's the same job in
any shop and a skill you acquire from experience'. Most telling of all was
the simple reply: 'part-time only'. It may be the general association of
part-time work with low skill and casual work, an association found
frequently in newspapers and in general discussions about employment,

which could be the main reason for part-timers' undervaluation of the skill
level of their job.

Conclusions

The first and perhaps most striking result of this comparison of the content
and skill of mens' and women's jobs is that the main cleavage in the quality
or skill level of jobs is not between all male and all female jobs but between
full-time and part-time jobs. The increasing share of part-time jobs in the
economy will therefore be likely to depress further the average quality of
women's jobs as measured in terms of job content and skill. In practice the
growth of part-time work is likely to result in a polarisation of skill levels
within the female labour force for at the same time more women are gaining
access to professional and other high quality jobs (Crompton and
Sanderson 1986). However we show elsewhere (Horrell *et al.* 1989) that
these differences in skill and job content are not the main cause of the
differences in pay between men and women, full-time women workers are
also systematically lower paid than men after adjusting for any differences
in skill composition of jobs.

The second main result is that there is evidence to support the view that
men's and women's jobs involve different skills or attributes and that
women are particularly likely to stress the personal and social relationships
which may be essential in service-type occupations. Here the difference is
found to be more one of gender and not between full- and part-time jobs.
It is thus essential for women to press for these types of attributes to be
included more widely and given greater weight in job evaluation schemes if
'female' job attributes are to be given similar weight to 'male' job attributes.

However, our results also suggest that perceptions of skills and job
content are very much influenced by the current status attached to the job,
so that rapid progress towards 'fairer' job evaluation of women's jobs may
be unlikely. Part-timers were found to be particularly prone to undervalue
the skill level of their job which may be because they are reflecting the
generally held attitude to part-time work as marginal employment. Perceptions of skill content are influenced not only by the status accorded the
job by their employer and by society but also possibly by the centrality of
wage work to the individual concerned. Men may attach a greater importance to their wage employment than women, leading to a tendency to see
their job as skilled, while part-timers may see their jobs as more marginal
to their lives and to their identity and thus be less concerned to see
themselves as doing a skilled job. The influence of these two factors cannot
be tested here, but the more important point for equal opportunities policy
is the importance of developing imaginative and diverse systems of measuring skill which aim to do more than reproduce the current grading and
status of jobs if there is to be any real progress towards the aim of equal pay
for work of equal value.

Notes

1. This paper is based on data collected under the Social Change and Economic Life Initiative funded by the ESRC at the Dept. of Applied Economics, Cambridge. The authors are indebted to all the other participants in SCELI who helped to develop the work attitudes questionnaire. We would particularly like to acknowledge the work of Carolyn Vogler, who managed the work attitudes survey from the centre, and the work of the other members of the Cambridge team both in developing the team-specific party of the questionnaire on which this paper draws and for their intellectual support in developing these areas of analysis. The work attitudes survey was conducted for the ESRC in Summer 1986 by Public Attitudes Surveys Ltd.

2. In another part of the SCELI project the Cambridge team has collected information from managers as well as employees on actual job content and skill which will be used in future publications to explore differences in perceptions of skill within organisations.

3. This sample is large enough to make more systematic comparisons of different aspects of skill reported in men's and women's jobs than has been the norm in studies of women's employment which have relied either on case-study material or on the other inadequate national data sources.

4. Some of the questions were specific to the Cambridge team questionnaire and were therefore asked only of Northampton labour market respondents, and not of respondents in the other five labour markets which participated in the work attitudes survey. These team specific questions were designed to ask about different components of skill, including types of skills which might be expected to be associated with women's jobs ever though these factors would not always be included in standard job evaluations. They therefore supplemented the questions on the more conventional aspects of skill asked about in the core survey.

5. As in almost all cases the differences between female full-timers and female part-timers was less pronounced than between male full-timers and female part-timers it was not felt necessary to repeat the analysis of variance between male full-timers and female part-timers.

6. Analysis of variance was used throughout this paper when testing for statistical significance of differences between groups of employees. In cases where, strictly speaking, the assumptions of analysis of variance were violated, e.g. skewed or dichotomous dependent variables, the results of these analyses were verified with non-parametric tests. For the sake of brevity and simplicity, these other analyses have not been presented here.

7. Indicated by the significant interaction term.

8. The only exceptions to this pattern were that there was no significant difference in training time between full and part-time women workers if one controlled for 'skill', although working-time was significant in the one-way analysis of variance. Also gender is only significantly associated with differences in the qualifications required for entry to jobs for the whole sample in the one-way analysis of variance. In this case the effect of comparing full-timers alone is not only to reduce the gender difference apparent in the aggregate distributions but to reverse it, so that women in full-time jobs on average require higher qualifications than men, although this difference is not statistically significant.

9. For employees this question was asked as part of a detailed battery of questions about their current job, whereas for the self-employed the only information came from the information collected in the work history schedule about their current job.

10. The existence of a significant interaction term between 'skill' and working-time should be noted. For part–timers it is much less likely that they would have responsibility for checking work if they were in an 'unskilled' job than is the case for full-timers.

11. These explanations as to why they said their job was 'skilled' or not 'skilled' refer only to the responses to that question in the 1988 survey. We include in table 7 not only those who were still in the same job and still made the same response, but also those who had changed jobs or entered the labour market since 1986 and those who had changed their answer as to whether their job was 'skilled' between 1986 and 1988.

12. The survey question allowed for open-ended responses which were subsequently categorised for analysis.

References

Armstrong, P. (1982) 'If it's Only Women's Work it Doesn't Matter So Much' in West, J. (ed.) *Work, Women and the Labour Market*, London: Routledge and Kegan Paul, 27–42.

Bettio, F. (1988) *The Sexual Division of Wage Labour: the Italian Case*, Oxford: Oxford University Press.

Blackburn, R. & Mann, M. (1979) *The Working Class in the Labour Market*, London; Macmillan.

Braverman, H. (1974) *Labour and Monopoly Capital*, New York and London: Monthly Review Press.

Craig, C., Rubery, J., Tarling, R. and Wilkinson, F. (1982) *Labour Market Structure, Worker Organisation and Low Pay*, Cambridge: Cambridge University Press.

Craig, C., Garnsey, E. & Rubery, J. (1985) *Payment Structures and Smaller Firms: Women's Employment in Segmented Labour Markets*, Department of Employment; Research Paper no. 48.

Coyle, A. (1982) 'Sex and Skill in the Organisation of the Clothing Industry' in West J. (ed.) *Work, Women and the Labour Market*, London: Routledge and Kegan Paul, 10–26.

Crompton, R. & Jones, G. (1984) *White-Collar Proletariat: Deskilling and Gender in Clerical Work*, London: Macmillan.

Crompton, R. & Sanderson, K. (1986) 'Credentials and Careers: Some Implications of the Increase in Professional Qualifications among Women', *Sociology*, 20, 1, 25–42.

Curran, M. (1988) 'Gender and Recruitment: People and Places in the Labour Market', *Work, Employment and Society*, 2, 3, 335–351.

Horrell, S., Rubery, J. & Burchell, B. (1989) 'Unequal jobs or Unequal Pay?', *Industrial Relations Journal*, 20, 3, 176–191.

Manwaring, T. (1984) 'The Extended Internal Labour Market', *Cambridge Journal of Economics*, 8, 2, 161–188.

Rubery, J. (1978) 'Structured Labour Markets, Worker Organisation and Low Pay', *Cambridge Journal of Economics*, 2, 1, 17–36.

Stieber, J. (1959) *The Steel Industry Wage Structure*, Cambridge, Mass: Harvard University Press.

Wood, S. (1982) *The Degradation of Work?*, London: Hutchinson.

Dept. of Applied Economics
University of Cambridge
CAMBRIDGE CB3 9DE

Name Index

The International Library of Critical Writings in Economics

Macroeconomics and Imperfect Competition
Jean-Pascal Bénassy

Labor Economics
Orley C. Ashenfelter and Kevin F. Hallock

Transaction Cost Economics
Oliver Williamson and Scott Masten

The Economic Analysis of Rent Seeking
Robert D. Tollison and Roger D. Congleton

The Economics of Ageing
John Creedy

Long Wave Theory
Christopher Freeman

International Trade
J. Peter Neary

Agricultural Economics
G.H. Peters

International Debt
Graham Bird and P.N. Snowdon

Small Firms and Economic Growth
Zoltan Acs

Business Cycle Theory
Finn E. Kydland

General Equilibrium Theory
Gerard Debreu

The Money Supply in the Economic Process
Marco Musella and Carlo Panico

Producer Cooperatives and Labor-Managed Systems
David L. Prychitko and Jaroslav Vanek

The Foundations of Public Finance
Peter Jackson

International Finance
Robert Z. Aliber

Welfare Economics
William J. Baumol and Janusz A. Ordover

The Theory of the Firm
Mark Casson

The Economics of Inequality and Poverty
A.B. Atkinson

The Economics of Housing
John M. Quigley

Population Economics
Julian L. Simon

The Economics of Crime
Isaac Ehrlich

The Economics of Integration
Willem Molle

The Rhetoric of Economics
Donald McCloskey

Ethics and Economics
Alan Hamlin

Migration
Oded Stark

Economic Forecasting
Paul Ormerod

The Economics of Training
Robert J. LaLonde and Orley Ashenfeiter

The Economics of Defence
Keith Hartley and Nicholas Hooper

Consumer Theory
Kelvin Lancaster

Law and Economics
Judge Richard A. Posner

The Economics of Business Policy
John Kay

Microeconomic Theories of Imperfect Competition
Jacques Thisse and Jean Gabszewicz

The Economics of Increasing Returns
Geoffrey Heal

The Balance of Payments
Michael J. Artis

The Economics of the Family
Nancy Folbre

Cost-Benefit Analysis
Arnold Harberger and Glenn P. Jenkins

The New Growth Theory
Gene M. Grossman

Economic Theory and Chaos Theory
W. Davis Dechert

The Economics of Unemployment
P.N. Junankar

Mathematical Economics
Graciela Chichilnisky

Economic Growth in the Long Run
Bart van Ark

Gender in Economic and Social History
K.J. Humphries and J. Lewis